THE CAMBRIDGE CO
TO SAPPHO

No ancient poet has a wider following today than Sappho; her status as the most famous woman poet from Greco-Roman antiquity, and as one of the most prominent lesbian voices in history, has ensured a continuing fascination with her work down the centuries. *The Cambridge Companion to Sappho* provides an up-to-date survey of this remarkable, inspiring, and mysterious Greek writer, whose poetic corpus has been significantly expanded in recent years thanks to the discovery of new papyrus sources. Containing an introduction and thirty-three chapters, the book examines Sappho's historical, social, and literary contexts, the nature of her poetic achievement, the transmission, loss, and rediscovery of her poetry, and the reception of that poetry in cultures far removed from ancient Greece, including Latin America, India, China, and Japan. All Greek is translated, making the volume accessible to everyone interested in one of the most significant creative artists of all time.

P. J. FINGLASS is Henry Overton Wills Professor of Greek in the Faculty of Arts at the University of Bristol.

ADRIAN KELLY is Tutorial Fellow in Ancient Greek Language and Literature at Balliol College, Oxford, and Associate Professor and Clarendon University Lecturer in the Faculty of Classics at the University of Oxford.

Authors

Edward Albee edited by Stephen J. Bottoms
Margaret Atwood edited by Coral Ann Howells
W. H. Auden edited by Stan Smith
Jane Austen edited by Edward Copeland and Juliet McMaster (second edition)
James Baldwin edited by Michele Elam
Balzac edited by Owen Heathcote and Andrew Watts
Beckett edited by John Pilling
Bede edited by Scott DeGregorio
Aphra Behn edited by Derek Hughes and Janet Todd
Saul Bellow edited by Victoria Aarons
Walter Benjamin edited by David S. Ferris
William Blake edited by Morris Eaves
Boccaccio edited by Guyda Armstrong, Rhiannon Daniels, and Stephen J. Milner
Jorge Luis Borges edited by Edwin Williamson
Brecht edited by Peter Thomson and Glendyr Sacks (second edition)
The Brontës edited by Heather Glen
Bunyan edited by Anne Dunan-Page
Frances Burney edited by Peter Sabor
Byron edited by Drummond Bone
Albert Camus edited by Edward J. Hughes
Willa Cather edited by Marilee Lindemann
Cervantes edited by Anthony J. Cascardi
Chaucer edited by Piero Boitani and Jill Mann (second edition)
Chekhov edited by Vera Gottlieb and Paul Allain
Kate Chopin edited by Janet Beer
Caryl Churchill edited by Elaine Aston and Elin Diamond
Cicero edited by Catherine Steel
J. M. Coetzee edited by Jarad Zimbler
Coleridge edited by Lucy Newlyn
Wilkie Collins edited by Jenny Bourne Taylor
Joseph Conrad edited by J. H. Stape
Dante edited by Rachel Jacoff (second edition)
Daniel Defoe edited by John Richetti
Don DeLillo edited by John N. Duvall
Charles Dickens edited by John O. Jordan
Emily Dickinson edited by Wendy Martin
John Donne edited by Achsah Guibbory
Dostoevskii edited by W. J. Leatherbarrow
Theodore Dreiser edited by Leonard Cassuto and Claire Virginia Eby
John Dryden edited by Steven N. Zwicker
W. E. B. Du Bois edited by Shamoon Zamir
George Eliot edited by George Levine and Nancy Henry (second edition)

Topics

THE CAMBRIDGE
COMPANION TO SAPPHO

EDITED BY

P. J. FINGLASS
University of Bristol

ADRIAN KELLY
University of Oxford

CAMBRIDGE
UNIVERSITY PRESS

University Printing House, Cambridge CB2 8BS, United Kingdom

One Liberty Plaza, 20th Floor, New York, NY 10006, USA

477 Williamstown Road, Port Melbourne, VIC 3207, Australia

314–321, 3rd Floor, Plot 3, Splendor Forum, Jasola District Centre, New Delhi – 110025, India

79 Anson Road, #06–04/06, Singapore 079906

Cambridge University Press is part of the University of Cambridge.

It furthers the University's mission by disseminating knowledge in the pursuit of education, learning, and research at the highest international levels of excellence.

www.cambridge.org
Information on this title: www.cambridge.org/9781107189058
DOI: 10.1017/9781316986974

First published 2021

Printed in the United Kingdom by TJ Books Limited, Padstow Cornwall

A catalogue record for this publication is available from the British Library.

ISBN 978-1-107-18905-8 Hardback
ISBN 978-1-316-63877-4 Paperback

Contents

The first plate section can be found between pp. 90 and 91.
The second plate section can be found between pp. 260 and 261.

Plates

Front Cover: *Sappho* (before AD 1909), sculpture by Auguste Rodin (1840–1917). Location unknown; photo © Alamy Images.

PART I

1 Red-figure *psykter* (*c.*505–500 BC) by Euphronius. St Petersburg, State Hermitage Museum, inv. ST 1670; photo © Vladimir Terebenin.

2 Red-figure *hydria* (*c.*510–500 BC) by Phintias. Munich, Antikensammlungen, inv. 2421.

3 Red-figure *kylix* (*c.*500 BC) by Onesimus. Malibu, Getty Museum, inv. 82.AE.14; photo © Getty Open Content Program.

4 Red-figure *kalpis* (*c.*510–500 BC), name vase of the Sappho Painter, with female figure labelled ΦΣΑΦΟ. Warsaw, National Museum, inv. 142333; photo © Piotr Ligier.

5 Red-figure *kalyx-kratêr* (*c.* 480–470 BC) attributed to the Tithonus Painter (obverse), with female figure inscribed ΣΑΦΦΟ. Ruhr-University Bochum, Kunstsammlungen, inv. S 508; photo © Beazley Archive, courtesy of the Classical Art Research Centre, University of Oxford.

6 Red-figure *kalyx-kratêr* (*c.* 480–470 BC) attributed to the Tithonus Painter (reverse). Ruhr-University Bochum, Kunstsammlungen, inv. S 508; photo © Beazley Archive, courtesy of the Classical Art Research Centre, University of Oxford.

xvi

Contributors

LUIGI BATTEZZATO is Professor of Language and Literature at the Scuola Normale Superiore, Pisa. He is the author of a commentary on Euripides' *Hecuba* (Cambridge University Press, 2018), two monographs on tragedy (*Linguistica e retorica della tragedia greca*, 2008[1], 2018[2]; *Il monologo nel teatro di Euripide*, 1995), one on Homer (*Leggere la mente degli eroi*, 2019), and many papers on ancient Greek literature, culture, language, and metre. He has been a Visiting Professor at the Istituto Universitario di Studi Superiori di Pavia and at the École Normale Supérieure de Lyon, and a Visiting Fellow at All Souls College, Oxford.

EWEN BOWIE, now an Emeritus Fellow of Corpus Christi College, Oxford, was Praelector in Classics there from 1965 to 2007, and successively Senior Lecturer, Reader, and Professor of Classical Languages and Literature at the University of Oxford. He has published on early Greek elegiac, iambic, and lyric poetry, Aristophanes, Hellenistic poetry, and many aspects of imperial Greek literature and culture. He recently completed a commentary on Longus, *Daphnis and Chloe* for Cambridge University Press and edited a collection entitled *Herodotus. Narrator, Scientist, Historian* (2018). He has co-edited collections of papers on Philostratus (Cambridge University Press, 2009) and *Archaic and Classical Choral Song* (2011).

VANESSA CAZZATO is a Marie Curie Post-doctoral Fellow in Paris at the Centre national de la recherche scientifique/Anthropologie et histoire des mondes antiques, where she is working on a project entitled 'A cognitively inflected aesthetics of the ancient Greek symposion'. She studied in Milan, Dublin, and Oxford, and has held post-doctoral positions in Oxford, Nijmegen, and Tokyo. She has (co-)edited several books on Greek lyric poetry and the symposion (*The Look of Lyric. Greek Song and the Visual*, 2016; *The Cup of Song. Studies on Poetry and the Symposion*, 2016; *The Symposion. Drinking Greek Style, Essays on Greek Pleasure 1983–2017* by Oswyn Murray, 2018; *Framing Hipponax*, Cambridge University Press, forthcoming). She has a monograph forthcoming on imagery in lyric poetry.

JINGLING CHEN received her PhD from Harvard University and teaches at the University of Illinois at Urbana–Champaign. Her research interests include Chinese and Greek comparative literature, modern and contemporary Chinese narrative, and modern Chinese intellectual history. She is completing a book on the Greek imaginary and Chinese cultural modernity.

LYNDSAY COO is Senior Lecturer in Ancient Greek Language and Literature at the University of Bristol. Her research focuses on ancient Greek drama, in particular the lost and fragmentary works. She is writing a commentary on the fragmentary Trojan plays of Sophocles, and has published on Greek tragedy and satyr play.

ROBERT DE BROSE is Professor of Classics and Head of the Postgraduate Programme in Translation Studies at the Federal University of Ceará, Brazil. He is the author of *Epikōmios Hymnos. Investigações sobre a performance dos epinícios pindáricos* (Diss. São Paulo 2014), and is currently working on a translation with commentary of all of Pindar's works.

FRANCO FERRARI taught, before retiring, Greek literature and classical philology at the Scuola Normale Superiore di Pisa (1976–2000) and at the University of L'Aquila (2001–12). Among his books are *Ricerche sul testo di Sofocle* (1983), *Oralità ed espressione. Ricognizioni omeriche* (1986), *Una mitra per Kleis. Saffo e il suo pubblico* (2007; English translation, *Sappho's Gift*, 2010), *La fonte del cipresso bianco. Racconto e sapienza dall'Odissea alle lamine misteriche* (2007), and *Il migliore dei mondi impossibili. Parmenide e il cosmo dei Presocratici* (2010).

P. J. FINGLASS is Henry Overton Wills Professor of Greek at the University of Bristol. Having recently completed terms as Director of the AHRC-funded South, West and Wales Doctoral Training Partnership and as Head of the Department of Classics and Ancient History, he now holds a Leverhulme Major Research Fellowship whose goal is a new edition with commentary of Sappho and Alcaeus. He has published a monograph *Sophocles* (2019) in the series 'Greece and Rome New Surveys in the Classics', as well as editions of Sophocles' *Oedipus the King* (2018), *Ajax* (2011), and *Electra* (2007), of Stesichorus (2014), and of Pindar's *Pythian Eleven* (2007) in the series Cambridge Classical Texts and Commentaries; has co-edited (with Adrian Kelly) *Stesichorus in Context* (2015) and (with Lyndsay Coo) *Female Characters in Fragmentary Greek Tragedy* (2020); and edits the journal *Classical Quarterly*, all with Cambridge University Press.

STUART GILLESPIE (University of Glasgow) is co-editor (with Philip Hardie) of *The Cambridge Companion to Lucretius* and (with Peter France) of *The Oxford History of Literary Translation in English*. His special interest in the reception and translation of ancient Greek and Latin literature is reflected in his monograph *English Translation and Classical Reception. Towards a New Literary History* (2011), and most recently in a large-scale edition of English translations taken from unprinted manuscripts: *Newly Recovered English Classical Translations, 1600–1800* (2018). He is also editor of the journal *Translation and Literature*.

BARBARA GOFF is Professor of Classics at the University of Reading, and Research Associate of the University of the Free State, Bloemfontein, South Africa. She has published extensively on Greek tragedy and its reception, especially in postcolonial contexts. Her most recent book is *'Your Secret Language'. Classics in the British Colonies of West Africa* (2013). She is currently working, with Michael Simpson, on a book provisionally titled *Working Classics. Greece, Rome, and the British Labour Movement*.

KATHERINE HARLOE is Professor of Classics and Intellectual History at the University of Reading. She is the author of *Winckelmann and the Invention of Antiquity* (2013) as well as of numerous articles on classical reception in literature, art, and historical scholarship, as well as three co-edited collections: *Thucydides and the Modern World* (Cambridge University Press, 2012), *Hellenomania* (2018), and *Winckelmann and Curiosity in the 18th-Century Gentleman's Library* (2018). She is joint editor of the *International Journal of the Classical Tradition*. She is currently working on a monographic study of classical rhetoric and ancient models of literary homoeroticism in Winckelmann's correspondence.

RICHARD HUNTER is Regius Professor of Greek at the University of Cambridge and a Fellow of Trinity College. His most recent books with Cambridge University Press include *Plato and the Traditions of Ancient Literature. The Silent Stream* (2012), *Hesiodic Voices. Studies in the Ancient Reception of Hesiod's Works and Days* (2014), *Apollonius of Rhodes. Argonautica Book IV* (2015), (ed., with A. Uhlig) *Imagining Reperformance in Ancient Culture. Studies in the Traditions of Drama and Lyric* (2017), and *The Measure of Homer* (2018). He is also an editor of Cambridge Greek and Latin Classics and of Cambridge Classical Studies.

ADRIANA X. JACOBS is Associate Professor of Modern Hebrew Literature and Cowley Lecturer in the Faculty of Oriental Studies, Oxford. She has published widely on modern Hebrew and Israeli poetry and translation, including articles in *Shofar*, *PMLA*, *Studies in American Jewish Literature*, and *Prooftexts*, as well as chapters in several edited volumes. She is the author of *Strange Cocktail. Translation and the Making of Modern Hebrew Poetry* (2018).

MARGUERITE JOHNSON is Professor of Classics at The University of Newcastle, Australia. An interdisciplinary cultural historian of the ancient Mediterranean, and a comparative cultural analyst, her methodology privileges literary-informed cultural paradigms, underpinned by praxes of both gender and postcolonial theories. Her research focuses on classical reception studies, particularly Australasian appropriations of ancient Greece and Rome in the early colonial period, as well as historical studies in sexualities, gender, and the body, extending to contemporary debates surrounding feminism, LGBTIQ histories, and related issues.

DIMITRIOS KARGIOTIS is Professor of Comparative Literature at the University of Ioannina in Greece and Tutor in European Literature and Creative Writing at the Hellenic Open University. He is the author of the following books in Greek: *Geographies of Translation. Spaces, Canons, Ideologies* (2017); *Critical Essays on Modern Greek Literature* (2018); and *Occasional Poetry. An Essay on the Emergence of a Category* (2021). He is completing a *Bibliography of French Translations of Modern Greek Literature (12th Century to the Present), with Annotations and Commentary*, as well as a collection of essays tentatively titled *Literary Studies, between Descriptivism and Ideology*.

ADRIAN KELLY is Tutorial Fellow in Ancient Greek at Balliol College, Oxford, and Associate Professor and Clarendon Lecturer in the Faculty of Classics, University of Oxford. He is the author of *A Referential Commentary and Lexicon to Homer, Iliad VIII* (2007) and *Sophocles. Oedipus at Colonus* (2009), and co-editor (with P. J. Finglass) of *Stesichorus in Context* (Cambridge University Press, 2015). He is completing a Cambridge Greek and Latin Classics commentary on Homer, *Iliad* 23 and co-editing (with Christopher Metcalf) *Gods and Mortals in Early Greek and Near Eastern Myth*, both for Cambridge University Press.

MAARIT KIVILO received her D.Phil. from the University of Oxford, after previously studying at the University of Tartu, Estonia. She is the author of *Early Greek Poets' Lives. The Shaping of the Tradition* (2010) and is now working on a book about using genealogical and biographical narrative patterns in early Greek hexametric poetry, especially in the *Iliad*.

LESLIE KURKE is Gladys Rehard Wood Professor of Classics and Comparative Literature at the University of California, Berkeley. Her research focuses on archaic and classical Greek literature and cultural history, with particular emphasis on archaic Greek poetry, Herodotus, and early prose. She is the author of *The Traffic in Praise. Pindar and the Poetics of Social Economy* (1991), *Coins, Bodies, Games, and Gold. The Politics of Meaning in Archaic Greece* (1999), and *Aesopic Conversations. Popular Tradition, Cultural Dialogue, and the Invention of Greek Prose* (2011). Her new book, co-authored with Richard Neer, is entitled *Pindar, Song, and Space. Towards a Lyric Archaeology* (2019).

ANDRÉ LARDINOIS is Professor of Ancient Greek Language and Literature at Radboud University in Nijmegen, and the Academic Director of OIKOS, the national Dutch research school in Classical Studies. His main field of study is early Greek poetry. Among his publications are (with L. McClure) *Making Silence Speak. Women's Voices in Greek Literature and Society* (2001), (with D. J. Rayor) *Sappho. A New Translation of the Complete Works* (Cambridge University Press, 2014), and (with A. Bierl) *The Newest Sappho. P. Sapph. Obbink and P. GC inv. 105, frs. 1–4* (2016).

LLEWELYN MORGAN is Leighton D. Reynolds Fellow in Classics at Brasenose College, Oxford. He is the author of *Musa Pedestris. Metre and Meaning in Roman Verse* (2010), and articles on various aspects of Roman literature, from metrical form to transhumance, with a particular focus on Virgil, Horace, Ovid, and Statius.

MELISSA MUELLER is Associate Professor of Classics at the University of Massachusetts, Amherst. She is the author of *Objects as Actors. Props and the Poetics of Performance in Greek Tragedy* (2016) and co-editor (with Mario Telò) of *The Materialities of Greek Tragedy. Objects and Affect in Aeschylus, Sophocles, and Euripides* (2018). She is also an editor of the series Ancient Cultures, New Materialisms.

CECILIA PIANTANIDA is Assistant Professor (Teaching) in Italian Studies at the School of Modern Languages and Cultures of Durham University. She holds a doctorate from the University of Oxford and has published on various aspects of the reception of Sappho in modern and contemporary Italy, including an edition of thirty autograph translations of her fragments by Giovanni Pascoli (2013). She is co-editor (with Teresa Franco) of *Echoing Voices in Italian Literature. Tradition and Translation in the 20th Century* (2018), and is completing a monograph on the reception of Sappho and Catullus in modern Italian and North American poetry.

FILIPPOMARIA PONTANI is Professor of Classical Philology at Ca' Foscari University of Venice. He is currently editing the ancient and medieval scholia to Homer's *Odyssey* (3 vols. to date, 2007–), and has published extensively on Greek and Latin texts, as well as on Byzantine, humanist, and Modern Greek literature. Beyond his commitment to the history of manuscript transmission (editions of forgotten or unknown poems; a new edition of Plutarch's *Natural Questions*, etc.), he has focused on the rise of ancient grammar and scholarship, on Byzantine philology, on the history of rhetoric and geography, on Homeric allegories, on Byzantine philology, and on the literary reception of ancient myths.

LUCIA PRAUSCELLO is Senior Research Fellow in Classical Literature at All Souls College, Oxford. She has variously published on archaic and classical Greek literature, language, and culture. Her monographs are *Singing Alexandria. Music between Practice and Textual Transmission* (2006) and *Performing Citizenship in Plato's Laws* (Cambridge University Press, 2014).

ALEX PURVES is Professor of Classics at UCLA, and the author of *Space and Time in Ancient Greek Narrative* (Cambridge University Press 2010) and *Homer and the Poetics of Gesture* (2019), as well as several articles on Greek literature and poetics. She is also co-editor, with Shane Butler, of *Synaesthesia and the Ancient Senses* (2013), and editor of *Touch and the Ancient Senses* (2018).

WOLFGANG RÖSLER is Professor Emeritus of Greek philology at Humboldt University, Berlin. His main fields of research include orality and literacy in ancient Greece, anthropological aspects and history of mentalities of early Greek culture, functions of archaic and classical Greek poetry and literature, ancient literary theory, theory and practice of the translation of Greek literature, and the history of classical philology.

RUTH SCODEL, educated at Berkeley and Harvard, is Professor emerita of Greek and Latin at the University of Michigan. Her books include *Credible Impossibilities. Conventions and Strategies of Verisimilitude in Homer and Greek Tragedy* (1999), *Listening to Homer* (2002), *Epic Facework. Self-Presentation and Social Interaction in Homer* (2008), and (with Anja Bettenworth) *Whither Quo Vadis? Sienkiewicz's Novel in Film and Television* (2009), and *An Introduction to Greek Tragedy* (2010). She is working on a monograph about theory of mind and attribution in archaic and classical Greek literature.

DEBORAH STEINER is Jay Professor of Greek at Columbia University. She has published extensively on Pindar and other lyric and iambic poets, and is the author of a Cambridge Greek and Latin Classics commentary on books 17 and 18 of the *Odyssey* for Cambridge University Press, which will also publish her forthcoming *Choral Constructions in Greek Culture. The Idea of the Chorus in the Poetry, Art, and Social Practices of the Archaic and Early Classical Period* (2021).

LAURA SWIFT is Senior Lecturer in Classical Studies at the Open University. She is the author of *Euripides. Ion* (2008), *The Hidden Chorus. Echoes of Genre in Tragic Lyric* (2010), *Greek Tragedy. Themes and Contexts* (2016) and *Archilochus. The Poems* (2019), and co-editor (with Chris Carey) of *Iambus and Elegy. New Approaches* (2016), as well as numerous articles on Greek tragedy and early Greek lyric poetry.

ROSALIND THOMAS is Tutorial Fellow at Balliol College, Oxford and Professor of Ancient Greek History at the University of Oxford. She has published *Oral Tradition and Written Record in Classical Athens* (1989), *Literacy and Orality in Ancient Greece* (1992), *Herodotus in Context. Ethnography, Science and the Art of Persuasion* (2000), and *Polis Histories, Collective Memories and the Greek World* (2019), all with Cambridge University Press. She has also written on Greek law, Thucydides, Greeks and the East, and performance in the Athenian democracy.

OLGA TRIBULATO is Associate Professor of Greek language and literature at Ca' Foscari University of Venice. Her main areas of interest are the Greek literary languages, Atticism, the linguistic history of ancient Sicily, and morphology. She is the author of *Ancient Greek Verb-Initial Compounds* (2015), the editor of *Language and Linguistic Contact in Ancient Sicily* (Cambridge University Press, 2012), and a contributor to *Storia delle lingue letterarie greche* (2008¹, 2016², edited by A. C. Cassio). Her current research focuses on the perception of the Greek dialects and literary languages in imperial scholarship, with a focus on Atticist lexicography.

RUTH VANITA, Professor at the University of Montana, was educated in India, where she taught at the University of Delhi. She works on the history of ideas, focusing on gender and sexuality. She co-edited the pioneering *Same-Sex Love in India. Readings from Literature and History* (2001), and is the author of many books, including *Sappho and the Virgin Mary. Same-Sex Love and the English Literary Imagination* (1996); *Gender, Sex and the City. Urdu Rekhti Poetry, 1780–1870* (2012); and most recently *Dancing with the Nation. Courtesans in Bombay Cinema* (2017). Her first novel, *Memory of Light*, a lesbian romance set in eighteenth-century India, was published in 2020. She is a well-known translator of fiction and poetry from Hindi and Urdu to English.

Abbreviations

A–B C. Austin and G. Bastianini (eds.), *Posidippi Pellaei quae supersunt omnia*. Biblioteca Classica 3. Milan 2002.

Adler A. Adler (ed.), *Suidae Lexicon*, 5 vols. Lexicographi Graeci 1. Leipzig 1928–38.

Austin C. Austin (ed.), *Menander. Eleven Plays*. Proceedings of the Cambridge Philological Society Suppl. 37. Cambridge 2013.

BAPD *Beazley Archive Pottery Database* (www.beazley.ox.ac .uk/pottery/).

B–C J. Bidez and F. Cumont (eds.), *Imp. Caesaris Flavii Claudii Iuliani epistulae leges poematia fragmenta varia*. Paris and London 1922.

Bekker^a I. Bekker (ed.), *Apollonii Sophistae Lexicon Homericum*. Berlin 1833.

Bekker^b I. Bekker (ed.), *Georgius Cedrenus Iohannis Scylitzae ope. Tomus primus*. Bonn 1838.

BNJ I. Worthington (ed.), *Brill's New Jacoby* (https:// referenceworks.brillonline.com/browse/brill-s-new-jacoby).

Campbell D. A. Campbell (ed., transl.), *Greek Lyric*, 5 vols. *Volume 1. Sappho. Alcaeus. Volume 2. Anacreon, Anacreontea, Choral Lyric from Olympus to Alcman. Volume 3. Stesichorus, Ibycus, Simonides, and Others. Volume 5. The New School of Poetry and Anonymous Songs and Hymns*. Loeb Classical Library 142, 143, 476, 144. Cambridge, MA and London 1982, 1990, 1991, 1993.

Criscuolo	U. Criscuolo (ed.), *Michele Psello. Autobiografia. Encomio per la madre*. Naples 1989.
De Borries	J. de Borries (ed.), *Phrynichi Sophistae Praeparatio Sophistica*. Leipzig 1911.
Dennis	G. T. Dennis (ed.), *Michael Psellus. Orationes panegyricae* and *Michael Psellus. Orationes forenses et acta*. Stuttgart and Leipzig 1994.
Dorandi	T. Dorandi (ed.), *Antigone de Caryste. Fragments*. Paris 1999.
Drachmann	A. B. Drachmann (ed.), *Isaac Tzetzes. De metris Pindaricis*. Det Kgl. Danske Videnskabernes Selskab Historisk-filologiske Meddelelser 9.3. Copenhagen 1925 and *Scholia vetera in Pindari carmina*, 3 vols. Leipzig 1903–27.
EGM	R. L. Fowler (ed.), *Early Greek Mythography*, 2 vols. (Oxford 2000–13).
Erbse	H. Erbse (ed.), *Scholia Graeca in Homeri Iliadem (Scholia vetera)*, 7 vols. Berlin 1969–88.
Finglass	P. J. Finglass, 'Text and critical apparatus', in Davies and Finglass 2014 (eds.), 93–205.
FGE	D. L. Page (ed.), *Further Greek Epigrams. Epigrams before* A.D. *50 from the Greek Anthology and Other Sources, Not Included in Hellenistic Epigrams or The Garland of Philip*, revised and prepared for publication by R. D. Dawe and J. Diggle. Cambridge 1981.
FGrHist	F. Jacoby *et al.* (eds.), *Die Fragmente der griechischen Historiker*. Leiden, Boston, Cologne 1923–.
Fischer	E. Fischer (ed.), *Die Ekloge des Phrynichos*. Sammlung griechischer und lateinischer Grammatiker 1. Berlin and New York 1974.
Gaisford	T. Gaisford (ed.), *Etymologicon magnum*. Oxford 1848.
Gautier	P. Gautier (ed.), *Michel Italikos. Lettres et discours*. Archives de l'Orient chrétien 14. Paris 1972.

GEF	M. L. West (ed.), *Greek Epic Fragments from the Seventh to the Fifth Centuries* BC. Loeb Classical Library 497. Cambridge, MA and London 2003.
GGM	K. Müller (ed.), *Geographi Graeci minores*, 3 vols. Paris 1855–61.
Giordano	D. Giordano (ed.), *Chamaeleontis Heracleotae fragmenta*². Edizioni e Saggi Universitari di Filologia Classica 45. Bologna 1990. [1st edn 1977]
GL	G. T. H. Keil (ed.), *Grammatici Latini*, 7 vols. with supplement by H. Hagen. Leipzig 1855–80.
GP	A. S. F. Gow and D. L. Page (eds.), *The Greek Anthology. The Garland of Philip and Some Contemporary Epigrams*, 2 vols. Cambridge 1968.
Harder	A. Harder, *Callimachus. Aetia*, 2 vols. Oxford 2012.
HE	A. S. F. Gow and D. L. Page (eds.), *The Greek Anthology. Hellenistic Epigrams*, 2 vols. Cambridge 1965.
Horna	K. Horna, 'Eine unedierte Rede des Konstantin Manasses', *Wiener Studien* 28 (1906) 171–204.
Hunger	H. Hunger (ed.), *Johannes Chortasmenos (ca. 1370–ca. 1436/37). Briefe, Gedichte und Kleine Schriften. Einleitung, Regesten, Prosopographie, Text.* Wiener byzantinistische Studien 7. Vienna 1969.
IEG	M. L. West (ed.), *Iambi et Elegi Graeci ante Alexandrum cantati*², 2 vols. Oxford 1989–92. [1st edn 1971–2]
IG XII/2	G. R. Paton (ed.), *Inscriptiones Graecae insularum Maris Aegaei. Fasciculus alter. Inscriptiones Graecae insularum Lesbi Nesi Tenedi.* Berlin 1899.
I.Kyme	H. Engelmann (ed.), *Die Inschriften von Kyme.* Inschriften griechischer Städte aus Kleinasien 5. Bonn 1976.
Janko	R. Janko (ed.), *Philodemus. On Poems. Book* I. Oxford 2000.
Keil	B. Keil (ed.), *Aelii Aristidis Smyrnaei quae supersunt omnia* II. Berlin 1898. [Orations 17–53 only]

Kolovou	F. Kolovou (ed.), *Die Briefe des Eustathios von Thessalonike*. Beiträge zur Altertumskunde 239. Munich and Leipzig 2006.
Koster	W. J. W. Koster (ed.), *Scholia in Aristophanem, Pars I. Prolegomena de comoedia, Scholia in Acharnenses, Equites, Nubes; Fasc. I A, continens Prolegomena de comoedia*. Groningen 1975.
Kühn	C. G. Kühn (ed.), *Claudii Galeni opera omnia*, 20 vols. Leipzig 1821–33.
LDAB	*Leuven Database of Ancient Books* (www.trismegistos .org/ldab/).
Lenz–Behr	F. W. Lenz and C. A. Behr (eds.), *P. Aelii Aristidis Opera quae exstant omnia*, 1 vol., 4 fascs. Leiden 1976–80. [Orations 1–16 only]
Littlewood	A. R. Littlewood (ed.), *The Progymnasmata of Ioannes Geometres*. Amsterdam 1972.
La–M	A. Laks and G. W. Most (eds.), *Early Greek Philosophy*, 9 vols. Loeb Classical Library 524–32. Cambridge, MA and London 2016.
LSJ[9]	H. G. Liddell and R. Scott, *A Greek–English Lexicon*[9], rev. H. Stuart-Jones *et al.* Oxford 1940.
Lu–M	C. M. Lucarini and C. Moreschini (eds.), *Hermias Alexandrinus. In Platonis Phaedrum Scholia*. Berlin and Boston 2012.
M–P[3]	Mertens–Pack[3], *Catalogue of Greek and Latin Literary Papyri* (http://web.philo.ulg.ac.be/cedopal/the-mertens-pack3-file/).
M–W	R. Merkelbach and M. L. West (eds.), *Fragmenta Hesiodea*. Oxford 1967. Supplemented in Merkelbach and West (eds.), *Fragmenta selecta, ap.* F. Solmsen (ed.), *Hesiodi Theogonia Opera et Dies Scutum*[3]. Oxford 1990.
Neri	C. Neri (ed.), *Erinna. Testimonianze e frammenti*. Eikasmos: Quaderni Bolognesi di Filologia Classica, Studi 9. Bologna 2003.

Palmieri	V. Palmieri (ed.), *Herennius Philo. De diversis verborum significationibus*. Naples 1988.
PCG	R. Kassel and C. Austin (eds.), *Poetae Comici Graeci*, 8 vols. to date. Berlin and New York 1983–.
PLF	E. Lobel and D. L. Page (eds.), *Poetarum Lesbiorum fragmenta*². Oxford 1963. [1st edn 1955]
P.Lond.Lit.	H. J. M. Milne, *Catalogue of the Literary Papyri in the British Museum*. London 1927.
PMG	D. L. Page (ed.), *Poetae melici Graeci*. Oxford 1962.
PMGF	M. Davies (ed.), *Poetarum melicorum Graecorum fragmenta*, 1 vol. to date. Oxford 1991–.
Polemis	I. D. Polemis (ed.), Θεόδωρος Μετοχίτης. Ηθικός ἢ Περὶ παιδείας. Κείμενα βυζαντινῆς λογοτεχνίας 1. Athens 1995.
P.Oxy.	B. P. Grenfell, A. S. Hunt *et al.* (eds.), *The Oxyrhynchus Papyri*, 83 vols. to date. London 1898–.
P.S.I.	*Papiri della Società italiana.*
Rabeᵃ	H. Rabe (ed.), *Scholia in Lucianum*. Leipzig 1906.
Rabeᵇ	H. Rabe (ed.), *Anonymi et Stephani in artem rhetoricam commentaria*. Commentaria in Aristotelem Graeca 21/2. Berlin 1896.
Rabeᶜ	H. Rabe (ed.), *Hermogenis opera*. Rhetores Graeci 6. Leipzig 1913.
Radt	S. L. Radt (ed.), *Strabons Geographika*, 10 vols. Göttingen 2002–11.
Reinsch–Kambylis	D. R. Reinsch and A. Kambylis (eds.), *Annae Comnenae. Alexias*, 2 parts. Corpus fontium historiae Byzantinae 40. Berlin and New York 2001.
RG	C. Walz (ed.), *Rhetores Graeci ex codicibus Florentinis Mediolanensibus Monacensibus Neapolitanis Parisiensibus Romanis Venetis Taurinensibus et Vindobonensibus*, 9 vols. Stuttgart, Tübingen, London, Paris 1832–6.
Romano	R. Romano (ed.), *Pseudo-Luciano. Timarione*. Collana di Studi e Testi 2. Naples 1974.

Rotstein	A. Rotstein, *Literary History in the Parian Marble.* Hellenic Studies 68. Cambridge, MA and London 2016.
RPC	*Roman Provincial Coinage Online* (http://rpc .ashmus.ox.ac.uk/).
R–W	D. A. Russell and N. G. Wilson (eds.), *Menander Rhetor.* Oxford 1981.
Schrader	H. Schrader (ed.), *Porphyrii Quaestionum Homericarum ad Iliadem pertinentium reliquias.* Leipzig 1880.
SEG	J. J. E. Hondius *et al.* (eds.), *Supplementum epigraphicum Graecum*, 64 vols. to date. Leiden, Amsterdam, Boston 1923–.
SH	H. Lloyd-Jones and P. J. Parsons (eds.), *Supplementum Hellenisticum.* Texte und Kommentare 11. Berlin and New York 1983.
Singer	P. N. Singer (transl.), *Galen. Selected Works.* Oxford and New York 1997.
SLG	D. L. Page (ed.), *Supplementum lyricis Graecis. Poetarum lyricorum Graecorum fragmenta quae recens innotuerunt.* Oxford 1974.
S–M	B. Snell and H. Maehler (eds.), *Pindari Carmina cum fragmentis*[8], 2 vols. Leipzig 1987–9.
Stählin	O. Stählin (ed.), *Clemens Alexandrinus*, 4 vols. Leipzig 1905–36.
Stallbaum	<G. Stallbaum> (ed.), *Eustathii Archiepiscopi Thessalonicensis commentarii ad Homeri Odysseam*, 2 vols. Leipzig 1825–6.
Thurn	H. Thurn (ed.), *Ioannis Malalae Chronographia.* Corpus fontium historiae Byzantinae 35. Berlin and New York 2000.
Treu	M. Treu (ed.), *Manuelis Holoboli orationes*, 2 vols. Potsdam 1906–7.
Van der Valk	M. van der Valk (ed.), *Eustathii Archiepiscopi Thessalonicensis commentarii ad Homeri Iliadem pertinentes*, 4 vols. Leiden, New York, Copenhagen, Cologne 1971–87.

Van Dieten   J. A. van Dieten (ed.), *Nicetae Choniatae orationes et epistulae.* Corpus fontium historiae Byzantinae 3. Berlin and New York 1972.

van Thiel   H. van Thiel (ed.), *Scholia D in Iliadem. Proecdosis aucta et correctior.* Cologne 2014. (https://kups. ub.uni-koeln.de/5586/).

Wehrli   F. Wehrli (ed.), *Die Schule des Aristoteles. Texte und Kommentar. Heft 11: Aristoxenos.* Basel and Stuttgart 1967^2. [1st edn 1945]

Westerink   L. G. Westerink (ed.), *Nicétas Magistros. Lettres d'un exilé (928–946).* Paris 1973.

Introduction

P. J. Finglass and Adrian Kelly

No ancient poet has a wider following today than Sappho; her status as the most famous woman poet from Greco-Roman antiquity has, down the centuries, ensured a continuing fascination with her work. The ancient edition of her poems, which filled probably nine books and thus over 10,000 lines, did not survive; but the fragments of those poems which have been preserved, both as quotations in authors whose works did outlast antiquity, and on ancient papyrus manuscripts recovered from the sands of Egypt, offer many glimpses of her poetic brilliance. The publication of quotation fragments from the sixteenth century onwards, and of papyrus fragments from the late nineteenth century, have inspired the imaginations of classical scholars and creative artists alike, but her reception within and beyond antiquity has always had a complicated relationship with her poetry and with the ancient biographical traditions that surrounded her.

The chapters in this volume show how every age both makes its own Sappho and reuses motifs identified and canonised by its predecessors. The Phaon theme, treated by several contributors, well illustrates this. The story originally held that Sappho became infatuated with Phaon, who piloted the ferry between Lesbos and the mainland; when he rejected her advances, she committed suicide by jumping from the Leucadian rock (Kivilo pp. 16–17). No fragments of Sappho refer to the story; the only ancient reference to her even writing about Phaon comes from an isolated and shadowy source, 'Palaephatus' (perhaps fourth century BC). Whatever the origin of their association, the very idea of a male lover, with the accompanying tale of suicide, authorised a reassuringly heterosexual Sappho for audiences unsettled by the openly homosexual orientation of her poetry (Mueller). This need, felt by audiences throughout the history of her reception, underlines how extraordinary the sexual and poetic perspectives found in Sappho's work were felt to be; the quality of her poetry demanded its transmission, but also a bio-graphical carapace to insulate audiences from its more unsettling aspects. The association between Sappho and Phaon also led to a bifurcated bio-graphical tradition – two Sapphos, one the famous poet and the other a courtesan linked with Phaon – which lived on well after antiquity: Guy Morillon, correspondent of Erasmus, detailed it in the preface to his edi-tion of Ovid's *Heroides* (GILLESPIE pp. 333–4).

In the Roman world, Plautus' *Miles gloriosus* modelled on Sappho the female character Acroteleium (literally 'cliff-top end', probably an allu-sion to the story of Sappho's suicide) in her apparent pursuit of the male hero, Pyrgopolynices, modelled in turn on Phaon (MORGAN p. 291). Sappho's most devoted Roman reader, Catullus, does not mention the Phaon story, but the positioning of his poetic self in an amatory relationship with 'Lesbia' invigorates a heterosexual narrative which the Phaon story had done so much to crystallise (*ibid.* pp. 296–9). The story also assimilated her to other literary types, such as the abandoned heroines who formed the basis for Ovid's *Heroides*. Though probably not by Ovid, the fifteenth letter in that collection (the *Letter to Phaon*) had an influential afterlife (GILLESPIE pp. 332–3, PIANTANIDA pp. 343, 345–55, 359, JOHNSON ch. 26 pp. 362–5, 367–9, 372). A late fifteenth-century manuscript of Octovien de Saint-Gelais's French translation of the *Heroides* contains an illumination depicting Sappho just before her leap (Oxford, Balliol College 383, fol. 167v, Plate 11): standing on the rock, her musical instruments abandoned on the ground, looking into the waters below. The roll held by Sappho in Raphael's fresco *Parnassus* (*c*.1509–11, Plate 12) is probably a copy of that same poem (Most 1995: 19 ≈ Greene 1996b: 17). Alexander Pope's poem 'Sapho to Phaon' (1712) draws on Ovid to tell the story of a woman who rejects all her other qualities and abilities for her love for the ferryman, while Maria Fortuna's play *Saffo* (1776) portrays Sappho as the wronged woman, abandoned to her death by an unworthy Faone; a similarly virtuous portrait in Alessandro Verri's novel *Le avventure di Saffo di Mitilene* (1782) was linked by the author with his horror at the bisexually pro-miscuous Sappho of antiquity, and Vincenzo Imperiali's *La Faoniade* (1780) had Sappho compose a ten-book poem in Phaon's honour. A painting *Sappho and Phaon* by Jacques-Louis David (1809, Plate 13) pre-sents a disturbing take on the story, with Phaon cradling Sappho's head as they both gaze directly at the viewer, with Sappho reaching for but separated from her lyre (Goldhill 2006: 260–1 ≈ 2011: 72–3).

Maria Rosa Gálvez's *Safo* (1804) used the tale as a paradigm for the author's life, as she struggled to assert independence and freedom as an artist (PIANTANIDA p. 348). Her Sappho was not afraid of her passion, though not redeemed by it either. Then Franz Grillparzer's *Sappho* (1818) reversed the relationship: now Sappho was the distant, artistically pure object of Phaon's affections (added to those of Anacreon and Alcaeus), won specifically by the quality of her poetry. The émigré English writer Adela Nicolson (1865–1904) was compared, approvingly, to Sappho in this respect (and others) by the Indian poet Kamala Das (1934–2009), herself a vital figure in the reception of Sappho (VANITA pp. 458–62). In the twentieth century more generally, Phaon retreated a little, though he was prominent in works as varied as Lawrence Durrell's *Sappho. A Play in Verse* (1950, GOFF AND HARLOE pp. 391–2), Christine Brückner's prose monologue 'Don't forget the kingfisher's name' (1983) (PIANTANIDA p. 359), and even Erica Jong's suggestively named novel *Sappho's Leap* (2004, GOFF AND HARLOE p. 393). Nowadays, given a change in attitudes to the expression of homosexuality and the discovery of papyrus fragments which openly expressed her desire for women, Phaon is a curious footnote in Sappho studies, a manifestation more of the desire to inoculate her sexuality than to appreciate and understand her poetry.

Contemporary mores thus shaped the themes and qualities of Sappho's poetry through an amatory biography that allowed her reputation to overcome the obstacles frequently put in its way. Phaon has been a comforting fiction, a source of heavy moralising, a symbol of triumphant heterosexism, and even the defeated rival left in Sappho's wake; but throughout he has served to conceal or reveal Sappho herself in ways that her audiences could understand and enjoy.

* * *

The volume is divided into four sections. The first, 'Contexts', examines Sappho in her own time and place: her biography, with all its unreliable traditions (KIVILO), the historical status and identity of her home, Lesbos, in the archaic world (THOMAS), Sappho's position in, and contribution to, ancient discourses on sexuality (MUELLER), and the relationship of her works to other poetry of the archaic period (KELLY, RÖSLER, STEINER). The second, 'Poetics', evaluates Sappho's poetic achievement from many different perspectives, considering questions of performance (KURKE), genre (FERRARI), metre (BATTEZZATO), and dialect

(TRIBULATO); of her poetic language (CAZZATO), self-construction (LARDINOIS), and lyricism (PURVES); and of the role of myth and the gods in her work (SCODEL, SWIFT). The third, 'Transmission', looks specifically at how (a fraction of) Sappho's poetry has made it to our own day: the ancient edition of her poetry (PRAUSCELLO); the discovery of the papyri and what they have told us about the survival and loss of her work in late antiquity (FINGLASS ch. 17); the editions which have popularised her work in the modern period (FINGLASS ch. 18).

The fourth, 'Receptions', is the biggest, containing over 40 per cent of the book. Classical reception has been a major part of Cambridge Companions in our discipline for over two decades now, thanks to the pioneering work of Charles Martindale in the 1990s (Martindale 2013: 170). Our volume follows in that tradition, while taking it further by emphasising Sappho's influence across the globe. It begins with her ancient and medieval receptions, which set up the major lines along which her poetry and persona would be handed on to subsequent ages: fifth- and fourth-century Athens (Coo), the Hellenistic world of the third and second centuries (HUNTER), Rome (MORGAN), the Greek world under Rome (BOWIE), and finally Byzantium (PONTANI).

We then move into an early modern and modern world, though still largely European in focus. From the fifteenth to nineteenth centuries, our contributors find Sappho's presence and influence in England and France (GILLESPIE, JOHNSON ch. 26), Italy, Germany, and Spain (PIANTANIDA), and Greece (KARGIOTIS). Finally, the volume expands its focus worldwide: to the United States and anglophone world more generally (JOHNSON ch. 26, GOFF AND HARLOE), Australia and New Zealand (JOHNSON ch. 29), Latin America (DE BROSE), Hebrew literature (JACOBS), India (VANITA), and China and Japan (CHEN).

Inevitably there are gaps: Africa, Russia, Poland, modern France; music, film, popular culture; more besides. A companion and not an encyclopedia, our book has no ambitions to completeness – something that the richness of Sappho's reception would in any case particularly resist. Nevertheless, we hope that the volume sketches at least some aspects of that reception in cultures diverse across time and space, and offers a stimulus to fill the many gaps that remain. Moreover, in our view it is high time that global reception becomes an established feature of classical Cambridge Companions. The old Eurocentric way of doing things is looking increasingly out of date; we must do justice to the worldwide impact of Greco-Roman antiquity if our subject is to flourish.

* * *

A note on the text. There is (remarkably) no complete critical edition of Sappho's fragments, or of her testimonia (that is, ancient evidence, whether textual or material, that sheds light on Sappho's life and work while not actually preserving text from her poetry). The most recent critical edition, by E.-M. Voigt, was published in 1971; a major work of scholarship, it is a rare and expensive book, and considerably out of date thanks to the publication of new papyri. As a consequence, our volume cites the fragments and testimonia of Sappho using the numeration of the Loeb Classical Library edition by D. A. Campbell (1982, reprinted with corrections 1990), since this book is easily available both in print and online (www.loebclassics.com), and because it is equipped with an English translation. (Fragments and testimonia are cited without 'Campbell' or 'C.' after the number; testimonia not in Campbell's edition are cited from Voigt's, with a 'V.', as are occasional poetical fragments which Campbell omits.) But a commitment to using Campbell's numeration does not imply a commitment to using his text. No edition of Sappho could be definitive; contributors to the volume take responsibility for the textual choices made in the fragments that they cite. (The above also applies to Sappho's contemporary Alcaeus, whose fragments and tesimonia are edited by Campbell in the same Loeb volume that contains the remains of Sappho's poetry; so too are those fragments found at the very end of Campbell's volume, which are by either Sappho or Alcaeus.)

Recent papyrological discoveries pose their own referencing problems. For instance, Sappho's poem on Tithonus (the 'New Sappho') was known in part, from several papyri, to Voigt and Campbell, who printed them as their fr. 58; but the most recent witnesses of this poem could not be included in their texts, and so a full reference to that poem would now look something like the cumbersome fr. 58.11–22+P.Köln 429+430. Equally, her poem on her brothers Charaxus and Larichus (the 'Newest Sappho') has no fragment number; although the relationship between Sappho and her brothers was known to Herodotus, we lacked an actual poem on the theme until the publication of this text in 2014 (P.Sapph. Obbink). Such a confusing situation means that the new papyri published after Campbell's edition are cited not by number but as the Tithonus Poem, Brothers Poem, and (for another new poem first published in 2014) Cypris Poem; where relevant, individual contributors specify a particular published text.

Some technical symbols necessitated by the printing of papyrological texts require explanation. ⊗ denotes the start of a poem. A dot printed under a letter indicates that the letter is doubtful; a dot printed under empty space indicates that ink is present, but the letter in question cannot be identified. Gaps on a papyrus are represented by square brackets, [ ]; attempts by scholars to fill in such gaps are found within the brackets. Letters printed that are not found on the papyrus are placed within angular brackets, < >; letters found on the papyrus that are not printed are placed within curly brackets, { }.

Cross references to other chapters are indicated by the use of small capitals for the chapter author's name. Translations from the Greek are by the author of the chapter unless otherwise indicated.

The treatise ascribed to Longinus which preserves Sappho fr. 31 is today generally regarded as pseudonymous, though in previous centuries Longinus was regarded as the author. In our book, therefore, the author is referred to as Longinus in discussions of historical contexts where Longinus' authorship of the treatise was not challenged, and as Pseudo-Longinus everywhere else.

* * *

The recent papyrological discoveries just mentioned are problematic in ways beyond mere referencing. The provenance of the 'Newest Sappho' papyri is unknown; the identity of the owner of one of these papyri, P.Sapph.Obbink (which contains the Brothers Poem and the Cypris Poem), is unknown; the location of that papyrus is unknown; whether Dr Dirk Obbink, apparently the only person (apart from its owner) who has seen this papyrus, is aware of its current location, is unknown. This lack of key information about priceless cultural artefacts is more than regrettable; see Mazza 2019, which links to earlier pieces documenting deep concerns over the uncertain origins of these papyri, and Sampson 2020, a detailed analysis of the situation published just as we were going to press.

Such uncertainty forces us to confront the question of whether these texts are in fact authentic. At the time of writing, six years after their original publication, no one has argued that they are not. Forging a new poem of Sappho would be no easy business, and if it is a forgery, it has fooled many leading scholars; it contains not a single linguistic or metrical slip. Accordingly, these papyri are treated as authentic throughout this volume. But we repeat that the circumstances surrounding the discovery and publication of these papyri fall very far short of ideal.

* * *

For advice on specific points in different chapters we are indebted to Dr Sofia Gil de Carvalho (Coimbra), Miss Martina Delucchi (Bristol), Dr Aneurin Ellis-Evans (Oxford), Dr John Gilmore (Warwick), Professor Stephen Harrison (Oxford), Dr Michael Hawcroft (Oxford), Professor Michel Hockx (Notre Dame), Professor Simon Hornblower (London), Dr Laura Jansen (Bristol), Dr Anna Lamari (Thessaloniki), Professor Elena Lombardi (Oxford), Professor Rana Mitter (Oxford), Professor Diane Rayor (Grand Valley State), Professor Yoshinori Sano (Tokyo), and Professor Alan Sommerstein (Nottingham). Two referees made valuable comments which improved the typescript. Cambridge University Press's production team, led by Nigel Graves, were a pleasure to work with; and our copy editor, Jane Burkowski, significantly improved the accuracy and presentation of the finished volume, as did the proofreader, John Jacobs. Finally, we thank Michael Sharp for seeing the volume through the whole publication process, and for suggesting that we undertake it in the first place.

PART I

Contexts

CHAPTER I

Sappho's Lives

Maarit Kivilo

The first largely comprehensive report of Sappho's life, from an ancient treatise entitled *On Sappho* preserved on a papyrus of the late second or early third century AD, mentions her home town and family members, and describes her appearance and character.[1] After that we must wait until the tenth-century Byzantine lexicon, the *Suda*, for short continuous biographies of Sappho.[2] Aside from those accounts, we have many brief statements about different aspects of her life scattered in ancient works from the fifth century BC onwards. This material together forms Sappho's ancient biographical tradition.[3]

Both ancients and moderns have drawn much information about Sappho from her poetry, although there are problems with using these poems as evidence in this way. In particular, we hardly ever know whether a poet at a particular moment is speaking of his or her own autobiographical experience and circumstances, or has taken the guise of some other person or fictional character.[4] Consequently, for example, it is unclear whether the 'brother' or 'daughter' mentioned in Sappho's poems is her actual brother or daughter. Ancient authors, however, did not doubt the autobiographical nature of Sappho's poems; with additional material from other authors' works and local traditions, they built an elaborate collection of stories and accounts about Sappho's life.

Biographical accounts tend to be loosely shaped according to conventional themes. Details – purely fictional, or gleaned from poems, local histories, genealogical accounts, and other sources – tend to be shaped into stories deemed characteristic of a particular occupation. Thus, traditions about tyrants frequently portray them leading armies to war,

---

[1] P.Oxy. 1800 fr. 1 (test. 1).
[2] *Suda* c 107–8 (testt. 2–3).
[3] Fairweather 1974, 1983, Kivilo 2010: 167–200, 2011, Lefkowitz 2012.
[4] Lefkowitz 1963 = 1991: 1–71, 1995, Rösler 1976: 304–8, Slings 1990a, E. Bowie 1993: 35–7.

supporting art, or receiving oracles about their future, whereas seers are reported as having a long life, taking part in contests of wisdom, and enjoying cults after their death. Traditions about poets tend to include information about their important ancestors, their initiation into poetry, travelling, quarrelling with the authorities, and being sent into exile. They are often presented as poor but wise, innovative, and accompanied by pupils; they are frequently associated with each other or with other famous people, and are likely to die under unusual circumstances and to have a grave that local people could point out. Such typical themes are further individualised according to the perceived character of the particular poet. In the case of Sappho, the fact that she was a woman and sang of love may have prompted the accounts that she had several male lovers and died as a consequence of unrequited love for young Phaon. Perhaps, too, the scarcity of stories of her travelling – otherwise common in the life traditions of poets – may have roots in the ancient authors' belief that women should not travel much.

Home, Parents, Husband, Daughter

Sappho mentions Mytilene on the south-east edge of Lesbos; Herodotus, taking his cue from this or another source, implies that it was her home town, and ancient authors follow his lead.[5] The only other settlement so described is Eresus at the other end of the island, but some authors associate it with a 'second' Sappho, a courtesan – perhaps after the 'second' Sappho was invented to safeguard the poet's good reputation.[6]

The name of Sappho's father is reported as Scamander or Scamandronymus ('Named after Scamander').[7] This suggests that Sappho's family was regarded as a part of the nearby Troad's complex genealogical system, since Scamander is the region's main river, names were frequently drawn from rivers, and important women often had a local river(-god) in their lineage.[8] The myths of the Troad also appear in

---

[5] Fr. 98(b).3, Herodotus 2.135 (fr. 202); Alcidamas cited by Aristotle, *Rhetoric* 1398b.10–14, Parian Marble A36 Rotstein (test. 5), etc. Mytilene as home of the 'second' Sappho: *Suda* c 108 (test. 3). Sappho was subsequently depicted on Mytilene's coinage: see e.g. the first/second-century AD coin from Mytilene (London, British Museum BNK, G.510, Plate 8).

[6] Dioscorides, *Greek Anthology* 7.407 (test. 58), *Suda* c 107–8 (testt. 2–3), Athenaeus, *Scholars at Dinner* 13.596e. A Hermaic pillar bust, a Roman copy of a Greek original, is labelled 'Sappho of Eresus' (Rome, Musei Capitolini, inv. MC1164, Plate 10).

[7] P.Oxy. 1800 fr. 1 (test. 1); Herodotus 2.135.1 (fr. 202), *Suda* c 107 (test. 2).

[8] Scamander in the lineages of Strymo (Apollodorus, *Library* 3.12.3) and Callirhoe (Apollodorus 3.12.2, Dionysius of Halicarnassus, *Roman Antiquities* 1.62.2); Simoeis in the lineages of Astyoche and Hieromneme (Apollodorus 3.12.2).

Sappho's songs: she describes Hector and Andromache's wedding, and may mention the return of the Atridae from Troy.[9] The *Suda* lists additional names for Sappho's father (Simon, Eumenus, Eerigyius, Ecrytus, Semus, Camon, and Etarchus) but nothing else is known of them.[10] In (Pseudo-?)Ovid's *Heroides* 'Sappho' mourns her father who had died when she was only six years old, but this is a one-off remark with no clear origin.[11]

A 'mother' is referred to in the fragments, but without a name; Sappho also mentions a daughter, Cleis.[12] Some testimonia state that Sappho's mother and daughter were both called Cleis.[13] The father of Cleis, and Sappho's husband, was said to be a wealthy man called Cercylas of Andros, whose name ('Prick [from the island] of Man') suggests his character may have been constructed in a comic context.[14]

Brothers; Rhodopis

According to ancient authors, Sappho had three brothers: Charaxus, Eurygius, and Larichus. Her extant poems do not give much information about them: fr. 5 mentions but does not name a 'brother' (line 2) and a 'sister' (line 9). Larichus is referred to disparagingly in the Brothers Poem, though he was reported to be Sappho's favourite brother, giving her a cause for praising him for serving as a cup-bearer (a post reserved for noblemen) at the town hall in Mytilene.[15] Nothing is known about Eurygius, but since a similar name is recorded for Sappho's father, the middle brother's name may have been constructed on that basis.[16]

In the Brothers Poem, Charaxus is a merchant seaman whose safe return is earnestly prayed for (1–9), but the poem does not make it clear whether he is the speaker's brother. Nor do we know whether the poem's narrator is the autobiographical Sappho or some fictional character.[17] Later authors reported that Sappho rebuked Charaxus in her poem(s) for

---

[9] Frr. 44, 17 with Obbink 2016a: 20–1.

[10] *Suda* c 107 (test. 2).

[11] (Pseudo-?)Ovid, *Heroides* 15.61–2 (test. 13).

[12] Fr. 98(a).1; frr. 132, 98(b).1. The Brothers Poem may feature Sappho's mother: Obbink 2014a: 41–2.

[13] P.Oxy. 1800 fr. 1 (test. 1), *Suda* c 107 (test. 2). Maximus of Tyre says that Sappho addresses a poem about lamenting in the house of the Muses' servants to her daughter (fr. 150). (Pseudo-?)Ovid mentions a little daughter adding to the poet's worries (*Heroides* 15.69–70 = test. 16).

[14] Parker 1993: 309–10 ≈ Greene 1996b: 146–7.

[15] Lines 17–20; Athenaeus, *Scholars at Dinner* 10.425a, Scholia T on Homer, *Iliad* 20.234d = V 41.82–4 Erbse (fr. 203).

[16] *Suda* c 107 (test. 2).

[17] Lardinois pp. 172–3.

being reckless,[18] but no such poem has survived. Herodotus' account is linked to a complex tradition of a courtesan Rhodopis/Doricha which has two independent strands. The first strand[19] tells the story of the beautiful Thracian woman Rhodopis[20] (or Doricha as Sappho calls her),[21] who became a slave to a man called Iadmon (or Admon).[22] At some point, another man, Xanthes or Xanthus, took Rhodopis to Egypt, where she worked as a slave-courtesan. When Charaxus came to Egypt with his wine-laden ship he fell in love with Rhodopis and bought her freedom for a great sum of money. According to one account, Charaxus married Rhodopis and had children,[23] whereas in others he returned to Mytilene alone, upon which Sappho violently railed against him (or the woman for fleecing him)[24] in her poems, and Charaxus became impoverished and had to roam the seas.[25] Meanwhile, Rhodopis lived on in Naucratis in Egypt, now as an 'extremely charming' free woman,[26] continued working as a courtesan, and grew very rich. Wishing to leave her mark in Greece, she spent a tenth part of her wealth in making iron ox-spits and sent them to Delphi as a dedication.

The other strand follows a Cinderella pattern.[27] While Rhodopis, the beautiful courtesan of Naucratis, was taking a bath, an eagle snatched her sandal, took it to Memphis, and dropped it into the king's lap. Amazed by the sandal's beauty, the king sent his men to find its owner, and when Rhodopis was found he married her. Later, when she died, a small but expensive pyramid was built in her honour (or, according to a variant, she built the pyramid, presumably for the king), which became known as the Tomb of a Courtesan. Neither Charaxus nor any other Greek seems to be a part of that strand; yet by the time of Herodotus the two had become conflated and Charaxus was firmly a part of her story.

---

[18] Herodotus 2.135.6 (fr. 202), etc.
[19] Herodotus 2.134–5 (test. 9, fr. 202), etc.
[20] *Suda* ρ 210–11 (IV 297.23–30 Adler).
[21] Strabo 17.1.33 (fr. 202) says that Sappho called her Doricha, while others gave her the name Rhodopis; cf. *Suda* ρ 211. Athenaeus (*Scholars at Dinner* 13.596c = test. 15) criticises Herodotus for mistakenly thinking that Doricha and Rhodopis are the same woman.
[22] Iadmon of Samos: *Suda* αι 334, 1 4 (II 182.27–9, 601.4–6 Adler), Iadmon: Tzetzes, *Prolegomena to Comedy* pp. 24.44–25.49 Koster (test. 254g V.); Admon of Mytilene: *Suda* ρ 211, α 496 (I 52.14 Adler).
[23] *Suda* αι 334, 1 4.
[24] Athenaeus, *Scholars at Dinner* 13.596b.
[25] (Pseudo-?)Ovid, *Heroides* 15.63–6 (test. 16).
[26] Herodotus 2.135.2.
[27] Strabo 17.1.33, Aelian, *Historical Miscellany* 13.33.

Sappho's Circle

In her songs of love and friendship, Sappho mentions fifteen female names (excluding gods and mythological characters), describing some of these women as friends and criticising others. Later authors add a few names, counting some among her friends or lovers, others as her pupils;[28] they also mention Damophyla, Gorgo, Andromeda, and Erinna as rival (or contemporary) female poets.[29] By contrast, all the males mentioned in Sappho are either mythological characters or left unnamed. Subsequent tradition, however, associated Sappho with many men. First, she was connected to the poets Alcaeus, Anacreon, Archilochus, Hipponax, and Stesichorus. Grouping famous poets is a staple biographical device, but only in Sappho's case did those links take the form of love affairs: Anacreon and Alcaeus were reported to be rivals for Sappho's attention, and Hipponax and Archilochus her lovers.[30] Aristotle reports a dialogue between Alcaeus and Sappho where she puts him in his place for being duplicitous, and Hephaestion cites a verse of Alcaeus mentioning Sappho.[31] The chronographers synchronised Sappho with Pittacus, the Lesbian tyrant who wrote poetry and was counted among the Seven Sages, but there is no extant story connecting them.[32]

Phaon and Sappho

Phaon was the man with whom Sappho was particularly associated. The legend goes that Phaon, a fair-minded ferryman working between Lesbos and the mainland, charged only the rich. Wishing to put him to the test, Aphrodite disguised herself as an old woman and asked to be ferried across. Phaon promptly obliged and requested no payment. Upon this the goddess either gave him some love unguent or made him young and

---

[28] (Pseudo-?)Ovid, *Heroides* 15.15–20 (test. 19), Maximus of Tyre, *Oration* 18.9 (test. 20), *Suda* c 107 (test. 2).

[29] Damophyla: Philostratus, *Life of Apollonius* 1.30 (test.21); Gorgo and Andromeda: Maximus of Tyre, *Oration* 18.9 (test. 20); Erinna: *Suda* η 521 (T 16a Neri).

[30] Hermesianax fr. 3.47–56 Lightfoot, an anonymous source cited by Chamaeleon fr. 25 Giordano, Diphilus fr. 71 *PCG*; their testimony is rejected by Athenaeus, *Scholars at Dinner* 13.599cd (test. 8), who cites them. Later associations were more decorous: so a third-century AD mosaic from Sparta depicts Sappho with Alcaeus, Alcman, and Anacreon (and Alcibiades), all in separate panels (Archaeological Museum, inv. 11584, Plate 9).

[31] Aristotle, *Rhetoric* 1367a7–15 (fr. 137); Hephaestion, *Handbook on Metres* 14.4 (Alcaeus fr. 384): ἰόπλοκ' ἄγνα μελλιχόμειδε Σάπφοι. The reading is contested: Rösler pp. 67–8.

[32] Strabo 13.2.3 (test. 7), *Suda* c 107 (test. 2). Diogenes Laertius synchronises Pittacus with Alcaeus (1.74 etc.).

exceptionally handsome – either way, the women of Lesbos fell in love with him. Sappho, too, was smitten, but as her love remained unrequited she travelled to the other end of Greece, to the island of Leucas, which was famous as a place where love was cured, and hurled herself from its cliffs.[33] The underlying aetiological myth of the healing powers of the Leucadian cliffs is old. Anacreon, Euripides, and, possibly, Stesichorus mention it, while Photius gives the whole account.[34] While searching for Adonis, Aphrodite found him dead in Argos. Grieving, she confessed her love for Adonis to Apollo, and he, having brought her to Leucas, advised the goddess to hurl herself from the cliffs. She did so and was freed from her longing. When she asked for an explanation, Apollo revealed that Zeus comes here whenever he is caught by desire for Hera, sits down on the cliffs and is freed from his desire. In the same passage, Photius presents a list of men and women who had jumped from the cliffs, of whom some had survived and some died, but all were cured of their passion – but Sappho is not there. The majority of accounts about her leap do not specify whether she died; only the *Suda* says that she drowned.[35] If she was thought to have done so, it would explain why there are no ancient accounts about her grave; usually a poet's tomb, even if invented long after their death, was known and talked about. The lack of a physical tomb, or a place (and cult) associated with it, suggests that the death leap was an early and influential part of the tradition.[36] Sappho's leap correlates with the logic of the biographical story pattern by which poets tend to die in extraordinary circumstances. The link between Sappho, Phaon, and the leap may have been based on her poems, since Pseudo-Palaephatus claims that she often sung about Phaon, though he is not mentioned in her extant fragments.[37]

---

[33] Aelian, *Historical Miscellany* 12.18, *Suda* φ 89, c 108 (test. 3). Pliny (*Natural History* 22.20 = fr. 211(c)) insists that Sappho fell for Phaon when he used a rare aphrodisiac, a male-organ-shaped root of sea holly. Menander claims Sappho was the first to leap from the Leucadian cliffs because of unhappy love, but Strabo gives that honour to a man called Cephalus; see Menander, *Leucadia* fr. 1 Austin, cited by Strabo 10.2.9 (test. 23), where Strabo also describes the scapegoat ritual connected to the tradition.

[34] Anacreon fr. 376 *PMG*, Euripides, *Cyclops* 166–7, Stesichorus fr. 326 Finglass (if Stesichorean), Photius, *Library* 190 (153a).

[35] *Suda* c 108 (test. 3). Ausonius (*Cupid Crucified* 22–5) seems to be of the same opinion.

[36] The references to Sappho's tomb in Hellenistic epigrams in the *Greek Anthology* – 7.14 (Antipater of Sidon, test. 27), 7.16 (Pinytus, 3939–40 *GP*), and 7.17 (Tullius Laurea, test. 28) – all seem purely literary; Platt 2018: 37–8.

[37] Pseudo-Palaephatus, *On Unbelievable Things* 48 (fr. 211(a)); Hunter 2016.

'Second' Sappho

Some sources insist that it was another Lesbian woman, a courtesan and harp-player also called Sappho, who loved Phaon. This 'second' Sappho emerges first in the Hellenistic period and may have roots in Middle and New Comedy. The first extant source to link Sappho with Phaon is Menander's *Leucadia*, and we know of at least six comedies entitled *Sappho* which probably influenced the reception of her character, but their exiguous remains do not allow even speculation.[38] One fragment presents Sappho as proposing riddles, suggesting that she was portrayed as a clever woman, and in another a character claims to have learnt all Sappho's love songs, confirming her poetic reputation.[39] On the other hand, Diphilus made her a lover of both Archilochus and Hipponax, something which may have fuelled, or even started, the tradition that Sappho was wanton, a 'hussily arrayed' and 'mannish' woman, a man-chaser and woman-lover female poet; Didymus, for example, is reported to have written a whole treatise about whether Sappho was a prostitute.[40] In that case, the 'second' Sappho may have arisen from the wish of ancient commentators to distance the poet from that (comic?) creature. The distinction between the two, however, was never clear; the *Suda*, for instance, claims that the 'second' Sappho may have composed lyric poetry, and mixes up their home towns in their respective entries.[41]

Reputation and Inventions

Ancient accounts about Sappho's love life and preferences are scarce compared to statements about her as a poet. Indeed, the ancients seem to have been quite considerably less interested in the former topic than modern commentators;[42] Maximus of Tyre (second century AD) encapsulates their rather relaxed view when he compares Sappho to Socrates:

---

[38] Menander, *Leucadia* fr. 1 Austin (test. 23); Ameipsias fr. 15 *PCG*, Amphis fr. 32, Antiphanes frr. 194 (test. 25), 195, Ephippus fr. 20, Timocles fr. 32, Diphilus frr. 70 (test. 26), 71. Sappho's love affair and demise may have also been touched upon in plays called *Phaon* (Plato frr. 188–98, Antiphanes fr. 213), *Leucadia* (Alexis frr. 135–7, Amphis fr. 26, Diphilus fr. 52), and *Leucadios* (Antiphanes fr. 130–40). See further Coo pp. 269–75.

[39] Antiphanes fr. 194 *PCG* (test. 25), Epicrates fr. 4.

[40] Hermesianax fr. 3.47–56 Lightfoot, Menander, *Leucadia* fr. 1 Austin (test. 23), Didymus *ap.* Seneca, *Letters* 88.37 (test. 22).

[41] *Suda* c 107–8 (testt. 2–3).

[42] Hallett 1979 ≈ Greene 1996a: 125–42, Stehle Stigers 1979 ≈ Stehle 1996, M. Johnson 2007: 77–101, Stehle 2009a: 69–71, Bierl 2016a, Boehringer and Calame 2016.

both had lovers, he loved men, she loved women, for both were capti-
vated by everything beautiful.[43] What the ancients were really interested
in was the quality of her poetry; her talent and style were constantly
praised, she was listed among the best poets and other famous people, she
was regarded as learned and refined, counted as one of the Muses, and
compared to Homer and to a nightingale; Solon is reported to have asked
his nephew, who had introduced Sappho's song to him, to teach it to him
'so that [he] could learn it and die'.[44] They were, however, less of one
mind about her looks. Some called her beautiful and sweet-smiling; her
skin was reported to be smooth, her eyes bright, her face both cheerful
and clever.[45] Others said she was ugly, contemptible, short, dark, and
with grey complexion – but always an excellent poet.[46]

   Like most early poets, Sappho was believed to have invented things
associated with music: the invention of the *pêktis* (harp) was ascribed to
her, as was the plectrum, and one of the Greek musical modes, the
Mixolydian.[47] There was a discussion about whether she or Alcaeus
invented the sapphic hendecasyllabic stanza, although it was agreed she
certainly used it more.[48]

Performance Context

At what occasions and in which contexts were Sappho's poetry sung? Her
poems about brides and bridegrooms were presumably composed for
wedding ceremonies; personal love poems and private prayers could have
belonged in symposia, and communal prayers and laments in public ritu-
als. Ancient authors, however, provide only a few, late mentions about
her performing her own songs: Dioscorides' epigram places her at wed-
dings and occasions of lament, and an anonymous elegist has Sappho
leading a dance at a festival to Hera.[49] The scarcity of such accounts may

---

[43] Maximus of Tyre, *Oration* 18.9 (test. 20).
[44] Aelian cited by Stobaeus, *Florilegium* 3.29.58 (test. 10); a similar account features Socrates and Stesichorus (Ammianus Marcellinus 28.4.15).
[45] Alcaeus(?) fr. 384, Plato, *Phaedrus* 235c, Damocharis, *Greek Anthology* 16.310.
[46] Chamaeleon fr. 26 Giordano, Maximus of Tyre, *Oration* 18.7, Scholia on Lucian, *Paintings* 18 (p. 186.13–15 Rabe[a]). The last of these compares her again to a nightingale, though this time because she was 'small and dark like a nightingale whose tiny body is wrapped in misshapen wings'.
[47] Menaechmus, *FGrHist* 131 F 4 (test. 38), Aristoxenus fr. 81 Wehrli = Pseudo-Plutarch, *On Music* 16.1136c (test. 37), *Suda* c 107 (test. 2), BATTEZZATO pp. 130–2.
[48] MORGAN p. 293 n. 19.
[49] Dioscorides, *Greek Anthology* 7.407 (test. 58); Anonymous, *ibid.* 9.189 (test. 59).

correlate with a relative lack of stories about travel in Sappho's tradition. While other poets were believed to have travelled regularly and performed for a living at contests, at kings' courts, and at panegyrics, or set up schools where the poems were taught, nothing of the kind is said of Sappho – perhaps because ancient authors did not deem that sort of activity suitable for women. The only other account of her travelling, apart from her journey to her death at Leucas, comes from the Parian Marble, which reports that she was exiled and sailed from Mytilene to Sicily. The strand of tradition of Sappho as a teacher of girls of noble families, both local and those from Ionia, seems to have developed late.[50]

The same performance contexts come up again when ancient authors report where Sappho's poems were sung in later times: Aelian recounts a story of Solon's nephew singing a song of Sappho at a private performance, while Aulus Gellius and Plutarch record her songs being performed at Roman symposia.[51] She is also depicted on some vases holding musical instruments used mainly at symposia.[52] But this is about all the ancient information on this matter, contrasting with its greater interest for modern scholarship.[53]

Sappho in Chronographical Framework

Ancient authors liked to link famous people and events, creating complex synchronisms which formed a kind of chronographical network. These considerations were not behind every such account: chronographical deliberation was not the only reason to make Sappho a contemporary of Archilochus, Hipponax, and Stesichorus, or of famous women such as Erinna, Telesippa, or Rhodogyne,[54] even if these accounts were used in

---

[50] Parian Marble A36 Rotstein. Fr. 214B.1.7–11, *Suda* c 107 (test. 2), Wilamowitz 1896 = 1913: 63–78, Parker 1993 ≈ Greene 1996b: 146–83.

[51] Aelian cited by Stobaeus, *Florilegium* 3.29.58 (test. 10), Aulus Gellius, *Attic Nights* 19.9.3–4 (test. 53), Plutarch, *Sympotic Questions* 622c.

[52] Black-figure *kalpis*, name vase of the Sappho Painter (Warsaw, National Museum, inv. 142333 = *BAPD* §510; 510–500, Plate 4), red-figure *kalathos-kratêr* attributed to the Brygos Painter (Munich, Staatliche Antikensammlungen, inv. 2416 = *BAPD* §204129; 480–470, on which see Rösler p. 65, Ferrari pp. 108–9, Battezzato p. 131), red-figure *kalyx-kratêr* attributed to the Tithonus Painter (Ruhr-University Bochum, Kunstsammlungen, inv. S 508 = *BAPD* §4979; 480–470, Plates 5–6), red-figure *hydria* in Athens attributed to the Group of Polygnotus (National Archaeological Museum, inv. 1260 = *BAPD* §213777; 440–430, Plate 7), red-figure *hydria* in the manner of the Niobid Painter (*BAPD* §11020; *c.*440).

[53] Stehle Stigers 1981 = H. Foley 1981: 45–61, Stehle 1997: 262–318, Yatromanolakis 2009: 214–26, Lidov 2016, Bierl 2016a, 2016b, Nagy 2016, Martin 2016, E. Bowie 2016a.

[54] Diphilus fr. 71 *PCG* (test. 8), *Suda* c 107 (test. 2) and η 521, [Dio of Prusa], *Oration* 64.2 (almost certainly by Favorinus).

later chronographical speculations.[55] Some story-level synchronisations can be wildly off the mark – for example, the link between Rhodopis (and therefore Sappho) and the Pharaoh Mycerinus (Menkaure) (*c.*2530–2500 BC), which Herodotus argues against (2.134).

Chronographical synchronisms correlate Sappho either with the Lydian king Croesus and the Pharaoh Amasis, or with Croesus' father Alyattes and Pharaoh Psammetichus II. The first set goes back to Herodotus: Rhodopis was freed by Sappho's brother Charaxus, which makes those three synchronous. Herodotus maintains that Rhodopis lived at the time of Amasis, adding him to the synchronism. Amasis, in turn, was a contemporary of Croesus. The latter received the Seven Sages as guests, among them Pittacus the tyrant of Lesbos who, in turn, was regularly synchronised with his fellow islanders Sappho and Alcaeus.[56] The *Suda*'s calculations lead to Croesus' time as well: it synchronises Aesop, Rhodopis, and Sappho, and on the other hand Aesop and Croesus, thus placing Sappho in the time of Croesus.[57] Rhodopis is not important enough to be mentioned in Eusebius' *Chronicle*; he clusters all the relevant figures in Sappho's chronographical accounts – Pittacus, Aesop, Psammetichus – into the reign of Alyattes (619–560), thus making her a generation older than suggested by Herodotus.[58] The modern dates for Alyattes and Croesus (595–*c.*546) thus place Sappho in the first part of the sixth century.

Conclusion

Since practically all sources are unreliable, we cannot determine if anything in the tradition reflects the life of the historical Sappho. However, it is a wonderfully rich and quirky tradition in its own right, with many variant stories and colourful details. It also conforms with the biographical story pattern for poets: Sappho is presented as a clever poet who had pupils, invented musical instruments, modes, and metres, was sent to exile, was associated with other famous people, and died under unusual circumstances – all common elements in poets' biographies. At the same time, some typical elements are missing. The most surprising omission is

---

[55] Kivilo 2010: 195–8.
[56] Strabo 13.2.3 (test. 7, Alcaeus test. 1), *Suda* c 107 (test. 2). Herodotus synchronises Sappho with Amasis (2.134.2 = test. 9), Amasis with Croesus (1.30.1, 77), and Croesus with Pittacus (1.27.2).
[57] *Suda* ρ 211, μ 116.
[58] For Eusebius on Sappho, see Mosshammer 1979: 246–54.

her initiation into song. Considering how prominent Aphrodite is in her poetry and how regularly Sappho was associated with the Muses, we would expect such a story to emerge quite early. Could it simply be lost? Some elements appear to be modified to suit her being a woman who sang of love: several men were represented as her lovers and her death was a consequence of unrequited love. The absence of travel stories may, as we have seen, reflect the relatively guarded position of women in ancient society. There are also no records of famous and important ancestors, although her father's name may suggest links with the nobility of the Troad. The latter may also indicate the high standing her family was believed to have in society, just like the detail that she married a very rich man, and that her brother Larichus was a cup-bearer in Mytilene's town hall. This may explain why ancient authors did not present Sappho as poor, which is sometimes the fate of other early poets. Her tradition also lacks a grave, probably reflecting an early manifestation of the leap from Leucas.

Many details in Sappho's ancient biography were already formed by the first part of the fifth century. Herodotus knows that she came from Mytilene and reports the names of her father and brother, the love story between her brother Charaxus and the courtesan Rhodopis, and a set of synchronisms that place Sappho in the time of Croesus. Her beauty and reputation as a heartbreaker may have been known by the beginning of the classical period as well. Other details were added one by one throughout antiquity, and are still being added and expanded by modern scholars, proving the enduring attraction of Sappho of Lesbos.

Further Reading

Lefkowitz 2012 (a revision of Lefkowitz 1981) provides a good overview of ancient poets' life traditions and explains the different ways in which ancient authors constructed biographies by using mythological patterns. Snyder 1989 discusses not only ancient but also Renaissance and later reception of Sappho; Kivilo 2010 examines the narrative patterns in biographical traditions of six archaic poets, including Sappho.

CHAPTER 2

Sappho's Lesbos

Rosalind Thomas*

The most recently discovered poem of Sappho, the Brothers Poem, opens with the image of chattering or gossip about Charaxus returning with a full ship, and ends with the hope that Larichus will grow into a man.[1] It thus propels us more overtly than most of Sappho's surviving fragments to consider the wider sociopolitical and economic world to which she glancingly refers. The women of an elite Greek family would be highly dependent on the status and success of their surrounding male relatives, and the anxiety or impatience of a sister concerning brothers not quite achieving the distinction they might would have added poignancy if the family's financial state was perilous (as in other eras too: we might also consider the Brontë sisters and their brother). What ship? What cargo? And what is she referring to, however vaguely, about the younger brother's role at home in Mytilene? A discussion of Sappho's Lesbos will involve the relations of the island, especially of Mytilene, with several parts of the eastern Mediterranean, and some consideration of the non-literary culture of Lesbos. In this wider picture it becomes most understandable that Sappho's family was engaged like many other Mytileneans in perilous, risky, and potentially profitable enterprises far beyond the shores of Lesbos. The storms of the Brothers Poem can be both real (the stormy risks of maritime enterprise) and metaphorical.

Geographical Situation and Cultural Identity

Like any Greek island, Lesbos is dominated by the sea. With its enclosed fan-like form and two inlets around which the land curves, it has an extremely long coastline relative to its area. All the six city-states of the archaic period were on the coast or very close, Arisbe and Pyrrha lying on

---

* I would like to thank most warmly Nigel Spencer, Hector Williams, and Gary Schaus for their guidance on the archaeological material; and André Lardinois and Felix Budelmann.
[1] Obbink 2016a.

the inner curve of the larger sheltered inlet. The island fits alongside the coast of Asia Minor in such a way that its obvious points of reference are the Troad and the Asian coastal area futher south. Methymna at the north of the island holds a commanding position looking north to the lower south-west bulge of the Troad (Cape Baba), and behind it to the south and south-west is a coastal plain, and (directly south) the high mountain of Mt Lepetumnos dividing it from the rest of the island. Yet the sea straits were open and visible, the Asian coast six miles away. The larger city, Mytilene, also lies close to the Asian coast and again it is a mere short crossing (as we are all now aware from the refugee crisis). It is located on the south-east side of the island with two harbours: the ample north harbour (and the ancient one) looks towards the narrow sea straits to Asia. The main modern south harbour also curves generously round towards the Asian coast.

It seems no coincidence that the two most powerful and prominent *poleis* of the archaic and classical times were Methymna and Mytilene: both had commanding positions over the sea straits along the Asian coast, and their prosperity must have been connected. Antissa on the north-west coast and Eresus in the west lay on the edge of the barren volcanic part of the island, though Eresus at least had a coastal plain. Methymna and Mytilene, on the other hand, had fertile land and high headlands which were easy to defend. The modern towns and Genoese castles basically lie over the ancient cities. Mytilene in classical times was, moreover, an island consisting of a rocky hill, with a narrow inlet between it and the main body of Lesbos, first bridged in antiquity and then silted up: the archaic town lay on either side of the inlet, but the inlet could act as a moat. There are Geometric remains on the hill, and it would be astonishing if the archaic town had not fortified it (though the Genoese castle now dominates). Bronze Age and Protogeometric remains have been found on the Acropolis, and a shrine to Demeter with hints of archaic architecture.[2] Harbour works of the same period have been found at the north harbour.[3] As for Methymna, beneath the Genoese castro there are signs of archaic Greek walling. Most of the archaic and classical town lies beneath the modern, with an apparent gap between Bronze Age and Geometric; short sections of fine Lesbian polygonal masonry (below, pp. 25–6) have emerged in rescue digs, indicating serious monumental

---

[2] C. Williams and H. Williams 1991: 176–9, H. Williams 1995, Spencer 1995a: 280, 299. The problem is that excavations reach bedrock rapidly, and it would seem that archaic buildings were swept away for later building: Schaus 1992: 356.

[3] With polygonal walls: C. Williams and H. Williams 1991: 179–81, Spencer 1995a: 296 with n. 171.

shoring up. It is inconceivable that Methymna did not also fortify itself seriously.

Mytilene and Methymna were separated from each other by upland forests, an extensive plain, the plain of Kalloni, and Mt Lepetumnos. Though it may seem surprising for Lesbos to support two such *poleis*, which often went their separate ways, the geographical layout helps explain this: they both looked out towards the sea, and the maritime world was essential.[4] The coast of Asia Minor was close and immediate, Troy far closer than Sparta, Corinth, and Athens; Lesbians were Trojan allies in the Homeric epic.[5] Alcaeus' use of the ship of state and storm metaphors would have had a natural and vivid force to his archaic hearers.[6]

The six *poleis* on the island were reduced to five when Methymna captured and destroyed Arisbe, the town in the centre, and enslaved the Arisbians (Herodotus 1.151.2). This presumably gave Methymna a huge territory like Mytilene, leaving the other *poleis* on their narrow coastal plains looking also towards the sea. There was, nevertheless, some common Lesbian identity. The shrine at Messon (now Mesa) is right in the centre of the island, situated on the fertile plain of Kalloni near the larger gulf and near wetlands (at least now), a tranquil place with ruins of the fourth-century Ionic temple within a larger *temenos* (sanctuary). The smaller archaic structure underneath has been partially found, and Alcaeus' verses mention it as the common sanctuary of the 'Lesbians', thus clearly encapsulating a shared cult:[7]

> the Lesbians established this great conspicuous precinct to be held in common, and put in it altars of the blessed immortals, and they entitled (κἀπωνύμασσαν) Zeus God of Suppliants and you, the Aeolian, Glorious Goddess, Mother of all, and this third they named Kemelios, Dionysus, eater of raw flesh. (Alcaeus fr. 129.1–8 (transl. Campbell))

The trio of deities is not only highly unusual, it is unique. Not yet explained, it may be the result of some amalgam of Greek and pre-Greek deities. At any rate, there is now little doubt that the 'Aeolian goddess' is Hera,[8] and the epithet shows her particular significance for the Aeolian portion of inhabitants, the Aeolian-speaking Greeks who had supposedly come to the island led by the Penthelids. Whatever the tangled situation

---

[4] Bresson 1983 = 2000: 101–8 stresses the trading base of this society.
[5] *Iliad* 9.128–30, 270–2, 663–5.
[6] Frr. 6, 208, 249.
[7] Robert 1960: 292–4, 300–15 = 1969: 808–10, 816–31 (he notes that it was also associated with a female beauty contest: Alcaeus fr. 130B), Caciagli 2010.
[8] Pirenne-Delforge and Pironti 2014.

on the ground – far more complex, we may be sure, than any colonisation myth – it is significant that the goddess was identified so early by this explicitly ethnic epithet. Hera is a protector of those at sea in the Brothers Poem (above), and the privileging of this deity in Sappho's prayers is not surprising, for Hera helped with seafaring elsewhere too.[9] Pirenne-Delforge has pointed out the remarkable dominance of Hera in later fourth-century Mytilene, so much so that Zeus was called *Heraios* ('of Hera').[10] A final point to make is that Alcaeus called the sanctuary 'conspicuous' (εὔδειλον, fr. 129.2). This common shrine was on the edges of the territory of the main *poleis*, a neutral place where they could meet in peace. The double loop of the island's two main wings makes it doubly significant as the middle, and its origin with the sons of Atreus returning from Troy, in the new text of Sappho fr. 17, gave it deep antiquity.

Nevertheless, we must wonder about the depth of Aeolian or even Greek identity and cultural habits. The island was settled and ruled by Makar in Homer (*Iliad* 24.544), an evidently non-Greek founder, and this was remembered and repeated in later island histories,[11] so the island sported two parallel foundation myths – first Makar, then the later Penthelids, who were supposedly the Aeolian newcomers, descended from Orestes. Did the island have a thick veneer of Greek-speakers alongside or mixed with non-Greeks? The archaeological remains can take us a great deal further and are essential for any deeper understanding of the society of archaic Lesbos, though we are not helped by the modern national divisions which separate the island from its nearest neighbour. In many respects Lesbian material culture shared characteristics with the material culture of the hinterland of western Asia Minor. In some respects, like burial, it shared practices with other eastern Greek cities, but the inhabitants carried on valuing their (rather grim) grey Lesbian pottery which had more affinities with the pottery of Asia Minor. The distinctive polygonal form of 'Lesbian masonry' implied a solid archaism. They never seem to have developed their own painted pottery, as other east Greek cities did. Other Anatolian features, like a fibula with affinities to Phrygian fibulae, seem to look showing the mainland as well as showing a long continuity with the centuries before the archaic period. An archaic cult of Cybele has been found in a curiously oval building in Mytilene,[12] and other hints in cultic architecture suggest an affinity to the

---

[9] Pirenne-Delforge and Pironti 2014: 28, de Polignac 1997; SWIFT pp. 208–11.

[10] It is still not clear what Dionysus is doing in this triad: see Pirenne-Delforge and Pironti 2014.

[11] E.g. the local historian Myrsilus (third century BC), who may also mention Dionysus Ômêstês, 'eater of raw flesh' (*BNJ* 477 F 18: Kaldellis 2018).

[12] Spencer 1995a: 296–9.

non-Greek areas of western Anatolia. The *thesmophorion* (shrine to Demeter and Kore) on Mytilene's acropolis seems shared with Cybele, the 'mother' goddess of Asia Minor.[13] In a groundbreaking article examining these phenomena, Spencer even went to far as to call Lesbos 'an island which in some respects is noticeably un-Greek in the Bronze Age and the early historical periods'; the literary evidence shows a side of life which 'one would hardly have believed existed at all if . . . one was making a judgement from the material record alone'.[14]

There are several non-Greek place names on the island (spelled with –*mn*–), and the close similarity of the name 'Myrsilus', the man repeatedly castigated by Alcaeus, to the Luwian and Neo-Hittite 'Myrsilis' (the name of a fourteenth-century Hittite king) seems to hint at some common culture of western Anatolia. As Herodotus states (oddly), the Lydian king Candaules 'was called Myrsilus by the Greeks' (1.7.2). An attractive recent suggestion is that 'Myrsilus' came to denote a 'throne name' as a relic of the Luwian substratum, and that when Alcaeus fr. 383 referred to a *myrsileion*, this was a building which was therefore a ruler's dwelling.[15] The early connotation of this name, however, should not be overblown: Myrsilus in Alcaeus repeatedly appears as an individual with this name, shared with a later Lesbian historian, and *myrsileion* is the result of an uncertain emendation.

The pre- and un-Greek elements are there, especially in the fabric of ordinary life and cult, and yet so is the extremely lively Greek culture, for this is an island which produced a large number of writers of Panhellenic stature in addition to Alcaeus and Sappho – Terpander, Lesches of Pyrrha or Mytilene who wrote the *Little Iliad*, Arion, Hellanicus, Theophrastus, Phaenias of Eresus. The cultured levels of society in Lesbos, particularly Mytilene, belonged recognisably to a sophisticated archaic Greek culture, while some of the fabric of ordinary life perhaps remained conservative and linked to its pre-Greek antecedents. This brings us to further contacts with areas of the Near East in the archaic period.

Overseas Contacts and Influences

Though much of our information derives from Alcaeus, the archaeological material and other sources like Herodotus and later writers help build up a picture of Lesbian, and particularly Mytilenean, expansion. Some of

[13] C. Williams and H. Williams 1991: 176–9.
[14] Spencer 1995a: 271, 305.
[15] Dale 2011b.

the testimony of Strabo or Aristotle may ultimately derive from Alcaeus, but what that means is that Alcaeus mentioned much in passing that had a bearing on Mytilenean activities. Thus, on the purely ceramic front, Lesbian grey-ware amphorae have been found in many far-flung locations from the Black Sea to Egypt, especially in the sixth century.[16] A Lesbian presence in Egypt is shown via the pottery,[17] and when Naucratis was more formally established after a less regulated Greek presence in Egypt, most of the cities from the east coast of the Aegean were represented there (Phocaea, Clazomenae, Chios, Teos, Samos, Miletus, Cnidus, Halicarnassus, Rhodes, Phaselis, and Aegina from further west). Amongst them was Mytilene, the only Aeolian city Herodotus mentions pointedly amidst so many Ionian and Dorian cities (2.178.2). So the story in Herodotus about the courtesan Rhodopis, bought her freedom at huge expense by Sappho's brother, may be mere sensational gossip, and the association with a small pyramid exotic fantasy,[18] but Mytilenean traders in Naucratis were a fact. Charaxus' activity probably focused first on tak-ing Lesbian wine there, as Strabo says (17.1.33 = fr. 202); and he would hardly bring back an empty ship with so many Egyptian luxuries on offer. There were 30,000 Greek and Carian mercenaries in Egypt serving under Apries (Herodotus 2.163.1). Charaxus would have been one of many Greeks, and we know of him only because he was Sappho's brother. Ex-mercenaries and other officials could make their fortune by serving the Pharaoh, as we learn from Pedon of Priene, rewarded by Psammetichus I and boasting of it on his statue.[19]

Perhaps just as significant were the ambitions of Mytilene on the Asian mainland opposite, where she gradually established a *peraia*, a series of mainland possessions, right up to the Hellespont near Sigeum. She had interests at Aenus in Thrace (hence Alcaeus fr. 45). Considering how little we know about archaic political developments in Lesbos, it is striking that the sources are relatively detailed on Mytilene's ambitions to take Sigeum, held by the Athenians. Mytileneans were established at Achilleum and attempted to seize Sigeum. As Herodotus has it, this was the battle in which Alcaeus lost his shield and wrote a poem about it (5.95 = Alcaeus fr. 428(b)). He adds that the arms were displayed in the temple of Athena at Sigeum itself, so we cannot quite dismiss this poem

[16] See the map at Spencer 2000: 77; add now Methone, in Northern Greece, c.700.
[17] Möller 2000 on Naukratis; also Villing and Schlotzhauer 2006.
[18] Coo pp. 263–6.
[19] Boardman 1999: 280–1, Şahin 1987; also Kaplan 2003, Luraghi 2006.

as simply generic play with revolving lyric topoi.[20] But with the help of
Plutarch, who saw this as a sign of Herodotus' malice, we learn that there
was also a famous conflict involving a bet between the Athenian leader
Phrynon and Pittacus of Mytilene, *aisymnêtês* or elected lawgiver (*On the
Malice of Herodotus* 858ab; pp. 33–4 below); in Plutarch, Pittacus killed
Phrynon, an Olympic victor, and was given land as a reward.[21] Strabo has
yet more details: Pittacus fought with a net, dagger, and trident and
killed Phrynon (13.1.38). It is likely that at least some of this cropped up
in Alcaeus, since he does mention Phrynon (fr. 167.17).[22] Some of this
may also have been retold by the main local historian of Lesbos, Myrsilus
of Methymna (*FGrHist* ~ *BNJ* 477), who was Strabo's source for the
foundation of Assos, and presumably for other possessions on the west-
ern Anatolian coast.

Setting aside the unusual details of this single-combat story, let us also
consider the implications of Mytilene, led by Pittacus, attempting to take
the strategically useful Sigeum on the south side of the Hellespont. The
relative dating is unclear, since the conflict continued in the sixth century
with the involvement of the Athenian Pisistratids, as Herodotus made
clear, and was eventually settled by the tyrant of Corinth, Periander
(5.94–5); but this episode is fixed chronologically by Alcaeus' and
Pittacus' presence. The conflict must have involved considerable commit-
ment and expense on the part of the Mytilenean elite, and most signifi-
cant of all, a clear eye to a useful position on the way to the Propontis
and Black Sea. It fits with the general acquisition of possessions on the
Troad and further south. Alcaeus also mentioned fighting between
Mytileneans and Erythrae, the Ionian city on the Asian coast just south
of south-east Lesbos: according to a scholiast to Nicander, Alcaeus says
that in the war against the Erythraeans, Apollo appeared to
Archeanactides and his companions in their sleep holding a tamarisk
branch (fr. 444). We know nothing more of this, but the tiny incident,
however fanciful, hints at a plausible background of military energy and
conflict outside the island.

From this evidence, Mytilene *c.*600 in the time of Alcaeus and Pittacus
was not only engulfed by periodic political struggles, but also attempted
ambitious overseas expansion and enterprise, and the two may not be
unconnected. Indeed, the evidence shows that Mytilene was considerably

---

[20] Herodotus is followed by Strabo 13.1.38 (= Alcaeus fr. 428(a)).
[21] According to Diodorus Siculus 9.12.1 he refused it.
[22] Page 1955: 159–61.

more outgoing and oriented towards the world beyond the island than the other cities of Lesbos; energy went into this rather than monumental building and display.[23] Archaic Lesbos hovered on the edge of the great Near Eastern kingdoms, looking towards them for help, livelihood, and cultural inspiration. Of these, Lydia was the closest. With its centre at Sardis, inland from Ephesus, it was a brooding or benign presence throughout much of the western part of Asia Minor. We do not know exactly how far and how deep Lydian dominance reached up to the Troad (much of which Mytilene also wanted), but Lydia's sphere of influence extended up to the Aeolian cities. Gyges had attacked Miletus and Smyrna (Herodotus 1.14.4); and Croesus subdued all Ionian and Aeolian cities on the mainland and eventually made a treaty with the islands, at least the Ionian ones (1.26–7). The archaeological affinities between Lesbos and the Anatolian hinterland hint at more interaction. At any rate, a surprisingly exact fragment of Alcaeus claims:

> Father Zeus, the Lydians, indignant at the turn of events, gave us two thousand staters in the hope that we could enter the holy city, although they had never received any benefit from us and did not know us; but he, with the cunning of a fox, predicted an easy outcome and thought we would not notice him. (Alcaeus fr. 69 (transl. Campbell))

The 'holy city' (a restoration of ἴρ[ ] | ἐc πόλιν, 3–4) is most probably Mytilene itself;[24] 'he' is Pittacus. The Lydians, then, seem to have engaged in financial enticements and entanglements on the edge of the Mytilenean internal struggles, perhaps inserting targeted funds to help the favoured side win. No wonder the set of anecdotes about the sages, Solon and Pittacus, gives them episodes where they resist the wealth of Croesus.[25]

Lydia must also have been a focus of admiration and a source of influence for its products and way of life, being by far the most sophisticated culture in western Asia Minor. There are hints in Sappho, who mentions a fine piece of Lydian leather sandal (fr. 39), and employed the beauty of Lydian women as a point of comparison (fr. 96). The Lydian cavalry and infantry are compared unfavourably to the sight of a loved one in fr. 16, where obviously the item of comparison would elicit general admiration

---

[23] Spencer 2000.
[24] Page 1955: 226–32.
[25] Solon in Herodotus 1.29.1–34.1; Pittacus in Diodorus Siculus 9.12.2, Diogenes Laertius 1.81. The traditions about the Seven Sages go back into the archaic period, but are much elaborated later: see Martin 1993.

and pleasure. A similar contrast occurs in fr. 132, where 'taking all of Lydia' is presumed to be highly desirable for most people, but not in the particular female world of Sappho's values.[26]

Were there links with the other Near Eastern kingdoms? We have mentioned Egypt, with the Greek camps at Daphne and elsewhere in the Delta, and the Egyptian Pharoah's desire for Greek mercenaries from the time of Psammetichus I. However, there are two tantalising fragments of Alcaeus which suggest that his brother Antimenidas was active on the Levantine coast at Askelon, just north of Gaza, and fighting, moreover, for the Babylonians in most interpretations. Fr. 350 consists of a couple of lines of verse from Alcaeus, and then a remark of Strabo which paraphrases something Alcaeus said:

> You have come from the ends of the earth with the hilt of your sword ivory bound with gold. (transl. Campbell)

Then, completely separately, but suggestively inserted under the same fragment number, is a section of Strabo (13.2.3 = Alcaeus test. 1):

> Mytilene produced famous men; in ancient times Pittacus, one of the Seven Sages, and the poet Alcaeus and his brother Antimenidas, who, as Alcaeus says, performed a great feat when he was fighting with the Babylonians (Βαβυλωνίοις cυμμαχοῦντα) and rescued them from trouble by killing a warrior who, as he says, was only one palm's breadth short of five royal cubits. (transl. Campbell, adapted)

Editions add verses 'reconstituted' from this short passage of Strabo, but note that they are entirely modern suggestions. Strabo was clearly paraphrasing Alcaeus (ὅν φηcιν, ὥc φηcι), but how loosely, and was he absolutely right about the whole context of this claim about a mighty single combat?

It would be tempting to see this as secure evidence for Alcaeus' brother fighting either as an ally or a mercenary ('ally' might be the diplomatic word for the latter) for the Babylonians, specifically on Nebuchadnezzar's campaign in 604 against Askelon.[27] The name of that city and the phrase 'from holy Babylon' appear in an exceedingly fragmentary scrap of papyrus which is too slight to see more than isolated words, including 'Hades', 'the sea', 'destruction', 'wreaths' – clearly not a peaceful context

---

[26] Page 1955: 226–33, especially 229–30 on Lydian contacts. There are hints in Alcaeus too, depending on the identity of the 'Allienoi', e.g. testt. 9(b), 9(c), with Campbell's note (p. 215). American excavations at Sardis now reveal massive structures: see Cahill's annual reports in the *American Journal of Archaeology* (especially 2011) and sardisexpedition.org.

[27] Raaflaub 2016: 136–7, though his 'spent some time in Mesopotamia' (137) goes too far.

(fr. 48). Page was more cautious, pointing out with the help of *Kings* II 24–5 that there were a series of conflicts along the southern half of the Levantine coast which might apply.[28] Nebuchadnezzar does not appear in any ancient source and is a purely modern conjecture; moreover, this would be the only evidence of Greek mercenaries fighting for the Neo-Babylonians, who tended to use subject peoples in their army.[29] However, their onslaught on Judaea and the coast is well attested.

As we can see even in the more numerous *stasis* (civic strife) poems of Alcaeus, his style does not spell things out in such a way as to explain to those who did not already know.[30] It is possible that Strabo and his sources read something into a poem or mistook a reference and ended up placing Antimenidas on the wrong side. There are other options, recently suggested by Fantalkin and Lytle, who note that Greek mercenaries served in the Egyptian army of the Saite dynasty and that some were probably stationed at Askelon in 604 when it was attacked by the Babylonians.[31] This lets Askelon back in as part of Alcaeus' brother's sojourn in foreign parts, or as a more generic element of an elite Mytilenean's world view. Askelon was under Egyptian control for some years before 604,[32] and so there is nothing implausible about Greek mercenaries being drawn into confict along the southern part of the Levantine coast.

The question can be reduced to whether we can rely on Strabo's rough paraphrase; and how might Askelon and Babylon have entered a fragment of Alcaeus which seems to have a warlike context? On the first question, Strabo is knowledgeable about Lesbos. He devoted a large section to the island, claiming that it was 'very worthy of account' (λόγου ἀξία πλείστου, 13.2.1), and the geographical surroundings are detailed. The paragraph on famous Lesbians did mention Pittacus, as well as the poets Alcaeus and Sappho (who received the hightest praise of all), and Alcaeus' brother is inserted as if he too was prominent. He talks about the several tyrants at that time, brought on by 'acts of sedition' (διχοστασίαι) and about whom Alcaeus wrote his 'poems of *stasis*, as they are called' (τὰ στασιωτικὰ καλούμενα τοῦ Ἀλκαίου ποιήματα, 13.2.3 = Alcaeus test. 1). He gives further details about Myrsilus, Melanchrus, the Cleanactids, and Pittacus, before moving on to other famous Lesbians,

---

[28] Page 1955: 223–4.
[29] Fantalkin and Lytle 2016: 96–7 with n. 31.
[30] E.g. frr. 69, 70, 72, 75, 112, 129, 130B, 208.
[31] Fantalkin and Lytle 2016: 102.
[32] Fantalkin and Lytle 2016: 104 with n. 64.

such as Theophrastus, Phaenias, Terpander, Hellanicus, and 'Callias who interpreted Sappho and Alcaeus' (13.2.4 = test. 41; cf. fr. 214B.11–15). It therefore seems hard to believe that he had not read the 'poems of *stasis*' and others, probably with the help of the Callias mentioned. Our knowledge of Mytilenean archaic politics is notoriously reliant on Alcaeus; he was the quick way into Lesbos' history. The simplest solution is to think that Strabo read the poems, probably with the help of commentators, and not just a biography of Alcaeus. He knew a poem about the brother Antimenidas and his supposed giant-slaying, and he was citing Alcaeus; but he may have mistaken the precise relationship of the Babylonians in the context.[33] The members of Mytilene's elite could be found serving abroad for other powers.

The possible fluidity and abstraction of the lyric 'I' is always a problem for literal interpretation; it cannot necessarily be translated literally into truthful biographical detail. But references to the Babylonians, or Askelon, or Lydian financial aid point to something more specific than generic topoi. Scholars nowadays emphasise the symposiastic context of Alcaeus' poems and the sociopolitical nature of that institution, and this context fits well with specific references to the activities of members of that circle as well as more loosely generic and imagined moments.[34] Claims to have slain a mighty warrior might equally be part of the semi-Homeric warrior ethos also visible in Alcaeus' evocation of gleaming armour in fr. 140; there we have a strangely old-fashioned medley of items, including a linen corselet which evokes the military garb of Egyptians or Trojans rather than Greek hoplites.[35] The elaborate sword of fr. 350 also evokes other exotic luxuries produced in or exported from the Near East in the late eighth and seventh centuries, which must have been highly prized objects for the aspiring elite of the archaic Greek cities.[36]

One final point: Aristotle stated that the Mytileneans elected Pittacus to supreme power 'to deal with the exiles who were led by Antimenidas and Alcaeus the poet' (*Politics* 1285a35–7). It is interesting that Aristotle – who had access to more of Alcaeus than we do, and whose school almost certainly wrote a *politeia* (constitution) of Mytilene – mentions Antimenidas as well as Alcaeus as a political exile and (no doubt) aristocratic agitator. Antimenidas was prominent along with Alcaeus either

---

[33] Cf. Fantalkin and Lytle 2016: 106 for other possible scenarios.
[34] Cazzato 2016.
[35] Page 1955: 209–23, with 215–16 on linen.
[36] Fantalkin and Lytle 2016: 105 even suggest it was a Saite gift in return for service.

before or after he had been in the Near East.[37] One suspects that if service in Egypt or the Levant could offer huge rewards as well as risks to Greeks who ventured there, those who returned might come back with destabilising wealth and honours.

Politics on Lesbos

Finally, we turn to the political situation within Lesbos. We can assume conflict between the different cities and jostling for the best land; Arisbe in central Lesbos was destroyed altogether. The large number of archaic towers in Lesbos cluster on the edge of the fertile land of the cities on the north of the island. They must be defensive as well as serving perhaps some symbolic and status-driven function.[38]

For Mytilene itself we are heavily dependent on the one-sided and often vitriolic poems of Alcaeus.[39] He was a member of the old aristocracy (or so he claimed) which traced itself back to the Penthelids claiming descent from Orestes, and they were regarded as leading the Greek settlers of Lesbos. There were clearly a series of tyrants and different configurations of alliances between factions. Pittacus in alliance with Alcaeus had expelled Myrsilus, then turned against Alcaeus. Pittacus himself, whom Alcaeus abused as being of low birth, may have had a Thracian father (Duris, *FGrHist* 76 F 75); if so, we would be seeing another sign of the wide links that Mytilene had with nearby areas. In any case, Pittacus was also accused of having married into the 'Atridae', that is, the Penthelids, the leading clan of Mytilene – 'let *him*, married into the family of the Atridae, devour the city as he did with Myrsilus' (fr. 70.6–7) – and this indicates a degree of social mobility and the same undermining of the ruling aristocracies' supposedly firm security that occurs all over the archaic Greek world as horizons and economies changed. Alcaeus' alternating expressions of regret, self-pity, and vitriol against Pittacus who, he admits, was elected *aisymnêtês* (p. 34 below) 'by the people', may in part be the frustration of an individual and a group whose status was being overshadowed by new opportunities for wealth and influence in a changing society. We should not forget, however, that Pittacus was remembered and then celebrated in the later traditions as one of the Seven Sages of archaic Greece (TT35.5, 37 La–M). For this we are at least not dependent on fragments of Alcaeus, though the poet offers some of

---

[37] Antimenidas is also mentioned in a commentary on papyrus, Alcaeus test. 9.
[38] See Spencer 2000, with the map at p. 69 for the towers, and Mason 2001 for Lesbian masonry.
[39] Page 1955: 149–243.

the most vivid and direct expressions belonging to actual contemporaries. While there was certainly later embroidery in the traditions of the Seven Sages, they were based on an archaic core of memories and traditions, perhaps even some sayings which would be more likely to be remembered. Pittacus was attributed with wise and sensible advice, much preserved in Diogenes Laertius (1.74–81) and Diodorus Siculus. According to Diodorus, he was asked by Croesus what was the best form of government he had seen, and he replied 'that of painted wood' – meaning the laws (9.27.4). He wrote laws but not a whole constitution, as Aristotle noted (*Politics* 1274b17–18). It is disappointing that there is virtually no epigraphic record from archaic Mytilene, and no trace of any of these laws; perhaps they were erected on perishable material.

Pittacus was, at any rate, chosen by the *dêmos*, the city, as *aisymnêtês*, apparently to resolve the problem of *stasis*.[40] This was a special high office with massive powers; the office holder was a kind of lawgiver who could turn into an authoritarian tyrant if he refused to stand down. Alcaeus called him 'tyrant' (fr. 348, cited by Aristotle), but this seems to be abuse from the party likely to lose most from the arrangement. The best way of understanding this situation is to see it as aristocratic infighting, and rivalry and alliances with other groups which might sometimes include the groups on the edge of the established aristocracy, all responding to demands for power within the developing city-state. This is characteristic of a time of rapid economic change which brought in its wake social and political pressures. As elsewhere in archaic Greece, we may assume that Mytilene was gradually shifting to become a 'state', a more ordered *polis* run on rules and with offices which were distinguishable from the calls of birth and charisma. We hear of the Penthelids, the Atridae (the same), the Cleanactids – all aristocratic families.[41] But then relative newcovers like Pittacus managed to marry into the circle, and his election was typical of a community in the process of state-formation: a formal high office was often created in time of political strife, like Solon's position as lawgiver, which could be abused and which enemies could claim was a tyranny. But even Alcaeus admits that the *dêmos* chose 'low-born' Pittacus (fr. 348), and he reveals reluctantly that there was an active (if small) citizen body which was beginning to demand more political influence in the *polis*.

---

[40] Aristotle, *Politics* 1285a29–40 with Diodorus Siculus 9.11–12, and below for Alcaeus' evidence.
[41] For the Cleanactids (to which Myrsilus belonged), see Sappho fr. 98(b).7, Alcaeus fr. 112.23, 306(a).13.

I have stressed the overseas activities of Mytilene as a *polis* and of Mytileneans as individuals, because they form an essential background to the factional strife; indeed, they were probably an important factor in the shifting social and economic changes. Though we do not know where Sappho's family stood in the factional fighting of Mytilene, such factional background must have been part of Sappho's Lesbos. The effects of *stasis* could be dramatic, leading to loss of land and exile, as Alcaeus lamented (fr. 130B), and to political instability. Moreover, while we can compare Mytilene with other cities of archaic Greece, Lesbos had its own character, and its proximity to the economic and political currents of Lydia and Phrygia deserves emphasis. The archaeological record suggests an island noticeably different from mainland Greece, or Samos or Miletus to the south, in its conservatism and links to the Anatolian hinterland. At the same time, Mytilene, led by its quarrelling elite families, had acquired overseas territory and was prepared to fight hard to protect it; its citizens, including the aristocracy, looked to Egypt and beyond. There are frustrating hints of Greek and non-Greek deities mixed together, and (on current evidence) a preponderance of prominent female deities. Thus, we do not really know what was lyric convention or non-convention for a high-born woman poet of Mytilene in *c.*600, let alone social convention. Archaeologists have not found a significant archaic town to match the song culture. What we do know was that the island was closely connected to great poets and musicians: the legendary figures of Terpander, Arion (of Methymna), and Orpheus in addition to the more readily identifiable Alcaeus and Sappho. We cannot fit Lesbos and its archaic society into a straitjacket derived from elsewhere in Greece.

Further Reading

For a compendium of sites and archaeological information, Spencer 1995c is essential; for Methymna, see Buchholz 1975. For the rural landscape of Lesbos, especially the towers, note also Spencer 1995b. For the relationship between the festival at Messon and Sappho fr. 17, see Caciagli 2016; and, for Lesbos as part of a cohesive, interlocking region within the Troad, Ellis-Evans 2019.

CHAPTER 3

Sappho and Sexuality

Melissa Mueller[*]

Few readers today would deny that Sappho's lyrics are intensely homoe-
rotic, yet there is little agreement on what, if anything, this tells us about
Sappho herself. In one camp are the radical constructivists, the heirs to
Foucault's legacy, who insist on the historical contingency of sexuality.
For them, 'homosexuality' and 'heterosexuality' are discursive inventions
of the modern world; they are cultural phenomena with no currency in
pre-modern societies. To refer to Sappho (or any of the female figures in
her lyrics) as lesbian is to project on to antiquity a binary opposition –
between hetero- and homosexuality – where none existed.[1] The ancient
Greeks, they claim, did not conceptualise their sexual acts in terms of
their partner's gender, whether this was the same or different from their
own. They were concerned instead with whether they were occupying an
active or passive position relative to their sexual partner, whether that
partner was male or female. In the opposing camp are the essentialists
who, seeking continuities between past and present, argue that even if the
discourse of sexuality had not yet been invented, the reality was there.[2]
Gays and lesbians, they claim, have always existed. Sappho and her con-
temporaries may not have been familiar with the binary axes of sexual
orientation that we use today,[3] but their passions and persuasions were
fundamentally the same as our own.

Naming is of course a political act. By naming, we legitimise and
affirm. We performatively call into being something that may not have
existed prior to its naming.[4] Calling Sappho a lesbian poet has political
ramifications. As a female poet, she has been a torchbearer for

---

[*] I am grateful to the editors and to Mario Telò for their help with this chapter.
[1] For a strong statement of the 'discontinuity' position, see Halperin 1990, Parker 2001.
[2] Davidson 2007.
[3] Although even today these orientations are questioned and malleable: Sedgwick 1990, Ahmed
2006.
[4] Judith Butler 1997.

36

generations of women writers. 'It is in Sappho's broken fragments', writes Ellen Greene, 'that the modern woman poet could reinvent Sappho's verse and thus inscribe feminine desire as part of an empowering literary history of her own'.[5] This is a literary history with numerous erasures. In the words of Susan Gubar, 'Sappho represents . . . all the lost women of genius in literary history, especially all the lesbian artists whose work has been destroyed, sanitized, or heterosexualized'.[6] There is a lot at stake, then, in these naming wars. To deny Sappho's homosexuality, to insist that she is not lesbian, is implicitly to acknowledge the power of that name. It is important, therefore, to be clear from the outset: the question of the poet's sexuality is not one that can be answered through a close reading of her lyrics.[7] Even if we read her lyrics biographically, or as personal poetry (LARDINOIS), what we see will be shaped by the conceptual horizon and theoretical tools which we bring to the page. For the followers of Foucault, the expressions of same-sex desire within Sappho's lyrics will continue to be disparate parcels of sexual experience which do not add up to a lesbian identity, while for others, they will continue to be the 'recovered voice of a long-suppressed lesbian consciousness'.[8]

My goal in this chapter, then, is neither to reaffirm nor to revoke Sappho's lesbianism. After brief general remarks on Sappho and female sexuality, I turn to the lyrics themselves. But rather than reading them as evidence for or against the poet's homosexuality, I instead trace the destabilising, 'queer affect' of Sappho's work:[9] the way that *erôs* as a force and a feeling captured in and created by her poetry eludes classification by inverting hierarchical relationships between self and other, human and environment, active and passive. Boundaries between sexually and intellectually inflected relationships are not always easily demarcated and may be deliberately blurred. In several Sapphic fragments, the defection of a member of Sappho's group to that of another woman inspires iambic rebuke of the sort more commonly associated with the spurned lover.

---

[5] Greene 1996d: 4. For Sappho and early twentieth-century lesbian poets, see Gubar 1984 = Greene 1996b: 199–217, GOFF AND HARLOE. For the contemporary politics of Sappho's lesbianism, see Haselswerdt 2016.

[6] Gubar 1984: 46 = Greene 1996b: 202.

[7] As Most 1995: 31 = Greene 1996b: 32 puts it, perhaps 'the most curious feature of Sappho's literary fortunes has been the contrast between the certainty attaching to the fact of her passion and the uncertainty attaching to the objects of that passion'. In nearly every place in the corpus where we seem to have evidence for the existence of a feminine gendered object of desire, alternative readings have been proposed. See FINGLASS ch. 18 pp. 254–5 on the feminine ἐθέλοιϲα at 1.24 and Most 1995: 28–31 ≈ Greene 1996b: 28–32 on fr. 31.7.

[8] Habinek 1996: xii.

[9] See Chen 2012, especially pp. 57–85 on the semantics and lexicography of the term 'queer'.

Likewise, the speaker of fr. 55 invokes the language of *erôs* to denigrate another woman's poetry, claiming lack of desire (*pothos*) to hear her songs reperformed. *Pothos*, with its sensual resonances, captures the intertwining of *erôs* and immortality, of sexual and poetic fortunes, whereas elsewhere in Sappho (in fr. 94, for example) its semantic remit is more narrowly sexual. It is these overlapping circles of desire that give us a sense of the expansive range of sexuality in Sappho.

Sappho and Female Sexuality

Female sexuality occupies at best a marginal place in the works of Dover and Foucault. Focused as they are on a pederastic and penetrative model of male sexuality, and on the norms governing relations between the *erastês* and *erômenos*, their findings do not map easily on to sexual relations between women.[10] Were sexual acts between women asymmetrical and age-differentiated, the way they were among men? Were women censured for engaging in sex with other women? I begin with the obvious and uncontroversial. Like their male counterparts, women in ancient Greece did not have the freedom to embrace a queer identity. They were expected to marry. Their social lives centred around domestic and ritual activities, including care for their husband, household (*oikos*), and children. These are the familial bonds neglected by Sappho's Helen when, pursuing what she loves, she leaves her husband and remembers neither her parents nor her child (fr. 16.10–11). Helen's object of desire, Paris, happens to be male. But the entire poem serves as a celebration of another woman's beauty – that of Anactoria, whose brightly glowing face and lovely step prompt Sappho to declare these things more valuable than the chariots and foot soldiers of the Lydians.

Sappho's celebration of female beauty and her frank depiction of female desire have led some scholars to argue that in the archaic period, 'female homoeroticism, far from being regarded as different from other erotic emotions, was suited for public art and performances'.[11] Sappho and Alcman both compose lyrics in which women openly express desire for other women, or lament not having their desire reciprocated. Alcman's *partheneia* (maiden songs) were composed in seventh-century Sparta for performance by choruses of maidens (*parthenoi*). Providing a

---

[10] Dover 1978, Foucault 1976–2018 ≈ 1978–86. For the reception of Foucault's *History of Sexuality* within the field of classics, see Holmes 2012: 84–91, Ormand 2018: 16–21. For feminist critiques of Foucault, see Richlin 1991, 1998, Greene 1996e, Holmes 2012: 100–2.
[11] Boehringer 2014: 152 – 156.

public platform for celebrating female beauty, the songs present a glowing portrayal of chorus leaders Agido and Hegesichora, and liken another woman, Astymeloisa, to a star unfolding in the radiant sky (fr. 3 fr. 3 (*sic*) col. ii.64–8 *PMGF*). In the visual sphere, a polychrome plate from Thera (*c.*625) shows two women facing one another, preparing to exchange garlands. One woman touches the chin of the other with her hand, in a 'readily identifiable erotic motif'.[12]

One Sappho fragment (fr. 213) even describes a woman, Archeanassa, as the 'yokemate' or wife – cύνδυγοc – of another woman, Gorgo. The image recurs in a later poem by Theocritus where it describes the homosexual union of two men.[13] In (Pseudo-?)Ovid's *Heroides* 15, Sappho's alleged relationship with Phaon is used to figure homoerotic relationships between men. Sappho has noticeably masculine qualities in this letter, particularly in comparison with the other epistolary heroines.[14] At least in part, the shift in Sappho's sexuality (and perhaps even her gender) has been produced in the process of textual reception. At different periods of the reception tradition different sexual profiles of the poet take centre stage. From female homoeroticism, to heterosexuality, to male homoeroticism: is our very obsession with naming what Sappho is (or was) perhaps 'queerer' than any classification?

Women from Lesbos may have begun to be associated in the cultural imaginary with same-sex sexual practices in the archaic period. Anacreon fr. 358 *PMG* features a male speaker lamenting that 'once again Eros hits me, forcing me to play with the girl with lovely shoes'.[15] He clarifies in the second stanza that she is from well-built Lesbos. Finding fault with him, she instead 'gapes at another person, a girl'. He suggests her being from Lesbos – ἔcτιν γὰρ ἀπ' εὐκτίτου | Λέcβου – motivates her choice of female lover. The verb 'she gapes' (χάcκει) can be understood in a sexual sense; taken together with the object of desire (ἄλλην τινά), also feminine, it affirms the homoerotic dynamic, reinforcing the idea, no doubt popularised by Sappho's lyrics, that women from Lesbos pursue other women.[16]

---

[12] Boehringer 2014: 152 – 156, on Thera Museum, inv. CE 34. See Dover 1978: 173, Rabinowitz 2002: 146–7, Boehringer 2014: 152–3 – 156–7, Hubbard 2014a: 139–40.

[13] Theocritus 30.28–9; thus Acosta-Hughes 2010: 103–4.

[14] Gordon 1997, Hallett 2005, MORGAN pp. 292, 298.

[15] Lardinois 2010: 23 suggests that Anacreon's girl from Lesbos likely reflects the reception of Sappho's poetry, which was 'very popular in this period and, despite its homoerotic content, interpreted as generally erotic'.

[16] Pfeijffer 2000b compellingly demonstrates that the Lesbian girl's preference is for a female; however, the terms *Lesbiades* and *lesbiazein* do not denote same-sex sexual practices (n. 22 below).

Our clearest case of same-sex erotic pursuit comes from Sappho fr. 1. The gender of the love object hinges on a single Greek form (which has been challenged). But the language of pursuit does, as Anne [Giacomelli] Carson has shown, appear to be consonant with that between a male *erastês* and his *erômenos*.[17] Having called on and been aided by Aphrodite in the past, the speaker of this poem, also named 'Sappho', prays again to the goddess of love and consoles herself by repeating the goddess's earlier speech to her. Even if the woman whom Sappho loves does not love her back, one day she will experience a similar sort of pain (1.21–4): 'For if she flees, soon she will pursue; and if she does not receive gifts, she will in turn give them; and if she does not love, soon she will love, even against her will.'

In her reading of these verses, Carson notes that Aphrodite's words omit a grammatical object, thus leaving unspecified to whom the unnamed girl will give gifts, and whom she will pursue, once the tables are turned. Aphrodite's consolation is, in Carson's words, not 'a specific program of revenge tailored to Sappho, but a general theory of lover's justice'.[18] The hope the goddess holds out is based on the principle that time will right all wrongs, that the younger beloved will inevitably become a lover herself, and her flight from passion be experienced as a compulsion eluding her rational capacity to control it: she will love in spite of herself, κωὖκ ἐθέλοισα (1.24). It is also a hope that, as Carson herself acknowledges, seems to allude to the realities of asymmetrical erotic roles – only to turn them on their head.[19] Assuming that women's sexual relationships mirrored the age-differentiated, pederastic pattern often traced for men,[20] the lover, in this case 'Sappho', is nominally in a position of power as the older woman. And yet, with her desire unreciprocated, she is more powerless than ever. She may enjoy the social privileges bestowed by age, but the power of *anangkê* (necessity) – for Greek lovers 'describe their experience as that of being coerced by a force outside oneself' – belongs to the younger woman.[21]

Sappho's poetry has featured prominently in modern discussions of ancient Greek lesbianism, but the name Sappho of Lesbos was not always associated with female homoeroticism. As Boehringer notes, 'the Greek

[17] Giacomelli 1980 = Carson 1996.
[18] Giacomelli 1980: 139 = Carson 1996: 230.
[19] Giacomelli 1980: 137 = Carson 1996: 227–8: 'There are clearly defined ages of life appropriate to the roles of lover and beloved. In the course of time the beloved will naturally and inevitably become a lover, and will almost inevitably experience rejection at least once.'
[20] Hubbard 2014a argues that this aspect of ancient sexuality has been overemphasised.
[21] Giacomelli 1980: 138 = Carson 1996: 229.

word *Lesbiades* designated geographical origin without any association with contemporary female "homosexuals", whereas the verb *lesbiazein* referred to various sexual acts performed with men, usually fellatio'.[22] And indeed, in Attic comedy Sappho was portrayed as aggressively heterosexual.[23] The most famous myth about Sappho in antiquity centred on her erotic obsession with a much younger man, the ferryman Phaon from Lesbos; the story is probably first told by Menander. In Ovid's *Heroides*, Sappho, having been spurned by Phaon, remembers her love affairs on Lesbos with Anactoria, Kydro, Atthis, and 'a hundred other women whom I loved'.[24]

Sexual acts in Greco-Roman antiquity were not classified, as mentioned above (p. 36), in accordance with the gender of one's partner, but rather by the active or passive position one occupied during sexual intercourse. Men sleeping with other men, or with boys or women, had nothing of which to be ashamed as long as they assumed a dominant role. Adult men who preferred the passive position were figured as socially inferior (to the dominant *erastês*) and sexually perverse. Women in a dominant role with other women – or with men – belonged to the special category of *tribades* and were thought of as usurping male social and sexual privilege. They were construed as transgressive, predatory, and lewd.[25]

This cultural bias may be what lies behind the Hellenistic testimony that that some (in antiquity) accused Sappho of being a 'woman-lover' and of leading a 'disorderly' life;[26] it may also have carried over into the *Suda*'s notice that she was slandered for being involved in the wrong kind of friendship.[27] The shameful and basically incomprehensible thing about lesbian affairs for the ancient reader was that they demanded that one woman take on an active role, a role that could only be properly occupied by the phallic male. The tribad was a woman playing at being a man, and in this regard an object of ridicule and scorn; in giving voice to strong erotic feelings in her poetry, Sappho clearly risked being seen as one of these dominant and pseudo-phallic women.

[22] Boehringer 2014: 150 ~ 154; also Gilhuly 2015 ≈ 2018: 92–116.

[23] For Sappho's representation in comedy, see Yatromanolakis 2007: 293–312, Coo pp. 269–75.

[24] (Pseudo-?)Ovid, *Heroides* 15.15–20 (test. 19); FINGLASS AND KELLY pp. 1–3.

[25] For the active–passive distinction as it relates to Sappho, see Parker 1997, Blondell and Ormand 2015a, Orrells 2015: 126–51. These 'real-life' protocols are, however, general tendencies, centred on the Athenian evidence, and derived mostly from literary sources, with all the problems which arise from extrapolating practices from textual constructions.

[26] P.Oxy. 1800 fr. 1 (test. 1).

[27] *Suda* c 107 (test. 2).

Circles of Desire

Nineteenth-century German scholars Friedrich Gottlieb Welcker and Karl Otfried Müller were reacting against a later iteration of this hyper-sexualised Sappho when they cast the poet into the role of 'a friendly spinster teacher at a boarding school'.[28] British scholars likewise contributed to the (re-)construction of a desexualised educator, eager to see the tribad and her lovers replaced by a more wholesome image of the school-teacher surrounded by eager pupils in an educational setting – albeit one that 'will hardly have had certification, course-credits, and graduation ceremonies, like modern [American] high schools or universities'.[29] And so was born the first iteration of Sappho and her circle.

The very idea of a poet's having a circle is a modern one. We have only to think of Percy Bysshe Shelley and his circle of fellow writers, friends, lovers, and readers – including, in Shelley's case, his wife Mary Shelley, and Lord Byron, all three of them major players in nineteenth-century romanticism.[30] But insofar as it designates the group of women surrounding Sappho, many of whose names appear in Sappho's verse, 'circle' derives, in the first instance, from a translation by way of the German of the Greek word *thiasos*. In Greek, *thiasos* typically refers to a cult or band of women involved in some sort of ritual activity; it can be applied, for instance, to the maenads who worship the god Dionysus. Wilamowitz describes Sappho as the leader of precisely such a 'circle' (*Kreis*) of women who came together to sing and celebrate Aphrodite.[31] Sappho herself does not mention a *thiasos* anywhere in her lyrics. Instead, she addresses herself to 'companions' (*hetairai*), and refers to 'children' (*paides*) and 'girls' (*parthenoi*), though nowhere to 'students'.[32]

Ancient witnesses report on Sappho's 'teaching in peace and quiet', while mentioning that girls came not only from Lesbos but from all over Ionia to study with her (fr. 214B). Additionally, the *Suda* names Anactoria (of fr. 16.15) as one of Sappho's pupils.[33] The romanticised view saw Sappho's female 'students' as on the cusp of marriage, even though

---

[28] Parker 1993: 313 ≈ Greene 1996b: 150; Welcker 1816, Müller 1840: 172–80 ≈ 1841: 1 310–25, Orrells 2015: 141–2.

[29] E. Robbins 1995: 229 = 2013: 127.

[30] A concept revised and decentred by B. Johnson 2014.

[31] Wilamowitz 1896 = 1913: 63–78; also Merkelbach 1957 = 1996: 87–114, Calame 1996 ≈ 2001: 210–14, 231–3, 249–52 ≈ 1977: 1 367–72, 400–4, 427–32, Parker 1993 ≈ Greene 1996b: 146–83, and, for Sappho and her community of women's devotion to Aphrodite, Gentili 1984: 120–1 ≈ 1988: 85–6.

[32] Frr. 160.1, 49.2, 30.2; E. Robbins 1995: 227 = 2013: 124–5.

[33] E. Robbins 1995: 228 = 2013: 127.

such a social reality is never explicitly articulated in her lyrics.[34] Apprenticeship is perhaps a better analogy than boarding school for the sort of didactic relationship Sappho is likely to have had with those in her group. Scholars who envision Sappho interacting with female 'trainees' in the role of choreographer or coach often cite as a parallel the relationship between the chorus girls and their leaders in Alcman's *partheneia*.[35]

Desire and longing (*himeros* and *pothos*) are aspirational feelings in Sappho. They occur in contexts both erotic and poetic, where they speak to the desire to be desired – to be remembered and not forgotten. This is demonstrated somewhat ironically in fr. 55 through the speaker's prediction that such an aspiration will *not* be fulfilled. Sappho's addressee here is an 'uncultivated' woman:[36]

> κατθάνοιςα δὲ κείςηι οὐδέ ποτα μναμοςύνα ςέθεν
> ἔςςετ᾽ οὐδὲ πόθα εἰς ὔςτερον· οὐ γὰρ πεδέχηις βρόδων
> τῶν ἐκ Πιερίας, ἀλλ᾽ ἀφάνης κἀν Ἀίδα δόμωι
> φοιτάςηις πεδ᾽ ἀμαύρων νεκύων ἐκπεποταμένα.

> You will lie there when you die, and there will be no memory of you ever, nor desire for you in the future: for you do not have a share of the roses of Pieria. Instead, you will go to and fro among the shadowy corpses, invisible also in the house of Hades, having flown away.

In the first several verses, Sappho asserts that neither memory (μναμοςύνα) nor desire (πόθα) will follow in the wake of this unnamed woman's death.[37] A first reading suggests that the woman's personal friends and family will forget her. But the predicted absence of 'desire' (πόθα) invites us to interpret the entire poem as a reflection on poetic mortality. The reference to the Pierian roses in the following *gar*-clause strengthens this reading. At issue is not so much the woman's network of personal friendships as her failure to cultivate, or to be cultivated by, a poetic Muse: οὐ γὰρ πεδέχηις βρόδων | τῶν ἐκ Πιερίας. She crafts

---

[34] In a rather unconventional reading of fr. 22, Schlesier 2013: 216 finds contrary evidence in the reference to a girl who comes back (*katagôgis*, 'she who returns'), which, Schlesier argues, makes little sense if marriage is the framework for transition and departure.

[35] As E. Robbins 1995: 229 = 2013: 128 remarks, 'Here cult, love, clothes, song, and perhaps even contests, come together in one exquisite amalgam. It would be perverse not to associate all these same things with Aphrodite in Sappho's world.'

[36] Thus Stobaeus, who cites the fragment.

[37] πόθα εἰς ὔςτερον, Bucherer's emendation for transmitted ποκ᾽ ὔςτερον, provides a noun to parallel μναμοςύνα (Wilamowitz 1913: 88 n. 2); for the synizesis cf. fr. 1.11 etc.

uninspired verse, easily forgotten songs. Currently unnamed, she will remain anonymous after her death, going down to Hades 'invisible' (ἀφάνης), where she will flit about among the shades.

There will be no 'remembering' (*mnamosuna*) of the unnamed woman insofar as her poetry will not be sung again, there being little 'desire' (*potha*) for her verses. The not-naming is in this sense a perlocutionary act, one that fulfils its promise by rendering the addressee as unseen to the singer's audience as she will be among the other shades of Hades.[38] And the *kai* in the third line drives home this point, by underlining that the woman will be invisible *also* in Hades. In other words, she is already *aphanês*. Somewhat paradoxically, she is rendered absent and anonymous, even while being sung. More pointedly, she will remain so, 'moving around unseen' – 'movements' that, as André Lardinois points out, 'may be contrasted with the radiant and memorable dancing of Anaktoria or Atthis, evoked in fragments 16 and 96'.[39]

The participle ἐκπεποταμένα ('having flown away') also merits comment, as the same verb is used in fr. 131 of Atthis' 'flight' to Andromeda:

> Ἄτθι, σοὶ δ' ἔμεθεν μὲν ἀπήχθετο
> φροντίσδην, ἐπὶ δ' Ἀνδρομέδαν πότηι

> Atthis, to think of me has grown hateful to you, and you fly away to Andromeda

Hardie and Lardinois read Atthis' departure as a personal betrayal of Sappho.[40] In fr. 55, the denial of *mnamosuna* to a woman who has 'flown from our midst' may conceal a similar narrative – Hardie, certainly, detects a 'vindictive tone' here. But whatever its external motivation happens to be, the denial of memory has poetic repercussions. The case of this anonymous woman serves as a stark reminder that *pothos* is a vital catalyst to reperformance. 'The roses of Pieria' reinforce what is at stake

---

[38] Carson 1997: 223–4 treats the poem itself as a kind of disappearing act and the crasis (*k'an*) in line 3 as a performative, suggesting that Sappho 'has used the syncopating action of crasis to speed up the meaninglessness and to introduce a lurch of hindsight into the reasoning process of her poem'. Approaching the same topos with an aural sensiblity, J. Clay 1993 notes the sound play of 'going, going, gone' in the repetition of –*pot*– in three words: *pota, potha, ekpepotamena*. See also Yatromanolakis 2006.

[39] Lardinois 2008: 87.

[40] A. Hardie 2005: 19–20, Lardinois 2008: 87. See Caciagli 2011: 212–16 for the suggestion that family politics, rather than individual *erôs*, may be the motivational force behind betrayals and changing alliances in Sappho's group.

in remembering (or not).[41] As the birthplace of the Muses, Pieria is a place redolent with the roses of song, the products of poetic craft. When a poet is 'remembered', she is made palpably present through the singing of her songs. And these songs in turn create the longer-term reputation of their author.[42] As we have seen with fr. 55, Sappho claims that the unnamed addressee will be forgotten.

Moreover, the Andromeda to whom Atthis flees in fr. 131 may be the same woman Sappho mocks in another fragment. It is her infatuation with a very unstylish 'country girl' that causes the speaker of fr. 57 to suggest that Andromeda has lost her mind:

> τίc δ' ἀγροΐωτιc θέλγει νόον . . .
> ἀγροΐωτιν ἐπεμμένα cτόλαν . . .
> οὐκ ἐπιcταμένα τὰ βράκε' ἔλκην ἐπὶ τὼν cφύρων;

> Who is this country girl who charms (your?) mind . . .
> dressed in a farm-girl dress . . .
> not knowing how to pull down her rags over her ankles?

Underlying this invective is the speaker's hurt at losing Atthis to Andromeda after (possibly) having lost Andromeda herself. The aspersions cast on the appearance of the other woman are an indirect attack on the questionable tastes of Andromeda (Sappho's rival). Whether the mockery targets Andromeda's sexual proclivities, her poetic style, or both, we have no way of knowing.

Sappho casts a living rival down into the shadows of Hades in fr. 55. In a move that mirrors this one in reverse, she makes the riverbanks of Acheron vibrantly alive in fr. 95.11–13:

> κατθάνην δ' ἴμερόc τιc [ἔχει με καὶ
> λωτίνοιc δροcόενταc [ὄ-
> χ[θ]οιc ἴδην Ἀχέρ[οντοc

> A certain longing seizes me to die, and to see the dewy lotus plants along the banks of Acheron

---

[41] Calame 1996: 119 n. 24 ≈ 2001: 232 n. 93 ≈ 1977: I 402 n. 93 assumes that this phrase must refer to 'Sappho's education', from which the uncultured addressee of fr. 55 has failed to benefit. For Lardinois 2008: 86, these roses 'stand for all of Sappho's poetic activities', a compelling reading. A. Hardie 2005: 18 suggests that the roses are meant to evoke a *stephanos*, such as might have been worn 'as a mark of the bearer's consecration and self-dedication' to various goddesses.

[42] Jarratt 2002: 23–6.

What inspires this desire for death? Is it the loss of a friend? A lover? Unexpectedly, Acheron is conjured as 'a place of life and nurture, with *erotic* overtones'.[43] The dewiness of the lotus plants, which grow lushly on the riverbanks of Acheron, connotes a remarkable fertility. This place of death is queerly animated in Sappho's topsy-turvy world.

In a provocative article, Renate Schlesier suggests that the girls who have traditionally been imagined in the role of pupils studying at Sappho's 'school' may actually be of a lower social class and, like Sappho herself, courtesans or *hetairai*.[44] Schlesier sketches a scenario in which the 'defection' of Atthis and Mika and other females 'might evoke rivalry not between different leaders of schools for adolescent girls, but different coteries of first-class *hetairai*, in control of their own *hetaireia*, not necessarily restricted to females'.[45] She proposes, moreover, the symposium as a likely occasion for the performance of many of Sappho's better-known songs, including fr. 31, which others have suggested might be a wedding hymn.[46] The sympotic context privileges homoerotic relations, for both sexes.[47] Moreoever, argues Schlesier, Sappho respects the convention of not revealing women's names in her wedding songs. When women are named, therefore, it is likely that the verses have been composed for a different occasion (i.e. not a wedding) and that the women themselves are not citizens.

Whether or not we agree that Sappho's poetry 'creates a glorious courtesans' cosmos, mixing pleasures with pains, heroism with baseness', there is something both brash and queerly compelling about Schlesier's idea – and it aligns remarkably well with the early reception history of Sappho's poems. For they were in fact recycled and reperformed at Attic symposia.[48] The ancient reception of Sappho (particularly the attraction that her lyrics held for male symposiasts) is, moreover, a compelling context for exploring the openness of these lyrics to non-heteronormative forms of desire. Any hypothesis about the social and performance context(s) of Sappho has to account for her continuing appeal to men and women of varying sexualities through the ages.

Taking a hint from the later reception history of Sappho, this time in Victorian Britain, we might even argue that the queer quality of the feelings represented enlarges the horizon of readerly expectations, allowing

---

[43] Boedeker 1979: 49.
[44] Schlesier 2013.
[45] Schlesier 2013: 211.
[46] Schlesier 2013: 213.
[47] Schlesier 2013: 215.
[48] Schlesier 2013: 217; for the sympotic reception of Sappho, see Yatromanolakis 2007: 213–20, 259–86, E. Bowie 2016a.

both male and female 'viewers' to project themselves into various sexual roles, as men desiring other men, men desiring women, or women desiring other women. Daniel Orrells has, for example, discussed the case of John Addington Symonds, a nineteenth-century English poet and literary critic, who mined his own homosexual affairs for poetic material.[49] Symonds returned to Sappho fr. 31 several times, first translating it so that the speaker's or poet's voice resembles that of a man who looks on jealously as another male ('equal to the gods') enjoys the sweet laughter of the woman he covets. In his memoirs, however, Symonds 're-fragments' the same poem, turning it into 'a male homoerotic fragment, in which Symonds identifies with the woman and desires the man'.[50] The numerous ellipses within Sappho's fragmentary poetic corpus have proven a boon to translators, poets, and readers, allowing them freedom 'to develop and enlarge upon the tattered remains in whichever direction they wished'.[51]

Queer Sappho

'Queer' is a term often used in connection with non-heteronormative forms of sexuality – sexual acts and identities that do not line up easily along the usual binaries of homosexual, heterosexual, bisexual, male, female, and so on. It is also a term that, as Dana Luciano and Mel Chen suggest, speaks to the precariousness of life and the precarity of all things.[52] 'Queer' applies to the dispersal of human emotions and affect among various senses, sensory objects and things that are in themselves non-material, such as the ephemeral 'objects' of memory. Given the impossibility of pinning down the sexual identities of the human figures in many of Sappho's poems it is appropriate to speak of 'queer' affect.

Ellen Greene argues of fr. 94 that the 'apostrophic structure of the poem . . . dramatizes an experience of desire as mutual recognition'.[53] Believing it possible for contemporary readers to discover in Sappho's representation of female desire 'an alternative to the competitive and hierarchical models of eroticism that have dominated Western culture', she and others have mapped on to Sappho's poetry an idealistically

---

[49] Orrells 2015: 142–5.
[50] Orrells 2015: 145; Symonds in Wharton 1885: 62.
[51] Orrells 2015: 145.
[52] Luciano and Chen 2015.
[53] Greene 1994: 42 = 1996a: 234; also Greene 1996c: 6–7.

egalitarian lesbianism, one which avoids the asymmetrical bias of male homosexuality as constructed by Foucault.[54]

Fr. 94 consists of a leave-taking between the speaker of the poem and another woman. Although the beginning of the poem is missing, it starts, for us, with a direct quotation: 'I sincerely wish to die', says 'the woman crying many tears, as she left me'. 'Sappho', who is in the position of the one who remembers, recalls the woman's words, and in doing so, she brings the dialogue between them to life, making the departed woman's intense feelings present once more: 'Oh, what awful things we've suffered, Sappho, and truly I leave you against my will', says the other woman. To which 'Sappho' replies, 'Go, happily, and remember me, for you know how I (literally "we") held you, and if you don't, I am willing to remind you . . . and we also experienced beautiful things'.

'Sappho' goes on then to remind this absent woman of the 'beautiful' things – *kala* – that they have experienced together, and from its earlier focus on I-to-you (speaker-to-addressee) relations,[55] the dialogue swivels the foreground into the background, just as it has collapsed the temporal planes of past and present:

> αἰ δὲ μή, ἀλλά c' ἔγω θέλω
> ὄμναιcαι [ ].[ ].εαι
> ὀc[ ] καὶ κάλ' ἐπάcχομεν·
>
> πό[λλοιc γὰρ cτεφάν]οιc ἴων
> καὶ βρ[όδων]κίων τ' ὔμοι
> κα. .[ ] πὰρ ἔμοι περεθήκαο
>
> καὶ πόλλαιc ὑπαθύμιδαc
> πλέκταιc ἀμφ' ἀπάλαι δέραι
> ἀνθέων ἐ[ ] πεποημέναιc.
>
> καὶ π. . . . .[ ].μύρωι
> βρενθείωι.[ ]ρυ[ ]ν
> ἐξαλείψαο κα[ὶ βαc]ιληίωι

---

[54] Greene 1994: 43 = 1996a: 236. Like much of the feminist scholarship on Sappho in the 1980s and 1990s, Greene compares Sappho's erotic strategies favourably to those of her male counterparts. Skinner 1996: 182, for example, finds Sappho's poetic discourse to be 'open, fluid, and polysemous – and hence conspicuously nonphallic'. Similarly Stehle Stigers 1979 ≈ Stehle 1996, L. Wilson 1996.

[55] Cf. Williamson 1996: 255: '"I", "you", and "she" (and in fr. 96 we should also add "we") are never clearly differentiated, securely demarcated positions, but are constantly linked in a polyphonic, shifting erotic discourse, a kind of circulation of desire in which the gaps between subjects, figured through time and space, are at the same time constantly bridged by the operations of love and memory.'

καὶ ϲτρώμν[αν ἐ]πὶ μολθάκαν
ἀπάλαν παρ[　　]ο̣ν̣ων
ἐξίηϲ πόθο[ν　　]. νίδων

But if not (i.e. if you do not remember), I wish to remind you . . . and the beautiful things we experienced. Many wreaths of violets and roses and . . . you put on by my side, and you put many plaited garlands around your delicate neck, made from flowers . . . and with costly myrrh you anointed yourself . . . and in a queenly way, on the soft sheets . . . you would satisfy your desire . . . for delicate . . .

The human subjects, the original loci for these feelings of sadness and desiring despair, give way to a more dispersed kind of animacy, one in which, partly due to the fragmentary state of the parchment, it is no longer possible to say who, or what, is satisfying whom. We hear only that 'in a queenly way, and on the soft sheets . . . you would satisfy your desire (ἐξίηϲ πόθο̣[ν] . . .' The addressee is the subject of the verb to 'exhaust' or 'satisfy', and desire (*pothon*) is its object.[56] But what it is she has desire *for* is irrecoverable. We simply have no idea what the noun is, in the genitive case, that 'tender' (ἀπάλαν) modifies. In this sense, the non-human objects, the things themselves that are being recalled, share the stage with the human speakers. All are objects of memory and entangled in the feelings and sensations to which remembering gives rise.

Violets, roses, plaited garlands, and myrrh, the soft sheets and other delicate things enable, through their encounter with human bodies, release from desire. And though these things are not apostrophised directly, it may still be appropriate to recall Jonathan Culler's insight into the capacity of apostrophic address 'to posit a world in which a wider range of entities can be imagined to exercise agency'.[57] The 'queerness' of fr. 94 lies, I propose, in its decentring of the human. Things both natural and crafted, living and remembered, impinge on the senses, and the poem's very language morphs from a human-centred discourse into object-oriented affect.[58]

But why 'queer', rather than 'lesbian' or 'gay'? 'Lesbian' is a sexual orientation. It is a term that one ascribes to the author of the lyrics (about

---

[56] Of the expression ἐξίηϲ πόθον, McEvilley 1971: 3 writes that it 'seems to provide a clear reference to homosexual acts – the only reference in our fragments'; in McEvilley 2008: 50 this has become 'possibly the only such reference in our fragments', accompanied by a footnote pointing to fr. 99(a).5, where the word ὄλιϲβοϲ, 'dildo', might be restored.

[57] Culler 2015: 242. For the animating effect of apostrophe, see Culler 2015: 211–43, B. Johnson 1986; for Sappho and lyric, see Purves.

[58] Compare McEvilley 1971: 9 = 2008: 61 on the fourth stanza of fr. 94: 'Images of beautiful objects and acts abound in what has been up to now an imageless poem.'

whom we know next to nothing) but not to the lyrics themselves. 'Queer' describes the affect, and the effect, of language; how it registers in relation to, or overturns and challenges, existing sexual and social norms. 'Queer' describes the feelings Sappho's lyrics elicit from audiences ancient and modern. And these feelings need not have anything to do with the sexual orientation of the writer or the reader. Luciano and Chen position queerness 'as primarily a tool of incessant unsettling, restless refusal of all forms of identity'.[59] Sappho's lyrics, then, can be queer, as can 'Sappho' the product or invention of her lyrics, without Sappho the author having a knowable, legible sexual identity. As Eve Kosofsky Sedgwick writes, queer is 'the open mesh of possibilities, gaps, overlaps, dissonances and resonances, lapses and excesses of meaning when the constituent elements of anyone's gender, of anyone's sexuality aren't made (or *can't be* made) to signify monolithically'.[60]

In proposing queer affect as a conceptual tool with which to read Sappho, I acknowledge the groundbreaking work of those who have emphasised the dissolution of boundaries between self and environment in both frr. 94 and 96.[61] Eva Stehle, for example, points to the diffusion of erotic affect whereby 'a woman's beauty is displaced onto the surroundings: song, scents, flowers, rich cloth, enclosed places all reflect the woman's erotic attractiveness'.[62] But the distribution of *erôs* beyond the borders of the human body should not in itself be taken as symptomatic of a gentler, more egalitarian form of sexuality. While the recollections of the sexual acts in fr. 94 (and the love affair between Atthis and another woman in fr. 96) are tinged with pleasurable remembering, elsewhere Sappho gives voice to the painful dynamics of domination and submission which characterise the unrequited desire of the speakers of frr. 1, 31, and the Cypris Poem.

Several times, a speaker is on the verge of death, uttering in Sappho's presence or in 'Sappho's' own voice, that she either wants to or seems to herself to be 'little short of dying'. The intensity of this wish – a 'metaphor for the rejection of present time, and memory' – nearly dissolves the unity of the speaker's body and voice.[63] The feelings of disempowerment and disintegration emerge that much more forcefully in the Cypris Poem, where

---

[59] Luciano and Chen 2015: 192.
[60] Sedgwick 1993: 8 (emphasis original).
[61] Greene 1994: 48–9 = 1996a: 241, Stehle 1996 (quoted below).
[62] Stehle 1996: 220; she remarks (*ibid.*) '94 V. is full of flowers and scent, and in 96 V. the woman's beauty is deflected onto the landscape'.
[63] McEvilley 1971: 8 = 2008: 59 on frr. 31, 94; also Stehle 1996: 220.

the speaker is fully in the clutches of Aphrodite's spell. And here too the language of domination and lovesickness captures our attention, although it is just one index of the intensity of the feelings ascribed to women in love.

Even when Aphrodite is neither mentioned nor invoked, the effects of *erôs* on the human body are vividly rendered. Take, for instance, the 'bittersweet' serpent, limb-loosening desire, against which one is powerless (fr. 130). Or the soul-shattering experience of desire which causes the singer to appear to herself little short of dying. It is this self-reflexive element, perhaps, that has inspired some to read into Sappho a more progressive, less binary form of eroticism than that found in the love poetry of her male counterparts. The subject, in Sappho, is objectified by its own gaze, rather than existing merely as a projection of the male gaze. Instead of a subject and an object, there are only subjects. Yet, even when the apostrophised 'other' is recognised as a 'subject', desire remains elusive and non-reciprocal. At best, it is a bittersweet memory.[64]

Songs record episodes of tenderness and gentleness between Sappho and her departed lover, moments shaded over with sadness. The joy the speaker takes in recalling past loves, kept alive through the songs and their reperformance, is itself ephemeral. There is a translation of carnal pleasure into the erotics of remembrance, made possible by the performance of Sappho's lyrics themselves.[65] If scholars have occasionally sought in Sappho the reflection of an idealised form of love, there have also been those who cannot help but be repelled but what they find. In writing about fr. 58 before it was supplemented with the Cologne papyrus, Winkler remarks: 'One of the fascinating aspects of studying fragments is to watch the Rorschach effect whereby scholars reveal their underlying attitudes about what is possible or acceptable in life and poetry.'[66] Winkler refers here to a scholar whose 'allusion to Ganymede and to Tithonos' supposed "congenital tendency" colors that old patriarchal attitude with the language of modern homophobia'. Making 'no secret of his contempt for a man who is carried away by a powerful woman', this scholar's attitude offers a useful reminder that 'Sappho and sexuality' is as much about the fears and fantasies of readers through the ages as it is about Sappho. One inevitably learns more about those who write about her than one can ever know about Sappho herself. And Winkler is no exception. He resists the idea that the myth of Tithonus is

---

[64] For Sappho's coinages connoting *erôs*, see Lanata 1966: 73–4 ≈ 1996: 20–1.
[65] Stehle Stigers 1981 = H. Foley 1981: 45–61, Snyder 1997: 45–61, Klinck 2005: 202, Boehringer 2007: 54.
[66] Winkler 1991: 230.

merely being used to exemplify the inevitability of growing old. He suggests that Dawn's role has been underappreciated and argues for an analogy between Sappho and Tithonus, as two figures constrained by mortality. In his view, Sappho, as a double of Tithonus, is also swept away in Dawn's arms:

> It is, like much in Sappho, a discrete but unmistakable lesbian image. Sappho allows us briefly to see herself in the role of Tithonos, wrapped in the rosy arms of Dawn and rapt away to the goddess' home in the Far East to be her 'spouse' (22) forever. It is a rather extraordinary picture of woman-to-woman passion and rapture.[67]

For Winkler, this is a lesbian image; but not all readers will see Sappho in the Tithonus figure. From a structuralist perspective, two primary oppositions deserve mention: that between male and female, and that between goddess and mortal. Heteronormative sex in ancient Greece subordinates the female to the male, but as a goddess the woman (i.e. Dawn) in this sexual pairing is unable to be fully dominated. Thus, 'the pairing of a goddess and a human man poses, within Greek hegemonic discourse, an irreconcilable conflict between the two established hierarchies, the hierarchy of male and female and that of divine and human'.[68] In the Tithonus Poem, Sappho once again destabilises the binaries underpinning established sexual and social relationships.[69] And this opens the door to all manner of queer readings.

Further Reading

Ormand 2018 treats Greco-Roman sexuality in general. Dover 1978 and Halperin 1990 are landmark studies of homosexuality in ancient Greece, while approaches tailored to the study of female homoeroticism are well represented by Boehringer 2007, 2014, and Rabinowitz and Auanger 2002; Lardinois 2010 is a sensible treatment of ancient views on Sappho's sexuality. DeJean 1989a and Prins 1999 remain unsurpassed as exemplary modern reception histories (in France and England) of Sappho and Sapphic sexualities; Orrells 2015 and Traub 2016 are excellent on the theoretical issues involved in writing pre-modern histories of sexuality.

---

[67] Winkler 1991: 232.
[68] Stehle 1996: 202.
[69] Compare fr. 140(a), which is addressed to Aphrodite and her young lover Adonis, as another pairing that destabilises the 'dichotomous construct usually inserted between gods and mortals' (L. Wilson 1996: 41).

CHAPTER 4

Sappho and Epic

Adrian Kelly[*]

οὔνομά μευ Σαπφώ, τόσσον δ᾽ ὑπερέσχον ἀοιδῶν
θηλειᾶν, ἀνδρῶν ὅσσον ὁ Μαιονίδας.

My name is Sappho, and so far did I surpass female
poets, as the (grand)son of Maeon the males.

Antipater of Thessalonica, *Greek Anthology* 7.15 (test. 57)

Ancient tradition readily sought to connect Sappho with the greatest of
all Greek epic poets, Homer,[1] and a particular and direct interplay
between the two has been prominent in recent scholarship. Yet Sappho's
relationship with epic poetry as a whole is a larger and more complex
issue, since neither figure was the first or only artist of their sort in the
earliest period, and Sappho certainly knew epics and stories not associ-
ated with the *Iliad* and *Odyssey*, and may not have known those two
poems at all.[2] When one considers the many sources, textualised or not,
with which Sappho and her audiences must have been familiar, then
one must be alive to the depth and range of possibilities for her interac-
tion with this material, and more than a little resentful that almost all of
it is lost.

Formally, archaic *epos* (epic poetry) and *melos* ('melic' or lyric poetry)
can be differentiated in several ways. The former uses the dactylic hexam-
eter and an artificial dialect which mixes Aeolic and Ionic forms from sev-
eral different periods, while the metres of Sappho's *melos* are more varied
in rhythm and arrangement, and her dialect is basically Lesbian

---

[*] I am grateful to Bill Allan, Felix Budelmann, Patrick Finglass, André Lardinois, Lucia Prauscello,
Henry Spelman, and to audiences in Cambridge and São Paulo, for their assistance with this chap-
ter.
[1] Maeon is named as either Homer's father (*Contest of Homer and Hesiod* 3) or grandfather (4).
[2] Cf. Burgess 2001: 65–7, 114–31, Kelly 2015a: 28–9, Spelman 2017a: 743–5. I do not rehearse my ear-
lier arguments against a direct relationship between Sappho and Homer, since Sappho is interact-
ing with epic poetry for broadly the sorts of reasons scholars have identified.

Aeolic.[3] As in other matters, an appreciation of definitional boundaries is useful, as long as they are not treated as impermeable. While, for instance, epic poets usually stand at a distance from the mythical content of their works, and lyric poets are inclined to refer directly to the contemporary world, some epic poets like Hesiod freely draw upon their own contexts (however fictively), and lyric poets can tell mythical tales (as we shall see). In terms of scale, *epos* generally fosters larger compositions than *melos*, and this may also be related to performance setting, with epic more readily associated with public contexts and lyric with private ones, though these too should not be considered strict boundaries: choral *melos*, for instance, straddled the public/private divide quite evenly, and the sixth-century lyric poet Stesichorus stands as a notable exception to almost all the above dichotomies. Now that scholarship has moved beyond mapping early Greek literary history into discrete periods (where *epos* simply precedes *melos*), the possibility for recognising cross-germination and mutual interaction can only increase if, as some have argued, Sappho and Alcaeus knew of local epic traditions more thoroughly Aeolic than those which have survived,[4] and we should also remember that the (probably sixth-century BC) *Little Iliad* was held in antiquity to have been composed by a Lesbian epic poet, Lesches of Pyrrha or Mytilene.[5] Add to this the island's geographical proximity to Troy and its profile in Homer,[6] and we might well think that Sappho's interaction with *epos*, particularly to do with the Trojan War, was unavoidable.

The complexity of that process is clear when we look more closely at Sappho's language.[7] Scholars have long noted similarities between her dialect and that of the (largely) Ionian epic poets, as for instance the genitive singular of masculine o-stem nouns in –οιο alongside Lesbian –ω, or ἐθέλω ('I wish') alongside Lesbian θέλω. These epicisms have been explained as traces of an older Aeolian dialect, simple borrowings from Ionian *epos*, or even as the common inheritance of Indo-European poetry but, whatever the truth,[8] the Lesbian singers interacted with epic language as an evolving and contemporary creature.

---

[3] Cf. TRIBULATO on language, BATTEZZATO on metre; also below, pp. 56–7, for Sappho's experiments with the dactylic hexameter.

[4] West 2002: 218 = 2011–13: I 406–7.

[5] Kelly 2015b: 318.

[6] *Iliad* 9.128–30, 664–5, 24.544–5, *Odyssey* 3.169, West 2002: 208 = 2011–13: I 393–4.

[7] Cf. TRIBULATO.

[8] This is not unconnected to the controversy surrounding the Aeolic elements in the epic language itself, which have been seen as evidence for a purely Aeolic phase in the evolution of *epos*: cf. Willi 2011: 460–2.

This applies to the most obvious sign of interaction, the shared posses-
sion of the noun–epithet combinations (e.g. ῎Εροc . . . λυcιμέλης, 'love
limb-loosening') so characteristic of hexameter epic.[9] Among the usual
links with Homer (Broger, for instance, lists 117 expressions held in com-
mon with the *Iliad* and *Odyssey*), a large proportion can be paralleled in
non-Homeric epic.[10] Indeed, one of the most famous of Sappho's epithets
for Aphrodite, ποικιλόθρον', usually translated 'with cunningly-wrought
throne' or similar, has also been interpreted to mean 'wearing a dress with
flowers woven in' and linked with the depiction of the goddess's beautifi-
cation with flowers in the *Cypria*.[11] Comparable too is the phrasing of
Aphrodite's promise for the human object of Sappho's prayer ('since if
now she flees, soon she will pursue'), which may be linked with Zeus's
pursuit of Nemesis in the *Cypria* ('for she fled and did not wish to mix in
love . . . she fled, and Zeus pursued, and desired in his soul to seize
her').[12] One need not assume that Sappho has drawn these expressions
directly from a fixed text – and our uncertainty about the date of the
Cypria, somewhere in the seventh and sixth centuries, allows the possibil-
ity that the influence ran the other way[13] – but it is a salutary lesson on
the limitations of the surviving evidence. We may see Sappho interacting
with the remains of non-Homeric epic poetry, but only by the merest
chance.

The *Iliad* and *Odyssey* dominate the extant records of early narrative
epos, and the former poem in particular plays a prominent role in the
study of Sappho's epic interactions,[14] though one notes the high propor-
tion of obviously formulaic expressions in any list one could compile, as
below for fr. 1:

---

[9] Fr. 130.1 ~ Hesiod, *Theogony* 120–1, 910–11. But cf. Archilochus fr. 196 *IEG*, ἀλλά μ' ὁ λυcιμελὴc
ὦταῖρε δάμναται πόθοc, 'but I, my friend, am tamed by limb-loosening desire'; associations with
non-epic poetry – much less well preserved in this period – need to be remembered throughout.

[10] Broger 1996: 253–69. Steinrück 1999: 146–9 argues that the *Iliad* and *Odyssey* were much less
important to Sappho than other texts, such as the *Homeric Hymn to Aphrodite*. Cf. below,
pp. 62–4 (on fr. 44).

[11] Fr. 1.1; *Cypria* fr. 5 *GEF*. Cf. Scheid and Svenbro 1994: 61–7 ≈ 1996: 53–8; *contra* Jouanna 1999
(with pp. 102–3 on the variant reading ποικίλοφρον', 'cunningly-minded').

[12] Fr. 1.21; *Cypria* frr. 10.4, 10.7 *GEF*.

[13] Cf. Currie 2015: 281.

[14] It is doubtful that the *Odyssey* was known to the Lesbian poets: cf. Meyerhoff 1984: 13, West 2002:
214 = 2011–13: I 401; *contra* M. Mueller 2016 (below). Winkler 1990: 178–80 reads the *makarismos*
('blessing') opening of fr. 31 next to Odysseus' praise of Nausicaa (*Odyssey* 6.158–61).

μή μ' ἄcαιcι μηδ' ὀνίαιcι δάμνα, | θῦμον (3–4)	οὐ γάρ πώ ποτέ μ' ὧδε θεᾶc ἔροc οὐδὲ γυναικόc | θυμὸν ἐνὶ cτήθεccι περιπροχυθεὶc ἐδάμαccεν (*Iliad* 14.315–16) δάμαcον θυμὸν μέγαν (*Iliad* 9.496)
ἄρμ' ὑπαcδεύξαιcα (9)	ζεύξειεν ὑφ' ἄρμαcιν (*Iliad* 24.14) ζεύξαθ' ὑφ' ἄρματ' (*Odyssey* 3.476) etc.
περὶ γᾶc μελαίναc (10)	γαῖα μέλαινα (8x Homer)
πύκνα δίννεντεc πτέρ' (11)	δινεύουcαν ὑπὸ πτερύγοc βάλε (*Iliad* 23.875) ἔνθ' ἐπιδινηθέντε τιναξάcθην πτερὰ πυκνά (*Odyssey* 2.151) etc.
ἀπ' ὠράνω‏ἴθεροc διὰ μέccω (11–12)	δι' αἰθέροc οὐρανὸν ἷκεν (*Iliad* 2.458) οὐρανὸν εἴcω | αἰθέροc ἐκ δίηc (*Iliad* 16.364–5) οὐρανὸν ἷκε δι' αἰθέροc (*Iliad* 17.425) etc.
αἶψα δ' ἐξίκοντο (13)	αἶψα δ' ἔπειθ' ἵκανον (*Iliad* 3.145) etc. αἶψα δ' ἵκοντο (*Iliad* 18.532) etc.
μειδιαίcαιc' ἀθανάτωι προcώπωι (14)	μειδιόων βλοcυροῖcι προcώπαcι (*Iliad* 7.212) ἐφ' ἱμερτῶι δὲ προcώπωι | αἰεὶ μειδιάει (*Hymn to Aphrodite* 10.2–3) φιλομμειδὴc Ἀφροδίτη (6x Homer, *Hymn to Aphrodite* 5.56) etc.
κὤττι μοι μάλιcτα θέλω γένεcθαι | μαινόλαι θύμωι· (17–18)	ὅccον ἤθελε θυμόc (*Iliad* 9.177) etc. ἤθελε θυμῶι (*Iliad* 16.255) etc. εἰ cύ γε θυμῶι | cῶι ἐθέλοιc (*Iliad* 17.488–9; cf. 23.894)
κωὐκ ἐθέλοιcα (24)	καὶ οὐκ ἐθέλουc' ὑπ' ἀνάγκηc (*Odyssey* 2.110) ὅc μ' ἔθελεν φιλότητι μιγήμεναι οὐκ ἐθελούcηι (*Iliad* 6.165) ἐμεῖο μὲν οὐκ ἐθελούcηc (*Iliad* 24.289) οὐκ ἐθελούcηι (*Odyssey* 2.50)

None of these parallels is so distinctive as to compel a particular intertextual reference to the Homeric passage(s),[15] but they have been taken to show how thoroughly immersed in epic language and phraseology this poem is – naturally, given its theme.

It is therefore no surprise that Sappho herself experimented with the hexameter, of which a few fragments survive.[16] Here the poet's

---

[15] Cf. *contra* Marry 1979, Rissman 1983: 1–4 (and below, n. 20).
[16] Frr. 105(a), 105(c), 106, 142, 143, perhaps frr. 107–9; see BATTEZZATO p. 125.

interactions extend to prosody and scansion: like the epic bards, she allows a regular pause ('caesura') in the middle of the verse, substitution of a spondee (two heavy syllables) for the dactyl (three syllables, one heavy + two light), and the treatment of an otherwise heavy open syllable as light ('epic correption') when that syllable is placed before another vowel ('hiatus'). None of these practices is typical in Aeolian versification and, their size notwithstanding, these fragments are illuminating examples of Sappho's epic interactions.

In fr. 105(a), perhaps from an *epithalamium* (wedding song),[17] Sappho deploys a vegetation simile reminiscent of epic examples to compare the object of her comparison to the 'sweet apple' which cannot be plucked (for lines 1–2, ἄκρωι ἐπ᾽ ὔϲδωι, | ἄκρον ἐπ᾽ ἀκροτάτωι, 'on the top branch, | top on the topmost', cf. *Iliad* 2.312, ὄζωι ἐπ᾽ ἀκροτάτωι, 'on the topmost branch'; also 4.484), but here the forceful polyptoton expresses the exquisite rarity of the fruit in an obviously erotic way, where martial epic mainly uses floral similes to suggest mortality and death.[18] Fr. 105(c) does it again, this time with the image of shepherds trampling the hyacinth, and the loss of its 'deep-red bloom' (πόρφυρον ἄνθος), to foreshadow the wedding itself.[19] Frr. 142 (Λάτω καὶ Νιόβα μάλα μὲν φίλαι ἦϲαν ἔταιραι, 'Leto and Niobe were true friends, companions') and 143 (χρύϲειοι δ᾽ ἐρέβινθοι ἐπ᾽ ἀϊόνων ἐφύοντο, 'and golden chickpeas were growing on the banks') do not give away much, but show an intriguing interchange of dialect forms (e.g. Aeolic Λάτω for epic-Ionic Λήτω, but also epic-Ion. χρύϲειοι for Aeol. χρύϲιοι) to suggest fruitful experimentation in cross-generic and -linguistic composition, seen again in fr. 106 (πέρροχος, ὠς ὄτ᾽ ἄοιδος ὀ Λέϲβιος ἀλλοδάποιϲιν, 'outstanding, as when a Lesbian bard among foreigners'), with specifically Aeolic vocalism (πέρροχος for Ionic περίοχος) and psilosis (ὠς / ὄτ᾽ / ὀ for ὡς / ὅτ᾽ / ὁ).

Sappho's recreation of themes found in epic poetry is not restricted to these few formally similar fragments; we can see a range of interactive possibilities throughout her corpus, stretching from appropriation to open opposition, sometimes within the same poem. Fr. 1 is the obvious

---

[17] For this genre, see McEvilley 2008: 186–214, F. Ferrari 2010: 117–33, Dale 2011a, FERRARI pp. 110–11, PRAUSCELLO pp. 227–9. Himerius, *Oration* 9.16 tells us that Sappho was here contrasting those who pick the 'fruit before its season' (i.e., before marriage) with those who wait until the proper moment: see BOWIE.

[18] Kelly 2007: 289–90; also Hesiod, *Works and Days* 681, Ibycus fr. 317(*a*) *PMGF*. For Sappho's other vegetation similes cf. frr. 115, 194 with Rissman 1983: 98–104. DuBois 1995: 46–7 suggests a direct intertext with the *Iliad* passage above, which would colour the fragment with intimations of death.

[19] For these two poems, see duBois 1995: 40–53, 2015: 70–1, Snyder 1997: 104–5.

example, especially given its saturation of epic language (above), and its theme – a request to Aphrodite for renewed aid in an erotic venture – invokes a widespread motif in epic narrative, where heroic males summon a helpful god at a moment of distress, and some scholars have suggested that Sappho is referring particularly to Diomedes' appeal to Athena in Book 5 of the *Iliad*.[20] With or without this direct link, Sappho relocates the usually male-dominated heroic associations of such an action into a female-centred and erotic context, endowing herself and her endeavours with an importance usually bestowed upon others.[21] *Epos* is not unaware of sex, as we can see in the rather prosaic frankness of the *Odyssey* or the seduction scenes throughout the tradition,[22] but it does not prioritise or foreground, as Sappho does here and throughout her work, the female experience and perspective of sexual desire.[23]

Repurposing of this sort is pervasive in the poem: the sparrows drawing Aphrodite's chariot (9–13) deliberately counterpart the more impressive beasts of burden we find in analogous circumstances in epic, as the horses (surrounded by sea beasts) drawing Poseidon's chariot to Aegae or those conveying Hera and Athena to the Trojan plain.[24] Sappho's playful relationship with her patron deity can be compared with that between Athena and Odysseus in the *Odyssey*, Athena and Diomedes in the *Iliad*, or even Helen and Aphrodite in the same poem; and Sappho's appeal 'be my ally' (cύμμαχος ἔςςο, 28) militarises the whole erotic programme.[25] The combined effect suggests the poetic seriousness of the theme, that love is an important endeavour, as well as showcasing the artist's and audience's ability to recreate and play off shared themes and expressions.

If fr. 1 seems to clothe erotic narrative in military garb, other more directly oppositional stances are possible, as in fr. 16, where Sappho

---

[20] For this poem, see Marry 1979, Rissman 1983: 1–29, Winkler 1990: 169–76, Greene 1994: 50–4 = 1996a: 243–6, duBois 1995: 7–10, Snyder 1997: 7–17, Stehle 1997: 296–9, M. Johnson 2007: 41–8, Blondell 2010: 373–7, SWIFT pp. 203–6.

[21] Thus Winkler 1990: 168–70 plausibly argues that fr. 1 is antipatriarchal in asserting Aphrodite's power and influence specifically as a response to her negative portrayal in this portion of the *Iliad*, but Aphrodite – unlike her various Near Eastern relatives – is generally treated in early Greek epic in negative and trivialising terms, so the point remains even without a direct link to this passage in Homer.

[22] Cf. Forsyth 1979 on seduction scenes, D. Campbell 1983: 1–4 for a summary.

[23] This common theme in Sappho's epic interactions is not evidence for the theory that her works were principally intended for and performed in women-only zones, or were only of interest to women; cf. Parker 1993: 343 = Greene 1996b: 180 ('there is no theme, no occasion, in Sappho that we do not find in other poets'), Bowman 2004: 13–15, LARDINOIS.

[24] *Iliad* 13.23–31, 5.730–2, 5.767–77. Cf. the swans for Apollo's chariot in fr. 208, Alcaeus fr. 307(c).

[25] For the unusual nature of Sappho's relationship with Aphrodite in the context of early Greek *melos*, see SWIFT.

memorably opens by contrasting the highest values of the military-minded (1–3) with her own valorisation of 'whatever someone loves' (κῆν' ὄττω τις ἔραται, 3–4).[26] Keeping in mind the multiform deployment of military themes in the personal poetry of her contemporary Alcaeus (and elsewhere in the Greek world, e.g. in Archilochus and Tyrtaeus), the contrast here may well include some epic poetry, and not necessarily just the *Iliad*, in its apparent dispreferral of the martial focus,[27] and some of its language may recall epic phraseology: ἰππήων στρότον . . . πέσδων, 'army of horsemen . . . of foot soldiers' (1) resonates with formulaic πέζοι θ' ἱππῆές τε, 'foot soldiers and horsemen' (3x Hom.), while ἐπ[ὶ] γᾶν μέλαι[v]αν, 'on the black earth' (2), unusual here as it comes straight after 'ships' in the same verse, may represent a fusion of the epic habit of so qualifying both earth (γαῖα) and, much more commonly, ships.[28]

Once more, whether referring to a single text or not, Sappho emphasises the independence of the female perspective and its power to create alternative modes of valuation in a male-dominated world. These reversals tap into the widespread early epic motif of feminine unsuitability for war,[29] and celebrate it as a positive, apparently even superior virtue, foregrounding the female experience of violence in the lives of Sappho and her contemporaries, while also suggesting once more that love is a powerful and serious topic for poetry (as also in frr. 31, 47, 130, etc.). Yet fr. 16 is not simply anti-*epos*.[30] Sappho deploys the story of Helen to explore the poem's opening contention about what is κάλλιστον ('fairest', 3), but the continuing presence of the epic background suggests that its apparent negation in the priamel is not straightforward. While the paradigm begins by suggesting that Helen is the love object referred to in lines 3–4, it is Aphrodite (and Paris) who led her to abandon husband and homeland (6–12) and, when the poet compares her beloved, *absent* Anactoria (15–16) to Helen, she concludes by casting herself effectively as Menelaus: Sappho's new, personalised and eroticised κάλλιστον, therefore, is not

---

[26] For this poem, see Winkler 1990: 176–8, Tzamali 1996: 130–65, Snyder 1997: 64–71, Pfeijffer 2000a, Hutchinson 2001: 160–8, Pallantza 2005: 61–79, E. Bowie 2010: 67–9, Blondell 2010: 377–87 (~ 2013: 111–16), Swift 2015: 105–6.

[27] As Hutchinson 2001: 161 puts it: 'The *Iliad* may be one element in the male militarism which the poem dismisses; but the structure of the stanza presents rather a crowd of contemporary men.'

[28] Cf. Rissman 1983: 34–8; *contra* Tzamali 1996: 135–6. These are, once more, formulaic expressions in epic, and hard to link with any specific Homeric passage. They are common in *melos* as well (e.g. fr. 20.6, Alcman fr. 89.3 *PMGF*, 'Theognis' 878), complicating any straightforwardly epic resonance.

[29] *Iliad* 8.163, Kelly 2007: 190.

[30] Cf. Hutchinson 2001: 160; *contra* M. Johnson 2007: 68, 'a rejection of the *Iliad* in particular and its martial heroism.'

unequivocally celebrated by the end of the poem. Thus, her relationship with the epic past is not just contrarian, since she relies on the audience to invoke its characters and their stories to explore the tensions and uncertainties in the poetic world that she constructs.

The dynamic between love and war tends to dominate discussions of Sappho's relationship with epic, but other themes at home in the latter's tradition played into the lives and concerns of her audiences. Travel and trade were vital for the prosperity and wealth of archaic Lesbos,[31] and here as well the epic heritage had something to offer. Narrating the voyage home of a stranded hero, the return song (*nostos*) was a type long thematised in epic poetry before Sappho, obviously in the *Odyssey* itself, and in archaic poems called *Nostoi*, one an epic, one a lyric by Stesichorus, which told the other heroes' returns from Troy.[32] Such a story pattern would have held particular resonance for Sappho and her audiences, however much Homer or his characters may seem to oppose the heroic with the mercantile (*Odyssey* 8.159–64), and her somewhat sceptical attitude towards sailing mirrors the tone with which Hesiod gives advice about sailing for the purposes of trade (*Works and Days* 618–94). In several poems, Sappho explores the roles allowed by this theme to those left behind, waiting for the return of the men upon whom their own safety and prosperity depended. The new Brothers Poem shows Sappho taking on a considerably authoritative role, not only rebuking the unreasonably hopeful attitude of someone (perhaps his lover Doricha; cf. fr. 15) towards Charaxus' current voyage (1–4), but also turning her ire upon the unimpressive brother Larichus, in the hope that he should live up to his potential and fulfil his duty towards his family (17–20). The bulk of the poem between these two points contains a reflection on the gods' power to save or destroy those whom they will (9–16) and advice to the unnamed addressee properly to consider that fact (5–9).

It has been suggested that Sappho may be reflecting Homer's Odysseus in her depiction of the absent Charaxus, channelling Penelope in her self-portrait as an anxious woman waiting for the male's return, even making Larichus into a Telemachus figure.[33] But many female characters in early

---

[31] See THOMAS.

[32] Danek 2015, Davies and Finglass 2014: 470–81.

[33] Obbink 2014b, 2016c: 212. Stehle 2016: 275–7 suggests an intertext between Odysseus' wish that he 'return *to find* his wife at home with her *steadfast* friends' (εὕροιμι . . . ἀρτεμέεσσι, *Odyssey* 13.43) and Sappho's desire that Charaxus 'find us *steadfast*' (κἄμμ᾽ ἐπεύρην ἀρτέμεας, 9), but the adjective is formulaic in the context of a warrior returning from battle (*Iliad* 5.515 = 7.308) and in a *nostos* setting likely to be an underrepresented formula. The influence of the *Odyssey* on the Lesbian poets is generally doubted in most recent scholarship (above, n. 14).

epic and myth – wives, mothers, and sisters – could just as well, or even better, be implicated in this role (Andromache, Clytemnestra, Electra, etc.). Sappho once more foregrounds the perspective on this situation of the family members and specifically, though not only, of the women left behind. These voices and views are not unheard in epic, since the situation of the absent hero's wife, family, and community are constant elements in epic *nostoi*, but once more Sappho puts this experience at the poetic centre, and makes it the determinative voice. She takes an active role in configuring Charaxus' activity for her addressee, and asserts an authoritative understanding of the gods' workings – a cautious attitude towards male behaviour once more familiar from epic, in Andromache's restraint of Hector (*Iliad* 6.407–39) or Hecabe's attempt to temper Priam's adventurism (24.200–16). However, unlike those cases, Sappho's view is not silenced by male counteraction. There is no attempt to put her back into a confined space, as Telemachus so forcefully represses Penelope (*Odyssey* 1.345–59); instead, Sappho continues by pronouncing on her other brother's shortcomings as well (Brothers Poem 17–20)! In doing so, she appropriates the conventions more readily associated with warning-figures like Nestor and Theoclymenus, and even with poets like Hesiod and Theognis.[34]

Sappho returns to the *nostos* theme several times.[35] In fr. 5, she prays to the Nereids directly for the safe homecoming of an unnamed brother (perhaps Charaxus once more), while in fr. 17 she focuses on Hera as the source of her family's safety and prosperity,[36] and gives a history for the goddess's cult established by the Atridae on Lesbos which differs from the Homeric version of the Greek army's *nostos* from Troy.[37] In fr. 15 Sappho turns her ire (once more? cf. above) on Doricha, expressing a desire that her boasting should end.

We cannot be certain that all of these cases engage with specific epic exemplars, any more than, say, any story about Helen must draw on the *Iliad*. At times, indeed, we may suspect that nothing is owed to *epos*, especially but not only when Sappho's language does not show the same kinds of saturation as fr. 1 (and even there the use of hymnic conventions need not only resonate with epic, since prayers and invocations have a lyric background too). Thus, for instance, there are many points of

---

[34] Cf. Swift 2018 on the brother theme, Kelly 2008 on paraenetic conventions.

[35] Boedeker 2016.

[36] Cf. P.Sapph.Obbink 5–9. For this devotional aspect, see RÖSLER, SWIFT.

[37] In Homer, the Atridae quarrel in Troy before they leave, and Menelaus comes to Lesbos without his brother: cf. *Odyssey* 3.167–9 with Meyerhoff 1984: 223–6, West 2002: 212–13 = 2011–13: I 399, Lidov 2004: 401–2, Spelman 2017a: 745–6.

agreement between her and Hesiod about 'poetic theology', including the notion that Pieria is the home of the Muses (frr. 55.3, 103.8; *Theogony* 52–4, *Works and Days* 1) or that Leto was the daughter of Coeus (fr. 44 A(a).2; *Theogony* 404–8), but it is not at all clear that this 'derives from Hesiod' rather than reflecting simply the same general store of tradition.[38] In fact, Sappho's poetry can sometimes help us to see more clearly the lively and varied discourse between and within other traditions, and flesh out our rather exiguous picture of early Greek storytelling. For instance, her emphasis on the weakness of the aged mortal Tithonus in the Tithonus Poem suggests a tension with his wife, the goddess Dawn, and aligns Sappho more closely with Mimnermus (fr. 4 *IEG*) and the *Homeric Hymn to Aphrodite* (218–38),[39] against the story assumed in the Homeric formulae (*Iliad* 11.1–2, etc.) where Dawn rises from Tithonus' side each day without any such hint.

But none of these qualifications seem to apply when it comes to fr. 44, 'Sappho's most Homeric poem',[40] which tells the wedding of Hector and Andromache.[41] Once considered an *epithalamium* even though it does not refer to any contemporary setting, it tells in deliberately epic language and style, and with a pronounced dactylic rhythm, the entrance of the couple into Troy.[42] Given that Homer mentioned their wedding on several occasions (*Iliad* 22.470–2, etc.), it is tempting to follow those scholars who see here Sappho drawing directly on several Homeric passages to create a pastiche of the *Iliad* in miniature, to herald their foreboding and unhappy future even at the moment of their happy marriage. Certainly, formular expressions abound, such as 'glory unperishable' (κλέος ἄφθιτον, 4; cf. *Iliad* 9.413, etc.) and 'over the brackish sea' (ἐπ' ἄλμυρον | πόντον, 7–8; cf. ἀλμυρὸν ὕδωρ, 8x Hom.) but these are formulae, while the epithet 'alike to the gods' (θεοεικέλο[ις, 34; cf. ἴ]κελοι θέοι[ς, 21), confined in the *Iliad* to Achilles (1.131) and so sometimes interpreted as a pointed reference to Hector's killer, is used in early hexameter for a number of figures (*Odyssey* 3.416, *Homeric Hymn to Aphrodite* 279, etc.). Similarly, the Trojan herald Idaeus, who marks the couple's arrival into the city

---

[38] West 2002: 215–16 = 2011–13: I 403, with more examples, going on to suggest that other similarities are 'Hesiodic in spirit, if not in the letter'.

[39] Cf. Faulkner 2008: 270–1. For the Tithonus Poem, see Obbink 2009 and the other essays in Greene and Skinner 2009.

[40] Rissman 1983: 121.

[41] For this poem cf. Rissman 1983: 119–41, Meyerhoff 1984: 118–39, Schrenk 1994, Suárez de la Torre 2008, E. Bowie 2010: 71–4, Kelly 2015a: 28–9, Sampson 2016, Spelman 2017a.

[42] Page 1955: 64–74, A. Bowie 1981: 32–5, Broger 1996: 54–73.

(fr. 44.3–11), is known to us only from the *Iliad*, where he conveys to the Greeks Paris' unsatisfactory peace offering in Book 7 and accompanies Priam to Achilles' tent in Book 24, yet he is also likely to be a traditional figure in any story concerned with the city before its sack.[43]

Perhaps, then, we might consider other stories and epic texts, such as the *Cypria* or its antecedents, as another or more likely background for this poem.[44] That narrative arc would have naturally included the story of this Trojan couple, but it definitely contained a far more foreboding pairing – Helen and Paris – an episode which left an early imprint on the visual traditions of the Trojan War.[45] Weddings in *epos* are in any case often rather ambivalent affairs:[46] for instance, the Lapiths and Centaurs quarrel at one (*Iliad* 1.262–8), the Trojan War was caused by two marriages involving Helen, first to Menelaus in the Hesiodic *Catalogue of Women* (frr. 196–204 M–W) and then to Paris in the *Cypria* (Argumentum 2 *GEF*) – not to mention her further marriage to Deiphobus after Paris' death (*Little Iliad* Argumentum 2, fr. 4 B) – while the slaughter of the suitors in the remarriage contest in the *Odyssey* is the most obvious extant case. More directly, the marriage of Hector and Andromache is inevitably bound up with the destruction of Troy and the death of Astyanax, which seems to have gained early purchase within literary and visual discourse on war, with e.g. the *Iliou persis* (Argumentum 20 B) and the *Little Iliad* (fr. 21 B) bothering to differ on the identity of the boy's killer (Odysseus/Neoptolemus).[47] Whatever the immediate inspiration of Sappho's narrative, fr. 44 still evokes Troy's destruction, a generic statement which pointedly contrasts epic subject matter with the apparent purpose of an *epithalamium*.

Aside from the question of its mythological sources, the poem shows us once more the fronting of the female experience, participation, and perspective: Idaeus' praise of Andromache's appearance and her dowry (8–10) finds its Trojan correspondence in the joyful participation of the women, including singing from maidens and older women as well

---

[43] Wathelet 1988: 1 598–600 (§157).

[44] Spelman 2017a; *contra* West 2002: 213 = 2011–13: 1 399–400. For other links with the *Cypria*, see above, p. 55.

[45] This story is also treated elsewhere in Lesbian *melos*, e.g. fr. 16 (above) and Alcaeus fr. 283, so that once more we should be wary of confining our conception of the poetic background to *epos*.

[46] Haubold 2000: 137–43, Cingano 2005: 124–7.

[47] Anderson 1997: 54–6, Burgess 2012: 176–82, Davies and Finglass 2014: 438–9. Scodel p. 198 and n. 21 suggests that Sappho may have known later attested stories of Scamandrius (i.e. a separate figure, and not simply Astyanax's original name, as in *Iliad* 6.402–3) in which he refounds Troy, intimating a less uniformly negative outcome.

(14–16, 25–7, 31). The pair's 'glory imperishable' (4) certainly encompasses the wife's contribution, and the gloomy future is contrasted with her promise, so that we can see Sappho positioning her recreations of epic stories and themes again in an ambitious way, juxtaposing the loss and violence of that world – in its entirety – through an unbearably heavy contrast with the hope and expectation represented in the figure of Andromache herself. Once more, as Sappho asks us to venture into her reframing of the epic world, it is a version where the female presence is as prominent, articulate, and visible as the male.[48]

* * *

Perhaps the gaps in the evidence do not matter: whether Sappho drew on her audience's knowledge of the *Iliad* (or any other text) and/or simply invoked a shifting and generic understanding of the stories and norms of *epos*, we can still see her thorough and varied engagement with that tradition. This is no straightforward process of rejection or preclusion, but an (ant-)agonistic and subtle appropriation of an avowedly patriarchal form to foreground the participation and determinative abilities of women. The epigraph to this chapter captures something of that reframing, but not all, since Sappho's attempts to reorient the epic world and its perspectives are redolent not so much of a separate poetic aimed at women, but a universalising encouragement to hear and appreciate the vibrant female voices otherwise kept behind the curtain of early Greek poetry and culture.

Further Reading

The fundamental intertextual examination of a direct relationship between Sappho and Homer is Rissman 1983 (with counterarguments in Steinrück 1999, Kelly 2015a), while the broader epic interaction of the Lesbian poets is surveyed by West 2002 = 2011–13: I 392–407. Graziosi and Haubold 2009 comment sensibly on the relationship between *epos* and *melos* in early Greek literary history; R. Fowler 1987 remains indispensible for the whole question. The treatment of fr. 44 in Spelman 2017a is particularly illuminating, as is the commentary on early lyric, including Sappho, in Budelmann 2018.

---

[48] The loss of Sappho's treatment of the story of Prometheus and Pandora (fr. 207) is to be regretted all the more keenly for this fact; SWIFT p. 213.

CHAPTER 5

Sappho and Alcaeus

Wolfgang Rösler

translated by Kathrin Lüddecke, with contributions by the author

Since antiquity, Sappho and Alcaeus have been considered contemporaries. Two pieces of evidence suggest that they also met in person. The earlier is a well-known red-figure *kratêr* in the shape of a *kalathos*, dated around 470, alternatively attributed to the Dokimasia Painter or the Brygos Painter, which shows both poets labelled with their names.[1] Alcaeus is addressing Sappho, though with his head bowed down, accompanying himself on the *barbitos* or lyre. Five small, very finely drawn bubbles emerging from his mouth represent his song.[2] Sappho is listening, while also holding a *barbitos* and looking straight at Alcaeus. Created a century after the poets' lifetimes, this depiction undoubtedly illustrates not a specific, 'historic' encounter but more generally the contemporaneity and close artistic affinity of the two poets, whose songs continued to be widely known and performed at this time.

Another century later, in the first book of Aristotle's *Rhetoric*, Sappho and Alcaeus are again presented as engaging with each other. Since it is an orator's task to praise what is good (*kalon*) and to criticise what is bad (*aischron*), Aristotle explains and provides examples for both. According to one of his definitions, 'good' is the opposite of what one is ashamed of; that is why Sappho had replied to Alcaeus' words 'I wish to say something to you but shame prevents me' by saying 'If you desired what is noble or good and your tongue were not stirring to say a bad thing, then shame would not hold your eyes, but you would talk about what you have a rightful claim to'.[3] Both speeches are rendered as a poem in Aeolic metre. Yet it is hardly conceivable that such a poem could have been

---

[1] Munich, Staatliche Antikensammlungen, inv. 2416 (*BAPD* §204129); Simon 1981: plate 150, Ferrari pp. 108–9, Battezzato p. 131.

[2] These are visible not on photographs but on the masterly drawing by Karl Reichhold (1856–1919) in the possession of the Munich Antikensammlungen, reproduced in Reichhold 1975: 50–1, Tafel 22. Cf. the more recent drawing by Valerie Woelfel in Nagy 2007: 264.

[3] Aristotle, *Rhetoric* 1367a7–15 (fr. 137); Page 1955: 104–9.

created in reality: it must be ruled out either that the two poets could
have composed it together, or that Sappho composed it in its entirety,
putting this compromising admission into Alcaeus' mouth. Rather, the
identification of the two participants in this dialogue as 'Alcaeus' and
'Sappho' may have been a secondary intervention, reframing a poem with
two speakers – but with different roles: a man in love and a young girl –
which may indeed have been by Sappho, in a new, no longer authentic
context. This hypothesis is an old one; it is first found in Stephanus'
commentary on Aristotle's treatise (fr. 137). The author of this change is
unknown; it probably predates Aristotle. What mattered to him in the
Rhetoric was the definition of *kalon* and *aischron* arising from the conver-
sation between the two speakers; it was no difficulty to him that such an
exchange would have been factually impossible, and therefore its prob-
lematic nature did not call for attention.

Hence, Aristotle's more recent testimony does not prove contact
between Sappho and Alcaeus either. However, such evidence is hardly
necessary, since every likelihood suggests that the two of them were
acquainted. As Page says: 'Sappho and Alcaeus certainly lived part of
their lives in the same city at the same era probably within the same aris-
tocratic circle'[4] – 'city' referring to Mytilene, Lesbos' main and Alcaeus'
home town. As for Sappho, while the smaller town of Eresus is also cited
as her birthplace, her family lived in Mytilene, at least later in her life. As
she herself mentioned, her brother Larichus held the office of cup-bearer
in the town's prytaneion.[5]

With time, the fascination and fame of the circle of girls which Sappho
founded and led made her a well-known personality on her home island.
A fragment from a Hellenistic treatise about Sappho, published in 1974,
notes 'she educated in seclusion the most noble girls not only from the
local (families) but also from (all of) Ionia and was held in such high
regard by her fellow citizens, as Callias of Mytilene states'.[6] In this role,
Sappho's task was to support the girls entrusted to her during the crucial

---

[4] Page 1955: 108 n. 1.
[5] Eresus: Dioscorides, *Greek Anthology* 7.407 (test. 58), *Suda* c 107 (test. 2). Mytilene: P.Oxy. 1800
fr. 1 (test. 1), Parian Marble A36 Rotstein (test. 3), fr. 98(b).3, etc. Larichus: Athenaeus, *Scholars at
Dinner* 10.425a (fr. 203).
[6] Fr. 214B.7–15; cf. Strabo 13.2.4 (test. 41). Callias, a grammarian of the third or second century BC,
and compatriot of Sappho's, may have had access to local traditions. The *Suda* (c 107 = test. 2) calls
the following girls Sappho's pupils: Anactoria from Miletus (cf. fr. 16.15, Maximus of Tyre, *Oration*
18.9 = test. 20), Gongyla from Colophon (fr. 95.4), Eunica from Salamis. Another connection was
with Sardis in neighbouring Lydia, where a former member of the circle was now resident (fr. 96);
perhaps she initially came from there.

period of their adolescence and to help them gain the knowledge and skills required of them after their initiation, i.e. the transition into adulthood, had been completed.[7] The cultivation of physical appearance and personal charm, artistic competence, and the expert observance of religion were all important areas, as was an induction to the erotic and sexual achieved by encouraging and fostering homoerotic relations within the circle. These are the areas which Sappho reviews in a poem whose extant part starts with the words τεθνάκην δ᾽ ἀδόλως θέλω (fr. 94.1). It pictures a situation which she experienced time and again when a girl had to leave Sappho's circle at the end of her education, usually because of an impending wedding, and was overwhelmed by the pain of separation. The creativity and empathy with which Sappho knew to give comfort in this situation, by imparting how the power of memory is able to overcome physical separation, gives a sense of her professional accomplishment to which Callias refers.[8]

Sappho's activity and her resulting renown could not have escaped Alcaeus' attention. The less so since lyric poetry and its performance as a recital with instrumental accompaniment, a core component of Sappho's programme, played an equally important role in his own activities, albeit in a completely different context: an all-male aristocratic club agitating and fighting for political goals and constituted in the social form of the time, the symposium. In spite of this difference, because of their standing and fame as poets, both must have not only known of each other but been connected in some way, as we will see. In this respect the vase painting on the Munich *kalathos*, which shows both as singers in festive dress and players of the *barbitos*, conveys not an evidential, but a general, basic truth. In fact, an honorific address transmitted as a single verse and categorised as Alcaean dodecasyllable in Hephaestion's metrical treatise, may, if attributable to Alcaeus, document his regard for Sappho:[9]

ἰόπλοκ᾽ ἄγνα μελλιχόμειδε Σάπφοι

With violets braided (in your hair), venerable gently smiling Sappho (Alcaeus fr. 384)

---

[7] 'Initiation' in this sense is to be found in various guises and for either gender in traditional peoples across the world; the standard ethnological account is Van Gennep 1909. Merkelbach 1957 = 1996: 87–114 first recognised initiation as key to understanding Sappho's social role and poetry.

[8] For this poem, see further Rösler 2016: 27–55. Its subtlety can be fully appreciated only since E. S. Bauer's liberating insight (*ibid.* 54 n. 161) that ἀδόλως has its literal meaning 'without guile' rather than 'honestly', 'davvero', 'ehrlich', etc.; this gives an entirely new complexion to the poem's sequence of thought and meaning.

[9] Page 1955: 108 n. 1.

Unfortunately we know little about the possible form or occasion of encounters between the two poets. It is generally likely (following Page's line of argument) that they met each other repeatedly in Mytilene, whether by chance or design. Yet we have more specific evidence for another place on Lesbos: the great common sanctuary of all islanders, i.e. one not belonging to just one *polis*, near Messon (modern Mesa) at the Gulf of Kalloni.[10] A poem by Alcaeus in the form of a prayer opens by recalling the foundation of the *temenos* (sanctuary) by the Lesbians:

Ὦ πότνι' Ἤ]ρα, τᾶ<ι>[11] τόδε Λέσβιοι
] . . . . εὔδειλον τέμενος μέγα
ξῦνον κά[τε]ςςαν, ἐν δὲ βώμοις
    ἀθανάτων μακάρων ἔθηκαν

κἀπωνύμαςςαν ἀντίαον Δία   5
cὲ δ' Αἰολήιαν [κ]υδαλίμαν θέον
πάντων γενέθλαν, τὸν δὲ τέρτον
    τόνδε κεμήλιον ὠνύμαςς[α]ν

Ζόννυςςον ὠμήςταν. ἄ[γι]τ̣' εὔνοον
θῦμον ςκέθοντες ἀμμετέρα[ς] ἄρας   10
ἀκούςατ', ἐκ δὲ τῶν̣[δ]ε̣ μόχθων
    ἀργαλέας τε φύγας ῥ[ύεςθε.

Lady Her]a, for whom the Lesbians ... this
great sanctuary at a widely visible place
founded as a common one, and inside they
set up altars of the eternal gods,

and they called Zeus 'Antiaos'   5
and you 'the Aeolian', powerful goddess,
origin of all, and him, the third,
this one they called 'Kemêlios',

him, Dionysus, who receives raw offerings. – Help,[12]
have a benevolent heart and hear our imprecations,   10
and from these troubles
and painful exile f[ree us.

Alcaeus fr. 129

The prayer invokes the divine triad to whom the sanctuary was dedicated, with Hera as the principal goddess, the only one addressed directly at the outset. In accordance with the attributive style of Greek prayers,

---

[10] Map at Boedeker 2016: 199; also THOMAS and SWIFT.
[11] Thus C. Gallavotti in Luppino 1950: 207, an unfairly disregarded supplement: Rösler 2016: 20–1.
[12] 'Help' is only an approximate rendering of ἄγιτ': Rösler 2016: 24 n. 61.

the cult names which the Lesbians gave their gods are also pronounced (rendered here in quotation marks),[13] as are further epithets.

It is in this sanctuary where Alcaeus had once made a solemn vow with his companions, among them Pittacus, never to abandon each other, as he recalls in what follows. He accuses Pittacus of having broken this oath and allied himself with Myrsilus, their mutual enemy; for this may the Erinys pursue him. Deictics such as 'this sanctuary' (τόδε . . . τέμενος) and 'our imprecations' (ἀμμετέρα[ς] ἄρας) signal that the circle of friends, now without Pittacus, has reunited in the same place at the moment presupposed by the poem.

In another song (fr. 130B) Alcaeus finds himself once more in the sanctuary. He has sought refuge there but is now without the company of his friends. To one of them, Agesilaïdas, addressed at its beginning (4), he conveys a poetic report of his situation recounting the mood in which he finds himself. In his loneliness, he says, he was '[warming his soul], even[14] in the gatherings of the women' (χλ[ιαίνω]ν ϲυνόδοιϲί μ' αὔταις, 15), which, as he seems to be hinting, he would not usually have frequented as a man.

Now he comes to mention a cultic ritual in the sanctuary (17–20):

> ὄππαι Λ[εϲβί]αδες κριννόμεναι φύαν
> πώλεντ' ἐλκεϲίπεπλοι, περὶ δὲ βρέμει
> ἄχω θεϲπεϲία γυναίκων
> ἴρα[ς ὀ]λολύγας ἐνιαυϲίας.

> where Lesbian women, for judgement of their figure,
> proceed in long dresses – but all around rings
> the sublime sound of the women
> during their annual sacred *ololugê*.

This ritual is also referenced and explained in the *Iliad* scholia: 'Among the Lesbians, a female beauty contest takes place within Hera's sanctuary, which is called the *Callisteia*.'[15]

As has been established only recently, Sappho, too, deals with the same celebration in a partially preserved poem about the sanctuary near Messon (fr. 17).[16] As in Alcaeus fr. 129, she initially addresses Hera alone

---

[13] For the significance of the names and designations, see Rösler 2016: 21–2.
[14] This translates αὔταις (Rösler 1980: 282–3).
[15] Scholia D on 9.129 (p. 344 van Thiel); cf. Scholia A on 9.129–30 (ii 425.78–9 Erbse).
[16] By supplementing the text known from earlier papyri with P.GC inv. 105, published by Burris, Fish, and Obbink 2014: 5–6; also in West 2014: 3–5, Obbink 2016a: 19–21.

as the main deity of this cult;[17] the other two divinities in the triad, Zeus and Dionysus, are included later in the third person (as in Alcaeus). In this context Sappho, again like Alcaeus, harks back to the early history of the sanctuary. Her focus, however, is not on its construction but on the creation of the women's festival, which we learn is attributed to the Atridae, Agamemnon and Menelaus. Returning from Troy,[18] they had been unable to chart the right course until they had visited the three gods on Lesbos and, as the poem seems to imply, had founded this festival to fulfil a vow,[19] a festival that is still celebrated. Here Sappho turns to the present day (11–14):

> νῦν δὲ κ[   ].._πόημεν[20]
>   κὰτ τὸ πάλ[αιον,
> ἄγνα καὶ κα[ὄ]χλος
> παρθέ[νων   γ]υναίκων

> Now also [   ] … we perform
> following tradition,
> pure and [   ]. a (great) throng
> of girls [and] women[21]

In contrast to Alcaeus, who experienced it chiefly as an interruption of his solitude, this festival must have been of immediate interest to Sappho and a pre-eminent and regular destination of cultic excursions which she undertook with the girls of her circle. For it combined two elements of the curriculum which they studied with Sappho: induction into cultic ritual as well as cultivating and refining their physical appearance, which was judged in the beauty contest. When Sappho recalls shared experiences in the above-mentioned poem addressed to a girl just about to leave her circle and notes that there had not been any cultic celebration 'from which we had stayed away' (ὄππ[οθεν ἄμ]μες ἀπέσκομεν, fr. 94.26), then this must have held true in particular for the *Callisteia*.

---

[17] The address πότνι᾽ Ἥρα (2), as we have seen, could be employed by Gallavotti for his reconstruction of the beginning of Alcaeus fr. 129.

[18] This is a variant of the traditional story according to which Agamemnon and Menelaus returned separately from Troy (Page 1955: 59–60, Caciagli 2016: 427–33).

[19] This led to the Hera of this Lesbian sanctuary permanently acquiring the function of protecting seafarers; her help is also invoked for Sappho's brother Charaxus in the Brothers Poem (5–9; Obbink 2014a: 37, 2016a: 25, Caciagli 2016: 434–5).

[20] The first person plural does not necessarily suggest that the song was destined for choral performance (despite Burris, Fish, and Obbink 2014: 5); in monodic lyric Sappho could speak on behalf of the group as a whole.

[21] In his translation of what follows Obbink 2016a: 30 also extracts this from the few remainders that have been transmitted: '[gather right here] | around [your altar, piously wishing to sing in] | measures the sacr[ed cry.]'

The reasons which led – in this one case where we can make an inference[22] – to Sappho and Alcaeus being present simultaneously at the sanctuary near Messon were quite different for each of them, as we have seen. We may, however, deem it plausible that they would have seized this unexpected opportunity for a meeting and mutual exchange, and indeed that both would have performed poems.[23] Alcaeus had access, as he himself mentions, to the women's cύνοδοι; it seems natural to assume that he sought a connection with Sappho's circle in particular.

A more precise indication of where the performances took place may be inferred from the poem's first word, πλάcιον, whose meaning Obbink reconstructs as follows: 'Nearby (i.e. in the context of this song/performance) let your charming festival be celebrated.'[24] This would imply that, in the presupposed situation, we would have to imagine Sappho, if not outdoors, then in one of those rooms within the *temenos* which, although not part of the immediate cultic area, were available nearby for meetings, including symposia.[25] Such rooms could also be used at times other than during official celebrations, e.g. for the meeting at which Alcaeus recited poem fr. 129 among his companions, for which a religious occasion is not apparent.

It may be that lyric performances took place frequently at Hera's sanctuary. Being held within the precinct clearly imbued such performances with a particular aura and solemnity. Messon was about thirty kilometres away from Mytilene,[26] as far as Eleusis from Athens – a journey that could be completed in half a day by carriage. Whether in Mytilene, Messon, both, or other places, it can hardly be doubted that, in their native region, it was at least possible for Sappho and Alcaeus to remain informed about each other's poetic activities. This is also suggested by what appear to be reflections, both content-related and thematic, of poetic communication and interaction between the two. The following

---

[22] There can be no ultimate certainty on this matter. Sappho may have been prevented from attending in this precise year, but what is important here is the possibility and plausibility of the encounter.

[23] Nagy 2007: 225 also proposes that Messon was the place where Sappho and Alcaeus met, in particular within the mimetic-dramatic context of a 'staged musical event'. Whatever this means, it is most likely to be considered part of the trend to fictionalise Greek lyric; see 'Further Reading', pp. 75–6 below.

[24] Obbink 2016a: 20.

[25] According to Leypold 2008 such facilities – banqueting houses with rooms equipped with dining couches – formed an important component of the infrastructure certainly of prestigious sanctuaries since the seventh century BC, which undoubtedly included the one near Messon.

[26] Caciagli 2016: 436.

illustrates this with the aid of the three poems – two by Alcaeus, one by Sappho – that treat the myth of Helen and Paris.

Each is concerned with an appraisal of Eros and the kinds of behaviour that he triggers, as well as the consequences that this spelled for others. In fr. 283 Alcaeus sharply castigates both Paris, 'who betrayed his host' and took his wife with him, and this wife, Helen herself, who fell victim to 'mania', i.e. lost her self-control (ἐκμάνεισα, 5), left husband and daughter, and followed the stranger across the sea. In one of the lacunae of the transmitted text, Aphrodite must also have been mentioned in her role as instigator of the suddenly kindled relationship.[27] In what follows, the catastrophic consequences resulting from this event are described with the same clarity. Repeated forms of πόλυς indicate the disproportionality between the initial action of two people and the countless victims to be lamented in the end: 'many brothers (of Paris) lay slain on the Trojan plain because of her (Helen), many carriages lay (broken) in the dust, many bright-eyed . . . were trampled' (12–17). The emphasis lies on the potentially immeasurable dangers of Eros and the enormous destruction that he can cause. To be beneficial, Aphrodite's operation requires a conscientious observance of legal principles and a prudent and controlled conduct by all involved. Alcaeus' *hetairoi* ('companions') will have understood this moral. Putting one's own life, as well as that of others, at risk could be legitimate when fighting for a just cause or against unscrupulous enemies, who like Pittacus did not shy away even from perjury, but not when combined with one's own hybris, exercised for selfish reasons.

By contrast, in fr. 16 Sappho assesses the relationship between Helen and Paris from a completely different perspective.[28] Paris is present in the poem only implicitly, and therefore indistinctly, as the person for whom Helen leaves her family and travels to Troy. His name is not even mentioned, and the Trojan War remains entirely out of view. Helen's desertion of her family is recounted, and in greater detail than in the fragment by Alcaeus, since Sappho also mentions her parents. Yet she refrains from any reproach regarding such behaviour, emphasising only what is astonishing: in spite of perfect living conditions in every respect, Helen has abandoned it all. Her decision was likewise initiated by Aphrodite according to Sappho's account, since a mention of the goddess is to be

---

[27] Aphrodite is a possible subject of ἐ]ππ[όαισε (3) and very likely of πεῖθ' (9): Barner 1967: 205, 209–10.

[28] This fragment is another one supplemented by P.GC inv. 105, published in Burris, Fish, and Obbink 2014: 9, as well as in Obbink 2016a: 19. But the new text does not affect the poem's introductory section, which is discussed in what follows.

assumed as the subject of παράγαγ' in a gap in the transmitted text, as in Alcaeus.[29]

The extraordinary subtlety of Sappho's argument can be appreciated through a single word: ἔραται (4), from the same stem as ἔρωc. Sappho had begun the poem with a set of replies which she puts into the mouths of different groups in response to the question of what they consider most beautiful on earth: an army of charioteers,[30] one of foot soldiers, or one of ships. Sappho counters this with an answer entirely different in kind: to her, the most beautiful thing is 'whatever one desires' (ὄττω τιc ἔραται). What she has in mind is the desire for closeness which must either be attained immediately or preserved during a process of change. The latter applies to the affair between Helen and Paris, which had started suddenly. Helen wishes to preserve it as Paris sets out to return to Troy; this is the reason she joins him. Once we have grasped this consideration – for it is, as Sappho notes (5–6), 'quite easy to make this understandable to everyone' (πά]γχυ δ' εὔμαρεc cύνετον πόηcαι | [π]άντι τ[ο]ῦτ') – it is obvious why Helen is willing to abandon her husband Menelaus as well as her daughter and parents. She is not connected to them, as she is to Paris, by Eros, by longing, by a dynamic relationship; rather, they are static elements in her world, like armies of charioteers, foot soldiers, or ships. In order to reinforce this explanation, Sappho adds a reflection on her own state of mind: Helen's example has reminded her of Anactoria of Miletus, who once belonged to her circle but no longer lives here.[31] Sappho has continued to harbour a dynamic relationship with her and would prefer the sight of her over that of the Lydians' war chariots and foot soldiers in their armour. If an introduction to the erotic and sexual was a fundamental part of the curriculum conveyed in Sappho's circle, then this poem may be read as a protreptic to allow the rise of such emotions. It makes sense that only the figure of Helen is of interest here. In Alcaeus' world, on the other hand, this would hardly have been acceptable.

Yet another surviving fragment of a poem by Alcaeus explores Helen and the suffering that she brought the Trojans (fr. 42). It does so by comparing two mythical female characters and the consequences of their actions: one is Thetis, who gave birth to Achilles after getting married to

---

[29] Lines 12–13; in Alcaeus, πεῖθ' (cf. n. 27). For a different reading of fr. 16, see Kelly pp. 58–60.
[30] This does not refer to 'riders' (frequently misunderstood thus), as ἄρματα (19) makes clear.
[31] Cf. n. 6.

Peleus; the other is Helen, where it is not her marriage to Menelaus but
the relationship with Paris that is used for the comparison. While the
poem presents Thetis as an altogether exemplary woman without any
moral flaw, Helen is condensed as a figure who brought utter ruin upon
Priam, his sons, and in the end the Trojans as a whole and their city,
which corresponds with the emphasis in fr. 283. In this respect, the Helen
section of what remains of this poem at first sight appears to be a the-
matic duplicate.

Yet the transmitted state of the poem would also allow a different inter-
pretation. It would recognise the extant text as part of a larger whole
which can be restored. This would yield a significantly different picture.[32]
As we have seen, in fr. 283 three actors were involved in the relationship
that developed in Sparta: Paris as 'the deceiver of his host'(ξ[εν]ναπάταις),
Helen as 'crazed' (ἐκμάνεισα), and Aphrodite as instigator who causes
something terrible to happen. In the contrasting configuration added by
fr. 42, i.e. of Peleus, Thetis, and once again Aphrodite, the goddess initi-
ates something good, while the configuration involving Helen and Paris
expresses her negative traits. Might not this very issue, the ambivalent role
of Aphrodite, once have been turned into the subject of a poem? Such a
question may appear entirely rhetorical and thus futile. Yet if one includes
fr. 41, which is part of the same papyrus fragment as fr. 42 (P.Oxy. 1233), it
is possible to make a hypothetical reconstruction of a poem composed of
ten sapphic stanzas with an address to Aphrodite in the first (fr. 41.17–
20):[33] 'You who have a sanctuary at the top of the town, with golden
wreath, Aphrodite.' The following five stanzas have been lost apart from
the three letters γυν – the stem of γυνή, 'woman' – in the next line
(fr. 41.21). Here the transition could have occurred to the ambivalent role
of Aphrodite and the varied character of women, a theme which we sug-
gested above as a mere possibility, but now deserving further exploration.
In the lost stanzas there would be room for a detailed portrayal of the
genesis of the liaison between Helen and Paris as a work of Aphrodite.
Fr. 42 would follow the missing stanzas as a continuation of the poem, in
which case the seeming introduction in fr. 42.1 would turn out to be a
closing résumé of the preceding narrative: 'Thus[34] goes the story! But
from terrible deeds arose, because of your influence, bitter (sorrow) for
Priam and his sons.' Linking ἐκ σέθεν (fr. 42.3) with Helen – which

---

[32] Rösler 1980: 221–38, 286–7, where this hypothesis was first made and expounded.
[33] See the reconstruction by Lobel 1923–5, which extends over two columns of the papyrus, together
      with the illustration in E. Turner 1987: 122–3 (§72).
[34] Reading ὤς (rather than ὠς), which would look backwards (its standard usage), not forwards.

appeared inevitable in an isolated reading of fr. 42 (even if the resulting abrupt change from the second, fr. 42.3, to the third person, fr. 42.15, for Helen seemed somewhat curious) – would be unnecessary. Instead, it would refer to Aphrodite, who is actually already addressed at the beginning of the other fragment (fr. 41.19).[35] The continuation provided by fr. 42 would provide a fitting ending to the hypothetically reconstructed poem. In contrast to the other two poems, it could be an attempt – over and above a negative (Alcaeus) or understanding (Sappho) portrayal of Helen – to represent the fundamentally indeterminate and open life journey of a woman, whose course and outcome is ultimately decided by Aphrodite.

Conclusions are difficult because we do not know the temporal order in which the three poems were composed. However, their manifold formal structures and different emphases, especially if we surmise a longer poem consisting of Alcaeus frr. 41–2, show that we are dealing with highly skilful texts that appear to be aligned with each other, whose quality may best be explained by assuming that their composers created them in mutual awareness, or even in artistic interaction.

Further Reading

The contributions in Bierl and Lardinois 2016 on the most recent (2014) Sappho fragments give manifold insights into the current trends in interpreting her work. Scholarship on Sappho has become increasingly difficult to follow, less so in Alcaeus' case. While assessments of Sappho have never been characterised by full consensus, views widely held and accepted only a few decades ago are now met with less approval and take their place among a multitude of diverging opinions.

As a consequence, a fundamental and longer-standing disagreement has intensified while at the same time becoming less clear-cut: after the Second World War, New Criticism in the United States established the view that in archaic Greek lyric, too, the 'I' should be considered as a persona as a matter of principle. While the assumption that texts by Sappho and Alcaeus represented their personal beliefs initially continued

---

[35] The argument may be developed further: in fr. 283 it is said the Trojans had perished 'because of her' (ἔν]νεκα κήνας, 14), in fr. 42 'because of Helen' (ἀμφ' Ἐ[λέναι, 15). Both prepositions reference the cause, that is, the object of the quarrel, in which the person in question (Helen) is viewed not as an active participant but a static figure; ἐκ, on the other hand, signifies an instigating active authority, and only Aphrodite, not Helen, may be considered in this role.

to dominate in Germany and Italy (Rösler 1985), the acceptance of assuming fictional elements has significantly increased since. A search for the term 'fiction' in the electronic version of Bierl and Lardinois 2016, including adjectives derived from it, allows a quick overview; it is surprising how many occurrences there are. The fictionalisation of Sappho's lyric is similarly advanced in other recent publications (Nagy 2007, on which see n. 23 above). However, clear criteria to distinguish fiction from non-fiction are not being established. The fact that Aristotle does not include lyric in his *Poetics* since he did not consider it to be mimetic, i.e. fictional poetry, is disregarded and does not seem to be considered as problematic.

Alongside the traditional view that Sappho's lyric primarily had a function within the circle of girls she led and should be interpreted in this context, a more recent approach regards it as a circle of women of no specific age, a female equivalent of Alcaeus' *hetaireia* or 'band of comrades'. (Parker 1993 ≈ Greene 1996b: 146–83 played a key part in initiating this discussion; see further Caciagli 2011, Selle 2012. It is now even considered possible that Sappho composed, and performed, erotic poetry directly for male symposia: E. Bowie 2016a.) This theory, however, fails to account for the various ways in which the poems reflect the girls' youth and, crucially, their transient, temporary membership of the circle, for example by recalling previous members in retrospect.

A book of great use for the study of Sappho's poetry deserves a final recommendation: Tzamali 1996. Anyone consulting this work – a linguistic and stylistic commentary on her most important fragments – will continue to be grateful for the plethora of instruction it offers.

CHAPTER 6

Sappho and Archaic Greek Song Culture

Deborah Steiner

According to Athenaeus, the New Comic playwright Diphilus wrote a
drama titled *Sappho*, which, the chronological impossibility notwith-
standing, introduced Archilochus and Hipponax as rival lovers of the
Lesbian poet.[1] Athenaeus also cites Diphilus for his portrayal of Sappho
in the act of toasting Archilochus, a gesture suggesting her possible con-
sent to his desires, a point to which I will return.[2] Indeed, so diverse is
the roster of Sappho's poet-inamorati that it is even contested at
Athenaeus' gathering: the speaker in Book 13 faults the early Hellenistic
elegiac poet Hermesianax for naming Anacreon as another aspirant, while
Alcaeus, who famously appears in company with Sappho in a visual rep-
resentation of *c.*470 where the two participate in an amorous poetic dia-
logue, forms a fourth frequent presence.[3] Since the ancient authors of the
testimonia mine the works of the poets themselves in fashioning their
'biographical' accounts, these accounts suggest that Sappho's early audi-
ences and readers were responding to elements within her poetry that
recalled or anticipated compositions by her poetic predecessors, contem-
poraries, and even those who would come after her. This chapter singles
out some of these multiple links and reciprocities, to demonstrate that
Sappho actively participated in and shaped contemporary sixth-century
song culture, and to illustrate the generic heterogeneity of the poetic tra-
ditions on which she drew and to which her poetry would in turn con-
tribute.

---

[1] Athenaeus, *Scholars at Dinner* 13.598d = Diphilus fr. 71 *PCG* (test. 8)
[2] Athenaeus, *Scholars at Dinner* 11.487a = Diphilus fr. 70 *PCG* (test. 26).
[3] Athenaeus, *Scholars at Dinner* 13.599c (test. 8). Cf. the vase Munich, Staatliche
Antikensammlungen, inv. 2416 (*BAPD* §204129) with RÖSLER p. 65, FERRARI pp. 108–9,
BATTEZZATO p. 131.

Sappho and Iambic Poetry

Recent work on Sappho, fuelled in part by the new Brothers Poem, has strengthened the case already made in antiquity for the poet as a composer in the iambic tradition.[4] Horace's observation that 'masculine Sappho tempers Archilochus' muse with [her choice of] metre' (*temperat Archilochi Musam pede mascula Sappho, Epistles* 1.19.28 = testt. 34, 17) and Sappho's supposed affair with Anacreon, as well as with the more canonical iambographers, add to her iambic profile: frr. 372 and 388 *PMG* are the best known among more extensive examples of iambic-style pieces composed by Anacreon,[5] whose *iamboi* are twice mentioned by the *Suda*,[6] and whose fr. 384 Athenaeus casts as Anacreon's table-turning rejoinder to Sappho after suffering a mocking amorous rejection at her hands (*Scholars at Dinner* 13.599cd = test. 8). Because there is no single defining hallmark of *iambos*,[7] Sappho's avoidance of the more outright aggression visible in Archilochus, Hipponax, and Semonides proves no stumbling block;[8] rather, the iambic label can be attached to works that run the gamut from vituperative attacks to the more indirect and humorous mockery and teasing visible in many of Sappho's compositions, whose iambic features more depend on their subject matter, context, tone, imagery, modes of discourse, and the poet's choice of diction.

When viewed through this wider lens, many Sapphic fragments reveal iambic dimensions,[9] even her familiar fr. 1, where, among the revisionary usages of epic,[10] we encounter both the larger iambic schema and the precise stratagems adopted by its participants to pay aggressors back in kind. Just as the poem's poetic 'I' presents herself as the victim of an outrage,[11] Sappho's retaliation has a 'by-the-book' character, and adopts a sequence

---

[4] Philodemus, *On Poems* 1 fr. 117 Janko, Julian, *Letter* 10 (p. 13.2–5 B–C). For a dissenting review of the evidence, see Dale 2011a.

[5] Martin 2016: 111.

[6] *Suda* α 1916.3, 1916.7–8 Adler.

[7] For the genre, see Carey 2016, Rotstein 2010, Andrisano 2001.

[8] Although see e.g. frr. 55, 57. Nor does the absence of iambic metre in Sappho's extant poetry prohibit her participation in this tradition; both Archilochus and Hipponax composed invective in a variety of metres in addition to iambics and choliambics, and Sappho's metrical flexibility was already noted in antiquity (Rosenmeyer 2006: 20–1). Some of the *epithalamia* (wedding songs) seem to have been polymetric: BATTEZZATO p. 131, PRAUSCELLO pp. 227–9.

[9] Rosenmeyer 2006; also Martin 2016, and Dale 2011a for the 'bawdy and scurrilous' (p. 51) in the *epithalamia*.

[10] KELLY pp. 55–8.

[11] According to the narrative recorded in numerous testimonia, Archilochus responds to Lycambes' reneging on their marriage agreement, and Hipponax to the humiliation inflicted by the sculptor brothers Bupalus and Athenis (*IEG* 1 pp. 63–4, 109–10).

of stylistic registers. Much as the fox in the Aesopic fable that Archilochus integrates into his Lycambes Epode curses the eagle for betraying their pact of hospitality by making a meal of the vixen's cubs and calls on Zeus for retribution, so the same motifs and registers of discourse shape the scenario in Sappho fr. 1.[12] Summoning Aphrodite, the deity best able to exact punishment from the perpetrator of an amorous injury, 'Sappho' paints herself as no less helpless than the beleaguered Aesopic fox and imagines her divine interlocutor styling her petitioner the one who has suffered a violation of *dikê* ('justice'; fr. 1.20). It is as guardian of justice, and the one concerned with its transgression, that Archilochus' vulpine alter ego appeals to Zeus (fr. 177 *IEG*). Much the same terminology recurs in the Strasbourg Epode – a work most probably by Hipponax, as a reference to Bu]pal[us in the margin suggests, and which clearly involves a curse on the malefactor – when the victim styles the target of his imprecation as 'he who has done me an injustice' (fr. 115.15 *IEG*).

Although the Aesopic fable omits the fox's curse, the retribution visited on the eagle, whose fledglings fall from the nest to be gobbled down by the fox, makes evident the tit-for-tat quality of the punishment effected by the imprecation, which typically asks that its object endure the manner of suffering that s/he has caused.[13] In the two final stanzas of fr. 1, where Aphrodite first declares the future fate of the beloved who has spurned the poetic ego's advances and 'Sappho' then reiterates her petition, both speakers adopt the language, syntax, and rhetorical devices typical not only of the erotic spells with which the lines have been equated,[14] but also of the ritualised discourse of ancient curses (21–8):

> καὶ γὰρ αἰ φεύγει, ταχέως διώξει·
> αἰ δὲ δῶρα μὴ δέκετ᾿, ἀλλὰ δώσει·
> αἰ δὲ μὴ φίλει, ταχέως φιλήσει
>   κωὐκ ἐθέλοισα.
>
> ἔλθε μοι καὶ νῦν, χαλέπαν δὲ λῦσον
> ἐκ μερίμναν, ὄσσα δέ μοι τέλεσσαι
> θῦμος ἰμέρρει, τέλεσον· cὺ δ᾿ αὔτα
>   cύμμαχος ἔcco.

---

[12] Aesop 1; cf. Archilochus fr. 177 *IEG*.

[13] This negative reciprocity maps on to the way that Archilochus attacks Lycambes through his offspring (Irwin 1998: 179–82): much as Lycambes' reneging effectively deprives Archilochus of progeny, so Archilochus' scurrilous attacks against Lycambes' daughters render them unmarriageable and cause their death, thereby wiping out the family line.

[14] Segal 1974: 149 = Greene 1996a: 67.

For if she flees, soon she will pursue, and if she does not receive gifts, nonetheless she will give them, and if she does not love, soon she will love and that even unwillingly. Come to me even now and release me from harsh cares, and whatever fulfilment my heart desires, fulfil it. And you yourself be my comrade in arms.

Typical of the highly conventionalised curses are the alliteration, assonance, homoeoteleuton, repetitions, conditional clauses, imperatives, and focus on speed and accomplishment.[15] The Sapphic Aphrodite's twofold request for details concerning the victimiser (albeit unsatisfied within the song) in the previous stanza also makes good sense: for the curse to be effective, its target must be carefully identified. The poem's seemingly sudden shift from its opening hymnal stance to the goddess's declaration of the revenge she will exact further confirms Sappho's incorporation of imprecatory conventions; the sequential re-enactment of several rituals, here a prayer supplemented by a curse, promotes the potency of the second of the speech acts together with the likelihood of its fulfilment.[16]

Alongside Sappho's deployment of the larger iambic paradigm, fr. 1 includes several of the genre's more particularised motifs and terms interspersed among Homeric language and formulaic expressions. The noun ἄcη ('distress'), coupled in line 3 with the ὀνίαι ('griefs') more familiar from hexameter poetry, is later used in the Hippocratic corpus of female physiological disorders,[17] and can refer to the nausea brought about by a surfeit or 'plenitude'. Aphrodite's subsequent portrayal of her interlocutor suits the later medical delineation of those prone to the condition: what 'Sappho' experiences is nothing new, but, as the goddess's twice-repeated δηὖτε ('again') affirms, the inevitable outcome of her overly active erotic career.

This focus on corporality and an alimentary register aligns the Sapphic speaker with the archaic iambographers and their victims on several counts. Hipponax not only parades his bodily miseries (e.g. frr. 34, 39, and 92 *IEG*), but gastronomic excesses and their resulting ailments are a leitmotif in the iambic fragments and testimonia.[18] Sappho's (partial) transformation of this iambic commonplace elevates her bodily disorder to a more lofty register, thus ridding ἄcη of something of its iambic sting.

Specific terms introduced by Sappho's iambic predecessors and contemporaries also punctuate fr. 1. At line 18, Aphrodite describes her interlocutor as 'raving', μαινόλης, selecting the same non-epic adjective that

---

[15] For the conventions of cursing, see Watson 1991.
[16] See Bachvarova 2007: 188, comparing fr. 1 to Alcaeus fr. 129, with a similar change in form.
[17] Schlesier 2011a: 424.
[18] E.g. Archilochus fr. 124(b) *IEG*, Hipponax frr. 118, 128.

Archilochus applied to the lust-crazed and (over)experienced Neoboule (fr. 196a.29–30 *IEG*). Adopting a gentler tone of mockery, the goddess similarly depicts 'Sappho' as another all-too-seasoned veteran on love's battlefield (so the δηὖτε noted above), and as the one who, much like Neoboule, has failed to spark an answering desire.

More striking still is the overlap with a second Archilochean fragment (fr. 108 *IEG*):

κλῦθ' ἄναξ Ἥφαιστε, καί μοι cύμμαχος γουνουμένωι
ἵλαος γενέο, χαρίζεο δ' οἷά περ χαρίζεαι

> Lord Hephaestus hearken, be a kindly ally to me as I supplicate you and grant the kind of favour that you grant

This is the first extant usage of the term cύμμαχος ('ally') that subsequently appears in verse-initial position (with emphatic enjambment) in the final declaration in Sappho's song, where the speaker calls on her tutelary deity to be her martial ally (28). Beyond its diction, further elements in fr. 108 *IEG* anticipate Sappho's appeal and most particularly its closing two stanzas: its petitionary character, the speaker's self-characterisation as suppliant, and the imperatives and repetitions deployed in Sappho's summary request. Were Archilochus' original composition a plea to avenge a wrong, then the resemblance with fr. 1 would be still more strongly marked.

Resistance ancient and modern to setting Sappho within the iambic tradition may stem in part from that genre's performance setting.[19] Although several late sources – all second century AD – suggest symposiastic (re)performances of Sappho,[20] nothing in the testimonia directly introduces her or her poems of mockery into this milieu.[21] Understandably: since only *hetairai* ('courtesans') and prostitutes frequented occasions from which all respectable women were excluded, 'Sappho's' sympotic presence would brand her a *demi-mondaine* or even workaday prostitute, the identity that seems to lurk at the edges of her ancient profile and needs to be argued away.[22]

---

[19] Rosenmeyer 2006: 33.

[20] Rosenmeyer 2006: 20; also E. Bowie 2016a.

[21] The several vases showing Sappho with a *barbitos*, the instrument of male sympotic poets, form a possible exception: Yatromanolakis 2007: 63–110, E. Bowie 2016a: 148–50.

[22] Most 1995 ≈ Greene 1996b: 11–35. Note particularly the view recorded in the *Suda* reference, echoing a theory that may date back to the Hellenistic author Nymphodorus of Syracuse (*FGrHist* 572 F 6), that there were two Sapphos, the second of whom was a Lesbian harp-player; this latter characterisation offers a softened representation of the poet as a courtesan. See, however, E. Bowie 2016a: 149–51 for the suggestion that *hetairai* on Lesbos could be 'upmarket' and enjoy a degree of social status.

But one among the many 'biographical' vignettes, the portrayal of
Sappho 'toasting' Archilochus cited above, runs counter to this prevailing
act of erasure. As both the visual and textual evidence affirms, individuals
performed such pledges at the drinking party, typically pronouncing
toasts while playing at *kottabos*: flicking the drops of wine left at the bot-
tom of their cup at designated targets, whether at the object of the play-
er's erotic affections or some inanimate goal, symposiasts would declare
the name of the desired boy or girl for whom the toast was destined.
Beyond the likely, and problematic, site for Sappho's enactment of her
pledge (Athenaeus cites the lines she delivered as she made her cast),
Diphilus' representation of Sappho as the instigator of the toast should
give us pause. In a comedy by Cratinus the pledge pronounced by a
female *kottabos*-player is patently obscene ('to my prick from Corinth'),
likely an indicator of the off-colour speech adopted by participants in
these wine- and *erôs*-spiked games.[23]

Supplementing this account are a series of well-known vase images from
the late sixth century that imagine women in sympotic settings, which
variously signal the game's consequent role reversals and upending of
decorum.[24] The interior of a red-figure *kylix* (broad, shallow cup) by
Onesimus (*c.*500 BC) features a nude female reclining in the manner of the
male symposiasts on the exterior as she prepares to make her cast,[25] while
the women celebrating symposia without men on a late archaic *psykter*
(bulbous vase for cooling wine) by Euphronius and an Attic red-figure
hydria by Phintias (*c.*510) are patently masculinised and even grotesque.[26]
Euphronius depicts four naked women reclining on mattresses on the
ground, variously occupied in playing the *aulos*, drinking (three of the fig-
ures hold two cups each, and the frontal figure looks as though she is
already inebriated) and making a *kottabos* cast; the vase's Dorian *dipinto*
records the toast spoken by one Smikra as she flicks the lees from her
kylix, 'I toss this for you Leagrus'. The dialect invites the viewer to identify

[23] Cratinus fr. 299 *PCG*. Granted, there is no hint of vulgarity in Sappho's pledge in Athenaeus' cita-
tion of Diphilus.

[24] Kurke 1999: 205–13, A. Steiner 2007: 206–10, Topper 2012: 105–35.

[25] Malibu, Getty Museum, inv. 82.AE.14 (*BAPD* §9023391, Plate 3). The oversized *skyphos* might
anticipate Aristophanes' frequent caricatures of women as inveterate drunkards (e.g. *Women at the
Thesmophoria* 630 with Austin and Olson 2004: 231, *Women at the Assembly* 14–15, 132–46); simi-
larly exaggerated are the proportions of the cup held by one of the women on Euphronius' *psykter*
described below.

[26] St Petersburg, State Hermitage Museum, inv. B 1650 (*BAPD* §200078, Plate 1); Munich,
Antikensammlungen, inv. 2421 (*BAPD* §200126, Plate 2). Note too the knotted walking stick – a
patently masculine accessory – behind the *kottabos*-player on Onesimus' *kylix*.

the player and her companions as Spartans,[27] members of a society often derided in Athenian humour for the licence it allowed its women. On Phintias' *hydria*, where two women play at *kottabos* on the shoulder of the vase, the painter suggests the women's subversive and parodic assumption of male roles and characteristics; by arranging the far right figure's *himation* (cloak) in a masculine style, and by giving both women prominent musculature, the picture 'mimics the masculine forms below'.[28]

The iambic invective included in Sappho's fr. 1 complicates the already vexed question of performance context. If this facet of the piece suggests delivery in the sympotic space,[29] where a female singer would necessarily rank among the *déclassées*, then the fragment's co-option of cletic conventions simultaneously advertises its suitability for a religious occasion and its possible performance by a female chorus within a ritualised setting. This 'bi-localism' and adaptability to both ritual and sympotic sites, as we will see, proves no less characteristic of Sappho's other works.

Sappho and the Choral Poetry of Alcman

Among the conceits in the Tithonus Poem, the poet includes an echo and reformulation of a motif in earlier hexameter and lyric repertoires. Following the opening appeal to the poem's addressees, the Sapphic speaker then laments the onset of old age, detailing its symptoms and ineluctable nature before citing the mythical exemplum of Tithonus to confirm her claim:[30]

]ποτ' [ἔ] οντα χρόα γῆρας ἤδη
ἐγ]ένοντο τρίχες ἐκ μελαίναν·

βάρυς δέ μ' ὀ] θῦμος πεπόηται, γόνα δ' [ο]ὐ φέροισι,   5
τὰ δή ποτα λαίψηρ' ἔον ὄρχησθ' ἴσα νεβρίοισι.

τὰ ⟨μὲν⟩ στεναχίσδω θαμέως· ἀλλὰ τί κεν ποείην;
ἀγήραον ἄνθρωπον ἔοντ' οὐ δύνατον γένεσθαι.

καὶ γάρ π[ο]τα Τίθωνον ἔφαντο βροδόπαχυν Αὔων
ἔρωι φ.. αθεισαν βάμεν' εἰς ἔσχατα γᾶς φέροισα[ν,   10

ἔοντα [κ]άλον καὶ νέον, ἀλλ' αὖτον ὔμως ἔμαρψε
χρόνωι πόλιον γῆρας, ἔχ[ο]ντ' ἀθανάταν ἄκοιτιν.

---

[27] G. Ferrari 2002: 19–20; further discussion in Topper 2012: 120.

[28] A. Steiner 2007: 208, citing Neer 2002: 106.

[29] E. Bowie 2016a: 154 also argues for performance at the symposium, but on different grounds.

[30] Text and supplemented translation from Obbink 2009: 14–15.

But me – my skin which once was soft is withered now by age, my hair has turned to white which once was black, my heart has been weighed down, my knees give no support which once were nimble in the dance like little fawns. How often I lament these things. But what to do? No being that is human can escape old age. For people used to think that Dawn with rosy arms took Tithonus fine and young to reach the edges of the earth; yet still grey age in time did seize him, though his consort cannot die.

In one respect, her weakened knees (legs), the aged singer's current state anticipates the subsequent turn to the myth of the Trojan youth and his abduction by Eos. As those familiar with the story as narrated in the *Homeric Hymn to Aphrodite* (conventionally dated to the last third of the seventh century) might recall,[31] among Tithonus' afflictions is the inability to move his limbs: 'there is no longer any vigour (literally "vital sap") such as there was in his curved limbs (γναμπτοῖϲι μέλεϲϲιν)' (237–8; see also 234). So too the former youth's now greying hair (228) spotlights another of the indignities endured by the Sapphic speaker.

But more immediate is Sappho's pronounced echo of the complaint made by Alcman, or his poetic persona, in fr. 26 *PMGF*:[32]

> οὔ μ᾽ ἔτι, παρϲενικαὶ μελιγάρυες ἱαρόφωνοι,
> γυῖα φέρην δύναται· βάλε δὴ βάλε κηρύλος εἴην,
> ὅϲ τ᾽ ἐπὶ κύματος ἄνθος ἅμ᾽ ἀλκυόνεϲϲι ποτήται
> νηλεὲϲ ἦτορ ἔχων, ἁλιπόρφυρος ἱαρὸς ὄρνιϲ.

No longer, honey-toned strong-voiced (or 'holy-voiced') girls, can my limbs carry me. If only, if only I were a cerylus, who flies along with the halcyons over the flower of the wave with resolute heart, strong/holy, sea-blue bird. (transl. Campbell)

The third-century BC author Antigonus Carystus, who preserves the lines, explains in his preface to the citation that the poet laments the weakness that renders him unable 'to whirl about with the choruses and with the maidens' dancing'.[33] Antigonus' gloss allows us better to understand the poetic wish: the capacity to fly with the female halcyons, the avian *comparanda* for the maidens (*parthenoi*) in the opening line, would signal the speaker's rediscovered ability to participate once more in choral dancing. When set within the most probable context for the composition, the conceit becomes not merely performative in effecting the

---

[31] Rawles 2006: 1–4.
[32] Gronewald and Daniel 2004a: 7, Bernsdorff 2004: 33–4, A. Hardie 2005: 27–8, Bierl 2016c: 323–4.
[33] Antigonus, *On Animals* fr. 54B Dorandi.

longing it articulates, but meta-performative insofar as it prefigures the chorus' coming action.[34] If the lines are a citharodic proem (i.e. sung to the accompaniment of the *kithara*) to a choral song, then viewers will shortly witness the moment when the youthful singer-dancers join their poet/musician/chorus leader. Whether they just dance while he continues to play and sing, or sing along with him, or assume the voice that formerly was his, the solo song becomes an ensemble performance with the opening speaker in the lead position. Alcman fr. 26 *PMGF* also offers our first instance of a scenario later echoed twice on the Attic stage,[35] first in the monodic passage from Aristophanes' *Birds*, where Tereus (in hoopoe form) invites his nightingale mate Procne to perform a summons to the other birds (209–22), and in the first song of Euripides' *Helen*, where the protagonist calls on the winged Sirens to accompany her lament. According to this aetiology of *choreia* (song/dance), the solitary mourner's cries stand as the foundational, pre-cultural form of song that precedes all more artful versions of the same and whose transition into fully developed *choreia* depends on the presence of a plurality of singer-dancers who can take up and transform the lamenting monodic voice into choral form.

Reading the Tithonus Poem alongside Alcman's fragment not only alerts us to their shared choral character, but also draws attention to several of the later work's motifs and its underlying claim. Dancing and flight are preoccupations common to both compositions. Foregrounded in Alcman, winged flight across the waves is also implicit in Sappho's choice of myth, which, like fr. 26, similarly sounds the notion of choral dancing first suggested by the weakened condition of 'Sappho's' knees.[36] While the poem declares impossible the escape from time that would permit participation in the dance, the subsequent lines' appeal to the myth of Eos and Tithonus keeps in play the idea of everlasting youth,[37] and more strictly rejuvenation in the context of *choreia*. Even as the seemingly sorry tale of the youthful abductee affirms that old age is inescapable, the poem's description of how Dawn carried off her beloved to

---

[34] Power 2010: 202–3.

[35] D. Steiner 2021; indebted to A. Ford 2010.

[36] See Bierl 2016c: 316–17 n. 35 for the suggestion that we supplement line 2 with ὄρχηϲθέ τε. Many scholars believe that the opening lines describe the benefactions of the Muses, but, following Bierl, I would instead suggest the Graces, patrons not just of music and song, but more particularly of choral dance (so too Schlesier 2011b: 12 n. 40); see Pindar, *Olympian* 14, *Pythian* 12.26–7.

[37] Schlesier 2011b: 13–14 suggests that the Tithonus story would call to mind the more unequivocally positive exemplum with which it was paired in the *Homeric Hymn to Aphrodite* (202–6, 218–38), where Ganymede achieves not just immortality, but the eternal youth that Eos forgets to request for Tithonus; see Greene 2009: 158.

'the edges of the earth' evokes a potentially different outcome. Not only is this the site where Oceanus flows, into whose waters the Sun sinks down before its dawn-time renewal and rebirth;[38] here too Eos has her 'house and χοροί' (*Odyssey* 12.3–4), both the dancing spaces and astral choruses over which the goddess presides.[39] Moreover, in the land of Aiai, the site to which (as Bierl suggests) Tithonus is transported by the winged goddess, Dawn would act as *chorêgos* to her company of dancing stars, leading them in performance as they enact their movements in the sky. Insofar as Sappho models herself on Eos no less than Tithonus – she too is captivated by the sight of her παῖδες and their youthful bodies, and conducts χοροί, for whom the mortal, like her divine counterpart, serves as *chorêgos*[40] – the goddess offers a model for just that rejuvenation or renewal that the poetic ego, 'being human', declares out of reach.

The overlap with Alcman's poems is several-fold: not just the obvious departure of strength from the speaker's limbs that prohibits choral dancing, but also the winged passage overseas to some fantastical site,[41] and the rejuvenation this could entail. In each instance, there is the possibility of endlessly prolonging that particular youthful activity from which the poetic ego finds itself excluded, and of allowing mortals, no less than gods, to enjoy an existence resembling that imagined by the *Homeric Hymn to Aphrodite*.[42] Here the miraculously mortal but ever unageing Nymphs exhibit precisely the conjunction that Sappho deems unattainable (259–60). Further linking the epic and lyric works is the signature pastime assigned to them, choral dancing ('they ply their limbs in the lovely choral dance with the immortals', 261).

If Sappho wishes listeners to have in mind not just the *Hymn*, but the part omitted in its story (viz., Tithonus' transformation into a cicada),[43] then her exemplum has, in fact, a happy resolution: the Trojan youth undergoes metamorphosis into a cicada, whose practice of sloughing off its old skin and acquiring a new carapace each year offers a model for perpetual revitalisation.[44] Tithonus' transformation is also relevant to

---

[38] Nagy 1973: 156 ≈ 1990: 241–2.

[39] Boehringer 2013: 38, Bierl 2016c: 321; also Zusanek 2005: 87–8, 138.

[40] Bierl 2016c: 320–1.

[41] E.g. Scheria, the land of the Hyperboreans, the Elysian fields and the region of the underworld set aside for initiates into mystery cults, as well as Olympus, where Apollo leads the Muses and Graces in their choral dances.

[42] Rawles 2006.

[43] Rawles 2006: 6.

[44] Janko 2005 sees the Tithonus paradigm as potentially positive insofar as the character's transformation into an eternally singing cicada supplies 'an ideal image for the aged poetess herself, with her well-attested wish to have her poetry win glory beyond the grave' (p. 19); see Janko 2017 and below, pp. 89–90.

Alcman's fr. 26 *PMGF*; by becoming both a singer and a winged creature, individuals escape unenviable conditions, whether old age or some other suffering. Those wings, furthermore, make the erstwhile Trojan beloved the mirror image of his divine abductor.

As for the fawns particular to Sappho's simile, confirmation of the creatures' affinity with choristers and their signal facility for dancing comes first by way of Bacchylides' ode for Pytheas of Aegina.[45] Evoking a maidenly *chorêgos* who leads her fellow dancers in celebrations of the island and its tutelary heroes, the epinician poet likens her to the gambolling animal introduced by Sappho (13.83–95):

> τό γε cὸν [κράτος ὑμ]νεῖ
> καί τις ὑψαυχὴς κό[ρα
>   ]ραν   85
> πόδεccι ταρφέωc
> ἠΰτε νεβρὸc ἀπεν[θήc
> ἀνθεμόεντας ἐπ[' ὄχθουc
> κοῦφα cὺν ἀγχιδόμ[οιc
>   θρώιcκουc' ἀγακλειτα[ῖc ἑταίρα]ιc·   90
> ταὶ δὲ cτεφανωcάμε[ναι φοιν]ικέων
> ἀνθέων δόνακός τ' ἐ[πιχω-
> ρίαν ἄθυρcιν
> παρθένοι μέλπουcι τ[   ]c, ὦ
>   δέcποινα παγξε[ίνου χθονόc   95

And some high-vaunting maiden [sings in praise] of your [might] . . . rapidly on feet . . . as she leaps lightly like a carefree fawn on to the flowery [banks] with her illustrious [companions] from close neighbours' homes. Crowning themselves with their local adornment of crimson flowers and reeds, the maidens sing and dance . . . , o mistress of the all-hospitable land

Bacchylides' analogy spells out what Sappho's briefer mention of the fawn leaves implicit. First underscoring the graceful and nimble motions of the fawn *qua* dancer, the epinician goes on to cite the flowery banks which anticipate the subsequent depiction of Bacchylides' choral celebrants who crown themselves in 'crimson flowers and reeds' (91–2). Also tying the tenor (the element being compared) to its vehicle (the element to which it is compared) is the intimation of the leaping fawn in the hapax ὑψαυχήc ('high-vaunting', 84) describing the maiden dancer, a compound which already carries the sense of height or elevation, perhaps conveyed through both vocal-cum-musical pitch and/or amplification, and which is then

---

[45] For a possible earlier usage, see the *Homeric Hymn to Demeter* 174–5 (the daughters of Celeus likened to fawns) with D. Steiner 2021.

transferred to the physical sphere and embodied with the introduction of the leaping deer. The near-dwelling 'companions' most obviously refer to the performer's fellow choristers, who stand in for the original parthenaic Asopid sorority of dancers,[46] but are also counterparts to the deer herd that would accompany the frolicking and *chorêgos*-like fawn. Adding to this textual chain is a stasimon in Euripides' *Alcestis*, where the chorus addresses Apollo and recalls his tutelage of Admetus' herds, supplying 'mating songs' for the pasturing animals.[47] Under the charm of the god's lyre and syrinx, wild animals join the domesticated groups, with the fawn rounding out this explicitly choral assemblage (583–7):

χόρευϲε δ' ἀμφὶ ϲὰν κιθάραν,
   Φοῖβε, ποικιλόθριξ
νεβρὸϲ ὑψικόμων πέραν
βαίνουϲ' ἐλατᾶν ϲφυρῶι κούφωι,
χαίρουϲ' εὔφρονι μολπᾶι.

and the dapple-haired fawn danced in choruses about your *kithara*, Phoebus, stepping with its light ankle beyond the fir trees with lofty foliage, rejoicing in your song-and-dance melody.

As for the concern of Sappho's Tithonus Poem with rejuvenation, achievable through the dancing that finds its analogue in winged flight, that recurs not only in the second stasimon of Euripides' *Heracles* (673–700), but also in the *Anacreontea*. In poem 53, composed at any point between the Hellenistic and Byzantine eras, the poetic ego locates himself in precisely the situation that Alcman and Sappho shared, as the (temporarily) excluded aged viewer of a company of dancers, here young men or boys who form the object of pederastic desires in sympotic contexts:

ὅτ' ἐγὼ 'ϲ νέων ὅμιλον
ἐϲορῶ, πάρεϲτιν ἥβα.
τότε δή, τότ' ἐϲ χορείην
ὁ γέρων ἐγὼ πτεροῦμαι,
παραμαίνομαι, κυβηβῶ.   5
παράδοϲ· θέλω ϲτέφεϲθαι·
πολιὸν δ' ἑκὰϲ τὸ γῆραϲ·
νέοϲ ἐν νέοιϲ χορεύϲω.

When I look at the company of young men, youth returns; and then, for all my age, I take wing for the dance; I am out of my wits, I am frantic. I

---

[46] D. Steiner 2021.

[47] Cf. Euripides, *Electra* 860–1, *Bacchae* 862–76; Aristophanes, *Lysistrata* 1316–19, *Women at the Thesmophoria* 1180, Bierl 2016c: 319 n. 38.

want to garland myself; hand me one. Grey old age is far away; I shall dance, a youth among youths. (transl. Campbell, adapted)

As in Alcman and Sappho, the sight of youthful bodies engaged in the komastic-style dance native to the Anacreontic symposium leads to the singer's desired, imagined, and even actualised rejuvenatory flight as he prepares to enter the choral company. The call for a wreath is significant; as at Pindar, *Pythian* 9.111–25, a passage that conflates choral dancing and a running race, the leaves and flowers of the circlet furnish symbols of youthful bloom (῞Ηβας | καρπὸν ἀνθήcαντ', 9.109–10), and the crowns are tangible representations of the 'blossoming' particular to the time of life best suited to *choreia*.[48] Also consistent with the earlier compositions is the amorous element permeating the Anacreontic text, which foregrounds what Alcman and Sappho's leave implicit;[49] in a deliberate echo of Anacreon's own fr. 378 *PMG*, to feel oneself airborne results from the sensation of desire that the sight of beautiful and youthful (dancing) bodies instigates from Homer on (e.g. *Iliad* 16.181–3, 18.603).

The reprise of Anacreon's own language, and the spelling out of what fr. 378 merely gestures at, viz. the speaker's old age, serves an additional purpose here. Insofar as these compositions seek to recover the persona and milieu of the earlier poet, the poem's visualisation of the Anacreontic ego participating in the dance deploys the powers of *choreia* to bring the necessarily aged – in fact long since dead – 'Anacreon' back to life. The choral garland is, again, integral: standing not just (as it does in the first poem in the collection) for the master's poetry with which the latter-day author is invested and imbued, but also for Anacreon in his role as *chorêgos*,[50] it allows this epigone to become chorus leader in his turn.[51] In an endlessly regenerative cycle (note 'I *will* dance'), this process of recovering what was lost will reach into the future each time the poem is resung (and danced?) and a new performer assumes the speaker/singer's voice.

The same concern with her poetry's *Nachleben* proves central to Sappho's Tithonus Poem, particularly with the additional four lines preserved on P.Oxy. 1787 that may have supplied the poem's (alternative) ending. In declaring that, because of Eros, the speaker has been granted the beauty

---

[48] Sappho's Tithonus Poem includes its own reference to (springtime) flowers with the opening mention of 'violets'. Note particularly the expression 'flourishing youth' in Bacchylides 3.89–90 in the context of a reflection on old age, and the discussion of this passage and of floral garlands of the type included in Sappho fr. 55 in A. Hardie 2005: 18–27.

[49] But see the introduction of Eros in the four lines that may complete the Tithonus Poem, discussed below.

[50] Ladianou 2005 shows that Anacreon was so characterised in later sources.

[51] Differently Ladianou 2005: 57.

and radiance of what Homer styles the 'unwearying' sun (*Iliad* 18.484), the poem seems to suggest that the poet's love songs partake of the brightness and implicit longevity proper to that celestial body. If Sappho's compositions also 'possess a contingent nature, in that they only have vitality so long as dynamic, mortal beings perform them',[52] then the opening of the Tithonus Poem supplies the necessary antidote to that evanescence: the injunction to the girls to sing and dance under the gods' sponsorship decked out in springtime flowers presents an invitation not only to those performing the piece now, but to all those encountering it in the future.

The Anacreontic reuse of this trope illustrates again the suitability of Sappho's songs for several performance contexts. Where the echoes of Alcman, combined with the plurality of addressees and the ensemble nature of their song and dance suggest a public and quite plausibly ritual site for the Tithonus Poem,[53] *Anacreontea* poem 53 aims to return the reader to the original sympotic setting. These diverse genres and performance venues recall the hybrid or bifurcated character of Sappho's fr. 1 (above), whose heterogeneous modes of discourse and diction likewise pointed simultaneously to a ritual (and feminine) sphere and the (masculine) symposium. Surrounded by wine cups, bowls, and jars whose images might display the abduction of the often lyre-equipped Tithonus by Eos (a scene which appears on countless vases from *c.*490 on) and by vessels depicting other motifs apparent in Sappho (the link between winged flight and *erôs*, dancers and fawns, choruses and komastic dancing among them), the symposiasts at the occasion might reperform a piece so apposite to their milieu.

Further Reading

For Sappho's presence in the visual tradition and exchanges with other lyric poets, see Yatromanolakis 2008; for Alcaeus, Race 1989 proves illuminating, particularly for Sappho fr. 16; for a different perspective, see Nagy 2007. For the Tithonus Poem, much of relevance appears in the essays collected in Greene and Skinner 2009 and, for both this and the Brothers Poem, the pieces in Bierl and Lardinois 2016. For lyric in the Hellenistic age more generally, see Barbantani 2010, Acosta-Hughes 2010.

---

[52] Greene 2009: 159–60.
[53] See Bierl 2016c and the bibliography at 311 n. 17.

Plate 1 Red-figure *psykter* (*c.* 505–500 BC) by Euphronius. St Petersburg, State Hermitage Museum, inv. ST 1670.

Plate 2 Red-figure *hydria* (*c.* 510–500 BC) by Phintias. Munich, Antikensammlungen, inv. 2421.

Plate 3 Red-figure *kylix* (*c.* 500 BC) by Onesimus. Malibu, Getty Museum, inv. 82.AE.14.

Plate 4 Red-figure *kalpis* (*c.* 510–500 BC), name vase of the Sappho Painter, with female figure labelled *ΦΣΑΦΟ*. Warsaw, National Museum, inv. 142333.

Plate 5 Red-figure *kalyx-kratêr* (*c.*480–470 BC) attributed to the Tithonus Painter (obverse), with female figure inscribed ΣΑΦΦΟ. Ruhr-University Bochum, Kunstsammlungen, inv. S 508.

Plate 6 Red-figure *kalyx-kratêr* (*c.*480–470 BC) attributed to the Tithonus Painter (reverse). Ruhr-University Bochum, Kunstsammlungen, inv. S 508.

Plate 7 Red-figure *hydria* (*c.* 440–430 BC) attributed to the Group of Polygnotus, with female figure labelled ΣΑΠΠΩΣ. Athens, National Archaeological Museum, inv. 1260.

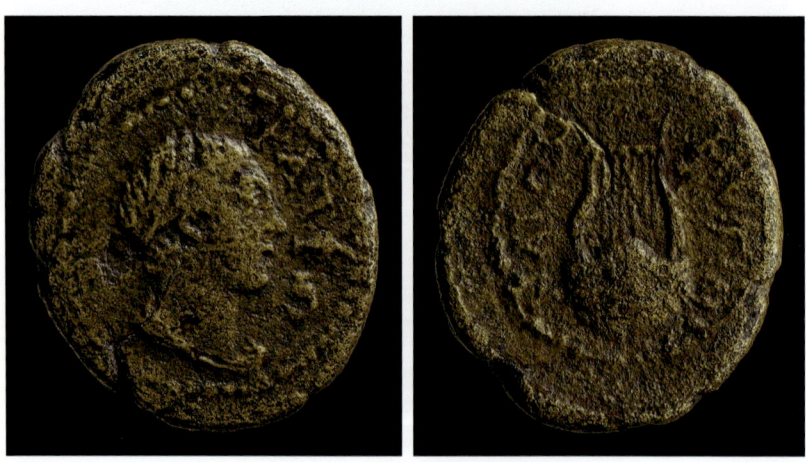

Plate 8 Bronze coin (1st/2nd century AD) from Mytilene, Lesbos, with head of female on obverse labelled ΨΑΠΦΩ. London, British Museum BNK, G.510.

Plate 9 Mosaic (3rd century AD) from the House of Kakaris, with female portrait labelled *ΣΑΦΦΩ*. Sparta, Archaeological Museum inv. 11584.

Plate 10 *Sappho of Eresos* (Roman copy of Greek original), Hermaic pillar bust. Rome, Musei Capitolini, inv. MC1164.

PART II

Poetics

CHAPTER 7

Sappho and Genre

Leslie Kurke

We tend to think of genre as a set of shaping norms or constraints – in this sense, opposed to the individuality of poetic talent or genius. This may be a false dichotomy, for all utterance requires norms or conventional constraints to be comprehensible, but, at the least, genre is about the social or conventional elements of verbal art that bind together the work of individual poets into structural groups. In the case of Sappho, the category of genre highlights how Sappho is both like and unlike the other canonical Greek lyric poets. As we shall see, Sappho participates in the genre system of archaic Greek poetry, but also stands aloof from it – hovering, as it were, on the threshold of genre.

Defining Genre in Archaic Greek Poetry

Genres are historically specific, internal to a given culture. Our approach to the context of genre and its definition is thus poised between the literary and the anthropological. In archaic Greece, all poetry was composed for performance and embedded in a social and/or ritual context, and these factors of performance and occasion were constitutive for genre in an anthropological sense (that is, emic genres within culture). At the same time, different genres were marked by specific formal features (e.g. metrical structure, length of stanza, elaboration of language, use of direct speech; for some genres, fixed refrain), that allow us to categorise and identify them, even absent the evidence for original performance occasion. We might also borrow from Bakhtin the notion of 'speech genres' or 'genres of discourse',[1] a dynamic oral system of shaping forms that leave their imprint on units of speech, familiar to (even if never explicitly articulated by) all competent speakers of a language. Finally, within a living, vibrant genre system, the mixing of genres or the embedding of more

[1] Bakhtin 1986: 60–102 (originally written 1952–3, originally published 1978).

informal genres of discourse within more formal poetic structures are common occurrences.

Throughout archaic Greece, a crucial performance (and therefore genre) distinction was monody versus choral song. The former, in which one person sang solo while accompanying him-/herself on the lyre, exhibited the formal features of short, fixed metrical structures (often used repeatedly by many singers); spare, simple language; occasional metaphor but only rarely simile; infrequent use of quoted speech; and short compass overall. Monody as a form was adapted to small-group performance settings like the symposium, in which the orderly rotation of speech or song and the regular sharing of the discursive floor were normative features. In contrast, choral poetry, sung and danced in unison by groups sorted by age and gender, exhibited a different set of formal features: specially designed and unique metrical patterns (often triadic); longer, more complex stanzaic structures; more elaborate, vividly imagistic language; use of extended simile; frequent use of quoted speech; and often more expansive length. Choral poetry was designed for larger, public performance venues – the great festivals of the gods, where notionally the entire city or an assembly of visiting pilgrims from a large catchment area served as audience for a given performance. Unlike monody, choral poetry was 'precious art' always intended for religious occasions, since a beautifully synchronised performance by a chorus was an offering to a god (or to the dead) analogous to a lavish sacrifice or costly dedication.

Traditionally, much of Sappho's preserved output, including her most familiar longer poems and fragments (frr. 1, 2, 16, 31, 94, 96) were assumed to be monody, since they conform in almost all particulars to the formal features associated therewith. Attempts have been made to claim these fragments and much of the rest of Sappho's preserved oeuvre as choral poetry;[2] but there is no evidence to support this claim, and it seems to be contradicted by the formal features noted above.[3] Likewise, scholars have long debated the performance context for Sappho's poetry, with one enduring theory assuming that she led a religious, initiatory group of girls (a *thiasos*).[4] As with choral performance, there is no

[2] Lardinois 1996.
[3] Calame 2001: 65, 212 ≈ 1977: I 126–7, 369–70 ≈ 1996: 115, 2009, Nagy 2007, 2016.
[4] The theory of Sappho 'schoolmistress' and the application of the term *thiasos* (which occurs nowhere in Sappho's corpus) go back to Wilamowitz 1896 = 1913: 63–78 and even earlier (Bornmann 1992); the model (with variations) is endorsed by Merkelbach 1957 = 1996: 87–114, Calame 1996 ≈ 2001: 210–14, 231–3, 249–52 ≈ 1977: I 367–72, 400–4, 427–32, Burnett 1983: 209–28, Lardinois 1994, 1996, F. Ferrari 2010: 33–7. See also MUELLER pp. 42–3, FERRARI.

internal evidence for such a religious function, and it seems to represent a confusion of categories within the anthropological modelling of genre, for it assumes that any occasion for which Sappho would have composed and performed must have been religious. This collapses what we know of the performance contexts of monody and choral poetry (only the latter of which invariably has a religious occasion), thereby imposing a ritual frame on Sappho's poetry not required of her fellow Greek monodists who are male (e.g. Alcaeus, Anacreon, Ibycus).[5] I therefore follow those scholars who assume that Sappho was first and foremost a poet, many of whose compositions were performed monodically for a small group of women in a context somewhat akin to the monodic performances of her contemporary poet Alcaeus. Scholars in general tend to assume that Alcaeus sang his songs solo to the small select group of his *hetaireia*, his combined political club/sympotic drinking group.[6] And while we cannot assume that Sappho and her 'circle' engaged in all-female drinking parties (after all, nowhere in Sappho's extant oeuvre is there any mention of wine), Sappho occasionally refers to female 'friends' or 'companions' (*hetairai*; frr. 126, 142 [referring to goddesses], 160). So we can imagine meetings of a group of like-minded aristocratic women that may have had no more formal purpose than the sharing of conversation and song.[7]

Sappho's Genres

The internal evidence of Sappho's poetry as well as later references to her corpus suggest a varied poetic output across at least three different genres: wedding songs, other ritual songs, and more private and informal compositions. These three categories of song are differentiated in Sappho's corpus by the age-classes of females mentioned, and by formal features of metre, language, and dialect – so therefore probably also by monodic versus choral performance. Sappho's *epithalamia* (wedding songs) could be monodic or choral, depending on when in the wedding ceremony they were performed.[8] The preserved fragments that are certain or likely to be

---

[5] This collapse of occasion into ritual is particularly clear in Merkelbach 1957 = 1996: 87–114 (cf. Calame 1996 ≈ 2001: 210–14, 231–3, 249–52 ≈ 1977: I 367–72, 400–4, 427–32), and is critiqued by Parker 1993 ≈ Greene 1996b: 146–83.

[6] For Alcaeus' performance context, see Rösler 1980, Rösler.

[7] For this view of Sappho, see Page 1955: 110–12, 126–40, Bowra 1961: 176–240, Kirkwood 1974: 101–2, Winkler 1990: 165–6 ('poetry readings'), Parker 1993 ≈ Greene 1996b: 146–83, Stehle 1997: 262–75.

[8] For multiple, different performance contexts within the wedding ceremony, see McEvilley 2008: 192–5.

epithalamia tend to feature mention of 'girls' (*parthenoi, korai,* or *paides*); a proliferation of comparisons and similes for bride and groom; certain distinct metres; and greater freedom in the use of non-Aeolic dialect forms and metrical licences.[9] As for Sappho's other ritual poetry, we have only tiny remnants of refrains and two lines of an apparently amoebean exchange between 'Cytherea' (Aphrodite) and a group of 'girls' (*korai*) whom she enjoins to mourn Adonis by beating their breasts and rending their garments (fr. 140(a); for refrains, see fr. 168, Sappho or Alcaeus fr. 24(b); cf. Sappho fr. 211). Given its dialogue form, fr. 140(a) also seems likely to derive from a choral song performed on a ritual occasion, wherein a chorus leader playing the role of Aphrodite would have interacted with a chorus of girls (or women playing *korai*).

Finally, the third category, which I have referred to as more private and informal compositions, represents the bulk of Sappho's preserved poems and fragments, including her most well-known and best-preserved songs (frr. 1, 2, 16, 31, 94, 96). I will focus on this group in a moment; for now, I simply note a few characteristic formal features and themes. These poems never mention 'girls'; they often use short, simple stanzaic forms, and conform more strictly to Aeolic dialect and metrical rules, while thematically they concern the first-person speaker's loves and losses, private family dramas, and assertions of poetic skill and immortality. Based on these formal and thematic elements, this group of poems seems most likely composed for monodic performance.

We may find support for this threefold division of Sappho's oeuvre in certain references in the later ancient reception of her poetry. Consider first a celebratory epigram by the Hellenistic poet Dioscorides:

> Sweetest prop of desires (ἐρώτων) for passionate young men, Sappho, together with the Muses Pieria or ivy-covered Helicon adorns you, breathing equally with those, the Muse in Aeolian Eresus. Or perhaps Hymen Hymenaeus, holding his bright torch, stands together with you over bridal chambers, or perhaps as fellow mourner for Aphrodite as she is lamenting the youthful offspring of Cinyras [Adonis], you look upon the holy grove of the blessed ones. Everywhere, mistress equal to the gods, hail, for we have your songs still now as immortal daughters. (*Greek Anthology* 7.407 (test. 58))

---

[9] Frr. 103B–117B; Lobel 1925: xxv–xxvii, Page 1955: 119–26, Stehle 1997: 278–82, McEvilley 2008: 186–214. I do not consider fr. 44 a wedding song; see Kakridis 1966, Nagy 1974: 118–39, Dale 2011a: 58–61, Sampson 2016.

Here the three different symbolic places where Sappho might be found correspond to three different categories of poetry – poetry of 'loves' (*erôtes*, significantly perhaps connected with the specificity of Sappho's home town of Eresus), wedding songs, and songs to help Aphrodite mourn Adonis (representing metonymically other ritual songs).[10] And once we notice that in Dioscorides' quasi-hymn to Sappho, her participation in the Adonia ritual allows her 'to see the holy shrine of the blessed ones', we may suspect that the same set of genre divisions informs the brief summary of Sappho's oeuvre in Demetrius' (Hellenistic or early Roman period) treatise *On Style*: 'Sometimes charm inheres in the subject matter, such as gardens of the nymphs, wedding songs, loves – in short, the whole of Sappho's poetry.'[11] Here, then, 'gardens of the nymphs' may represent the same poetic domain figured by the 'holy shrine of the blessed ones' in Dioscorides' epigram – signifying the possibility of communion with supernatural beings conjured by choral ritual song. Read thus, Demetrius' list offers the same three categories as Dioscorides' epigram, in inverse order: other ritual songs like the Adonia, wedding songs, and songs of love.

The third and largest category of Sappho's preserved songs – non-ritual monody, or what I have termed more informal and personal compositions – is much more elusive, in ways that seem to be deliberate on Sappho's part. For all the major fragments are unmoored from specification of place, time, and particular occasion, which means also nearly impossible to categorise generically.[12] Thus, we tend to refer to fr. 1, Sappho's longest completely preserved poem, as a 'Hymn to Aphrodite', but the poem is entirely bare of indications of where, when, and who (the object of the speaker's unrequited affection). And as the song proceeds, it surprisingly morphs into a narrated epiphany of Aphrodite in the past, complete with her quoted direct speech to 'Sappho', so that what begins as a hymn becomes a narrative with 'Sappho' as a quasi-heroic character, only to return to prayer form in the final stanza.[13] It is perhaps more difficult to assess what is going on in fr. 2, another apparent cletic hymn to Aphrodite, since the four stanzas we have may not be complete at either end. Nonetheless, this poem teases us with a

---

[10] Stehle 1997: 275.
[11] Demetrius, *On Style* 132 (test. 45), εἰcὶν δὲ αἱ μὲν ἐν τοῖc πράγμαcι χάριτεc, οἷον νυμφαῖοι κῆποι, ὑμέναιοι, ἔρωτεc, ὅλη ἡ Cαπφοῦc ποίηcιc.
[12] D'Alessio 2018 makes a similar point about frr. 1, 2, 5, 17, and 31.
[13] Excellent treatment of these surprising moves and effects in Hutchinson 2001: 149–60.

proliferation of detail about its 'pretty grove', while remaining entirely elusive about place, time, participants, and specific occasion. In fact, the poem itself thematises the dissolve from concrete to abstract within each preserved stanza,[14] forcing us to recognise that abundance of detail does not correspond to or guarantee 'reality'.

Fr. 31 (φαίνεταί μοι κῆνος), preserved by Pseudo-Longinus and imitated by Catullus, is equally elusive. Scholarly debate has long raged over the topic and purpose of this poem: is it an account of jealousy? Is it rhetorical praise of the woman heard 'sweetly speaking and desirably laughing' in its opening lines? Critics committed to the ritual and/or choral reading of Sappho's songs have even claimed fr. 31 as a wedding song, sung by Sappho herself at the wedding banquet to honour the 'godlike' groom and his bride.[15] But this over-rigid application of an anthropological model of genre and occasion exposes the pitfalls of this approach, for such a reading can be secured only by dint of ignoring all of the fragment's specific language and formal structure beyond the first stanza. This enduring scholarly debate itself arises from and indexes the poem's profound under-specification – no place, no time, no names, while even the other two principals in the song's imagined erotic triangle dissolve after the first stanza and a bit. As Anne Carson formulates it,

> It is a strangely theatrical poem . . . The action of the poem is in a true sense spectacular. We see the modes of perception reduced to dysfunction one by one; we see the objects of outer sense disappear, and on the brightly lit stage at the center of her being we see Sappho recognize herself: *emmi*, 'I am', she asserts at verse 15.[16]

Again fr. 16 (which seems likely to be complete in twenty lines) is weirdly unmoored, beginning abruptly with a priamel of value and beauty wherein an unnamed lyric 'I' disputes the preferences of whole groups for massed military armaments, asserting instead that 'the most beautiful thing is whatever someone passionately desires'. To make this claim 'entirely easy for everyone to understand', the ego invokes Helen in a mythological exemplum that cascades through two and a half stanzas and somehow reminds the speaker of Anactoria 'who is absent'. It is symptomatic that many critics have been tempted to read this poem as

---

[14] Burnett 1983: 264.

[15] Thus Wilamowitz 1913: 56–8, followed by Snell 1931 = 1966: 82–97, Merkelbach 1957: 6–12 = 1996: 92–7; see the devastating critique of this position in Page 1955: 30–3. Long discredited, this reading has been revived by Lardinois 1996: 167–9 to support his theory of choral performance.

[16] Carson 1990: 149–50.

'philosophical', not just as a radical *Umwertung aller Werte* ('re-evaluation of all values'), but in fact as a disquistion on one and many – on singularity (the ego, Helen, Anactoria) and multiplicity or 'all' – that turns out also to be a disquisition on concrete and abstract.[17]

Finally, to give just one more example, fr. 94 offers what appears to be a personal recollection, a remembered private dialogue of two. And yet again, there is no specification of time or place, or the identity of the woman who has left (unless she was named in the poem's lost opening line(s)). In the apparently detailed reminiscences that 'Sappho' offers the departing woman to remember as talismans of the good times they shared, the profusion of sensual details – of flowers, unguents, scents, and bodily sensations – again progressively dissolves into generic 'shrine' and 'grove' and 'chorus'.[18]

So, paradoxically, what emerges is that these 'more informal and personal' songs are not personal at all, but artfully abstracted around the still point of the occasionally named character 'Sappho'. What goes along with this (perhaps) is yet another form of elusiveness – elusiveness about the gender of the speaker or the object of his/her (its?) desire. Several poems contain no gender specification at all (frr. 2?, 16, the Tithonus Poem), while others seem deliberately to defer the gender 'reveal' as long as possible (gender of beloved in fr. 1; gender of speaker in fr. 31).[19] If indeed the studied impersonality of these seemingly profoundly personal poems and their coyness about gender are connected, it may encourage us to speculate on the motivation for this combination of qualities. For, as such, these songs become eminently portable and reperformable by anyone, anywhere, of any gender.

Narrativising Genre, or Sappho in the Antechamber of Genre

Given the (apparently deliberate) elusiveness in several of Sappho's best-known poems, I would like to propose a different model for the poet's use of and relation to genre. This alternative model derives principally from Sappho's Brothers Poem, but noticing the pattern in this newly

---

[17] For the philosophical qualities of this poem, see Wills 1967, duBois 1978 = Greene 1996a: 79–88, Hutchinson 2001: 167–8.
[18] Thanks to Erin Lam (unpublished seminar paper) for this point about fr. 94.
[19] Several scholars have noted this for individual poems: see Most 1995: 27–31 ≈ Greene 1996b: 27–31 on fr. 31, Janko 2005, 2017 on the Tithonus Poem. I am indebted to Renate Schlesier for pointing out this phenomenon in Sappho in general (Public Lecture, University of California, Berkeley, September 2015).

discovered song helps us see a similar conjunction of features in other (often more fragmentary) poems. This set of poems represents a slightly different, but related calibration of the relation of specificity and generality; of the personal to the abstract. Whereas some of the poems already surveyed seem to have no identifiable emic genre (e.g. frr. 16, 31, 94), the set I will consider briefly now instead appear to contain too many genres within each given song. In what seems a distinctive feature of several of Sappho's songs (for which I can find no parallels in the other Greek monodists), each poem presents a complex amalgam of different genres and speech registers such that we can track a development from intimate, private scenes to a focus on public political issues or communal ritual action (or both). The poems that exhibit these features tend to concern the speaker's private family issues, but in a way that opens out to broader political and/or religious settings.

We might offer two reasons for such genre mixture and experimentation, which are not mutually exclusive. First, in Sappho's poetry, gender overwrites and complicates genre. That is to say, Sappho's gender excludes her from the public sphere; one response in her non-ritual monodic compositions is to fold the public sphere and its attendant genres into her monodic song, producing a conflation or crossing from the intimate genres of monody and mimed colloquial speech to the imitation or evocation of choral song out in the *polis*.[20] Second, within some of Sappho's poems, genre is narrativised to create a fictional 'storyworld'. Thus, individual poems present scenes and interacting characters in snapshot or fragmentary form within a non-sequential cluster that can be heard or read and understood in more or less any order. Scholars have tended to assume that such conjuring of shards of a sustained 'storyworld' over a disconnected sequence of poems represented an innovation of Roman poets like Catullus, Propertius, and Ovid, but Sappho's Brothers Poem and the poems that seem to pattern with it raise the possibility that Sappho was already engaged in a similar aesthetic project.[21] Read thus, the Brothers Poem turns out not to be an outlier in the Sapphic corpus, or the insipid juvenilia of a teenage Sappho, but instead a *Paradebeispiel* ('prime example') of Sappho's sophisticated experimentation with genre and 'storyworld' narrative.

---

[20] For a similar hypothesis for what he calls 'Sappho's parachoral monody', see Power 2020.

[21] For these kinds of effects in the Roman poets Catullus, Horace, and Propertius, see McCarthy 2010, 2013, 2019 – an inspiration for my own thinking about Sappho.

But you are always chattering about Charaxus coming with full ship. These things, I think, Zeus and all the other gods know, but you ought not to think about these things,

But instead you ought to send me and bid me pray many times to queen Hera that Charaxus arrive here guiding his ship safe,

And find us safe and sound. As for all the rest, let us entrust it to the divinities, for periods of good weather come suddenly from great storm-blasts.

For of whomever the king of Olympus wishes a divinity as helper now to turn them around from toils, those men are fortunate and richly blest.

Just so for us, if Larichus only raise his head and finally become a man, then we would suddenly be released from great heavinesses of spirit that weigh us down.

This poem explicitly mentions for the first time in Sappho's corpus two brothers we had only known about from the later biographical tradition – Charaxus and Larichus (hence its name). It thereby clarifies the situation as the poet's own family drama and the first-person speaker as 'Sappho' herself. We have lost one or two stanzas at the start of the song. It picks up in the midst of a private domestic scene, with the ego reproaching somebody (mother? sister-in-law?) for the wrong kind of speech. This behind-the-scenes disagreement of family members uses markedly colloquial language (*thrulêstha*, 'you are always chattering'; parenthetic *oiomai*, 'I think'), but then shifts as the speaker teaches the addressee the right kind of speech and ritual action: 'send me and bid me pray many times to queen Hera'. The proposed prayer to Hera for Charaxus' safe return seems to conclude with the enjambed line at the beginning of the third preserved stanza, 'and find us safe and sound'. But it may in fact continue beyond this point (across the transition from indirect to direct discourse) to the end of the poem, folding in the pious resignation of stanza three, the gnomic reflections of stanza four, and finally the wish that the younger brother Larichus 'raise his head and finally become a man': that is, become an active, responsible figure within his household and broader community.

Thus, in brief compass, the poem kaleidoscopically plays through multiple different voices, discourses, and genres – colloquial speech, imagined prayer, and gnomic reflection more at home in choral poetry. At the same time, it subtly and indirectly reaches out through the proper religious activity of women (prayer to Hera) to the high god Zeus beyond and to the doings of men out in the public sphere. Likewise, it mobilises the form of (imagined) prayer as a cover or alibi to reproach one or both

brothers for their lacklustre performance.[22] Through this complex amal-
gam of voices and discourses, the Brothers Poem narrativises genre to
offer us a storyworld snapshot of a family poised at a moment of crisis,
one brother at sea, the other inert at home.

In the light of the Brothers Poem, we can track the same blending of
multiple voices and/or splicing of different discourses and genres in
other, less well-preserved fragments. So, for example, frr. 98(a) and (b),
from a poem ostensibly about a girl's headband:

> 98(a): . . . for my mother [once said/used to say] that in her youth, if
> someone had her hair bound with a purple ribbon, this was a very great
> ornament indeed. But she who has hair yellower than a torch [and hair]
> fitted with wreaths of flowers in bloom [(is) beautiful to see; or (is) con-
> spicuous to behold].
>
> But a headband just now, an embroidered one from Sardis . . . [Ionian?]
> cities . . .
>
> 98(b): But for you, Cleis, an embroidered headband – I don't know
> where I can get one. But [take it up with?] the Mytilenean . . . child . . . to
> have . . . if . . . embroidered . . . These things the city has in abundance as
> memorials of the exile of the Cleanactids. And [these things? or these
> men?] have terribly flowed away to ruin[23]

The first-person speaker, presumably addressing her daughter, quotes her
own mother's sage words about the modesty of personal ornament when
she (the mother) was young, and then bemoans her inability to procure
for her daughter the latest fashion accessory, an embroidered Lydian
headband. The address to the daughter as 'Cleis' again confirms that the
first-person speaker is 'Sappho', since, according to later biographical tra-
dition, Sappho's mother and daughter were both named 'Cleis'.

Fragmentary as it is, the poem combines to a striking degree elaborate
poetic word order and complex nested syntax in its first three preserved
stanzas with abrupt anacolouthon that seems to mime colloquial speech
in the first three lines of fr. 98(b).[24] It also (apparently) exhibits a shift

---

[22] Martin 2016.

[23] Like all scholars, I assume that these two fragments very probably derive from a single poem. At
the end of fr. 98(a).7 I have translated two possible supplements proposed by D. Squire 2018:
17–18: either προ[cίδην κάλα or προφ[άνης ἴδην. Both these suggestions are preferable to Page's
πρό[φερει πόλυ or Ferrari's προ[φέρην πόλυ since (as Squire notes) this verb does not otherwise
take an impersonal construction. For the reconstruction of fr. 98(b), especially lines 7–9, I follow
F. Ferrari 2010: 9–10, who in line 8 reads ἄλιθ' (an unpublished conjecture of Carlo Grassi) and
the transposition ἔχει πόλις (Vogliano) for the unmetrical πόλις ἔχει.

[24] In fact, these three lines appear at the bottom of the column, marked as displaced in the Milan
papyrus; by convention, scholars place them as the first three lines of fr. 98(b).

from indirect to direct discourse within the quoted speech of the mother (lines 5–7).[25] The first and third of these features produce the effect of the intertwining and merging of the voices of grandmother ('Cleis') and mother ('Sappho'), affectionately passing on a single family tradition to daughter ('Cleis'). The colloquial anacolouthon – 'I do not have – from where it will be – a headband' (fr. 98(b).2–3) – in turn conjures up a private, behind-the-scenes colloquy of mother and daughter.

And yet, here too, as in the Brothers Poem, this intimate, apparently trivial conversation opens out to much more consequential political commentary: 'These things the city has in abundance as memorials of the exile of the Cleanactids. And [these things? or these men?] have terribly flowed away to ruin.' The political details here are obscure: powerful families (Cleanactidae), warring factions, possibly sumptuary legislation against Eastern luxuries, certainly exile.[26] But what we can be sure of is that the impossibility of attaining the longed-for Lydian headband has become a symptom or register of broader civic crisis. The poem itself hints at the expanding circles of order (or disorder) it addresses in the early mention of *kosmos*, which can designate a girl's hair ornament, but also signifies civic and cosmic 'order'.[27]

We find a similar layering or superimposition of genre and progressive development from private to public in fr. 5 (newly supplemented by P.GC inv. 105):

> Mistress Nereids, grant that my brother arrive back here unharmed, and whatever he wants to happen in his heart, let that be accomplished,
> And all the wrongs he did before, let him atone for them, and let him become a joy to his family and friends and a pain to his enemies – and then may there never be even one [enemy/pain?] for us.
> And may he wish to hold his sister in greater honour, and may he [release me from the many things] with which he [used to master (my?) spirit,] grieving it formerly.
> . . . listening to [the rhythmic beat of the (shaken)] millet seed . . . through the [censure] of the citizens . . . just as much as ever, but it was not long before he came to realise it.

---

[25] This is true of most supplements, except Lobel's ἀλλά . . . ἔχην . . . προ[φέρην. Cf. F. Ferrari 2010: 5 n. 7, who also prefers προ[φέρην.

[26] For a reconstruction of the historical/political situation behind this fragment, see F. Ferrari 2010: 6–14.

[27] Cf. Carson 2002: 372, and thanks to Dylan Kenny for calling my attention to the multiple meanings of κ]όϲμον at fr. 98(a).3.

And honour(?) . . . if . . . but you, reverend Cypris, having made . . .
bad/evil . . .[28]

Here, in what appears to be a complete poem of five stanzas, the
unnamed first-person speaker prays for the safety of her unnamed
brother, conjuring a situation that scholars have long assumed reflects
Sappho's concern for the wayward Charaxus, away (perhaps) trading
Lesbian wines in Egypt and squandering his resources on the courtesan
Doricha.[29] As in the Brothers Poem, the genre of prayer serves as a cover
or alibi, enabling the sister's indirect blame of her brother's irresponsible
behaviour and proffering a model for improvement. Striking too is the
poem's careful pattern of oscillation of levels of community or human
interrelation.[30] In the first stanza, there is only brother and sister, 'me' and
'him', while the second stanza expands to include the broader circle of
'kith and kin', *philoi*, and 'us'. The third stanza narrows the focus again to
brother and sister, while the fourth abruptly opens out to the level of the
citizens (whether 'by the reproach of the citizens' or 'at their command',
we cannot say). It is intriguing, though, that this public or civic level may
be accompanied by 'the rhythmic beat of the [shaken] millet-seed', signi-
fying some kind of summons to assembly or perhaps a public ritual or
musical performance(?).[31] Thus the discreet private prayer of a sister for a
brother's safety and proper behaviour expands subtly and incrementally
to gesture towards (perhaps warn against) the broader circuit of civic con-
sequences for his actions. Again, fr. 5 narrativises genre to offer us an
instantaneous, vivid flash of family drama and its larger implications.

All these poems and fragments concern (or stage) the speaker's family,
and that is suggestive for my final example. Fr. 27 was identified by Page
1955: 125 as an *epithalamium*, but certain elements within its tattered two
and a half preserved stanzas should give us pause:

. . . she/he –s (third-person singular verb?);
[But,] since you too were once a child and you [loved] to sing and
dance, come discuss [all] these things [with me? with yourself?] and give
us freely abundant . . . [from this time? from these?] . . . ,

[28] Most of the supplements included in the translation derive from Burris, Fish, and Obbink 2014:
11; for 'through the [censure] of the citizens', see West 2014: 6, Lidov 2016: 72 n. 23.
[29] Cf. fr. 15, Herodotus 2.135 (fr. 202), Strabo 17.1.33 (fr. 202), Athenaeus, *Scholars at Dinner* 13.596bc
(test. 15).
[30] Thanks to Dylan Kenny for this point.
[31] Burris, Fish, and Obbink 2014: 25 (emphasising sound as an essential feature); for a suggested con-
nection with religious ritual, see Lidov 2016: 71–2 n. 22.

> For we are going to a wedding; and you also [know] this well. But send away/dispatch the maidens as quickly as possible, [and] may the gods have
>
> . . .
>
> [There is no?] road to great Olympus for mortals . . .[32]

This fragment may look like *epithalamium*, but, unusually for that genre, seems to contain a moment of reminiscence, recalling to someone a time in the past when he or she 'was once a child and [loved] to sing and dance', followed by a pair of second-person imperatives. The 'you' here is unlikely to be the bride or groom; instead it seems to be an older person of some authority, who is in a position to supply 'us' with something we need for a wedding ceremony in prospect, and to 'send out' or 'dispatch' the maidens. All this suggests a moment of private conversation between 'I' and 'you', a behind-the-scenes vignette of negotiation and preparation for a wedding ceremony about to take place in the public sphere. The poem then proceeds with a prayer to the gods and a gnomic sentiment very much at home in choral poetry, as if miming in its progression the choral voicing of the wedding song.[33]

Read thus, the remains of this poem suggest something like an imagined personalised narrative from inside a genre scene from the Shield of Achilles – the wedding festivities depicted in the 'city at peace':

> And on it [Hephaestus] made two cities of mortal men, both beautiful. In one there were marriages and revels, and they were leading brides (νύμφας) from the chambers through the city, accompanied by burning torches, and a loud hymeneal song rose up. And the young men were whirling in the dance, and among them the pipes and lyres resounded. But the women (αἱ δὲ γυναῖκες) were marvelling, each standing in her doorway (ἐπὶ προθύροιϲιν ἑκάϲτη). (*Iliad* 18.490–6)

It is almost as if our speaker turns aside to one of the 'women' hovering in her doorway, to conduct a private conversation complete with reminiscence of the woman's own girlhood.[34] We might even suggest that, like the other poems in this group, this represents a family scene: perhaps the

---

[32] I owe the supplement ἀλλά in line 4 (implying impatience), along with the interpretation of καὶ γάρ as introducing a parenthesis, to D. Squire 2018: 15–16. Other supplements introduced into the text *exempli gratia*: 4 [ἔϲϲα or [ἦϲθα Voigt; 5: κἀφ]ίληϲ Di Benedetto, [πάντα Treu; 6 coὶ] Treu or μοὶ] Kurke; 8 δ' ἐ[πίϲτεαι Snell.

[33] Cf. Alcman fr. 1.16–17 *PMGF*, Pindar, *Pythian* 10.27. Alternatively, Snell 1944: 287 assumed that a new poem began with the gnomic utterance at line 12; in that case, our poem would end right on the verge of the wedding ceremony with a final prayer to the gods.

[34] Di Benedetto 1987: 51–2 and F. Ferrari 2010: 31–2 compare this passage, but in the service of supporting a much older, biographical reading of fr. 27: these are Sappho's words directed at her rival 'schoolmistress' Andromeda, encouraging her to let her pupils join in, as Sappho and her group

addressee is the speaker's mother, reminded of her own girlish pleasure in festival song and dance to cajole her to 'give us freely an abundance [from these ornaments?] (ἀπὺ τῶ⟨ν⟩δε κόcμων(?)), for we are going to a wedding . . .'

Whether we accept this further hypothesis or not, Sappho's song seems to figure the anticipatory private moment right before the public festival begins, which is to say that it portrays genre, like the women on Achilles' shield, hovering on the threshold of public performance. Hence we might think of this group of poems as representing 'Sappho' – or Sapphic song – in 'the antechamber of genre'.

In the end, Sappho's artful lyrics, including the unusual new finds, demand close reading to supplement anthropological models of genre. When we read them attentive to language and form, these poems always surprise us and unsettle our expectations.

Further Reading

For genre(s) in Sappho in general, see Page 1955: 119–30, Parker 1993 ≈ Greene 1996b: 146–83, Stehle 1997: 262–88, Yatromanolakis 2004, D'Alessio 2018. In addition to these, for wedding songs, see McEvilley 2008: 186–214. For the Brothers Poem and genre, see Martin 2016, M. Mueller 2016, Peponi 2016.

---

sweep by on their way to a wedding. For an interpretation closer to that offered in the text, see Caciagli 2009: 77–9, reading fr. 27 as the 'missing link' between Sappho's private *hetaireia* poems, but 'in proximity to' a public wedding. My reading comes closest to that of D'Alessio 2018: 46–56, who considers this fragment and others as 'stage directions' set at 'the margins of a ritual frame' (pp. 46, 54).

CHAPTER 8

Performing Sappho

Franco Ferrari

Viewpoints

For a few of Sappho's poems we can say with some certainty how and where they were performed. This is the case with the *epithalamia* (wedding songs) and the *contrasto* (dialogue poem) for Adonis' death (fr. 140), both of which can be safely assigned to choral performance before a large audience. In this way, fr. 104 (on Hesperus bringing back everything that Dawn scattered but leading away the child from her mother) was taken up by Catullus (62.20–4) as part of a dialogue between two choral groups; fr. 111 alternates descriptive sequences on the carpenters who must raise up the architrave and the bridegroom equal to Ares with the iambic wedding refrain *hymenaon* (sung with one collective voice); and fr. 112 is a dialogue with an exchange of praises addressed to the groom and bride (cf. frr. 116, 117). Therefore, the choral and public nature of the *epithalamia*, also attested in Pseudo-Hesiod, *Shield* 273–80 and elsewhere, cannot be doubted, although their performance could be variously articulated with exchanges between semi-choruses or between a single and a collective voice.

For the performance of most of the other remains of Sappho's poetry, scholars have taken different positions. For Fränkel, Sappho and her followers worshipped the gods with songs and dances not only during festive occasions but also according to sudden, personal impulses; for Page, Sappho performed her poems 'informally to her companions'; Merkelbach suggested that nearly all Sappho's poems were intended for a group of girls (*Mädchenbund*) that she directed; West summarised her work as 'music and song, for public as well as private performance'; and Aloni thought there were three groups of poems: ritual songs, poems destined to heterogenous people, poems addressed to a narrow female audience.[1] But the existence of such a circle, whatever form it is envisaged as taking – whether a cultic association (*thiasos*)[2] or a school to guide young girls from virginity to marriage[3] – has been denied by Stehle (1997: 262–78). It has been also argued that Sappho maintained emotional and artistic relationships not with girls but with peers. Parker, Stehle, and Schlesier have suggested as an occasion for many poems a kind of meeting replicating forms and modes of the male symposium (Stehle additionally imagined for some cases written communication on a personal basis); by contrast, Lardinois has claimed that all (or almost all) of Sappho's poetry was choral.[4]

That teenage girls, not peers, were Sappho's privileged interlocutors and customary emotional reference can be inferred from clues like the apostrophes 'girls' (παῖδες) in the Tithonus Poem line 1 (cf. Sappho or Alcaeus fr. 18(c)) and 'virgins' (κόραι) in fr. 140(a).2, and from witnesses like fr. 214B (a biographical sketch), (Pseudo-?)Ovid, *Heroides* 15.15–16 (test. 19), Ovid, *Tristia* 2.365 (*Lesbia quid docuit Sappho, nisi amare, puellas?*, 'What did Sappho of Lesbos teach her girls except how to love?', test. 49), Philostratus, *Life of Apollonius* 1.30 (test. 21), Himerius, *Oration* 28.2 (test. 50).[5]

Although it is impossible in archaic Greece to draw a neat distinction between monodic and choral lyric, the voice that says 'I' is defined many times in this corpus as an individual entity opposed to a group or to another individual figure, and in a few cases is explicitly mentioned as 'Sappho'.[6] Nor is there any reference to a context somehow comparable with male symposia.

Night Parties

Iconography provides some relevant evidence, although the figure of Sappho appears only rarely.[7] On an Attic red-figure *kalathos* dating to 480–470 from Agrigento alternatively attributed to the Dokimasia Painter or the Brygos Painter, the poet, upright and with the *barbitos* in her hand,

---

[1] Fränkel 1969: 198 ≈ 1975: 175, Page 1955: 119, Merkelbach 1957: 6 = 1996: 91, West 1970: 325 = 2001–13: II 46, Aloni 1998: 220.
[2] Gentili 1984: 108–25 ≈ 1988: 77–89.
[3] The 'Mädchenpensionat' of Wilamowitz 1905: 26 = 1912: 41; the idea is already found in Nietzsche and in Welcker 1816 (Bornmann 1992).
[4] Parker 1993 ≈ Greene 1996b: 146–83, Stehle 1997: 262, 282–318, Schlesier 2014, Lardinois 1994, 1996.
[5] Lardinois 1994, F. Ferrari 2010: 33–7.
[6] Frr. 1.19–20, τίϲ ϲ’, ὦ Ψάπφ’, | ἀδίκηϲι;, 65.5, 94.5, 133(b).
[7] Yatromanolakis 2007: 51–164.

is listening to a bearded Alcaeus who plays the *barbitos* and sings.[8] This dialogue between the two singers already seems to presuppose the tradition of Alcaeus' courtship of Sappho known from Aristotle and a red-figure *hydria* from Vari dating to 440–430, where Sappho sits on a *klismos* (chair) surrounded by three female figures, according to a typology that recalls the music lessons often portrayed on fifth-century Attic pottery.[9]

More significant clues emerge from some surviving songs. In fr. 23 a female figure is compared not only to Hermione but even to Helen. It is indeed possible that the object of this message was, in the context of a marriage rite, the bride-to-be, as also seems to be confirmed by the frequency with which in *epithalamia* bridegroom and bride are assimilated to divinities, heroes, or natural elements. However, references to Eros and to the gaze (1–3), and to 'all these anxieties' (8), show a markedly subjective mood that recalls both fr. 31.7 ('indeed as soon as I look on you') and the 'oppressive anxieties' of fr. 1.25–6. Then, if the speaker trusted his/her anxieties to a female figure, the distance between a poem such as this and ritual songs such as those the Alexandrian scholars gathered in a book of wedding songs is obvious. Although the references to an open space (the 'banks' of line 11) and to a *pannychis*, a nocturnal feast (13), hint at a ritual frame, and notwithstanding the frequently attested connection between nocturnal rites and performances of female choruses, yet within the festival Sappho produces a decidedly monodic poem, at least in the sense that it features a personal, subjective voice, able to open a close dialogue with a woman as lovely as Helen.

A partially similar communicative situation emerges in fr. 27. What remains of the poem allows us to assume an appeal to some mature woman who ought to be persuaded with a recollection of a youth cheered by songs and dances in order that she may decide to send the girls of her circle to a wedding to which the speaker is going. What emerges is, in the wake of *Iliad* 18.490–6, 'a glimpse of everyday life: we could imagine that the scene takes place on the street, with the other "teacher" before her door looking at the procession of Sappho and her pupils'.[10]

The lyric dialogue involves two groups respectively identifiable with the 'we' of line 6 and the girls of line 10, with the speaker imparting directions to arrange the beginning of the festival. The phrase 'once you

---

[8] Munich, Staatliche Antikensammlungen, inv. 2416 (*BAPD* §204129); Rösler p. 65, Battezzato p. 131.

[9] Aristotle, *Rhetoric* 1367a7–15 (fr. 137); Athens, National Archaeological Museum, inv. 1260 (*BAPD* §213777); West 1992: 36–8. For Sappho's 'relationship' with Alcaeus, see Rösler.

[10] Di Benedetto 1987: 51 (my translation).

too [were] a girl' (4) shows that the addressee is not a girl on the day of her wedding but a mature woman standing in front of the door of her house, where Sappho's group pauses on its way to the wedding place.

References to a nocturnal rite together with stage directions of the kind just noted in fr. 27 also appear in fr. 30 (lines 1, 3). At the poem's close, the 'I' addresses the groom and first tells him that a group of young girls is celebrating, in a ceremony held at night, the love that binds him to his violet-bosomed bride, then urges him to rise and summon a group of his age-mates so that '[we] may look upon a sleep [more brief] than that of the clear voiced-one' (the nightingale). Scholars have frequently opined that this poem is an 'epithalamium on waking' (diegertikon),[11] but it has been objected that the verb ἐγέρθεις 'after rising' has nothing to do with the morning arousal of the spouses;[12] we should also bear in mind that the wedding banquet took place in the house of the bride's father before the beginning of the wedding procession, and that at such a banquet both the spouses and their relatives and friends took part in two separate groups of men and women (cf. Catullus 62.1–4).

If this is the context for Sappho's ode, the 'I' alerts the groom that the girls have already begun to sing the hymeneals and therefore urges him to rise from the banquet and to start the final phase of the feast by calling his friends together. The 'I' could belong to a choral group referring to itself first in the third person plural ('they sing') and then in the first person plural ('we see'), but we cannot exclude the possibility of a monodic voice maintaining an equal distance from the choruses of young men and women before merging with the plurality of the female group put under its direction.

We may compare the end of another poem, this one containing instructions relevant to the conclusion of the ceremony (fr. 43). The silent rustle of the leaves at the soft breath of the wind, the toil that seizes the soul, the sleep that settles on the eyes (which can be glimpsed in the lacunose lines 3–7) promote the exhortation to a group of 'friends' (line 8) to accomplish an action, now lost in the lacuna, that should have taken place near the end of the night.

The Book of *Epithalamia*

The poems with nuptial overtones analysed so far, where a monodic or choral voice imparts stage directions to a group or a single figure and converses on confidential terms with the groom, belonged either to the

---

[11] Contiades-Tsitsoni 1990: 100–1.
[12] Aloni 1997: 61.

first or second book of Sappho's Alexandrian edition, in sapphic stanzas and Aeolic pentameters (gl²ᵈᵃ) respectively.[13] It is commonly held that the Alexandrian scholars did not include all Sappho's nuptial songs in the book of *Epithalamia* (whether the eighth or the ninth, we do not know), but only those composed in a metre different from that of the *epithalamia* scattered through the other books.[14] Yet, as far as the nuptial content is concerned, only the small sub-corpus consisting of frr. 104–17, which modern editors arrange by putting together poems explicitly mentioned by ancient sources as *epithalamia* (frr. 113, 116) and poems with evident nuptial themes, provides us with songs whose 'ritual purpose seems always obvious, concrete, and often achieved by means of direct, folk-like tones and forms of address such as, for instance, apostrophe, dialogue, or straightforward mockery'.[15] Demetrius, a literary critic from the Hellenistic or early Roman period, already observed that, against the general tenor of her poetry, 'it is in a different tone that she mocks the rustic bridegroom and the doorkeeper at the wedding, using very ordinary language, in the diction of prose rather than poetry'.[16]

The arrangement of a book of *Epithalamia*, then, did not happen mechanically, merely by inserting in one and the same place nuptial songs not already assigned to other books; it involved instead a careful awareness of this poetic genre rooted in stylistic and performative features found in the texts.

Interiors and Externals

The two last remaining strophes of fr. 94 focus precisely on the destination and the occasions of this poetry. Sappho, whose name appears in the vocative at line 5, recalls her parting from a young woman who shortly before left her in tears, perhaps for a marriage in Lydia. Sappho would now like to be dead but – she recalls – at the actual moment of parting was able to utter words of comfort to soothe the crying girl. The recollection of a shared past consists of three pictures. First (12–14) the garlands of violets, roses, and crocuses with which the young woman frequently plaited her own hair; then (15–17) the floral necklaces that the girl placed about her delicate neck; finally (18–20) the precious ointment with which she perfumed her skin. The scene places Sappho and the young woman in the former's home, since already in Homer (e.g. *Odyssey* 11.490) a

---

[13] First: frr. 24, 27, 30; second: fr. 43. For the metres, see Battezzato.

[14] Prauscello pp. 227–9.

[15] Pernigotti 2001: 15 (my translation).

[16] Demetrius, *On Style* 167 (fr. 110(b)).

locution such as πὰρ ἔμοι (14) usually denoted, like French *chez moi*, finding oneself not only near but in someone's house.

A strophe follows (21–3) in which the girl satisfied some 'longing' (her own or that of her young friends) on 'soft covers', and this strophe, whatever its exact meaning, with καί ('and') at its beginning and its syntactic development shows itself to be analogous to the three that precede it. Thus, the whole sequence of lines 12–23 is one homogenous distillation of memories. With the opening of the next strophe (24–6), the poem's cadence undergoes a quick acceleration: through a dissemination of negative particles, a series of spaces or situations is enumerated from which the lyric subject and the girl who dominates the scene were never absent.

Some references are certain – a sanctuary (25), grove (27), sound (28, perhaps castanets, depending on a supplement) – while others are conjectural but very likely, such as dancing (27). The dichotomy that characterises the unravelling of the poem was therefore accompanied by a contrast between spaces internal and external to Sappho's house – an opposition between private activity related to elegance, beauty, and the pleasure of sleeping together, and activities tied to festive occasions and musical performances.

Cretan Aphrodite

A confirmation of one of these scenarios (the sacred grove) comes to us in the ode from the Florentine *ostrakon* or potsherd (fr. 2). The 'graceful grove of apple trees' of lines 2–3 echoes the 'grove' of fr. 94.27, and the whole poem unfolds as the fulfilment of a rite that involved Aphrodite's epiphany. The goddess is arriving from Crete to a sacred space gladdened by the vegetation dear to her (apple trees, roses, perhaps lotuses), while altars are smoking with incense and a feeling of deep sleep falls on the place.

The ode does not contain explicit references to poetic and musical performances, but Sappho addresses her prayer to Aphrodite as she sings and plays (perhaps accompanied by the dancing performance of her pupils) and replaces wine with nectar (on the model of the Homeric scenes of heavenly symposia, *Iliad* 1.598, 4.2–3) and water with a term (θαλίαισι, 15) connoting the joy of the feast and the feast itself: a game of substitutions that emphasises the symbolic value of Sappho's role as cup-bearer.[17] Since Sappho is playing and singing, it is not so much the wine that she intends to distribute to her internal audience involved in the rite as the

---

[17] For the textual problems at the end of the poem and my reading δός μ' . . . οἰνοχόαισα[ι, see F. Ferrari 2000: 40–4.

nectar of the initiatory rebirth. More specifically, the sacred shrine, the insistence on vegetation, the presence of a group of devotees celebrating a rite that includes a state of trance (κῶμα, 8), the sharing of a drink connected with immortality – all these elements suggest a mystery rite in honour of Aphrodite.

This perspective well explains the reference to Crete as the place from which Aphrodite should arrive, since in western Crete the goddess was worshipped at Kato Simi, in the district of Víannos, in a sanctuary where young Cretan aristocrats celebrated, under the protection of Hermes Cedritas, the *rite de passage* from adolescence to manhood described in Ephorus (*FGrHist* 70 F 149 §§20–1). Young females coming from all Cretan cities performed in the name of the goddess of love the pre-nuptial rite replicated in the Mytilenean ceremony organised and managed by Sappho herself through this song.[18]

Worries for Charaxus

Fr. 5, a poem recently increased by P.GC inv. 105 and addressed to the Nereids for the return from Egypt of Charaxus, Sappho's brother, refers to the sacred space of a temple. Here we do not have any explicit indication about the specific occasion of the ode, yet the information provided by the third-century BC historian Myrsilus of Methymna about a cult to the Nereids and Poseidon dedicated at Lesbos in a harbour of the bay of Pyrrha supports the hypothesis that our poem was performed in the same temple in front of a large audience.[19]

The prayer, with its apostrophe to divinities at the beginning (Nereids) and end (Aphrodite), involves in its wish not only Sappho's *philoi* ('family/friends') but also the entire civic community (line 14). There is no reference in the poem to a choral performance, and only Sappho could speak of her brother in the first person. Whether or not the ode was accompanied by a dancing chorus, it is in any case subjectively oriented, and the same is true for another poem (fr. 15) addressed to Cypris, a prayer not for returning home but for a safe landing at Naucratis for Charaxus without rekindling his erotic flame for Doricha.[20]

---

[18] Lebessi 2009, F. Ferrari 2011.

[19] Plutarch, *Moralia* 163ad, likely to derive from the same passage as Myrsilus, *FGrHist* 477 F 14; cf. Lasserre 1989: 189–93.

[20] See F. Ferrari 2014: 10–12 on the intertextual link, discovered by H. Fränkel, between fr. 5.5, ὄccα δὲ πρόcθ' ἄμβροτε πάντα λῦcα[ι ('and the mistakes he once made, that he may wipe them all out') and fr. 15.5, ὄccα δὲ πρ]όcθ' [ἄμ]βροτε κῆ[να ('and the mistakes he made in the past, those . . .').

The Brothers Poem returns to the impact of the reckless behaviour of Charaxus on his family group – Sappho, her mother (as it seems), her younger brother Larichus. Now that her elder brother Charaxus is away on business and Larichus has not yet become an adult, the mature mother and younger Sappho are in a state of social and economical uncertainty, or at least feel that they are.

The poem does not contain any directional signal about its performance, but the remains of what the *coronis* (symbol marking the end of a poem) shows to be the final line of fr. 17, line 20 (Ἥ]ρ’, ἀπίκε[cθαι, 'o Hera, to come'), suggests that the reference to the supplication to Hera in the Brothers Poem (πόλλα λίccεcθαι βαcίληαν Ἥραν | ἐξίκεcθαι τυίδε, 'strongly to supplicate queen Hera that he may come here', 6–7; cf. fr. 5.2, τυίδ’ ἴκεcθα[ι, 'to come here') concerned the rite of which the invocation of Hera in fr. 17 was an integral part, a rite which, we may imagine, took place in the pan-Lesbian Heraion of Mesa dedicated to the 'Lesbian triad' of Hera, Zeus, and Dionysus.[21] This coincidence shows, in the context of what we may call the 'cycle of Charaxus', the use of quasi-formulaic locutions to underline connections between some of these poems, activating in the same kind of audience the memory of previous lyric moments.

The intersection between cultic dimension and personal suffering, between conventions and actual experience (highlighted by the personal pronoun μοι at lines 17, 25, and 26 and by the apostrophe ὦ | Ψάπφ’ at 19–20), comes to the fore in the prayer to Aphrodite in fr. 1 as well, where the cultic aspect is recognisable not only in the liturgical scheme of the cletic hymn but also in the first word of the text, since the epithet ποικιλόθρον’ suggests the very presence of Aphrodite's statue within her temple. Whether we should interpret this epithet as 'sitting on a skilfully wrought throne' or 'of the dress sprinkled with colourful flowers' is hotly debated.[22] But for either meaning this unique compound implies a deictic value linked to the poem's actual performance; compare Nossis, *Greek Anthology* 9.332.1–2 = 2803–4 *HE*, where we find a similar deictic value in the reference to a wooden image of Aphrodite in a Locrian temple and to the gold that embellishes it.

---

[21] Fr. 17 is now substantially augmented by P.GC inv. 105 (West 2014: 3–5, Obbink 2016a: 19–21). For this rite, see THOMAS pp. 24–5, RÖSLER pp. 68–71, SWIFT pp. 209–10.

[22] KELLY p. 55; also Pironti 2014 on –θρονοc compounds.

Old Age

The intertwining of singing solo and choral dance finds a confirmation in the Tithonus Poem, where Sappho laments the presence on her body of the signs of old age (wrinkles, grey hair, wobbly knees) and yet, referring to the mythological example of Dawn and Tithonus, accepts all this as an inescapable result of the human condition. The new papyrus has confirmed the presence, already suspected by Edmonds, of the verb ὄρχηϲθ(αι), 'to dance', in line 6; the enumeration of the symptoms of old age culminates in the impossibility of dancing on the part of the speaker. Sappho must therefore have been inviting the young girls of her group not to listen or play but to dance, just as Abanthis is invited to dance in Sappho or Alcaeus fr. 35.8 V. Old age prevents the poet from leading the dances of the chorus as she once used to do, as in an anonymous Hellenistic epigram (*Greek Anthology* 9.189 = test. 59):

> Come to the splendid sanctuary of ox-eyed Hera, girls of Lesbos, whirling the delicate steps of your feet. Form there a beautiful chorus in honor of the goddess; Sappho will lead you with the golden lyre in her hands. Blessed you in the joy of your dance: surely you will believe you are listening to the sweet song of Calliope herself.

Sappho's poem on old age thus replicates the picture alluded to by Alcman's famous lines on the cerylus and the halcyons (fr. 26 *PMGF*), but whereas Alcman's poem in dactylic hexameters must have been part of a citharodic proem (i.e. one sung to the accompaniment of the *kithara*) which led the way to a *partheneion* (maiden song) sung and danced by the maidens addressed in the proem, in Sappho's poem the chorus of girls limits itself to dancing.

Sing for Us!

We find an invitation to take the lyre and sing in two passages involving the succession of songs as in the case of *skolia* or elegies in the male symposium. In fr. 21 (just as in the Tithonus Poem), the invitation expressed by the speaker is connected with the theme of old age, though here it is directed not to a choral group but to a single figure in a communicative situation in which the lyrical 'I' places itself, in the near future, as part of a group ('sing for us!', 12). Despite the textual gaps, we can recognise the opposition between something that moves around (7) and something that 'flies away chasing' (8): a negative mood (sadness or anxiety) envelops the mind of the subject while charm flies off chasing other young figures. These lines and the following exhortation to take up the lyre and to sing, we can imagine, introduced the performance of a song in honour of a figure with violet bosom, probably Aphrodite. Here it is not her age that deters Sappho from playing and singing as she is now doing, but the years and perhaps also a woeful event (4) distract her from themes dear to the goddess. She nevertheless wishes for the celebration to take place and therefore invites one of her pupils to sing.

On the other hand, a reference to a present performance can be seen in fr. 22, a poem that shares with fr. 31 the theme of the shock caused by the sight of a stunning beauty. A girl, probably called Abanthis, is invited to take the *pêktis* (harp) and to praise Gongyla, and this Abanthis must do as soon as she can, until the charm of desire flies around herself. Abanthis' dress has excited Gongyla and Sappho is pleased about this, especially since, as far as we can infer from the last extant words, Aphrodite had once faulted Abanthis' garment and extended her reproach to Sappho herself.

One would expect that it is the girl who is praised (Gongyla) who wears the charming dress, and several ineffectual attempts have been made to reconcile the text with this interpretation; but if it is Abanthis who is wearing the garment, and Gongyla becomes troubled by its sight, Sappho does not intend to instruct Abanthis on the theme of the poem shortly to be sung. Rather, she suggests that she should take advantage of the astonishment which her own garment has just aroused in her friend. In other words, music and song should combine with physical beauty and charming clothing as seduction tools. Even if Sappho's focus is on the triangle involving herself, Abanthis, and Gongyla, this does not imply that the performative scenario is of a private nature. This seems to be excluded by the object that is the visual focus of the scene, namely the garment called κατάγωγις (13): a long-sleeved cloak coming down to the feet, an expensive *himation* (cloak) suitable to wear in public for a young girl who knew how to sing and play the *pêktis*.

Similarly, the varied colours of crocuses, purple *peploi*, Persian mantles, and garlands mentioned in fr. 92 all refer to an outdoor scene (whether nocturnal or not, we cannot say), while in another lost poem (fr. 177) there was a reference to a diaphanous mantle (βεῦδος) of oriental origin, the poem to which fr. 39 belonged told about an intricate leather sandal-strap, and in the first poem of the Cologne papyrus Sappho claims the privilege of taking her *pêktis* and singing in a festival (line 3, νῦν θαλ[ί]α) as well as one day, under the earth, of enjoying the admiration of the souls of the dead as she keeps on singing before them.[23]

In the context of songs performed in succession during a party for a group or an individual we can also place fr. 160, where 'I will sing my companions' sounds like a variation of 'sing for us!' in fr. 21.12, and the double deictic 'now this' (τάδε νῦν) seems to refer to a sequence of songs. Still, when in fr. 98(b).1–3 Sappho tells her daughter Cleis that she cannot get her a Lydian headband, this should not be an embarrassed confession uttered sotto voce, but a statement with a pragmatic function. If Cleis is not covered by a headband suitable to the specific occasion, but is instead wearing a garland of flowers such as her grandmother recommended for blonde girls while the other girls each wear a scarlet ribbon (fr. 98(a).4), it is easy to think of a female group that Cleis herself led in her role of chorus leader. To such a choral spectacle Sappho's poem could be offered as a monodic prelude: almost an excuse, in times of austerity, for the simplicity in dress and hair arrangement of the chorus leader and the dancers. Some confirmation of this comes from fr. 81.4–7, where the same perspective is expressed in the form of an instruction with which the poet, who here too takes on the role of chorus teacher, tells Dica to bind her head with a crown of anise.

Erotic Pathography

Not even the famous pathography of passion that appears in fr. 31 must be understood, given its obvious analogy with the description of old age in the Tithonus Poem, as a signal of a communication within the boundaries of a narrow private audience. The ode seems to be structured along the opposition between 'seems to me' (φαίνεταί μοι, 1) and 'I seem to myself' (φαίνομ' ἔμ' αὔτ[αι, 16): to the initial 'that man', κῆνος . . . ὤνηρ (1–2) – a *deixis* of absence – corresponds a retreat to monologue at the end of the description of the pathological symptoms.[24]

It has often been asked whether 'that man' is to be envisaged as present or not at the time of its first performance: a question linked to the long-standing question whether 'equal to gods' at line 1 repeats the traditional nuptial wish (μακαρισμός) by which the new spouses were declared

---

[23] Cf. Horace, *Odes* 2.13.21–32, Di Benedetto 2005 = 2007: II 925–46.
[24] For *deixis*, see PURVES pp. 186–9.

'blessed'.[25] There is a tension within the lyric discourse: whereas the indicative mood in 'appears' (1), 'sits' (3), and 'attends' (4) implies by itself a contemporary perspective, the demonstrative 'that' (κῆνοc, 1) and the indefinite 'who(ever)' (ὄττιc, 2) distance the man blessed by the girl's smile and blur his profile almost into the evanescent symbolic figure in Odysseus' wish for Nausicaa, 'and that man is very blessed beyond all others in his heart | who will prevail with gifts and lead you to his house' (κεῖνοc δ' αὖ περὶ κῆρι μακάρτατοc ἔξοχον ἄλλων | ὅc κε c' ἐέδνοιcι βρίcαc οἶκόνδ' ἀγάγηται, *Odyssey* 6.158–9), where 'that man' (κεῖνοc) identifies a hypothetical, future spouse. Sappho elsewhere calls the groom (or the spouses) 'godlike' or compares him to a specific deity (frr. 44.21, 44.34, 111.5), yet in this case the comparison with Odysseus' praise of the man who will have Nausicaa as his bride confirms the nuptial overtone of the poem's opening but refutes an epithalamian contextualisation of the song as a whole.

The scene cannot refer either to a wedding procession (with bride and groom proceeding side by side on foot or on a wagon) or to the banquet at the bride's paternal house, where the couple did not sit in front of each other but separately, the tables of the men being distinct from those of the women; the intimacy evoked by man and woman sitting in front of each other is instead consistent with a scene of courtship, if it is true that, from the Cologne Epode of Archilochus (fr. 196a *IEG*) to the *Ephesian Tales* of Xenophon (3.1–2), courtship of a high-born girl usually could occur in Greek society only within the space of a sanctuary during a religious festival.

Mourning Becomes Not Sappho

An apparent exception that actually corroborates the trends emerging thus far appears in fr. 150, where Maximus of Tyre says that Sappho reproached her daughter Cleis, as Socrates did with Xanthippe, for excessive lamentation connected with bereavement: 'For it is not permitted in the house of the Muse's servants | that there be the song of mourning: this would not suit us.' The textual tradition of Maximus of Tyre does not clarify for us whether Sappho intended programmatically to ban the *thrênos* (understood as a disorderly expression of grief) from the houses of those who were the Muse's servants or limited herself to stating that ritual lament should not suppress the practice of other types of song even after

---

[25] Wilamowitz 1913: 56–61; also (for an account of scholarship on the question) Race 1983.

a sorrowful event. Yet the *thrênos* was part of the Muses' archive, a lyric genre meant to be sung by professional singers (*Iliad* 24.720–1), and Sappho herself composed a *thrênos* on the death of Adonis (fr. 140), whereas an epigram of Posidippus directed to Carian girls (51 A–B) alludes to mourning songs composed by Sappho in its final exhortation: 'and to your tears let songs of Sappho be joined'.[26]

Unless we give the word *thrênos* a diverse and more generic value than its use from Homer to Aeschylus and Pindar – a ritual funeral song different from spontaneous lamentation (*goos*) – Sappho could not say that funereal song is unsuitable to a house animated by the cult of the Muses. Instead, all this takes on a coherent sense if we imagine an exhortation to stop a mourning song that risked becoming endless: Sappho should have suddenly said something like 'Enough with the lament!' and our distich should itself have been a part of a *thrênos* conceived by Sappho for a funeral involving her familiar group. Then it is wholly understandable that this poem be sung on such an occasion in the house of the poet at a time that this house became something that it habitually was not, i.e., the scenario of a ritual event, the focus of a ceremony in which a family of the Mytilenean aristocracy made the community a participant in the grief that had smitten it.

Towards a Conclusion

The stage directions emerging from Sappho's remains do not refer, as far as we can see, either to home performances within a small circle of girls or to those sympotic meetings reflected in the poems of Alcaeus and elsewhere in Greek lyric poetry. Instead, references to night festivals, temples, shrines, groves, altars, sacrifices, musical instruments, choral groups, cloaks, crowns, and so on seem organically linked to the festivals – weddings, rites in honour of Aphrodite, the Adonia, cultic ceremonies for Hera at Messon and for the Nereids in the bay of Pyrrha, and so on – which animated the communal life of Mytilene and of the island of Lesbos. Within these festive occasions, however, we encounter two different communication modes: on the one hand, poems, usually choral, marking the key moments of public events; on the other, monodic (eventually with dancing accompaniment) or choral poems related to emotions, situations, and relationships that interested Sappho and her adepts in the context of cultic occasions.

---

[26] Battezzato 2003: 37–40.

Further Reading

The main scholarly trends relating to the context(s) of Sappho's songs are mentioned at the start of this chapter; see in addition F. Ferrari 2003, Tedeschi 2015: 11–14, Neri in Neri and Cinti 2017: xliii–l, and Loscalzo 2019, who states, in line with the sympotic perspective adopted by H. Parker and others, that Sappho and her followers were *hetairai*, polite and cultured women used to meeting male guests and exchanging various feelings and topics with them on equal terms. For the likely audience of Sappho's iambic poetry, see Rosenmeyer 2006.

CHAPTER 9

Sappho's Metres and Music

Luigi Battezzato

Metrical Terminology

Greek is a quantitative language: its syllables are either long or short. In Greek, a syllable ending in a short vowel is short; all other syllables are long. All syllables which include a long vowel or a diphthong are long; the same applies to syllables that end in a consonant.[1] Greek poets combined short and long syllables in imaginative ways; their inventiveness created a large number of rhythmical structures.

The metres of Sappho and Alcaeus are peculiar within the Greek metrical system, and probably maintain features that date back to the Indo-European tradition.[2] They used the Aeolic dialect;[3] their metrical tradition too, by extension, is regularly called 'Aeolic', and can be usefully contrasted with the Ionic tradition of Homer (who composed his poetry in dactylic hexameters) and Archilochus (who used elegiac distichs, iambs, trochees, among other metres), and the Doric tradition of Alcman, Stesichorus, Pindar, and Bacchylides.[4]

The main peculiarity of Aeolic metre is 'isosyllabism'. In the earliest poems of the Ionic poetic tradition, under certain conditions two short syllables can be used instead of a single long syllable (a phenomenon called 'resolution'); conversely, in dactylic hexameters and pentameters a long syllable can be used instead of two short ones ('contraction'). By contrast, in the Aeolic tradition of Sappho and Alcaeus, each line contains a fixed number of syllables (i.e. is 'isosyllabic'); it is not possible to substitute two short syllables for a long element, or a long syllable for two short ones.

A second peculiarity of Aeolic metre is the 'Aeolic base'. The first two elements of many Aeolic metrical structures are completely free: they can

---

[1] West 1982: 7–18.
[2] Battezzato 2009: 133–4.
[3] Tribulato.
[4] West 1982: 29–56.

be two short syllables, two long syllables, a long and a short, or a short and a long. An element that can be either short or long is called 'anceps' (plural 'ancipitia', symbol ×). The Aeolic base is thus made of two ancipitia. The number of syllables, not their length, is what matters in the Aeolic base: this characteristic is coherent with isosyllabism, and in contrast with the rest of the Greek tradition.

Four other general metrical concepts should be taken into account: synapheia, responsion, catalexis, and acephalia. These concepts apply to Greek metre in general, not simply to Sappho's poems.

Synapheia ('connection', 'conjunction') means that all words within a verse are prosodically connected; this connection stops at the metrical pause that ends the verse. In some cases, for practical purposes, some longer verses are split between two lines on the written or printed page (below, p. 128); this means that e.g. a word can be split between two lines, because the line break on the page does not correspond to a pause in ancient poetical performances.

Sappho composed her poems in strophic form: the metrical pattern of the strophe was repeated several times throughout the poem. This is called 'responsion': two or more metrical sequences are in responsion if they can be analysed according to the same metrical pattern, making allowances for anceps and indifferent elements, and (rarely in Sappho) for resolution/contraction.[5] Some specific cognate, rather than identical, metrical sequences, having the same number of elements, occasionally occur in responsion: in Sappho this happens with the choriambic dimeter and the glyconic.[6]

The two final elements of a metrical structure are often substituted by a single long element; this phenomenon is called catalexis ('termination', 'cadence'). A catalectic version of a metrical structure is thus one element shorter (at the end) than the 'original' metrical structure. Catalectic structures frequently occur at the end of strophe or of verse; they often give a sense of rhythmical closure. The symbol ^ at the end of a metrical structure indicates that the structure is catalectic (e.g. the trochee is *tro* = – ∪ – ×; a catalectic trochee is *tro*^ = – ∪ –). The term 'hypercatalectic' is often used to designate a metrical structure in which the final long element is substituted by two long elements.

---

[5] The final element before end of verse is termed the *elementum indifferens* or 'indifferent element' (symbol ∩). It means that the length of the final syllable before the pause (marked by ‖) does not matter. Other scholars mark the element before the pause with the symbol for a long syllable (i.e. –) in order to indicate that long and short syllables, when followed by a pause, are considered equivalent.

[6] Battezzato 2009: 132.

Acephalia ('headlessness') occurs when the first element of a metrical structure is omitted. An 'acephalous' ('headless') version of a metrical structure is thus one element shorter (at the beginning) than the 'original' metrical structure. The symbol ^ at the beginning of a metrical structure indicates that the structure is acephalous (e.g. the iambic metron is *ia* = x – ∪ –; an acephalous iambic metron is ^*ia* = – ∪ –).

Basic Metrical Structures

One of the most important Aeolic structures is the glyconic.[7] Its basic structure is:

x x – ∪∪ – ∪ –   *glyc* or *gl*

The pherecratean is a catalectic version of the glyconic:

x x – ∪∪ – –   *pher* or *ph*

The hipponactean is a hypercatalectic version of the glyconic (that is, it has one syllable more than the glyconic):

x x – ∪∪ – ∪ – –   *hipp* or *hi*

The resulting ending ∪ – – is often called 'pendant' (West 1982: 19) and probably suggested a sense of rhythmical termination.

Glyconics, pherecrateans, and hipponacteans start with the Aeolic base, and are built around the central rhythmical structure – ∪ ∪ –, a structure called the choriamb (*cho*). Sappho already uses a variant of the glyconic destined to be popular with later poets, especially Euripides. The variant is variously called 'choriambic dimeter' or 'wilamowitzian'.[8] Its structure in Sappho is:

x x – ∪ – ∪∪ –   *dim cho* or *wil*

The structure is similar to the glyconic, except that the fifth and sixth element switch place through 'anaclasis' (literally 'bending back'). Sappho, like many later poets, uses this structure in responsion to the glyconic (frr. 95.9, 96.7); it is thus viewed as a variant of glyconic.[9]

---

[7] The names of the cola are often derived from the name of the ancient poet who first (supposedly) used each structure as a verse in a stichic composition (i.e. in a poem composed of identical verses): Glycon, Pherecrates, Hipponax, Telesilla, Asclepiades. They may also derive from the name of the modern scholar who studied them (Reiz, Wilamowitz), or from the text of ancient poets who used these structures (West 1982: 30 with n. 3 named the 'hagesichorean' after the Hagesichora mentioned in Alcman fr. 1.57 *PMGF*).

[8] So-called because the first detailed study of it is in Wilamowitz-Moellendorff 1921: 210–44 (although he gave it a different name).

[9] For later usage, see Itsumi 1982, 1984.

Aeolic poets often used acephalous versions of these cola:

$\times - \cup\cup - \cup -$ $^{\wedge}glyc$ = telesillean (*tel*)

$\times - \cup\cup - -$ $^{\wedge}pher$ = reizianum (*reiz*)

$\times - \cup\cup - \cup - -$ $^{\wedge}hipp$ = hagesichorean (*hag*)

If ancient poets omit the Aeolic base altogether, we have 'doubly acephalous' cola; Sappho uses the structure:

$- \cup\cup - -$ $^{\wedge\wedge}pher$ = adonean (*adon* or *ad*)

Aeolic poets created expanded versions of these metres by adding more choriambs next to the one at the nucleus of the colon, or by lengthening the choriamb into a series of dactyls ($- \cup\cup$, *da* or *d*). This process is often called 'internal expansion' and affects the choriambic nucleus. It is normally designated with a raised symbol printed next to the main structure.[10] For instance, Book 3 of Sappho was written in a metre that can be symbolised as $glyc^{2cho}$; that is, a glyconic ($\times \times - \cup\cup - \cup -$) expanded by two choriambs ($- \cup\cup -$ and $- \cup\cup -$) to give $\times \times - \cup\cup - - \cup\cup - - \cup\cup - \cup -$. This is the resulting strophe:[11]

$\times\times - \cup\cup - -\cup\cup - -\cup\cup - \cup\cap \|$ $glyc^{2cho} \|$

$\times\times - \cup\cup - -\cup\cup - -\cup\cup - \cup\cap \|\|$ $glyc^{2cho} \|\|$

This metre was often used by ancient poets, including Horace, and has a special name, 'greater asclepiad', after the poet Asclepiades; it is contrasted with the 'lesser asclepiad' or $glyc^{cho}$ ($\times \times - \cup\cup - - \cup\cup - \cup -$), in which the glyconic is expanded by a single choriamb.[12]

Book 2 of Sappho was written in a metre that can be symbolised as $glyc^{2da}$; that is, a glyconic ($\times \times - \cup\cup - \cup -$) expanded by two dactyls ($- \cup\cup$ and $- \cup\cup$), giving $\times \times - \cup\cup - \cup\cup - \cup\cup - \cup -$.[13] This is the resulting strophe:

---

[10] The concept of expansion and the relevant symbols are mainly due to Bruno Snell (1982: 44–5, especially 45 n. 23), but Caesius Bassus (first century AD, VI 306.4–6 *GL*) already interpreted the lesser asclepiad as a choriambic expansion of a glyconic. Some modern scholars (e.g. Gentili and Lomiento 2003: 154–5) object to the idea of expansion, which, however, should not be conceived as a description of the historical process that generated these metrical structures, but simply as a synchronic description of the rhythms within archaic and classical performing practice.

[11] The symbol $\|\|$ indicates end of strophic structure.

[12] Sappho may have used $glyc^{cho}$ in frr. 120, 166.

[13] Ancient scholars called this line the 'sapphic line of 14 syllables', an unhelpful name rarely used in modern scholarship: Hephaestion, *Handbook on Metres* 7.7 (test. 227 V.). Gentili and Lomiento 2003: 106–7 interpret it as an Aeolic form of a dactylic pentameter (with Aeolic base and cretic ending $- \cup\cap \|$).

$$\times \times - \cup\cup - \cup\cup - \cup\cup - \cup \cap \parallel \qquad glyc^{2da} \parallel$$

$$\times \times - \cup\cup - \cup\cup - \cup\cup - \cup \cap \parallel\parallel \qquad glyc^{2da} \parallel\parallel$$

Grenfell and Hunt observed that all the lines in P.Oxy. 1787 (= frr. 58–87) are compatible with the following metrical pattern:[14]

$$\times - \cup\cup - - \cup\cup - - \cup\cup - \cup - \cap \parallel \qquad {}^{\wedge}hipp^{2cho} \parallel$$

$$\times - \cup\cup - - \cup\cup - - \cup\cup - \cup - \cap \parallel \qquad {}^{\wedge}hipp^{2cho} \parallel\parallel$$

It is plausible that these structures occurred in Book 4 of the Hellenistic edition of Sappho (frr. 82(a), 91), along with other types of strophes.[15] These examples offer an illustration of internal expansion of Aeolic cola.

Sappho writes lines that can be interpreted either as dactylic hexameters or expanded pherecrateans (fr. 142; also fr. 143):

$$\times \times - \cup\cup - \cup\cup - \cup\cup - \cup\cup - \cap \parallel \qquad pher^{3da} \parallel \text{ (or } 6da \parallel)$$

Λάτω καὶ Νιόβα μάλα μὲν φίλαι ἦσαν ἔταιραι

Here the shortening of the final diphthong of φίλαι in front of the following vowel is a type of prosody that strongly recalls epic, and reinforces the dactylic interpretation.[16] Sappho also writes verses that can only be interpreted as true hexameters, for instance fr. 105(c).2:

$$- \cup\cup - - - \cup\cup - \cup\cup - \cup\cup - \cap \parallel \qquad 6da \parallel$$

πόσσι καταστείβοισι, χάμαι δέ τε πόρφυρον ἄνθος

Here an Aeolic interpretation is impossible: the base would be a dactyl (– ∪ ∪), but this implementation of the Aeolic base, although possible in later poets (e.g. Euripides), is unattested in Sappho and Alcaeus. Moreover, we find a contraction of the double-short rhythm in the fourth and fifth syllable (–αcτει–), which would be impossible in the double-short rhythm of Aeolic cola, at least in Sappho and Alcaeus.[17] Some scholars actually suggest that structures such as *pher*[3da] gave origin to the hexameter.[18] The rhythmic and (possibly) genetic affinity explains why Sappho used actual hexameters in her poetry (and found them as part of the Aeolic poetic tradition).

---

[14] Grenfell and Hunt 1922: 26.

[15] Liberman 2007: 48–50, Prauscello 2016, Battezzato 2018: 9–11, PRAUSCELLO p. 223.

[16] See also frr. 44.5, 105(a).1, 143, Lobel 1925: lix–lx.

[17] These phenomena are attested in the Aeolic cola of later poets: West 1982: 116, Itsumi 1984: 77–8, Lourenço 2011: 93.

[18] Nagy 1974: 27–149, Battezzato 2009: 140.

These specifically Aeolic cola are often prefixed or followed by other types of structures common in the Ionic and/or Doric metrical traditions:

× – ∪ –   iambic metron or iamb (*ia*)

– ∪ –   ^*ia* = cretic (*cr*)

∪ – –   *ia*^ = baccheus (*ba* or *b*)

× – ∪ –   trochaic metron or trochee (*tro* or *tr*)

– ∪ ∪   dactyl (*da* or *d*)

Snell calls this process 'external expansion'.[19] Sappho uses structures that are not specifically Aeolic in sequences 'kata metron', that is in sequences where the same metron occurs twice or more (e.g. 2*tro* – – ‖ and 3*tro* – ‖ in test. 243 V.). In addition, Sappho also uses other types of cola, including the Ionic metron:

∪ ∪ – –   ionic metron (*io*)

Ionics are used as trimeters (3*io*: frr. 113, 135). Like other, later Greek poets, Sappho combines ionics with a cognate rhythm ∪ ∪ – ∪ – ∪ – –, normally called 'anacreontic' (*anacr*), after Anacreon, who used it often. The anacreontic can be seen as an anaclastic version of the ionic dimeter.[20] In Sappho we find:

∪ ∪ – ∪ – ∪ – – ∪ ∪ – ∪ – ∪ – – 2 anacreontics (or 'anaclastic ionic tetrameter') (test. 238 V.; cf. *anacr io* at fr. 134)

She also uses the 'ithyphallic' (*ith*: – ∪ – ∪ – –) and the choriamb as repeated metra (e.g. fr. 127 2*ith*, fr. 128 3*cho ba*).

Strophic Structures

The Alexandrian editions ordered Sappho's poems mostly on the basis of metrical criteria.[21] The standard ancient edition can be usefully taken as the starting point to explore the types of strophes used by Sappho.

The most famous structure is the so-called 'sapphic stanza'. All her poems written in this metre were collected in Book 1 of the Hellenistic edition of her poems. An ancient manuscript (fr. 30) attests that this book included 1,320 lines, which amount to 330 sapphic stanzas. The general pattern is as follows:

---

[19] Snell 1982: 44.
[20] West 1982: 31. For responsion between anacreontics and ionic dimeters in tragedy, see West 1982: 124. For anacreontics in lyric and tragedy, see Zuntz 1984: 28–58.
[21] Liberman 2007, Battezzato 2018, PRAUSCELLO.

– U – x – U U – U – ∩ ‖	*cr* ^*hipp* ‖
– U – x – U U – U – ∩ ‖	*cr* ^*hipp* ‖
– U – x – U U – U ⋮ – x ⋮ – U U – ∩ ‖‖	*cr* ^*hipp adon* ‖‖
	= *cr* ^*glyc* ^*pher* ‖‖

A tradition dating from the Hellenistic and imperial age presented the sapphic strophe as a four-line structure, writing the last five syllables of the third verse as a separate fourth line, but lines 3 and 4 are not separated by a metrical pause. The disposition over four lines had several practical advantages: it makes it easier for readers and performers to perceive the recurrence of the identical sequence *cr* ^*hipp* at the beginning of lines 1–3, and it saves space in manuscripts, avoiding a long third line.

The final sequence, – U U – ∩ ‖, called 'adonean', is often preceded by word end (caesura: symbol |). A word may be split between line 3 and 4 of the strophe (fr. 31.3–4 φωνείϲαϲ, 11–12 ἐπιρρόμ|βειϲι); we also find elision (fr. 31.7–8 φώναιϲ' οὐδ') or other signs of prosodical continuity (fr. 1.7–8 λίποιϲἄ | χ'ρύϲιον, 19–20 ὦ | Ψάπφ'). There are also cases where elision occurs between lines 1 and 2 (fr. 31.9–10 λέπτον | δ' αὔτικα). This phenomenon, called 'episynaloephe', does not imply the absence of metrical pause: the same phenomenon occurs in Sophocles between recited iambic trimeters.[22] Ancient scribes wrote the elided monosyllable at the beginning of the following line, avoiding ending a line with an elision.[23]

The third verse of the stanza begins with the same rhythm as the first two, and it is probably simpler to memorise it as *cr* ^*hipp adon*. The interpretation *cr* ^*glyc* ^*pher* makes better metrical sense, however: the pherecratean is a shortened (catalectic) version of a glyconic, and often used to suggest the sense of an ending after glyconics.[24] Additionally, the caesura after the anceps of the acephalous pherecratean (x ⋮ – U U – ∩) is in accordance with Irigoin's observation that the caesura occurs a syllable after the beginning of the new colon, a phenomenon called 'dovetailing' by West.[25]

Sappho often used strophic structures made of two identical verses. This occurred in Book 2 (*glyc*²ᵈᵃ ‖ *glyc*²ᵈᵃ ‖‖) and Book 3 (*glyc*²ᶜʰᵒ ‖ *glyc*²ᶜʰᵒ

---

[22] E.g. Sophocles, *Oedipus Tyrannus* 29–30, μέλαϲ | δ' Ἅδηϲ; see Battezzato 2008: 127–8, 130, Finglass 2018 *ad loc.*

[23] Thus Sophocles, *Oedipus Tyrannus* 523–4, τάχ' ἂν | δ' ὀργῆι in P.Oxy. 2180.

[24] The sequence *glyc pher* is so common that it receives a specific name, 'priapean': see e.g. Euripides, *Heracles* 357–8, 362–3, 378–9 with G. Bond 1981: 147.

[25] Irigoin 1956, West 1982: 6, 60, 117.

|||) of the Alexandrian edition in their entirety; it also occurs in many poems in Book 4 (^*hipp*^2cho || ^*hipp*^2cho |||).[26]

Some poems from Book 5 display a structure where the first and/or last line, as presented in ancient manuscripts, are longer, as in the sequence preserved in the Berlin parchment (P.Berol. inv. 9722: frr. 94–6) and in other fragments:[27]

> fr. 94 *glyc* || *glyc* || *glyc*^da |||
> fr. 95 *cr* [*glyc*] / *glyc* / *glyc* [*ba*] |||
>
> fr. 96 *cr glyc* / *glyc* / *glyc ba* |||
>
> fr. 98 *glyc* | *glyc* | *cr glyc* |||

The combination of rhythms is perfectly normal and the three-line distribution, with a longer third colon, is well balanced. In frr. 95.9, 96.7, in the second line of the strophe, the glyconic (× × – ∪ ∪ – ∪ –) is substituted with a wilamowitzian (× × – ∪ – ∪ ∪ –).

The strophe of fr. 96 is unusual in that it is made of a single verse: no metrical pauses occur within the strophe and all lines are linked in synapheia, as attested by the numerous cases where a word is split between two lines. Some scholars object that it is impossible to sing thirty syllables without a metrical break.[28] In fact Alcaeus fr. 140 has a one-verse strophe, with an uninterrupted sequence of twenty syllables (2*glyc ia* ||).[29] The third verse of the alcaic strophe (described below) has nineteen syllables. Pindar has sequences of twenty-two and twenty-three metrical positions (the fifth verse of the strophe of *Isthmian* 7: *glyc tel* ^*wil*; the fourth verse of the strophe of *Nemean* 2: || 2*glyc pher* ||).[30] The technical problem of delivering this long sequence without metrical pauses was probably solved by using some kind of rubato delivery,[31] and the length of the verse is paralleled in the examples from Pindar and Alcaeus. It is probably better to admit that Sappho occasionally wrote a one-verse strophe.

---

[26] Battezzato 2018: 3–11.

[27] The sign / indicates that the line end in the ancient layout is incompatible with verse end; | that line end in the ancient layout is compatible with verse end; [ ] that the metrical structure is not completely preserved in the manuscript.

[28] Thus Privitera 2009, 2011, whose colometry does not correspond to the metrical practice of archaic poets (so rightly Giannini 2010: 22–4).

[29] West 1982: 33 mentions Sappho fr. 141 and Alcaeus fr. 10B, and Giannini 2010: 24 Bacchylides 17, but it is not certain there that synapheia is unbroken.

[30] Itsumi 2009: 11, 73. The structure of *Isthmian* 7 is followed by a sequence of another six syllables, which may or may not be in synapheia with the preceding sequence.

[31] So-called 'fiato rubato' or 'stolen breath' (Gentili and Lomiento 2003: 12, Giannini 2010: 24); i.e. the performer takes breath 'by stealth', in such a way that the audience does not perceive the interruption of the sound sequence (a well-known performance technique).

For Book 6, no information is extant. We have one fragment from Book 7, fr. 102, which runs *ia glyc ba* || *ia glyc ba* ||. It is impossible to know whether or not this was part of a longer strophe, or to determine the exact strophic structures of the fragments written in hexameters, ionics, and *pher*[3da]. Fr. 137.1–2, if authentic, may be part of an alcaic strophe.

A fragment of an *epithalamium* or wedding song (fr. 111) presents the sequence *pher* || *ia* || ^*pher*[da] || *ia* || ^*pher*[da]? || < *ia* || > ^*pher*[da] || <*ia* ||>. We cannot reconstruct the length and structure of the strophe as a whole, but the sequence of short verses suggests a lively performance by a chorus that did not need lengthy training.

The Music of Sappho: Scales and Rhythms

Sappho's poetry was song. But her music remains elusive for us. For most of what we think we know about the music of archaic Greek lyric, we have to rely on prose sources, often written centuries later than the lyric texts themselves. Lasus of Hermione (sixth century BC) was the first to write a treatise on music, about which we have minimal information (fr. 1 Campbell). A system of musical notation probably did not exist before the fifth century BC.[32] It is therefore extremely unlikely that Sappho's music survived until the classical age. Some reasonably reliable information might have reached scholars writing in the fifth and fourth century thanks to the transmission of performance habits and traditional tunes; many performance practices, such as musical scales, were probably preserved somewhat faithfully over long periods of time. Classical writings on music are preserved only scantily, and we rely on authors of the imperial era, such as Pseudo-Plutarch or Aristides Quintilianus, who base their statements on now lost earlier works from the late classical or Hellenistic age.

We thus have some technical information about the organisation of intervals in ancient Greek music.[33] Greek scales (*harmoniai*) were not built on the octave but on 'tetrachords', that is the distance of a fourth. This distance was divided into smaller steps, but these steps were often greater than a tone and smaller than a semitone.[34]

---

[32] The notation consisted in pitch-symbols derived from modifications of Greek letters. This system was firmly established in the third century BC: Hagel 2010: 1–102. Aristoxenus (fourth century BC) attests that some system already existed (probably identical to the standard system known to us). See Aristides Quintilianus, *On Music* i.11 (Barker 1989: 424–30), West 1992: 254–65.

[33] West 1992: 160–89, Hagel 2010: 1–256.

[34] 'Modes' or 'genera' (diatonic, chromatic, and enharmonic) introduced further variations in the scales: West 1992: 166–72.

Harmoniai built on different notes did not have the same succession of intervals. As a result, they had different characters and names. The instruments were built to suit one or, when possible, more than one specific *harmonia*: lyres played a limited number of notes, and had to be tuned to a particular mode. This explains the term *harmoniai*, 'tunings' (i.e. 'scales').[35]

Sappho and Terpander of Lesbos (a *kitharôidos* active in the seventh century BC) are said to have used the Mixolydian *harmonia*, a mournful mode that 'mixed' the *harmonia* from neighbouring Lydia with other elements.[36] Ancient sources may have inferred this from passages of Sappho and Terpander known to them.[37] We do not know whether Sappho used other *harmoniai*, but it is plausible that she did, in accordance with the rhythm, content, and performance context of each poem, as certainly did Pindar and other archaic and classical poets.

In ancient Greek music, the accompanying instrument(s) mostly repeated the singer's notes, or doubled them in the upper or lower octave (a musical phenomenon called 'homophony').[38] The practice whereby instruments and the voice play different melodies ('heterophony') is attested in Plato, *Laws* 812de; this practice was in use in late classical and Hellenistic times,[39] but we have no evidence that it occurred in archaic music.

Many ancient and modern scholars have attempted to reconstruct the exact values of syllables in the musical performance, starting from the premise that, in most Greek verse types, a long syllable is equivalent to two short ones. This is problematic in Aeolic lyric: the Aeolic base (××) can be implemented by any combination of long and short syllables (– –, – ∪, ∪ –, and even ∪ ∪). Many modern scholars have suggested possible rhythmical reconstructions, using, for practical purposes, the musical notes of modern Western tradition.[40] These attempts can give a sense of ancient rhythms, but reconstructions of archaic music remain speculative.[41]

---

[35] West 1992: 160–89, 223–42.

[36] Aristoxenus fr. 81 Wehrli = Pseudo-Plutarch, *On Music* 16.1136c (test. 37) (used by Sappho and in tragedy: Barker 1984: 221) and Plato, *Republic* 398de (mournful: West 1992: 179, 182). For modern reconstructions and discussion of ancient sources on Mixolydian, see West 1992: 174–5, 230–3, Hagel 2010: 372–3.

[37] Cf. what Pindar says about the Lydian *harmonia* in *Olympian* 14.17–18, a poem in Aeolic metres.

[38] Barker 1995.

[39] West 1992: 103–4, 205–7, 359, Prauscello 2006: 140–2, Hagel 2010: 220 with n. 4.

[40] E.g. ♩♩ and ♪ in West 1992, Silva Barris 2011: 108–29.

[41] West 1982: 18–25, Lidov 2012, Lomiento 2013.

The Music of Sappho: Voices and Instruments

Sappho wrote both for solo singers and for choruses. Scholars normally agree that *epithalamia* (frr. 104–17) were meant for choral performances, even if we may imagine that a soloist could alternate with a chorus, and/ or that choruses were split into semi-choruses: see the dialogue in fr. 114, which can be divided between two singers or two groups of singers.[42] It is debated whether some of the non-epithalamic poems were performed by a chorus;[43] many scholars suppose that the Tithonus Poem was meant to be performed by Sappho as a soloist, accompanying the dance of a silent chorus, as some have interpreted the performance(s) described in *Odyssey* 8.250–384.[44]

Musicians of the late classical age started the practice of having different notes sung to one long syllable of text (a musical phenomenon called *melisma*). Some classical sources criticised this practice; it is thus probable that in Sappho, and in archaic Greek lyric as a whole, each syllable was sung to a single note.[45]

Sappho mentions several musical instruments in her poems which accompany the performanc: the lyre (λύρα), the 'tortoise' (χελύννα), and the *pêktis*, a harp of Lydian origin.[46] Athenaeus attributes to Sappho the use of the words βάρβιτος and βάρωμος, apparently as synonyms.[47] The *barbitos* was a version of the lyre, playing at a deeper pitch, and with long, curved arm.[48] A famous fifth-century vase alternatively attributed to the Dokimasia Painter or the Brygos Painter depicts Sappho and Alcaeus holding *barbitoi*.[49] Pindar states that the *barbitos* was introduced into

---

[42] West 1992: 21–2, F. Ferrari 2010: 117–28; also Contiades-Tsitsoni 1990: 68–109 on Sappho's *epithalamia*.

[43] Lardinois 1996: 167–9 argues for a choral performance of fr. 31; for these hypotheses, see FERRARI, LARDINOIS.

[44] For the *Odyssey* passage, see West 2015, Finglass 2017: 75–81 and cf. *Iliad* 18.569–72. For the Tithonus Poem, see West 2005 = 2011–13 II 53–66, F. Ferrari 2010: 194–8. For choral performance, see also Lardinois 1996. 164 on fr. 1 and 165–6 on fr. 5 (a controversial hypothesis); for a different approach, see D'Alessio 2018.

[45] Aristophanes, *Frogs* 1314, 1348; West 1992: 201.

[46] Frr. 103.12 (lyre), 58.12 (tortoise), 22.11, 156.1 (*pêktis*, in the former a plausible supplement). On the *paktis* (Aeolic)/*pêktis* (Attic), see West 1992: 71–2.

[47] Athenaeus, *Scholars at Dinner* 4.182e (fr. 176).

[48] West 1992: 57–8. The attribution to Sappho of the use of the word βάρωμος, also reported in fr. 176, is not certain: the word βάρμος is simply associated with βάρβιτος by Athenaeus (*Scholars at Dinner* 14.636c) without attribution to Sappho. Other sources, also reported in fr. 176, mention the supposed Aeolic (not necessarily Sapphic) variant form βάρμιτος.

[49] Munich, Staatliche Antikensammlungen, inv. 2416 (*BAPD* §204129); cf. West 1992: plate 19; F. Ferrari 2010: 74, RÖSLER p. 65, FERRARI pp. 108–9. For similar images, see Yatromanolakis 2005, F. Ferrari 2010: 99–107.

Greece by Terpander of Lesbos in imitation of a Lydian instrument.[50]
The usage of the *barbitos* is another musical item which links Terpander
to Sappho.[51] The invention of the lyre with seven strings is often associ-
ated with Terpander, but the instrument is attested much earlier, and has
Near Eastern parallels.[52] Close to the Anatolian coast, Lesbos was an
important centre for music, both in the archaic and in the classical era.

The *aulos* was a wind instrument, having two pipes, each one with a
reed. *Auloi* were the most widespread wind instruments in ancient Greece,
and were normally used in symposia and (later) in the performance of
comedies and tragedies. They are never mentioned by Sappho as accom-
panying the actual performance of her poems, although she says that they
accompanied the 'song of the young women', along with castanets
(κ]ροτάλω[v) at the wedding of Hector and Andromache (fr. 44.24–6).

Sappho mentions musical performances that accompany her songs (the
Tithonus Poem), but the text of her poems locates itself at the margin of
the musical or ritual performance, which she describes as something that
has just taken place or is about to (frr. 9, 17), or has taken place a long
time ago (frr. 6, 27, 30), or that takes place elsewhere (fr. 44). This is a
general characteristic of her textual strategies.[53]

Sappho's Metrical and Musical Style

Ancient critics considered 'charm' (χάρις, χάριτες; *gratia*) to be the main
characteristic of Sappho's poetry.[54] As for her metres, Dionysius of
Halicarnassus stressed that Sappho, like Alcaeus, used short stanzas, and
for that reason 'they did not introduce many variations in their few
cola'.[55] By this Dionysius meant that the cola used in the poems were
rhythmically similar, and that Sappho and Alcaeus did not show the vari-
ety and complexity of the metrical structures used by Stesichorus and
Pindar.

This sense of homogeneity and regularity is further enhanced by isosyl-
labism, yet Sappho uses her skilful placement of word end (caesura) and
syntactic boundaries (especially enjambment) to create an 'inner metre'

---

[50] Pindar fr. 125 S–M; Barker 1984: 296.
[51] See above, p. 130, on the Mixolydian *harmonia*.
[52] For the Greek lyre and its connections with the Near East, see J. Franklin 2015. For Terpander and
      the lyre, see Gostoli 1990: XXXIX–XLIII, J. Franklin 2002, Power 2010: 350–5 (and *passim*).
[53] D'Alessio 2018.
[54] Demetrius, *On Style* 132 (test. 45), Apuleius, *Apologia* 9 (test. 48); also HUNTER.
[55] *On the Arrangement of Words* 19.7 (test. 36).

that deftly interacts with and varies the fixity of the verse structure.[56] For instance, we normally find a caesura either after the fourth or the fifth syllable in the three first lines (as written on the page) of the sapphic stanza, in roughly similar percentages.[57] In the description of Sappho's pathological symptoms (fr. 31), however, almost all word breaks occur after the fourth, not the fifth, syllable.[58] This striking and unusual pattern is broken at the very end of the description, at the climactic word 'to die' (τεθνάκην). This unusual pattern of caesurae is highlighted by the very extensive use of enjambment, linking the first and second lines of each strophe (e.g. 13–14 τρόμος δὲ | παῖσαν ἄγρει): the syntax of the second line of the stanza is thus often broken into two shorter units separated by caesura (– ∪ – × and – ∪∪ – ∪ – ∩ ‖).

Similar strategies are used in the strophic structures of Books 2, 3, and of most of Book 4. These strophes are in fact distichs in which the same verse is repeated.[59] Many scholars suppose that the musical pattern was repeated in each strophe,[60] but others argue that the melody varied in accordance with the pitch accent of the words of each line.[61]

Sappho uses enjambment and caesurae to introduce subtle variations into these homogeneous structures. For instance, in fr. 44 (Book 2) the syntax is often enjambed across strophic divide.[62] In fr. 44.26–7, ἴκα]νε δ᾽ ἐς αἴθ[ερα] | ἄχω θεσπεσία ('a divinely inspired sound reached the sky'), Sappho divides across the strophic boundary an epic phrase (ἠχὴ δ᾽ ἀμφοτέρων ἵκετ᾽ αἰθέρα, *Iliad* 13.837), combining it with the imitation of another epic phrase which is normally enjambed (τοὶ δ᾽ ἄμ᾽ ἔποντο | ἠχῆι θεσπεσίηι, 12.251–2).

---

[56] Hagel 1994–5, and below, n. 66.

[57] Lidov 1993: 510 gives 41 per cent and 37 per cent as figures for end of word groups respectively after fourth and fifth syllable. Recent finds (Obbink 2016a) give us, in my calculations, 33 new analysable lines, which display a higher number of word group end after the fifth syllable: 27 per cent after the fourth (9 instances); 42 per cent after the fifth (14 instances). If we combine old and new finds, we have 153 lines and the figures for word group end after the fourth and the fifth syllable are identical: 52 instances for each of these two possibilities, i.e. 34 per cent of all lines (104 instances in total, 68 per cent of all lines).

[58] Lidov 1993: 511–12.

[59] See above, pp. 127–8.

[60] See Dionysius of Halicarnassus, *On the Arrangement of Words* 19.4, 'the composers of lyric poems cannot change the melodies of strophes and antistrophes' (τοῖς δὲ τὰ μέλη γράφουσιν τὸ μὲν τῶν στροφῶν τε καὶ ἀντιστρόφων οὐχ οἷόν τε ἀλλάξαι μέλος); also West 1992: 198–9, 209–12, 339, Fassino and Prauscello 2001: 13–19, Prauscello 2006: 196–202; see, however, Ruijgh 2001: 303–4.

[61] Ruijgh 2001: 300–4, 312–14, D'Angour 2006: 277–82; differently, Gagné 2013: 310–13.

[62] E.g. fr. 44.8–9, 14–15 with Fassino and Prauscello 2001: 13–19, Prauscello 2006: 196–202.

The interaction of 'inner metre' and meaning is especially striking in the Tithonus Poem, a poem from Book 4.[63] In the description of Sappho's old age and inability to dance (lines 1–6), the ninth and tenth syllables (which must be long) are always part of the same word, a rhythmic effect that we may interpret as 'spondaic' and 'heavy' (see –ηται, in line 5 of the poem):

βάρυc δέ μ' ὁ [θ]ῦμος πεπόηται, γόνα δ' οὐ φέροιϲι

and my heart has become heavy, my knees do not support me

The pattern suddenly changes at line 7, where word- and sentence-end separate elements 9 (the final syllable of θαμέωϲ) and 10 (the first syllable of ἀλλά), precisely where 'but' marks the end of the description of Sappho's old age,

τα<ῦτα> ϲτεναχίϲδω θαμέωϲ, ἀλλὰ τί κεν ποείην;

I often bewail this: but what could I do?

Hermann Fränkel observed that the Homeric hexameter is as complex and varied as a small strophe.[64] Sappho varies her less flexible isosyllabic strophes with the skilful use of caesura and enjambment, creating a series of rhythmic ripples not obvious at first sight, which subtly intensify crucial shifts in meaning and content.

Further Reading

For the metres of Sappho, see Page 1955: 318–23 (somewhat dated), Snell 1982: 43–8 (the best and most influential approach on Aeolic metres), West 1982: 29–34 (an excellent short survey), Sicking 1993: 135–8 (somewhat idiosyncratic), M. Martinelli 1997: 238–41 (main strophic types only). For a complete list of metres used by Sappho, with minimal discussion, see Voigt 1971: 15–20. West 1992 and Hagel 2010 offer excellent surveys of ancient Greek music.

---

[63] For the text and translation printed below, see F. Ferrari 2010: 194–5; also West 2005: 5 = 2011–13: II 60. For a general discussion of 'inner metre' in Sappho's Books 2–4 and in this fragment, see Lidov 2009.

[64] Fränkel 1968: 113 ≈ 1995–6: 191.

CHAPTER 10

Sappho's Dialect

Olga Tribulato

Sappho's Dialect and Its Historical Context

Sappho's literary language is based on the local dialect of Lesbos. Lesbian is a variety of East Aeolic, the dialect spoken in some centres of Asia Minor and the east Aegean. Linguists nowadays use the term 'East Aeolic' for the language of this region, Lesbos included. East Aeolic shares features with the other Aeolic dialects, Thessalian and Boeotian, but also shows many characteristic innovations which set it apart. The most notable phonetic and morphological phenomena of Sappho's East Aeolic dialect are described later in this chapter.

Sappho's adherence to the local dialect may derive from the unique setting of archaic Lesbos, which experienced intense contact with the non-Greek cultures of Asia Minor but which at the same time – and for much of its history – was keen on the promotion of local traditions, including the Aeolic dialect. This vibrant cultural environment also determined another trait of Sappho's poetry: its continuous dialogue with the epic legacy, be it through its images, style, or language. In this respect, Sappho provides an excellent example of how interpreters' perceptions of a lyric poet's language can dramatically change over time. Until the mid-twentieth century, under the influence of great nineteenth-century dialectologists such as H. L. Ahrens, scholars assumed that Sappho wrote in a form of pure 'vernacular'. Epic legacies were duly noted but quickly dismissed as elements uncharacteristic of 'authentic' Sapphic poetry: Lobel's downgrading of compositions such as fr. 44 to the status of 'abnormal poems' is indicative of such an approach.[1]

Nowadays the issue is viewed in different terms.[2] Advances in the knowledge of the Greek local varieties have led to a reappraisal of their use in literature: literary dialects are never linguistically 'pure' and

---

[1] Lobel 1925: xxv–xxvi, Gallavotti 1948: 81–6, Page 1955: 120–1.
[2] A. Bowie 1981: 60–7.

authentically 'local' since they always partake of the poetic tradition, itself supraregional and hence partly artificial.[3] As a consequence, Sappho's language is now rightly viewed as a literary product, which often reuses epic material while also possibly drawing upon an unattested Aeolic poetic tradition.[4] In examining Sappho's East Aeolic features, the next section will also note the major non-Aeolic elements of her poetry, both of which have been confirmed by the most recent papyrological findings.

Much modern perception of Sappho's language depends on the way her poetry was transmitted in antiquity, and therefore on the mutual influence of editorial practice and grammatical thought. To date, there is no comprehensive study of this aspect: this chapter offers a brief sketch of the issues. The grammarians' approach to the Greek dialects was quintessentially literary and their understanding and description of Aeolic were therefore profoundly dependent on the Lesbian poets; three case studies – the ancient handling of accentuation, digamma, and 'Aeolic ā' – show how the linguistic mindset of the Hellenistic and imperial ages has shaped the perception and written representation of Sappho's language until this very day.

Sappho's East Aeolic: A Phonological and Morphological Sketch

The most notable traits which East Aeolic shares with Thessalian and Boeotian are widespread in the language of Sappho. In phonology, these are:

(1) preservation of the /a:/ inherited from Indo-European (e.g. Ἀφροδίτᾱ, fr. 96.26), with no exceptions;

(2) /o/ outcome of the inherited resonant *r̥ (e.g. στρότος for στρατός 'army', fr. 16.1: for the accent, see pp. 143–4 below);

(3) initial /w/ is usually lost (on some graphic remains of digamma, see p. 142 below);

(4) forms such as ξένος, 'stranger', κάλος, 'beautiful' from ξένϝος, καλϝός: the first vowel remains short because, as in Attic, no compensatory lengthening takes place. Compare the opposite treatment in the Ionic forms ξεῖνος, κᾱλός;

---

[3] This theoretical shift also resulted from the advances in the fields of dialectology, sociolinguistics, and stylistics: Silk 2009: 11–17, 2010.

[4] A. Bowie 1981, West 2002 = 2011–13: I 392–407, Kelly 2015a: 28–9.

(5) forms such as πέμπε from *penkʷe* (labial outcome of inherited labio-velars).

Notable morphological traits include:

(1) third-declension datives of the type πόδεccι for ποcί, which end up looking like those of the type γένεccι.[5] Sappho also uses some 'regular' –cι datives (e.g. πόccι, fr. 105(c).2; χέρcιν, fr. 81.5), which could be due to epic influence;

(2) the analogical spread of present endings to the active perfect participle (e.g. ἐκγεγόνων for Attic ἐκγεγονώc);

(3) the use of patronymic adjectives to signify filiation (whereas Attic employs the genitive of the father's name with the same function).

Four Typical Phonetic Features: Gemination, Diphthongisation, Secondary Long Vowels, and Psilosis

Apart from these shared traits, the most important phonetic phenomena characterising East Aeolic concern the outcome of certain old consonantal groups and the treatment of secondary long vowels (i.e. those long vowels resulting from lengthening or contraction). The former is the source of the widespread phenomena of gemination (consonantal doubling) and 'diphthongisation', which are described below.

The first person ἔμμι (= εἰμί, 'I am') contains a double /m/, which results from the loss of inherited /s/ in the group /sm/. In the reconstructed Early Greek form *esmi*, loss of /s/ triggers compensatory lengthening in Attic (which in εἰμί is signalled by the spurious diphthong ει, which stands for a long vowel) but the doubling of /m/ in East Aeolic: hence ἔμμι. Common geminated forms in Sappho include ἄμμες, 'we' (= ἡμεῖς), ὔμμες, 'you' (= ὑμεῖς), and ἔμμεναι, 'to be' (= εἶναι).

The same treatment affects /ln/, so that East Aeolic has cτάλλα (< *stālnā) for Attic cτήλη, 'stele'. Gemination also concerns nasal or liquid roots followed by *j: thus e.g. κρίννω, 'I judge', from *krin-jō (Alcaeus fr. 130B.17) for κρίνω.

'Diphthongisation' derives from the loss of consonantal groups containing a secondary sibilant and nasals (/m/, /n/) or liquids (/l/, /r/): the same consonantal groups in other dialects produce secondary long vowels. A typical 'diphthongised' element is the ending of the feminine

---

[5] The origin of this innovation (which is not limited to Aeolic) is studied by Morpurgo Davies 1976.

participle –οισα (from –ονσα, itself from *–ont-ja) as in λίποισα (fr. 1.7), which corresponds to Attic λίπουσα. Two other common diphthongised elements are the active third person plural ending –οισι (Attic –ουσι, both from –ονσι < –οντι) and the adjective παῖς, παῖσα for πᾶς, πᾶσα (< *pant-s, *pant-ja).

As regards the secondary long vowels resulting from contractions, the most noteworthy outcomes concern /e/ and /o/ vowels, which in East Aeolic are open: /ɛ:/ (η) and /ɔ:/ (ω).[6] Common forms showing these secondary vowels are the second declension genitive singular ending –ω (< –οο), as in προσώπω (fr. 16.18 = Attic προσώπου), and the thematic infinitive ending –ην (< –εεν, e.g. ἴδην, fr. 16.18 = Attic ἰδεῖν). The contraction of /a/ with short or long e- and o-sounds is always /a:/ (ᾱ). This is responsible for the first declension plural genitive ending in –ᾱν (e.g. μερίμναν, fr. 1.26 = Attic μεριμνῶν) and the first declension masculine genitive singular in –ᾱ from –ᾱο (e.g. Κρονίδᾱ, fr. 103.6).

Another important phenomenon concerning the pronunciation of East Aeolic is the lack of initial aspiration ('psilosis') which – although typical of other dialects as well, such as Ionic and Cretan – was identified as a typical Aeolic feature by ancient grammarians. There is no reason to doubt that this was an authentic trait of Sappho's language: late classical inscriptions already show unaspirated stops where Attic has aspirated ones, such as the perfect participle κατεστακόντων for καθεστηκότων in IG xii/2 645.21, dated to c.318 BC.[7]

The final notable phonetic trait is the apocope of disyllabic prepositions, through which κατά, παρά, περί, and ἀνά become κατ, παρ, περ, and ὀν (the latter with the typically East Aeolic /o/ vocalism). P.Sapph.Obbink confirms that Sappho used the adverbial form ἄϊ for ἀεί.[8] This had previously been conjectured by Ahrens in fr. 44A.5 on the basis of ancient grammatical information; on the basis of the parallel in P.Sapph.Obbink, ἄϊ has also been restored in the Sapphic fragment P.Oxy. 4411 fr. 84.5.[9]

Noteworthy Traits of Nominal Morphology

The main phonological traits above have an impact on declensions, which are summarised in the table below with an eye to aiding the understanding of a large part of Sappho's language. The first and second

---

[6] In the archaic script in which Sappho's poems are likely to have originally circulated, these sounds would have been written with epsilon and omicron respectively.
[7] Hooker 1977: 13–17, Hodot 1990: 51.
[8] Line 1 of the Brothers Poem.
[9] Prauscello and Ucciardello 2015: 22–3.

declensions are exemplified by forms of the adjective χαλεπός, 'difficult' (in East Aeolic, χάλεποc: note the recessive accent throughout).

First declension		Second declension	
Singular	Plural	Singular	Plural
χαλέπᾱ	χάλεπαι	χάλεποc	χάλεποι
χαλέπᾱ	χάλεπαι	χάλεπε	χάλεποι
χαλέπᾱc	χαλέπᾱν	χαλέπω	χαλέπων
χαλέπαι	χαλέπαιcι	χαλέπωι	χαλέποιcι
χαλέπᾱν	χαλέπαιc	χάλεπον	χαλέποιc

In the singular, the first declension retains inherited /a:/ (ᾱ) throughout (see too the genitive plural χαλέπᾱν < χαλεπάων); the second declension genitive ends in –ω. Accusative plural endings are diphthongised: χαλέπαιc (< χαλέπανc) and χαλέποιc (< χαλέπονc). In the dative plural, East Aeolic employs the 'long' endings –αιcι and –οιcι, also used in other Greek dialects.

As concerns the third declension, the most important difference is the already noted extension of –εccι to consonantal stems (e.g. fr. 96.6–7 γυναίκεccιν, here with epic-Ionic *nu ephelkystikon*, a literary feature which Sappho sometimes employs). Stems in –ευ– tend to preserve the original long diphthong of the suffix; this produces forms such as βαcίληοc (genitive singular, Alcaeus fr. 387), βαcίληεc (nominative plural, fr. 17.4), ἱππήων (genitive plural, fr. 16.1), τόκηαc (accusative plural, Alcaeus fr. 6.14). Forms with shortened /e/, which invariably occur in personal names, seem to be due to epic influence: e.g. Νηρεΐδων in Alcaeus fr. 42.11, against nominative Νηρήϊδεc in Sappho fr. 5.1 (< Νηρήϝιδεc).[10]

The declension of first- and second-person plural pronouns is also noteworthy. The nominatives ἄμμεc and ὔμμεc show: (1) psilosis (vs ἁ–, ὑ– of other Greek dialects: in Attic ἁ– becomes ἡ–); (2) gemination, ensuing from the loss of the inherited consonantal group /sm/ (*asmes); (3) retention of the archaic pronominal ending –εc (Attic generalised the nominal ending –ειc). The first two features return in the genitives ἀμμέων and ὑμμέων, as well as in the accusatives ἄμμε and ὔμμε, the latter retaining the inherited ending –ε, which Attic replaces with –αc (ἡμέαc).

[10] Hamm 1958: 159.

In spite of this peculiar aspect, the East Aeolic pronominal declension is more conservative than the Attic one. The demonstrative pronoun αὐτόϲ does not replace the inherited third person singular pronoun, which survives in forms such as ϝέθεν (genitive) and ϝοι (dative).

Two Typical Verbal Features: Infinitives and the Athematic Conjugation of *verba vocalia*

East Aeolic verbal morphology shows a number of unique traits. The athematic infinitive ending –μεναι is particularly remarkable: it derives from the fusion of the Aeolic (and Doric) ending –μεν with the Attic-Ionic ending –ναι. It is widespread in Homeric language, where it also artificially features in thematic verbs (ἐλθέμεναι, etc.). The thematic present infinitive ending –ην is extended to the perfect active conjugation (e.g. τεθνάκην, fr. 31.15 = τεθνηκέναι), in which, as already noted, the participle too is analogical on the present. Analogy with thematic infinitives affects the ending of athematic verbs with roots ending in a vowel (ἴϲτᾱμι, τίθημι, δίδωμι, etc.): their present infinitive does not show –μεναι but simply adds –ν to the full-grade root, yielding ἴϲτᾱν, τίθην, δίδων, etc.

The overlap and mutual influence of the thematic and athematic conjugations, which variously affects other Greek dialects as well, produces one of the most remarkable phenomena of East Aeolic morphology: the athematic conjugation of the so-called 'contract verbs' (*verba vocalia*) (e.g. τιμάω, φιλέω, δοκιμόω).[11] On the whole, in Sappho these verbs do not show the thematic vowel before the endings and their root vowel tends to be long; this is most evident in first-person forms of –ημι (= –εω) and –ωμι (= –οω) verbs, such as κάλημι (fr. 60.4), δοκίμωμι (fr. 52), and οἴκημι (Alcaeus fr. 130B.16). The phenomenon tends to be viewed as a dialectal development arising from the fact that in Aeolic the contraction occurring in the thematic 'contract verbs' produced long vowels identical to those of the original athematic presents ἴϲτᾱμι, τίθημι, and δίδωμι.[12]

The second and third persons of the singular, however, end in –αιϲ, –ειϲ, –οιϲ, and –αι, –ει, –οι. These could be remnants of the old thematic conjugation, later replaced (though not fully) by a new athematic

---

[11] Hamm 1958: 138–44, 171–2.

[12] An alternative explanation is that these athematic 'contract verbs' result from a much older reorganisation of morphological classes which affected the whole of Greek, producing athematic formations in Thessalian, East Aeolic, Arcadian, and Cypriot (the position of Mycenaean is debated) and thematic ones in the remaining dialects.

conjugation. Alternatively, they could be the regular phonetic outcome of older athematic second and third person forms.[13] The mixed character of the conjugation of these verbs is also suggested by the Sapphic forms ποθήω (fr. 36) and ἀδικήει (fr. 1.20, albeit textually suspect). Overall, the impression is that Sappho chose different conjugational types according to the metre or content of her compositions: in fr. 16.20 she uses the athematic participle πεϲδομ]άχενταϲ (Attic πεζομαχέω), but in fr. 44.33 (one of her most epicising pieces: KELLY pp. 62–4) she has the thematic participle ὀνκαλέοντεϲ.

Sources for Sappho's Dialect: Ancient Editions, Papyri, and Inscriptions

Sappho's dialect and its reception in antiquity can be studied through the combined evidence of the ancient text itself, its transmission in papyri and ancient authors, and inscriptions from the East Aeolic area. It is conceivable that the poetry of Sappho and Alcaeus was entrusted to writing in a period close to its original composition.[14] A turning point in Sappho's transmission was the Alexandrian edition, the knowledge of which has been greatly improved by the papyrological findings of the last 140 years.[15] To date, Sapphic papyri span from the third century BC (P.Köln inv. 21351+21376, containing the 'New Sappho') to the seventh century AD (P.Berol. inv. 5006).[16] However, the papyri containing traces of exegetical (including lexicographical and grammatical) work are extraordinarily few; exegesis of Alcaeus on papyrus is much better represented.[17]

Ancient grammatical sources have much to contribute to the understanding of Sappho's reception in antiquity, but are often a neglected type of evidence. Part of the material which surfaces in the grammatical treatises of the imperial age probably derives from local Lesbian erudition; we know that, in the period when the Alexandrian philologists started editing the lyric poets, Callias of Mytilene (third–second centuries BC) produced a commentary on Sappho and Alcaeus, and this kind of exegetical

---

[13] Willi 2012a: 272–4.

[14] For Sappho's early reception and the possibility that her poetry was transmitted in writing as well as orally, see Yatromanolakis 2007: 210–11.

[15] For the genesis of the Alexandrian edition, the fluidity of this concept, and the role played by Aristophanes of Byzantium and Aristarchus, see PRAUSCELLO; for the papyri, see FINGLASS ch. 17.

[16] The Cologne papyrus, which predates the Alexandrian edition, shows a different arrangement.

[17] Porro 1994, 2004, 2007.

activity probably started soon after the poets' lifetime.[18] The beginnings of Greek dialectology in antiquity were based on direct knowledge of the local varieties, but later, when the *koinê* replaced the dialects, it necessarily became a bookish enterprise: only those varieties which had risen to the status of literary languages made their way into the linguistic treatises of this period.[19] It follows that the grammarians use the collective term οἱ Αἰολεῖς, 'the Aeolians', when in fact they have only a passage from Sappho or Alcaeus in mind: 'Aeolic' equals East Aeolic.

The grammarians' interest in Aeolic is predominantly devoted to phonology. Barytonesis, gemination, contractions, and digamma are common topics, while notes on morphology focus mostly on the declension of personal pronouns and the athematic conjugation of 'contract verbs', *verba vocalia*. 'Diphthongisation' – which modern readers immediately single out as a characteristic East Aeolic phenomenon – is never properly discussed in ancient texts.

The third important source for the study of Sappho's language is in East Aeolic inscriptions, which provide insights into the phonology and morphology of certain phenomena and allow the comparison of the writing conventions in the papyri with epigraphic practice. Epigraphy, however, has little to contribute to East Aeolic in the seventh–sixth centuries BC, since no documents from this period have survived and few others date to before the end of the fifth century BC. In assessing Sappho's language, scholars necessarily compare sets of data unequal in both chronology (archaic vs late classical) and typology (literary vs epigraphic). For example, there are no means to verify the status of the /w/ sound and the use of digamma in archaic Lesbos; late classical inscriptions bear no traces of the letter itself and scholars generally assume that East Aeolic, like Ionic, lost the sound early on. In ancient copies of Lesbian lyric, digamma is often written in forms of the third-person pronoun and adjective (e.g. ϝε, ϝοι), and this depends on the grammarians' belief that in Aeolic these forms were pronounced with initial /w/. As a *sound*, initial /w/ is usually ignored in Sapphic prosody.[20]

---

[18] See Cassio 1986: 142–3 on Antidorus and Ephorus, both from Cyme, and Zopirus of Magnesia.
[19] For the literary inclination of ancient dialectology, see Cassio 1993.
[20] Cf. fr. 22.14 ἐπτόαις' ἴδοιϲαν, with the elision showing that /w/ was not pronounced in ἴδοιϲαν, and A. Bowie 1981: 69–79. Compare the writing of initial ρ as βρ in βρόδον, 'rose', βράδινοϲ, 'soft', and βραϊδίωϲ, 'easily', generally explained as an editorial signal that the syllable preceding some words beginning with ρ (from *wr–) was to be scanned long: Hooker 1977: 27–30, A. Bowie 1981: 82–3.

A well-known characteristic of Lesbian epigraphy is that a large number of dialectal traits are still employed in inscriptions dated to the period when the *koinê* was already the standard Greek variety (second–first century BC). In the Hellenistic period this could be based on an authentic persistence of the local dialect, but as time progressed it also reflected an ideologically charged revival, whereby the dialect was showcased in official documents as a marker of local identity and pride, additionally fuelled by the prestige of Sappho's and Alcaeus' poetry in Greco-Roman culture.[21] The promotion of Aeolic reached its peak towards the end of the first century BC, when antiquarian and archaising trends swept Greece and Rome. Dionysius of Halicarnassus argued that Latin was a form of Aeolic, a fanciful theory which also surfaces in contemporary grammatical sources.[22] The strong ties between Rome and Lesbos, which underpinned the Roman career of Lesbian celebrities such as Potamon of Mytilene, have a cultural counterpart in the Roman fascination with all things Aeolic, of which Julia Balbilla is an enthusiastic representative: the travelling companion of the empress Sabina, Hadrian's wife, she had four epigrams in East Aeolic incised on the statue of Memnon at Thebes in Egypt in November AD 130.[23] In such a climate, it is not surprising that the official inscriptions of the Roman-led Lesbian chancellery continued using the local dialect, a linguistic perpetuation which endows modern scholars with precious information on the evolution and ancient perception of East Aeolic.

Between Language and Writing, Grammars and Papyri

Papyri constitute the most important source for Aeolic accentuation, given that the fragments of the indirect tradition are influenced by the Byzantine system, which did not preserve traces of dialectal accentuation. Aristophanes of Byzantium (mid-third/second century BC) is traditionally credited with having introduced diacritics for accents into the literary texts he edited; it is probable that he played a role in the representation of Sapphic accentuation as well. Given that neither inscriptions nor pre-Alexandrian texts contained written accents, the Alexandrian scholars

---

[21] E.g. the honorary decree for L. Vaccius Labeon issued by Cyme between 2 BC and AD 14 (*I.Kyme* 19): Hodot 1975, Cassio 1986: 133, 137, 138–9.

[22] *Roman Antiquities* 1.90.1; Gabba 1963 = 2000: 159–64, Ascheri 2011: 65–71.

[23] The standard edition is Bernand and Bernand 1960; see further Rosenmeyer 2008, BOWIE p. 317.

must have derived their knowledge of Aeolic accentuation from informa-
tion pertaining to the spoken dialect, probably collected by the first
experts on local traditions. Accentuation therefore provides an ideal field
to follow the circulation of linguistic theories among the professionals of
the ancient 'book industry' and therefore to observe the mutual influence
between grammar and editorial practices. In East Aeolic all accents
become recessive as long as they still comply with the general 'antepenult
rule': the result is that there are no oxytone words in the text of the
Lesbian poets.[24]

Some papyri also use accents to draw attention to peculiar prosodic phe-
nomena. One of these concerns vocalic sequences ending in /i/, which
may be marked with either diaeresis on the *iota* (e.g. τυϊδ' in P.S.I. 123,
rendering the adverb τυίδε, 'hither', of fr. 17.7) or an acute accent on the
first vowel (e.g. τύιδ' in P.Oxy. 1231).[25] Such usages can only be understood
by considering the parallel evidence of ancient grammarians, who observed
that in Aeolic poetry (including Theocritus) some vocalic sequences end-
ing in /i/ were disyllabic: e.g. δάϊδος. Such hiatuses are due to the loss of
intervocalic /w/ (here < δάϝιδος, from δαΐς 'torch'), but the grammarians
seem to have drawn a general rule according to which most vocalic
sequences ending in /i/ must be scanned and accented as if they were disyl-
labic: hence treatments such as τυϊδ' or τύιδ'. In fr. 17.7 – as in many other
cases – the vocalic sequence in fact scans long, i.e. it is a diphthong. Both
the accentuation of the papyri and the grammatical theory on which it is
based are therefore wrong, but the example illustrates the degree to which
the graphic layout of ancient editions may be based on a linguistic reason-
ing which deserves to be known if one wishes to appreciate the impact of
ancient grammar on the transmission of a 'dialectal' author.

Vocalic sequences ending in /i/ also provide a good practical example
of the ancient grammarians' analogical mindset, according to which
forms which have similar traits (e.g. sequences containing ι) will behave
in a similar way (i.e. by being disyllabic). Another example of analogical
reasoning of this kind is the treatment of East Aeolic /a:/ (ᾱ). The gram-
marians observed that Aeolic may show αι where standard Greek had ᾱ:
e.g. in the Aeolic adjective παῖς, where αι is the result of regular diph-
thongisation, vs πᾶς. By analogy, the grammarians were able to state that
Aeolic had forms such as Κρονίδαις (Alcaeus fr. 38A.9) and φαῖμι (Sappho

---

[24] E.g. a trisyllabic oxytone word with a short last syllable becomes proparoxytone (σύνετον <
συνετόν, 16.5), a perispomenon word becomes paroxytone (ἔμας < ἐμᾶς, 1.6); Hamm 1958: 43–4.
[25] García Teijeiro 1993: 151–2.

fr. 88.17).[26] These, however, are nothing more than artificial inventions, in which the regular Aeolic ᾱ is replaced by αι by a false analogy with regular diphthongised forms such as παῖς.

In the case of αι for ᾱ the comparison between papyri and inscriptions is not particularly helpful, since East Aeolic inscriptions bear almost no traces of analogical αι replacing ᾱ.[27] A different case is provided by another phenomenon involving both writing and phonology: the replacement of intervocalic ζ with cδ, attested (albeit with inconsistencies) in both papyri and ancient quotations of Lesbian poetry.[28] This is supposed to reflect the grammarians' knowledge that in Aeolic the sound represented by ζ was pronounced [zd]: cδ would therefore be a sort of analytical spelling to draw the readers' attention to the Aeolic pronunciation of the sound, given that in post-Classical Greek ζ represented the voiced sibilant [z] instead.[29] Intervocalic cδ was thus introduced in lieu of ζ not only in the text of the Lesbian poets, but also in that of authors thought to have employed Aeolic in their compositions, such as Theocritus and Alcman. Epigraphy unmasks the grammatical nature of cδ, since this spelling is attested only once in Aeolic inscriptions: tellingly, in the honorary decree for L. Vaccius Labeon (*I.Kyme* 19.7–8), which also contains other artificial elements (see n. 21). The influence of grammar on textual editing also emerges from the use of cδ by Julia Balbilla, who in her four epigrams displays the full range of the Aeolic and hyper-Aeolic linguistic apparatus. The slavish adherence to imperial editorial practices of this Roman imitator is a fascinating example of the enduring prestige of Sappho's dialect.

Further Reading

The standard reference grammar of the language of Sappho (and Alcaeus) is still the excellent Hamm 1958, though it is not very informative on ancient sources on Aeolic and obviously requires updating in the light of new papyrological discoveries. Other works, more limited in scope, are

---

[26] P.Oxy. 1233, 2290 respectively.

[27] A rare instance is the accusative singular ταὶν πόλιν ταὶν Καλχαδονίων for τὰν πόλιν τὰν in an inscription from Chalcedon found in Tenedos (*SEG* 4.720, third century BC); cf. Hodot 1990: 98.

[28] Hodot 1990: 45. The earliest papyri are not consistent: P.Köln inv. 21351 (third century BC) has cτεναχίζω in the Tithonus Poem line 7, whereas the Florentine *ostrakon* or potsherd (second century BC) bears traces of –cδ– in ὔcχων (fr. 2.5), clearly a corruption of ὔcδων 'branches'. An example from indirect transmission is ἐικάcδω in fr. 115.1 (from Hephaestion's *Handbook on Metres*).

[29] Lejeune 1972: 112–16. The grammatical evidence for this phenomenon is generally late.

Gallavotti 1948 and Hooker 1977. A. Bowie 1981 analyses language in view of his theory of a native Lesbian tradition, while Tribulato 2016 provides an overview of the language of East Aeolic poetry in the context of monodic lyric. The publication of the 'New' and 'Newest' Sappho has not added much to the overall picture of the dialect; a work specifically dealing with linguistic features of the 'New' Sappho is Bettarini 2005.

The East Aeolic (i.e. Lesbian) epichoric dialect is described in standard works such as Bechtel 1921: 1–130, Buck 1955, and Colvin 2007; see also now Finkelberg 2018 and Hodot 2018. Blümel 1982, a study of the Aeolic group within a generative framework, is a difficult work, which should only be approached by experts. The most up-to-date study of the dialect as transmitted by inscriptions is the excellent Hodot 1990.

There is no comprehensive and up-to-date overview of the passages in which ancient grammatical and dialectological sources discuss Sappho's language. This can still be studied only by scanning the whole apparatus and *index auctorum* of Voigt 1971. Individual studies dealing with some aspects of the grammarians' handling of ancient lyric (and thus also of Sappho) are García Teijeiro 1993, Cassio 1993, 2007.

CHAPTER II

Sappho's Poetic Language

Vanessa Cazzato

Perhaps the most immediate impression one gets on leafing through an edition of Sappho's fragmentary poetry – all the more on account of its fragmentariness – is of flashes of beauty, scattered sequences partially preserving sensuous snapshots. This impression is compounded by the contrast between the poetry and the context in which it is preserved, either on scraps of papyrus or, when in the indirect tradition, often in dry treatises on metrics or grammar, so that Sappho's verses, with their numerous mentions of ποικιλία ('dappling' or 'intricate decoration'),[1] gold, silver, and purple, seem to reach us like pebbles of coloured glass washed up by the tide of time. To a lexicographical scholion on the Hellenistic epic poet Apollonius of Rhodes we owe the mention (fr. 152) of a tunic 'mixed with all kinds of colours [or textures]', παντοδάπαιϲι μεμειχμένα χροίαιϲιν, where the root meaning of that last word is 'skin', as if to underline the sensual dimension; the scholia to Aristophanes preserve for us the isolated image of (dancing?) 'feet covered by intricate sandal-straps, fine Lydian handiwork' (πόδαϲ δὲ | ποίκιλοϲ μάϲληϲ ἐκάλυπτε, Λύδιον κάλον ἔργον, fr. 39). The sensual vividness which the fragments build up goes beyond the visual sphere to include all the other senses. There is touch: 'I lay down my limbs on soft cushions', fr. 46, preserved by Herodian's *On Anomalous Words* (second century AD); or fr. 126, 'may you sleep on the bosom of your soft companion', preserved in the *Etymologicum genuinum*, a ninth-century Byzantine dictionary. Taste can be literal or metaphorical: 'I'll have neither the bee's honey nor her sting' (μήτε μοι μέλι μήτε μέλιϲϲα, fr. 146), quoted by Tryphon (late first century BC / early first century AD) as a proverb, but where the opposition between the two concepts melts into a common sweetness through the

---

[1] A difficult word to translate: LSJ⁹ s.v. offers 'marking with various colours', 'embroidering', 'variety', 'intricacy', and 'ornamentation', among other possibilities. For a study of ποικιλία from the point of view of archaic Greek aesthetics, see Grand-Clément 2015.

alliteration of the soft, humming *m*; or the famous definition of Love as 'sweet-bitter' (γλυκύπικρος, fr. 130), which we owe to Hephaestion's *Handbook on Metres*. The sense of smell is often invoked by mention of perfumes and incense. Most significant is sound, specifically the sound of voices and musical instruments. Sappho's own poems were sung, of course, but they also often evoke in words the sound of singing voices and music – or, at a further remove, the echoing memory of the singing voices of those who have left her, just as Sappho's voice lives on as a mental echo for us today. Often the girls whose voices Sappho mentions are named, and these many names studded throughout the corpus also add a layer of ornamentation: Anactoria, Abanthis, Atthis, Gongyla, Gorgo, Gyrinno . . .[2] A scrap of papyrus preserves many broken syllables and just three recognisable words: 'robes . . . the necklaces . . . Gorgo . . .' (fr. 29).

So this surface of sensory brightness is what strikes us first, exciting our imagination for all that is lost from this distant world that flourished at the Asiatic edge of Greece two and a half millennia ago. But even in the original performance setting of these poems there was probably a point to this accumulation of beautiful detail. In fr. 44, the climax of the messenger speech describing Andromache's arrival at Troy as bride to Hector is a catalogue of precious items (7–10):

> ἄβραν Ἀνδρομάχαν ἐνὶ ναῦσιν ἐπ' ἄλμυρον
> πόντον· πόλλα δ' [ἐλί]γματα χρύσια κάμματα
> πορφύρ[α] καταΰτ[με]να, ποίκιλ' ἀθύρματα,
> ἀργύρατ' ἀνάριθμα ποτήρια κἀλέφαις.

> [Hector comes bringing . . .]
> soft Andromache in his ships over the salt
> sea; and many coiled golden bangles and
> purple-dyed ?perfumed? garments, intricate adornments,
> and innumerable silver drinking cups and ivory.

Here, frequent elision and crasis and the absence of a verb produce an imposing sequence of assonant nouns and adjectives describing Andromache's dowry; such a list acts as a verbal counterpart to her treasure. This technique of accumulation is reprised a few lines later, when the wedding procession is described:

> αῦλος δ' ἀδυ[μ]έλης [κίθαρίς] τ' ὀνεμίγνυ[το
> καὶ ψ[ό]φο[ς κ]ροτάλ[ων, λιγέ]ως δ' ἄρα πάρ[θενοι   25
> ἄειδον μέλος ἄγν[ον, ἴκα]νε δ' ἐς αἴθ[ερα

---

[2] For the names, perhaps alluring pseudonyms, see Schlesier 2013.

ἄχω θεσπεσίᾳ γελ[
πάνται δ᾽ ἦς κὰτ ὄδο[ις
κράτηρες φίαλαί τ᾽ ὀ[. .]υεδε[. .]εακ[.].[
μύρρα καὶ κασία λίβανός τ᾽ ὀνεμείχνυτο·   30
γύναικες δ᾽ ἐλέλυσδον ὄσαι προγενέστερα[ι
παντες δ᾽ ἄνδρες ἐπήρατον ἴαχον ὄρθιον

and the sweet-sounding *aulos* and the *kithara* were blended
and the rattle of castanets, and maidens sang clearly
a holy song, and a divinely inspired sound
reached the sky . . . ?laughter?
and everywhere along the streets was . . .
bowls and cups . . .
myrrh and cassia and frankincense were mingled.
The elder women cried out joyfully,
and all the men let forth a lovely high-pitched strain

In this description sound and smell 'mix' together – using the same verb but phonetically varied (ὀνεμίγνυ[το . . . ὀνεμείχνυτο, also the same verb, incidentally, as had been used of colour or texture in fr. 152 above) – in a surfeit of sensory detail which adds expressive force to the scene of festivities at the same time as it complements the experience of the poem's own performance by stirring the imagination to aesthetic response. Sappho's poetry, then, displays a dense, intricate, lively patina of sensuous beauty, which goes hand in hand with vividness, and this accumulation of sensory data and insistence on beauty both characterises Sappho's poetic world and lends a sense of preciousness to her poetry.

Beauty in Sappho is not just a quaint idea but an oft reprised theme that has programmatic force; cognates of κάλλος ('beauty') occur numerous times, as do cognates of χάρις ('grace') and ἀβροσύνα ('delicacy'), and beauty is often an overt concern of the poet/speaker and her characters. Fr. 16 opens with a quasi-philosophical argument about what is κάλλιστον (3),[3] where the idea of that which is 'most beautiful' is emphasised by the poetic syntax that builds up to the predicate with a tricolon of alternative subjects (an army of cavalry, one of foot soldiers, one of ships), and only after that gives the real subject ('what one loves'). This deferral of the true object of interest by one or more elements acting as foil, commonly referred to as the 'priamel', is a favourite of Sappho's.[4] It

[3] Several scholars have viewed this abstract argument on competing notions of beauty as the precursor of later philosophical works: see especially Race 1989: 16–20 (Gorgias' *Helen*), H. Foley 1998 (Plato's *Phaedrus*).
[4] For the priamel, see Race 1982.

defines her conception of what is desirable against other, prevailing notions, and its repeated use in the corpus builds up a sense of the distinctiveness of the poet's world view, whether this be idiosyncratic or, as much scholarship has it, pointedly feminine in opposition to a masculine world. In fr. 16, this sense of a distinctive world view is reinforced by an element of surprise (the rhetorical technique *aprosdokêton*) when the military-themed list is capped by talk of love.[5] Elsewhere the poet returns again and again to beauty, approaching the theme from all angles. In fr. 50 beauty is once more the object of philosophical-sounding reflection in an abstract argument defining the relationship between moral and aesthetical qualities: ὁ μὲν γὰρ κάλος ὄccον ἴδην πέλεται ⟨κάλος⟩, | ὁ δὲ κἄγαθος αὔτικα καὶ κάλος ἔccεται ('For he that is beautiful is beautiful as far as appearances go, but he that is also good at once is all the more beautiful'). Beauty is paronomastic for life in fr. 58.25–6, καί μοι | τὸ λάμπρον ἔρος τὠελίω καὶ τὸ κάλον λέλογχε ('and for me love has obtained the brightness and beauty of the sun'). Above all, beauty – whether present and overwhelming or absent and remembered – is the stimulus to desire, and beauty and desire together are the richest sources of imagery, similes, and metaphors in Sappho. They excite alike the imagination of the speaker and her addressees in the world of the poems, and that of the poet and her addressees, the audience, in the framing world of the performance. Take fr. 22.9–14:

.] . ε . [. . . .] . [. . . κ]έλομαι c' ἀ[είδην
Γο]γγύλαν ['Άβ]ανθι λάβοιcαν α [
πᾶ]κτιν, ἄc cε δηὖτε πόθοc τ [
ἀμφιπόταται
τὰν κάλαν· ἀ γὰρ κατάγωγιc αὔτα[c
ἐπτόαιc' ἴδοιcαν, ἔγω δὲ χαίρω·

I bid you [sing] of Gongyla(?), Abanthis(?) – take up your lyre, since desire for her flutters about you once again, the beautiful one.[6] Her outfit excited you when you saw it, and I rejoice.

Here Abanthis' excitement at the sight of Gongyla beautifully dressed (perhaps in a garment like the one described in fr. 152 above) models the audience's reaction to all the beauty in Sappho's own songs as well as providing the stimulus to song within the poem. Desire (πόθοc)

[5] Pfeijffer 2000a.
[6] Referring to Gongyla or perhaps to Abanthis, either way in stark hyperbaton.

metaphorically 'flies about' Abanthis, in keeping with an established metaphor – Eros is commonly winged in poetry and in painting, and the variation with πόθος here perhaps suggests some gentle wordplay with the verb (ἀμφιπόταται, whose root echoes in sound that of the noun). The topical δηὖτε for succumbing 'once again' to desire,[7] normally employed of the speaking 'I''s own experience, here refers to a second person; this departure from convention underlines Sappho's observant remove in her own action of 'rejoicing', which is in turn the stimulus of *this* lyric, and thus reinforces the play on a song within a song. In fr. 23 the sight of the beautiful beloved occasions not so much a simile as an explicit poetic comparison, since a girl in the 'here and now' is compared to famous beauties from mythology sung in other poems: 'of love . . . I see you(?) before me . . . liken you to Hermione herself or blond-haired Helen . . .' (3–5).

Beauty is the stimulus for imagery again in fr. 132:

> ⊗ ἔcτι μοι κάλα πάιc χρυcίοιcιν ἀνθέμοιcιν
> ἐμφέρην ἔχοιcα μόρφαν Κλέιc ⟨ ⟩ ἀγαπάτα,
> ἀντὶ τᾶc ἔγωὖδὲ Λυδίαν παῖcαν οὖδ' ἐράνναν ...

> I have a beautiful child with an aspect
> like golden flowers, beloved Cleis,
> for whom I would not [take in exchange] even the whole of
> Lydia or desirable ...

Here simile and metaphor are entwined, since the flowers are golden; precious metals, especially gold,[8] are among Sappho's favourite vehicles,[9] and here they afford a link to the idea of luxury implicit in the mention of Lydia.[10] Here also, as in fr. 16 and often elsewhere, we find Sappho's special take on beauty contrasted with a more commonly acknowledged ideal (Lydian luxury) as a foil.

A favourite metaphor of Sappho's to express the idea of beauty involves comparison with the moon. Fr. 34 preserves only the vehicle of what must have been an extended metaphor – perhaps an implied metaphor? – for a woman's beauty outshining that of her companions.

---

[7] For δηὖτε as a topos of erotic lyric, cf. Alcman fr. 59(a).1 *PMGF*, Anacreon frr. 358.1, 376.1, 394(*b*) *PMG*; in Sappho, cf. frr. 1.15, 1.16, 1.18, 130.1, Carson 1986: 117–22, Mace 1993.

[8] Even chickpeas are 'golden' in fr. 143; even gold is not 'golden' enough in fr. 156.2.

[9] With reference to metaphors and similes 'tenor' refers to the element being compared, 'vehicle' to element to which it is being compared.

[10] Cf. frr. 39 (cited above, p. 147), 98a, Alcman fr. 1.67–9 *PMGF*, Archilochus fr. 19 *IEG*.

ἄστερες μὲν ἀμφὶ κάλαν ϲελάνναν
ἂψ ἀπυκρύπτοιϲι φάεννον εἶδοϲ
ὄπποτα πλήθοιϲα μάλιϲτα λάμπη
γᾶν

* * *

ἀργυρία

the stars about the beautiful moon
hide away their shining face
when at her fullest it/she shines
on the earth

* * *

silvery

The moon itself (or *her*self) is in turn the tenor of another vehicle, as we know from the testimonium telling us that it/she is termed 'silvery', so that here again the precious metals adorning Sappho's beautiful women return even in the metaphors for them. The image of the moon for a beautiful woman recurs in fr. 96, here explicitly (ὤϲ ποτ', 7) and with remarkable elaboration (6–17):

νῦν δὲ Λύδαιϲιν ἐμπρέπεται γυναί-
κεϲϲιν, ὤϲ ποτ' ἀελίω
δύντοϲ ἀ βροδοδάκτυλοϲ <ϲελάννα>

πάντα περρέχοιϲ' ἄϲτρα. φάοϲ δ' ἐπί-
ϲχει θάλαϲϲαν ἐπ' ἀλμύραν   10
ἴϲωϲ καὶ πολυανθέμοιϲ ἀρούραιϲ·

ἀ δ' ἐέρϲα κάλα κέχυται, τεθά-
λαιϲι δὲ βρόδα κἄπαλ' ἄν-
θρυϲκα καὶ μελίλωτοϲ ἀνθεμώδηϲ·

πόλλα δὲ ζαφοίταιϲ' ἀγάναϲ ἐπι-   15
μνάϲθειϲ' Ἄτθιδοϲ ἰμέρωι
λέπταν ποι φρένα κ[.]ρ... βόρηται·

And now she stands out among the women
of Lydia like (after the sun
has dipped) the rosy-fingered moon

as she surpasses all the stars; and her light
encompasses alike the salt sea
and many-flowered fields;

and the beautiful dew is distilled,
and roses are in bloom
and soft cow parsley and flowering clover.

And often as she goes to and fro, turning
her mind to gentle Atthis, doubtless,
is consumed in her tender heart … with desire

The female subject is implied and her place taken by the moon, prominently positioned at the end of the stanza and qualified with the epic epithet for dawn (βροδοδάκτυλος), which, following on from the idea of the sun (ἀελίω) conjured up at the end of the previous line, redoubles the woman's radiance by conflating the two heavenly bodies. The extended image is held together by syntactical runover across the three stanzas as well as by the woven repetition of sounds and concepts: the strikingly applied βροδοδάκτυλος anticipates βρόδα (13) just as πολυανθέμοις (11, same position in the line) anticipates ἀνθεμώδης (14). This passage can be compared to a Homeric simile, a sustained imaginary excursion, for the way it marks a departure from the tenor;[11] but, in contrast to the manner of Homeric similes, the return to the 'here and now' is artfully unobtrusive: after a series of parallel clauses (φάος δ' . . . ἀ δ' ἐέρσα . . .) in the image, πόλλα δὲ ζαφοίταις' leaves the new subject implied, and we do not immediately realise that there has been a return to the tenor. A certain indirectness or mobility of thought is manifested in other ways too: differences between vehicle and tenor win prominence, as polarities of time and place are elided by the unifying light of the moon, and lack and lamentation turn to fertility and rejoicing.[12] The whole builds up to extraordinary poignancy. What is most striking of all is the way in which the image gains substance in the elaboration. It seems to acquire a life of its own, which is key to the purpose of the poem: the moon reunites the girl who has gone and the girls left behind in its all-encompassing light.

We find a similar conjuring up of an imaginative world in fr. 2, another poem that includes an extended description of a landscape rich in symbolic meaning:[13]

δεῦρύ μ' ἐκ Κρήτας ἐπ[ὶ τόνδ]ε ναῦον
ἄγνον, ὄππ[αι τοι] χάριεν μὲν ἄλσος
μαλί[αν], βῶμοι δὲ τεθυμιάμε-
νοι [λι]βανώτωι·

ἐν δ' ὔδωρ ψῦχρον κελάδει δι' ὔσδων
μαλίνων, βρόδοισι δὲ παῖς ὀ χῶρος   5

---

[11] Hutchinson 2001: 182.
[12] Hutchinson 2001: 182–5.
[13] Kurke pp. 97–8, Ferrari pp. 112–13, Purves pp. 183–4, Swift p. 214

ἐϲκίαϲτ', αἰθυϲϲομένων δὲ φύλλων
    κῶμα κατέρρει·

ἐν δὴ λείμων ἱππόβοτοϲ τέθαλεν
ἠρίνοιϲιν ἄνθεϲιν, αἰ δ' ἄηται   10
μέλλιχα πνέοιϲιν [
        [   ]

ἔνθα δὴ ϲὺ ... ἔλοιϲα Κύπρι
χρυϲίαιϲιν ἐν κυλίκεϲϲιν ἄβρωϲ
ὀμμεμείχμενον θαλίαιϲι νέκταρ   15
    οἰνοχόαιϲον

Hither to me from Crete to this holy
temple, where yours is a graceful grove
of apple trees, and altars smoking
with frankincense;

and in it cool water chatters through apple
branches, and the entire place is shaded
by roses, and unconsciousness drips
from quivering leaves;

and there a pasturing meadow blooms
with flowers of spring, and the breezes
breathe honey-like ...
...

there you ... taking ... Cypris
in golden cups elegantly
pour nectar blended with
festivities

This poem evokes a *locus amoenus* or garden of delights whose surfeit of
sensuousness builds up to a hypnotic effect. It is not clear to what extent
this landscape is literal or figurative. Does it mirror a space of worship in
the context of a cultic hymn? Or is this something more akin to an
extended metaphor, an eroticised symbolic scenario? (Cf. pp. 151–2
above on fr. 34.) Something tending towards the latter is suggested,
most explicitly, by the metaphor of 'unconsciousness dripping from
quivering leaves' (7–8) placed in coordination with the other descriptors
and without anything to distinguish it from them; moreover, the cups
(κυλίκεϲϲιν, 14) in the return to the 'here and now' of the prayer are spe-
cifically sympotic rather than cultic, while the fact that they are made of
gold suggests their extraordinariness.[14] Distinctive of Sappho is also the

---

[14] Budelmann 2018: 126 *ad loc.*

playful or idiosyncratic use of conventional ritual language; here the poet appropriates the conventions of a cletic hymn (as in fr. 1, discussed below, pp. 159–61), from the opening address to the deity (though her name is delayed to the end of the poem) to the reiteration of the request in the closing. The syntactically self-contained stanzas add to the impression of cultic simplicity. But the poem turns traditional form to tongue-in-cheek playfulness by ending with a petition for Aphrodite to act as wine-server.

Related to stimulation of all the senses by manifestations of beauty is Sappho's arresting insistence on the emotions and sensations instigated by the beauty of the beloved. The sensations of love's pain and pleasure are metaphorised into vivid physical phenomena: whereas it had been deep sleep that dripped from quivering leaves in Aphrodite's grove in fr. 2, it is pain that is 'a dripping', ϲτάλυγμον, at fr. 37.1. Love 'shakes' the speaker 'like the wind assaulting oaks on a mountainside' (fr. 47). Extremes of sensation are employed to express love's irresolvable contradictions: 'you came, and I desired you, and you cooled my heart which was burning with desire' (ἦλθεϲ, ἔγω δέ ϲ' ἐμαιόμαν, | ὄν δ' ἔψυξαϲ ἔμαν φρένα καιομέναν πόθωι, fr. 48). This insistence on sensations is famously in evidence in fr. 31:[15]

> ⊗ φαίνεταί μοι κῆνοϲ ἴϲοϲ θέοιϲιν
> ἔμμεν' ὤνηρ, ὄττιϲ ἐνάντιόϲ τοι
> ἰϲδάνει καὶ πλάϲιον ἆδυ φωνεί-
>   ϲαϲ ὐπακούει
>
> καὶ γελαίϲαϲ ἰμέροεν, τό μ' ἦ μὰν   5
> καρδίαν ἐν ϲτήθεϲιν ἐπτόαιϲεν·
> ὠϲ γὰρ ἔϲ ϲ' ἴδω βρόχε', ὤϲ με φώναι-
>   ϲ' οὐδ' ἒν ἔτ' εἴκει,
>
> ἀλλὰ κὰμ μὲν γλῶϲϲά <μ'> ἔαγε, λέπτον
> δ' αὔτικα χρῶι πῦρ ὐπαδεδρόμηκεν,   10
> ὀππάτεϲϲι δ' οὐδὲν ὄρημμ', ἐπιρρόμ-
>   βειϲι δ' ἄκουαι,
>
> κὰδ δέ μ' ἴδρωϲ κακχέεται, τρόμοϲ δὲ
> παῖϲαν ἄγρει, χλωροτέρα δὲ ποίαϲ
> ἔμμι, τεθνάκην δ' ὀλίγω 'πιδεύηϲ   15
>   φαίνομ' ἔμ' αὔτ[αι.
>
> ἀλλὰ πὰν τόλματαον, ἐπεὶ †καὶ πένητα†

---

[15] Kurke p. 98, Ferrari pp. 117–18, Battezzato p. 133, Lardinois pp. 170–1, Purves pp. 185–9.

That man seems to me equal to gods
the man who opposite you
sits and listens close to your sweet
voice and lovely laugh. It truly
shook the heart in my breast:
for when I set eyes on you even momentarily
I have no voice left in me,
but my tongue is shattered, at once
a subtle heat races under my skin,
my eyes see nothing,
my ears whirr
sweat pours down me, a tremor
seizes me all over, greener than grass
I am, a little short of being dead
I seem to me.
But all must be endured [or dared], for …

Here the description of the effect on the speaking subject of the appear-
ance and sound of the loved one is rendered entirely in physical terms;
we find no abstract words for love or desire but only a list of 'symptoms'
involving the sympathetic listener in this extraordinary keenness of physi-
cal sensation. The use of a long list – here it takes up nearly three whole
stanzas of a poem that probably did not stretch beyond five – recalls the
technique already noted in fr. 44, where, too, accumulation enacted
something in the world of the poem; but here the effect is more pointed
still, since the idea that is enacted is that of sensory overload and emo-
tional overwhelm. This effect is reinforced by the emphatic climax of the
list ('I seem to myself to be a little short of dying')[16] as well as by the play
with tempo: the rise into perception of the agent of erotic disturbance is
delayed by a priamel,[17] as the 'godlike' man of the opening swiftly deflects
our gaze to the woman sitting opposite him, the addressee of this love-
lorn utterance. Then the woman in turn recedes from view as the
speaker, unable to engage with a situation that is experienced as over-
whelming, turns inward with such fierce concentration that we feel as
though we are absorbed into her interiority and are privy to the physical
sensations that only she can know. The hyperbaton in the word order in
that first stanza mirrors the roundabout way in which we are led to the
speaker's real concern: the subject of the main clause (ὤνηρ) is delayed,
while the description of the woman opposite whom he sits, with its

---

[16] For the metrical effects of this expression, see BATTEZZATO p. 133.
[17] Furley 2000.

pleasing chiasmus (ἄδυ φωνείϲαϲ – γελαίϲαϲ ἰμέροεν) trailing into the second stanza, is suggestive of her beauty. Next, the clause introducing the list – τό μ' ἦ μάν | καρδίαν ἐν ϲτήθεϲιν ἐπτόαιϲεν, 'it truly shook the heart in my breast' – acts as a kind of pivot. The aorist marks the moment that sets in motion the cascade of sensations at the same time as the indefiniteness of the phrase (does τό in line 5 refer to the woman's demeanour, the man's imperviousness, or both, or something else?) maintains the enigmatic atmosphere set up by the priamel. The language of this clause is markedly conventional (Voigt's apparatus lists parallel passages); in contrast to this, the list of 'symptoms' that follows exhibits distinctive and arresting language. The Homeric trope of the 'heart in my chest' is taken to an extreme as other parts of the body or physical phenomena are made grammatical subjects for most of the list. The transmitted text of line 9 – κἀμ μὲν γλῶϲϲα ἔαγε, 'my tongue is shattered' – where the hiatus is striking enough as to have drawn attempts to emend the text, can be construed as enactment of broken speech.[18] In this context the primary meaning of πῦρ (line 10) is 'heat' or 'fever', but the root meaning 'fire' is also reactivated, conjuring up the image of tongues of fire running under the skin. The verb ἐπιρρόμβειϲι ('whirr') is also distinctive: it is all but unparalleled, an ad hoc formation from a noun (ῥόμβοϲ) denoting whirling motion. Its use in this context, applied to the speaker's ears, is particularly expressive: it combines the onomatopoeic association of rumbling sound (cf. the frequent emendation ἐπιβρόμειϲι 'roar') with the spatial connotation of 'whirling', vividly to convey the sensation of vertigo.[19] The expression 'greener than grass' is an instance of a striking expressive quirk of Sappho's, her frequent use of so-called 'supra-superlatives' (cf. 'on the top branch, top on the topmost', frr. 105(a).1–2; 'more golden than gold', 156.2; 'far whiter than an egg', 167; 'hair more blond than a flaming torch', 98(a).6–7).[20] The distinctiveness of the expressions in the list, then, conveys the shock of unmediated experience, while the prosaic word order, arranged in a series of short clauses following upon each other in quick succession and with frequent enjambment, creates an impression of immediacy. This leads us to the climax in lines 15–16: 'a small way away from dying I seem to me', which also jolts us back through a ring composition to the opening 'he seems to me' and underlines the contrast between the godlike man and the

---

[18] B. Ford and Kopff 1976.
[19] Prauscello 2007.
[20] See Demetrius, *On Style* 127, 162 (on hyperbole), Zellner 2006.

speaker. This contrast has meanwhile been suggested through other details also: he sits 'opposite' and 'close by' the woman but the speaker is overwhelmed if she looks at her 'even for a short moment' (7), he listens to her but the speaker's ears no longer hear anything, he simply 'sits' but the speaker has fire 'running' under her skin, 'whirling' in her ears, and her whole body is seized with tremor.

There is irony in this exquisite expression of the incapacity to process experience. This gap between poet and speaker leaves room for the suspicion that the speaker is not as entirely transported by her experience of love and beauty as she would have us believe, and this in turn makes us wonder about the tone of the poet's voice. There is in fact a great variety of tone in Sappho, and it would be misleading to suggest that all is beauty and exquisite expressions of desire. We have already noted how the earnestness of some of the love fragments can give way to playfulness (in fr. 2 above, and cf. fr. 1 below); moreover, praise can give way to invective, so that an ancient tradition has Sappho as the author of *iamboi*.[21] To this variation in tone correspond variations in register, elevation sometimes giving way to remarkable lowness. Fr. 57 (introduced by Athenaeus with the verb ϲκώπτει, an iambic generic marker):

> τίϲ δ᾽ ἀγροΐωτιϲ θέλγει νόον ...
> ἀγροΐωτιν ἐπεμμένα ϲτόλαν ...
> οὐκ ἐπισταμένα τὰ βράκε᾽ ἔλκην ἐπὶ τῶν ϲφύρων;

> What country bumpkin beguiles your mind ...
> clad in a country bumpkin's cloak ...
> who does not know how to drag her rags over her ankles?

The fragment is clearly corrupt since it is unmetrical, but we might still remark that word order and diction are prosaic (with the single exception of the absence of the article before νόον), while the prodding repetition ἀγροΐωτιϲ ... ἀγροΐωτιν in polyptoton compounds the impression of coarseness. In every way the fragment strikes a contrast with all the beautiful girls in beautiful garments discussed above. The different skoptic (i.e. ritually abusive) tone of, for instance, fr. 110(a) (on the doorkeeper's grotesquely large feet) belongs with the ritual language of marriage ceremonies; in other marriage songs the ritual imprint on the language is felt in the frequent recourse to anaphora (frr. 105(a), 114–17). In any case, Sappho's range is wide enough that many have not shied away from

---

[21] *Suda* c 107 (test. 2); Rosenmeyer 2006, Dale 2011a: 51–5, Martin 2016, STEINER.

ascribing the bizarre compound ὀλιϲβόδοκοϲ, 'receiver of dildoes', to her corpus (fr. 99(a).5).[22] At the higher end of the range, fr. 44 expands to accommodate epic Iliadic subject matter: the diction often departs from the Aeolic poetic dialect to include epic forms (e.g. in the genitive ending –οιο in line 16), it riffs on epic formulaic language (e.g. in the enjambed conflation of two epic formulae at lines 7–8, ἐπ' ἄλμυρον πόντον, 'on the briny sea' ≈ ἐπὶ οἴνοπα πόντον, 'on the wine-faced sea' and ἄλμυρον ὕδωρ, 'briny water'),[23] and the metre (stichic rather than stanzaic, and with a marked dactylic lilt) also reinforces the elevation.[24] Between these extremes of high and low register there is also a middle range most clearly identifiable in the subset of fragments dealing with domestic subjects, which has prompted talk of 'a poetics of the familial'.[25] These display a relatively colloquial or prosaic register, as in the recently discovered Brothers Poem, addressed to a family member and concerning the vicissitudes of her brothers: ἀλλ' ἄϊ θρύληϲθα Χάραξον ἔλθην ('but you are always babbling on that Charaxus will come') begins the extant text, setting the standard for the diction, tone, and content of the rest of the fragment.

Considerable stylistic movement is evident even within the scope of a single composition in Sappho's only extant complete poem, fr. 1. In this prayer to Aphrodite, the 'manifesto' poem at the head of the Alexandrian edition, the dazzling interplay of style and structure helps us imagine what we might be missing elsewhere in poems only partially preserved. The opening is couched in the conventional language of prayer, with an invocation (including the name of the divinity accompanied by epithets) followed by a petition ('I pray of you', λίϲϲομαί ϲε, 1), a reminder of the existing relation of favour ('if ever', αἴ ποτα, 5), and the reprisal of both these elements in the closing ('come to me on this occasion too', ἔλθε μοι καὶ νῦν, 25). The epithets too are coherent with a ritual utterance: their poetic connotations go hand in hand with cultic function, since real-life prayers borrowed ornamental epithets from poetic hymns to increase their effectiveness.[26] But, as she is wont to do, Sappho turns this conventional framework to her own poetic purposes, leavening it with language that has different associations.

[22] Voigt however ascribes the papyrus to Alcaeus (fr. 303Aa.5); West 1970: 324 = 2001–13: II 45 argues that ὄλιϲβοϲ here has the unparalleled meaning 'plectrum'.
[23] Budelmann 2018: 142 *ad loc.*
[24] For epic language and themes in fr. 44, see KELLY pp. 62–4.
[25] Peponi 2016: 227.
[26] Pulleyn 1997: 52–3.

The language of prayer is related to that of magic – performative incantations often involve prayerful invocation – and Sappho here plays up this relation. The verb ἄγην ('lead', 19, if that is the true text) is pertinent to *agôgê* spells (spells of attraction), and the verbs τέλεccαι/τέλεcον ('fulfil') and the reference to 'all those things my heart desires' (26–7) are common features of standard hexametrical erotic spells. The same is true of the syntax of Aphrodite's predictions (21–4), with the performative implication of its repetitions and oppositions, as well the emphasis on the swiftness with which they will occur and the unwillingness of the target.[27]

A further layer is added by a dense set of allusions to epic poetry.[28] The vignette describing Aphrodite's journey and shading into the present to effect her epiphany (7–13) resonates with descriptions of goddesses descending to earth on chariots, for instance Hera and Athena's elaborate descent in the *Iliad* in response to Diomedes' prayer (5.115–32, 720–77). The reference to 'dark earth' (γᾶc μελαίναc, 10) is at least traditional if not specifically epic. The description of the sparrows' flight finds a strikingly close parallel in *Odyssey* 2.151, 'wheeling around with a close beating of wings' (ἐπιδινηθέντε τιναξάcθην πτερὰ πυκνά), where the birds in question are majestic eagles rather than the frivolous sparrows, suggesting playfulness in this allusive turn. In a similar vein the participle 'smiling' (μειδιαίcαιc', 14) evokes Aphrodite's traditional epithet 'laughter-loving' (φιλομμειδήc)[29] but turns it to idiosyncratic effect to suggest Aphrodite's actual presence before Sappho's eyes.

Within this web of language conveying different associations we can discern multiple voices corresponding to the characters of 'Sappho' and Aphrodite. Aphrodite's speech shades cleverly from indirect to direct to enact the goddess's epiphany, but in both cases it is syntactically distinctive: short, punchy questions and statements accumulate in parallel constructions and the stanzas culminate in the short final line with emphatic words and ideas. At the same time, repetition weaves together the different voices: the 'heart' (θῦμοc) on which Sappho insists (4, 27) is picked up in her report of Aphrodite's speech, 'for your maddened heart' (μαινόλαι θύμωι, 18), where the addition of the adjective is pointed. Throughout, repetition underlines the idea of recurrence at the heart of the poem and weaves together so artfully its many frames. The petition 'come' in the

---

[27] Petropoulos 1993, Faraone 1999: 136–7; cf. Segal 1974: 149 = Greene 1996a: 67.
[28] KELLY pp. 55–8.
[29] Budelmann 2018: 119 *ad loc.*

present (ἔλθ', 5) resonates with the successful petition 'you came' in the past (ἦλθες, 8) and leads with a suggestion of inevitability to the imminent future in 'come to me on this occasion too' (ἔλθε μοι καὶ νῦν, 25). The emphasis on repeated experience is given an ironic twist in the refrain 'once again now' (δηὖτε, 15, 16, 18), which is reported by Sappho in the present to have been said to her in the past, and is then picked up in Aphrodite's direct speech (cf. p. 151 above on its topical erotic connotations). This significant repetition only adds to the diffuse, almost incantatory, repetitive sound patterns throughout the poem: *poikilo–* . . . *doloploke . . . lissomai se me m'asaisi med' oniaisi damna potnia* . . . and so on. There may be some clever play with sound and meaning in Aphrodite's naming of Sappho too: τίc c', ὦ Ψάπφ', ἀδίκηcι; 'who wrongs you, Sappho?' (19–20). That Sappho's name should occur in the vocative in her own poem, a cletic hymn, is striking enough; in this particular phrasing the elision of the ending and the echo of an 'unrealised rhyme' (*ô psapf[ô]*) reinforces the reversal of syllables, and underlines the reversal of speaking personas.[30]

Sappho's language, then, is artful and yet flexible. The poet's overt interest in beauty and its sensuous manifestations often translates into an intensity that is nevertheless tempered by elegance or wit. Her language owes much to ritual and poetic traditions but it is never too formalised, on the contrary being remarkable for its dexterity. Related to this dexterity is Sappho's distinctive mobility of thought, discernible in the longer fragments such as frr. 1 and 31, and her elusiveness in the use of figures by analogy, such as in fr. 96 discussed above. Fr. 16 exemplifies both mobility and elusiveness. As we have seen, the priamel on what is 'most beautiful' leads into a mythical exemplum in which Helen exemplifies not beauty but the subjectivity of judgement on what is beautiful; she leaves behind her husband and chooses to go far away with Paris instead, and this in turn reminds the speaker of beautiful Anactoria, who is far away. The relevance of the priamel to the exemplum, and of these in turn to the 'here and now', keeps shifting, and yet this surplus of correspondences, the multiple but elliptic points of relevance, maintain an air of naturalness, and the whole is held together by ring composition (1–4 ~ 17–20, desirability and armies). Sappho has a peculiar way with omissions and absences more generally. The notion of absence lies at the heart of erotic love: the object of intentionality is always elusive, the loved one always an

---

[30] Cf. Purves 2014: 188–90.

absent presence;[31] we see this explored in different ways in frr. 96, 31, and 16 among others. Some of Sappho's most remarkable passages are those in which she expresses feelings of longing and the heightening of the imagination these feelings engender. The paradox of capturing so precisely in language what is so elusive in experience is part of the enduring fascination of Sappho's poetry.

Further Reading

Silk 2010 is a helpful introduction to the language of lyric poetry in general. Two excellent commentaries are most perceptive on Sappho's poetic language: Hutchinson 2001: 139–86 and Budelmann 2018: 113–52; Tzamali 1996 is useful on points of detail. Several of the chapters in section I ('Language and literary context') of Greene 1996a have a lot to say about Sappho's poetic language. Zellner 2010 has an axe to grind but brings out the playfulness of Sappho's rhetorical style.

[31] Carson 1986: 10–17 and *passim*.

CHAPTER 12

Sappho's Personal Poetry

André Lardinois

In her survey of the reception of Sappho in Europe Joan DeJean observes:

> in the four centuries of Sappho commentaries that I analyzed for this project, I encountered only three instances in which Hellenists call for the application to the study of Sapphism of what literary critics today consider the most elementary principles: a distinction between the speaking subject or narrator of a literary work and the biographical individual known or presumed to have authored that work, and the concomitant distinction between literary word and actual deed.[1]

Interpretations of Greek lyric poetry since the Second World War are generally more careful in identifying the speaking voice in this poetry with the author,[2] but in the case of Sappho an exception is made: many scholars, implicitly or explicitly, consider her poetry to be personal and largely autobiographical. This chapter will argue that there are reasons to be sceptical about such an interpretation. I do not deny that Sappho's personal experiences influenced her poetry (they influence the work of any artist), but that is different from saying that her poetry is *about* her personal experiences. I will first provide an overview of the different speakers that are found in the extant fragments. Next I will discuss the limitations of genre and occasion on the expression of personal feelings that we may expect to find in Sappho's poetry; and finally I will examine Sappho's songs about love and family, which are most often identified as dealing with her personal life.

---

[1] DeJean 1989a: 9.
[2] Slings 1990a; further Diller 1962/3 = 1971: 64–72, Rösler 1985 ≈ Rutherford 2019: 80–93, Lardinois 1994: 60 n. 13, Calame 2005a, especially 1–7 and 55–69, Hedreen 2016, Bakker 2017.

Different Speakers

Sappho regularly introduces in her poetry speaking characters who are different from herself. In fr. 1, for example, she cites the words of Aphrodite (18–24), in fr. 94 those of a woman who is going away (4–5),[3] and fr. 137 consists of a dialogue between a man and a woman.[4] This already should make us cautious about attributing single fragments, often consisting of not more than one or two lines, to 'Sappho' as speaker. (I distinguish between Sappho, the poet and possible performer of her songs, and 'Sappho', the speaking character given that name in some of these songs.)

We know, furthermore, that Sappho composed choral as well as monodic songs. Among her fragments are examples of religious hymns and marriage songs most likely performed by choruses, and there is evidence of mixed performances as well, where Sappho is speaking as poet-performer and a chorus responds.[5] Denys Page argued that Sappho's choral poetry was easily distinguishable from her monodic compositions: 'There is nothing to contradict the natural supposition that, with this one small exception [i.e. marriage songs], all or almost all her poems were recited by herself informally to her companions.'[6] However, his most important support, the linguistic evidence, has since been questioned. Page followed Edgar Lobel in his assessment that Sappho wrote in her Lesbian vernacular, 'uncontaminated by alien or artificial forms and features', with the exception of some 'abnormal' poems,[7] but Hooker and Bowie have shown that all of Sappho's poetry is a complicated mix of old Aeolic, epic, and her local dialect.[8]

There seems to be no clear metrical division between Sappho's choral and monodic fragments either, since we possess a cultic hymn most likely performed by a chorus (fr. 17),[9] wedding songs (frr. 27, 30), and songs that appear to be monodic (fr. 1) in the same sapphic stanza.[10] Sappho

---

[3] I am convinced that most of the women mentioned in Sappho's poetry were young and of marriageable age (Lardinois 1994: 58–60), but because this is controversial (Parker 1993 ≈ Greene 1996b: 146–83, Stehle 1997: 262–78), I will refer to them simply as women, unless explicitly identified as children (παῖδες) or girls (κόραι). The question does not affect my argument.

[4] For more examples, see Tsagarakis 1977: 77–82.

[5] Lardinois 1996.

[6] Page 1955: 119.

[7] Page 1955: 327.

[8] Hooker 1977, A. Bowie 1981, TRIBULATO.

[9] Burris, Fish, and Obbink 2014: 5.

[10] The poems in Book 1 were arranged alphabetically, not by genre or subject: Obbink 2016b: 41–5, PRAUSCELLO pp. 221–2.

also composed frr. 94 and 96 in a similar metre, but while fr. 94 appears to be monodic, fr. 96 is more likely choral.[11] Finally, Sappho used the dactylic hexameter for wedding songs (frr. 105, 106, 143) and for such a song as fr. 142, perhaps the opening line of one of her amorous songs. Hence we cannot deduce from language or metre whether any first-person speaker represents a chorus or a soloist.

Not every singer of the monodic songs needs to have been Sappho either. The fragments sometimes refer to other women who sing songs about each other.[12] These songs may have been compositions by the women themselves, but it is also possible that Sappho composed them, in the same way she composed the marriage songs or hymns for others to sing. There are, in other words, various different persons who may appear as first-person speakers in Sappho's songs. The fact that ancient authors, who quote these fragments, sometimes identify the speaker as Sappho herself does not help, because ancient commentators are notorious in identifying the first-person speaker of archaic Greek poetry with the poet him- or herself. Thus, the autobiographical reading of Sappho's poetry had already started in antiquity.

Occasion

The occasion for which Sappho's poetry was composed can help to determine the degree of personal statement we might expect in them. It is often assumed that Sappho performed her poetry before a small group of pupils or female friends during a kind of private symposium, in which case the chance that (some of) her poetry would contain her personal thoughts becomes more likely.[13] With others I have argued against this view.[14] I consider it much more likely that (most of) Sappho's poetry was performed before substantial audiences of both men and women. We are furthermore dealing with songs: all poems of Sappho were intended to be performed to music, either by Sappho herself or others. This already implies a public persona and the possibility, if not expectation, of

---

[11] Lardinois 1996: 161–4.

[12] Frr. 21, 22. In fr. 96.4, we are told that a (Lydian?) woman used to compare the addressee to a goddess, and it is not unlikely that she did so in a song. The addressee herself performed a song-dance (μόλπα) when she was praised.

[13] Diller 1962/3: 564–5 = 1971: 69–71, Skinner 1996, Stehle 1997: 262.

[14] Merkelbach 1957 = 1996: 87–114, Calame 1996 ≈ 2001: 210–14, 231–3, 249–52 ≈ 1977: 1 367–72, 400–4, 427–32, Lardinois 1994, 1996, F. Ferrari 2010, FERRARI.

reperformance. I will argue below that Sappho probably took account of this in the creation of the first-person speaker of her songs.

The genres to which Sappho's songs can be assigned suggest where they may have been performed. There are love songs (*erôtika*), some of which may have functioned as praise poems (*enkômia*) as well.[15] We further possess songs about her family (discussed below), religious hymns,[16] wedding songs,[17] satirical songs,[18] a song about old age (the Tithonus Poem), and an epic-like fragment (fr. 44). In the case of the religious hymns or marriage songs, one expects the first-person speaker, whether a chorus, the poet, or another soloist, to express sentiments shared by the community on behalf of which s/he speaks. Such a speaker, the 'representative I',[19] need not reflect sentiments of the whole community, but can also represent just a part of it, for example women.[20] This may account for feminine perspectives expressed by speakers in Sappho's poetry.[21]

The satirical songs, mostly about other women who left the first-person speaker against her wish or about the women to whom they subsequently turned, presuppose a semi-public setting and, probably, reperformance in order to be effective. Here, too, it cannot be excluded that in some cases the first-person speaker is not 'Sappho', but another woman or a chorus, for example in fr. 55, where the first-person speaker describes someone who will not be remembered, because she did not share in 'the roses of Pieria' (songs like Sappho's), but after flying away from her/them (ἐκπεποταμένα) she 'goes to and fro among the shadowy corpses of the dead'. This throng, among which the woman now wanders, may be implicitly contrasted to the bright chorus that performs this song of Sappho above the earth.[22]

The song about old age (the Tithonus Poem) was probably also performed in public with the help of a chorus, which is addressed as 'children' (παῖδες) in line 1: they dance 'like young fawns' (6) while Sappho or

---

[15] This has been argued for fr. 16 (Howie 1977 = 2012: 102–25) and suggested for fr. 31 (Lardinois 2001: 90–1 = Rutherford 2019: 304–6). See also Lasserre 1974.

[16] E.g. frr. 17, 140; testt. 21, 47, 58, 59.

[17] E.g. frr. 27, 30, 103–17B; testt. 45, 58.

[18] E.g. frr. 55, 57, 71, 99, 131; test. 20.

[19] Slings 1990a: 2–4; cf. Stehle 1997: 28.

[20] Lardinois 2011.

[21] 'Feminine' here refers to a concept or behaviour that a given culture typically associates with women, 'female' to the state of being a woman, and 'feminist' to a critical stance towards the dominant (masculine) culture. For Greek concepts of the feminine, see Zeitlin 1985 ≈ 1996: 341–74 ≈ Winkler and Zeitlin 1990: 63–96. For the feminine (almost feminist) perspective in Sappho's epic interactions, see KELLY.

[22] Lardinois 2008: 87.

another performer is singing.[23] The epic-like fragment (fr. 44), finally, may have been composed for solo performance at a wedding banquet,[24] or for more general entertainment.[25] Most fragments of Sappho are, however, too small to determine which genre they belonged to, let alone where or by whom they were performed, and it is better to acknowledge this than to try to fit them all into the mould of personal poetry. In the following paragraphs I will discuss the first-person speaker in the fragments of Sappho's love songs and in her songs about family members, because they in particular have been associated with Sappho's personal experiences.

Love Songs

If any piece of evidence has contributed to the idea that Sappho is the speaker in her own poetry, it is fr. 1, the 'Hymn to Aphrodite', in which the first-person speaker is explicitly identified by her interlocutor, the goddess Aphrodite, as 'Sappho' (fr. 1.20). Before the discovery of the papyri, this poem was the only substantial sample of her poetry to survive, together with fr. 31, in which Sappho is also the speaker, according to Pseudo-Longinus, who cites the fragment. We therefore should not be surprised that scholars for a long time assumed that Sappho was the speaker in (most of) her songs. Now we know, however, that fr. 1 is exceptional. Hellenistic scholars placed this song out of its alphabetical order as a signature poem (*sphragis*) at the beginning of their collection probably because of the rare mention of her name.[26] Sappho further identifies herself explicitly as first-person speaker only three times elsewhere (frr. 65, 94, 133(b)). Nevertheless, we have here a series of poems in which 'Sappho' appears as speaker, and must therefore consider if here at least we are dealing with personal, autobiographical songs.

Fr. 1 takes the form of a typical Greek prayer, including an invocation, a narration, and a request.[27] It is, however, not a real prayer but a song, composed in stylised poetic language and metre and intended for an audience of mortals. It qualifies as an *erôtikon* (a song about passionate

[23] Lardinois 2009: 43, 51–3, F. Ferrari 2010: 197–8.
[24] Rösler 1975, Contiades-Tsitsoni 1990: 107.
[25] Kirkwood 1974: 144–5, M. Johnson 2007: 65–6.
[26] Obbink 2016b: 42. Dale 2015: 23–4, 29–30 argues that fr. 1 was placed in its alphabetical order before the Brothers Poem, but fibre traces connect the Brothers Poem papyrus (P.Sapph.Obbink) to papyrus fragment P.GC inv. 105 fr. 1, which preserves traces of Sappho fr. 9 (Obbink 2016b: 40). Sappho fr. 9 therefore must have stood before the Brothers Poem, as West 2014: 1–2 already suspected. Cf. PRAUSCELLO p. 222 n. 17.
[27] Pulleyn 1997: 132.

love), not a *hymnos* (a song for a god). The fictional character of the song is clear because the woman whom 'Sappho' loves is not named: this makes the poem highly ineffective as a prayer, but works well for a song, making it easier to perform on different occasions.[28]

Another fictional element is the close encounter that 'Sappho' had with Aphrodite, not once but at least twice in the past (cf. 15–18). True, the ancient Greeks believed in epiphanies, but Sappho's audience would hardly have believed that she was visited by the goddess whenever she experienced problems with her beloved. Such encounters were considered more typical of the mythical age of heroes, as described by the epic poets; and Sappho here portrays 'Sappho' as a Homeric hero, similar to Diomedes who prays to Athena.[29]

Finally, interpreters of this song have rightly questioned what it is that Aphrodite exactly promises to 'Sappho' in lines 21–4:

κα὎ γὰρ α὎ φεύγει, ταχέως διώξει·
α὎ δὲ δῶρα μὴ δέκετ', ἀλλὰ δώσει·
α὎ δὲ μὴ φίλει, ταχέως φιλήσει
κωὺκ ἐθέλοισα.

If now she flees, soon she'll chase.
If rejecting gifts, then she'll give.
If not loving, soon she'll love,
even against her will.[30]

The object of the woman's chase, gift-giving, and love is not expressed. Aphrodite therefore does not necessarily promise that the woman will chase, give gifts to, or love 'Sappho' again in the future; she could also be saying that the woman will chase, give gifts to, and love *someone else* against her will, just as 'Sappho' loved this woman in vain.[31] This is not what the speaker in the poem expects: she believes the goddess will help her, but Sappho the composer and likely performer of the song may not: 'Sappho' in the song is a persona, with whom Sappho the poet/performer can disagree.

Of the other three fragments in which Sappho is named, two more seem to come from conversations between 'Sappho' and Aphrodite

---

[28] West 1970: 310 = 2001–13: II 31.

[29] *Iliad* 5.115–32; thus Svenbro 1975, Winkler 1981: 68–72 = H. Foley 1981: 66–71 ≈ Winkler 1990: 169–70, 175–6 ≈ Greene 1996a: 93–6, KELLY.

[30] Translation by Rayor cited by Rayor and Lardinois 2014: 26.

[31] Giacomelli 1980 = Carson 1996, Calame 1999: 23–7. This interpretation helps to explain why Aphrodite is described as 'weaving wiles' (δολόπλοκε) in line 2. It also helps to explain why 'Sappho' does not list the actual help she received from Aphrodite in the past, as is common in prayers, but only what the goddess promised her (cf. Diller 1962/3: 565 = 1971: 70).

(frr. 65, 133(b)), and must therefore be imaginary and probably fictional as well. Fr. 94, however, records 'Sappho' as first-person speaker consoling a woman who must leave her by reminding her of the good things they did together. This conversation could be based on the poet Sappho's real experience, although even then we must allow for a degree of fictionalisation: it has, after all, become part of a public song. The woman in the song may have been named in the lost opening part, but it is just as likely that Sappho left out the name, as in fr. 1, making it a song that could be performed on different occasions.[32] 'Sappho' is not speaking entirely for herself, either: she uses a first person plural to remind the woman that 'we cared for you' (cε πεδήπομεν, 8), including others perhaps present during performances of the song.[33] This fragment may be derived from a wedding lament, in which friends of the bride sing a formal farewell as companions of her youth;[34] 'Sappho' in that case would be speaking for them and for Sappho.

What fr. 1 talks about is the capriciousness of love, both on the human level (the persona 'Sappho') and on the divine (Aphrodite). Although Sappho voices this idea artfully, it was not new: this is generally how the Greeks looked at *erôs* and the workings of the goddess.[35] What is new, however, is that Sappho illustrates these workings through a woman passionately desiring another woman. Since antiquity, this choice has generally been attributed to her personal love of women,[36] but another explanation is possible. As Stehle Stigers has remarked:

> The formal problem facing Sappho was to find a way of presenting the female persona as an erotic subject. Culturally acceptable models presumably did not include woman's pursuing man. Sappho's solution, to direct the erotic impulse toward other women, was perhaps a traditional one.[37]

Furthermore, by using as her example a homoerotic relationship, Sappho, like other archaic Greek poets, indicates that she is talking about the passionate love of Aphrodite, not the measured form of love that was the domain of Hera and expected to prevail between a man and a woman in

---

[32] If the woman was named at the beginning of the poem, one perhaps might have expected 'Sappho' to repeat the name in her address of the woman in her speech that begins at line 7; cf. Archilochus fr. 196a.10 *IEG*.

[33] Page 1955: 78, Lardinois 1996: 163–4.

[34] Lardinois 2001: 85–6 = Rutherford 2019: 298–300.

[35] Calame 1999: 3–9 and *passim*. Compare Aphrodite's treatment of Helen in *Iliad* 3.383–420.

[36] P.Oxy. 1800 fr. 1 (test. 1), for example, speaks of Sappho being accused by some of being irregular in her ways and a 'woman-lover' (γυναικε[ράc]τρια); see further MUELLER.

[37] Stehle Stigers 1981: 47 = H. Foley 1981: 45.

marriage.[38] Sappho may well have loved other women; certainly, her poetry marks a memorable moment in the history of sexuality and testifies to the fact that the ancient Greeks recognised the possibility of love between two women and were not too shy to sing or listen to songs about it. But I doubt that we can deduce Sappho's personal feelings from statements made about this in her poetry.

The next love song in the corpus is fr. 16. In this song the situation as regards the speaker and her beloved is reversed from fr. 1: here the beloved is identified, as Anactoria (fr. 16.15), but the speaker is not. This means that this song could have been performed (and reperformed) by anyone, and the speaker may represent Sappho, another woman, or even a chorus.[39] This, however, would not make much difference for the interpretation of the song, because we seem to be dealing again with a 'representative I': the singer wants her audience to experience together with her the painful absence of Anactoria. Although the wording of the song does not reveal the gender of the speaker, it was probably intended to be performed by a woman or a female chorus, because it advocates a perspective that the ancient Greeks would have recognised as feminine. The opening stanza contrasts 'some (men)' (οἰ μὲν . . . οἰ δὲ . . . οἰ δέ), who say that the most beautiful thing on earth is an army of horsemen, foot soldiers, or ships, with the first-person speaker (ἔγω), who proclaims that it is whatever one loves.[40] This contrast between the sexes, that men are preoccupied with war and women with love, is again not new: it permeates Greek literature from the laments of the women in the *Iliad* to the *Lysistrata* of Aristophanes and beyond. What makes this song special is that it privileges the feminine position over the masculine.

In two other love songs of which substantial portions have been preserved (fr. 31 and the Cypris Poem), neither the first-person speaker nor the beloved is named, at least not in the parts that survive. In both cases, however, the speaker is identified as a woman through the grammar.[41] These songs could therefore have been performed by any woman and Sappho may well have intended them that way.[42] We do not know where

---

[38] Merkelbach 1957: 16 = 1996: 101.

[39] Lardinois 1996: 166–7.

[40] οἰ μὲν . . . οἰ δὲ . . . can refer either to some men (male gender) or some people (gender unspecified); the meaning 'some men' presents itself strongly because of the objects listed that are considered beautiful. See Winkler 1981: 73–4 = H. Foley 1981: 71–2 ≈ Winkler 1990: 176–7 ≈ Greene 1996a: 97, Williamson 1995: 167.

[41] Fr. 31.14, Cypris Poem 11 (αὔται; text at Obbink 2014a: 49).

[42] This does not preclude that men could also have reperformed these songs, but they would then be adopting in their performance a female persona, as we sometimes see in other lyric poetry, composed by male poets for performances by men, as well: Martin 2001.

Sappho's love songs were performed, but one possibility is the wedding banquet, which constituted one of the few occasions on which men and respectable women feasted together and sang songs.[43] Sappho composed other songs for the wedding ceremony (see above); 'serious love songs' (ἐρωτικὰ cύντονα) were performed during the wedding banquet;[44] and men and women could take turns singing songs from a masculine and feminine perspective at weddings.[45] This may be reflected in a song like fr. 16 that adopts a feminine perspective. This song then speaks for all the women in the audience, not only for Sappho.

Family Songs

Another set of songs commonly associated with Sappho's personal experiences are about family:[46] they include songs in which the first person mentions a mother,[47] a daughter named Cleis,[48] and brothers.[49] In none of these, as far as we can tell, does the first-person speaker identify herself as 'Sappho'. If she is nevertheless the first-person speaker, we have to assume that the audience could infer this from the performance context (Sappho herself performing the songs) and/or because they knew the persons she was singing about. The latter is not impossible in a relatively small town like Mytilene, where Sappho's songs were presumably first performed. However, Sappho tells more in these songs than the story of her life. In fr. 98, for example, the first-person speaker uses her inability to obtain a decorated headband for her daughter to comment on the island's political situation.[50] She may well have intended these songs to be reperformed by anyone who agreed with this political assessment, just as people were expected to reperform the political songs of Alcaeus or Solon.

---

[43] Oakley and Sinos 1993: 22–4, J. Burton 1998: 158–9.

[44] Aristoxenus fr. 125 Wehrli (Scolia test. 2 Campbell).

[45] Compare Catullus 62 and the wedding laments mentioned above. Catullus 62 reflects Greek wedding practices and seems to be based on earlier Greek wedding songs, including Sappho's (Bowra 1961: 219–21).

[46] KIVILO pp. 12–14.

[47] Fr. 98(a).1. West 2014: 2, 7–9 assumes that fr. 9 and the Brothers Poem were addressed to Sappho's mother as well.

[48] Fr. 98(b), 132; cf. P.Oxy. 1800 fr. 1 (test. 1), *Suda* c 107 (test. 2), (Pseudo-?)Ovid, *Heroides* 15.63–8 (test. 16). The context in fr. 98 and a single word in fr. 132 (Hallett 1982) suggest that in these fragments the first-person speaker is referring to her own child, not another child that she cares about.

[49] Frr. 5, 15, 203, Brothers Poem. Frr. 3, 7, 9, 20, and test. 209 V. may also be related to the story about Charaxus and Doricha: F. Ferrari 2014, Lardinois 2016: 172–3.

[50] F. Ferrari 2010: 3–11, Caciagli 2016: 437–40. For Sappho's political poetry, see Parker 2005.

Another set of songs deals with 'her' brothers Charaxus, Larichus, and, possibly, Eurygius.[51] Ancient sources tell us of songs in which Sappho praised Larichus for serving the wine in the town hall of Mytilene and in which she criticised Charaxus for his affair with a woman named Doricha.[52] Thanks to the Brothers Poem we are much better informed about the character of these songs. Sappho's songs about her brothers differed considerably from each other, however, at least in presentation. In fr. 5, recently augmented by P.GC inv. 105, neither the sister, who presumably is the first-person speaker,[53] nor the brother is explicitly named, making it possible for any woman with a brother at sea to perform this song. In the Brothers Poem, on the other hand, Charaxus and Larichus are named, but the first-person speaker and the addressee are not, although the addressee was probably identified in the missing opening strophe(s) of the song.[54] If Charaxus and Larichus were Sappho's real brothers, we must assume that Sappho is talking about personal experiences.

But were Charaxus and Larichus her real brothers?[55] They could be fictional characters.[56] For one thing, they never seem to change or to grow up. It is tricky to argue from silence, when so much of the work of a poet is lost, but it is striking that when Charaxus is mentioned in Sappho's extant poetry or in the biographical tradition, it is always in connection with his absence from home and his affair with Doricha. Similarly, Sappho 'often' (πολλαχοῦ) praised Larichus for serving the wine in the town hall of Mytilene, according to Athenaeus,[57] but neither in the biographical tradition nor in the extant fragments of Sappho do we hear anything else about him. He seems to be frozen in this state of being a 'Ganymede'. Such persistence of character is more suggestive of fictional characters than of real brothers whom Sappho had occasion to sing about in the course of her life.

---

[51] Eurygius, also spelled Erigyius or Eurygyius, is mentioned as a third brother in P.Oxy. 1800 fr. 1 (test. 1), *Suda* c 107 (test. 2), P.Oxy. 2506 fr. 48 (test. 213a.40–1 V.).

[52] Athenaeus, *Scholars at Dinner* 10.425a (fr. 203); Herodotus 2.135 (fr. 202).

[53] Lidov 2016: 69 argues that the speaker in fr. 5 does not have to be the sister, since she is spoken of in the third person (line 9), but if the speaker is not the sister mentioned in this line, he or she is never identified and the song would become hard to understand.

[54] West 2014: 8, following Obbink 2014a: 41–2, 2016c: 217–19, identifies the addressee as Sappho's mother. I have proposed that it could also be her third brother, Eurygius (Lardinois 2016: 182–4). For a list of suggested addressees, see Neri 2015: 58–9.

[55] The following three paragraphs are based on Lardinois 2016: 185–7.

[56] Bierl 2016a, Lidov 2016, and Obbink 2016c: 214–17 argue that Charaxus and Larichus were cultic figures, associated with the cult of Hera at Messon (cf. Dale 2011a: 70–1); *contra* Lardinois 2016: 184–5.

[57] Athenaeus, *Scholars at Dinner* 10.425a (fr. 203).

Furthermore, if Charaxus was Sappho's real brother, it is difficult to understand why she would publicly scold him in her poetry, as Herodotus reports and fr. 15 seems to suggest. It would be an extreme case of airing the family's dirty laundry and Sappho herself would contribute to the bad reputation of the family which she expresses concern about in fr. 5 and in the Brothers Poem.[58] Someone wishing to maintain that Charaxus was Sappho's real brother has to postulate a performance situation in which such a critical stance towards a real brother would be permissible and accepted. One could think of a small, intimate setting for the first performance of these songs, but even in that case Sappho must have been aware that at some point these songs would circulate, as they ultimately did. Such is the nature of songs.

The difference between fictional and real, historical brothers may ultimately not be so great, however, for the interpretation of these songs, because even real-life persons are necessarily abstracted and fictionalised in the process of composing a song. For if Sappho's songs about her brothers were based on real-life persons, we should ask why ancient audiences would be interested in listening to such songs? It must be because she generalises from her own experiences. As Chris Carey, who argues for the historicity of Lycambes and his daughters in Archilochus' poetry, puts it:

> As a general rule, the archaic solo poet uses his own person and represents the events he narrates or judges as belonging to his own life or the lives of those around him. But though he writes about himself he usually sees two aspects to his experience, the individual and the general. It is as a rule true that the archaic monodists use their own experience to express a truth of general validity. The poet rarely concentrates upon the details of his life; he seeks rather to use his own experience to inform others.[59]

What then is the meaning of Sappho's songs about 'her' brothers? They served as exempla that address a number of anxieties haunting aristocratic Greek families: the loss of family capital and reputation, the risks of trading at sea, the allure of foreign courtesans, and strife between family members. Some of these themes are reminiscent of Hesiod's *Works and Days*, such as the quarrel with a bad brother or the risk of trading at sea;[60] others of Theognis, such as the loss of family capital and reputation. These are themes that transcend Sappho, her family, and Lesbos.

---

[58] Cf. P. Freeman 2016: 101.
[59] Carey 1986: 67.
[60] Dale 2011a: 69–71, KELLY pp. 60–2.

Conclusion

This chapter takes a critical stance towards a personal or autobiographical reading of Sappho's poetry. Providing an overview of the different first-person speakers in Sappho's poetry and discussing the occasion where the poems could have been performed, I have focused in particular on her love songs and family songs, arguing that most of her songs were intended to be publicly performed, which limits the degree of personal detail we may expect in them. Often the first-person speaker in her poems consists of a 'representative I', who speaks on behalf of the community or of parts of it, in particular the women. Even in cases where we might suspect her songs to deal with personal experiences, as in fr. 94 and perhaps in some of her family songs, we must account for a degree of fictionalisation, which helped to make them relevant for others to sing, and to enjoy.

Further Reading

The complexities of the first-person speaker in Greek lyric poetry are well described by Slings 1990a and further discussed in a collection of essays edited by Bakker 2017. Calame 1996 ≈ 2001: 210–14, 231–3, 249–52 ≈ 1977: I 367–72, 400–4, 427–32, Lardinois 1996, and F. Ferrari 2010 argue for the public performance of Sappho's songs. For Sappho's love songs, Winkler 1981 = H. Foley 1981: 63–89 ≈ Winkler 1990: 162–87 ≈ Greene 1996a: 89–109, Snyder 1997, and Boehringer and Calame 2016 may be consulted. For the songs about her brothers, see F. Ferrari 2014, Lardinois 2016, and Peponi 2016. Lidov 2016 discusses both types of song.

CHAPTER 13

Sappho's Lyric Sensibility

Alex Purves

The papyrus discoveries of the early twenty-first century, which provided us with two sizeable and relatively complete new poems in the Tithonus Poem and Brothers Poem, allow us to consider anew the question of how Sappho's composition of individual poems falls within the larger poetic category of the lyric. These new finds, like the complete fr. 1 and like the relatively well-preserved frr. 2, 16, 31, 44, and 94, share a number of poetic devices – such as deixis (defined below, pp. 186–7), second-person address, and the 'lyric present' – which have been identified as key figures of lyric expression, and which I will discuss in relation to Sappho in this chapter.

These devices are not unique to Sappho; indeed, they can be understood as definitive of lyric as a long-standing poetic category. Jonathan Culler identifies lyric as (among other things) focused on experience over narrative, as operating usually though some form of a triangular relationship between poet, addressee, and audience, and as expressing a form of enunciation tied to the idea of the present place and moment, where the poem itself *is* the event, rather than the attempt to represent an event.[1] His work addresses lyric from antiquity to the present day, with an emphasis on the Romantic period and beyond, but it also applies well to Sappho, whose language is densely vivid and sensory, turning on 'the paradox of capturing so precisely in language what is so elusive in experience' (CAZZATO p. 162). This chapter offers examples of how Sappho's poetry achieves those effects by considering (1) her deployment of, and resistance to, narrative strategies; (2) her use of tense, mood, and voice in the evocation of a lyric present; and (3) the role of deixis in her work. Each of these stylistic devices, as I show, is connected to lyric's central preoccupation with the articulation of the self.

---

[1] Culler 2015. I do not subscribe to the belief that Greek lyric must be understood fundamentally differently from private or written lyric (*pace* P. Miller 1994, W. R. Johnson 1982).

Lyric and Narrative

Sappho's poetry employs certain key narrative markers through its engagement with the mythological tradition and its practice of naming recurring characters.[2] But these narratival elements are often left undeveloped, whether due to a withholding of information (who is the woman Aphrodite asks about in fr. 1?) or because narrative in the past tense is never fully sustained. Memory, through which Sappho transports her listener into the past, features prominently, yet it affords only glimpses of an incomplete history.[3]

In fr. 16, Sappho moves from general statement (priamel) to mythological exemplum (Helen) to the memory of past experiences (Anactoria), before returning to the chariots and foot soldiers of the poem's beginning. The exemplum begins with the clear narrativisation of past events activated by participles and aorist indicatives ('leaving behind . . . , [Helen] went, sailing, to Troy . . . she did not remember, . . . but [Cypris?] led her astray', 9–11). Yet this rapid succession of action-verbs is called to a halt just a few lines later, as Helen's story 'reminds me now (νῦν) of Anactoria' (15), and Sappho's mind is diverted to her own personal memories.[4] In an ironic overlaying of time frames, therefore, Helen's 'complete' (11) forgetfulness of the person she loved causes Sappho to forget Helen and remember Anactoria, and in doing so leads to the poem resurfacing in the present.[5]

Rather than structuring her recollection of Anactoria in terms similar to those in which she described Helen, Sappho uses the potential optative and a comparative construction, shifting her mode of expression from ἔβα, '[Helen] went', to the elusive image of Anactoria's βᾶμα, or 'step' (15–18; text from Obbink 2016a: 18):

> . .]με νῦν Ἀνακτορί[ας] ὀνεμναι-
> ϲ' οὐ] παρεοίϲαϲ,
>
> τᾶ]ϲ κε βολλοίμαν ἔρατόν τε βᾶμα
> κἀμάρυχμα λάμπρον ἴδην προϲώπω
>
> reminds me now of Anactoria,
> who is not present,

[2] Purves 2014, SCODEL.
[3] Fr. 16, 55, 94, 96; Burnett 1983: 277–313, Lardinois 2008, MUELLER pp. 43–4, 47–52.
[4] 'νῦν marks the shift from myth to the here and now, as repeatedly in epinician' (Budelmann 2018: 131 ad loc.), but the 'I' here is distinctive. Cf. Calame 2005b: 60–1, Stehle 2009b.
[5] Rosenmeyer 1997: 144, Stehle 2009b: 119–20, Culler 2015: 283–7.

> whose lovely footstep and the bright sparkle of whose face
> I would rather see

While ἔβα anchors a story to which prepositions, participles, and further verbs are attached, its cognate βᾶμα stands as its own isolated event. In settling on the 'sparkle' of Anactoria's face and her 'step', Sappho returns to the focus on things (or 'that thing', κῆνο, 3) with which the priamel began, providing a formal structure which draws her language back to the present moment of the poem's utterance and to the immediacy of its speaker's experience.

Memory in fr. 94 also offers a particularly lyric or non-narrative voicing of the experiences which Sappho has shared with a departing lover. The fragment begins with (presumably) the lover articulating her despair at having to leave, but in the fourth stanza Sappho moves the poem away from the straightforward recounting of a conversation and into a markedly different register with the phrase 'I wish to remind you . . .':

τεθνάκην δ' ἀδόλως θέλω.
ἄ με ψιςδομένα κατελίμπανεν

πόλλα καὶ τόδ' ἔειπέ [μοι·
ὤιμ' ὠς δεῖνα πεπ[όνθ]αμεν,
Ψάπφ', ἦ μάν ς' ἀέκοις' ἀπυλιμπάνω.   5

τὰν δ' ἔγω τάδ' ἀμειβόμαν·
χαίροις' ἔρχεο κἄμεθεν
μέμναις', οἶσθα γὰρ ὤς cε πεδήπομεν·

αἰ δὲ μή, ἀλλά ς' ἔγω θέλω
ὄμναιςαι [. . . .]. [. . .]. εαι   10
ὸς[   ] καὶ κάλ' ἐπάςχομεν·

πό[λλοις γὰρ ςτεφάν]οις ἴων
καὶ βρ[όδων . . .]κίων τ' ὔμοι
κα. . [   ] πὰρ ἔμοι περεθήκαο

καὶ πόλλαις ὐπαθύμιδας   15
πλέκταις ἀμφ' ἀπάλαι δέραι
ἀνθέων ἐ[   ] πεποημέναις.

καὶ π. . . . . [   ]. μύρωι
βρενθείωι. [ ]ρυ[. .]ν
ἐξαλείψαο κα[ὶ] βαςιληίωι   20

καὶ ςτρώμν[αν ἐ]πὶ μολθάκαν
ἀπάλαν παρ[   ]ονων
ἐξίης πόθο[   ]. νίδων

κωὔτε τις[οὔ]τε τι
ἶρον οὐδ᾽ ὐ[ ]   25
ἔπλετ᾽ ὄππ[οθεν ἄμ]μες ἀμέσκομεν,

οὐκ ἄλσος.[   ].ρος
                  ]ψοφος
                  ]...οιδιαι

'Truly I wish to die',
weeping very much she was leaving me,

and she said this to me,
'Alas how terribly we have suffered,
Sappho, and indeed I leave you unwillingly.'   5

But I answered her in this way:
'Go from me rejoicing and
remember me, for you know how we cared for you.

If not, I wish to remind you,
...   10
... and we experienced beautiful things,

many wreaths of violets
and roses and crocuses[?] together
... you put on beside me

and many garlands   15
plaited around your soft neck
made from flowers ...

and ...   with costly
royal perfume ...
you anointed ...   20

and on soft beds ...
for[?] tender ...
you satisfied your[/my?] longing ...

and neither anyone ... nor some ...
holy nor ...   25
was there from which we were absent

nor grove ...
... sound ... '

In the first section (1–11), the fragment is crowded with verbs, qualifying participles, and personal pronouns, which together recreate a narrative event: a real-time conversation between two characters that cycles through first, second, and third person during what is – for the one leaving at least – a moment of crisis. The couple's constant self- and cross-referencing leads to ten changes of subject in the first four stanzas, with a verb occurring in every one of the first eleven lines except for the very fragmentary line 10. But with the shift induced by Sappho's call to remember in line 12, the poem takes on an additive structure (καὶ . . . καὶ . . . καὶ . . . καὶ . . . καὶ . . . κωὔτε . . . οὔτε), with each verse now shaped by the appearance of nouns and adjectives. As we saw in fr. 16, here a specific kind of erotic memory is constructed through a reflection on things, while the volleying between *I, she, we,* and *you* with which the fragment began is now streamlined into just four occurrences of second-person verbs, each placed in the final line of the stanza to secure the abundance of items listed ('you put on', 'you placed', 'you anointed', 'you released') and each bringing to light a recurrent, playful, and non-specific practice, where desire is renewed and released in what appears to be a gentle (ἄπαλος x2, μόλθακος) cycle. Here, as in fr. 16, Sappho shifts temporal registers to interweave a vivid sense of immediacy and presence amidst a countervailing impression of absence and distance: Anactoria is notably 'not present' in fr. 16, and the objects of memory in fr. 94 become increasingly evanescent, from flowers to perfumes to a kind of vanishing with the release of desire.[6]

In these examples we see a back-and-forth between narrative and lyric elements, as well as an illustration of how simple shifts in the formal categories of words and their properties create different poetic effects. Whenever Sappho uses a concentration of past tenses, she almost always, elsewhere in the poem, will work to undo or attenuate that sense of linear movement through time in order to create a focus on the here and now. We can see this also in fr. 1, where the mini-narrative of Aphrodite's descent (note the past tenses and absence of any reference to Sappho in lines 7–15) is contrasted with the imperatives and present or future indicatives in the surrounding stanzas.

In each of these cases, moreover, the shift in temporal registers from narrative to lyric is caused by a moment of self-reflection – what we might call the insistent surfacing or presencing of Sappho herself within the poem: 'you asked . . . what I most wanted to happen to me' (fr. 1.15– 17); 'which reminds me now of Anactoria' (fr. 16.15–16); 'but I wish to remind you' (fr. 94.9–10). Indeed, the strong preference throughout Sappho's corpus for infinitives, imperatives, and optatives, as well as for

---

[6] For absence and presence in Sappho, see duBois 1978 = Greene 1996a: 79–88, Carson 1997: 224. For the structure of fr. 94, see McEvilley 1971 ≈ 2008: 48–64.

present or future tenses of the indicative, speaks to her use of certain lyric forms of expression as disrupters of typical narrative sequences.[7]

Even fr. 44, which focuses exclusively on Andromache's arrival in Troy,[8] shows the same movement from action to experience and a centripetal pull towards the description of objects and the repetition of small-scale events, so that by the end the choral celebration of the bridal couple merges with Sappho's own act of singing the poem. Here, perhaps more clearly than in any other example, the fragment begins with a decisive, epic representation of events (κᾱρυξ ἦλθε, 'the herald arrived', 2), followed by further decisive, epic action on the part of the Trojans (ἀνόρουσε . . . ἆγον . . . ἐπ[έ]βαινε . . . ὔπαγον . . . , 'he leapt up . . . they yoked . . . stepped aboard . . . they yoked . . . ', 11–17) before an anomalous (historical?) present appears (ὄρμαται, 'sets out', 23), and linear time becomes unmoored, drifting back into the lyric present of song and celebration.

In a 2016 article on the Brothers Poem, Peponi suggests that Sappho constructs narrative vignettes from her own immediate surroundings. She identifies in Sappho's use of named characters and familiar scenes a triangulated form of narrative which plays out between a first-person speaker and a second-person listener (both situated within the poem's *hic et nunc*) and a displaced, absent third party, such as Atthis' companion in fr. 96 or Charaxus in the Brothers Poem. This kind of triangulation is a classic device of lyric expression, and shows Sappho adapting and creating her own forms of storytelling in conjunction with the special properties of her lyric voice. But Peponi's analysis also reveals an important aspect of Sappho's negotiation between 'lyric' and 'narrative' discourse, insofar as we see the poet drawing on characters from her real or imagined life who, like Sappho herself, bring forms of their own histories into her poetry.

We might think here also of the Tithonus Poem, where Sappho's tracing of the development of her own old age transitions into the story of Tithonus' senescence beside an 'immortal wife' (12). The separation she draws earlier in the fragment between her own time of life and those of the girls (παῖδες) whom she addresses calls various forms of temporality into play, from the timeless present of lyric song (the 'beautiful gifts of

---

[7] The sequence of infinitives in the Brothers Poem is particularly remarkable; see also frr. 5, 16.21–2 (probably the start of a new poem).

[8] Two or three lines are missing from the start of the poem, which would not seem to create enough space for extra-mythological material (Budelmann 2018: 137).

the violet-bosomed [Muses]' and the 'song-loving, sweet lyre', 1–2) to her own time-marked body (3–6), to her 'frequent' lamentations and the sudden interjection 'but what can I do?' (7). Sappho's persistent returning to forms of 'to be' (ἔ]οντα . . . [ἐγ]ένοντο . . . ἔον . . . ἔοντ' . . . γένεσθαι . . . ἔοντα), moreover, underpins the lesson which both Eos and Tithonus must together determine, of what time 'is' and how change occurs between the past and the present. What I have referred to here as a lyric resistance to narrative time on Sappho's part, therefore, should also be understood as her own necessary entanglement within it.[9]

Apostrophe

Apostrophe denotes the practice of addressing an absent person or thing using the second person. There have been several studies on its importance as a triangulating device between poet, addressee, and reader, some of which have focused on its animating potential, especially in relation to lyric's call for a response from the non-human world.[10] In Sappho's poetry, second-person address is hardly ever directed at the actual audience of her songs but rather calls on various forms of 'you' as a means of involving the reader and opening up the poem's sphere of experience beyond the single lyric 'I'.

In fr. 114, for example, the speaker (a bride in a wedding song) calls to her own virginity using second-person address to accentuate what once was here and has now departed. Her act of addressing an absent entity summons it back into a form of presence in the space of the verse, especially as here the virginity itself responds:

> παρθενία, παρθενία, ποῖ με λίποισ' ἀποίχηι;
> †οὐκέτι ἤξω πρὸς σέ, οὐκέτι ἤξω†.

> 'Virginity, virginity, where have you gone leaving me?'
> 'No longer will I come to you, no longer will I come.'

The apostrophe plays on the paradox of virginity's survival outside or beyond the body. For the *parthenia* (also translated 'maidenhood' – the stage of a girl's life before marriage) existed only as part of who the bride was, and thus can only take on an existence as something other than herself

---

[9] Stehle 2009b, Ormand 2020.
[10] B. Johnson 1986, Greene 1994 = 1996a: 233–47, Waters 2003, Jackson 2005: 118–65, Payne 2007, Culler 2015: 186–243.

('you') after it has disappeared.[11] Similarly, the response of *parthenia* back to the speaker, 'No longer will I come to you', itself expresses an improbable concept: the virginity did not 'come' to the bride when it was part of her either, just as it will not come for a second time after it has gone. Time is again at issue, for in the woman's decisive transition from *parthenos* (virgin) to *gynê* (wife), *parthenia* denotes the temporal category of *before* or *not yet* in relation to marriage. Through the figure of apostrophe, however, Sappho draws both sides of that divide into the same temporal space, allowing the speaker's virginity to co-exist as both 'gone' and 'here' at the same time.

The addressee in fr. 114.1 possesses an indeterminate status, therefore, hovering somewhere between abstract and concrete, present and absent, person and thing. The dialogic structure of the fragment within the ritual-ised setting of the wedding song articulates the split in the woman's iden-tity as she transitions into marriage. What is 'impossible' about this act of second-person address thereby emerges as an important factor in lyric com-position, insofar as it is able to open up a different and more flexible form of time and a reframing of experience, both of which capture the contra-dictory status and impulses of the bride on the night of her marriage.[12]

Finally, the fragment – like all instances of apostrophe – blurs the line between listener/reader and addressee. Although we are certainly not the speaker's virginity, we cannot help but somehow be summoned into the 'you' of the fragment's first verse. Likewise, the *parthenia* itself, which has 'left' the bride and 'gone away', invites a personified reading insofar as its actions imitate those of characters elsewhere in the fragments who have similarly left their loved ones and homes (e.g. Helen, Anactoria, the woman in fr. 94).

It is no surprise that this example of apostrophe should come from Sappho's wedding songs, for it is in this category of poems that we find the clearest examples of Sappho calling directly upon characters from the immediate context of the song's performance (frr. 112–16 address brides and grooms in the vocative). Elsewhere, Sappho uses second-person address with great regularity, but not usually to call on members of her audience explicitly, as Alcman appears to do in his first *Partheneion*.[13] Typically, Sappho will address members of her circle, or she will address

---

[11] Cf. fr. 107, ἦρ' ἔτι παρθενίας ἐπιβάλλομαι; ('Do I still yearn for virginity?'); also Sissa 1987 ≈ 1990 on the possibility of virginity's return.

[12] For the 'impossible addressee' of lyric, see Culler 2015: 187.

[13] Alcman fr. 1.50 *PMGF* (with Peponi 2004). As D'Alessio 2018 argues, little suggests that Sappho's frequent second-person addresses to members of her community were sung directly *to* those char-acters in her audience during performance.

deities, such as Aphrodite, Hera, or the Muses. In what follows, I will briefly reflect on how her address to both of these groups may be conceptualised as lyric apostrophe, before turning to some examples of how Sappho engineers the role of 'you' in her poetry.

Lyric apostrophe, as Culler points out, relates to the 'I–Thou' structure of hymnic address, and the call or prayer to a deity or deities (especially frr. 1 and 5, which begin in that way) provides a contextual underpinning for Sappho's use of the second person in general.[14] When she summons Aphrodite in fr. 1, for example, Sappho mimics the form of a traditional cletic hymn in the opening stanza, yet as the poem proceeds we can also trace the abandonment of that form in favour of a dynamic interplay between subject and object, predicated on the exchange of speaking positions between herself and Aphrodite.[15] As touched on earlier, the second and third stanzas of the poem (Aphrodite's descent) at first appear to present an account of a single occurrence in the past, but with δηὖτε ('once again') in lines 15–18 and the open, generalising conditions in lines 21–3 ('if she flees . . . if she does not receive . . . if she does not love . . .'), we come to understand that all of fr. 1 operates in a special temporality created through apostrophe. Every time an imperative or the word for 'you' is sung in the hymn (lines 2, 9, 13, 19, 27), it binds speaker, addressee, and audience within a shared quality of lyric time that the three construct and participate in together.[16] The use of imperatives, in particular, lends urgency to the discourse, opening up the present into a time that extends to the brink of the future within the collected 'nows' and 'yous' of the poem's utterance.

In fr. 2 the shared or participatory quality of apostrophe is drawn out through a lingering scene of apple trees, sweet breezes, and scented flowers. The entire scene is set within a call to Aphrodite, for the fragment begins δεῦρύ μ' ('here . . . to me', 1) but completes the address only in the last stanza, with the vocative Κύπρι ('Cypris', 13). For the intervening three stanzas, embedded within the apostrophe, we have an extended description of the sacred grove, whose timeless qualities have often been noted.[17] The entire scene's framing first by the deictic markers 'here' and 'to me', and by the call to Cypris at the end, makes it more than just a description,

---

[14] Culler 2015: 186–243. While scholars of modern poetry sometimes understand apostrophe as a private form of address 'overheard' by the reader, in Sappho's case the ritualised prayer to a god is the more appropriate model.

[15] Cameron 1939; cf. Winkler 1990: 171 on fictional speaker and fictional audience changing places.

[16] See Payne 2007, 2018 on the shared temporality created by apostrophe.

[17] McEvilley 1972 ≈ 2008: 28–46, Burnett 1983: 259–76, E. Robbins 1995: 232–6, 237–9 = 2013: 136–9, 141–4.

however. Like fr. 1, the fragment falls within the category of 'apostrophic temporality', where lyric address is understood as part of a larger call for responsiveness from the non-human world, and in which elements from that world 'resist being organized into events' in the manner of a narrative.[18] In frr. 1 and 2, as with the bride's *parthenia* in fr. 114, Sappho's act of summoning the god into the space of the poem's utterance is paradigmatic of the epiphanic power or efficacy of lyric apostrophe in general – its ability to make possible or present what is impossible or absent, and to open up a responsive space within the discursive logic of address.

By calling 'you', therefore, Sappho not only recalls us to the time *of* the poem but also creates a special form of time *for* the poem, a time that is a combination of hers, 'yours', and ours.[19] This may be an invitation into the space of song, as with fr. 22.9–12 –

> κ]έλομαι σ᾽ ἀ[είδην
> Γο]γγύλαν [Ἄβ]ανθι λάβοισαν ἀ.[
> πᾶ]κτιν, ἆς σε δηῦτε πόθος τ.[
> ἀμφιπόταται

> I call on you [to sing?]
> Abanthis, of Gongyla, taking your
> lyre, while desire once again
> flies around you

– or of reminiscence, as with the woman in fr. 94, where the second half of the fragment, as we have seen, uses second-person address to suggest both intimacy and distance. Sappho places herself next to the woman in these remembrances ('by my side', πὰρ ἔμοι, 14), and the four stanzas are bookended by an anagrammatic pair of first-person plurals: ἐπάσχομεν and ἀπέσκομεν ('we suffered', 'we were [not] absent', 11, 26). When Sappho sings 'we' at those moments she is speaking directly to her beloved in the fiction of the poem's representation, but when she sings 'you' in verses 12–23 she is using indirect address as a circuit through which she can involve and include her audience, as well as calling back to life the 'leaving' and 'dying' woman from the opening lines (1–2). This second-person experience is key to the creation by lyric of a triangulated mode of expression and its animating potential goes some way to recuperating the effects of separation and loss.[20]

---

[18] Culler 2015: 226.
[19] Cf. Payne 2018.
[20] Greene 1994 = 1996a: 233–47.

But lyric address can also work in reverse, as it were. Sometimes Sappho's use of apostrophe is ironic, as in fr. 55, where the woman addressed becomes increasingly distanced and shadowy as Sappho takes on the aggressive, iambic 'you' to cast her out of her environment and render her invisible.[21] At other times, as in fr. 16, there is no 'you' at all, unless one counts the c' hidden within the phrase Ἀνακτορί[ας ὀ] ν̣έμναι[c' οὐ] παρεοίcας ('reminded – ὀνέμναιc̱ε – me of Anactoria, who is not present', 15–16).

Sappho's celebrated account of love-sickness in fr. 31 addresses the object of her desire with 'you' (τοι) at the end of the second line, and c' in line 7:

⊗ φαίνεταί μοι κῆνος ἴcος θέοιcιν
    ἔμμεν' ὤνηρ, ὄττις ἐνάντιός τοι
    ἰcδάνει καὶ πλάcιον ἆδυ φωνεί-
    cας ὐπακούει

    καὶ γελαίcας ἰμέροεν, τό μ' ἦ μὰν   5
    καρδίαν ἐν cτήθεcιν ἐπτόαιcεν·
    ὠς γὰρ ἔς c' ἴδω βρόχε', ὤς με φώναι-
    c' οὐδ' ἒν ἔτ' εἴκει,

    ἀλλὰ κὰμ μὲν γλῶccά <μ'> ἔαγε, λέπτον
    δ' αὔτικα χρῶι πῦρ ὐπαδεδρόμηκεν,   10
    ὀππάτεccι δ' οὐδὲν ὄρημμ', ἐπιρρόμ-
    βειcι δ' ἄκουαι,

    κὰδ δέ μ' ἴδρως κακχέεται, τρόμος δὲ
    παῖcαν ἄγρει, χλωροτέρα δὲ ποίας
    ἔμμι, τεθνάκην δ' ὀλίγω 'πιδεύης   15
    φαίνομ' ἔμ' αὔτ[αι.

    ἀλλὰ πὰν τόλματαον, ἐπεὶ †καὶ πένητα†

    He seems to me equal to the gods,
    that man who sits opposite you
    and listens closely to you speaking
    sweetly

    and laughing beautifully, which truly   5
    has struck my heart within my chest.
    For whenever I look at you, even for a moment,
    it is not possible for me to speak anymore,

> but my tongue is broken, a thin
> fire runs straight away under my skin,   10
> with my eyes I can see nothing, my
> ears ring,
>
> sweat drips down on me, trembling
> seizes all of me, I am greener than
> grass, and I seem to myself to be little short   15
> of dying.
>
> But everything must be endured, since †even a poor man†

One element that makes this fragment so effective is its suppression of the usual apostrophic devices. Although the 'you' of fr. 31 has such a powerful effect on the speaker, she is overshadowed by both Sappho herself (μοι) at the fragment's opening and 'that man' who is the subject of the entire beginning stanza. The 'you' in this poem, therefore, is seen only through her deflection via other characters, and as the poem progresses she becomes increasingly invisible.[22] With the phrase 'whenever I look at you, even for a moment' (itself the result of emendation; an alternative would give the sense 'whenever I look upon', εἰςίδω, without any 'you' at all),[23] Sappho stages her own attempts to visualise the beloved in glimpses before her speech and body give way. Yet as she details the effects of the love object's overwhelming presence, Sappho's own body crowds the woman's out of the poem (μ' . . . c' . . . με . . . <μ'> . . . μ' . . . ἔμμι . . . ἐμ' αὔτᾳ, 5–16). The result is a kind of anti- or auto-apostrophic move, which leaves the beloved unspoken and Sappho almost dead. This double reversal – failure, even – of apostrophe's animating potential mirrors Sappho's apparent failure to speak.[24] In both cases, the artfulness of her expression lies in her careful masterminding of poetic and lyric strategies.

Deixis

In the examples above we have seen a number of formal or poetic devices placed in some kind of temporal relation not only to ourselves, as readers, but also to Sappho's poetic voice and body. This concluding section will consider how deixis – the pointing to *this* – can help us think through both proximity and temporality in Sappho's poetry. Deixis, according to Felson, centres on 'linguistic forms that point in a variety of ways to

[22] Carson 1986: 16, Williamson 1996: 257–9.
[23] Most 1995: 29–31 ≈ Greene 1996b: 29–31.
[24] For the animating potential of apostrophe, see B. Johnson 1986.

diverse kinds of objects . . . In the act of pointing to or creating such objects, deixis establishes orientation points between which the characters of the textual universe move' (2004: 254). In the Tithonus Poem, for example, one finds in the trifold occurrence of πότα ('once', 3, 6, 9) two different articulations: on the one hand, what is 'over there' or 'not now', i.e. Sappho's youth, and on the other hand, the moment long ago when Dawn carried Tithonus to the ends of the earth.[25]

The deictic structuring of the fragment thus points to two instances of the past which take place in distinct temporal frames, and the effect is to orient the poem's 'now' (ἤδη, 3) around alternately biological and mythological concerns. This in turn affects how we understand the temporal dimensions of the adverb θαμέως in the statement 'I lament these things often', as well as the optative ποείην in 'what should I do?' (7), within the 'now' of the poem's enunciation. Following West's supplements, we can surmise that the fragment begins with three clear deictic markers: a second-person pronoun, a vocative, and an imperative:

> ὔμμες πεδὰ Μοίσαν ἰ]ο̯κ[ό]λπων κάλα δῶρα, παῖδες,
> σπουδάσδετε καὶ τὰ]ν̯ φιλάοιδον λιγύραν χελύνναν·

> You for] the beautiful gifts of the violet-bosomed [Muses], girls,
> Be zealous, and for] the song-loving sweet lyre.

The message of these lines appears to be 'dance and sing now before you're too old', but it could also mean 'seek out immortality from the Muses' gift of song'.[26] As noted earlier, its temporal structure is far from straightforward. A reconsideration of that structure through the lens of deixis shows how we can uncover new aspects of its lyric effect through the concrete indices of its spatial and temporal coordinates. Indeed, we might add a spatial overlay on to the πότα that separates Tithonus from the 'now' of the poem, since he is said to have been taken by Eos 'to the edges of the earth' (10). The phrase creates a deictic effect which contrasts strongly with Sappho's own proximity to the girls whom she exhorts.[27]

We have already discussed several examples of other deictic markers in Sappho's corpus, such as δεῦρυ in fr. 2 and the personal pronouns ἔγω and σύ. To close, let us briefly consider a different form of deictic, the intratextual use of the demonstrative pronoun 'this' (τό, τόδε, and τοῦτο) to denote the circumstances or state of affairs just (or about to be)

---

[25] Stehle 2009b.
[26] Rawles 2006: 4.
[27] Rawles 2006: 3.

recounted in the poem. For example, 'it is easy to make this (τοῦτο) understood by all' (16.5–6), 'I know this (τοῦτο) for myself' (fr. 26.11–12), 'she said this (τόδε) to me' (fr. 94.3), or 'I lament these things (τά) frequently' (Tithonus Poem line 7). These uses of the deictic serve to anchor the poem in its own reality, reinforcing the frame of reference and the immediate context of the poetic statement. In fr. 31, however, the referent of the neuter pronoun τό in τό μ' ἦ μὰν | καρδίαν ἐν cτήθεcιν ἐπτόαιcεν ('which truly has struck my heart within my chest', 5–6) is intriguingly vague.[28] There is no specific antecedent for it to refer to in the first stanza; rather, it points towards an event ('this thing') whose temporal and spatial coordinates are hard to discern. For although the godlike man is anchored by the words for 'that' (κῆνοc), 'opposite' (ἐνάντιοc), and 'near' (πλάcιον), our relationship to the scene is set at one remove, so that we feel far from close to the couple ourselves.[29] Perhaps one of the reasons why scholars have worried so much about the identity of the man is because Sappho's deictics in this opening stanza do not work in the expected way. If they point to anything, it is to a 'thatness' which is hard to visualise and – for all Sappho's initial efforts at orienting us – hard to express in referential language.

Zhang has argued that modernist literature's relation to sensory experience and the 'what-it-feels-like' qualities of first-person experience often brings the author to the limits of description. In those cases, the demonstrative pronoun 'this' is the best resource for naming not the object which one sees, but 'the subject's *feeling* of being unable to express her vision' (2014: 56). Just as Zhang's 'this' points to an experience that cannot be shared, through a word that changes its meaning based on who says it and in what context, so Sappho's τό in fr. 31 marks the limits of her attempt to bridge the gap between her own experience and the outside world through the process of naming. As others have shown (starting with Pseudo-Longinus), Sappho in fact brilliantly expresses herself by itemising the breakdown of different parts of her body, but the τό in line 5 also captures lyric's special quality of knowing when and when not to name.[30] In the fragments we have considered in this chapter, things play a special role in capturing certain aspects of the lyric experience ('that thing' in fr. 16, the accumulation of objects in fr. 44, the flowers in

[28] Furley 2000: 11–14.
[29] S. Stewart 2002: 145–95.
[30] Porter 2016: 118–24, on the account of this poem by Pseudo-Longinus.

fr. 94). In fr. 31, Sappho uses something still smaller – the shifting deictic τό – to trace the line between experience and event, or between the thing that one feels and lyric modes of expressing it.

Further Reading

Culler 2015 is an excellent resource for an overview of modern lyric, as is Jackson and Prins 2014, while Prins 1999 addresses Sappho's place within the genre. For recent 'literary' approaches to Sappho, see Budelmann and Phillips 2018, and for helpful discussion on the idea of the lyric in Pindar, Payne 2007, 2018. For apostrophe in Sappho, see Greene 1994 = 1996a: 233–47, and for deixis, Felson 2004, Peponi 2004 (in Alcman), and D'Alessio 2018. For readings of Sappho which engage with body, time, and language, see Burnett 1983: 209–313, duBois 1995, Carson 1986, 1996, 1997, Winkler 1990: 162–87, Greene and Skinner 2009.

CHAPTER 14

Myth in Sappho

Ruth Scodel

History, for Sappho, appears only as the legendary past that we call 'myth'. Because stories about long-ago heroes were both widely shared and open to variation and adaptation, Sappho could use them to ground the present in the past, but could also interpret them as she chose to argue for her own understanding of her present. Two features of Sappho's use of myth in the extant fragments are especially salient. First, mythical examples often serve as a consolation when she considers mortal limits – even the legendary figures of the heroic past lived under the same conditions of inevitable loss and error that still prevail. Stories about the ancient heroes were useful because they were familiar, and because the poetic tradition often made the engagement of the gods apparent, while in everyday life the gods might be omnipresent but unknowable.

In addition, the successes of past heroes could be models for the present. Sappho selects a particular moment of celebration within a larger story. She presents her own version of the archaic Greek ethical attitude that because mortal life is so uncertain and brief, occasions of success, joy, or divine favour need to be appreciated fully, and it is an important function of song to make these times splendid and joyous, and simultaneously to remind audiences of the uncertainties that surround mortal life. According to the fourth-century AD orator Himerius, Sappho compared a bridegroom to Achilles 'in his deeds'.[1] Perhaps the bridegroom had already shown himself a brave warrior. Achilles did not achieve the long and happy life that everyone wishes for the nuptial pair, so his full story would not be an ideal paradigm, but the marriage was a moment of splendour at which the glamour of the ancient hero could appropriately be attributed to the bridegroom. If, however, the brevity of Achilles' life reminded the audience that bridegroom and bride might suffer

---

[1] Fr. 105(b); West 2002: 211 = 2011–13: 1 398 suggests at Sigeum.

misfortune, the appropriate response would be to savour even more the happiness of this moment.

Second, the extant fragments and testimonia suggest that although Sappho's repertory was not narrow, her myths were typically connected to her own region or narrated travel between East and West. She also emphasised particular themes, especially erotic stories, notably those of the loves of goddesses for mortals: Phaon, Adonis, Tithonus, probably Endymion.[2] Stories with connections to Troy are prominent in the extant fragments.[3] She was not necessarily consistent in choosing versions of mythological stories. Even in the relatively few surviving mythological passages, Sappho twice introduces a mythological narrative with 'they say' (fr. 166.1) or 'they used to say' (Tithonus Poem line 9). Sappho does not present her knowledge of the remote past as divinely inspired, as the epic poet does. She relies on tradition, as her contemporary Alcaeus also does when speaking about Helen and Thetis (fr. 42). Such allusions to earlier tellings may refer to particular poems familiar to Sappho and her audiences, but may also indicate only that the story is not the poet's own. In both cases, the story is outside normal human experience: fr. 166 told how Leda found an egg (from which Helen was born), and the Tithonus Poem of the abduction of Tithonus to the ends of the earth by Dawn. So Sappho may use 'they say' to avoid staking her own poetic authority, since she claims no supernatural source. Song and dance are gifts of the Muses (Tithonus Poem line 1) and she is their servant (fr. 150.1), but she does not invoke them as sources.

Sappho frequently uses epic expressions, and her one extended mythological poem (fr. 44) shows that she was not only familiar with performance in epic dialect, but deliberately distinguished it from her own usual poetic practice. She clearly knew Trojan War stories in forms similar to those familiar to us. Her contemporary Alcaeus echoes the *Iliad*'s narrative so closely that he must know something close to our *Iliad* (fr. 44), but knowledge of our *Odyssey* is less certain.[4] When, in fr. 1, Sappho asks Aphrodite to be her 'ally' in an erotic crisis, she may subtly evoke the help that gods give heroes in battle. She thereby reminds both goddess and audience that the alliance sought here belongs to Aphrodite's proper sphere, while her intrusions into heroic action in the *Iliad* were not successful.[5]

[2] Phaon: fr. 211; Adonis: frr. 140, 168, 211(b)(ii–iii); Tithonus: Tithonus Poem; Endymion: fr. 199.
[3] Frr. 16, 17, 44, 166, Tithonus Poem.
[4] West 2002: 209 = 2011–13: I 394–5; contrast Kelly 2015a: 25–30.
[5] Rissman 1983: 1–29; KELLY pp. 57–8.

She shows little interest in non-Trojan heroic epic, however. She seems to have mentioned Medea, who is both the protagonist of an erotic narrative and a character who travels from East to West. Fr. 142, Λάτω καὶ Νιόβα μάλα μὲν φίλαι ἦσαν ἔταιραι ('Leto and Niobe were very dear companions'), implies a version of the story of Niobe somewhat different from those found elsewhere before late antiquity, and especially pathetic. Niobe had a regional connection: her petrified form, already mentioned at *Iliad* 24.614–17, is on Mt Sipylus (Spil Dağı), not far south-east of Lesbos, while as daughter of Tantalus she belonged to the family from which the Penthelids, formerly rulers of Mytilene, claimed descent. Sappho apparently gave her own genealogies of Eros, in which his father was Ouranos (Heaven), his mother Gê (Earth) or Aphrodite, and was said by Pausanias, in the context of genealogies, to have 'sung many inconsistent things about Eros' (fr. 198). In Hesiod's *Theogony*, Eros comes into being along with Gaia (116–22), but Greek poetry in general gives Eros different genealogies for different contexts – he becomes the son of Aphrodite where he serves her purposes, but as a cosmic force he is primeval. Sappho seems to have told a version of the Prometheus story (fr. 207). For most of these myths, we have only the briefest of testimonia or short fragments.

Sappho may have composed more than one Adonis poem, since frr. 140(a) and 168 are in different metres.[6] In fr. 140(a), there are two distinct voices:

κατθνάσκει, Κυθέρη᾽, ἄβρος Ἄδωνις· τί κε θεῖμεν;
καττύπτεσθε, κόραι, καὶ κατερείκεσθε χίτωνας

He is dying, Cytherea, tender Adonis. What should we do?
Strike yourself, maidens, and tear your dresses

While the first verse is addressed to Aphrodite, the second verse answers the question just posed. The speakers could shift within a chorus, but the goddess herself answers in the second line. The poem is dramatic, bringing the participants into the long-ago time of Adonis' death. If the poem was performed within the ritual of mourning for Adonis, all the women present were participants – even if they did not all sing, they could all enact the gestures. In such a performance, the present truly re-enacts the past.

This ventriloquism of this song, where the voice of Aphrodite and the performer merge without any marking of a shift, may help explain the

---

[6] The authenticity of fr. 168, however, is not certain. Pausanias says that Sappho sang of Adonis and Linus ('Oetolinus') together (9.29.8 = fr. 140(b)).

strangest aspect of Sappho's mythology. By the late fourth century, there was a legend about Sappho: desperately in love with Phaon, who did not return her passion, she was the first to leap from a cliff into the sea at the White Rocks of Leucas; this leap is treated as a potential cure for love in the (pseudo-?)Ovidian *Letter to Phaon*.[7] Nothing in Sappho's surviving fragments suggests erotic desire for men, let alone legendary men. In archaic and classical poetry, however, leaping from the White Rock into the sea indicates an ecstatic loss of consciousness, from alcohol or sex.[8] According to Pseudo-Palaephatus, Phaon was a generous ferryman, apparently between Lesbos and the mainland. When he ferried Aphrodite, disguised as an old woman, without payment, Aphrodite restored the old man to youth and beauty, and 'Sappho often sang of her desire for him'.[9] Phaon, however, is attested as a beloved of Aphrodite (fr. 211(b)), and in Hesiod's *Theogony* (984–91, possibly post-Hesiodic) Phaethon, son of Eos and Cephalus, is abducted by Aphrodite and made her temple-keeper (a subordinate divinity). Sappho was certainly concerned with old age. If Sappho spoke in the voice of the goddess, that would be enough to prompt a biographical tradition of her passion for Phaon.

In her Trojan narratives, like Homer, she shows sympathy for both sides, selecting *exempla* from both Greek and Trojan perspectives. This is not surprising. The southern Troad, dominated by Mt Ida, is visible across the water from the north coast of Lesbos. In the *Iliad*, Lesbos is within the Trojan sphere of influence: Achilles defines it as the limit by sea of Priam's pre-eminence (24.544–5), and himself sacked it (9.128–30). For Sappho, the Trojan past called for identification with both sides. Archaic Lesbos was a contact zone between Greek and Anatolian cultures; Mytilene had territory on the mainland, the *peraia*.[10] Its material culture shows strong connections with the east, and these imported luxury goods are important for Sappho.[11] At the sanctuary of Hera, Zeus, and Dionysus at Messon (modern Mesa), shared by all the *poleis* of

---

[7] Pseudo-Palaephatus, *On Unbelievable Things* 48 (fr. 211(a)), Menander, *Leucadia* fr. 1 Austin (test. 23), *Suda* c 108 (test. 3), (Pseudo-?)Ovid, *Heroides* 15.163–72; FINGLASS AND KELLY pp. 1–3. The unreliable mythographer Ptolemaeus Chennus, cited by Photius (*Library* 153), gives a catalogue of those who sought the cure, beginning with Aphrodite.

[8] Anacreon fr. 376 *PMG*, Euripides, *Cyclops* 164–7; Nagy 1973 ≈ 1990: 223–62 ≈ Greene 1996a: 35–57.

[9] Pseudo-Palaephatus, *On Unbelievable Things* 48 (fr. 211(a)); Hunter 2016.

[10] Spencer 1995a, THOMAS pp. 27–8.

[11] Kurke 1992: 97, THOMAS pp. 26–33.

Lesbos,[12] Hera was in all probability identified with the Great Mother. Sappho's emphasis on a Trojan past that combines Greek and Trojan is entirely coherent with her social and religious milieu.

Fr. 166 gives a version of Leda's story:

> φαῖcι δή ποτα Λήδαν ὐακίνθιον
> . . . ὤϊον εὔρην πεπυκάδμενον

They say that once Leda found an egg of hyacinth colour, shaded . . .

This must be a variant of the story of Helen's birth found in Apollodorus, where Nemesis, raped by Zeus, gives birth to the egg, and a shepherd brings it to Leda. If Nemesis, the personification of divine anger at wrongdoing, is Helen's mother, the Trojan War as a whole is either divine vengeance for human crimes or (more likely) the act of massive folly it avenges.[13]

In contrast, fr. 17 mentions a visit of the Atridae to Messon. In her account, the Atridae were the first to celebrate a festival that is the present occasion of her song.[14] They came, however, because after their long-delayed conquest of Troy they were unable to navigate home without approaching the three divinities:

> Πλάcιον δη μ[   ]. . .οιc ἀ[γέcθ]ω
> πότνι' Ἥρα, cὰ χ[αρίε]ςς' ἐορτα
> τὰν ἀράταν Ἀτρ[έϊδα]ι πϼήcαν-
> τ' οἰ βαcίληεc,
>
> ἐκτελέccαντεc μ[εγά]λοιc ἀέθλοιc   5
> πρῶτα μὲν πὲρ Ἴ[λιον]· ἄψερον δέ
> τυίδ' ἀπορμάθεν[τεc, ὄ]ϼον γὰρ εὔρη[ν
> οὐκ ἐδ[ύναντο,
>
> πρὶν cὲ καὶ Δί' ἀντ[ίαον] πεδέλθην
> καὶ Θυώναc ἰμε[ρόεντα] παῖδα·   10
> νῦν δὲ κ[ἄμμεc ταῦτα]. . . πόημεν
> κὰτ τὸ πάλ[αιον,
>
> ἄγνα καὶ κα[ὄ]χλοc
> παρθέ[νων   γ]υναίκων

---

[12] Robert 1960: 292–4, 300–15 = 1969: 808–10, 816–31, Caciagli 2010, RÖSLER pp. 68–71, THOMAS pp. 24–5, SWIFT pp. 209–10.

[13] Apollodorus, *Library* 3.10.7; Sammons 2017: 43–5.

[14] Calame 2009 takes this poem as exemplary of poetry's evocation of the past in ritual performance, but there may be no single type.

> Near here, indeed, [. . . let be celebrated]
> your [charming] festival, revered Hera,
> which the Kings, the Atridae, performed
> on a vow,
>
> since they had accomplished heroic exploits
> in the beginning at Troy, but later on
> putting in just here: for they could not
> find their way
>
> before they had approached you, and Suppliant
> Zeus and Thyone's soothing child.
> Now we, too, [continue] to perform [these things]
> just like of o[ld]
>
> Pure and . . . crowd of maidens . . . of women

In this poem, the defeat of Troy seems to be a heroic achievement. At *Odyssey* 3.165–83, Nestor tells Telemachus how Diomedes and he, joined by Menelaus, fearing divine anger because of the Achaeans' actions in the sack of Troy, fled, but stopped at Lesbos to seek a sign from 'the god' about the best way to sail homeward. They received a sign warning them to cross over the open sea to Euboea. Reaching Euboea, they sacrificed to Poseidon, and Nestor and Diomedes reached their homes safely. Menelaus, however, had to stop at Sunium because his helmsman had died (3.278–85), and was caught off Cape Malea and driven off course. Agamemnon, Menelaus later tells Telemachus, reached home (4.512–23) thanks to the help of Hera, only to be murdered by Aegisthus. Sappho's version is evidently a local variant.

Although the translation of 3–4 is very uncertain, it seems likelier that Ἀτρ[έϊδα]ι is nominative plural than dative singular. Especially since the Penthelids claimed descent from Orestes, it is not surprising that a Lesbian version would both put Agamemnon along with his brother on the island and narrate more than a portent. 'They could not find their way' suggests not uncertainty about the best route, but an insurmountable obstacle, and the poem narrates the first celebration of a recurring festival, vowed as thanksgiving if the obstacle were removed. But another characteristic is just as typically Sapphic. Although the Atridae received the help for which they asked and crossed the sea successfully, neither had an entirely successful return. For Sappho, however, the moment at which they created the festival after receiving the requested sign is important, and the larger, unmentioned narrative context does not change that success. The full story, for Sappho, would include not just the bad fortune of the Atridae, but the return to Lesbos of Agamemnon's descendants.

Past and present are analogous in the poem, but Sappho makes no claim of actual continuity. While the place has evidently always been holy to the triad, Sappho says nothing of the intervening generations.

In the Tithonus Poem, Tithonus exemplifies the impossibility of avoiding old age. The first eight lines of the song, addressed to a group of 'children' (παῖδες, a girls' chorus), express the speaker's unhappiness because she can no longer dance. Depending on how we supplement the opening of the second line, she either urges the chorus members to pursue the gifts of the Muses or explains that she can still engage in music even if she cannot dance.

> καὶ γάρ π[ο]τα Τίθωνον ἔφαντο βροδόπαχυν Αὔων
> ἔρωι φ. . αθεισαν βάμεν' εἰc ἔcχατα γᾶc φέροιcα[ν,   10
> ἔοντα [κ]άλον καὶ νέον, ἀλλ' αὖτον ὔμωc ἔμαρψε
> χρόνωι πόλιον γῆραc, ἔχ[ο]ντ' ἀθανάταν ἄκοιτιν.

For in fact people used to say that once rosy-armed Dawn, overcome by desire, came and carried Tithonus to the ends of the earth, beautiful and young as he was. But all the same eventually grey age seized him, though he had an immortal wife.[15]

In Mimnermus (fr. 4 *IEG*) and the *Homeric Hymn to Aphrodite* (218–38), Dawn had Zeus make Tithonus immortal but not ageless, so he endures far worse than ordinary mortals as he shrivels away; contrast Homer, where Dawn rises from his bed (*Iliad* 11.1–2, *Odyssey* 5.1–2, etc.). Most interpreters believe that Sappho alludes to the story of the *Hymn*. However, she ignores Tithonus' misery, and presents a curious contrast between the part of the story narrated in the voice of unidentified people of the past and the straightforward aorist of the speaker. The use of the imperfect to introduce an exemplary story is very unusual. Some interpreters have suggested that it contrasts how Sappho understood the story when she was young, in contrast to her present understanding, or see it as marking the *Hymn* as her source, or regard it as marking an older view later displaced by the true version.[16] However, she could be following a different version of the story. When Tithonus vanished, people said that

---

[15] In P.Köln inv. 21351, the poem ends here, while it continues for an additional four lines in P.Oxy. 1787.
[16] Edmunds 2006, Rawles 2006: 3, C. Brown 2011.

Dawn had taken him to the ends of the earth. They sound a little like the envious neighbours of Pindar's *Olympian* 1, although in this case they were right. They were probably envious, assuming that his happiness would be permanent. But they did not know how the story would turn out. Sappho's version does not require that Tithonus be deathless; it would make perfect sense if, when he grew old, Dawn simply returned him to the mortal world, and he died. Tithonus had his time of exceptional favour from a god, the greatest good the poet can imagine. Yet the speaker of the poem may even be better off than Tithonus, even though he enjoyed a sexual relationship with a goddess, since the Muses may be better divine patrons than the Dawn.

The Tithonus Poem sets its mythical example in a vague past, with π[ο]τα ('once'). The past represented by the visit to Messon of the Atridae seems close and precise, part of local social memory. Tithonus belongs to the generation before the Trojan War and is a much hazier figure. Still, he is a Trojan, at *Iliad* 20.237 son of Laomedon and, according to Hesiod (*Theogony* 984–5, possibly post-Hesiodic), father of Memnon and Emathion.

Fr. 44, the last poem in the second book of the Alexandrian edition, is closer to epic than any other poem of Sappho. It uses some Ionic forms that did not belong to Sappho's regular Aeolic dialect, and its metre, though distinctly Aeolic, has a dactylic component that makes it sound a little like a hexameter. It is missing two or three lines at its beginning, and six or seven after line 20.[17] The extant portion is entirely narrative, and if the missing proem and end connected the narrative to a present occasion, the framing was short. Because it narrates a wedding, scholars have speculated that, like Sappho's *epithalamia*, it was composed for a wedding, but there is no evidence about its original occasion.[18]

The poem narrates the journey of Hector to bring his bride Andromache to Troy. Andromache's native town of Thebe is south of Mt Ida, and is usually identified with Mandra Tepe, inland from modern Edremit. The voyage from Thebe to Troy would go along the northern coast of Lesbos. For Sappho and her Lesbian audience, Hector and Andromache, like Tithonus, belong to their own past. The herald Idaeus announces the imminent arrival of Hector with Andromache, promising 'imperishable fame'. He describes the precious objects she is bringing.

---

[17] Sampson 2016.

[18] Nagy 2010: 239–40 suggests a ritual at the Messon, but the only god mentioned is Apollo, who had no cult there.

Then the Trojans all prepare to go on chariots and mule-wagons to meet the bridal party. The lacuna must have told the actual arrival, since the concluding lines describes the wine, song, and ritual of their reception. Many details belong not to the epic world, but to the most splendid occasions of Sappho's own milieu.[19]

Throughout the extant lines, the emphasis lies on the Trojan community. There is no attention to the emotions of the bridal pair. The young men's song calls them 'godlike', θεοεικέλο[ιc (34; the speaker probably uses a similar epithet at 21, ἴ]κελοι θέοι[c), but nothing says that they are happy. Aphrodite does not appear, although in the *Iliad* she gave Andromache a headband, κρήδεμνον, on the day Hector brought her to Troy (22.470–2). Even the joy of the Trojans must be inferred from their actions. It is obvious enough, as they rush to their vehicles, and then as incense, wine, and music are everywhere. Young women sing 'a pure song' (26), and men sing a paean. Yet there is not a single emotive word in the extant text.

The poem tells of an occasion of supreme felicity for a couple that the epic tradition presents as loving but doomed. The poem seems to be deliberately reviving a 'before' for an audience that know what is to come. By the time in which the *Iliad* is set, Achilles has already destroyed Thebe and killed the men of Andromache's natal family. Within the *Iliad* Hector is killed, and Andromache predicts the murder of their son, Astyanax (24.734–9). Achilles in the *Iliad* plays a lyre that he took from Thebe (*Iliad* 9.186–8); in Sappho, the herald catalogues the splendid ornaments and banquetware that Andromache brings. The herald himself is a 'swift messenger', although in the *Iliad* he is an old man, and Priam leaps up energetically. One interpretation of the poem sees such ironic allusion to the *Iliad* as central to its meaning.[20] However, the *Iliad* represents only some of the stories available to Sappho, who may have been familiar with Scamandrius, son of Hector and Andromache, as a legendary founder of cities in the Troad.[21]

The narrative could allude to other events in the Trojan story, such as the arrival of Paris and Helen.[22] Then, the Trojans welcomed a bride arriving by sea with great wealth (stolen from Menelaus), and, by

---

[19] Page 1955: 71.

[20] Kakridis 1966, Nagy 1974: 135–9, Rissman 1983: 119–48, Schrenk 1994.

[21] Such traditions are found on Lesbos in the fifth century: Hellanicus of Lesbos fr. 24b *EGM*. Dionysius of Halicarnassus has Scamandrius released by Neoptolemus, and restored as ruler of Troy by Ascanius (*Roman Antiquities* 1.47.5). This too probably depends on Hellanicus.

[22] Spelman 2017a.

receiving her happily, doomed themselves. Another possible subtext of fr. 44 is the reception of the Wooden Horse. In narratives of the Horse, Trojans would have come out of the city in crowds and probably sung a paean.

Just as the later misfortunes of the Atridae do not erase their success in getting help for their return when they conducted a festival on Lesbos, the later disasters of Troy do not necessarily cancel the splendour of the wedding. Sappho's description emphasises what she loves most: elegance, luxury (myrrh and frankincense), and song. If her audience thought of the child of this wedding as the ancestor of important families in the towns of the Troad, the wedding of Hector and Andromache may stand in contrast to the bad receptions of Helen and the Horse. Despite all the external signs of joy, perhaps the Trojans did not sufficiently appreciate their own happiness, or realise that only such truly valuable outsiders should be welcomed.

In fr. 16, the exemplary function of the myth is explicit. Again, the material is Trojan. The opening lines claim that the most beautiful/noble/fine thing is whatever someone desires. Sappho's word κάλλιςτον (3) encompasses not just aesthetics, but moral and social qualities, and she inverts the usual assumption that being καλόν makes a thing desirable, as in the Muses' song according to Theognis 17 ('what is beautiful is dear, what is not beautiful is not dear'). Sappho further promises to make this point comprehensible, and presumably convincing, to anyone. By introducing the example with the particle γάρ ('for', 6), she marks it as the evidence for her claim and her explanation of why this claim is easy for anyone to accept: the story of Helen, as Sappho presents it, is all the demonstration required. Helen, despite her excellent husband, abandoned family to go with Paris, thinking of neither daughter nor parents. Although the end of the example is fragmentary, it is clear that the speaker refers it explicitly to herself. As Helen thought only about the object of her desire, Paris, the speaker thinks about Anactoria, who is not nearby. Yet this apparently simple mythic example is not nearly as straightforward as it appears.[23]

The Helen of this poem is not the Helen implied by fr. 166. A Helen who does not think of her beloved parents (φίλων το[κ]ήων, 10) is unlikely to be the child of Zeus and Nemesis, adopted by Leda and Tyndareus, or to be the daughter of Zeus at all. The mortal genealogy makes Helen a better analogy for Sappho or any other person, but also

---

[23] Pfeijffer 2000a.

has implications for the myth itself, since it does not require any divine causality for the Trojan War. Although Sappho erases any more cosmic causes, she may bring a supernatural power into Helen's story, for Helen did not remember her family, 'but rather [... Cypris?] led her astray' (ἀλλὰ παράγαγ' αὔταν | [ ]ϲαν, 11–12). Only παράγαγ' indicates a moral judgment. The participle ending in]ϲαν described Helen's state of mind, probably some kind of resistance, but the subject of the sentence is lost at the opening of the next stanza (it must have been short, since γάρ in the middle of the next line is the second word of a new sentence). That sentence explained why Helen could not resist: P.GC inv. 105 shows that it contained a generalisation about the weakness of mortals: ἄγν]αμπτον γάρ [∪ –] νόημμα | – ∪ –] κούφωϲ τ[∪∪ –] νοήϲηι, 'for she (sc. Cypris) easily [overcomes] an unbending mind . . . thinks'.[24]

The poem begins with a priamel, a rhetorical device that lists rejected alternatives before climaxing with the real topic: some people say that the most beautiful thing in the world in an army of cavalry, some of infantry, and some a fleet, but the speaker says that it is what a person desires. 'What is the most beautiful thing in the world?' is exactly the kind of theme Greek men might debate in a symposiastic game, but it is hard to imagine that even men would typically select military formations as the most beautiful (though they could certainly debate what was most beautiful within the military category). The poem invents its own rejected possibilities, so that it can establish an opposition between the masculine sphere of war and the universal realm of desire.

It then seems to contradict its own endorsement of subjectivity by calling Helen 'she who excelled all human beings in beauty' (ἀ . . . πόλυ περϲκέθοιϲα | κάλλος [ἀνθ]ρώπων, 6–7). If the most beautiful is what someone desires, how can the poet say that an individual woman was the most beautiful? Since the entire tradition agrees that Helen was the most beautiful, perhaps everyone desired her, so that the distinction between objective and subjective criteria would be irrelevant. Yet the emphasis on Helen's beauty, and the poem's repetition of *kal*- sounds, points to another complication. The opening opposition between military and erotic worlds invites the hearer to expect the example to concern Helen as object rather than subject of desire. Yet Helen's own desirability is irrelevant to the example as Sappho presents it, unless we infer that Helen's choice demonstrates the arbitrary nature of desire – Helen, being the

[24] West 2014: 2–3.

most beautiful, could arouse reciprocal desire in anyone she desired, yet chose a man inferior to the one she already had. Greek literature, as early as Homer, repeatedly wonders why Greeks and Trojans should have fought a terrible war for Helen. So it would be a simple argument for Sappho to have said that the Trojan War proves that erotic desire is the strongest of all forces. Such an argument may be implicit in the example of Helen, and may be a criticism of men for failing to understand their own motives, or of epic poetry for celebrating war instead of the *erôs* that impels it.

Explicitly, however, the poem considers only the choice of Helen, and does not even mention the consequences of her choice. Still, the consequences were so well known that nobody could fail to think of them, especially since the song primes the hearer by mentioning armies and fleets. After the example, when the speaker turns to her own emotions, she speaks of the absent Anactoria, whose 'alluring' (ἔρατον, 17) step and 'brilliant gleam of her face' the speaker would rather see than the chariots and infantry of the Lydians. Prompted by the mention of Lydians, the hearer may guess that Anactoria is now in Lydia (like the absent beloved of fr. 96). Like Helen's beauty, Anactoria's is not just the effect of the speaker's desire, but seems to be its impetus, and again the speaker contrasts her own desire with the imagined spectacle of an army. The audience must remember the war Helen caused, even though the song elides it. That may be part of the point. Sappho names as the reasonable constraints on Helen's behaviour her husband, her child, and her parents. Another woman whose desire led her to violate social norms would not start a war, but she, like Helen, would have a family. Sappho pointedly describes Helen's choice in universalising terms.

The exemplum has two different points of comparison. The speaker, like Helen, is overwhelmed by desire. But it is Anactoria who resembles Helen in beauty, and Anactoria who has left, probably for the East. Nothing implies that she has abandoned any social obligations. The speaker herself imitates neither Helen nor Menelaus, seeking instead consolation in memory and poetry. So the example may implicitly criticise both Helen and Menelaus. Desire creates beauty, but this desire can be transmuted into the beauty of song instead of becoming social transgression and violence.

Brief comparison to a mythological figure could also serve as a shorthand. Even a single epithet may allude by 'traditional referentiality' to a wider narrative (the name Thyone for the mother of Dionysus in fr. 17 probably implies her immortalisation), while calling the swallow

'Pandion's daughter' (fr. 135) evokes the entire story of the swallow's meta-morphosis.[25]

Finally, contemporary events could evoke underlying mythological patterns even without explicit references. Many readers see an epic model behind the Brothers Poem, in which Sappho's brother Charaxus is away at sea and the family's situation is precarious.[26] The immediate problems of the speaker are vivid and familiar enough that no hearer would need to remember Odysseus to understand – but such comparisons are always available. An audience can appreciate Sappho 1 without hearing echoes of an epic Aphrodite-in-battle, but the resonance gives the poem even more wit and depth.

Sappho, then, has varying techniques for evoking the mythic past, from extended narrative to brief or even implicit allusion. Her sources were also varied – Ionian epic, the poetry of Lesbos itself, local traditions grounded in ritual. She selects and adapts, choosing primarily erotic sto-ries and those relevant to contemporary Lesbos. The relationship between present occasion and mythic past is dynamic, as mythic exempla help elucidate the present even as the present situation influences how Sappho presents the past.

Further Reading

A discussion of myth in Greek lyric that would show Sappho's common-alities and differences would be useful, but Nagy 2007 is idiosyncratic and already outdated. Meyerhoff 1984 compares Sappho and Alcaeus, and although the newer fragments are of course absent and some inter-pretations are forced, the book offers many good observations. There are excellent studies of the myths in particular poems and fragments: on fr. 16, Pfeijffer 2000a is especially helpful; on the Tithonus Poem, see Greene and Skinner 2009; on fr. 44, Spelman 2017a offers an interesting interpretation and gives a good view of the discussion.

---

[25] 'Traditional referentiality', a term created by J. Foley 1991 for Homeric interpretation, refers to the ability of expressions in a stylised language to carry meanings from their traditional contexts.

[26] Nünlist 2014, M. Mueller 2016, Obbink 2016c: 212, Bierl 2016a: 310. Kurke 2016 argues that the brothers are associated with the Dioscuri instead. Swift 2018 sees a traditional pattern of contrast between siblings and advice from one to another, in both mythical and contemporary settings.

The Gods in Sappho

Laura Swift

The gods are a constant presence in the world of early Greek poetry, and Sappho's work is no exception. Sappho's presentation of the gods draws on tradition, as we see her reworking the tropes of religious poetry or epic to create a relationship with the divine that suits her persona and interests. Since desire is the primary theme of her poetry, it is not surprising that the central deity in her work is Aphrodite, and this chapter will begin by exploring the complex and personal relationship that Sappho constructs with this goddess. However, Aphrodite is not the only god in Sappho's poetry, and her treatment of the rest of the pantheon has been less thoroughly treated. The second section will therefore examine the relationship Sappho constructs with other deities through prayer. Finally, we shall investigate how Sappho uses religious and cultic myth, and what this reveals about her poetry's preoccupations and its performance.

The Patronage of Aphrodite

The special connection between Sappho and Aphrodite is one of the major strands of her poetry.[1] Not only is Aphrodite frequently named and invoked, but Sappho's poetic persona imagines herself as enjoying an intimate relationship with the goddess, as set out most clearly in fr. 1. The poem consists of a prayer to the goddess to save Sappho from the anguish of unrequited love, and she imagines Aphrodite hearing and responding. As well as giving us insight into Sappho's relationship with her patron goddess, the poem's sophisticated play on the conventions of the Greek hymn demonstrates her creativity with the tropes of traditional religious song.

---

[1] Aphrodite is mentioned by name (or a known cult title) in frr. 1, 2, 5, 15, 22, 33, 65, 73(a), 86, 90, 96, 102, 112, 133, 134, 140(a), and the new 'Cypris Poem'. It is almost certain that she is mentioned (though her name does not survive) in frr. 35, 44, 101, 159, and there is a good case for her presence in frr. 16, 40, 58, 103.

Sappho draws on the form known as the cletic hymn, a religious poem which invokes a god to appear and requests a favour. Such hymns are known from our earliest sources and usually follow a tripartite structure (for example, *Iliad* 1.37–42). They begin by summoning the god through the use of his or her names, powers, and favourite places. Next they remind the deity of past deeds, either favours the god has previously granted or honours the mortal has paid the deity, or they promise honours in the future. Finally, once the god has been suitably prepared, the petitioner requests his or her assistance. Here Sappho follows this structure, though adapts it to suit her own purposes. The poem begins with an invocation of the goddess by her traits and genealogy: she is 'Ornate-throned immortal Aphrodite, daughter of Zeus, weaver of guile' (ποικιλόθρον' ἀθανάτ' Ἀφρόδιτα, | παῖ Δίος δολόπλοκε). These opening words show Sappho's blend of tradition and innovation. Aphrodite is regularly depicted on thrones in Greek art, but the epithet ποικιλόθρον' ('ornate-throned') is, as far as we know, Sappho's own invention, and makes an impact as the first word of the poem.[2] By addressing Aphrodite as the daughter of Zeus, Sappho nods to her Homeric depiction as the daughter of Zeus and Dione, rather than the tradition preserved in Hesiod where she is born from the foam of the castration of Ouranos ('Heaven'; *Theogony* 176–206). Aphrodite's deceitfulness is well known in myth, but putting the adjective 'weaver of guile' (δολόπλοκε) at the end of the sequence draws attention to it, and ends the description of the goddess on a note that stresses her ambiguous nature and the dangers of trusting her.

The middle section of the hymn is an embellishment on the usual requirement that a petitioner list past deeds, since Sappho gives an extended description of Aphrodite's visits to her in the past, beginning with a vignette of her departure from Olympus (5–12):

αἴ ποτα κἀτέρωτα
τὰς ἔμας αὔδας ἀίοισα πήλοι
ἔκλυες, πάτρος δὲ δόμον λίποισα
χρύσιον ἦλθες

ἄρμ' ὑπασδεύξαισα· κάλοι δέ σ' ἆγον
ὤκεες στροῦθοι περὶ γᾶς μελαίνας

---

[2] Some manuscripts preserve ποικίλοφρον' ('intricate-wiled'), but this is likely to be corrupt, and adds nothing new to δολόπλοκε: Hutchinson 2001: 151, Budelmann 2018: 117 *ad loc.* Andromache at *Iliad* 22.441 works θρόνα ποικίλ' into her weaving, and θρόνα must mean flowers or other forms of decoration. Some scholars have therefore argued that ποικιλόθρον' is derived from θρόνα not θρόνος: Lawler 1948, Putnam 1960, KELLY p. 55.

πύκνα δίννεντες πτέρ’ ἀπ’ ὠράνωῖθε-
ρος διὰ μέccω·

If ever in the past you heard my voice from afar and you heeded it and
came, leaving your father’s golden house and yoking your chariot; lovely
swift sparrows drew you over the dark earth with their wings whirring
quickly from heaven through the air.

The detail of the sparrow-drawn chariot adapts Aphrodite’s assocation
with doves or geese, and elevates the birds into noble steeds (the adjective
‘swift’, ὤκεες, in 10 is normally used of heroic animals such as horses and
eagles). The image of the little sparrows beating their wings fast to pull
the chariot is amusing, as is the juxtaposition of the tiny birds with the
vast journey they make. Again, Sappho hints at her awareness of tradi-
tion,[3] but signals that the portrait of the goddess is very much her own.

In the lines that follow, Sappho emphasises the close relationship with
the goddess that she enjoys. Homeric gods often have favourite mortals,
but the affection and familiarity with which Aphrodite speaks to Sappho
is striking (13–20):

cὺ δ’, ὦ μάκαιρα,
μειδιαίcαιc’ ἀθανάτωι προcώπωι
ἤρε’ ὄττι δηὖτε πέπονθα κὤττι
δηὖτε κάλημμι

κὤττι μοι μάλιcτα θέλω γένεcθαι
μαινόλαι θύμωι· τίνα δηὖτε πείθω
ἄ]ψ c’ ἄγην ἐc cὰν φιλότατα; τίc c’, ὦ
Ψάπφ’, ἀδικήει;

Blessed one, with a smile on your immortal face you asked me what the
matter was this time, why I was calling this time, what I most wished to
happen for myself in my mad heart. ‘Who is it this time that I am to per-
suade to lead you back to her love? Who, Sappho, is wronging you?’

Sappho styles herself as Aphrodite’s favourite and protégée. The goddess
not only manifests herself directly to her, but greets her affectionately by
name and acts as a confidante. This presentation of Aphrodite differs
from the typical portrayal of *erôs* in Greek lyric either as an overwhelm-
ing force (e.g. fr. 47), or as a god who subjugates the hapless speaker (e.g.
Anacreon fr. 413 *PMG*). In fr. 1, Aphrodite is both anthropomorphised
and approachable, and her relationship with Sappho is surprisingly equal

---

[3] See KELLY for epic interactions more generally.

(though the goddess's power is still made clear). Aphrodite's calm and supercilious manner also contrasts with the idea that *erôs* is a disruptive force. In fact, Sappho appeals to the goddess's power to instil peace and asks her to 'release me from harsh cares' (χαλέπαν δὲ λῦσον | ἐκ μερίμναν, 25–6). Thus Aphrodite stands in opposition to the emotions she creates, as emphasised by her teasing description of Sappho's 'mad heart' (μαινόλαι θύμωι, 18).

The repetition of 'this time' (δηὖτε, 15, 16) refers to the idea commonly found in erotic poetry that being in love is an endlessly repeated experience, but also suggests the ongoing relationship between god and mortal. While Aphrodite may tease Sappho for being in love yet again, she nevertheless responds to the poet's prayers each time. Whereas the Homeric Aphrodite first deceives and then threatens her favourite, Helen (*Iliad* 3.390–420), in Sappho Aphrodite's terrifying power is used to the poet's advantage, as she promises to inflict desire upon Sappho's beloved against her will if needs be (24). This sense of alliance between god and mortal is summarised in the final words of the poem, where Sappho calls upon Aphrodite to be her 'ally' (cύμμαχος, 28). The relationship Sappho constructs with Aphrodite is reminiscent of the exceptional closeness depicted, for example, in the *Odyssey* between Athena and Odysseus. Here too we find a familiar and close relationship, where the deity teases her favourite as well as promising her allegiance (13.287–310). Just as Athena admires Odysseus because he represents her qualities of intelligence and cunning to an exceptional degree, so too Sappho is the lover par excellence, who feels the emotions represented by Aphrodite more frequently than others.

While fr. 1 is Sappho's most extended description of Aphrodite, the goddess features throughout her poetry. The frequency of her presence itself attests to the importance she holds in Sappho's world view, and the smaller fragments reinforce the special relationship apparent in fr. 1. For example, in fr. 22, we are told that Aphrodite has 'found fault' with Sappho (ἐμέμφ[ετ', 15) for a prayer she has made (perhaps lusting after a new beloved and forgetting the old one), a phrase which evokes the teasing familiarity of fr. 1. Other fragments report further conversations between Sappho and her patron: thus, Aphrodite seems to name Sappho in fr. 65, while an ancient rhetorician tells us that fr. 159 (consisting only of the words 'you and my servant Eros', cύ τε κἄμος θεράπων Ἔρος) were spoken by the goddess to Sappho. In fr. 133(b), a speaker (plausibly either poet or goddess) asks Sappho a question about her behaviour towards Aphrodite, though sadly the verb is missing that would supply the crucial ingredient, while fr. 134 reports a conversation that Aphrodite and the narrator had in a dream. Fr. 86 seems to present a situation similar to fr. 1, as the poet calls upon Aphrodite to 'hear my prayer' (κλ]ῦθί μ' ἄρας, 5) and describes her leaving [one of her haunts] (6), presumably to visit Sappho. Aphrodite also seems to play a role in the saga of Sappho's brother Charaxus, since she is probably invoked at the start of a poem dealing with his adventures (fr. 15). She is called 'blessed one' (μάκαι[ρα, 1), and is asked to watch over Charaxus' return but to refuse assistance to his girlfriend Doricha.[4] As the goddess of love, Aphrodite is invoked in the context of an unsuitable love affair that will cause damage to Sappho's family. Here too, she is presented as the poet's ally, who will harm her enemies.

The latest papyrus discoveries have further expanded our knowledge of Sappho's relationship with Aphrodite through the preservation of the 'Cypris Poem', so collad because of the address to the goddess under her cult title Cypris ('Cyprian one'):[5]

> ⊗ πῶς κε δή τις οὐ θαμέως ἄσαιτο,
> Κύπρι, δέσποιν', ὄττινα [δ]ὴ φίλ[ησι,
> κωὐ] θέλοι μάλιστα πάθαν χάλ[ασσαι;
>   ποῖ]ον ἔχησθα

> νῶν] σαλοισί μ' ἀλεμάτως δαΐσδ[ην
> ἰμέ]ρω⟨ι⟩ λύ{ι}σαντι γόν' ωμε[
>   ].α.α.[ ]αιμ' οὐ προ [ ].ερης[
>   ]νεερ.[ ]αι

>]...[ ] σέ, θέλω[
>   τοῦ]το πάθη[ν
>   ].αν, ἔγω δ' ἔμ' αὔται
> τοῦτο σύνοιδα

> How can someone not be hurt and hurt again,
> Cypris, Queen, whomsoever one really loves,
> and not especially want respite from suffering?
> What sort of thoughts do you have
> to pierce me idly with shiverings
> out of desire that loosens the knees [
>   ] not [
>   ] . . .
>   ] you, I wish [

---

[4] The details of this reconstruction are not certain, but this interpretation is widely accepted. For the text and translation, see Obbink 2016a: 17, 28; for discussion, see Bierl 2016b, Schlesier 2016.

[5] Text and translation from Obbink 2016a: 26–7, 33.

] to suffer this [
]. This
I know for myself.

If Obbink's interpretation is correct, the situation is not dissimilar to that of fr. 1: Sappho is suffering from unrequited love and beseeches Aphrodite as a result of her suffering. However, Aphrodite is less friendly here and more menacing than in the other poem, as Sappho emphasises her power (and willingness) to hurt her. Conversely, Martin West interpreted the opening as a lament that Aphrodite no longer loves Sappho, translating the first lines as 'How can a woman help being regularly heartsick, my Lady, if you do not love her?' – but here too, we find a less beneficent Aphrodite than elsewhere.[6] In any case, the same presumption of a close relationship between mortal and goddess underlies the poem on either interpretation: Sappho can address Aphrodite in familiar terms, and can complain about her mistreatment. The idea that the favour of the gods is unreliable is also a theme of epic: we might think, for example, of Odysseus' rebuke to Athena that she failed to protect him during his travels (*Odyssey* 13.318–21) and his fear that she is mocking him (13.326–7), or the Iliadic Aphrodite's threat to Helen that defiance will turn the goddess's favour into hatred (3.414–17). Equally, the poem's tone may have become more optimistic as it continued, and Sappho's fears that Aphrodite has abandoned her may turn out to be as unfounded as Odysseus' accusations against Athena. To be a favourite of the love goddess means to experience the pains as well as the delights that she brings, and in Sappho, as elsewhere in Greek lyric, her gifts are not straightforward.[7]

Prayer and Gender

Compared to the frequency with which Aphrodite appears, mentions of other gods are relatively few, and the discrepancy underscores the importance of Sappho's relationship with her patron. However, we do find prayers to other deities in Sappho's poetry, and a full understanding of her theology requires us to venture beyond her erotic songs. We find some evidence of a preference for Hera, and for a difference in the way Sappho expects women and men to worship the gods.

[6] West 2014: 10.
[7] Cf. Homer, *Iliad* 3.64–6.

Here too, recent papyrological discoveries have enhanced our understanding, since we now have additions to a poem long known to be a prayer to Hera (fr. 17), as well as a new poem in which the goddess is mentioned (the Brothers Poem). Fr. 17 describes a festival for Hera on contemporary Lesbos.[8] The poet addresses the goddess as 'revered Hera' (πότνι᾽ ῞Ηρα, 2) and tells how the festival was established by Agamemnon and Menelaus, who vowed to found it in return for finding a route home from Troy (3–10). The festival is in honour of Hera, Zeus, and Dionysus, an unusual combination of gods also attested in Alcaeus (fr. 129) and referred to by scholars as the 'Lesbian triad' for this reason.[9] In Sappho's poem she emphasises the connection between the festival's foundation myth and its practice in her own day, claiming that 'now . . . we perform [these things?] in accordance with ancient tradition' (νῦν δὲ . . . πόημεν κὰτ τὸ πάλ[αιον, 11–12). Sappho also refers to the active role that women play in this festival, whereby a 'crowd of maidens and wives' (ὄ]χλος | παρθέ[νων . . . γ]υναίκων, 13–14) are gathered to perform some sort of ritual activity. The details of what was involved are unclear, but line 16 probably began with a part of the word *ololugê*, a ritual cry performed by women, which may suggest female choral performance. It is striking that women of all generations are involved, including married women, who feature less frequently in ritual or choral occasions than young girls. The ritual seems to cross the boundaries between life stages, involving the whole female community.

Women's rituals in honour of Hera are also attested in Alcaeus fr. 130B, where the poet describes a sanctuary where the women of Lesbos participate in beauty competitions; an ancient scholar tells us that the sanctuary in question belonged to Hera.[10] This also fits with an anonymous Hellenistic epigram which invites Lesbian women to a dance led by Sappho at a sanctuary of Hera.[11] It seems, then, that women played an active role in the worship of Hera on Lesbos, and that this is reflected in Sappho's poetry, some of which (such as fr. 17) may well have been composed for performance at these festivities.[12] Scholars have mostly agreed that all these references relate to the same sanctuary, and that this was a pan-Lesbian shrine at Messon (modern Mesa).[13] Hera appears to have

---

[8] For the augmentation of fr. 17 by P.GC inv. 105, see Obbink 2016a: 19–21, West 2014: 3–5.
[9] Thomas pp. 24–5, Rösler pp. 68–71, Scodel pp. 194–6.
[10] Scholia D on 9.129 (p. 344 van Thiel); cf. Scholia A on 9.129–30 (II 425.78–9 Erbse).
[11] Anonymous, *Greek Anthology* 9.189 (test. 59).
[12] L. Wilson 1996: 181–2, Calame 2009: 3–7, Caciagli 2016.
[13] Robert 1960: 292–4, 300–15 = 1969: 808–10, 816–31, Caciagli 2010.

been the most prominent of the three deities worshipped there: in both Sappho fr. 17 and Alcaeus fr. 129 all three are mentioned, but it is she who is directly addressed. A festival for Hera seems also to be mentioned in fr. 9, though too little survives to give any certainty.

The sanctuary at Messon may be the shrine the poet has in mind when she imagines appealing to Hera at the start of the Brothers Poem (1–16):

ἀλλ' ἄϊ θρύλησθα Χάραξον ἔλθην
νᾶϊ cὺν πλήαι. τὰ μὲν οἴομαι Ζεῦc
οἶδε cύμπαντέc τε θέοι· cὲ δ' οὐ χρῆ
    ταῦτα νόηcθαι,

ἀλλὰ καὶ πέμπην ἔμε καὶ κέλεcθαι   5
πόλλα λίccεcθαι βαcίληαν Ἤραν
ἐξίκεcθαι τυίδε cάαν ἄγοντα
    νᾶα Χάραξον

κἄμμ' ἐπεύρην ἀρτέμεαc. τὰ δ' ἄλλα
πάντα δαιμόνεccιν ἐπιτρόπωμεν·   10
εὔδιαι γὰρ ἐκ μεγάλαν ἀήταν
    αἶψα πέλονται.

τῶν κε βόλληται βαcίλευc Ὀλύμπω
δαίμον' ἐκ πόνων ἐπάρωγον ἤδη
περτρόπην, κῆνοι μάκαρεc πέλονται   15
    καὶ πολύολβοι·

but you are always babbling about Charaxus coming with a full ship. It is Zeus and all the other gods who know these things, I think. You ought not to be thinking like this, but you should be sending me and instructing me to pray repeatedly to Queen Hera that Charaxus should return here, bring his ship undamaged, and find us safe and sound. As for the rest, let us leave it to the gods, for fair weather quickly arises from huge storms. Those whom the king of Olympus wishes to have a divine helper to turn them from troubles, it is they who become blessed and fortunate.

The poem distinguishes between Hera, who can be approached and influenced through prayer, and the other gods, who appear inaccessible. Zeus and the other gods know of Charaxus' fate, but it is impossible for humans to share this knowledge. Zeus can choose to make mortals prosper, but the poem gives no indication of what humans can do to win his favour, and Sappho advises her addressee to give up trying to influence what is beyond mortal power.[14] Conversely, praying to Hera for

---

[14] Stehle 2016: 278–9.

Charaxus' safety is imagined as a positive and pragmatic course of action, and is contrasted with the empty chatter offered by the addressee.

Hera is not usually responsible for seafaring, and so it is noteworthy that she is the goddess uppermost in Sappho's mind in this context. She is singled out from the mass of 'all the gods', and appears to be more open to influence than her consort Zeus. The implication of Sappho's advice is that, if approached appropriately, Hera might intervene on the family's behalf. This may reflect her prominence on Lesbos, but probably also relates to the role that women played in her worship there, in that she is the god with whom a young girl would naturally be sent to intercede. This gendered aspect of prayer reflects the gendered division within the poem more broadly, whereby the poet and her (probably female) interlocutor are powerless to act themselves and must depend on their male relatives to restore the family fortunes.[15] In the absence of suitable male protectors, however, a female deity is a suitable conduit for the women's hopes and fears, and supplicating her is the closest step to public action the youthful Sappho can achieve.

This gendered approach to the gods is also reflected in fr. 44, a description of the wedding of Hector and Andromache. As would be customary in a Greek wedding, the public celebrations involved groups of men and women, and the poem ends with the prayers and choral songs performed to honour the couple (31–4):

> γύναικες δ' ἐλέλυϲδον ὄϲαι προγενέϲτερα[ι,
> πάντεϲ δ' ἄνδρεϲ ἐπήρατον ἴαχον ὄρθιον
> Πάον' ὀνκαλέοντεϲ ἐκάβολον, εὐλύραν,
> ὔμνην δ' Ἔκτορα κ' Ἀνδρομάχαν θεοεικέλο[ιϲ.

The older women cried out 'eleleu', and all the men sent forth a lovely orthian melody, calling upon the Healer, the Far-shooter skilled in the lyre, and they praised the godlike Hector and Andromache.

Here men and women sing to the same god, but do so in distinct groups and fashions. The women's cry of 'eleleu' refers to the *ololugê* (as in fr. 17 above) – the female equivalent to the *paian* cry that the men perform.[16] Just as marriage itself symbolises the mixing of male and female in society, yet upholds the separation of man and wife into their proper spheres, so too do the religious songs that accompany it reflect how men and women must approach the gods in different ways, even when praying for the same ends.

[15] Kurke 2016.
[16] For the gendered nature of paeanic singing, see Rutherford 2001: 59, A. Ford 2006: 285–6.

Religious Narratives and Cult

Fr. 44, with its extended mythological content, leads us on to the question of how the gods feature in embedded religious narratives, as opposed to direct prayers. The fragmentary nature of Sappho's work means that we cannot be sure whether a religious myth is told for its own sake or whether it is embedded in a paradigm to illustrate some other (and perhaps more personal) situation. However, examining which myths Sappho chooses and how she tells them can still be revealing.[17] Once again we see a preference in what survives for female-oriented narratives that contain female protagonists and often focus on sex, marriage, and family relationships, the primary focuses of women's lives.

Given the importance of marriage to Sappho's poetry, it is not surprising that several of her religious narratives touch on this theme. Thus, for example, fr. 141 describes the gods' participation at a wedding (possibly that of Peleus and Thetis), where like mortal banqueters they pray for the good fortune of the bridegroom. This may come from a wedding song, in which case the good will of the gods and their beneficence towards the marriage would be a positive image for the contemporary bridegroom. Fr. 27, which is certainly a wedding song, expresses some kind of wish for divine favour (lines 10–11), and the fragment as we have it concludes with a theological moral: 'there is no road to great Olympus for mortals' (ὄδος μ[έ]γαν εἰς Ὄλ[υμπον | . . . ἀ]νθρω[ποιϲιν, 12–13). To a modern audience this may seem a surprising message to give at a wedding, though we find a similar idea in Alcman's first *partheneion* (maiden song), where the chorus of girls advise their audience 'let no man fly to heaven nor try to marry queen Aphrodite' (fr. 1.16–18 *PMGF*). On an occasion such as a wedding, where humans were at the peak of their physical desirability and their blessedness, it was appropriate to sound a note of caution, and to remind the audience that even the most exalted and godlike couple were only frail mortals.[18] Sappho expresses a similar idea in the last surviving lines of fr. 96, where she warns that 'it is not easy for us to rival goddesses in the beauty of their figures' (εὔμαρ[ες μ]ὲν οὐκ ἄμμι θέαιϲι μόρφαν ἐπή[ρατ]ον ἐξίϲωϲθαι, 21–3). If this is the same poem as the earlier part of the fragment, this warning perhaps acts as a corrective to the praise of the woman's beauty in what has come before.[19]

---

[17] SCODEL.

[18] A parallel is found in epinician poetry, another genre which praises its recipient while countering the praise with reminders of mortality to avoid it becoming dangerously excessive: cf. Pindar, *Olympian* 1.30–4, *Pythian* 3.80–3. For the tradition of praise in wedding poetry, see Hague 1983.

[19] For the importance of distinguishing between mortal and immortal beauty, cf. *Odyssey* 5.215–18.

Female sexuality is explored through a different religious myth in fr. 44A, where the poet recounts how Artemis vowed to remain a virgin and persuaded her father Zeus to agree. The story is reminiscent of the opening of the *Homeric Hymn to Aphrodite*, which explains Aphrodite's dominion over everything on earth except three goddesses: Athena, Artemis, and Hestia. In the *Hymn*, it is Hestia who swears an oath to remain a virgin and has her status ratified by Zeus (25–32), though Artemis' preference for the wild places of the earth is also mentioned (18–20). Sappho's poem depicts a more assertive Artemis, who swears the oath apparently on her own initiative. Nevertheless, Zeus's permission is required for this oath to be fulfilled, and her speech ends with a plea that he should 'assent for my sake' (τά]δε νεῦσον ἔμαν χάριν, fr. 44A.7). Thus, her behaviour reminds Sappho's audience of the social hierarchy, whereby young girls are subject to male authority. Artemis' desire for perpetual virginity reflects a theme we find elsewhere in Sappho's poetry of sadness at the ending of girlhood (frr. 107, 114), yet we are also reminded that this is a necessary part of the life cycle, and that it is only Artemis' special status that allows her to avoid it. Thus, by choosing the myth of how Artemis assumed her role as the virgin huntress, Sappho raises issues relevant to the women whose lives she sings of elsewhere.

Later authors preserve descriptions of other poems that contained a religious myth. Thus, Aulus Gellius refers to Sappho's version of the story of Niobe (fr. 205), where she apparently put the number of Niobe's children as nine of each sex, rather than the six of each found in Homer. This poem may be connected with fr. 142, which describes the friendship between Leto and Niobe, and is usually thought to have been a personal poem that used the myth to reflect upon one of Sappho's own friendships. The detail that Leto and Niobe were friends adds poignancy to the myth, as this friendship turns sour and leads to terrible consequences. Niobe's friendship with the gods, and her acceptance on equal terms by Leto may also be part of the moral, as it leads Niobe to overstep the mark.[20] Sappho is also said to have told the story of Pandora (fr. 207), concurring with Hesiod's version, where the creation of women is a punishment for Prometheus' theft of fire. Given the prominence Sappho's world view gives to women's lives and concerns, it would be fascinating to know how her perspective differs from the misogynistic account of Hesiod.[21]

---

[20] Gantz 1993: 537.
[21] Hesiod, *Theogony* 570–602, *Works and Days* 49–105; West 1978: 155, Marquardt 1982, duBois 1992.

While we can only guess at the performance context of most of Sappho's poetry,[22] some of her religious fragments show signs of having been composed for cultic performance. Fr. 2, a description of an idealised sanctuary of Aphrodite, is probably a song to be performed at a real shrine. If the opening of the poem has been correctly restored, the goddess is summoned 'here to this temple' (δεῦρυ . . . ἐπ[ὶ τόνδ]ε ναῦον, 1), which makes the ritual and physical context clear. Here the setting is idealised, and what Sappho describes as features of the sanctuary are in fact poetic constructs, imbued with symbolism. Thus, the shrine at which the poem was performed may or may not in fact have had apple trees, rose bushes, and cool springs, but in poetic terms an idealised sanctuary of the love goddess must have these features, as they are associated with *erôs* and turn the sanctuary into the perfect 'meadow of love', where erotic activity can occur.[23] Aphrodite is imagined as participating in festivity with the singer (or singers), and acts as a cup-bearer, a role that she seems also to adopt at the end of fr. 96. The goddess is imagined as present at whatever ritual activity has prompted the song, and the description of her shrine praises the goddess and also reminds the listeners of the powers she holds.

In fr. 140(a) Sappho goes beyond simply narrating a religious story, and instead represents it as a dialogue between performers:

> – κατθνάσκει, Κυθέρη', ἄβρος Ἄδωνις· τί κε θεῖμεν;
> – καττύπτεσθε, κόραι, καὶ κατερείκεσθε κίθωνας.

> – Delicate Adonis is dying, Cytherea, what shall we do?
> – Beat your breast, maidens, and tear your clothing!

The singers are presumably a chorus of maidens and a soloist representing Aphrodite (here addressed by her cult title Cytherea), and the occasion they imagine is the death of Adonis, the lover of Aphrodite. Elsewhere in the Greek world this myth is associated with a women's festival, the Adonia, which in classical Athens involved ritual lamentation and dancing.[24] It is tempting to take this fragment as a cultic performance as part of the Adonia, where the women re-enacted the story of Adonis as they mourned his death. The laments they sing are presented as the original ones mandated by Aphrodite, sorrowful at the death of her lover, and the group take on a mimetic persona which links the current

---

[22] FERRARI.
[23] For the features of the *locus amoenus*, see Haß 1998. For its poetic symbolism as a place of erotic activity, see Bremer 1975: 268–74, H. Foley 1994: 33–4, Swift 2009.
[24] Burkert 1985: 176–7, Detienne 1994 ≈ 2007, Reed 1995, Reitzammer 2016.

rites to their aetiology. Sappho also treats the theme of a goddess's sexual relationship with a mortal man in the Tithonus Poem, where Tithonus' inability to escape old age is contrasted with the immortality of his wife Eos.[25] Here Tithonus is not evoked in a ritual context but as an exemplum to illustrate the impossibility of avoiding old age, just as Sappho contrasts herself to a group of young girls. The relationship between god and mortal in both examples highlights human vulnerability, since both mortals come to disaster despite the best efforts of their partner. In both cases, there is also a contrast between female sexual power and male weakness: a combination that leads to sad consequences.

Conclusion

Sappho, like all other Greek early poets, does not have a single model for how to think about the gods, and her poetry demonstrates the range of ways in which poetry could engage with the divine. However, some central strands run through her surviving work. First, in matters divine, as in other aspects of her poetry, Sappho shows particular interest in the world of erotic love. This is clear above all in her dedication to Aphrodite, who is presented as patron and confidante, and with whose cult worship Sappho also appears to be involved. Sappho's personal relationship with Aphrodite is unlike anything we find elsewhere in Greek lyric: she styles herself as the goddess's protégée and favourite, and depicts affectionate conversations between them. While the boundary between goddess and mortal is made clear and Sappho maintains suitable respect for the deity, Aphrodite's fondness for the poet, and the teasing way she addresses her, create a feeling of intimacy. An examination of the fragments shows that this closeness is not confined to fr. 1, its most famous example, but rather seems to have been a trope of Sappho's work. By presenting herself as Aphrodite's favourite, Sappho marks herself out as the supreme example of the lover: she has special access to Aphrodite's favours, yet feels the goddess's pains acutely. Sappho's imaginative portrayal of her relationship with Aphrodite showcases her ability to recast traditional motifs to suit her own purposes.

When we look beyond Aphrodite, we see a clear interest in how religion affects women's lives. Just as Sappho puts a female-oriented spin on traditional stories such as the abduction of Helen (fr. 16), so too in religious matters, women's preoccupations take centre stage. Women's role in

---

[25] For literary discussion of this fragment, see Greene and Skinner 2009, SCODEL pp. 196–7.

prayer and their role in the cult of Hera seem to be important strands, and prayer is one way in which Sappho reflects gender differences in her world. The religious myths she chooses are ones that reflect her own concerns, in particular marriage, virginity, and female friendships. Thus, in matters of religion, as elsewhere, Sappho gives us a tantalising insight into women's lives in archaic Lesbos.

Further Reading

The hymnic elements in Sappho's prayer to Aphrodite in fr. 1 have been much discussed. For the conventions of Greek hymns, see Pulleyn 1997, Furley and Bremer 2001. For fr. 1's relationship to cultic hymns, see Cameron 1939, Stanley 1976, B. Thomas 1999. For Sappho's relationship with Aphrodite more generally, see Martyn 1990, Schlesier 2016. The recent papyrus finds have led to increased interest in the role of Hera in Sappho's poetry: Boedeker 2016, Kurke 2016: 242–9.

PART III

Transmission

CHAPTER 16

The Alexandrian Edition of Sappho

*Lucia Prauscello**

In archaic, classical, and Hellenistic times Sappho's poetry enjoyed an unparalleled fortune. All the evidence (papyri, *ostraka* or potsherds, vase-paintings, the indirect and biographical traditions) seems to confirm Wilamowitz's *obiter dictum* that Sappho had already acquired 'pan-Hellenic renown' during her lifetime.[1] In this sense, Aelian's anecdote of Solon listening to, and being fascinated by, Sappho's song at a symposium testifies to the credibility, for a second- or third-century AD audience, of Sappho's widespread popularity in sixth-century Athens.[2] An anonymous epigram, probably our earliest evidence for the existence of the canon of lyric poets, shows that the canonisation of Sappho as one of the nine lyric poets (ἐννέα λυρικοί) was already firmly established by the third or second century BC.[3] This is supported by the Sappho papyri (mostly dating to the imperial period): their homogeneous layout suggests that Sappho's text underwent the editorial care (collation of manuscripts, evaluation of their variants, emendation, marginal annotations, and diacritical signs) of the Alexandrian philologists.[4] It was Alexandria, the Egyptian capital of the Ptolemies and main cultural centre of the whole contemporary Greek world, that saw the flourishing of systematic philological activity on archaic and classical authors, including the canonical lyric poets, between *c.*285 and 145 BC. This gigantic effort to produce a collection of the whole of Greek literature resulted also in the establishment of a scholarly text of each author, written on papyrus roll and arranged in cola (shorter metrical units), with the aid of diacritical

---

* My sincerest thanks to the editors for their observations and criticism.
[1] Wilamowitz 1913: 82.
[2] Aelian cited by Stobaeus, *Florilegium* 3.29.58 (test. 10). For the transmission of Sappho in the fifth and fourth centuries BC, see Nicosia 1976: 32–3. For her reception in that period, see Coo.
[3] Anonymous, *Greek Anthology* 9.184 (1194–203 *FGE*); Barbantani *ap.* Acosta-Hughes and Barbantani 2007: 429–31, 438–42. For Sappho in Hellenistic poetry, see Hunter.
[4] For the papyri, see Finglass ch. 17. For the nature and scope of a 'grammarian's edition' (ἔκδοσις) in antiquity, see Montanari 2015.

signs. Throughout this chapter the Alexandrian edition of Sappho will be referred to as the 'standard' scholarly edition of Sappho's text.

Notwithstanding this uninterrupted chain of interest in Sappho and her poetry, establishing more precisely what the Alexandrian edition of Sappho looked like confronts us with some basic, yet disputed or unanswerable questions: was there only one such edition, by Aristarchus of Samothrace (*c*.216–145), or also an earlier one by Aristophanes of Byzantium (*c*.257–180)? What were its organising principles and how far back in time can they be traced? How many books did Aristarchus' edition comprise? Did it include a separate book entitled *Epithalamia* (*Wedding Songs*)? A major concern of recent scholarship has been to emphasise the existence, in both Hellenistic and later times, of 'multiple editions' or 'collected poem editions' of Sappho competing with the standard Alexandrian edition.[5] This issue deserves closer attention for its potential impact upon the history of transmission of ancient texts in general and of Sappho in particular, since it has been used, among other arguments, to deny the existence of a book entitled *Epithalamia* as part of the Alexandrian edition of our poet.

From Lesbos to Alexandria

The anonymous compiler(s) of the Byzantine lexicon, the *Suda*, record(s) nine books of lyric poetry by Sappho.[6] This roughly compares with what we know about the poetic productivity of the other archaic lyric poets: at least six books by Alcman, seven by Ibycus, ten by Alcaeus, with Stesichorus' twenty-six and Pindar's seventeen book-rolls representing exceptions.[7] The sheer quantity of Sappho's poetic production and its early circulation through the Hellenic world make it inherently likely that already from a very early period, possibly still during Sappho's lifetime, her poetry circulated in both oral and written form.[8] Some scholars have emphasised the role of Athens in the pre-Alexandrian transmission to the quasi-exclusion of other centres.[9] Yet it is far more likely that by the second half of the fourth century BC local written copies of Sappho's

---

[5] Yatromanolakis 1999, 2008, Pernigotti 2001: 12–14.
[6] *Suda* c 107 (test. 2).
[7] Finglass 2014: 19–20 with n. 123.
[8] Liberman 1999: I xxxv–ix, Yatromanolakis 2007: 210–11, De Kreij 2016: 60.
[9] Edmonds 1922b: 9, Lobel 1925: xiv, Nagy 2004: 39–40.

and Alcaeus' poetry were preserved at Mytilene and that this copy was a primary source of the Alexandrian edition.[10]

It is often assumed that Aristophanes of Byzantium was the editor of all the canonical nine lyric poets, Sappho included.[11] Since all Sappho's extant papyri that are not anthological present a uniform editorial layout, it is reasonable to assume that they all go back to the Alexandrian edition. Did the two leading Alexandrian scholars, Aristophanes and Aristarchus, each produce an edition of Sappho, or only one of them?[12] The second-century AD metrician Hephaestion tells us that in the editions of the lyric poets the asterisk was most commonly used to signal that the following poem was in another metre, a practice that occurred in particular in the monostrophic poems (i.e. poems consisting of repetitions of the same strophic structure) of Sappho, Anacreon, and Alcaeus. He then specifies that Aristophanes, in his edition of Alcaeus, marked with the asterisk the end of a poem only when the following composition was in another metre, while in the current edition of Aristarchus the asterisk marked the end of *any* poem whatsoever.[13] Strictly speaking, this passage tells us only that both Aristophanes and Aristarchus edited Alcaeus and him alone. Yet the same Hephaestion tells us elsewhere that Anacreon too was edited twice, presumably by Aristophanes *and* Aristarchus.[14] The cumulative mention of Sappho together with Anacreon and Alcaeus suggests that Sappho's poetry too was edited by both Alexandrian scholars.

The Ordering of Books in the Alexandrian Edition

Whereas Alcaeus' books were ordered by Alexandrian scholars according to their content and/or internal chronology,[15] the prevailing ordering principle of book-division in Sappho's Alexandrian edition, with the exception of the book entitled *Epithalamia*, was metre. Direct and indirect evidence concur unanimously in this direction. Books 1–3 were metrically homogeneous, whereas Books 5 and 7 were not; so the transition from metrical homogeneity to relative polymetry probably occurred in Book 4.

---

[10] Liberman 1999: I xxxix, xliv–v, Pöhlmann 1994: 15.
[11] Pfeiffer 1968: 205.
[12] Aristophanes: Dale 2015: 25 n. 25. Both: Liberman 1999: I xlvi–vii with n. 148, 2007: 41–2. Agnostic: Yatromanolakis 1999: 180 with n. 4.
[13] *On Signs* 2–3 (test. 236 V.); Liberman 1999: I xlvi–vii with n. 147 and his T XLVII.
[14] *On Poems* 4.8.
[15] Respectively Pardini 1991, Liberman 1999: I xlviii–lx.

However, metre was not the only criterion. Already before the publication of the 'Newest Sappho' in 2014, and especially on the basis of what we knew from Books 1 and 2, it had been suggested that multiple principles of arrangement could be found within a given book, such as alphabetical order by first letter only or thematic clusters.[16] The discovery of P.Sapph.Obbink and P.GC inv. 105 has further confirmed this state of affairs for Book 1, allowing us for the first time to reconstruct a sequence of ten poems by an archaic poet as they must have appeared in the Alexandrian edition.[17] According to Obbink, in this series we can detect within the alphabetical ordering a 'roughly chronological' criterion based on subject matter.[18] The ordering posited by Obbink – *first* alphabetical order, *then* thematic clusters within the alphabetical series – has been doubted by Neri, according to whom poems in Book 1 were *first* arranged thematically: that is, the alphabetical criterion was applied only secondarily, within thematic clusters.[19] Both interpretations present difficulties, yet the priority of alphabetical ordering seems beyond question.[20]

Metrical and thematical ordering are certainly visible in our earliest extant Sapphic papyrus, the Cologne Sappho (P.Köln 429+430), from the early third century BC, before any Alexandrian edition. In this anthology, perhaps to be used in the symposium, the Tithonus Poem, otherwise known from P.Oxy. 1787 (late second/early third century AD), is preceded by a poem in the same metre ($^\wedge hipp^{2ch}$) but different from that which precedes the Tithonus Poem in the Oxyrhynchus papyrus.[21]

As often in ancient editions of canonical authors, the first and last ode of a book might have stood out of alphabetical sequence thanks to their perceived programmatic importance, as with Pindar's *Olympian* 1, which commemorated victory in a single horse-race, even though the arrangement of the *Epinicians* generally placed chariot-race victories first as being the more prestigious competition.[22] This is clearly also the case with

---

[16] Liberman 2007: 46–7, Obbink 2016b: 41–5. For alphabetisation as an Alexandrian principle of arrangement, see Dale 2015: 26–30.

[17] The evidence strongly supports the suggestion of West 2014: 2 (against Dale 2015: 20–5) that P.GC inv. 105 fr. 1 (= fr. 9) fell in the fifth column of the roll (that is, fr. 9 would be preceded by fr. 5): Obbink 2016a: 24, 2016b: 40, D'Alessio 2019.

[18] Obbink 2016a: 51.

[19] Neri 2015: 71–2.

[20] D'Alessio 2019.

[21] For the use of the papyrus, see Yatromanolakis 2008, Liberman 2016: 61–2. For Sappho's metre, see BATTEZZATO.

[22] The 'abnormal' placement of *Olympian* 1 is credited to Aristophanes of Byzantium: Prodi 2017: 553–60.

Sappho fr. 1 in Book 1 (the hymn to Aphrodite: Hephaestion's quoting practice strongly suggests that this was the first poem of the first book).[23] Likewise, the final poems of Books 1 (frr. 27, 30) and 2 (fr. 44), as confirmed by P.Oxy. 1231 and 1232, are also out of the alphabetical sequence: in both cases we are dealing with poems that were 'epithalamian in character', without having necessarily to be classified as wedding songs proper.[24]

Each book-roll must have contained between 1,000 and 2,000 lines, since the direct tradition, the *subscriptio* (title found at the end of a work) of P.Oxy. 1231 fr. 56 (= fr. 30) tells us that Book 1 of Sappho included 1,320 lines, and comparison with book-rolls of other lyricists suggests a similar figure.[25] Here follows a brief prospectus of the metrical arrangement of the books for which something is known:

> **Book 1** (test. 29; frr. 1–42) was composed entirely in sapphic stanzas (eleven syllables), comprising 1,320 lines: so 330 sapphic stanzas divided into fifty-something poems, given an average of seven stanzas per poem.
>
> **Book 2** (test. 227 V.; frr. 43–52) was composed entirely in glyconics with double dactylic expansion (fourteen syllables).
>
> **Book 3** (test. 229 V.; frr. 53–7), also metrically homogeneous, was composed in glyconics with double choriambic expansion (sixteen syllables).
>
> What is currently considered **Book 4** (frr. 58–91), for us mainly represented by P.Oxy. 1787 and the indirect tradition, was dominated by a scheme built around the hipponactean, in both doublets and three-line stanzas.[26]
>
> **Book 5** (test. 31, test. 231 V.; frr. 92–101) was also metrically heterogeneous. For this book Roman metricians attest the use of phalaecian hendecasyllables, both as repeated individual lines (κατὰ δίϲτιχον - *continuati*) and as a colon within a broader metrical unit formed by different cola (*dispersi*), and of lesser asclepiads. The heavily corrupt fr. 101 is explicitly attributed by Athenaeus to Sappho's fifth book,

---

[23] Obbink 2011: 33–8 has argued that fr. 1 might not have been the first poem of the book, since the underlying layer of writing in P.Oxy. 2288 suggests that another poem of Sappho must have preceded in the roll; Dale 2015: 23–5 reaches a similar conclusion from different premises (alphabetical ordering). But, for a refutation of Obbink's hypothesis, on the basis of a new assessment of the position, within the roll, of the overlying layer of writing of P.Oxy. 2288, see D'Alessio 2021.

[24] Obbink 2016b: 45 with n. 37.

[25] Finglass 2014: 20 n. 123.

[26] Prauscello 2016.

and its likeliest metrical structure is a glyconic stanza, which is also
the metre of fr. 94. Fr. 96 (from the Berlin parchment, like fr. 94)
exhibits a stichic sequence centred on the glyconic, as does fr. 98.[27]

Book 6 is a total blank.

Book 7 (test. 232 V.): Hephaestion's formulation, though corrupt,
about Sappho's use of what he calls the antispastic catalectic tetram-
eters (fifteen syllables) at the beginning or end of this book also
suggests metrical variety.

As for Book 8, as we shall see, the evidence of fr. 103 does not allow us to
draw any safe inference. It stands to reason that the book of *Epithalamia*
(frr. 104–17) must also have been metrically heterogeneous, including
dactylic hexameters.[28]

How Many Books?

According to the *Suda*, Sappho 'wrote nine books of lyric songs. She was
also the first to invent the plectrum. She also wrote epigrams, elegies,
iamboi, and monodies.'[29] The only other piece of evidence mentioning
the number of books written by Sappho (nine again) is a first-century BC
epigram by Cicero's freedman Tullius Laurea.[30] Ventriloquising Sappho's
voice from the underworld, Laurea refers to her 'set of nine (books)' in a
baroque conceit relating the number of Sappho's books to the number of
Muses. Since elsewhere the *Suda* seems to know Laurea's epigram, the
Suda entry might derive from Laurea and so have little independent
worth.[31] Does, then, Laurea's number of nine books find any supporting
evidence elsewhere?

What at first sight would seem the most promising candidate, a
work containing a section *On Sappho* transmitted by a late second-/early
third-century AD papyrus unfortunately breaks off just where we would
expect the numbers of Sappho's books to be mentioned.[32] However,
ancient authors – mostly metricians and grammarians – cite from or refer
to what they unanimously mention as the first (test. 29), second (test. 30,

---

[27] BATTEZZATO.
[28] Page 1955: 123–5, KELLY.
[29] *Suda* c 107 (test. 2).
[30] Tullius Laurea, *Greek Anthology* 7.17 (test. 28).
[31] Lobel 1925: xiv.
[32] P.Oxy. 1800 fr. 1 (test. 1).

fr. 49), third (test. 30), fifth (test. 31, fr. 101, test. 231 V.), seventh (fr. 102), and eighth (test. 32) books of Sappho, and also to a book entitled *Epithalamia* (frr. 103, 116). As seen above, these sources also tell us explicitly that, at least for the books referred to by number, Sappho's Alexandrian edition privileged metre as the overarching criterion for book-division. Direct and indirect evidence thus concur in attesting eight books of Sappho's poems consistently referred to by book number, and in addition a book entitled *Epithalamia*, probably occupying a single papyrus roll. This would not have included all Sappho's wedding songs (some poems with 'epithalamian character' can be found already at the end of Books 1 – frr. 27, 30 – and 2 – fr. 44), but those that, mostly for metrical reasons, were not included in the previous books, called by Page 'the miscellaneous remainder'.[33] This reconstruction brings us to a total of nine books, as attested in the *Suda* and in Laurea's epigram.

Yet recently most scholars, with the exception of Liberman, have wholeheartedly embraced Lobel's radical scepticism about the trustworthiness of Laurea's epigram and the *Suda* entry.[34] In particular, they have reached the conclusion that Book 9 of the Alexandrian edition is a phantom, that the edition included only eight books, and that the eighth contained mostly or solely wedding songs.[35] Lobel's scepticism, though, is unjustified. His reasoning is twofold: (1) the 'stichometric notation' of the *Suda* entry, that is, the numeral θ′, must be in the Attic (i.e. meaning 'eight') and not in the Ionian (i.e. meaning 'nine') notation, since Athens was the primary context for book-culture before Hellenistic Alexandria; (2) Laurea thus mistook the numeral θ′, interpreting it as nine instead of as eight; the book of *Epithalamia* must have been the last because it entails an ordering principle which is not metrical; Wilamowitz already suggested this (as we shall see), and so it must be. But we have already noted that Athens was by no means the only possible source of Sappho's text, and Lobel's presumption about the use of the 'Attic notation' in the *Suda* is not supported by what we know to be the common practice, at least from the early fourth century BC onwards, of referring to books' numbers using Ionian notation, not Attic.[36]

Moreover, Wilamowitz's suggestion that the eighth book of Sappho's Alexandrian edition must coincide with the book of *Epithalamia* was not

---

[33] Page 1955: 126.
[34] Lobel 1925: xiv.
[35] Yatromanolakis 1999, Acosta-Hughes 2010: 99–102, Dale 2011a: 55–67.
[36] For the Aristotelian exception, see Primavesi 2007: 63–7.

advanced without reservations.[37] He believed that the 'Sappho's eighth
book' excerpted by the fourth-century AD sophist Sopater (test. 32) might
be the book of *Epithalamia* because the sixth-century AD rhetor
Choricius also quotes from an *epithalamium* by Sappho (fr. 112.3–5) and
so does the fifth-century AD Neoplatonist Syrianus (fr. 105(a)) in his com-
mentary on Hermogenes. Yet this inference presupposes the almost total
loss of classical texts in the imperial period, whereby Choricius and
Syrianus, when quoting Sappho, must necessarily depend on Sopater
because no other copy of the eighth book of Sappho could have survived
or have been available in the Greek world.[38] This hypothesis runs against
the evidence: Sappho's latest surviving fragments of the direct tradition,
the two Berlin parchment codices usually dated to the late sixth/early sev-
enth century AD, testify that Sappho's text, at least as far as Book 5 is con-
cerned, was still available in Roman Egypt in its entirety a century after
the lifetime of Himerius or Syrianus, and there is no reason to suppose
that this was unusual in other parts of the Greek world.[39] Furthermore,
our present state of knowledge about ancient editorial practices of lyric
poets does not seem to support the existence of 'double titles' of the type
μελῶν α΄ = Ἐπιθαλάμια.[40]

A further argument against the trustworthiness of Laurea's epigram has
been put forward:[41] that the mention of a 'set of nine (books)' could be
motivated by merely literary reasons (that is, the long-standing associa-
tion of Sappho with the Muses), or that Laurea was using not the stand-
ard Alexandrian edition of Sappho but an alternative contemporary
'collected poems' edition which included the 'elegy' book mentioned by
P.Oxy. 1800 fr. 1 (test. 1; see above). Again, the arguments do not seem
decisive: it is highly unlikely that Laurea, while showing off his learning,
would refer to an 'alternative' edition in nine books of Sappho's poetry if
it was widespread knowledge among the literati that Sappho's
Alexandrian edition included only eight.[42] As to the coincidence of the
number of the books (nine) with that of the Muses, this may well be an
artificial ordering imposed by the Alexandrian editors out of the desire to
match Sappho's poetic production with the nine Muses, but the

---

[37] Wilamowitz 1900: 72–3. He did not doubt that Sappho's Alexandrian edition contained nine
books (p. 71).
[38] PONTANI p. 322 n. 12.
[39] P.Berol. inv. 5006 ([= Sappho frr. 3–4), 9722 ([= frr. 92–7).
[40] Pardini 1991: 261–5; *pace* Yatromanolakis 1999: 188 n. 35.
[41] Yatromanolakis 1999: 181–4, 194, followed by Dale 2011a: 55.
[42] Page 1955: 113.

'artificiality' of this solution does not invalidate the trustworthiness of Laurea's epigram.[43]

Sappho's Book of *Epithalamia*

Let us now have a closer look at the two pieces of evidence attesting a book of *Epithalamia* by Sappho, frr. 116 and 103. In the former, Servius Auctus (an ancient commentator on Virgil, henceforth SA) in his commentary on Virgil, *Georgics* 1.31 says

> many accept the use of the word *gener* ('son-in-law') instead of *maritus* ('husband'), following the example of Sappho, who in the book entitled[44] *Epithalamia* says 'rejoice bride! Rejoice, many-honoured son-in-law' (χαῖρε νύμφα, χαῖρε τίμιε γάμβρε πόλλα) instead of the word νυμφίος ('groom'). Likewise also Pindar in the *Paeans*.

The mention of a book of wedding songs by SA has been dismissed as 'elusive', since either SA was not using the Alexandrian edition, or he was confusing single poems with a whole book, as Pseudo-Dionysius of Halicarnassus does when he states 'also by Sappho there are some instances of this kind of composition, namely the so-named epithalamic songs'.[45] The latter hypothesis is unnecessary, since Pseudo-Dionysius is simply speaking of a *type* of composition, which may be in prose or in verse, as exemplified by some poems by Sappho, without paying attention to the collocation or arrangement of this type of poems within her collection. Moreover, as to the former hypothesis, two considerations suggest quite the opposite. First, differently from Servius, SA had access to exegetical activity prior (and in some cases superior) to Donatus, dating back to the first or second centuries AD, a period where authors less well known than Sappho still had common currency in school curricula. Secondly, the very fact that SA refers above to Pindar's *Paeans* (and not just to Pindar in general) to support the usage of γαμβρός for νυμφίος seems to suggest that SA is indeed quoting from the 'standard', that is, Alexandrian editions of both poets, even if at second hand.

The evidence of fr. 103 (= P.Oxy. 2294) is more difficult to assess.[46] Carefully written on a sheet of good-quality papyrus, this second-century

---

[43] Cf. Liberman 2007: 43–4.
[44] Thus Heinsius (<*in*>*scribitur*) for transmitted 'it is written' (*scribitur*), a virtually certain supplement that employs a word frequently used by Servius Auctus elsewhere.
[45] [Dionysius of Halicarnassus], *Rhetoric* 4.1; Yatromanolakis 1999: 193.
[46] Puglia 2008: 1–3.

AD witness belongs to the fluid category of 'paraliterary' texts, that is, products like catalogues or lists that have grown out of and on the margins of primary literary texts.[47] Fr. 103 contains a list of ten incipits (first lines) from Sappho's poems; the first incipit (line 4) has a dactylic rhythm, whereas the other nine, with some editorial intervention, have been generally reconstructed as either acephalic hipponacteans with double choriambic expansion (the metre of Book 4) or as catalectic choriambic tetrameters. There is no guarantee that the metre of these nine incipits is homogeneous. After these ten opening verses, at line 14 we have traces of a letter with a superscript horizontal bar alternatively supplemented as either]ῆ and so meaning 'from Book 8 (of the μέλη)', indicating the number of the book from which the incipits are taken,[48] or]ῑ and meaning 'ten poems'.[49] In the same line, after a blank space we find the number of verses (presumably of the ten poems) as cτι(χοι) ρλ[, ('verses: 13[0–9]'). Then at line 15 follows an observation that something was the case 'after the first (poem)'; at line 16 we are told that the above quoted poems(?) 'are 'transmitted under the title', and in mid-column at line 17 we have the term ἐπιθα]λάμια, with horizontal strokes below and above the final letter, to indicate that this was a 'formal' title. Finally, at line 18 we have the mention of 'the/a book' or of something which was 'even better than the/a book' (βυβλίου καὶ βέλτιο[ν); at line 20 follows a blank line and at line 21 some illegible traces of ink. While the incipits of lines 5 and 11 have an unmistakably epithalamian character, this is not certain for the others; here again Sappho's poetics of 'indeterminacy' allows for a certain lassitude as to how a wedding song may be framed and/or introduced.[50]

What should be made of all this? Hypotheses by modern critics about the value of fr. 103 for the reconstruction of Sappho's Alexandrian edition vary greatly.[51] One interpretation argues that fr. 103 represents a 'collection of *incipits* of Sapphic poems' from Book 8, hence indirectly supporting a claim 'about the circulation – public or private – of several

[47] Dubischar 2015: 570–3.
[48] Yatromanolakis 1999: 190 n. 46, after Lobel and Page 1955.
[49] Puglia 2008: 4.
[50] Yatromanolakis 2009: 216.
[51] Page 1955: 116–19 thought that P.Oxy. 2294 demonstrated that Book 8 of Sappho's Alexandrian edition totalled between 130 and 139 lines inclusive and that the title *Epithalamia* of line 17 referred forwards, not backwards – that is, to the ninth book – whereas Treu 1954: 167–9 suggested that the 13(0–9) lines of fr. 103 must refer to a selection of incipits of wedding songs to be used as a script for a wedding ceremony.

"editions" of Sappho in later antiquity'.[52] Another sees in our fragment a bibliographical record (*pinax*) by a 'grammarian or a passionate reader of poetry' who has selected the ten most beautiful odes of Sappho, nine of which come from a book entitled *Epithalamia* which is, however, not the eighth, but possibly the fourth or an unspecified book (not the last) of the Alexandrian edition.[53] The lacunose state of the fragment does not allow anything like certainty (what is the most plausible reading for line 14:]ῑ or]ῆ? Does the title *Epithalamia* refer backwards or forwards?[54] Do lines 18–21 still refer to Sappho or not?). Yet some points of reference nevertheless emerge. First, the physical characteristics of P.Oxy. 2294 (good-quality papyrus roll, elegant and orderly handwriting) strongly suggest that we are dealing not with an impromptu performance script but rather with a paraliterary product (a list of incipits for a bibliographical purpose). Second, as already noted, we have a further ancient witness (second century AD) attesting the title *Epithalamia* as the title of one book by Sappho. Third, if we are indeed dealing with an accurate bibliographic piece of work, it is inherently more likely that the source of the list/collection of incipits of P.Oxy. 2294 too was an erudite one, that is, Sappho's 'standard' Alexandrian edition.[55]

Epigrams, Elegies, and *iamboi*

After the mention of nine lyric books of Sappho in the *Suda* entry, another sentence suggests, almost as an afterthought, that 'she also wrote epigrams, elegies, *iamboi*, and monodies'.[56] The transition between these two sets of information (the nine lyric books and the more generic reference to a miscellaneous poetic production) is provided by the mention of Sappho's invention of the plectrum. The overall structure of the *Suda* entry indicates that this second chunk of the entry relies on a different kind of source(s) from those used in the first part, most probably on 'less known writings or even doubtful ones that circulated separately from the

---

[52] Yatromanolakis 1999: 191, 192.
[53] Puglia 2008: 5.
[54] Ancient scribal practices allow for either possibility: see P. J. Parsons *ap.* Contiades-Tsitsoni 1990: 74–5.
[55] Likewise, when Hephaestion (*On Poetry* 1.2 = test. 30) mentions παλαιὰ ἀντίγραφα with reference to the metrical articulation of Sappho's Books 2 and 3, it is unnecessary to suppose that he is drawing on pre- or non-Alexandrian editions. The context itself (book-division according to metrical principles) argues in favour of an Alexandrian origin of these 'ancient manuscripts': Battezzato 2018: 4–5.
[56] *Suda* c 107 (test. 2).

nine books of the Alexandrian edition'.[57] Sapphic material of doubtful authenticity circulated already at the time of Meleager (130–70 BC), who included in his *Garland* Sappho's 'few' epigrams;[58] the *Greek Anthology* ascribes three almost certainly spurious epigrams to Sappho.[59] It is, however, remarkable that two of these already show a marked connection between Sappho's poetry and funeral lament, visible elsewhere in Hellenistic epigram.[60] Threnodic elements or poems were present in Sappho's lyric production (e.g. fr. 140(a), the ritual lament for Adonis), and this is probably why elegies are attributed to Sappho in the biographical tradition.[61]

The mention of *iamboi* in the *Suda* entry among Sapphic or pseudo-Sapphic production is more puzzling. Traces of iambic metres are scanty in Sappho's extant lyric poems (fr. 117, from a wedding song), yet the 'iambic mood' – i.e. mockery, invective – is not absent, especially but not only in her *epithalamia*, where she deploys the traditional mockery of the bridegroom.[62] Two ancient sources, one Hellenistic (Philodemus, first century BC) and one late antique (Julian, fourth century AD), also mention Sappho in connection with *iambos*. In the first passage, Philodemus quotes the example of Sappho, who 'composes some poems in an iambic manner', to exemplify the thesis of those who believe that poets compose in a given genre by convention and not by nature.[63] 'In an iambic manner' must refer not to the metre but to the perceived mocking content of some of Sappho's poetry.[64] The second piece of evidence is more difficult to reconcile with this 'generic' interpretation, since it seems to assume that Julian knew of Sappho's use of iambic metres and not just mocking tones. Julian thanks Alypius for sending him a geographical treatise which his friend has embellished with some iambic verses of his own (προσθεὶς τοὺς ἰάμβους), which are, however, not 'singing the fight with Boupalos, as the Cyrenean poet (i.e. Callimachus) would put it' – that is, iambics not violent as those of Hipponax – 'but such as those that the

---

[57] Rotstein 2010: 35.
[58] Meleager, *Greek Anthology* 4.1.6 (test. 43).
[59] [Sappho], *Greek Anthology* 6.269, 7.489, 7.505 (frr. 157D, 158D, 159D; 672–83 *FGE*).
[60] [Sappho], *Greek Anthology* 7.489, 7.505; Dioscorides, *ibid.* 7.407 (test. 58), Posidippus 51 A–B.
[61] Thus the second-century papyrus P.Oxy. 1800 fr. 1 (test. 1), referring to 'one' book of 'elegies'; cf. Yatromanolakis 1999: 185–6. Aristoxenus fr. 81 Wehrli = Pseudo-Plutarch, *On Music* 16.1136c (test. 37) says that Sappho composed in the Mixolydian harmony, a scale often associated with lament (cf. West 1992: 182). For a 'threnodic' Sappho in Latin literature, see Bessone 2003.
[62] STEINER.
[63] Philodemus, *On Poems* 1 fr. 117 Janko.
[64] Yatromanolakis 1999: 186–7, Rosenmeyer 2006, Dale 2011a: 51–5, Martin 2016, STEINER.

fair Sappho wishes to accommodate to her poems' (οἴους ἡ καλὴ Caπφὼ βούλεται τοῖς ὕμνοις ἁρμόττειν).[65] We cannot rule out the idea that Julian is referring here to 'iambics' as isolated metrical elements in some of Sappho's odes, or that some later iambic poems may have been credited to Sappho.[66] A further possibility is that Julian wants to underline the literary quality of Alypius' verses: they are metrically iambics but like Sappho's poems from the point of view of the style and content.[67] All in all, it seems reasonable to suppose that Sappho's Alexandrian edition did not include elegies/epigrams and 'proper' iambic poems.[68]

Further Reading

The most up-to-date treatment of Sappho's Alexandrian edition remains Liberman 2007. For new insights provided by the 'Newest Sappho' into the articulation of Book 1, see Obbink 2016b, D'Alessio 2019. For the vexed issue of Sappho's *Epithalamia*, the most recent contributions are Yatromanolakis 1999, Puglia 2008, and Dale 2011a. For the early reception, textual and visual, of Sappho in the fifth and fourth centuries, see Yatromanolakis 2007 and Coo. For the direct and indirect transmission of Aeolic poetry, see Nicosia 1976.

---

[65] Julian, *Letter* 10 (p. 13.2–5 B–C).
[66] See Dale 2011a: 49–51 for the former, Yatromanolakis 1999: 187 for the latter.
[67] Rotstein 2010: 37–8.
[68] For a different view, see Martin 2016.

CHAPTER 17

Sappho on the Papyri

P. J. Finglass[*]

She nearly made it. The first papyrus of Sappho to be discovered, rescued
from the City of Crocodiles (Krokodilopolis, in the modern Fayum) and
published in 1880 as P.Berol. inv. 5006 by Friedrich Blass, showed the
world how tantalisingly close Sappho's poetry had come to making it to
the modern world.[1] This unprepossessing scrap could be dated on the
basis of its script to the seventh century, roughly twelve hundred years
after Sappho was composing her poetry: so late that its scribe might have
been born after the Arab invasion of his country. Since Sappho was still
being read in Egypt at this time, it is odds on that her works were accessi-
ble in Constantinople and other major cultural centres around the
Byzantine Empire, too. She had done well to make it this far. The works
of Stesichorus, another major lyric poet from the archaic period much
praised in antiquity, leave no trace in the papyrological record beyond the
third century;[2] Sappho's contemporary and fellow Mytilenean, Alcaeus, is
not securely attested past the third.[3] Indeed, none of the nine canonical
lyric poets seems to have survived as long. If her works had lasted just a
bit longer, we might today possess a medieval manuscript, say from the
tenth century, containing dozens of entire poems, or more; the history of
Sapphic scholarship, indeed of world literature, would look very different
as a result.[4] So, from the beginning of the discovery of Sappho's works on
papyrus, it was clear that the story of the survival of her poetry would be
a particularly remarkable one, if also tinged with disappointment.
Sappho called love 'bitter-sweet' (fr. 130.2); she might have said the same
of her own textual transmission.

[*] I am grateful to Adrian Kelly and Lucia Prauscello for helpful comments.
[1] Blass 1880a: 36–7, 40, 1880b: 287–90; Sappho frr. 3–4. In fact this fragment is written on parch-
ment, not papyrus, but for the sake of convenience parchment fragments are conventionally
included under the general heading 'papyri', and I adopt that usage in this chapter.
[2] Finglass and Kelly 2015b: 1.
[3] See Porro 2007, especially the table on p. 179.
[4] For the failure of Sappho's poetry to survive down to the high Byzantine Empire, see PONTANI.

'Sappho on the papyri' is a broad title; indeed, it could be the title of this volume as a whole, or of any modern book on Sappho, given the central place of papyrological evidence for almost any assertion or argument that we might seek to make about this poet. This chapter, however, has a more modest compass. In it I first sketch the discovery of the papyri from 1880 down to the most recent finds of 2014.[5] That brief narrative, intended to show how our knowledge of Sappho has steadily increased over the past hundred and forty years or so, and how readers have had to deal with a rapidly changing corpus, is followed by a synoptic presentation of those papyri in tabular form. That table introduces a few remarks on the papyri as historical documents: apart from restoring passages of Sappho's poetry that had been lost, what else can they tell us?

After the Berlin papyrus, the next fragment to appear was P.Oxy. 7, a third-century papyrus published by Bernard Grenfell and Arthur Hunt in 1898: the first literary papyrus in the first volume of their series *The Oxyrhynchus Papyri* (P.Oxy. 1–6 are all biblical texts). As well as the text proper, they print a 'brilliant restoration' (p. 11) of the text by Blass, and a verse translation.[6] Such a presentational style was natural enough given that this was the first substantial fragment of Sappho to be discovered. But subsequent papyrus publications would tend to be more austere; the appearance in *The Oxyrhynchus Papyri* of a full reconstruction of a fragmentary text, even if labelled *exempli gratia*, could lend it an authority that it was never intended to have, with disastrous effects for subsequent interpretation. Another parchment followed in 1902, P.Berol. inv. 9722, from the late sixth or early seventh century.[7] The three codex folia making up this document contained a great deal of text, including two substantial passages (each about thirty lines) vividly expressing the emotional impact of Sappho's separation from her companions, which are likely to be close to full poems. Like P.Berol. inv. 5006, this new parchment was evidence that people were reading Sappho in very late antiquity. Moreover, we now could see that substantial amounts of Sappho had made it down to that period; the earlier papyrus was no freak survivor.

The next few papyri to appear were less dramatic. In 1903 a third-century papyrus, P.Oxy. 424, was published which was later identified as containing the same poem as P.Berol. inv. 5006.[8] A decade later followed

---

[5] For another account of the discovery of the papyri, see Casanova 2007: 1–9.
[6] Grenfell and Hunt 1898; fr. 5.
[7] Schubart 1902: 195–206; frr. 92–7.
[8] Grenfell and Hunt 1903: 68, 71–2; fr. 3.

P.S.I. 123, probably a roll, from Oxyrhynchus, dated between 50 and 150, containing scraps of two poems later illuminated by richer papyri.[9] The same year also saw the publication of P.Halle 3, another fairly short fragment.[10] In 1914, fragments of two papyrus rolls appeared: P.Oxy. 1231, from the second century, and 1232, from the third.[11] Both are extremely substantial, the former including (among other texts) the major part of the poem 'Some praise an army of horses . . .' (fr. 16), the latter the wedding of Hector and Andromache (fr. 44). P.Oxy. 1231 prompted a major encomium in the *New York Times*:

> Out of the dust of Egypt comes the voice of Sappho, as clear and sweet as when she sang in Lesbos by the sea, 600 years before the birth of Christ. The picks and spades of Arab workmen, directed by Bernard P. Grenfell and Arthur S. Hunt of the Egypt Exploration Fund, have given the world a hitherto unknown poem by the greatest woman poet of all time . . . It is already a classic, this little song, whose liquid Greek syllables echo the music of undying passion.[12]

The year 1922 saw the publication of P.Oxy. 1787, a second- or third-century papyrus roll,[13] with fragments, some quite substantial, of at least eight different poems; it was recognised that P.Halle 3 was a fragment of the same papyrus. Five years later came P.Oxy. 2076, an early second-century papyrus roll providing further evidence for Sappho's account of the wedding of Hector and Andromache.[14] Both these papyri would later be associated with others discovered at Oxyrhynchus containing lyric poetry, apparently from the same library, with some written in the same hand.

The *ostrakon* (potsherd) from between 225 and 150 BC published in 1937 and later designated P.S.I. 1300 was the first, and so far the only, piece of her poetry to appear in this medium; it preserves a beautiful description of a *locus amoenus* (literally 'lovely place') to which the goddess Aphrodite is summoned.[15] The next year a section of a papyrus roll followed, from the first century BC, P.Mil.Vogliano 40,[16] to which three years later was added P.Haun. inv. 301, a fragment of the same papyrus.[17]

---

[9] Vitelli 1913; frr. 16–17.
[10] Bechtel *et al.* 1913a; fr. 60.
[11] Grenfell and Hunt 1914a; frr. 15a–30. Grenfell and Hunt 1914b; frr. 43–4.
[12] J. Kilmer, 'Poem by Sappho, written 600 B.C., dug up in Egypt', *New York Times*, 14 June 1914: 59 (a detailed piece, including a text and translation).
[13] Grenfell and Hunt 1922; frr. 58–87. See pp. 237–9 below.
[14] Hunt 1927.
[15] Norsa 1937, 1953; fr. 2.
[16] Vogliano 1938, Gallavotti 1961; fr. 98.
[17] Vogliano 1941.

In 1941 came the publication of P.Oxy. 2166;[18] this was not a single new papyrus but a series of overlooked fragments belonging to previously published papyri, including two of Sappho, P.Oxy. 1231 and 1787. Fresh material now would not come for a decade, until in 1951 fully eight papyri were published containing poetry definitely, probably, or possibly by Sappho. These were P.Oxy. 2288, a papyrus roll from the first or second century;[19] P.Oxy. 2289, a second-century papyrus roll, which provided a small amount of text from a handful of poems;[20] P.Oxy. 2290, a papyrus, perhaps a roll, from the second or third century;[21] P.Oxy. 2291, a third-century papyrus roll;[22] P.Oxy. 2308, a late second- or third-century papyrus;[23] P.Oxy. 2292 and 2293, second-century papyrus rolls, each containing a commentary;[24] and P.Oxy. 2294, a second-century papyrus, perhaps a roll, containing 'bibliographical details about a book of Sappho'.[25] Thanks to this hoard, for the first time scholars had access to papyri not just of Sappho's poetry, but of the commentaries on her work written by scholars in antiquity: precious documents that preserve traces of how some ancient readers reacted to Sappho, and thus a vital part of the story of her reception.

In the same year appeared addenda to previously published Oxyrhynchus papyri of Sappho,[26] and in the following year a papyrus of uncertain provenance, P.Fouad inv. 239, from the second or third century.[27] This bumper crop was the result of Lobel's particular concern with this poet ahead of the edition of Sappho (and Alcaeus) that he and Denys Page published in 1955; the Lesbian poets were given priority in the publication schedule to ensure that the forthcoming major edition would contain as much of their work as possible.[28] Yet, even after these labours, Lobel had not exhausted the Oxyrhynchus collection (not to speak of others). New papyri from that source appeared in 1956 (P.Oxy. 2357, a second-century papyrus roll,[29] and P.Oxy. 2378, a papyrus roll from between 50 and 150, containing poetry that could be by Sappho or

---

[18] Lobel 1941: 38, 44.
[19] Lobel 1951a; fr. 1.
[20] Lobel 1951b; frr. 5–9, 12, 17.
[21] Lobel 1951c; fr. 88.
[22] Lobel 1951d; fr. 99.
[23] Lobel 1951h; fr. 103B.
[24] Lobel 1951e; fr. 213. Lobel 1951f; fr. 90.
[25] Lobel 1951g; fr. 103.
[26] Lobel 1951i.
[27] Lobel and Page 1952 (although they leaned towards attributing it to Alcaeus); fr. 44A.
[28] Lobel and Page 1955.
[29] Lobel 1956a; fr. 103C.

Alcaeus[30]) and 1963 (P.Oxy. 2506, a papyrus roll or rolls from the early second century, containing an anonymous commentary on lyric poets written between *c.*150 BC and AD 100[31]), followed by another in 1965 (P.S.I. inv. 51 = P.S.I. 1470, a papyrus of unknown provenance from between 150 and 250).[32] The 1956 papyri (though not the 1963 one) were added at the end of the revised 1963 version of the edition by Lobel and Page, but no further updates of that book were issued; the reprint by Sandpiper Books in 1997 was simply a reissue of the 1963 edition. But all the papyri mentioned up to now were published in time to be included in Voigt's edition of 1971, which today, nearly half a century on, remains the most recent critical edition of Sappho.[33]

Anyone relying solely on Voigt's edition for a text of Sappho will be missing a good deal of material, however, since the publication of papyri over the last half century has continued, if not quite at the rate of the fifty years before that. In 1967 (though not included in Voigt's edition, which seems to have been completed several years before publication) appeared P.Oxy. 2637, a second-century papyrus roll or rolls containing another commentary on lyric poetry, which includes three fragments (frr. 27, 35, 38) that discuss Sappho.[34] Some Aeolic verses which may belong to Sappho, perhaps with a commentary, were published in 1972 as P.Oxy. 2878, a papyrus from the late first or early second century.[35] The following year saw the publication of a papyrus roll from the second century BC, P.Mich. inv. 3498, which contained several line-beginnings, including a couple from Sappho.[36] Two papyri from Cologne, both from the second century, were published in 1974: P.Köln inv. 8 = P.Köln 60, a scrap of Sappho's poetry,[37] and P.Köln inv. 5860 = P.Köln 61, a commentary on her work.[38] Almost all the papyri so far mentioned would find a place in Campbell's edition, published by the Loeb Classical Library in 1982.

More than two decades would pass before further additions to Sappho's corpus would see the light, the longest such gap since the

---

[30] Lobel 1956b; Sappho or Alcaeus fr. 42.
[31] Page 1963; fr. 213A, test. 14. For the nature of this papyrus, see Finglass 2014: 81.
[32] Manfredi 1965, then Bastianini 2008; fr. 213B.
[33] For these and other modern editions of Sappho, see the next chapter.
[34] Lobel 1967; fr. 214A.
[35] Lobel 1972; also Page 1973; frr. 287–312 *SLG*.
[36] Merkelbach 1973; fr. 213C. The papyrus was subsequently joined with P.Mich. inv. 3250; see C. Borges and Sampson 2012.
[37] Merkelbach 1974, Kramer 1978a; fr. 214C.
[38] Gronewald 1974, Kramer 1978b; fr. 214B.

publication of the first fragment in 1880. When such an addition was finally published, it was not immediately recognised as belonging to Sappho: such is the recalcitrance of the material that papyrologists often have to deal with that identifying the author of a new papyrus is sometimes a baffling task. In 1997 P.Oxy. 4411, a papyrus roll or rolls from between 125 and 175, was published as a new text of Old Comedy; while most of the pieces are indeed from this genre, it was pointed out three years later that several fragments of the papyrus (now clearly identified as coming from more than one roll) overlapped with the Sappho papyus P.Oxy. 2290, and subsequent work has revealed new, tiny Aeolic (and in this context therefore presumably Sapphic) fragments from P.Oxy. 4411.[39]

The twenty-first century has seen three discoveries of Sappho papyri; two, from 2004 and 2014, are particularly famous, but the other, from 2005, should not be overlooked. In 2004 appeared the 'New Sappho', P.Köln 429+430.[40] This was the oldest papyrus of Sappho yet discovered, dating as it does to the third century BC, perhaps only three centuries after Sappho's death, and probably reflecting an arrangement of Sappho's poetry that predates the Alexandrian edition being put together at that time or not much later.[41] The papyrus was recovered from cartonnage (pieces of papyrus and linen glued together to fashion mummy masks and cases) and comes from a roll – naturally, since codices were not in use at that time – containing parts of two successive columns. The first eight lines preserved in the first column represent the end of a new poem by Sappho. They are followed by a twelve-line poem, straddling the first and second columns, which overlaps with the earlier Sappho papyrus P.Oxy. 1787 fr. 1.11–22. The final poem in the papyrus is not by Sappho, as can be discerned from its metre.

The overlap between the Cologne fragment and P.Oxy. 1787 gives us a virtually complete poem by Sappho, in which she laments her old age before concluding with the myth of Tithonus, who was taken away by the goddess Dawn to be her husband, but grew old alongside his ever-young wife. But it also allows us to correct assumptions made by many scholars about the beginnings and ending of poems in P.Oxy. 1787. In the editions of Lobel and Page, Voigt, and Campbell, P.Oxy. 1787 fr. 1.26 is marked as the last line of a poem, although there is no evidence for this

[39] Haslam 1997, Steinrück 2000, Ucciardello 2001, Steinrück 2010, Prauscello and Ucciardello 2015.
[40] Gronewald and Daniel 2004a, 2004b, 2005, 2007a, 2007b. The key analysis of the papyrus is West 2005 = 2011–13 II 53–66.
[41] Thus Liberman 2007: 51–2; for that edition, see PRAUSCELLO.

on the papyrus. Thanks to the Cologne fragment, we can see that the poem's ending came rather at line P.Oxy. 1787 fr. 1.22, and that line 23 begins a fresh poem which contains the rest of P.Oxy. 1787 fr. 1 followed by P.Oxy. 1787 fr. 2, which in the editions just mentioned is given a separate fragment number altogether. So, as well as giving us more Sappho, the Cologne fragment has significant implications for the interpretation of a papyrus discovered decades ago; it additionally highlights the dangers of overconfident editorial decisions.

In 2005 P.S.I. inv. 1357 was published, a papyrus dating to between 150 and 300 which contains a commentary on poems by Sappho; this commentary is written on the verso of a papyrus that has a table of accounts on its recto, a fact which, together with the rather casual nature of the script, suggests that this is a personal commentary written by a reader of Sappho's poetry rather than a full transcription of a scholar's commentary.[42] As such, the text is a reminder of the range of different types of text which we gather under the single heading 'commentaries', which can include amateur efforts just as much as scholarly productions: all of them shed light on the reading of Sappho in the past.

In 2014 appeared P.GC inv. 105 (four separate pieces)[43] and P.Sapph. Obbink (one piece),[44] both written by the same scribe in the same format, and probably from the same roll, between the late second century and first half of the third. Together, the fragments preserve parts of nine poems; two are new, with the other seven known in part from previous sources (P.Oxy. 1231, 2289, and P.S.I. 123, with which the new fragments overlap), but often helpfully augmented by the new finds, which additionally provide new information about the ordering of poems in the Alexandrian edition of Sappho.[45] Christened the 'New New Sappho' or the 'Newest Sappho', the latter the title of a major edited collection on the papyrus which appeared in 2016,[46] these documents had an immediate impact greater than that of any previous discovery of a Sappho papyrus. Emendations and supplements were published on social media, a resource with a turnaround even faster than the *Zeitschrift für Papyrologie und Epigraphik*; newspapers and radio programmes covered the discovery; the papyri were hailed by an authoritative source as 'a still greater

---

[42] Prauscello 2005, especially pp. 53–4.
[43] Burris, Fish, and Obbink 2014.
[44] Obbink 2014a; also Burris 2017, which joins P.GC inv. 105 fr. 4 with P.Sapph.Obbink.
[45] The key analysis of the papyrus is West 2014. For the provenance, see FINGLASS AND KELLY pp. 6–7.
[46] Bierl and Lardinois 2016.

enrichment [than the Cologne Sappho], the greatest for 92 years'.[47] The two new poems are now generally known as the Brothers Poem (since in it Sappho refers to her brothers Charaxus and Larichus) and the Cypris Poem (which contains an early invocation of that goddess); both, especially the longer Brothers Poem, have generated intense discussion.

Let us now look at these fragments in tabular form. I begin with a table detailing papyri containing fragments of actual texts of Sappho, and follow this with a table describing all other relevant papyri – those containing commentaries on Sappho, for instance, that cite her works but are not primarily texts of her poetry. Details of the texts are laid out in Table 1, and of the commentaries in Table 2.

The papyri in these tables are arranged not by date of discovery and/or publication (a contingent datum of interest to the story of Sappho's modern reception but not to the fate of her texts in antiquity), or by the ordering of fragments in any modern edition (which would give too much weight to an editor's inevitably subjective decisions), but by the approximate date when they were written. We have already noted the two latest papyri, one from the seventh century, one from the late sixth or early seventh. The next oldest papyri of Sappho's poetry are from the third century – at least three, and up to nine. Six definitely come from the second century, with six more from the third or second, and three more from the second or first. Before then the number of papyri falls away, with one from the first, one from the first BC, one from the third or second BC, and one from the third BC. In all there are twenty-four papyri, a high number for a writer in this genre; that includes two papyri containing texts that could be by Alcaeus.[48]

The peak in the second century is not an unexpected pattern for a classical poet. What is interesting is how the number of papyri do not fall away much in the third century and may in fact increase, depending on the date of the six papyri assignable to either third or second century; this is consistent with what we would have deduced from the existence of papyri from late antiquity, namely that Sappho's poetry proved unusually resilient at a time when the works of other poets were beginning to disappear. Crucially, Sappho's works successfully navigated the transition from roll to codex, a process which began in the first century and was mainly complete by the third; less popular authors were finished off by this change of technology, since they were not recopied into the new format.

---

[47] West 2014: 1, implicitly referring to the 1922 publication of P.Oxy. 1787.
[48] For Pindar, see Ucciardello 2012.

Table 1 *Papyri containing texts*

Papyrus	Fragment Number(s)	Bookform	Provenance	Date	Handwriting/Other Comments
P.Berol. inv. 5006 (M–P³ 1440, *LDAB* 3902)+P.Oxy. 424 (M–P³ 1441, *LDAB* 3896)	frr. 3–4	parchment codex	Krokodilopolis, Fayum	VII	uncial
P.Berol. inv. 9722 (M–P³ 1451, *LDAB* 3901)	frr. 92–7	parchment codex	Egypt	VI ex./VII in.	small careful uncials
P.Oxy. 7 (M–P³ 1442, *LDAB* 3897)	fr. 5	papyrus roll	Oxyrhynchus	III	square sloping uncial
P.Oxy. 1232 (M–P³ 1447, *LDAB* 3900)	frr. 43–4	papyrus roll	Oxyrhynchus	III	'rapidly formed sloping uncials'
P.Oxy. 2291 (M–P³ 1901, *LDAB* 3898)	fr. 99	papyrus roll	Oxyrhynchus	III	could be by Alcaeus: Voigt labels it Alcaeus fr. 303A
P.S.I. inv. 1357 (M–P³ 1949.01, *LDAB* 10353)	n/a	papyrus roll	Egypt	150–300	verso
P.Fouad inv. 239 (M–P³ 1900, *LDAB* 175)	fr. 44A	papyrus roll	Egypt	II/III	

Papyrus	Fragments	Material	Provenance	Date	Script
P.Oxy. 1787+P.Oxy. 2166+P.Halle 3 (M–P³ 1449, LDAB 3899)	frr. 58–87	papyrus roll	Oxyrhynchus	II/III	'rapidly formed uncial'
P.GC inv. 105+P.Sapph.Obbink (LDAB 341738)	Brothers Poem, Cypris Poem, additions to frr. 5, 9, 15–18, 26	papyrus roll	Egypt?	II ex./III in.	calligraphic uncials
P.Oxy. 2290 (M–P³ 1450, LDAB 3895)	fr. 88	papyrus, perhaps roll	Oxyrhynchus	II ex./III	
P.Oxy. 2308 (M–P³ 1902, LDAB 5090)	fr. 103B	papyrus; format unknown	Oxyrhynchus	II ex./III	'of the angular type'
P.Oxy. 2357 (M–P³ 1446, LDAB 3888)	fr. 103C	papyrus roll	Oxyrhynchus	II ex.	'not very well executed . . . early example of the angular type'
P.Oxy. 2289 (M–P³ 1443, LDAB 3887)	frr. 5–9, 12, 17	papyrus roll	Oxyrhynchus	II ex.	'small uncial'
P.Köln 60 (M–P³ 1452.1, LDAB 3885)	fr. 214C	papyrus	Egypt	II	
P.Oxy. 1231+P.Oxy. 2166 (M–P³ 1445, LDAB 3893)	frr. 15a–30	papyrus roll	Oxyrhynchus	II	informal upright hand
P.Oxy. 4411 (M–P³ add., LDAB 372036)	n/a; adds text to Sappho fr. 88	papyrus rolls (at least three)	Oxyrhynchus	125–175	formal round (rounded majuscule)

Table 1 *(cont.)*

Papyrus	Fragment Number(s)	Bookform	Provenance	Date	Handwriting/Other Comments
POxy. 2076 (M–P³ 1448, *LDAB* 3889)	fr. 44	papyrus roll	Oxyrhynchus	II in.	'not far removed from cursive'
POxy. 2378 (M–P³ 1903, *LDAB* 4491)	Sappho or Alcaeus fr. 42	papyrus roll	Oxyrhynchus	50–150	
POxy. 2288 (M–P³ 1438, *LDAB* 3886)	fr. 1	papyrus roll	Oxyrhynchus	I/II	
POxy. 2878 (M–P³ 1903.1, *LDAB* 4500)	frr. S287–312 *SLG*	papyrus roll	Oxyrhynchus	I ex./II in.	Aeolic verses, perhaps with a commentary; 'medium-sized upright round book-hand'
P.S.I. 123 (M–P³ 1444, *LDAB* 3894)	frr. 16–17	papyrus roll	Oxyrhynchus	I ex.	
P.Mil.Vogliano 40+P.Haun. inv. 301 (M–P³ 1452, *LDAB* 3903)	fr. 98	papyrus roll	Egypt	I BC	
P.S.I. 1300 (M–P³ 1439, *LDAB* 3904)	fr. 2	*ostrakon*	Egypt	225–150 BC	
P.Köln 429+430 (M–P³ 1449.01, *LDAB* 10253)	n/a; adds text to fr. 58	papyrus roll	Egypt	III BC	

Table 2 *Papyri containing commentaries*

Papyrus	Fragment Number(s)	Bookform	Provenance	Date	Handwriting/Other Comments
P.S.I. 1470 (M–P³ 1455·2, *LDAB* 3883)	fr. 213B	papyrus roll	Egypt	II/III	commentary on Sappho; 'una libraria informale di tipo rotondo' (P.S.I. p. 41)
P.Oxy. 2292 (M–P³ 1453, *LDAB* 3890)	fr. 213	papyrus, perhaps roll	Oxyrhynchus	II ex.	commentary on Sappho; 'neat specimen of the upright angular type'
P.Oxy. 2637 frr. 27, 35, 38 (M–P³ 1949·3, *LDAB* 4820)	fr. 214A	papyrus roll(s)	Oxyrhynchus	II med.	commentary on choral lyric; 'a rather small upright uncial, practised but by no means handsome' (Lobel p. 138).
P.Oxy. 2293 (M–P³ 1454, *LDAB* 3891)	fr. 90	papyrus roll	Oxyrhynchus	II	commentary on Sappho
P.Köln 61 (M–P³ 1455·1, *LDAB* 3884)	fr. 214B	papyrus roll	Egypt	II	commentary on Sappho
P.Oxy. 2294 (M–P³ 1455, *LDAB* 3892)	fr. 103	papyrus, perhaps roll	Oxyrhynchus	II	'bibliographical details about a book of Sappho'
P.Oxy. 2506 (M–P³ 1950, *LDAB* 193)	fr. 213A, test. 14	papyrus roll(s)	Oxyrhynchus	II in.	from a work on lyric poets
P.Mich. inv. 3498 (M–P³ 1596·1, *LDAB* 7079)+P.Mich. inv. 3250	fr. 213C	papyrus roll	Oxyrhynchus	II a.C.	work containing several line-beginnings, including two by Sappho

Moreover, although most of the papyri are from the second century or later, at least four, and perhaps up to seven, are from before that date – a respectable number for a lyric poet. The provenance of the papyri, where known, is always Oxyrhynchus, except that one, as noted above, comes from Krokodilopolis in the Fayum, and several are said to come simply from Egypt.

The Sappho commentaries are less chronologically disparate: of seven papyri, five are from the second century, with one from the third or second, and another from the second century BC. Naturally, these are the dates of the papyri, but not necessarily of the works which they contain, for which they provide only *termini ante quos*; at least they do permit us to discern the demand for Sapphic exegesis on the part of readers in the high Roman empire. And as already mentioned, the level and intended audience of these commentaries varies, suggesting the wide readership that Sappho's poetry continued to enjoy.

Further information on that subject comes from one of the most intriguing of these texts, the *ostrakon* from the third or second century BC (fr. 2). This may have been a school text: that is, the result of a teacher dictating a poem, which the student would attempt to reproduce faithfully on a potsherd, though in this case he made many mistakes.[49] If so, the object would provide not just a welcome additional poem of Sappho, but evidence for her presence in the Ptolemaic schoolroom, where her work was evidently thought suitable for a lesson of this kind. The poem in question is a divine invocation; it would be interesting to know if more obviously emotional poetry by Sappho was put to similar use. On the other hand, this interpretation has been questioned: the presence of plenty of phonological mistakes, but no real mistakes of dialect, has led one scholar to view the scribe of the *ostrakon* as a cultured amateur rather than a schoolboy.[50] The debate reminds us of how difficult these inferences can be.

People reading ancient texts of Sappho rather than listening to them via the dictation of a schoolmaster will have read them in the order in which they appeared in ancient books. As we have seen, papyri provide vital information as to what that order was. For instance, Hephaestion's citation of fr. 1 as his example of the sapphic stanza suggests that this poem appeared first in the Alexandrian edition of Sappho, and two

---

49 Cribiore 2001: 152–3.
50 F. Ferrari 2011: 445 n. 14.

papyri provide independent support for this deduction: P.Oxy. 2288, where the beginning of that poem coincides with the top of a column, and P.S.I. inv. 1357 verso, a commentary which seems to be dealing with the end of that poem before turning to a new poem explicitly labelled 'two'. The Cologne fragment in particular indicates that, at least before the Alexandrian edition became standard, poems of Sappho could appear in a very different order, indeed accompanied by poems that were not by Sappho at all, with no indication of change of authorship from one poem to the other beyond what readers could deduce for themselves from language, style, or metre. That papyrus reminds us of how little we know about the ancient reading experience, especially in the centuries immediately after Sappho's lifetime.[51]

Towards the other end of antiquity, the evidence afforded by papyri is richer still, and sometimes permits fascinating glimpses into the fate of individual books and libraries. P.Oxy. 2076 belonged to a rich collection of literary texts disposed of at Oxyrhynchus about AD 300, which, thanks to documentary papyri found intermingled with the literature and dating between 186 and 265, can be identified as belonging to a particular family, one of whose members was called alternatively Sarapion or Apollonianus, a local official in the first quarter of the third century.[52] P.Oxy. 1787(+P.Oxy. 2166+P.Halle 3) is thought to have been written by the scribe of several papyri of Pindar, as well as one of Alcaeus and possibly one by Alcman – and this group of papyri may have been written by Spartas, a member of that Sarapion/Apollonianus family, on the basis of the similarity of their script to that of a document written by Spartas in AD 186.[53] If that hypothesis is correct, the texts owned by this family were extensive indeed. It is a tantalising thought to imagine spending a busy afternoon in the library of this house, surrounded by so many precious texts of ancient lyric poetry, the vast majority of which have not come down to us; quite a thought to imagine, too, the day around AD 300 when somebody decided to take all these precious books and cast them in the rubbish heap. Yet that casual act of destruction was, unknown to its perpetrator, one of the greatest ever acts of historical preservation: for it was from that rubbish heap that most of the discoveries of Sappho's poetry would derive nearly two millennia on.

---

[51] Prodi 2017: 572–82.

[52] Houston 2014: 143–56.

[53] Funghi and Messeri Savorelli 1992; see further Ucciardello 2012: 115–16, and also W. A. Johnson 2004: 26–7, who argues for two distinct scribes.

Further Reading

Janko 2005 (on the New Sappho) and Obbink 2014b (on the Newest Sappho) offer approachable guides to newly discovered papyri. The major problems with the provenance of the latter papyri are treated by Mazza 2019 and Sampson 2020; this is a fast-moving area which has attracted considerable international press attention. An outstanding account of the discovery of papyri from the nineteenth century onwards is provided by Parsons 2007.

CHAPTER 18

Editions of Sappho since the Renaissance

P. J. Finglass[*]

The coming of the printing press had a transformative impact on the transmission of Sappho's poetry. Previously, would-be readers of what remained of her writings would have had to track down and hunt through manuscripts of ancient authors who quoted her: a laborious task for a reader, still more for an editor, and (not surprisingly) there is no evidence that anyone ever undertook it. But once editions of Greek texts began to be published in the last quarter of the fifteenth century, Sappho's poetry became steadily more accessible, at least to those capable of reading her in Greek. True, the first collections of her fragments were still decades off. But readers could now at least encounter her poetry embedded in published texts; no longer was it confined to handwritten books hidden away in monastic libraries.

The historic moment when a major fragment of Sappho appeared in print for the first time was in 1508, when the Venetian scholar–printer Aldus Manutius published a collection edited by the Byzantine scholar Demetrios Doukas of Greek rhetorical works that included Dionysius of Halicarnassus' *On the Arrangement of Words*;[1] this text contains the substantial piece of poetry by Sappho known today as fr. 1, the 'Hymn to Aphrodite'. The text as it appears in Doukas's edition can be found in Plate 14; here are a transcription of the Greek and my own translation:[2]

---

[*] I am grateful to Stuart Gillespie and Adrian Kelly for helpful comments.

[1] Some smaller ones were published even earlier; for example, the *editio princeps* of Apollonius Dyscolus' grammatical works, which contain several fragments of Sappho's poetry, appeared in 1495.

[2] Doukas 1508: 537; for this edition and its editor, see Sicherl 1992, and for its significance for Sappho, see Williamson 1995: 44. DeJean 1989a: 30 (and in the title of her justifiably influential book) puts the date of the first printing of this poem nearly four decades later, in Robertus Stephanus's 1547 edition of Dionysius' treatise (which she dates to 1546, the date of the first volume of Stephanus's edition of Dionysius' works).

ποικιλόθρον' ἀθάνατ' ἀφροδίτη,	Ornate-throned immortal Aphrodite,
παῖ διὸς δολοπλόκε λίccομαί cε,	daughter of Zeus, weaver of wiles, I beg you:
μή μ' ἄccαιcι μήδ' ἀνίαιcι δάμνα	do not conquer my heart, lady,
πότνια θυμόν·	with pains and anguish,
ἀλλὰ τύ δ' ἐλθέ που κατ' ἔρωτα,	but you come somewhere according to love, 5
τὰc ἐμὰc αἰδῶc ἀΐοιc ἀπόλαc,	may you hear my voice, which many times
ἐκλύεc πατρὸc δὲ δόμον λιποῖcα	you heard and, leaving your father's golden
χρύcειον ἦλθεc	house, you came
ἄρμα ὑποζεύξαcα· καλοὶ δέ c' ἄγων,	after yoking your chariot. Fair swift sparrows
ὠκέεc cτρουθοὶ πτέρυγαc μελαίναc,	brought you, thickly whirring their dark 10
πυκνὰ δινῆντεc πτέρ' ἀπ' ὠρανῶ;	wings, feathers from the sky?
θέροc δ' ἄμεc πω,	Summer us yet,
αἶψ' ἄλλ' ἐξίκοντο· τὺ δ' ὦ μάκαιρα,	immediately but they came. And you, blessed one,
μειδιάcαc ἀθανάτωι προcώπωι,	the man having smiled with immortal face,
ἦρε' ὄττι δ' ἦν, τό, πέπονθε κ' ἄττι δ'	asked what it was, that, he suffered and what 15
ἦν τε κάλημμι;	which woman I call?
κ' ὄττ' ἐμῶι μάλιcτα θέλω γενέcθαι	And what I want to happen most of all for
καινόλα θυμῶι· τίνα δ' εὖτε πείθω-	my heart … What when I am to persuade
μαι cαγηνεύcαν φιλότατά τιc cω	they caught friendship with a dragnet some
ψαπφαδίκη·	. . . 20
καὶ γὰρ εἰ φεύγει ταχέωc διώξει·	For if he flees, he will soon pursue;
αἱ δὲ δῶρα μὴ δὲ κέτ' ἄλλα δώcει·	They he gifts not but … but he will give.
αἱ δὲ μὴ φιλεῖ, ταχέωc φιλήcει,	They but he loves not, he will soon love,
κὠϋκ ἐθέλοιc,	even if you would not want,
ἐθέλοιμι καὶ νῦν· χαλεπὰν δὲ λῦcον	may I want now too. And release grim 25
ἐκ μέριμναν· ὄcα δέ μοι τελέcαι,	care from; and what my heart desires
θυμὸc ἱμείρει, τέλεccον cύ δ' αὐτά,	to accomplish, accomplish but you yourself,
cύμμαχοc·	ally.

To anyone familar with Sappho's poem today this version may come as a surprise. The first stanza, at least, is recognisable, but after that much is beyond comprehension, and overall it is hard to see what the poem is about. Metre and dialect are faulty throughout, too, and the presentation of the text falls short of what we would expect in a modern edition: cursive script and tiny print make it hard to read, and instead of being set as poetry it is written as prose, with only marginal quotation marks to indicate its different status. None of this is meant as a criticism of Doukas, Sappho's first modern editor, or Manutius, his printer. They were pioneers, editing texts for the first time which had long lacked due scholarly attention; it is only thanks to centuries of scholarship – a process which they began – that we can see further than they.

The next appearance of this poem in print was nearly four decades later, in the edition of Dionysius by the Parisian scholar–printer Robertus Stephanus:[3]

Ποικιλόθρον᾽, ἀθάνατ᾽, ἀφροδίτα,	Ornate-throned, immortal, Aphrodite,
παῖ διὸς δολοπλόκε, λίccομαί cε,	daughter of Zeus, weaver of wiles, I beg you:
μή μ᾽ ἄταιcι μήδ᾽ αὐίαιcι δάμνα	do not conquer my heart, lady,
πότνια θυμόν.	with destruction and …
ἀλλὰ τῆιδ᾽ ἐλθέ ποτε κατ᾽ ἔρωτα·	but come here some time according to love; 5
τὰc ἐμὰc αὐδὰc ἄῖοιc, ἄc πολλάκ᾽	may you hear my voice, which many times
ἔκλυεc· πατρὸc δὲ δόμον λιποῖcα	you heard; and, leaving your father's golden
χρύcειον ἤλυθεc	house, you came
ἄρμα ὑποζεύξαcα. καλοὶ δέ c᾽ ἄγον	after yoking your chariot. Fair swift sparrows
ὠκέεc cτρουθοὶ πτέρυγαc μελαίναc,	brought you, thickly whirring their dark 10
πυκνὰ δινεῦντεc πτέρ᾽ ἀπ᾽ ὠρανῶ, αἰθέρ-	wings, feathers from the sky, through the
οc διὰ μέccω·	middle of the air;
αἶψα δ᾽ ἀρ᾽ ἐξίκοντο. τὺ δ᾽ ὦ μάκαιρα,	and they arrived immediately. And you blessed one,
μειδιάcαc᾽ ἀθανάτωι προcώπωι	smiling with immortal face
ἤρε᾽ ὄ, τι δ᾽ ἦν τὸ πέπονθα, κ᾽ ὦτῖ	asked what it was that I suffered and what 15
δεῦρο καλοῖμι.	I would call here.
κ᾽ ὦτι γ᾽ ἐμῶι μάλιcτα θέλω γενέcθαι	And what I want to happen most of all for
μαινόλαι θυμῶι. τινὰ δ᾽ εὖτε πύθω-	my frenzied heart. Whom when I am to
μαι cαγηνεύcαι φιλότητόc c᾽ ὦ	learn to catch you with a dragnet justice
Cαπφώ, δίκην.	of friendship, Sappho. 20
καὶ γὰρ αἰ φεύγει, ταχέωc διώξει·	For if he flees, he will soon pursue;
αἰ δὲ δῶρα μὴ δέχετο, τἄλλα δώcει·	if he does not receive gifts, he will give the others;
αἰ δὲ μὴ φιλεῖ, ταχεώc φιλήcει.	if he does not love, he will swiftly love.
κ᾽ ὦτι καὶ θέλειc,	And what you even want,
ἐθέλοιμι. καὶ νοῦν χαλεπᾶν λῦcον	may I want. And release my mind from 25 difficult
ἐκ μεριμνᾶν· ὄcα δέ μοι τελέcαι	worries; and whatever my soul desires
θυμὸc ἱμείρει, τέλεcον. cύ δ᾽ αὐτὰ	to accomplish, accomplish. You yourself
cύμμαχοc ἔcο·	be my ally.

---

[3] R. Stephanus 1547: 36–7.

Again the poem is printed as prose, again with marginal quotation marks; again the text is often difficult to follow. But there are signs of critical engagement with textual problems. So, in line 5, in place of the meaningless ἀπόλας the editor has written πολλάκ' ('many times'), which must be his (or someone else's) conjecture rather than the reading of a manuscript. It happens to be wrong; subsequent manuscript evidence allows us today to see what Sappho's text actually read at this point, and greater understanding of the Greek language means that we can see that the word is improperly elided and does not fit the metre. But when Robertus Stephanus was writing, that emendation was a decent enough attempt to make sense of the mysterious letters on the page. In other places, such as the recovery of the word αἰθέρος in lines 11–12, or the writing of μαινόλαι in place of the meaningless καινόλα in line 18, the improvements probably result from better manuscript evidence, or more careful consultation of that evidence.

A second major fragment of Sappho first appeared in August 1554, when the Italian humanist Franciscus Robortellus published the *editio princeps* (first printed edition) of the treatise *On the Sublime* ascribed to Longinus; that treatise preserves fr. 31, φαίνεταί μοι κῆνος ἴϲος θέοιϲιν ('He seems to me to be equal to a god').[4] In the same year, only a couple of months later, the French humanist Marcus Antonius Muretus published an edition of Catullus that printed a text of the same poem to illustrate Catullus' poem 51.[5] Muretus's text is better than that offered in Robortellus; he says that the text that he prints has been improved by the Cretan scholar Franciscus Portus.[6] The impact of the piece was swift: it appears in the first vernacular translation of poetry by Sappho, Rémi Belleau's French rendering of 1556,[7] and is incorporated into a collection of Sappho's fragments published in the same year by Robertus Stephanus's son Henricus, who followed his father as a printer and scholar of classical texts.[8]

---

[4] Robortellus 1554: 20–1.
[5] Muretus 1554: 56v–58r.
[6] Morrison 1962.
[7] Belleau 1556: 61–2 = Demerson *et al.* 1995–2003: 1 124–5; *pace* Fabre-Serris 2016: 78, who claims that Le Fèvre 1681 was the first French translation of Sappho. Anne Le Fèvre herself (later Anne Dacier) was naturally aware of Belleau's work, as can be seen from the unpaginated first and second pages of her preface. For other French translators of Sappho preceding Anne Le Fèvre, see Aulotte 1958, Reynolds 2000: 97.
[8] H. Stephanus 1556: 69.

Henricus Stephanus first published poems by Sappho in 1554; two poems, to be precise, frr. 1 and 168B.[9] These fragments come at the end of a book devoted to the fragments of Anacreon (spurious, it turns out, but that is another story), after which the editor sets a few fragments by Alcaeus and then these two by Sappho. Few in number though they are, this is the first time since antiquity that anyone had gathered together poems by Sappho: a momentous point in her transmission. Yet it is ironic that the first collection of a fragmentary Greek poet known and admired beyond any other today should have appeared as a mere appendix to a book dedicated to another author entirely, without even her name on the title page.

Stephanus's edition of the 'Hymn to Aphrodite' is worth comparing with that of his father. The passage in lines 18–20, where Robertus had printed the nonsensical τινὰ δ' εὖτε πύθωμαι caγηνεύcαι φιλότητός c' ὦ Caπφώ, δίκην, becomes τινὰ δ' αὖτε πειθώ, | καὶ caγηνεύcαν φιλότητα· τίc c' ὦ Caπφοῖ ἀδίκει; ('[and asked me] what persuasion, one more time, and catching with a dragnet friendship. Who, Sappho, is treating you unjustly?').[10] This is far from perfect – caγηνεύcαν ('catching with a dragnet'), for instance, continues to puzzle – but the basic form of the concluding question has been discerned correctly. Then in lines 23–5 Robertus's text αἲ δὲ μὴ φιλεῖ, ταχέωc φιλήcει. κ' ὦτι καὶ θέλειc, ἐθέλοιμι. καὶ νοῦν ... becomes αἲ δὲ μὴ φιλεῖ, ταχέωc φιλήcει, κ' ὄττι κελεύηιc. ἐλθέ μοι καὶ νῦν ... ('but if he does not love, soon he will love, and whatever you command. Come to me now too ...'). Here too the overall articulation has been much improved: the beginning of the final stanza is now recognised as a fresh command to Aphrodite, not a meaningless appendage to the previous idea. Yet problems remain. In line 24, κ' ὄττι κελεύηιc, 'and whatever you command', seems to be Stephanus's conjecture, but while it fits the metre, the sense is rather abrupt (we would need in addition a phrase meaning 'he will perform'), and the supposed corruption lacks obvious rationale. Nor are we given an apparatus criticus, or any footnote, to indicate that Stephanus has changed the manuscript reading.[11] With its successes and faults, Stephanus's text of this poem is

---

[9] H. Stephanus 1554: 62–3, 84.

[10] The incorrect form ἀδίκει, found in the 1554 edition, is corrected into ἀδίκεῖ in the second of 1556.

[11] According to Fabre-Serris 2016: 86, at this point '[Stephanus's] Greek allowed (that was the aim) a heterosexual reading of the text'; but the textual reading which makes it clear that Sappho here reveals that her beloved was female was conjectured (and then discovered in a manuscript) only in the nineteenth century (pp. 253–5 below).

largely the same as the text found in the subsequent Renaissance editions
described below; this, then, was the text of this famous poem that readers
would encounter for years to come.

The second edition of Stephanus's popular book, which appeared in
1556, added to the two fragments a further one, fr. 31, which (as we have
seen) had been first published only two years before.[12] The same year saw
an edition by Michael Neander of two of Sappho's fragments, which
formed part of his collection of maxims provided by different lyric
poets.[13] Then, in 1560, Stephanus published a substantial edition contain-
ing the works of Pindar and fragments of the lyric poets. This, the earli-
est major collection of Sappho's work, presents dozens of fragments
culled from other ancient authors read by Stephanus. The edition itself,
equipped with a Latin translation, is preceded by a Latin introduction
that gives details of Sappho's family and attempts to absolve her of the
charge of having sexual relations with women; it cites in particular
(Pseudo-?)Ovid's *Letter to Phaon*, in which the character Sappho expresses
her passion for Phaon, and which is taken as evidence for a poem by the
real Sappho on the same subject.[14] Of the fragments gathered by
Stephanus for this edition, nearly thirty appear here in a collection of
fragments for the first time.[15] Intermixed with the fragments are a few tes-
timonia, with no attempt to distinguish actual quotations and para-
phrases of Sappho's poetry from comments by ancient writers about her.
The final fragments printed by Stephanus are the epigrams attributed to
Sappho in the *Greek Anthology*, poems today known to be spurious, but
which thanks to Stephanus were presented to readers as genuine Sappho
for hundreds of years.

The fragments offered by Stephanus's 1560 collection were further aug-
mented in its second edition, published in 1566.[16] Two years later a more
substantial collection, including both testimonia and fragments, was
gathered by Fulvius Ursinus, as part of an edition of nine female poets,
and of nine lyric poets from antiquity; Sappho was the only member of

---

[12] H. Stephanus 1556: 67–9, with a few notes on p. 100.
[13] Neander 1556: 427–30; the new fragments (cited by Voigt number) are frr. 55 and 121.
[14] H. Stephanus 1560: second part, pp. 33–71, 421–2. The introduction, as Stephanus indicates, is
  influenced by the account of Sappho's life found in Gyraldus 1545.
[15] The fragments in question are frr. 42, 49, 54, 100–2, 104(a), 106, 111, 112, 114, 118, 120, 127, 128, 130,
  133–5, 137, 138, 141, 148, 152, 154, 156, 163.
[16] H. Stephanus 1566: 33–71; the new fragments are frr. 81, 122, 136, 166, 167.

both groups.[17] Nevertheless, Stephanus's collection retained its influence, being issued in subsequent editions such as one from 1586.[18]

For decades to come, editions of Sappho were significant neither for adding new fragments nor for improving the text of fragments already known; the selection published in 1614 by Jacobus Lectius, for instance, contains nothing novel.[19] Substantial progress in these areas waited until 1733, when the first edition of Sappho' works in their own right, not as part of an edition including a variety of poets, was published by Johann Christian Wolf, Professor at the Hamburg Gymnasium. His text, preceded by a detailed introduction, offers not just more than a dozen new fragments,[20] but also a substantial critical commentary, explaining textual choices and commenting on points of language; the commentary often consists of passages taken wholesale (with acknowledgement) from other scholars, thus giving readers access to a variety of views, sometimes in contradiction to the editor's own. So in the 'Hymn to Aphrodite', at the end of line 5 Wolf prints κατ' ἔρωτα ('according to love') as in previous editions, but includes in his notes Vossius's suggestion that the true text is κατερῶτα, i.e. καὶ ἑτερῶτα 'even on another occasion';[21] this reinterpretation of the transmitted letters makes excellent sense in the context (reminding a deity that s/he has heard the worshipper in the past is a typical feature of ancient prayer), and has (in the form κατέρωτα, with correct Lesbian accentuation) been near-universally accepted by subsequent editors.

Further editions followed in the first half of the nineteenth century with increasing philological sophistication, thanks to greater understanding of Lesbian dialect and metre, and better editions of the authors quoting Sappho: by Volger in 1810, the first editor to admit in passing that the 'Hymn to Aphrodite' could be expressing love for a woman as much as for a man,[22] by Blomfield in 1814, by Neue in 1827, the last edition before the

---

[17] Ursinus 1568: 2–36, 281–95; the new fragments are frr. 34, 35, 39, 47, 49, 50, 53, 57, 105(a), 110, 113, 115, 117, 119, 123, 124, 132, 142–5, 148, 150, 155, 159, 160, 168A. Contrast DeJean 1989a: 37, who claims that Stephanus 1566 constituted 'the most complete Sappho corpus available before 1733'.

[18] H. Stephanus 1586: 22–47.

[19] Lectius 1614: second part, pp. 96–9.

[20] The new fragments are frr. 32, 37, 38, 40, 45, 116, 126, 129, 147, 149, 151, 158, 162, 164.

[21] Vossius 1684: 115–16.

[22] Volger 1810: 15, 'sed quomodo, quaeso, poetria Venerem ita loquentem inducere potuisset, cum antea agat de fervidissimo ipsius in iuvenem vel puellam amore?' ('but how, I ask, could the poetess have presented Venus speaking in this way, when before she was dealing with her intense love for a young man or girl?').

advent of papyri to add a significant number of previously unnoticed fragments,[23] and by one of the great nineteenth-century German philologists, Theodor Bergk, in 1843.[24] Bergk's second edition a decade later added a few more fragments, containing 120 in all, followed by 50 testimonia;[25] those numbers remained constant in the third and fourth editions of Bergk's collection, which appeared in 1867 and 1882.[26] This outstanding scholarly work is the culmination of a tradition of collecting and editing Sappho's fragments which began in the 1550s. The impact of that tradition is evident if we consider once again the very first poem of Sappho to be published, this time reading it in Bergk's first edition of 1843:

Ποικιλόθρον’, ἀθάνατ’ Ἀφρόδιτα,	Ornate-throned, immortal Aphrodite,
παῖ Δίος, δολόπλοκε, λίccομαί ce,	daughter of Zeus, weaver of wiles, I beg you:
μή μ’ ἄcαιcι μήδ’ ὀνίαιcι δάμνα,	do not conquer my heart, lady,
πότνια, θῦμον.	with pains and anguish.
ἀλλὰ τυῖδ’ ἔλθ’, αἴ ποτα κἀτέρωτα	but come here ever, if according on another occasion 5
τὰc ἔμαc αὔδωc ἀΐοιcα πήλυι	you heard my voice
ἔκλυεc, πάτροc δὲ δόμον λίποιcα	from afar, and, leaving your father’s golden
χρύcιον ἦλθεc	house, you came
ἄρμ’ ὑπαζεύξαιcα· κάλοι δέ c’ ἆγον	after yoking your chariot. Fair swift sparrows
ὤκεεc cτροῦθοι πτέρυγαc μελαίναc	brought you, thickly whirring their dark 10
πύκνα δινεύεντεc ἀπ’ ὠράνω αἴθε-	wings from the sky, through the
ροc διὰ μέccω.	middle of the air.
αἶψα δ’ ἐξίκοντο· τὺ δ’, ὦ μάκαιρα,	And they arrived immediately; and you blessed one,
μειδιάcαιc’ ἀθανάτωι προcώπωι,	smiling with immortal face
ἦρε’, ὄττι δηῦτε πέπονθα κὤττι	asked what it was that I suffered again and for what 15
δηῦτε κάλημι,	I was calling on her again,
κὤττι ἔμωι μάλιcτα θέλω γένεcθαι	and what I want to happen most of all for
μαινόλαι θύμωι· τίνα δηῦτ’ ἀπείθην	my frenzied heart. Which disobedient person
μαῖc ἄγην ἐc càν φιλότατα, τίc c’, ὦ	again do you seek to bring into your friendship, who
Ψαπφ’, ἀδίκηει;	Sappho, is treating you unjustly? 20
καὶ γὰρ αἰ φεύγει, ταχέωc διώξει,	For if she flees, she will soon pursue;
αἰ δὲ δῶρα μὴ δέκετ’, ἀλλὰ δώcει,	if she does not receive gifts, she will give others;
αἰ δὲ μὴ φίλει, ταχέωc φιλήcει	if she does not love, she will swiftly love.

---

[23] These are frr. 33, 37, 40, 46, 52, 104b, 107, 146, 157.
[24] Bergk 1843: 598–632.
[25] Bergk 1853: 664–702.
[26] Bergk 1867: 874–924, 1882: 82–140.

κωὖκ ἐθέλοιϲα.	even if she does not want to.
ἔλθε μοι καὶ νῦν, χαλεπᾶν δὲ λῦϲον	Come to me now also, and release my mind from difficult
ἐκ μεριμνᾶν, ὄϲϲα δέ μοι τελέϲϲαι	worries; and whatever my soul desires
θῦμοϲ ἰμέρρει, τέλεϲον· cὺ δηὖτε	to accomplish, accomplish. You once again
cύμμαχοϲ ἔϲϲο·	be my ally.

This version of the poem shows major improvements on earlier attempts. One stands out: for the first time since antiquity, readers can discern that Sappho's beloved is a woman. The text of line 24 printed here was suggested by Bergk himself in an earlier article;[27] albeit only a conjecture, it nevertheless was instantly persuasive, suiting sense, dialect, and metre, and not straying far from what had been transmitted. The subsequent collation of further manuscripts of Dionysius of Halicarnassus (from whose work the poem is taken) revealed that Bergk's text actually has manuscript support.[28] For over three centuries Sappho's poem had been presumed to be an account of heterosexual passion; since 1843, thanks to Bergk's brilliant editorial work, readers have been able to appreciate the poem as an ode of specifically lesbian desire. As so often, without textual criticism there can be no gender studies.

From 1880 onwards Sappho's corpus has steadily increased thanks to the recovery of fragments of her poetry written on papyrus, parchment, and even one potsherd.[29] From Stephanus until Bergk, the editor's task involved attempting to discover new fragments of Sappho in those surviving ancient authors who quoted her poetry; the majority of these fragments had been discovered by the mid-eighteenth century, but some remained to be found as late as the nineteenth, including by Bergk himself. Bergk died in July 1881, only a few months after Friedrich Blass's publication of the first Sappho papyrus. The great editor nevertheless managed to incorporate it into what would be his final edition of lyric poetry, albeit as an unattributed fragment, since he thought that it was not by Sappho.[30]

In his publication of the papyrus, Blass expressed the wish that others would follow.[31] That wish would be fulfilled, but not for nearly two

---

[27] Bergk 1835: 211; Calder 1986: 146–7, Most 1995: 32 n. 85 ≈ Greene 1996b: 33 n. 79.
[28] Piccolomini 1892: 10.
[29] Casanova 2007: 1–9, FINGLASS ch. 17.
[30] Lyr. Adesp. frr. 56a–b in Bergk 1882: 704–5.
[31] Blass 1880b: 287.

decades. New papyri published in 1898 and 1902 offered substantial frag-
ments of Aeolic poetry, and this time their content permitted no doubt
about Sapphic authorship; new texts, several quite substantial, followed
in 1903, 1913, 1914, 1922, and 1937, with more to follow in succeeding dec-
ades. Editors coped with these succcessive waves of fresh material by pub-
lishing collections of all the papyrus fragments as supplements to Bergk's
edition, which remained unchallenged as the scholarly publication of
choice for the quotation fragments: thus Ernst Diehl's *Supplementum
Lyricum*, new editions of which came out in 1908, 1910, and 1917.

J. M. Edmonds published a new complete edition of Sappho, includ-
ing both papyrus and citation fragments, in 1922. Unfortunately, this edi-
tion was rather too complete, its editor being excessively quick to fill in
the many gaps found in the fragmentary papyrus texts;[32] he referred to
these supplements as 'restorations which, though they are far from being
mere guesses, are only approximations to the truth',[33] an altogether too
self-complimentary description. The volume received a devastating
review from the great papyrologist Edgar Lobel, a key figure in the publi-
cation of the Oxyrhynchus papyri.[34] With biting irony, Lobel describes
Edmonds as 'the fortunate possessor of a pair of eyes which enable him
to discern, sometimes from a mere photograph, what has often deceived
or totally escaped the vision of the most expert decipherers working on
the manuscript itself', and as moreover 'endowed with powers of divina-
tion not ordinarily vouchsafed to humanity'; he further suggests that the
dialect of Edmonds's Sappho is not wholly Aeolic, labelling it 'Triballian'
instead, the name of a barbarous Thracian tribe satirised by Aristophanes.
Lobel described his own preferred approach to editing Sappho in the
preface to his edition:

> But for the caution which I have laid upon myself in handling a text usu-
> ally either fragmentary or corrupt, though it will appear pusillanimous to
> the more swashing spirits among those who may be at the pains of criticiz-
> ing me, I am not at all disposed to apologize, remembering the word of a
> wise king, with which I have steeled myself against the seductive appari-
> tion of Conjecture, that a fool can throw a stone into the Sea of Spain and
> all the wise men in the world not manage to get it out.[35]

The faults in Edmonds's Sappho were quickly recognised by the academic
community; Lobel's Sappho, by contrast, still stands as an enduring and

---

[32] Edmonds 1922a: 140–307.
[33] Edmonds 1922a: viii.
[34] Lobel 1922.
[35] Lobel 1925: v.

influential monument of scholarship, thanks to the prudence with which he supplemented the papyrus fragments edited in that book, and the detailed account given in his introduction of Sappho's transmission and dialect.

In 1955 Edgar Lobel joined forces with Denys Page, Regius Professor of Greek at Cambridge, to publish a fundamental new edition of the fragments of both Sappho and Alcaeus, *Poetarum Lesbiorum Fragmenta*; a corrected reprint of the volume in 1963 incorporated addenda from a papyrus published in 1956, and an affordable reprint of the 1963 edition was published by Sandpiper Books in 1997. For much of her history, Sappho had been linked to Anacreon; setting her alongside Alcaeus, a contemporary poet writing in the same dialect, made much more sense, not least as fragments that could not be safely attributed to either poet, but which on grounds of language were likely to come from one of them, could be included in their own section at the end rather than running the risk of being overlooked entirely. With such distinguished editors, this book looked destined for a long career as the edition of choice for the discerning reader. Yet the austerity of its approach to supplementation, doubtless in reaction to the excessive creativity of Edmonds and earlier editors, made it less useful than it otherwise might have been.

Within a few years Eva-Maria Voigt, Professor (like Wolf before her) at Hamburg, and author (under her maiden name) of an outstanding grammar of the language of Aeolic lyric,[36] was at work on a fresh *editio maior* of Sappho and Alcaeus, which appeared in 1971; despite the publication date, the book seems to have been completed before 1967, since a papyrus published in that year does not make it into her text. Voigt's text, in the words of Martin West, 'is thoroughly prudent, without the gymnosophist tendencies of L<obel>–P<age>: where a reading or supplement is probable she is prepared to print it in the text';[37] three decades after the book's publication, he noted how the book 'ha[d] remained unchallenged as the edition of first recourse'.[38] Voigt's edition includes the testimonia to both poets, and much fuller assistance to the reader than is found in Lobel–Page. Each poem has three critical apparatuses: one setting out the sources for the poem and their readings (since different sources, and different manuscripts of the same source, often disagree), another giving an account of parallel passages for linguistic and literary phenomena found

[36] Hamm 1958.
[37] West 1977: 161–2.
[38] West 2001: 4.

in the poems, and another surveying useful bibliography on each line. The use of Latin made the book accessible to the international scholarly community, if not to the general reader; the only English is on the dust jacket.

Since Voigt, no editions of fundamental importance have appeared, although editorial work has certainly continued. Papyrus fragments published between 1963 (the date of the revised impression of *PLF*) and 1974 inclusive were included in Page's *Supplementum lyricis Graecis*.[39] This book, in combination with either *PLF* or Voigt's edition, once again gave readers easy access to the entirety of Sappho's poetry, at least for a while. The edition published in 1982 by Campbell in the Loeb Classical Library series brought together almost all the fragments then known, with the exception of the smallest;[40] the incorporation of testimonia and an English translation were naturally welcome, but the most welcome thing of all was the replacement of Edmonds's Loeb with a work that scholars, students, and general readers could rely on. Italian editions have subsequently been published by F. Ferrari in 1987 and Aloni in 1997, and a German one by Bagordo in 2009. But these rely on Voigt for their text, rarely including anything not found in her edition, even the later papyri; for instance, Bagordo incorporates the papyrus finds of 2004 but none of the others from 1967 on, even those found in Campbell. A new edition published in 2017 by Neri, with translation by Cinti, is based on a reconsideration of the fragments, though it lacks an apparatus: Neri is at work on a full critical edition. A recent monograph, Benelli 2017, contains detailed analysis of several papyri on the basis of painstaking autopsy.

So half a century after it was completed, and after the publication of many subsequent papyri, not to speak of fresh textual studies of existing poems, Voigt's edition still stands as the most recent fundamental engagement with the text of Sappho. Long out of print, it is rare and expensive, however; the edition by Lobel and Page, by contrast, is more readily available, and that fact, together with (I suspect) the enduring magic of its editors' names, has ensured that despite being even more out of date it is nevertheless still frequently cited. Moreover, neither of these books has the kind of detailed commentary, dealing with textual matters but also with literary interpretation and the social and historical context, that we would expect for a major ancient author; it is curious that Sappho should be less well served in this regard than, say, Lycophron. A

---

[39] Page 1974: S259–261a, S273–312, S476.
[40] See West 1983 for a review.

new edition of Sappho would need to incorporate all the new material that has appeared since Voigt in the 1960s; in the case of fragments already in Voigt, it would need to reconsider all textual points afresh, making full use of a fresh collation of the papyri, improvements in our understanding of Sappho's language, and developments in the editing of classical texts since the 1960s; it would need a detailed introduction and commentary that drew on all good scholarship on Sappho to provide new pathways for better understanding of her poetry and her contexts. As this chapter has shown, we are the inheritors of a long tradition of editing Sappho that has transformed our understanding of her poetry; that tradition urgently needs to be updated if Sappho – all the Sappho that we have – is to be read and appreciated in the years to come.

Further Reading

DeJean 1989a remains central to this topic, as does Most 1995 ≈ Greene 1996b: 11–35; both demonstrate how philological problems and the interpretation of Sappho's life and poetry are intertwined.

Plate 11 'Sappho contemplating her leap' (AD 1500), illustration from *Épîtres d'Ovide* (translation of Ovid's *Heroides*) by Octovien de Saint-Gelais (1468–1502), Paris. Oxford, Balliol College, MS 383 fol. 167v.

Plate 12 *Parnasso* (AD 1509–11), fresco painting by Raphael (1483–1520). Stanza della Segnatura, Vatican Museums, Rome.

Plate 13 *Sappho and Phaon* (AD 1809), painting by Jacques-Louis David (1748–1825). St Petersburg, State Hermitage Museum, inv. GE 5668.

ὅμοι πάλιν λέγειν.ἀκόλουθοι δ' αἱ ἔη καὶ τὰς ἐν αὐτῇ προτιθύσαντας κατα
ειδημόσας.ἀπὸ ποιῶν μὲν ἰδίων ἐμοί γε μάλιστα τουτωνὶ δοκεῖ δ' ὁ χαρακτήρ ἐ
πεξεργάσασθαι ἡ ὁσιόδε.μᾶλον ποιῶν δὲ σαπφὼ καὶ μᾶλ ταύτης ἀνακρέων τε
καὶ σιμωνίδης.ζαγωδοποιῶ ἢ μόνος ὡς ἐπίδης.συγγραφίων δ' ἀκειβῶς μὲν οὐ
λῶς.μᾶλον δὲ τῶν πολλῶν ἔφορός τε Θεόπομπος.ῥητόρων τε ἰσοκράτης.δηλώ
δὲ καὶ ταύτα παρακλείγματα τῆς ἁρμονίας· φωνητῶν μὲν προχειρεισαίμενος
σαπφῶ.ῥητόρων δὲ ἰσοκράτης.ἄρξομαι δὲ ἀπὸ τῆς μελοποιὲ.ποικιλόθρον' ἀθά

ι νατ' ἀφροδίτη, παῖ διὸς δολοπλόκε λίσσομαί σε, μή μ' ἄσαισι μή δ' ἀνίαισι
ι δάμνα πότνια θυμόν· ἀλλὰ τυΐδ' ἔλθ' που κατ' ὄρωτα, τὰς ἐμὰς αὔδως ἀΐοις ἀ
ι πόλας, ἐκλύθ' παῖδὸς δὲ δόμον λιποῖσα χρύσεον ἤλθεθ' ἅρμα ὑπαζ̇ύξασα· κα
ι λοὶ δέ σ' ἀπω, ὠκέθ' σφαθοὶ πέριγας μελαίναθ', πυκνὰ δίηντις πτέρ' ἀπ' ὠρα
ι νῶ· ἤρεος δ' ἄμθὺ πω, αὶ ψ' ἅμ' ὀξίκοντ, τὺ δ' ὧ μάκαιρα, μειδίασις ἀθανάτω
ι προσώπω, ἤρε' ὅττι δ' ἦν, τὸ, πέποθε κ' ἄτι δἤυτε κάλημμι, κ' ὅτι ἐμῶ μάλιστα θί
ι λω γενέαθ, καινόλα θυμῶ· τίνα δ' ἀυτε πειθώμαι σαγηνῦσαι φιλότατά τις σω
ι ψ̇καφαλίκη· κ' τὴ ἐ φὐγει ταχέως διώξει· αἰ δὲ δῶρα μὴ δὲ κετ' ἄλλα δώσει· αἰ
ι δὲ μὴ φιλεῖ, ταχέως φιλήσει, κ' ὠνικὶθέλοις, ἐθέλοιμι κ' νῶ· χαλεπαὶ ἡ λῦσον
ι ἐκμερίμναν.ὅσα δέ μοι τελέσαι, θυμὸς ἱμέρει, τέλεσον σὺ δ' ἄ αὐτά, σύμμαχος.

ταύτης τ' λέξεως ἡ δύ πειακὴ ἡ χάρεις ἐν τῇ ποιι ἐπείᾳ κ̇ λεό
τη τι λέγει τ̇ αρ μονίαν·παρχκεῖ τ̇ ἅ ἀμήλοις τὰ ὀνόματα κ̇ σιωνυφαι̇ κ̇ τὰ
πιλα οἰκειότητας καὶ συζυγίας φισικὰς τῶν γραμμάτων·τὰ γῶ φωνίεντα
τοῖς ἀφώνοις τε κ̇ ἡμιφώνοις σιωμπτετοι μικροῦ δεῖ δι' ὅλης τῆς φώνης· ἐστι
προστάσεθαί τε κ̇ ὑπο τάσεσθαι, ἐμφώνων δὲ πρὸς ἡμίφωκ, κ̇ φωνη
έντων πρὸς ἄμηλα συμπτώσεις αἱ διωσκελεύουσαι τὺς ἤχους, ὀλίγαι τὴν ἐ
σὶν·ἐτων̇ ὄν ὅλην τὴν ἐσθὶ αὐσκασὸ πούμενος, πίντε κ̇ εἴ ἴσως ὅρον ἐν τοῖς τοι
τοῖς ὀνόμασι καὶ ῥήμασι καὶ τοῖς ἄλλοις μυείοις ἡ μιφώνων τε ἀπιλάτων συμπλο
κας τῶν μὴ τελεύσουσον ἀμήλοις κεράννυσθαι·καὶ οὐ δὲ ταύτας ἐπὶ πολὺ βαχύ
ιοῦσις τὴν δύ πειαν·φωνι̇ έντων δὲ παρακβίσεις, τὰ μὲν ἐν τοῖς κώλοις αὐτοῖς
γινομέναθ·ἐπι ἐλάττους ἢ τὸ σαύτατε·τὰ δὲ σιωαπεύσας τὰ κώλαἀμήλοις·
ὀλίγω τιν̇ τούτων πλεῖοσα̇·εἰκότως δὴ γέγονεν ἡ λέξις ἱδεους κ̇ μαλακή τ̇
αρμονίαθ·τῶν ὀνομάτων μηδὲν ἀ ποκυμπτιζούσης τ̇ ν ἤχον·ἰλεῖον δ' αὖ καὶ τὰ
λοιπὰ τῆς σιωθείσαις ταύτης ἰ δεῖματα·καὶ ἀπιλεῖκον ἰδὴ τῶν παραδειγμ
μάτων τοιαῦτα ὄντα οἶκιῶ φημι, εἰμὶ μακρὸς ἔμαλεν ὁ λόγος γενήσεαθ·καὶ
των πλοῖσκς τὴν δόξαν παρέχειν·δίξαι γάρ σοι παντὶ ἄμφ καθ' ἓν ἕκαστον τ̇
ὀθεριβημηκαισν ὑπ' ἐμοῦ κατὰ τὴν προέκθεσι τ̇ χαρακτήρος ἐπιλέγεσθαί τε
καὶ σκοπεῖν ἐδὴ παρακλίγμάτων κατὰ πολὺν δίκαιείαν καὶ σρ λὴν· ἐμὸς δ'
οὐκ ἐγχωρεῖ τ̇τ' θ̇ φιάν·ἀλλ' ἀπὸ χοὶ τῶν λέξαι μόνον ἀσκαιωπος ἃ βούλομαι τοῖς
δυνησομένοις παρακολουθήσαι·εἰδε ἐπι παρακθῷ λέξιν ἀφόρως ἐς τῆν αὐτῆν
κα ποκλααμίον χαρακτήρα·ἰσοκράτους τὸ ῥήθρος ἐπὶ μάλιστα πάντων οἴο
μαι τὴν πεζὴ τῇ λέξει χρωσιμένου,ταύτην ἀκριβείω τὴν ἁρμονίαν· ἔστι δὲ ὁ λέ
ξεις ἐκ τὴ ἀριστφαγητικοῦ ὑδὴ· τ̇ ο Μουδ' ὑμῶν οἴομαι θαυμάζειν ἣν πᾶ ᾠ τε γνώ
μῃ τ̇ χρ̇ ἐπιστειλμ̇ τὴν πλείσθν ἐφιπωισμ̇ τ̇ περ τῆς πόλεις οὐ κινδύ
νοις οὔσης, ἢ σφκλῶς αὐτὴ τῶν πραχμ̇των κα̇ θεσώπον,ἀλλ' οὐ πλέιος κα̇
τελέσεις,ἢ διαισθαιᾶ κεκτημένα,έρήνη δὲ καὶ τὰ πεδὶ τὴν χώρα ἐχούσης,
καὶ τὴ κα̇τὰ θάλατ]αν ἀρχούσησ,ἔτι δὲ συμμάχους ἱ χούσης,πολλοὺς μὲν τὺς
ἑτοίμως ἡ μᾶν̇ ν τι δέη βοηθήσοντας,πολὺ δὲ πλέονο τὺς σιωστάξεις ὑ ποτε
λοως ἱας,καὶ ἐν προσταθόμεσω ποιεῖωπας.ἐν ὑ παρχόντων, ἡμᾶς μὲν αἴ τις

venetis hymnus

PART IV

Receptions

CHAPTER 19

Sappho in Fifth- and Fourth-Century Greek Literature

Lyndsay Coo

Perhaps no writer from classical antiquity has appeared in as many differ-
ent guises as Sappho. The varied accounts of her life and the fragmenta-
tion of her work have combined to produce a figure both alluring and
elusive, whose modern reception is characterised by malleability and
defined by loss. As much as her words, it is the gaps – in our knowledge
of Sappho's biography, and in the remnants of her poetry – that have
shaped the way in which we think about her, allowing readers to fill in
the empty spaces with their own (pre)conceptions.[1] This chapter traces
such questions of Sappho's representation back to antiquity by examining
three moments in her literary reception, in Herodotus, Plato, and
Antiphanes. Spanning the genres of history, philosophy, and comedy,
these authors offer insights into what it meant to represent Sappho at a
time when variant accounts about her life and poetry were already taking
shape. The diverse roles that Sappho plays in the literature of this period
suggest that her tradition was already defined by the ability to assume dif-
ferent, sometimes contradictory, personas. Nonetheless, these three exam-
ples all present her as a figure possessing an unusual authority, in each
case inextricable from her unique status as the canonical female poet.

Sappho the Poetry-Maker

In the second book of his *Histories*, Herodotus turns to Mycerinus' con-
struction of the smallest pyramid at Giza, which 'some Greeks'
(μετεξέτεροι ... Ἑλλήνων, 2.134.1) mistakenly attribute to the famous
hetaira (courtesan) Rhodopis. In fact, Herodotus notes, she lived much

---

[1] The flexibility of Sappho's tradition is much emphasised in scholarship; see e.g. Most 1995 ≈
Greene 1996b: 11–35, Pitts 2002, Yatromanolakis 2007. The entry on Sappho in *Brouillon pour un
dictionnaire des amantes*, translated as *Lesbian Peoples. Material for a Dictionary*, is, famously, a
blank page (Wittig and Zeig 1976: 213 = 1979: 136).

later, during the reign of Amasis, and he goes on to relate this account of her life:[2]

> Rhodopis arrived in Egypt after being brought there by Xanthes of Samos, and having come to follow her profession she was freed at great expense by a Mytilenean man, Charaxus, the son of Scamandronymus and brother of Sappho the poetry-maker (τῆς μουσοποιοῦ). And so Rhodopis was set free and remained in Egypt and, being very alluring, she acquired great wealth – enough for the purposes of being Rhodopis, at any rate, but not so as to arrive at such a pyramid. For it is possible even to this day for anyone who wishes to see a tenth of her wealth; and there is no need to attribute great wealth to her. For Rhodopis desired to leave behind a memorial of herself (μνημήιον ἑωυτῆς) in Greece, by making a work (ποίημα ποιηcαμένη) which no one else had ever come up with or dedicated in a temple, and dedicating this at Delphi as a memorial to herself (μνημόcυνον ἑωυτῆς). And so from a tenth of her wealth she made (ποιηcαμένη) many iron ox-spits, as many as this tithe would allow, and sent them to Delphi. And even today these are piled up behind the altar that the Chians dedicated, opposite the temple itself. And somehow it seems that the courtesans of Naucratis do tend to be alluring. For the woman about whom this story is told became so famous that all Greeks knew full well the name of Rhodopis (οἱ πάντες Ἕλληνες Ῥοδώπιος τὸ οὔνομα ἐξέμαθον). And later a woman whose name was Archidice became an object of song throughout Greece, but she was less talked about than the other. When Charaxus, after freeing Rhodopis, returned home to Mytilene, Sappho taunted him violently in song (ἐν μέλεϊ Cαπφὼ πολλὰ κατεκερτόμηcέ μιν).[3] But now that is enough about Rhodopis.

Later sources record that Sappho wrote songs about her brother's affair with a Naucratite woman named Doricha, and according to Strabo this was the same person that others called Rhodopis.[4] Many discussions have aimed at reconciling the information in Herodotus with that found in other accounts of Sappho's family, focusing on questions such as the identity of Rhodopis/Doricha, how to deal with the chronological disparity (with Sappho generally thought to have died around the start of

---

[2] Herodotus 2.135 (fr. 202).

[3] μιν could refer to Rhodopis rather than Charaxus, but the sentence structure makes this much the less likely option; see Lardinois 2016: 170.

[4] Strabo 17.1.33 (fr. 202); cf. P.Oxy. 1800 fr. 1 (test. 1), Athenaeus, *Scholars at Dinner* 13.596bd (test. 15, preserving Posidippus 122 A–B), (Pseudo-?)Ovid, *Heroides* 15.63–8 (test. 16). The name 'Doricha' has been restored at frr. 7.1, 9.17, and 15.11, the last being (*pace* Lidov 2002: 203, 2016: 79) the most plausible: see Yatromanolakis 2007: 330–2, Burris, Fish, and Obbink 2014: 16, Lardinois 2016: 171–3.

Amasis' reign), and whether Herodotus' source was Sappho's own poetry.[5] Such questions are important but have been treated thoroughly elsewhere; this discussion focuses instead on analysing Herodotus' digression on its own terms, and will try to establish what role the reference to Sappho plays within the wider concerns of his narrative.[6]

The first occurrence of Sappho's name is when Charaxus is introduced as 'the son of Scamandronymus and brother of Sappho the poetry-maker'. Men were not usually identified in relation to their female family members, and so this citation highlights her unusual status and fame: Charaxus, not his sister, is the one who requires glossing. Sappho appears alongside the earliest known instance of the word μουϲοποιόϲ ('poetry-maker'), and this epithet lays the ground for the reoccurrence of her name at the end of the passage, where she rebukes Charaxus ἐν μέλεϊ ('in song'). Herodotus thus bookends the story of Rhodopis with two instances of naming Sappho, both times foregrounding her ability to commemorate events through poetry.

By concluding with a reference to Sappho's abusive song, Herodotus positions her poetry within his narrative as proof for Charaxus' actions, just as he cites the iron spits still visible at Delphi as proof for the correct valuation of Rhodopis' estate. The parallelism of these two types of evidence is strengthened through the association of both women with the language of 'making' (ποιεῖν): Sappho μουϲοποιόϲ makes poetry, and Rhodopis, in commissioning her memorial, is described as ποίημα ποιηϲαμένη.[7] The song of Sappho thus becomes a poetic counterpart to the material evidence of the spits, and Herodotus illustrates his own ability to draw accurate conclusions from both types of material.

Sappho's song fits into this episode's wider exploration of how evidence for the past can become distorted and neglected over time. Herodotus begins by relating the belief of 'some Greeks' that Rhodopis was responsible for the construction of the pyramid, an error that he finds incredible: 'they seem to me to speak without even knowing who Rhodopis was'

---

[5] Page 1955: 48–51, Di Benedetto 1982: 226–30, Lloyd 1988: III 86, Lidov 2002, Kivilo 2010: 175–7. Herodotus' tale has received renewed attention in the light of the publication of the Brothers Poem (Obbink 2014a: 32; the Herodotean passage is mentioned in numerous chapters in Bierl and Lardinois 2016); but for a sceptical approach to the relationship between the two, see Bär 2016: 10–13.

[6] For this approach, see Kurke 1999: 220–7, Yatromanolakis 2007: 312–37, Beecroft 2010: 129–43, Raaflaub 2016: 127–32.

[7] Yatromanolakis 2007: 320.

(2.134.2). He explains how Rhodopis determined the form of her own memorial (μνημήιον/μνημόσυνον ἑωυτῆς), and that she was universally famous. And yet, despite this, she was unable to control her biographical tradition: Mycerinus' pyramid is still misinterpreted as that of Rhodopis, and while all Greeks may know her name, some Greeks do not even know who she really was. The attempts of both Mycerinus and Rhodopis to attain accurate self-memorialisation are shown to be unsuccessful, and these failures contrast with the role that Sappho plays within Herodotus' narrative, with her implicit authority in preserving the 'true' story of Charaxus.

Throughout this tale we see Herodotus' interest in the value of different forms of evidence: the pyramid, the ox-spits, the songs composed about Rhodopis and Archidice, and the lyrics of Sappho may all be read (or misread) to uncover the facts of the past. Herodotus' demonstration of his ability to interpret such data correctly relies on his construction of Sappho's lyric as an authoritative source. Like the tangible proof of the ox-spits, the mere fact of the song's existence – at least within the world of the story – is sufficient evidence for the veracity of his account. Sappho thus stands in contrast to Rhodopis as a woman able to control the facts relating to her own life, in this case through the accurate testimony of her song. In this, our earliest direct literary reference to Sappho herself, we find the first of many moments in her ancient reception where she is characterised by the authority of her poetry. In Herodotus' tale, she is a poet of invective; in our next example, we will see Sappho in her more familiar role as a poet of *erôs*.

The Beautiful Sappho

In Plato's *Phaedrus*, the young man of that name enthuses over a speech by the orator Lysias arguing that it is better for the beloved to gratify a non-lover than a lover. When Phaedrus insists to Socrates that no one could possibly speak better on the topic, his friend's reply is that he cannot agree without being refuted by 'the wise (coφoí) men and women of old who have spoken and written about these things'; their conversation continues (235cd):

| PHAEDRUS: | Who are they? And where have you heard anything better than this? |
| SOCRATES: | Right now I am unable to say, but it is evident that I have heard something, either from the beautiful Sappho |

(Cαπφοῦϲ τῆϲ καλῆϲ) or the wise Anacreon or from one of the prose-writers. What grounds do I have for saying this? Why, my friend, I sense that my bosom is full and that I could make another speech on this topic, different and no worse [than Lysias]. Conscious of my own ignorance, I know perfectly well that I have come up with none of these things myself, but there remains the possibility, I think, that I have been filled up through my ears by the flowing streams of another, like a pitcher; but again, owing to my stupidity, I have forgotten how and from whom I heard it.

At Phaedrus' insistence, Socrates goes on to deliver a speech of his own on the superiority of the non-lover, but then, in what he terms his 'palinode', proceeds to argue at length for the reverse. In this second speech, Socrates expounds on his theories of divine love: both the lover and the beloved (so long as they are philosophically inclined) are able, through recollection of the Form of beauty, to transcend their desire for sex and turn instead to the practice of philosophy.

The well-known hostility towards poets that Plato attributes to Socrates elsewhere in his writings raises several questions here: to what extent should the apparent praise of Sappho and Anacreon at 235c be understood as ironic or sincere, and, more generally, how are we to interpet the relationship between erotic lyric and the ideas about *erôs* presented in the *Phaedrus*?[8] Criticism may be implied by the deliberate vagueness of the reference, with Socrates' uncertainty over the source of his proposed speech and his claim to have been filled up like a water vessel. The latter is a gentle mockery of Phaedrus' uncritical enthusiasm for Lysias, and also recalls the unflattering portrait in Plato's *Ion* of the rhapsode as merely a passive receptacle for poetic inspiration. The picture is complicated, however, by the many lyric echoes in Socrates' second speech, itself inspired by the palinode of Stesichorus (243a = fr. 91a Finglass), where he repeatedly employs the established language and imagery of erotic poetry to convey his ideas about divine love. Even his central philosophical concept, the celebrated image of

---

[8] For the use of Sappho in the *Phaedrus*, see Fortenbaugh 1966, duBois 1985: 99–100, 1995: 85–8, Nightingale 1995: 157–62, H. Foley 1998, Pender 2007, 2011, M. Johnson 2012: 19–21, Capra 2014: 69–87, 2019. This is the only mention of Sappho in the Platonic corpus, although an ancient epigram naming her as the tenth Muse (*Greek Anthology* 9.506 = test. 60) was spuriously attributed to Plato.

the soul as a winged chariot drawn by two horses, may be related to erotic motifs found in the lyric poets Sappho, Anacreon, Theognis, and Ibycus.[9]

The most striking direct correspondence with Sappho's poetry occurs when Socrates describes the experience of the lover gazing at his beloved, a process by which he may begin to recollect the Form of beauty (251ab):

> whenever he sees a godlike face which is a good imitation of beauty, or some bodily form, first he shivers and then something of that fear comes over him, and then, as he gazes on, he reveres him like a god … And as he looks at him, a change comes over him from the shivering, and sweat and unfamiliar heat grips him. For as he receives the emanation of beauty through his eyes, he heats up …

The parallels have long been noted between this passage and Sappho's famous depiction of *erôs* at fr. 31.7–14:

> When I look at you for a moment, I am
> no longer able to speak
> but my tongue is broken and a delicate
> fire runs straight away beneath my skin,
> in my eyes there is no sight,
> my ears fill with humming,
> cold sweat pours from me and trembling
> takes hold of me completely

The *Phaedrus* employs recognisable motifs from Sappho and the other lyric poets – the combination of viewing the beloved and experiencing heat, sweat, and trembling – but puts them to different use. Here, the primary effect of beauty and its corresponding heat is not on the body of the lover, but on his soul.[10] Socrates goes on to explain how, moistened and warmed by the sight of beauty, the lover's soul begins to regrow the feathers and wings that will eventually enable its movement upwards towards contemplation of the Forms.

Even if Sappho's vocalisation of the erotic experience stops short of addressing the soul, her language effectively captures the overwhelming sensation caused by perception of the beloved. For Socrates' speech to

---

[9] Sappho fr. 1.8–13; Pender 2007: 20–7.
[10] See e.g. G. R. F. Ferrari 1987: 154 on 'the radically different way in which Socrates relates the symptoms to the sufferer'; but cf. H. Foley 1998: 68, who argues that 'for both Plato and Sappho erotics involves far more than the body'.

communicate the transformative effect of viewing beauty, Plato can only resort to the lofty and thrilling effects already codified by the erotic language of the lyric poets. The act of naming Sappho and Anacreon thus conjures up an established lyric mode of writing about the experience of *erôs* against which, and through the language of which, Socrates can go on to define his own ideas about divine love. At the same time as it expounds a theory of *erôs* quite different from that of Sappho and Anacreon, the Platonic text seems to acknowledge the impossibility, and indeed the undesirability, of writing on this theme without recourse to the essential and effective tropes of the lyric poets.

The antipathy towards poets demonstrated elsewhere in Plato is to some extent present in the *Phaedrus*, which places poets sixth (out of nine) in the hierarchy of reincarnated souls, above only farmers and craftsmen, sophists and demagogues, and tyrants (248e). Nonetheless, even as it highlights the limitations of using Sappho's poetry for philosophical understanding, the dialogue evinces sincere respect for the power of her writing, acknowledging her as 'the beautiful' for her authoritative poetic expertise on the relationship between beauty and *erôs*.[11] Plato thus invokes Sappho as one of the original authors of a cultural lexicon able to articulate the connection between sight, beauty, memory, and desire central to his own philosophical project.

Sappho, Woman of Letters

Sappho became a particularly popular figure on the ancient comic stage. The earliest known comedy entitled *Sappho* was by the fifth-century playwright Ameipsias, and in the fourth century comedies of that name are attested for Amphis, Antiphanes, Diphilus, Ephippus, and Timocles. Little is known about the plot of any of these works with the exception of Diphilus' *Sappho*, which portrayed the poets Archilochus and Hipponax as rival suitors of Sappho (fr. 71 *PCG*) and included a sympotic scene (fr. 70). An ancient biographical tradition told that Sappho died by leaping from the Leucadian rock out of unrequited love for a local ferryman named Phaon (fr. 211(a)); she may therefore have featured in plays entitled *Phaon* by Plato comicus and Antiphanes, *Leucadia* by Alexis, Amphis, Diphilus, and Menander, and *Leucadios* by Antiphanes. Even if she did not appear as a speaking character, Sappho could be invoked as

---

[11] Pender 2007, 2011.

an example of ill-fated love, as in Menander's *Leucadia* (fr. 1.1–4 Austin = test. 23):

> where it is said that Sappho first,
> chasing the arrogant Phaon,
> in her frenzied desire, flung herself from the rocks
> that can be seen from far away.

The presence in these plays of several potential lovers of Sappho has often been taken to indicate that comedy stereotyped her as sexually promiscuous, and that this had a decisive influence in shaping her later reception.[12] For example, it is often assumed that salacious details in Sappho's biography must have originated in comedy, such as the *Suda*'s claim that she married a rich husband named Cercylas (from κέρκος, 'tail', slang for 'penis') from the island of Andros ('Man').[13] However, others have rightly emphasised the paucity of the evidence, arguing that we cannot say much for certain about the comic portrayal of Sappho beyond the mere fact of her popularity as a character.[14]

The best-preserved comic appearance of Sappho – indeed, her most extensive literary representation to survive from this period – does not concern amorous adventures, but rather offers an intriguing exploration of her relationship to both private and political discourse in the fourth century. In the tenth book of the *Scholars at Dinner* (early third century AD), Athenaeus turns to the topic of riddles and offers a series of examples taken from comedy, including the following from Antiphanes:

> In *Sappho*, Antiphanes represents the poet herself as posing riddles in this manner, while someone tries to solve them, as follows. For she says:
>
> 'There is a female being that keeps her children safe in her womb;[15]
> despite being voiceless, they raise a resounding cry
> over the swell of the sea and over the whole mainland,
> to whichever mortals they like, and it's possible for those not present
> to hear them; they possess a deaf sense of hearing.'
>
> The man trying to solve it says this:

---

[12] See Lardinois 1989: 22 (the comic Sappho as an 'extreme heterosexual'), Most 1995: 17 = Greene 1996b: 14 ('a favourite stage figure . . . but one who exemplified insatiable heterosexual promiscuity'), Kivilo 2010: 190 ('she was probably treated in these plays as a stock-character of a lascivious woman with many partners'), duBois 2015: 90 ('Giving Sappho many male lovers seems to have been one of the great jokes of the Athenian comic writers of the classical age').

[13] *Suda* c 107 = test. 2.

[14] Yatromanolakis 2007: 293–9.

[15] This phrase might also be translated as 'in the folds of her robe'.

'The being of which you speak is a city (πόλιϲ),
and the children that she rears inside herself are the rhetors.
These with their shouting draw over here overseas
revenues from Asia and from Thrace.
And while they're dealing it out
and constantly reproaching each other,
the people sit nearby and neither hear nor see anything.'

(SAPPHO): '... for how, father,[16] might a rhetor be voiceless?'

(B): 'If he's convicted three times of transgressing the law.
... and yet I thought I'd figured out exactly
what you said. But tell me.'

And then he portrays Sappho as solving the riddle like this:

'The female being, then, is an epistle (ἐπιϲτολή),
and the children that she carries around inside herself are letters.
Although they are voiceless, they speak to those far away,
to whomever they want. And if someone else happens
to stand nearby when it is being read, he will not hear.'

Antiphanes fr. 194 *PCG* (Athenaeus, *Scholars at Dinner* 10.450e–451b = test. 25)

This tantalising passage has generated much discussion.[17] The opposition of gender is clear: the public, male world of politics represented by the rhetors and the male speaker conflicts with the private, female world represented by epistolary writing and Sappho. Scholars have emphasised how Sappho's unusual status as a woman writer makes her ideally placed to pose a riddle that relies on the identification of maternity with literary creation, while the description of silent reading has been understood as an allegory for interpreting Sappho's own poetry. We might also see a model for Sappho-as-riddler in her fr. 16, where the priamel recalls the form of a 'superlative riddle', a riddle which poses the question of what person or thing possesses a given quality to the highest degree (in this case: what is most beautiful?).[18] Yet there has been a strong tendency to excerpt the text and interpret it as an isolated fragment, rather than to examine it within the context of the other comic riddles quoted by

---

[16] The man is not necessarily Sappho's biological father, since the term could be used as a respectful address to an older man. It was also used by symposiasts, and by *hetairai* ('courtesans') to their clients: Konstantakos 2000: 161–2.

[17] Williamson 1995: 15–16, Prins 1996: 46–8 (~ 1999: 25–7), Konstantakos 2000: 157–80, Martin 2001: 73–4, Pitts 2002: 116–28, Olson 2007: 200–3, Yatromanolakis 2007: 300–12, Ceccarelli 2013: 244–57, Hauser 2016: 148–50.

[18] Konstantakos 2004: 125–7 (with n. 80 for other examples in archaic lyric).

Athenaeus. These offer a glimpse into the wider tendencies of riddle-composition in comedy, and hence into what it is that makes this particular example distinct. Although this chapter is interested in the fourth-century BC perspective of Antiphanes rather than the early third-century AD concerns of the *Scholars at Dinner*, the particular significance of Sappho's riddle is thrown into sharper relief when set against some other examples selected by Athenaeus.

Athenaeus begins this section by stating (10.448b): 'But let us first inquire as to the definition of a riddle, and what Cleobulina of Lindus put forward in her *Riddles*.' Cleobulina was the daughter of Cleobulus, one of the Seven Sages renowned for both posing and solving riddles, and was known in antiquity for her skill as a creator of riddles in hexameter verse. She appeared in comedy: Cratinus wrote a *Cleobulinas* (nothing is known of the plot, but the title suggests a group of riddle-posing women), and Alexis a *Cleobulina*. Athenaeus then quotes an exchange from Alexis' *Sleep*, in which an older woman puts a riddle to a younger one (10.449de = fr. 242 *PCG*). Later, immediately following his citation of Antiphanes' *Sappho*, he recalls an example from Diphilus' *Theseus* (451bc = fr. 49 *PCG*), in which three Samian girls at the Adonia festival give successive answers to the riddle proposed by one of them, 'What is the strongest thing of all?', with the final, and presumably best, answer being 'a penis'.

We can thus fit Antiphanes' Sappho into a wider pattern of comic female riddlers, but it is striking that in these last two instances, and in Athenaeus' later example of Callias' *Alphabet Tragedy* (discussed below), the riddles are both proposed and answered by women. Sappho's posing of the riddle to a male interlocutor creates a different kind of context, activating a gendered confrontation not only between the content of the two solutions, but between the views and experiences of the interlocutors. One of the few real-world situations in which women might propose riddles to men was in the case of *hetairai* and their male clients at the symposium. It has been suggested, and is certainly plausible, that this was the setting of Antiphanes' scene and that Sappho was represented as a courtesan posing a riddle to a client.[19] Sappho would then intrude into the male realm of the symposium, just as the answer to her riddle replaces the male-ruled *polis* with the female world of the epistle.

---

[19] Konstantakos 2000: 162–3, Olson 2007: 201.

Sappho's riddle maintains a higher tone and has more complex impli-
cations than many others cited in the *Scholars at Dinner*. This is particu-
larly noticeable since key elements of her riddle echo other examples
quoted by Athenaeus. The solution involves correct identification of both
the 'female being' (both ἡ πόλις and ἡ ἐπιστολή are grammatically femi-
nine) and the 'children' whom she nourishes. The 'parentage' of inani-
mate objects is a very common feature in riddles: just prior to this
passage, Athenaeus cites one from Antiphanes' *The Sex-Fiend*, which
refers to a cooking pot as 'baked in a different chamber of its mother' and
'pregnant' with food (10.449b = fr. 55 *PCG*). However, the association of
pregnancy and *letters* is found in only one other classical text, which is
also quoted by Athenaeus in this section of the *Scholars at Dinner*. This is
Callias' comic *Alphabetic Tragedy*, a play whose chorus consisted of
twenty-four women, each representing a different letter of the alphabet.
In the relevant passage preserved by Athenaeus (10.454a = *PCG* test. 7), a
woman states that she is pregnant and describes the name of her baby
through a riddle spelling out the letters ΨΩ. It is evident from her open-
ing line ('For I'm pregnant, ladies; but, friends, out of embarrassment I
will tell you the name of the baby by spelling it'), as well as Athenaeus'
claim that the solution to her riddle is ἀκολαστότερον ('rather crude'),
that she resorts to this in order to avoid directly naming something that
is vulgar and shameful. A plausible conjecture is that her 'baby' Ψώ is
actually flatulence (cf. ψῶα, 'putrid stench').[20] The play seems also to
have had some connection to the idea of Sappho. In another scene, a
character – very probably female – instructs a group of women on how to
pronounce the vowels (Athenaeus, *Scholars at Dinner* 10.453f–454a =
PCG test. 7), and Gagné has suggested that even if this teacher is not
Sappho herself, she is modelled on facets of Sappho's traditional charac-
terisation.[21] The *Alphabetic Tragedy*, with its similar combination of a
female riddler and the association of pregnancy with letters, thus offers a
striking contrast to Antiphanes' *Sappho*. While Callias' woman employs
her riddle to obfuscate a humiliating bodily secret, Antiphanes' Sappho
celebrates the maternal body as a metaphor for the creative power of the
epistle. This contrast between the crude and dignified is further illus-
trated by another element of Sappho's riddle, the paradox of the shouting
yet speechless babies. This finds a parallel in a riddle just cited by

[20] Ruijgh 2001: 327.
[21] Gagné 2013: 314–16.

Athenaeus (10.449e–450a) from Eubulus' *Sphinx-Carion* (fr. 106 *PCG*) where another speaker also asks what is 'tongueless, but speaking'; here, the answer is 'an anus'.

In Sappho's riddle, the solution is not vulgar, nor banal, nor merely ingenious. It demonstrates her intellectual superiority over her male interlocutor, who misses a fundamental element of the riddle in his answer.[22] While his answer veers in a more obviously comic direction, with the butt of his joke being both the ineffective rhetors and the people who neither see nor hear them, Sappho's solution returns us to an apparently serious reflection on the potency of the written and read word. By focusing on women's bodily experience – the *grammata* ('letters') are nurtured and carried within the maternal 'body' of the epistle – Sappho evokes a private and feminine form of writing, contrasting its silent vitality with the loud but empty brawling of the male rhetors. Leitao has shown that the metaphor of male pregnancy appears suddenly in the 420s, when we find an explosion, especially in drama, of the metaphor of men 'giving birth' to ideas, laws, and poetry; the female experience of childbirth is appropriated to express male creative potential.[23] Sappho's riddle can thus be seen as an attempt not only to reclaim for women the state of pregnancy, but also to claim the creativity of thought and language with which it has been metaphorically connected. If Sappho's answer itself seems apolitical, in the sense that it concerns the private world of the epistle rather than the public world of the *polis*, the construction of Antiphanes' scene, bringing the two realms of experience into tension with one another, is anything but. The second answer is spoken by a woman, concerns a 'female' object, and feminises the world of the epistle. Male knowledge of the *polis* is here outwitted by female understanding of the creative power of letters.

Despite our ignorance of the context of this scene, we can see that Antiphanes' Sappho possesses an authoritative stature, expressed through the dignified and thoughtful construction of her riddle. In her role as female riddler she may recall the figure of Cleobulina, but the content of her riddle is carefully matched to the specifics of the construction of Sappho as a historical figure. As a poet, Sappho's skill explains her witty understanding of the power of words; as a female poet, she deploys

---

[22] The man's answer is not 'wrong' (for both answers as simultaneously valid, see Ceccarelli 2013: 250–1), but the power relations inherent in riddle scenes tend to position the riddler as superior to the recipient; see Potamiti 2015: 143–51.

[23] Leitao 2012: 100–2.

metaphors of maternity as literary creation; as a female poet of immense renown, she is uniquely placed to pose this riddle's particular challenge to the world of male experience. Antiphanes' scene thus offers an intriguing portrait of the artist as a figure embedded within explorations of male and female authority, public and private discourse, and poetic creation and dissemination.

Citing Sappho

In antiquity, so many and such contrasting accounts of Sappho circulated that some writers solved the discrepancy by concluding that there were actually two different women of the same name: one a poet, the other a *hetaira* ('courtesan').[24] The three texts analysed in this chapter have sketched some of these Sapphic variations. In the *Phaedrus*, we find Sappho in her best-known role as a poet of *erôs*, whereas both Herodotus' tale of how she attacked Charaxus in song and Antiphanes' comic Sappho besting her male interlocutor present a writer of confrontational verse whose poetic voice could engage directly, publicly, and successfully with the world of men. These texts demonstrate the variety of her receptions by showing that she could be characterised not only as one of the original voices of erotic lyric, but also as a blame poet or riddler, while still remaining recognisably Sappho.[25] Yet across these divergent accounts we can discern a similar underlying methodology on the part of the authors. In each case, the inherent authority – factual, erotic, or intellectual – associated with the persona and poetry of Sappho is crucial for the role that she plays within the text. To cite Sappho is thus to mobilise her name as a recognised shorthand for an authoritative system of poetic language.

These are selected accounts out of a vast cultural reception, and other writers of this period emphasised different aspects of her tradition: the Sappho who attacks her brother over his unseemly love for a courtesan may seem incongruous with the love-crazed Sappho leaping from the Leucadian rocks. Yet these sources are three important points on the spectrum of her representation, as the earliest literary reference to Sappho, her sole extant mention in Plato, and the most substantial portrayal to survive from comedy. All offer suggestive insights into what it

---

[24] Nymphodorus of Syracuse, *FGrHist* 572 F 6, Aelian, *Historical Miscellany* 12.19 (test. 4); Most 1995: 17–19 ≈ Greene 1996b: 15–16, KIVILO pp. 12, 17.

[25] For iambic themes in Sappho, see Rosenmeyer 2006, Dale 2011a: 51–5, Martin 2016, STEINER.

could mean to represent Sappho, and serve as testament to her unique status and rich versatility, characterised by both contradiction and continuity.

Further Reading

For the early reception of Sappho, the most extensive and detailed study is Yatromanolakis 2007; pp. 287–361 focus on fifth-century and later writers. For Sappho's reception in the three genres covered in this chapter, see Lidov 2002 (on Herodotus), H. Foley 1998, Pender 2007, 2011, Capra 2014: 69–87, 2019 (on Plato's *Phaedrus*), Ceccarelli 2013: 244–57 (on comedy).

CHAPTER 20

Sappho and Hellenistic Poetry

Richard Hunter

Remembering Sappho

I begin from three Hellenistic testimonia to Sappho's life and poetry:

(1) ἀφ᾽ οὗ Cαπφὼ ἐγ Μιτυλήνης εἰc Cικελίαν ἔπλευcε φυγοῦcα [ἄρχο]ν-
τοc Ἀθήνηcιν μὲν Κριτίου τοῦ προτέρου, ἐν Cυρακούccαιc δὲ τῶν
γαμόρων κατεχόντων τὴν ἀρχήν.

From the time when Sappho sailed in exile [or 'in flight'] from
Mytilene to Sicily [. . . years], when the earlier Kritias was archon at
Athens,[1] and at Syracuse the Gamoroi held office. (Parian Marble A36
Rotstein (test. 5))

(2) Naucratis too produced famous *hetairai* ('courtesans') who were
exceptionally beautiful, including Doricha, who became a lover of
Sappho's brother Charaxus when he sailed to Naucratis for trade;[2] in
her poems the lovely Sappho abuses (διαβάλλει) Doricha for having
taken a great deal from Charaxus. Herodotus, however, calls her
Rhodopis (2.134–5 = test. 9, fr. 202), being unaware that this is a differ-
ent person from Doricha ... Posidippus composed the following epi-
gram on Doricha ...

Δωρίχα, ὀcτέα μὲν cὰ πάλαι κόνιc ἦν ὅ τε δεcμὸc
    χαίτηc ἥ τε μύρων ἔκπνοοc ἀμπεχόνη,
ἧι ποτε τὸν χαρίεντα περιcτέλλουcα Χάραξον
    cύγχρουc ὀρθρινῶν ἧψαο κιccυβίων.
Cαπφῶιαι δὲ μένουcι φίληc ἔτι καὶ μενέουcιν
    ὠιδῆc αἱ λευκαὶ φθεγγόμεναι cελίδεc
οὔνομα cὸν μακαριcτόν, ὃ Ναύκρατιc ὧδε φυλάξει
    ἔcτ᾽ ἂν ἴηι Νείλου ναῦc ἐφ᾽ ἁλὸc πελάγη.

---

[1] The date is a few years either side of 600 BC.
[2] Strabo 17.1.33 (fr. 202), a passage which seems to share a source with Athenaeus, *Scholars at Dinner*
13.596bc (test. 15, if it is not a source itself), reports that Charaxus traded Lesbian wine in
Naucratis.

Doricha, your bones have long been dust, and the band for your hair and the shawl which breathes out perfume with which you once enfolded the lovely Charaxus, skin on skin, and took hold of the wine-cups at dawn. Sappho's white columns of her dear song, however, still remain and will remain; they speak your name and make it celebrated. Naucratis here will keep it safe as long as a ship sails out from the Nile over the stretches of the sea. (Athenaeus, *Scholars at Dinner* 13.596bd (test. 15 = Posidippus 122 A–B))[3]

(3) Contemporary with [Alcaeus and Pittacus] was Sappho, an extraordinary person (θαυμαστόν τι χρῆμα): in all of recorded history, I know of no woman who could rival Sappho, in even the slightest degree, as far as poetry goes. (Strabo 13.2.3 (test. 7))

For literate Greeks of the Hellenistic age, as for the Romans who followed, the very idea of Sappho creates θαῦμα 'wonder';[4] she is almost a τέρας, a phenomenon defying the normal parameters in which we understand the world. Pseudo-Longinus, author of *On the Sublime*, another critic apparently poised, like Strabo, between Greece and Rome, also identifies θαῦμα as the appropriate reaction to Sappho's art in what was perhaps her most frequently echoed poem in antiquity, φαίνεταί μοι κῆνος.[5] The sources of our wonder, in this ancient view, are several. First, and most obviously, Sappho was a woman; there is a significant corpus of Hellenistic and later epigrams which celebrates her poetry, but the fact she was a woman, perhaps indeed the 'female Homer', is almost always foregrounded.[6] She was, however, not just a female poet, but one whose poetry had survived in considerable quantity, far greater than it is easy for us to imagine today;[7] that sense of wondrous survival and of Sappho's presence 'still among us' is another leitmotif of the poems about her.[8] In part, this is presumably a transference to poems about Sappho of what was very likely a repeated motif of her poetry, namely the survival of

---

[3] There are serious problems of text and interpretation in this poem, but I hope that they do not impede the relatively simple use to which it is put here. For a recent interpretation, see Bing 2018: 157–63.

[4] Strabo's θαυμαστόν τι χρῆμα is usually underplayed as being, as indeed it is, an example of a not uncommon colloquial periphrasis in Hellenistic prose (so Bergson 1967: 105, followed by Radt on Strabo *ad loc.*, VII 525); here, however, the sense of 'wonder' is important.

[5] Fr. 31, Pseudo-Longinus, *On the Sublime* 10.3; cf. below, pp. 284–8.

[6] Rosenmeyer 1997: 133–6.

[7] For the extent of Sappho's poetry and the form of the Alexandrian edition, see PRAUSCELLO.

[8] Cf. 'Sappho's white columns of her dear song, however, still remain and will remain' in Posidippus above, Dioscorides, *Greek Anthology* 7.407.9–10 (test. 58), etc.

poetry after death, a survival which grants κλέος ἄφθιτον, 'immortal renown', to the poet no less than to the subjects of his or her song, whether that be an Achilles or even a Doricha, as in Posidippus' epigram. Aelius Aristides (second century AD) claimed to know a poem or poems in which Sappho said that 'the Muses had made her fortunate and blessed, and that there would be no forgetting of her even after death',[9] and we can sense this confidence in four lines which survive in more than one ancient quotation:

κατθάνοισα δὲ κείσηι οὐδέ ποτα μναμοσύνα σέθεν
ἔσσετ' οὐδὲ †ποκ'† ὕστερον· οὐ γὰρ πεδέχηις βρόδων
τὼν ἐκ Πιερίας, ἀλλ' ἀφάνης κἀν Ἀίδα δόμωι
φοιτάσηις πεδ' ἀμαύρων νεκύων ἐκπεποταμένα.

In death you will lie and there will never be any memory of you in future time, for you have no share in the roses from Pieria. Unseen in the house of Hades once you have flown away, you will flitter about with the shadowy dead. (Sappho fr. 55)

Whether or not the object of Sappho's scorn was indeed unnamed in the poem from which this fragment comes, the nature of the survival of these verses has certainly ensured the truth of Sappho's prophecy; if it is true (cf. Athenaeus cited above) that Sappho 'abused Doricha' in her poems, then she has also, perhaps ironically, as Posidippus realised, made the *hetaira*'s name 'celebrated'.[10]

The motif of the eternal survival of poetry is not, of course, restricted to Sappho and her *Nachleben*. It is, for example, central to Callimachus' funerary poem for Heraclitus (*Epigr.* 2 Pfeiffer = *HE* 1203–8), which shares more than one motif with Posidippus' poem on Doricha,[11] allowing the suspicion that Callimachus' poem too may be indebted to Sapphic motifs. Nevertheless, the motif of the survival to the present day of poetic 'immortal daughters' may have particular force in Sappho's case.[12] Her poetry produces an overwhelming sense of the poet's almost

[9] *Oration* 28.51 = fr. 193; BOWIE p. 308.
[10] Cf. Christian 2015: 63–4, who sees a direct allusion in Posidippus' poem to fr. 55, an allusion pointed by the naming of Doricha with the first word of Posidippus' epigram. These Sapphic verses seem also to resonate (along with Asclepiades, *Greek Anthology* 7.11 = 942–5 *HE* and Callimachus fr. 1 Harder) in Antipater of Sidon, *Greek Anthology* 7.713 (560–7 *HE*) about Erinna (often associated with or compared to Sappho).
[11] The Callimachean parallel is cited by Austin–Bastianini in their edition.
[12] Dioscorides, *Greek Anthology* 7.407.10 (test. 58).

physical presence through her voice, that sense that Pseudo-Longinus describes as evoked by fr. 31 and that Catullus too captures in his translation of that same poem, addressed to the 'Lesbian woman' (poem 51); this sense of presence cannot be divorced, in antiquity any more than now, from the fact that Sappho was a woman. For readers of poetry after the classical period it was, above all, the style of a famous poet, that is the audience's knowledge of, and familiarity with, a 'classical' voice, still existing and repeatedly ventriloquised, which brought the writers of the past 'close' to that audience; in antiquity there was no more distinctive or individual poetic voice than that of Sappho, even within the markedly personal world of archaic lyric. Whoever originally chose to place first in the 'Alexandrian edition' the poem which we call Sappho fr. 1, the prayer to 'elaborately throned immortal Aphrodite', in which Sappho recalls a previous epiphany of the goddess to her, certainly recognised the power of that signature voice.[13]

Sappho's powerful presence is partly acknowledged and partly deflected by the echoes and reworkings of her poetry with which Hellenistic poetry is filled and which this chapter will briefly survey.[14] Virtually every new papyrus of her poetry reveals Sapphic echoes lurking unnoticed in the high poetry of the third century BC and beyond, and this too is an area where there seems room for unprovable speculation. It is, for example, hardly rash to suspect that there are evocations of Sappho's poetry in Posidippus' epigram quoted above; the quatrain concerning the lovemaking of Doricha and Charaxus is one obvious candidate,[15] and the suspicion is not lessened by the similarity of these verses to the lovemaking of Dionysus and Ariadne in Apollonius of Rhodes' *Argonautica*, recalled through the marvellous cloak on which they lay:

> τοῦ δὲ καὶ ἀμβροσίη ὀδμὴ ἄεν ἐξέτι κείνου
> ἐξ οὗ ἄναξ αὐτὸς Νυσήιος ἐγκατέλεκτο
> ἀκροχάλιξ οἴνωι καὶ νέκταρι, καλὰ μεμαρπὼς
> στήθεα παρθενικῆς Μινωίδος, ἥν ποτε Θησεὺς
> Κνωσσόθεν ἑσπομένην Δίηι ἔνι κάλλιπε νήσωι.

An ambrosial scent hovered over it ever since the time when the Nysaean lord himself, tipsy with wine and nectar, lay upon it as he pressed against

---

[13] For other consequences of the placing of fr. 1, cf. Hunter 2007: 219–21 = Thorsen and Harrison 2019: 158–60, Prodi 2017: 572–82, and below p. 284.
[14] The fullest recent account is Acosta-Hughes 2010.
[15] Obbink 2016c: 221.

himself the lovely breasts of the maiden daughter of Minos, whom Theseus once abandoned on the island of Dia after she had followed him from Knossos. (Apollonius of Rhodes, *Argonautica* 4.430–4)

Posidippus' poem illustrates a further way in which Sappho's particularity was felt: much of the surviving Hellenistic and later discussion of her has a biographical slant, whether that be focused on the girls addressed in her poems or on her relations with her brothers, a subject already highlighted by Herodotus and forcefully brought home to us by the recent publication of the Brothers Poem. Biographical criticism in antiquity is (again) far from limited to Sappho, but her femaleness gave the details of her life an enduring fascination, and almost inevitably led to the assumption that the voice of her poems was indeed a strongly autobiographical one. Sappho, moreover, names herself with a marked frequency, and real events and people seem to fill her poetry; Sappho's presence was also the presence of a whole world of intrigue, erotic suffering, and cultic observance. Moreover, Charaxus' dalliance with the lovely Doricha at Naucratis and its immortalisation first in Sappho's own poetry and then in Herodotus gave Sappho a direct presence in the Greek culture of North Africa, and Posidippus' poem incorporates her within that culture in its confident Ptolemaic manifestation.[16]

No ancient notice about Sappho is more surprising than the entry in the Parian Marble (erected 264/3 BC) that records her exile (or perhaps 'flight') from Mytilene to Sicily at the end of the seventh century or the beginning of the sixth. This event is not recorded anywhere else in the biographical or historical record,[17] but Cicero claims that Verres stole a statue of the poet by Silanion (late fourth century) which had stood in the town hall of Syracuse, and it is an easy guess that this was commissioned by the city to celebrate its belief that Sappho had visited or lived in the city.[18] Cicero says that the loss of the statue deeply affected the Syracusans:

---

[16] Barbantani *ap.* Acosta-Hughes and Barbantani 2007: 439 suggests that Posidippus' poem 'subtly celebrates the edition of Sappho's poems, now in the process of being produced in the Alexandrian Library'.

[17] Parian Marble A36 Rotstein (test. 5), with p. 111; the source was perhaps Phaenias of Eresus (second half of the fourth century; thus Mosshammer 1979: 253).

[18] Cicero, *Against Verres* 2.4.125–7 (test. 24). This is the standard assumption, though other scenarios are possible; Rosenmeyer 2007: 295, 280 assumes (probably rightly) that 'the statue was meant to remind the citizens that their city had once offered asylum to this famous poet' and thus Sappho is 'a famous adopted daughter of the city'. Cicero's report about Silanion's statue, a work which would fit with what else we know of his bronzes, is supported (or at least not undermined) by Tatian, *Oration to the Greeks* 33; cf. Coarelli 1972, A. Stewart 1990: I 296–7, 1998: 278–81.

atque haec Sappho sublata quantum desiderium sui reliquerit dici vix potest.

The depth of the longing which the removal of the statue of Sappho caused can hardly be expressed. (Cicero, *Against Verres* 2.4.127 (test. 24))

It is tempting to see Cicero here employing a Sapphic motif: we may be reminded of her poems (frr. 94, 96) for female friends no longer present. However that may be, there are good reasons to believe that in the late fourth and early third century there was a tradition that Sappho had visited Sicily, and that the Syracusan Theocritus may well have known of this tradition, may indeed have seen Sappho's statue on display in his home city. Sappho, then, would have been an 'honorary Syracusan'; she too, like the Cyclops, was 'one of us' (Theocritus 11.7). For Theocritus, Sappho took her place alongside the great figures of the Sicilian poetic heritage – Stesichorus, Epicharmus, Sophron – all of whom are echoed in his poetry.[19] When, therefore, the opening verses of the Sicilian Cyclops' address to Galateia (11.19–24) are replete with echoes of Sappho,[20] the Sicilian, or indeed Syracusan, lover is made to echo *the* (honorary) Sicilian love poet, and we might guess that more Sapphic echoes lie behind the close of his speech; ὦ Κύκλωψ Κύκλωψ (11.72) may imitate Sappho's habit of using her own name, particularly as the Cyclops' break-off has reminded more than one modern reader of the final (*otium*, 'leisure') stanza of Catullus 51, which probably imitates, rather than translates, a Sapphic pattern.[21]

For Theocritus, then, Sappho was not just one more poet of the past to be echoed and incorporated, but rather part of a closely felt local poetic heritage. The situation has something in common with the epigrams of Nossis from Locri (in the toe of Italy) which seem to recreate a female Sapphic world in the west in conscious mimesis of Sappho's eastern Lesbian world.[22] In *Idyll* 15, two women proud of their Syracusanness listen at the royal palace in Alexandria to a hymn in honour of Aphrodite and Adonis performed by a female singer of (in the judgement of the Syracusan women) amazing skill (τὸ χρῆμα σοφώτατον ἁ θήλεια, 145). The Adonis cult makes its first appearance in a few Sapphic

[19] Willi 2012b: 285–8.
[20] Hunter 1999: 229–31.
[21] D. Fowler 1994: 245–9 = 2000: 22–7; Hunter 2019: 54–5.
[22] Nossis, *Greek Anthology* 7.201 (2831–4 *HE*); Skinner 1989, Gutzwiller 1998: 85–8, Bowman 1998.

fragments,[23] but Dioscorides' epigram for Sappho suggests that the theme was felt to have some prominence in her poetry, alongside the wedding songs for which she was so renowned;[24] the *epithalamia* are richly echoed and evoked in *Idyll* 18, the wedding song for Helen and Menelaus,[25] and it is a reasonable suspicion that echoes of Sappho's poetry on Adonis lurk in the Adonis hymn of *Idyll* 15, perhaps, particularly, in the opening lines 100–5.[26] About *Idyll* 28, 'The Distaff', however, there can be no doubt. This poem is in Sapphic language and metre and debts of motif and specific verbal echoes have long been identified.[27] The distaff is to travel with the poet to Miletus as a gift to the wife of his ξέννος ('guest-friend') Nicias (lines 5–9), and the distaff and the 'Distaff' poem are thus essentially identified: both are gifts for, and celebrate the virtues of, Theugenis. Both come from Syracuse, 'from', as the poet puts it, 'my land' (16–18); this is Theocritus of Syracuse speaking as Sappho of Syracuse. In celebrating a woman and female virtues, Theocritus chooses to ventriloquise not just any female poet, but the one who can most obviously speak for him, namely one with a (real or believed) claim to belong to Syracuse.

Theocritus is likely also to have been conscious of an earlier imitation of Sappho, though one very different from his own. The 'Distaff' of Erinna (? late fourth century BC), though it is not certain that the title is original, was a poem of three hundred hexameters, in which Erinna, a female poet from the eastern Aegean, seems to have lamented the death of her childhood friend Baucis, who died shortly after marrying. Some fifty-four badly damaged verses of this poem, which was much admired in the Hellenistic period, survive on a papyrus.[28] This was a poem of memory and loss, suffused with Sapphic echoes and an evocation of a now shattered world of female friendship and closeness.[29] It is a great pity that we cannot trace in detail how Erinna presented the relationship between Baucis' marriage and her death; were they fused so as to become all but synonymous? Erinna's themes of separation and regret were an inheritance from Sappho, and we see them again in the marked Sapphic

---

[23] Fr. 117Bb Voigt = Sappho or Alcaeus fr. 24(b) Campbell, frr. 140, 168 C., test. 211c V.

[24] Dioscorides, *Greek Anthology* 7.407.5–8 (test. 58).

[25] Hunter 1996: 151–2, 2015b: 158–60.

[26] For other possible Sapphic resonances in *Idyll* 15, cf. Acosta-Hughes 2010: 16, 72–3.

[27] Spelman 2017b, with new arguments for Sapphic echoes; Papadopoulou 2016: 224–37 argues for an essentially political and Ptolemaic motive for the form of this poem.

[28] Erinna fr. 401 *SH* = fr. 4 Neri.

[29] We may be reminded particularly of Sappho fr. 94; cf. Rauk 1989, Rayor 2005.

colouring of the lament by the lock of hair which Berenice II dedicated for her husband's safe return but which is now forever sundered from the royal head, a poem which brought Callimachus' four-book *Aitia* to an extraordinary conclusion (fr. 110 Harder). The lock is grammatically masculine (contrast the *coma* of Catullus' translation, poem 66), but its experience is very female,[30] and as such it borrows the voice of *the* female poet to protest at its fate.

Erotic Suffering

Dioscorides opens his epigram on Sappho (p. 283 above) by calling her 'the sweetest support for the desires of young men in love',[31] thus foregrounding that theme of her poetry which was always given the greatest prominence in the Hellenistic period. Desire and the repeated sufferings that it brings were advertised by the placement of fr. 1 at the head of the Alexandrian edition.[32] At issue was not just subject matter, but also style, as the author of *On Style*, ascribed to Demetrius (Hellenistic or early Roman period), makes clear:

> When Sappho sings of beauty (κάλλος), her words are beautiful and sweet, and when she sings of loves and springtime and the halcyon. Every beautiful word is woven into her poetry, and some she herself has created (εἰργάσατο). (Demetrius, *On Style* 166 = fr. 195)

Sappho was, then, the 'natural' poet to whom to turn when later poets sought to depict erotic suffering, particularly female suffering. Fr. 31, the famous poem whose survival we owe to Pseudo-Longinus (*On the Sublime* 10.1–3) and which was translated by Catullus (poem 51), seems to have been singled out from a relatively early date as a particularly memorable description of erotic suffering. Echoes of this poem are very frequent in Greek and Latin literature.[33] It was, for example, to this

---

[30] Fantuzzi and Hunter 2004: 87–8, Acosta-Hughes 2010: 68.

[31] Dioscorides, *Greek Anthology* 7.407.1 (test. 58), ἥδιστον φιλέουσι νέοις προσανάκλιμ' ἐρώτων. Cf. Demetrius, *On Style* 132 (test. 45) on *charis* arising from subject matter: 'gardens of the nymphs, wedding songs, loves, all of Sappho's poetry'.

[32] Above, p. 280. It is, however, always worth remembering that we owe the preservation of this poem to Dionysius of Halicarnassus (*On the Arrangement of Words* 23.10–15), who does not cite it for its erotic subject matter.

[33] Costanza 1950, Acosta-Hughes 2010: Index locorum s.v. Sappho. Plutarch, perhaps roughly contemporary with Pseudo-Longinus, is an important witness to the fame of this poem: Bowie pp. 305–6.

poem (though not to this Sapphic poem alone) that Apollonius in the *Argonautica* turned to chart crucial moments in the progress of the Colchian princess Medea's desire for the handsome Greek stranger, Jason, who had arrived in her land.[34] When Eros first shoots Medea with his arrow, the effect is described with an evocation of Sapphic motifs:

ἧκ' ἐπὶ Μηδείηι· τὴν δ' ἀμφασίη λάβε θυμόν.
αὐτὸς δ' ὑψορόφοιο παλιμπετὲς ἐκ μεγάροιο
καγχαλόων ἤιξε, βέλος δ' ἐνεδαίετο κούρηι
νέρθεν ὑπὸ κραδίηι φλογὶ εἴκελον. ἀντία δ' αἰεὶ
βάλλεν ἐπ' Αἰσονίδην ἀμαρύγματα, καί οἱ ἄηντο
στηθέων ἐκ πυκιναὶ καμάτωι φρένες· οὐδέ τιν' ἄλλην
μνῆστιν ἔχεν, γλυκερῆι δὲ κατείβετο θυμὸν ἀνίηι·

He shot at Medea, and her spirit was seized by speechless stupor. Eros darted back out of the high-roofed palace with a mocking laugh, but his arrow burned deep in the girl's heart like a flame. Full at Jason her glance shot, and the wearying pain scattered all prudent thoughts from her chest; she could think of nothing else, and her spirit was flooded with a sweet aching. (Apollonius of Rhodes, *Argonautica* 3.284–90)

When Jason and Medea meet at the temple of Hecate, it is again echoes of Sappho which describe the sickness of desire:

ἐκ δ' ἄρα οἱ κραδίη στηθέων πέσεν, ὄμματα δ' αὔτως
ἤχλυσαν, θερμὸν δὲ παρηίδας εἷλεν ἔρευθος·
γούνατα δ' οὔτ' ὀπίσω οὔτε προπάροιθεν ἀεῖραι
ἔσθενεν, ἀλλ' ὑπένερθε πάγη πόδας.

Her heart within her breast dropped, her eyes grew misty, and a hot flush seized her cheeks; she had no strength at all to move her legs, but her feet were held fast beneath her. (Apollonius of Rhodes, *Argonautica* 3.962–5)

For Medea, however, there is no turning back once she has betrayed her father. At the beginning of Book 4 Apollonius describes her panic as she assumes that her father knows about her assistance to the Argonauts:

ἐν δέ οἱ ὄσσε
πλῆτο πυρός, δεινὸν δὲ περιβρομέεσκον ἀκουαί·
πυκνὰ δὲ λαυκανίης ἐπεμάσσετο, πυκνὰ δὲ κουρίξ
ἑλκομένη πλοκάμους γοερῆι βρυχήσατ' ἀνίηι.

---

[34] For what follows cf. Acosta-Hughes 2010: 49–57 and the relevant sections of Hunter 1989, 2015a.

Fire filled her eyes, and in her ears was a terrible roaring; often she felt her throat, often she screamed in pain and lamentation, pulling her hair out by the roots. (Apollonius of Rhodes, *Argonautica* 4.16–19)

The causal link between her love and her panic is thus marked through different reworkings of Sappho fr. 31.

A strikingly similar pattern occurs in Simaetha's narrative of her love affair with Delphis in Theocritus 2.[35] Simaetha's first sighting of Delphis on his return from the gymnasium led to a 'Sappho fr. 31 experience':

καί μευ χρὼς μὲν ὁμοῖος ἐγίνετο πολλάκι θάψωι,[36]
ἔρρευν δ' ἐκ κεφαλᾶς πᾶσαι τρίχες,[37] αὐτὰ δὲ λοιπὰ
ὀcτί' ἔτ' ἧc καὶ δέρμα. καὶ ἐc τίνος οὐκ ἐπέραςα,
ἢ ποίαc ἔλιπον γραίαc δόμον ἅτιc ἐπᾶιδεν;

Often my skin became pale like fustic, all the hair was falling from my head, and all that was left of me was bones and skin. To whose house did I not go, or what dwelling of an old woman who knows incantations? (Theocritus 2.88–91)

When Delphis enters her house, Simaetha describes her reactions with a further reworking of Sappho fr. 31:

πᾶca μὲν ἐψύχθην χιόνος πλέον, ἐκ δὲ μετώπω
ἱδρώς μευ κοχύδεcκεν ἴcον νοτίαιcιν ἐέρcαιc,
οὐδέ τι φωνῆcαι δυνάμαν, οὐδ' ὅccον ἐν ὕπνωι
κνυζεῦνται φωνεῦντα φίλαν ποτὶ ματέρα τέκνα·
ἀλλ' ἐπάγην δαγῦδι καλὸν χρόα πάντοθεν ἴcα.

My whole body was colder than snow, and from my forehead sweat flowed like the damp dews, and I could say nothing, not even as much as children mumble in the sleep as they call to their dear mothers. My fair body was stiff all over like a doll. (Theocritus 2.106–10)

Roberto Pretagostini argued that whereas the first reworking of fr. 31 marked the onset of love, the second marked 'the fear of love' (and love-making),[38] though he did not go on to suggest that this reflected two different ways in which fr. 31 had been understood in ancient tradition,

---

[35] Acosta-Hughes 2010: 17–29, Hunter 2014: 142–4.
[36] There is no firm evidence (*pace* Acosta-Hughes 2010: 27) that Sappho used the word θάψος (cf. fr. 210), though there may well be a thicker literary texture than we can now recover.
[37] Simaetha is here perhaps made (comically) to evoke Hesiod's lustful Proetides: Hunter 2019: 56.
[38] Pretagostini 1984: 114 (see also 114–16).

as indeed it has in modern discussion.[39] The study of ancient interpretations of fr. 31 offers rich material, but here I would like rather to explore a link between these passages which may shed light on how the poetry of Sappho might be seen within the wider context of the literary heritage.

When she can bear her passion for Delphis no more and can find no remedy for it (we are perhaps reminded of Euripides' Phaedra), Simaetha sends her slave Thestylis to fetch him:

κἠπεί κά νιν ἐόντα μάθηις μόνον, ἄσυχα νεῦσον,
κεῖφ' ὅτι "Ϲιμαίθα τυ καλεῖ", καὶ ὑφαγέο τεῖδε.
ὣς ἐφάμαν· ἀ δ' ἦνθε καὶ ἄγαγε τὸν λιπαρόχρων
εἰς ἐμὰ δώματα Δέλφιν·

'And when you see that he is alone, sign secretly to him, and say "Simaetha calls you" and bring him here.' So I spoke. She went and brought Delphis of the gleaming skin to my house. (Theocritus 2.100–3)

Nancy Andrews attractively suggested that Simaetha here recalls (with appropriate reversal – Delphis is a kind of Paris) Aphrodite's opening words to Helen in the famous scene which concludes *Iliad* 3:[40]

δεῦρ' ἴθ', Ἀλέξανδρός ϲε καλεῖ οἶκόνδε νέεϲθαι.

'Come hither: Paris calls you to come to your home.' (Homer, *Iliad* 3.390)

The servant Thestylis then brings Delphis to Simaetha, as Aphrodite disguises herself as one of Helen's aged retainers to bring the couple together. This same Homeric scene is also recalled when, on sitting down next to Simaetha, Delphis 'fixes his eyes upon the ground', as Helen 'turns her eyes aside' when faced with Paris,[41] and perhaps also when Delphis notes that 'thanks are first owed to Cypris' (line 130). The reworking of Sappho fr. 31 as Delphis enters the house thus follows on from an evocation of Aphrodite's summoning of Helen, in such a way

---

[39] F. Ferrari 2010: 171–92.
[40] Andrews 1996: 33.
[41] *Iliad* 3.426–7; cf. Lentini 2012: 185–6. Delphis' gesture is more usually associated with Odysseus as described in *Iliad* 3.217; cf. Andrews 1996: 36–41. What Theocritus has done, and this technique is familiar elsewhere in Hellenistic and Roman poetry, is to substitute one phrase from elsewhere in the poetic model for a similar one found in the scene which is being imitated; in this case, Theocritus has not only taken a phrase from the same book of the *Iliad*, but also one which suggests a character (Odysseus) who is also very appropriate in the new context.

as to suggest that fr. 31 may (at least in part) be read as an exploration of that Homeric scene.[42] This is, in other words, how such a scene may be reimagined in lyric mode, and we may even speculate that the object of desire in such a reading of fr. 31 would be Helen, who, as is well known, figures prominently and unusually in Sapphic poetry; in another critical mode we would say that *Iliad* 3 is 'read through' fr. 31. Some support for such a reading is perhaps found in the fact that Aphrodite places a chair so that Helen sits 'opposite Paris' (*Iliad* 3.424–6), just as fr. 31 initially focuses on 'that man … whoever sits opposite you'.

As for Simaetha's 'Sapphic symptoms' at lines 88–91, they result from an experience partly modelled on Zeus's reaction to the sight of Hera in *Iliad* 14:

χὼς ἴδον, ὣς ἐμάνην, ὥς μοι πυρὶ θυμὸς ἰάφθη

I saw, I went mad, my heart burst into flame. (Theocritus 2.82)

ὡς δ᾽ ἴδεν, ὥς μιν ἔρος πυκινὰς φρένας ἀμφεκάλυψεν

He saw, desire enveloped his wise mind . . . (Homer, *Iliad* 14.294)

Theocritus' Simaetha thus associates both her reworkings of fr. 31 with the two most prominent scenes of desire in the *Iliad*, whose close verbal and thematic similarity to each other was often noted in the later critical tradition. Theocritus thus becomes an early witness to this tradition, and this serves to remind us of how poets helped to fashion that tradition, as much as they also reflected it. The two greatest moments of male desire in the *Iliad* are reshaped as female desire through reworkings of the most famous poetic description of such an emotion, but so as to intimate that the Sapphic poem itself is a response to the Iliadic scenes. This is not a matter of finding the 'source' of Sappho's poetry in the epic poet from whom all culture was thought to derive, but rather of exploiting what was most distinctive about the Sapphic voice when set against the Homeric, even those erotic scenes of Homer which might be thought closest in spirit to her.

---

[42] Winkler 1990: 178–80 reads fr. 31 in the light of the meeting of Odysseus and Nausicaa in *Odyssey* 6 (cf. especially lines 242–5), but there seem fewer signals of such a model text than in the reading proposed above for Theocritus. See further Rosenmeyer 1997: 137–40.

Further Reading

The principal echoes of Sappho in Hellenistic poetry, at least before the recent additions to the corpus, are recorded in the major commentaries to the poets. Acosta-Hughes 2010 is the fullest survey covering third-century poetry as a whole. For Sapphic influence on particular poets, cf. Rauk 1989 (Erinna), Skinner 1989 (Nossis).

CHAPTER 21

Sappho at Rome

Llewelyn Morgan

Sappho's prominence in the Roman imaginary, greater than that of any other Greek lyric poet, is perhaps best illustrated by some less familiar instances of allusion to her work, spanning the classical period of Roman poetry. In Juvenal the shocking betrayal of aristocratic dignity represented by Eppia (6.82–114), the senator's wife who has left her privileged life behind to follow Sergius the gladiator to Egypt, is sharpened by reminiscence of Sappho fr. 16.[1] Like Helen, Eppia has abandoned her children and noble husband, but surpasses her mythical counterpart by abandoning even Paris, too (in this case, the Domitianic-era *pantomimus*). In a different style, Statius' poem *Silvae* 4.7 seems to be guided by the sapphic metre Statius adopts for it (if we discount the hendecasyllable,[2] this is one of only two poems in Aeolic metres in the five books of the *Silvae*) to emulate not only Horace, the most energetic composer of sapphics in Latin, but also Horace's model, Sappho herself. Addressed to Vibius Maximus, Statius' poem carries hints, for instance in the myrtle garland identified with Statius' poetic exercise at 10–11,[3] that evoke Sappho's status as 'the erotic poet *par excellence*';[4] and in the *torpor* ('paralysis') that Statius claims afflicts him in Maximus' absence (*Silvae* 4.7.21) he seems to allude to fr. 31.9, ἀλλὰ κὰμ μὲν γλῶσσά <μ'> ἔαγε ('but my tongue is broken'), as mediated by Catullus' translation of the line at 51.9, *lingua sed torpet* ('but my tongue is numb').[5]

---

[1] M. Edwards 1991.
[2] West 1982: 151, 167 identifies the phalaecian (hendecasyllable), used extensively by Martial and Statius in his *Silvae*, both in imitation of Catullus, as an Aeolic metre based on the glyconic, one of the most common Aeolic cola (Battezzato p. 123).
[3] K. Coleman 1988: 200.
[4] Hunter 1989: 27.
[5] Morgan 2010: 189–99.

Two centuries before Statius, fr. 1 Courtney of Valerius Aedituus, a poet of the first century BC,[6] 'is strongly reminiscent of Sappho fr. 31[7] in its attention to the physical symptoms of love, although Courtney comments on the jarringly un-Sapphic quality of the rare word *subidus* ('in heat'):

> dicere cum conor curam tibi, Pamphila, cordis,
>   quid mi abs te quaeram, uerba labris abeunt,
> per pectus manat subito \<subido\> mihi sudor:
>   sic tacitus, subidus, dum pudeo, pereo.

> When I try to speak of my heart's pain to you, Pamphila, what shall I ask of you? Words fail my lips, a sudden sweat pours over my aroused breast. Thus silent and in heat, I restrain myself and am lost.

Earlier still, in the late third or early second century, Plautus in the *Braggart Soldier* (*Miles gloriosus*) models the scene of Acroteleutium's pretended infatuation with Pyrgopolynices (1216–83) on the legend of Sappho's passion for Phaon (mentioned explicitly at 1246–7), while Acroteleutium's supposed physical reaction to setting eyes upon Pyrgopolynices (1260–2, 1270–3) once again recalls Sappho fr. 31.[8] There is extended play with Pyrgopolynices as Phaon throughout the comedy, even potentially encompassing Acroteleutium's name, and in all likelihood this aspect of the play derives from the lost Greek comedy *The Braggart* (*Alazôn*), which was Plautus' model.[9]

If we ask what more general picture of Sappho's reception in Rome we gain from these allusions to her poetry across the centuries and genres, Sappho is treated as a poet exclusively concerned with love – not unexpectedly – but also as a poet exploring a somewhat extreme manifestation of that emotion. 'What is more uninhibited (*lasciuius*) than Sappho?', asks Ovid (*The Art of Love* 3.331), and she is typically associated with an overwhelming, physically debilitating onset of erotic passion. Reinforcing that characterisation in the Roman reception of Sappho are the mythological accretions that she had gathered. The story of her fatal infatuation with Phaon no doubt had its origins in an actual poem expressing her own (or maybe Aphrodite's) devotion to Adonis,[10] but it seems that Attic

---

[6] Nisbet 2019: 269–70 discusses the background of Gellius' quotation of this and two other 'early poets' at *Attic Nights* 19.9.10–14.
[7] Courtney 1993: 72.
[8] Traill 2005.
[9] Traill 2005: 531–2.
[10] Bowra 1961: 213–14, Detienne 1994: 68–71 ≈ 2007: 103–7, Kivilo 2010: 179–81.

comedy, in which Sappho regularly featured, did most to make passionate, unrequited love a feature of her biography.[11] The Sappho inherited by the Romans was thus in some respects a fictionalised and pruriently embellished figure. But in other respects her poetry was, in the way of literary traditions, simplified and essentialised in its reception. In my opening illustrations from Plautus, Valerius Aedituus, and Statius, for instance, the narrow focus of allusion, and the prominence of Sappho fr. 31, are striking, and easily paralleled: aside from Catullus' translation in poem 51, fr. 31 seems to be a presence in Lucretius' account of the influence of *animus* on *anima* in *On the Nature of Things*,[12] in an epigram of Lutatius Catulus,[13] in the blush of Lavinia in Virgil's *Aeneid*,[14] and in the pseudo-Ovidian *Sappho's Letter to Phaon*, where the departure of Phaon elicits from Sappho an all-too-familiar physical response.[15] But as well as being a putative model for Plautus' *Miles* (and *Alazôn* before it), fr. 31 is an important presence in Theocritus 2 and Apollonius of Rhodes, *Argonautica* 3,[16] indicating that it had long achieved a representative status in Sappho's poetry. We must be careful: fr. 31 is far from the only Sapphic text we find Roman poets alluding to,[17] and even if it were, we would need to consider the distorting effect of our very partial knowledge of Sappho's oeuvre.

That we would we see a richer intertextual engagement with the Greek poet in Latin if more of her work survived is certain,[18] but a flattening of Sappho's complexity comparable to the focus on fr. 31 is evident enough in other aspects of her reception, not least metrical. Only one of nine books of her Alexandrian edition, which was organised by metre, was in sapphics, but it was the metre of that first book that came to be

---

[11] Traill 2005: 518–19; Coo pp. 269–75.

[12] 3.152–8; Kenney 2014: 99.

[13] Q. Lutatius Catulus fr. 2.4 Courtney with Granarolo 1971: 48–50.

[14] Virgil, *Aeneid* 12.67–9; F. Cairns 1989: 154, Harrison 2019: 137.

[15] *Heroides* 15; see lines 111–12. Debate about its authorship persists, but its lack of quality tells against ascription to Ovid: Tarrant 1981, Rosati 1996, Bessone 2003.

[16] Hunter 1989 on Apollonius of Rhodes, *Argonautica* 3.284, 296–8, and, for Theocritus 2, Hunter 2019: 55–6, HUNTER.

[17] Fr. 16 is at issue in Juvenal (above, p. 290), while Morgan 2010: 198–9 proposes an allusion to fr. 1 in Statius' sapphic ode *Silvae* 4.7; Traill 2005: 527–8 finds a precedent for the olfactory aspects of Acroteleutium's play-acting elsewhere than fr. 31, for example in fr. 94, and a more general Sapphic character in prayer. Courtney 1993: 72 wonders if Sappho fr. 137 is behind *dum pudeo* in Valerius Aedituus fr. 1.4. For an allusion to Sappho frr. 96, 98 in Laevius' *Protesilaudamia* (fr. 18 Courtney), see Fantuzzi 1995, Barchiesi 2009: 320–1. Spelman 2017b identifies a reminiscence of Sappho fr. 101 in Catullus 12.

[18] Phillips 2014, Morgan 2016.

considered her signature form,[19] whether Alexandrian scholars created or merely sustained that perception. In turn, the metre named 'sapphic' could on its own evoke the poet and her work,[20] a phenomenon discernible in Statius' *Silvae*, but more clearly still in Catullus' deployment of the form in poems 11 and 51.

To Catullus we shall return, but another conclusion to be drawn from Plautus and Juvenal, at least, is Sappho's susceptibility to parodic treatment. The fourth-century comic poet Diphilus, in his play *Sappho*, 'made Archilochus and Hipponax her lovers, forcing two plain-speaking poets of blame to court the epitome of aristocratic refinement', to comic effect.[21] What Sappho also seemed to represent was a poetry of notable finesse which made it and its author a productive target for subversive forms such as comedy or Juvenalian satire. The extensive literary criticism that Sappho attracted in antiquity, and that also shaped the Roman reception of her poetry,[22] confirms this impression that Sappho was felt to represent refinement, in style as well as content.

In the literary criticism of Demetrius (Hellenistic or early Roman period), Dionysius of Halicarnassus, and no doubt in Dionysius' Augustan contemporary Caecilius of Caleacte, 'Sappho is a classic of the smooth or elegant style, her subjects, language and cύνθεcιc [arrangement of words, Latin *compositio*] all contributing to a general effect of charm.'[23] A key term to define this style or χαρακτήρ that Sappho was felt to exemplify is γλαφυρόc ('elegant, smooth, polished, refined, neat, delicate, pretty') and a consistently cited characteristic of this style, as here, is χάριc ('charm'), a quality associated with lyric in general but most insistently with Sappho's poetry.[24] For these ancient critics, τὸ πρέπον ('propriety'), the ideal of a style of expression matched to the chosen topic, is a fundamental criterion. How far χάριc arises from the subject matter, and how far from its presentation, is thus, as Demetrius suggests, hard to define precisely:

---

[19] See Woodman 2002: 214 n. 9 for the designation of this system as 'sapphic'; also BATTEZZATO pp. 126–7. The attribution met resistance. Referring to the 'sapphic hendecasyllable' (the metre of the first three lines of the sapphic stanza, as usually set out), Hephaestion states that 'it is uncertain which of [Sappho or Alcaeus] invented it' (14.1); cf. 'Marius Victorinus' (Aphthonius, fourth century AD, VI 161.18–20 *GL* = test. 33), claiming that the sapphic stanza was invented by Alcaeus but called 'sapphic' 'because Sappho used it more regularly than its inventor Alcaeus.'

[20] Morgan 2010: 181–283.

[21] Traill 2005: 532, referring to Diphilus fr. 71 *PCG* (test. 8); Coo pp. 269–70.

[22] Hunter 2019: 51–9 sets both Catullus 51 and Lucretius, *On the Nature of Things* 3.152–60 in the context of ancient academic discussion of fr. 31.

[23] Russell 1981: 77–8; also HUNTER.

[24] Demetrius, *On Style* 132 (test. 45).

εἰcὶν δὲ αἱ μὲν ἐν τοῖc πράγμαcι χάριτεc, οἷον νυμφαῖοι κῆποι, ὑμέναιοι, ἔρωτεc, ὅλη ἡ Cαπφοῦc ποίηcιc. τὰ γὰρ τοιαῦτα, κἂν ὑπὸ Ἱππώνακτοc λέγηται, χαρίεντά ἐcτι, καὶ αὐτὸ ἱλαρὸν τὸ πρᾶγμα ἐξ ἑαυτοῦ· οὐδεὶc γὰρ ἂν ὑμέναιον ἄιδοι ὀργιζόμενοc, οὐδὲ τὸν Ἔρωτα Ἐρινvὺν ποιήcειεν τῆι ἑρμηνείαι ἢ γίγαντα, οὐδὲ τὸ γελᾶν κλαίειν. ὥcτε ἡ μέν τιc ἐν πράγματι χάριc ἐcτί, τὰ δὲ καὶ ἡ λέξιc ποιεῖ ἐπιχαριτώτερα ...

Charm may reside in the subjects, such as gardens of the nymphs, mar-
riage songs, loves, all Sappho's poetry. Themes like these, even in the
mouth of Hipponax, possess charm, and the subject matter is light-
hearted in and of itself. No one could sing a marriage song in a state of
rage, or make Love a Fury or a Giant, or laughter tears, by stylistic
means. So charm does reside in the subject matter itself, but diction can
sometimes give an added charm ... (Demetrius, *On Style* 132–3 (≈
test. 45))

Suggestive in Demetrius' account is both Sappho's treatment as an
embodiment of these qualities and Hipponax's role as their antithesis.
Later Demetrius explains how propriety applies also to the iambic poetry
(poetry of criticism) that Hipponax wrote (with special reference here to
Hipponax's signature metre, the *scazôn* or limping verse), and what he
gives us is, naturally enough, an account of a style or a character opposite
to Sappho's:

καὶ ὥcπερ τὸ διαλελυμένον cχῆμα δεινότητα ποιεῖ, ὡc προλέλεκται, οὕτω
ποιήcει ἡ διαλελυμένη ὅλωc cύνθεcιc. cημεῖον δὲ καὶ τὸ Ἱππώνακτοc·
λοιδορῆcαι γὰρ βουλόμενοc τοὺc ἐχθροὺc ἔθραυcεν τὸ μέτρον καὶ
ἐποίηcεν χωλὸν ἀντὶ εὐθέοc καὶ ἄρρυθμον, τουτέcτι δεινότητι πρέπον καὶ
λοιδορίαι· τὸ γὰρ ἔρρυθμον καὶ εὐήκοον ἐγκωμίοιc ἂν πρέποι μᾶλλον ἢ
ψόγοιc.

And just as the figure of disjointedness produces harshness, as has been
said before, so also will disjointed composition in general. Hipponax's
practice is illustrative: for, wanting to abuse his enemies, he shattered his
metre, making it lame instead of upright, and irregular, and thus suitable
for harshness and abuse. Regular, harmonious rhythm would be more suit-
able for eulogy than invective. (Demetrius, *On Style* 301)

Elsewhere, somewhat similarly, Demetrius contrasts the laughable (τὸ
γελοῖον) and the charming (τὸ εὔχαρι) as subject matter, with gardens of
the nymphs and loves again representing the latter, while Irus and
Thersites, Homer's beggar and ill-favoured common soldier, illustrate the
former (163). We have seen Juvenal, with satirical inappropriateness,
evoking Sappho in connection to Eppia's passion for a gladiator,

a Hyacinth (6.110), an ideal of male perfection, in her eyes, despite a wounded arm, 'many facial blemishes, a furrow made by his helmet, a huge wart in the middle of his nose, and the severe complaint of a constantly weeping eye' (6.106–9), and Diphilus achieving comic impact by making Archilochus and Hipponax Sappho's lovers. Both clearly trade on a tangible contrast between what Sappho's poetry represented and the invective of Hipponax or Juvenal.

That this amounts to an 'essentialisation' of Sappho, a reduction of her poetry by the tradition to what were perceived to be its most salient features, is indicated by another passage of Demetrius that gives more attention to Sappho's poetic style, perfectly suited as it is to her charming subject matter:

> διὸ καὶ ἡ Σαπφὼ περὶ μὲν κάλλους ἄιδουσα καλλιεπής ἐστι καὶ ἡδεῖα, καὶ περὶ ἐρώτων δὲ καὶ ἔαρος καὶ περὶ ἀλκυόνος, καὶ ἅπαν καλὸν ὄνομα ἐνύφανται αὐτῆς τῆι ποιήσει, τὰ δὲ καὶ αὐτὴ εἰργάσατο. ἄλλως δὲ σκώπτει τὸν ἄγροικον νυμφίον καὶ τὸν θυρωρὸν τὸν ἐν τοῖς γάμοις, εὐτελέστατα καὶ ἐν πεζοῖς ὀνόμασι μᾶλλον ἢ ἐν ποιητικοῖς, ὥστε αὐτῆς μᾶλλόν ἐστι τὰ ποιήματα ταῦτα διαλέγεσθαι ἢ ἄιδειν, οὐδ' ἂν ἁρμόσαι πρὸς τὸν χορὸν ἢ πρὸς τὴν λύραν, εἰ μή τις εἴη χορὸς διαλεκτικός.

> This is why Sappho sings of beauty with beautiful and attractive words, or of loves or spring or the halcyon. Every beautiful word is woven into her poetry, and she has created some herself. But it is in a very different style that she mocks the awkward bridegroom and the doorkeeper at the wedding [fr. 110], in very ordinary language and prosaic rather than poetic words. Consequently these poems of hers are better spoken than sung, and would not suit the chorus or the lyre, unless there were a chorus that spoke in prose! (Demetrius, *On Style* 166–7)

Even as he cites poetry by Sappho that does not meet the stereotype, 'loves or spring or the halcyon' are still what Demetrius cites as the essence of her verse. In Dionysius' account of 'the polished style of composition' (ἡ γλαφυρὰ σύνθεσις, *On the Arrangement of Words* 23.1), broadly comparable to Demetrius' classification, Sappho functions similarly as a model of the category. Dionysius' vivid summary of the effect of fr. 1, the survival of which we owe to him, parallels Demetrius' characterisation of her style: 'The natural result is a smooth-flowing and soft diction, the coordination of the words causing no upheaval in the sound' (εἰκότως δὴ γέγονεν εὔρους τις ἡ λέξις καὶ μαλακή, τῆς ἁρμονίας τῶν ὀνομάτων μηδὲν ἀποκυματιζούσης τὸν ἦχον, 23.15). Aptness of style (τὸ πρέπον) remains a watchword: the quality of χάρις, in particular, is an ideal for girls of marriageable age, a typical subject of Sappho's verse, as well as a characteristic of the poetry she wrote about them.[25]

Equipped with a feeling for the strong and widespread perception of the nature of Sappho's poetry in the Roman period, we can properly address what may count as the most creative Roman response to Sappho.[26] Catullus was the first of the Roman poets to couple imitation of Sappho with adoption in Latin of her signature metre:[27] two poems of Catullus, 11 and 51, are composed in the so-called sapphic stanza. Poem 11, despite its position in the Catullan text that has come down to us, asks to be read as the poet's second venture in sapphics. Catullus 51, as far as the end of its third stanza at least, is a faithful translation of Sappho fr. 31, and the overtly Sapphic atmosphere of the poem, in content and metre, also yields a pseudonym for Catullus' lover, 'Lesbia'.[28] The poem thus styles itself the starting point of the cycle of poems about 'Lesbia' within Catullus' collection. To associate his lover with Sappho in this way claims Clodia as a literary ally, like Caecilius' lover in Catullus 35, 'girl more learned than the Sapphic muse' (*Sapphica puella | musa doctior*, 16–17 = test. 56), a woman who shares Sappho's (and thus Catullus' and Caecilius') literary sophistication.[29] Sappho's poetry had a brevity and intricacy that made it very compatible with Catullus' Callimacheanism;[30] the assimilation of Catullus to Sappho implied by this poem also establishes a (not uncontroversial) point of reference for Catullus' self-presentation more widely.[31]

If poem 51 celebrates the beginning of the relationship between Catullus and Lesbia, poem 11 seems to mark its end, as Catullus requests his friends to deliver to his lover the brutal news of its termination; and the relationship between two poems with little stylistically in common is strongly signalled by the metrical form they share. Poem 11 is 'designedly

---

[25] C. Brown 1989, on fr. 16. Cf. Himerius, *Oration* 28.2 (test. 50) 'Sappho alone among women loved beauty along with the lyre, and therefore devoted all her poetry to Aphrodite and the Loves (τοῖς Ἔρωσι), making a girl's beauty and charm the pretext for her songs.'

[26] Morgan 2010: 200–12.

[27] Barchiesi 2009: 322.

[28] Alfonsi 1950, Holzberg 2000, Gram 2019. Barchiesi 2009: 322–3 compares the name that Varro Atacinus, a first-century BC poet, gave to the girl who was the focus of his love poetry, Leucadia; cf. Courtney 1993: 236–7.

[29] Fitzgerald 1995: 22, 245 n. 14.

[30] Hunter 2019: 51 ponders other commonalities between Sappho and Callimachus.

[31] For Sappho as a means for Catullus to play with Roman gender expectations, see Greene 2011, Woodman 2002: 58–61. One potential source of the hendecasyllabic metre, an obscure form before Catullus' generation but extremely popular with him and his contemporary poets, is Sappho (Morgan 2010: 80–1). Catullus' debt to Sappho is illustrated also in the epithalamic poems 61 and 62 (Barchiesi 2009: 322). See also Spelman 2017b.

composed in the metre of [Catullus'] first poem to [Lesbia] ([51], which we are presumed to recognize – the sapphics would otherwise not be an appropriate medium for invective – and which it echoes in the word *identidem*, 19)'.[32] But there is more to be said than that 11 would not, without its connection to 51, justify its sapphic form. There is an *impropriety* about Catullus' composition, a mismatch of subject matter and sapphic form that is most marked in the fifth stanza, which represents the 'unpleasant message' (*non bona dicta*) that Catullus has entrusted to Furius and Aurelius to take to his lover (11.17–20):

> cum suis vivat valeatque moechis,
> quos simul complexa tenet trecentos,
> nullum amans vere, sed identidem omnium
> ilia rumpens.

> Farewell and long life to her with her adulterers, three hundred at once, whom she embraces and holds, loving none truly but time and again bursting the balls of all of them.

The scene is repellent, and in various ways contradictory of the aesthetic that contemporary critics attributed to Sappho. There is no *erôs* here, indeed a clear suggestion of prostitution,[33] and despite attempts to argue that the language is compatible with lyric propriety,[34] the issue is not so much whether terms like *moechis* ('adulterers') or *ilia* ('groins') are imaginable in Sappho's actual poetry as whether they are compatible with the idea of Sappho's poetry projected by ancient scholarship, and they clearly are not. Nor is the broader style of these lines, its exaggerated expression ('three hundred', 'all of them'), intense alliteration, and above all the string of elisions or synaloephae at 19–20, *null(um) amans vere, sed identid(em) omni(um) | ilia rumpens*. A high incidence of synaloepha has stylistic affinities with less elevated genres of poetry such as the verse satire Juvenal, among others, wrote: it is 'a metrical irregularity, an obstacle to the neatness (*netteté*) of the rhythm … a phenomenon that could seem barely compatible with a refined art'.[35] If Sappho is perceived to be anything, it is refined.

[32] Goold 1983: 238.
[33] Syndikus 1984–90: I 126.
[34] Jocelyn 1999: 346–8, Heyworth 2001: 131.
[35] Soubiran 1966: 269, 613. The synaloepha *between* lines 19 and 20 might be felt in Latin as especially transgressive. In Greek usage the stanza is best analysed into three periods, two identical verses followed by an amplification of that length: West 1982: 32–3, BATTEZZATO pp. 126–7. In Latin the so-called 'adonius' was treated as a discrete length, albeit more closely related to the preceding line than in stichic verse.

Fundamentally, as a metrical embodiment of the essential character attributed in antiquity to Sappho's poetry, sapphics can never be an appropriate vehicle for invective, but in that resides the power of Catullus' poem. These are indeed *non bona dicta* (literally, 'not good words', 16), not only a brutal repudiation of his lover, but also a thuggish abuse of sapphic form. A poem announcing the end of a love affair enacts also a violent rejection of the poetic medium most redolent of *erôs*. We see again the invitation that Sappho's high refinement offered to subvert it, whether in Diphilus or Juvenal or in this invective by Catullus.

A further twist in the play with the Sapphic tradition represented by Catullus 11 and 51 involves the matter of marriage. The image of Sappho as pedagogue, and specifically as pedagogue of girls in some kind of archaic version of a finishing school, is not currently popular.[36] But it is present in the Roman reception of Sappho, for example in the *Letter to Phaon* ascribed to Ovid, where the women of Lesbos are addressed, rather pointedly, as *nupturaque nuptaque proles*, 'offspring yet-to-be-married and already-married' (*Heroides* 15.199), and in Ovid's *Tristia* (*Lesbia quid docuit Sappho, nisi amare, puellas?*, 'What did Sappho of Lesbos teach her girls except how to love?', 2.365 = test. 49), where Ovid's point seems to be lost unless the perception at least was that Sappho *taught* the girls she names in her poetry. Underlying Catullus 11 is the pattern of a Roman divorce 'by missive' (*per nuntium*),[37] the friends of Catullus fulfilling the role of the *nuntii* ('messengers') delivering the message to his 'wife'. That sits well with an interpretation of Catullus 51, inversely, as a poem in some sense marital, but again renders poem 11's contradiction of those circumstances, at every level of the poetic artefact, shattering.[38]

The two concluding stanzas of 11 and 51 exert an interest on their own account, in 11 restoring the poem to a satisfactory lyric propriety as it ends (alluding to Sappho fr. 105(c)), and at 51.13–16 also, perhaps, in its jaundiced dismissal of *otium*, debunking the ethos Sappho was felt to represent: the notion of ἡϲυχία (both *otium* and ἡϲυχία can denote 'detachment' or 'seclusion') is easily associated with Sappho.[39] Horace

---

[36] Parker 1993 ≈ Greene 1996b: 146–83; MUELLER pp. 42–3, FERRARI pp. 107–8. Contrast Lasserre 1974, Lardinois 2001: 89–90 = Rutherford 2019: 304–6, for whom the erotic appeal of the girl praised in fr. 31 is a form of public praise of her as an ideal bride.

[37] Mayer 1983.

[38] Traill 2005: 533 argues that the comic parody of fr. 31 in *Miles* 'must … put to rest the notion that the poem was widely received as a wedding song in antiquity', but as a spoof it does no such thing: Acroteleutium does claim to be seeking marriage with Pyrgopolynices (1239–41), and the context is in fact intensely marital. See also the excellent good sense of T. Wiseman 1985: 153.

[39] Barchiesi 2009: 322–3, Morgan 2010: 244–7.

Odes 2.16, in sapphics, with its similar anaphora of *otium* at 1–8, looks in turn like a correction of Catullus' disenchantment and a reassertion of the values that the sapphic stanza was felt to embody.

Horace's *Odes*, at the beginning and end of the first collection (1.1.34, 3.30.13–14), assert a particular debt to the two 'Aeolic' lyric poets, Sappho and Alcaeus, even if the reference in 3.30 to Aeolian song and Italian measures, when the *Odes* are Italian *song* in predominantly Aeolian *measures*, is hard to parse: perhaps Horace is deliberately confusing material and metre so as to imply his absolute mastery of lyric form. A further implication in the claim to primacy among Latin lyric poets that he makes in 3.30 is that Catullus' ventures in sapphics in the previous generation had lacked the systematic character of his own realisation of a Roman lyric. As for Sappho, the echo of her status as the tenth Muse gives her a special prominence at the end of *Odes* 1.1,[40] while *Odes* 1.2 introduces sapphics to his collection well in advance of the alcaics (the signature metre of Alcaeus) that first appear in 1.9. But as ancient scholars insisted, Alcaeus had his own claim on the sapphic stanza.[41] *Odes* 1.32, a poem in sapphics, is a programmatic exercise in associating the lyric Horace with the model of Alcaeus, represented as a figure experienced in the political realm (*Lesbio ... civi*, 5) and in war (*ferox bello*, 6), but whose poetry encompassed lighter subject matter,[42] and thus excludes Sappho simultaneously from Horace's all-important self-definition and from her own characteristic metre. While the explicit comparison of Alcaeus and Sappho at *Odes* 2.13.21–32 (= Alcaeus test. 22 ≈ Sappho test. 18) can be read as a more balanced assessment of the two poets than it is generally understood to be (it is the crowd, the *vulgus*, that prefers Alcaeus' poetry, not as a rule the most respected arbiter of taste),[43] in Horace's self-construction across the collection it is Alcaeus who is the more assertive presence.

What Sappho does represent to Horace may perhaps be illustrated by the elusive poem 3.27, the farewell to Galatea. It is again in sapphics, but also reminiscent of Sappho is the scenario of a farewell to a loved one, and the model represented by Sappho is advertised at 13–14, *sis licet felix*

---

[40] Woodman 2002: 53–4.
[41] See n. 19.
[42] The (deplorable) diversity of Alcaeus' output was a conventional observation in later antiquity: Cicero, *Tusculan Disputations* 4.71, Quintilian, *Institutes of Oratory* 10.1.63 (test. 21), 'but he also stooped to triviality and love poems, although more suited to higher topics'.
[43] Woodman 2002: 55. The polarity between the domestically focused Sappho and Alcaeus *sonantem plenius* ('singing more resonantly') that Horace presents is readily paralleled: (Pseudo-?)Ovid, *Heroides* 15.29–30 (test. 44), fr. 214B with Gronewald 1974. Davis 1991: 85–6 offers a particularly subtle analysis of the vignette in 2.13.

ubicumque mavis, | *et memor nostri, Galatea, vivas,* 'May you be happy wherever you choose to be, Galatea, and may you remember me', a reminiscence of Sappho's 'Go in happiness and remember me' (χαίροις᾽ ἔρχεο κἄμεθεν | μέμναις᾽, fr. 94.7–8), also addressed to a departing girl. David West insightfully characterises this poem as playful but affectionate, a light and self-deprecating last word to a loved one.[44] What Sappho seems to represent within Horatian lyric is both a guarantee of authentic emotion, the *commissi calores* | *Aeoliae fidibus puellae* ('passion entrusted to the lyre of the Aeolian girl', 4.9.11–12 = test. 51), and an indication that the poetry may occupy the less momentous end of the lyric spectrum. That is a subtle message, nevertheless, as Horace's decision to concentrate on monodic models has already defined his lyric as modest and small-scale: the 'small measures', *modi parvi,* that are an inadequate vehicle for the divine matter of *Odes* 3.3 (at 69–72) are the *minores gyri,* 'narrower circuits', of Statius' unique exercise in sapphics (*Silvae* 4.7.3–4) and the μικραὶ στροφαί, 'little stanzas', of Dionysius of Halicarnassus[45] – the less expansive poetic forms of both Alcaeus and Sappho that insist, by the principle of propriety, on literary expression that is correspondingly less ambitious. In his fourth book of *Odes,* Horace 'is careful to realign the intertextual connections he makes, and stress thematic links with e.g. Pindar and Simonides, more than with the guiding inspirations of the previous books, Alcaeus and Sappho',[46] although his metrical forms remain what they were.

It has been suggested that Sappho exerts her presence in Horace's lyric in a more subtle way, that the metre known as sapphic carried with it at least some of the ethos the ancients associated with her.[47] In *Odes* 4.2, for example, Steinmetz saw a tension between the celebration of the Pindaric inspiration of Iullus Antonius and the sapphic form of the poem.[48] In this poem Horace's setting of his language within the sapphic stanzas, along with other aspects of the poem's metrical style, plays on the collision of Pindaric exuberance and Sapphic restraint, and distinguishes the divergent aspirations of the two poets.[49] In other sapphic odes of Horace, and in the *Carmen saeculare,* a significance in the choice of metre may be more elusive, but in the latter case Putnam finds a rationale for the (at

[44] D. West 2002: 222–35.
[45] *On the Arrangement of Words* 19.7 (test. 36).
[46] Barchiesi 2009: 328.
[47] Morgan 2010: 224–74.
[48] Steinmetz 1964.
[49] Syndikus 2001: II 286; cf. Morgan 2010: 224–37.

first sight) abnormal form of a chorally performed paean partly in the way it identifies the source of Roman success:

> But the *Carmen* embraces a whole populace, women as well as men, and views it at a universal celebration for the city's domestic well-being. It is to their homes, after all, that the chorus carries the thoughts behind their prayers once the Palatine festivity is past. For such purposes Sappho and her warmth of personal expression are entirely suitable.[50]

The notion that Sapphic poetry has a special affinity for enclosed, domestic space is an appealing one – she was 'the woman singing about private life in public occasions', as Barchiesi puts it[51] – and we potentially find it at work elsewhere in Horace's lyric. *Odes* 3.14, *Herculis ritu*, opens with material seemingly too momentous for its sapphic metre, the return of Augustus to Rome, which is likened to the advent of Hercules, but it finds its way to the more personal focus of Horace's private party arrangements, in the process offering a powerfully innovative assessment of Augustus as benefactor of the domestic realm.[52] In metrical terms, a form potentially expressive of the domestic carries in its own way the dilemma posed by a poem in Aeolic 'little stanzas' of which the first word is a mighty 'Hercules', and what seemed a metrical anomaly at the start of the poem is revealed as a satisfyingly appropriate match of metre and matter as it approaches its conclusion.

A broadly similar trajectory might be identified in *Odes* 1.22, *Integer vitae*, a poem that moves from an apparently serious opening to an unexpectedly light conclusion. Again, we might be tempted to see the character of the sapphic metre drawing the poetic artefact towards a less public or more feminine – in a word, Sapphic – aesthetic. *Odes* 1.22 is 'a poem which flirts with the possibility that it has something solemn to say about ethics',[53] but the message of its closing lines, that the invulnerable man of which he speaks is a lover, not a philosopher, reveals it as a much more whimsical piece. It has also been suggested that in its sober *incipit* and elsewhere 1.22 alludes to Alcaeus,[54] and that would increase the impact of

---

[50] Putnam 2000: 107. For further thoughts on its sapphic form, see Putnam 2000: 106–8, Barchiesi 2009: 332, Morgan 2010: 221–74. Becker 2010 and Rossi 1998 ≈ 2009 offer alternative interpretations of Horace's relaxation of his own rule regarding the caesura in the sapphic hendecasyllable in the *Carmen*. Beyond the *Carmen*, Cucchiarelli 1999 interprets Horace's account of the metrical relationship between Sappho, Alcaeus, and Archilochus at *Epistles* 1.19.23–31, drawing out Horace's debt to contemporary metrical analysis.

[51] Barchiesi 2009: 333.

[52] For discussion of this poem, the fundamental issue being in what its unity might consist, see La Penna 1963: 129–31, Brink 1971: 460, D. West 2002: 126–33, Morgan 2005, 2010: 237–48.

[53] Morgan 2010: 211.

[54] Burzacchini 1976.

what is undoubtedly a richly Sapphic coda, both capping and improving on Catullus' version (51.5) of Sappho's 'sweetly speaking . . . and laughing charmingly' (ἄδυ φωνείϲαϲ ... | καὶ γελαίϲαϲ ἰμέροεν, fr. 31.3–5), and (above all) selecting as its final image a female object of erotic attraction:

> pone sub curru nimium propinqui
> solis in terra domibus negata:
> dulce ridentem Lalagen amabo,
>   dulce loquentem.

Set me beneath the chariot of a sun too close at hand in a land denied to human habitation – I shall love my Lalage, sweetly laughing, sweetly speaking.

Further Reading

Traill 2005 is an excellent introduction to the reshaping of Sappho by her posthumous tradition, comedy especially, and Kivilo 2010: 167–200 investigates the legends about her in more detail. Barchiesi 2009 sets Roman reception of Sappho in the context of the Latin afterlife of Greek lyric, while D. West 1995, 1998, 2002 are full of informed insights into Horace's practice, including his debts to Sappho. Feeney 1993 offers an excellent overview of the challenge facing Horace in replicating Greek lyric. Woodman 2002 is a stimulating turn against the consensus regarding the relative importance of Alcaeus and Sappho in Horace's poetry, offering many insights into Sappho's status in Rome. Thorsen and Harrison 2019 is a collection of essays on the reception of Sappho in Rome tackling a range of Roman authors with up-to-date bibliography. Morgan 2010 discusses many of the issues broached here at greater length, discussing (metrically) sapphic poetry by Catullus, Horace, and Statius. This important metrical dimension of Roman Sappho, the character of the stanza bearing her name, is taken in interesting directions by Rossi 1998 ≈ 2009 and Becker 2010, who both consider Horace's use of the caesura, something that he himself introduced in a strong form to Latin sapphics in *Odes* 1–3, but relaxed in the *Carmen saeculare* and *Odes* 4; Becker 2010 is particularly concerned with the interplay of metre and accent in the stanza. Cucchiarelli 1999, meanwhile, investigates how contemporary metrical theory influenced Roman use of the form.

CHAPTER 22

Sappho in Imperial Greek Literature

Ewen Bowie

High evaluations of Sappho's poetry are spread across almost every genre of Greek writing in the Roman empire and are comparably documented in Latin. Just as the term 'the poet' (ὁ ποιητής) could usually be taken to refer to Homer, so 'the poetess' (ἡ ποιήτρια) would always mean Sappho.[1] Most telling, perhaps, are the judgements of writers who were themselves critics, and in at least one case teachers, of literature, two of whom were indeed the only witnesses to complete or near-complete poems of Sappho until our knowledge of her oeuvre was greatly augmented by papyri from Roman Egypt. I shall begin with these critics, then review the knowledge or use of Sappho by philosophers, rhetors, lexicographers, and novelists, concluding with a few words on Christian writers and on late antiquity.

Critics

The earliest critic, writing in Augustan Rome, is Dionysius of Halicarnassus, who quotes all twenty-eight lines of Sappho's prayer to Aphrodite, fr. 1, whose first line's citation by the second-century AD metrician Hephaestion (14.1) to exemplify the sapphic stanza demonstrates that it stood first in the standard Alexandrian edition. Dionysius chooses Sappho among poets and Isocrates among orators to illustrate the style he

---

[1] So Galen, *Mental Faculties Follow Physical Temperaments* IV 771 Kühn = p. 152 Singer (cf. Antipater of Thessalonica, *Greek Anthology* 7.15 = test. 57), one of only three references to Sappho's poetry in that polymath's known work. The others are at *A Commentary in Three Books on Hippocrates' Prorrhetic* XVI 566 Kühn, where he recalls a literary scholar thinking he was reading a book of Bacchylides or Sappho when delirious, and *Exhortation to Study Medicine* I 16 Kühn = p. 41 Singer, where he endorses 'the Lesbian woman' for commending goodness as superior to beauty. More knowledge of Sappho may be shown by his use of the plural ἄσαι ('vexations') at *Commentaries on Hippocrates' Aphorisms* XVIIb 859 Kühn. Although the singular is common in medical writing, this rare plural may recall Sappho fr. 1.3.

terms 'polished and flowery' (γλαφυρά καὶ ἀνθηρά) and draws attention to how the poem's 'charm' (χάρις) is created by the sounds and juxtaposition of its words:[2]

> The euphony and charm of this diction are created in the cohesion and smoothness of the combinations. Words are juxtaposed with each other and woven together according to natural affinities and pairings of their letters.

Dionysius' other reference and citation are similarly focused on the sound of her poetry,[3] and, unlike one of his judgements of Alcaeus,[4] say nothing of the power of Sappho's ideas.

Very different is our other critic to quote a whole poem, the author of *On the Sublime* whom his manuscripts name Longinus, writing perhaps late in the first century AD. He too, citing fr. 31, praises Sappho's selection and combination, but of ideas related to erotic frenzy, not of words and sounds:

> on each occasion she chooses the emotions that go with the madness of desire from what accompanies it and from the actual reality. And in what does she demonstrate her excellence? By the fact that she is clever at picking out and combining with each other their crucial and extreme elements.[5]

A third critic to admire Sappho was a Demetrius (Hellenistic or early Roman period) who wrote *On Style*, and who cites Sappho and her poetry no less than eight times. Like Dionysius he is interested in how she creates charm (χάρις). This he finds partly in her subjects – 'some elements of charm are to be found in subject matter, like gardens of nymphs, marriage poems, desires: all Sappho's poetry'[6] – partly in verbal techniques like hyperbole, repetition, comparison, and 'change of expression' (μεταβολή).[7] Similar ideas are expressed by the late second-century sophist Hermogenes of Tarsus: he observes that 'sweetness' (γλυκύτης) can be achieved by describing 'a beautiful place, varieties of plants, a diversity of streams', citing phrases from fr. 2; or by attributing agency to inanimate things, as when Sappho tells her lyre to speak in fr. 118.[8]

---

[2] Dionysius of Halicarnassus, *On the Arrangement of Words* 23.1, 10, 12.

[3] *Demosthenes* 40.11, where Sappho is again mentioned, here alongside Hesiod and Anacreon, as an example of the elegant and refined style; and *On the Arrangement of Words* 25.19, which cites fr. 113 to exemplify a metrical pattern also found in Demosthenes.

[4] *On Imitation* 2.8 on Alcaeus' magnanimity (τὸ μεγαλοφυές).

[5] Pseudo-Longinus, *On the Sublime* 10.1.

[6] Demetrius, *On Style* 132 (test. 45); cf. 166.

[7] *On Style* 127, 162 (hyperbole), 140 (repetition), 146 (comparison), 148 (change of expression).

[8] Hermogenes, *On Ideas* 2.4 (pp. 331, 334 Rabeᶜ).

Philosophers

Plutarch

Plutarch felt both the power and the sweetness of Sappho's poetry, and though sharing Plato's worries about poetry's capacity to corrupt, his *On How Young Men Should Listen to Poetry* shows that he had a strategy to deal with it.[9] His awareness of its power is reflected in Philippus' remark in *Sympotic Questions* (711d) that 'he would put his cup down out of respect if he heard Sappho and the poems of Anacreon being sung' in a symposium, just as he would be embarrassed hearing Platonic dialogues read there. Plutarch's feeling for the charm that accompanies that power comes across when Serapion remarks in *On Pythian Oracles* (397a) 'do you not see how much *charis* Sappho's songs have, bewitching and charming their hearers?'[10] Fr. 31 made an especially powerful impression on Plutarch, as it did on Pseudo-Longinus. Plutarch quotes it twice in the *Moralia*. In *On Desire* (763a) Autobulus' narrative presents his father – i.e. Plutarch earlier in his life – persuading Daphnaeus to recite lines from this poem of 'beautiful Sappho', and then Plutarch himself commenting on the power of desire that they attest. In *How to Detect One's Ethical Progress* (81d) the same passage is mischievously drawn into a comparison between erotic arousal and excitement at sensing philosophical progress:

> In the case of a young man who has tasted true progress in philosophy these Sapphic symptoms attend him:
>
> > His tongue breaks, and a delicate fire at once courses beneath his skin,
>
> but you will see his eye undisturbed and calm, and you would wish to hear him uttering.

Fr. 31 also surfaces in the *Demetrius*, when Plutarch (naming Sappho) lists the symptoms of desire Antiochus betrayed in Stratonice's presence (38.4).[11]

---

[9] E. Bowie 2014.

[10] Similarly another Platonist, Apuleius, *Apologia* 9 (test. 48): Greek love poets include 'also the woman from Lesbos, [who wrote] lasciviously and with such charm that she commends her unfamiliar dialect by the sweetness of her songs'.

[11] With the exception of a possible allusion to fr. 130.2 at *Sympotic Questions* 681b (the term γλυκύπικρον), all Plutarch's citations of Sappho identify her as their poet: as well as those discussed, cf. *Recommendations for Marriage* 146a (fr. 55). Might this imply that Sappho is not a 'respectable' poet whose work one might be expected to recognise in a high-minded context?

Plutarch, it seems, knew Sappho moderately well. Another passage too, fr. 55, is cited twice, once by Eraton discussing garlands in *Sympotic Questions* 646ef, and more fully by Plutarch himself in *Recommendations for Marriage* 145f–146a. But neither citation offers all four lines later found in Stobaeus (3.4.12), an anthologisation that, together with their quotation by Clement of Alexandria,[12] suggests they were quite widely known. Plutarch perhaps got them from an anthology, as too the exhortation cited in *On Controlling Anger* 456e: 'and in anger nothing is more dignified than keeping quiet, as Sappho recommends [fr. 158] "when anger spreads in your breast guard against an idly barking tongue"'. His glossing of the line cited in *On Desire* 751d (fr. 49.2), 'you seemed to me to be a little girl and without charm', as addressed to a girl not yet ready for marriage, casts doubt on whether he knew the line that may have preceded it (fr. 49.1): 'Once long ago did I feel desire for you, Atthis'.[13]

We might conclude that Plutarch was very familiar with fr. 31, knew some other lines of Sappho's poetry, perhaps out of context, but that he was not fully conversant with her corpus at first hand, as he was with Homer and the Attic tragedians.

Dio of Prusa

The Stoic Dio of Prusa, despite a Platonist streak, is much less sympathetic. He mentions Sappho only once, when in *Oration* 2.28 his character Alexander rejects her poetry, like Anacreon's, as unsuitable for singing by kings:[14] rather they should sing poems of Stesichorus and Pindar (though in a very un-Stoic way Dio proceeds to quote in full an erotic poem by Anacreon).[15]

There is no such lapse in the hard-core Stoic whose lectures we owe to Arrian's reworking, Epictetus. Indeed, when he insists that attaining higher status does not quell hankerings for what one still lacks, his use of Sappho's term for a such pangs, ἡ ἄση, may be a snipe at her admirers: 'the burning is similar, the tossing is the same, the craving, the desire for

---

[12] See below p. 317 with n. 51.

[13] From Hephaestion, *Handbook on Metres* 7.7 (test. 227 V.).

[14] [Dio], *Oration* 64.2, almost certainly by Favorinus, not Dio, also mentions Sappho as a μουσική among the distinguished women of antiquity. For taking Anacreon and Sappho as similar in their production of love poetry, cf. Plutarch, *Sympotic Questions* 711d, discussed above; Menander, *On Display Speeches* 333.8–10 (pp. 6–7 R–W, discussed below, p. 317); and Gellius (cited below, n. 40).

[15] E. Bowie 2016b.

what is not there' (Arrian, *Lectures of Epictetus* 4.1.174–5). It is no surprise, then, that whereas Dio's Platonist pupil Favorinus, concluding his speech to the Corinthians when they decided to pull down his statue, quotes fr. 147 to support the greater importance of γνώμη than of being remembered,[16] Sappho is mentioned by none of the great philosophers of the following century – Marcus Aurelius, Sextus Empiricus, Alexander of Aphrodisias – nor by Diogenes Laertius. Nor indeed is she of interest to historians or geographers of the high empire. Arrian, Appian, Cassius Dio, and Herodian are silent, with the exception of the passage in the *Lectures of Epictetus* just discussed. Earlier, Strabo (13.2.3 = test. 7) at least praised her: 'a contemporary with these was Sappho, an extraordinary phenomenon: for in the whole of recorded history we know of no woman attested who was even in the least comparable with her in respect of her poetry'. But he offers only one quotation from her poetry, understandably geographical (1.2.33 = fr. 35): 'either you (are at?) Cyprus or Paphos or Panormus'. In his references too topography dominates: the place she leapt into the sea out of 'maddening longing' for Phaon (10.2.9 = test. 23, citing Menander, *Leucadia* fr. 1 Austin), her calling a promontory in southern Lesbos 'Aiga' (Αἰγᾶ, 13.1.68 = fr. 170). But Strabo was not a sloppy reader,[17] and picks up Herodotus' misidentification of Rhodopis as her brother Charaxus' mistress: Sappho, he points out, calls her Doricha (17.1.33 = fr. 202).

Late in the second century, Pausanias likewise has little. It is hardly credible that he saw no sculptures of Sappho, but he mentions none, and is interested chiefly in mythology she touched on. As often linking Sappho with Anacreon, the first poet after her whose poetry was chiefly about *erôs* (1.25.1), he is irritated by her contradictory presentation of the god Eros ('the Lesbian Sappho sang many inconsistent things about Eros', 9.27.3), and suggests that she got the name Oetolinus from Pamphos (9.29.8 = fr. 140(b)).

Rhetors and Sophists

Sappho gets much more attention from the rhetors Aelius Aristides, Lucian, Maximus of Tyre, and Philostratus.

---

[16] [Dio], *Oration* 37.47.
[17] Unless he got this from the scholar Callias of Mytilene, whose commentary on Sappho and Alcaeus he knows (13.2.4 = test. 41; cf. fr. 214B.11–15).

Aristides' three Sappho quotations are admittedly few by comparison with those of several other early poets, above all of Pindar.[18] He knows she was honoured at Mytilene (12.85 Lenz–Behr), and she joins many other writers cited to excuse his self-praise (28.51 = II 158.13–16 Keil): here, in referring to Sappho's claims that she will not be forgotten even after her death, Aristides may be thinking of frr. 55, 65, or 147. A possible allusion to fr. 34 (at 1.11 = I/I 11.22 Lenz–Behr) and to fr. 31.11 in the monody for Smyrna, destroyed by an earthquake in AD 177 (fr. 196 at 18.4 = II 9.19–20 Keil), complete the tally.

Lucian never actually quotes Sappho, and only twice mentions her. For him she is a μελοποιός like Anacreon or Stesichorus to whom one may allude to establish one's claims to *paideia* – much like the rich women of *On Salaried Retainers* who are pleased 'if it is said that they are educated, are philosophers, and compose songs almost as good as Sappho's'.[19]

But Lucian's other reference shows he knows critical assessments of Sappho. In *Paintings* 18 the interlocutor Polystratus recommends that the depiction of Pantheia, consort of the Emperor Verus, should draw on Sappho: 'The second and third models should be the famous Theano and the song-writer from Lesbos ... Theano contributing magnanimity to the painting, and Sappho her polished *modus vivendi*.' The last phrase (τὸ γλαφυρὸν τῆς προαιρέσεως) is probably a reference to the style of which Dionysius of Halicarnassus saw her as representative.[20]

It is unlikely, however, that the Lesbia of Lucian's *Dialogues of Courtesans* in any way evokes Sappho,[21] but not impossible – Aelian may protest too much in distinguishing Scamandronymus' daughter from another Sappho of Lesbos who was a *hetaira* ('courtesan').[22] But it is also to Aelian that we owe the famous story of Solon so struck by a song of Sappho that he said he wanted to learn it and then die.[23]

Maximus of Tyre refers to no fewer than twelve poems of Sappho at the end of *Oration* 18, developing a virtuoso comparison between Socrates and his lovers and Sappho and hers; six of his citations are our only text of two epithets and four longer fragments, totalling six lines of poetry, indicating a good, possibly first-hand knowledge.[24]

---

[18] E. Bowie 2008a.
[19] *On Salaried Retainers* 36: cf. below on Balbilla and the song to the rose in Achilles Tatius 2.1.2–3.
[20] *Demosthenes* 40 (test. 42).
[21] *Dialogues of Courtesans* 2.2–3, 5.
[22] Aelian, *Historical Miscellany* 12.19 (test. 4).
[23] Aelian cited by Stobaeus, *Florilegium* 3.29.58 (test. 10).
[24] Schlesier 2017.

Good knowledge of Sappho is also expected by Philostratus in three places where he plays entertainingly with her poetry and her reputation. Most unexpected is the scene early in his *Life of Apollonius* (1.30 = test. 21) where, conversing with his 'disciple' Damis in the Parthian king's palace, Apollonius conjures up a bogus Pamphylian female poet, allegedly Sappho's pupil: 'This skilled woman was called Damophyle and she is said to have been like Sappho in having young girls as her pupils and composing poems both erotic and hymnic. And her songs to Artemis are refashionings based on those of Sappho.'[25] This division into erotic and hymnic poetry suggests a reasonable knowledge of Sappho's poetry. Each genre is represented in Philostratus' other two engagements with Sappho.

One is in his *Letter* to Cleonides (51), opening: 'Sappho loves the rose and always garlands it with a word of praise, likening lovely maidens to it; and she likens it also to the arms of the Graces when she bares their arms to the elbow.' Here Philostratus alludes to a line (fr. 53) known from an ancient introduction to Theocritus poem 28: 'Holy Graces with rosy arms, hither, daughters of Zeus'; and his claim that Sappho repeatedly praised roses may show that he knew all or some of several poems.[26] But in none of these does Sappho compare girls to roses, so Philostratus probably evokes lines still unknown to us but drawn on by Longus for the phrase 'lips softer than roses' (χείλη ... ρόδων ἀπαλώτερα) and still known in the twelfth century to Gregory of Corinth, and perhaps to Michael Italikos.[27]

That other phrases in this letter also evoke Sappho might be argued from some similarities with a letter of Alciphron:

> I am no longer myself, mother; I cannot endure the thought of being married to the boy from Methymna ... He is beautiful, mother, beautiful, the sweetest thing, and his locks are curlier than sea-moss, and his smile is more charming than the sea in a calm, and the radiance of his eyes is like the dark blue of the sea, as it appears in the first moment of illumination by the sun's rays. And his whole face – you might say the Graces themselves have left Orchomenus and, after washing themselves in the Argaphian fountain-house are dancing in his cheeks; and his lips – he has plundered the roses from the bosom of Aphrodite and set their blossom upon them. I shall be joined with this man, or, if I can't, I shall

---

[25] E. Bowie 2009: 58, 60–1.
[26] See frr. 2.6, 55.2, 74a.4 V., 94.13, 96.13.
[27] Longus, *Daphnis and Chloe* 1.18.1 (below, p. 315); Gregory of Corinth, *On Hermogenes' Method of Forcefulness* 13 (VII/2 1236.14 *RG*) = Sappho fr. 156; Michael Italikos, *Oration* 2 (pp. 68.14–69.4 Gautier) = fr. 117A. See PONTANI pp. 326–7.

follow the example of Lesbian Sappho: not from her Leucadian cliff but from the Piraeus' jutting rocks shall I hurl myself into the surf.[28]

If, as I suspect, the concluding reference to Sappho is there partly to confirm alert readers' identification of Sapphic material, the letter sets Alciphron alongside Philostratus as familiar enough with her poems to play allusive games.

This Philostratus certainly does in the opening of his second book of *Paintings* (Eἰκόνες), descriptions of pictures purportedly viewed in a gallery at Naples.[29] In this *Painting*, entitled 'Hymn-singers' (ὑμνητρίαι), the epithet 'rosy-armed' (ῥοδοπήχεις) reappears (§3; cf. fr. 53), and other poems too are evoked: fr. 2 by the altar and frankincense, perhaps by the myrtle grove;[30] the Tithonus Poem by the remark on the teacher's advancing age; fr. 96 by the dew; fr. 35 by the reference to Paphos:

> An Aphrodite, made of ivory, delicate maidens are hymning in delicate myrtle groves. The chorister who leads them is skilled in her art, and not yet past her youth; for a certain beauty rests even on her first wrinkle . . . Do you wish us to pour a libation of discourse on the altar? For of frankincense and cinnamon and myrrh it has enough already, and it seems to me to give out also a fragrance as of Sappho ... For the maidens are singing, are singing, and the chorister frowns at one who is off the key ... For as to their garments, they are ... for instance, the close-fitting girdle, the chiton that leaves the arm free, and the way they enjoy treading with naked feet on the tender grass and drawing refreshment from the dew; and the flowered decoration of their garments, and the colours used on them – the way they harmonise the one with the other ... As to the figures of the maidens, if we were to leave the decision regarding them to Paris or any other judge, I believe he would be at a loss how to vote, so close is the rivalry among them in rosy arms and flashing eyes and fair cheeks and in 'honeyed voices', to use the charming expression of Sappho.

> Eros, tilting up the centre of his bow, lightly strikes the string for them ... What, then, is the song they are singing? For indeed something of the subject has been expressed in the painting; they are telling how Aphrodite was born from the sea through an emanation of Ouranos (Heaven). Upon which of the islands she came ashore they do not yet tell, though doubtless they will name Paphos ...

I have quoted this text extensively because it probably plays as much with Sapphic poetry still unknown to us as with what we already recognise.

---

[28] Letter 11 in Benner and Fobes 1949: 60–3; their translation, adapted.
[29] For 2.1, see Platt 2011: 1–7, Bachmann 2015: 69–99, M. Squire 2016.
[30] For myrtles, cf. Philetas' garden in Longus 2.4.1.

Philologists and Lexicographers

A good knowledge of Sappho also characterises both lexicographers and a writer with an *anima naturaliter lexicographica*, Athenaeus of Naucratis.

Athenaeus' *Scholars at Dinner* has some twenty-three citations of a poem's text, or references to a poem's content, offering around thirty-five lines – admittedly few by comparison with his thousands from comedy. Those of Sappho are prompted by an interest not in the quality of her poetry but in its testimony for sympotic practice and accessories – cups, garlands, perfumes, wine-pourers – and for some associated linguistic features. Although Athenaeus only twice attributes a quotation to a book (fr. 44.10 to Book 2 at 11.460d, fr. 101 to Book 5 at 9.410de), he probably had access to a complete edition, though he sometimes offers a text different from that elsewhere transmitted.[31] Four lines of one poem, fr. 141, featuring Hermes mixing and pouring ambrosia for the gods into drinking vessels called *karchêsia*, are quoted at two different points (2.39ab, 10.425d); four more from the same poem elsewhere (11.475a); and in a fourth passage Athenaeus refers to it for Hermes' role as an *oinochoos* ('wine-pourer', 5.192c). One other sequence of four lines that he cites is still our only text of the poem from which they come: fr. 101 at 9.410de. In other cases what he transmits has been supplemented by texts on papyri (e.g. fr. 44 at 11.460d, the Tithonus Poem at 15.687ab) or an *ostrakon* or potsherd (fr. 2 at 11.463e).

Pollux too (Julius Polydeuces) was from Naucratis, but taught as a sophist in Athens. His lexicon cites Sappho from Book 3 onwards. First, accusing poets of confusing terminology, he criticises Sappho for using the term γαμβρόν for a husband (3.32).[32] Then he cites her twice in Book 6, for 'cups ornamented with golden knuckle-bones' (φιάλαι ... ὡς αἰ Cαπφοῦς χρυσαστράγαλοι, 6.98, fr. 192) and a garland of anise (6.107), referring to fr. 81, four lines of which Athenaeus cites, while other scraps survive on a second- or third-century papyrus. She is then cited three times in Book 7: at 7.49 (fr. 177) for a woman's garment called βεῦδος, apparently a short, diaphanous dress; then at 7.73 (fr. 100) he quotes from her fifth book 'and covered her well with soft, fleecy material'; finally at 7.93 he pounces on her unusual word μάcληc: 'a many-coloured sandal of fine Lydian workmanship' (fr. 39). At 10.40 he ascribes a non-Attic word τύλαι for 'cushions' or 'quilts' to Sappho (fr. 46), and finally at

---

[31] De Kreij 2016.

[32] Her surviving uses of γαμβρόc seem to be of a bridegroom, with fr. 161 a possible exception.

10.124 reports that she is credited with the first use of χλαμύc for a cloak – one worn by Eros 'coming from the heavens, girt in a bright red cloak' (fr. 54). Pollux also observes at 9.84 (test. 11) that Mytilene put Sappho on its coins – something confirmed by extant examples, which also exist for Eresus.[33]

The smaller surviving corpus of Pollux's contemporary Phrynichus has two citations: one, in the *Preparation for Rhetoric*, for the term γρύτα, a box for 'perfumes and certain women's perquisites' (fr. 179).[34] The other, at *Ecloga* 272 (p. 89 Fischer), concerns natron, called by Sappho νίτρον (fr. 189), a luxury from Egypt probably used to wash both person and garments.[35]

Herennius Philo shares the interest of Athenaeus and Pollux in *Realien*. Thus he notes that in her second book Sappho calls frankincense not λίβανον but λιβανωτόν; but he also has a broader linguistic interest, criticising her for using ἀρτίωc in the line 'Golden-sandalled Dawn had just …' (ἀρτίωc μὲν ἀ χρυcοπέδιλοc Αὔωc), whereas in his view she should have used the purely temporal term ἄρτι.[36]

Lexicographers' ability to quote pertinently from Sappho is matched by the good but obviously necessary knowledge of her corpus shown by the mid-second century metrician Hephaestion. His ten citations,[37] most of more than one line, involve assignation of different metres to Books 2, 3, and 7.

Novels

It might be expected that the prose fiction texts we call novels, given their focus on *erôs*, would evoke Sappho's poetry. Most do not. In Chariton Goold claims echoes of fr. 44 at 1.1.13 (Callirhoe's wedding)[38] and fr. 44A at 1.1.16.[39] But neither passage has a close verbal echo, nor is fr. 1 discernable in Callirhoe's several prayers to Aphrodite. Given Sappho's frequent references to roses (cf. Philostratus, *Letter* 51, pp. 309–10 above) it might be

[33] *RPC* §§1785, 1787, 2649, 3145 (Mytilene), 2482, 2622 (Eresus).
[34] Phrynichus, *Praeparatio sophistica* p. 60.16–18 De Borries on γρυμεῖα.
[35] E. Bowie 2016a: 162–3.
[36] Herennius Philo λ 108, α 33 Palmieri (Sappho frr. 44.30, 123).
[37] Of frr. 49.1, 82(a), 102, 110(a), 112, 115, 117, 130, 131, 168B; also test. 229 V.
[38] Goold 1995: 34 n. a, presumably seeing especially 1.1.13 as evoking fr. 44.29–30.
[39] Goold 1995: 35 n. d. At 1.1.16 Callirhoe's appearance awes, as when Artemis appears to hunters in the wild; but fr. 44A.9, on Artemis' birth, simply describes her as πάρθενον δ' ἐλαφάβ]ολον ἀγροτέραν (*suppl.* Page).

guessed that the praise of the rose sung by Leucippe to the accompaniment of her *kithara* (Achilles Tatius 2.1.2–3) might evoke Sappho, whose poetry we know from Philodemus might be sung by a *hetaira* and from Lucian by would-be-educated ladies.[40] But again there are no verbal echoes.

By contrast, Longus' *Daphnis and Chloe* is shot through with refashioning of Sappho. 'In Lesbos', Longus' first words, prompts thoughts of that island's most famous love poet. Its next phrase, 'in a grove of the Nymphs', corroborates: a grove is the setting of a poem in Sappho Book 1 (fr. 2) and groves figured in another poem in Book 5 (fr. 94.27) – both poems known to Longus' near-contemporary Athenaeus,[41] as was fr. 2 to Hermogenes.[42] The trees, flowers, and water (πηγή, pr. 1) of Longus' gove (ἄλcοc) pick up those of Sappho fr. 2.2–9: 'your delightful grove of apple-trees . . . therein cold water babbles through apple-branches, and the whole place is shadowed by roses, and from the shimmering leaves the sleep of enchantment comes down; therein too a meadow …' Shortly the shepherd Dryas discovers the baby Chloe near a cave of the Nymphs somehow related to the grove (1.4.1). It too has a spring (πηγή) watering a meadow (λειμών) of soft grass, whose relation to Sappho's λείμων is hinted at by its epithet 'smooth' (γλαφυρόc) (1.4.3) – the epithet used together with 'flowery' (ἀνθηρόc) by Dionysius of Halicarnassus for the style he chooses Sappho to exemplify.[43] The Nymphs, crucial to Longus' story, have no immediate ancestor in Sappho, for whom νύμφα always means 'bride', but are iconographic cousins of the Graces (Χάριτεc): Longus' presentation of them as bare-armed (1.4.2) may follow Sappho's invocation of the Graces as rosy-armed (fr. 53), a feature picked up by Philostratus (*Paintings* 2.1, above).

I now return briefly to two earlier details. First, again, the preface. Its concluding phrase, 'for assuredly nobody has escaped desire, nor shall escape it, so long as beauty exists and eyes see' (pr. 4), may echo Posidippus' claim for the immortality of Sappho's poetry, cited by Athenaeus, 'so long as a Nile ship goes down to the briny sea'.[44] Second,

---

[40] Philodemus, *Greek Anthology* 5.132.7 (test. 55), Lucian, *On Salaried Retainers* 36 (above, p. 308). Singing is also envisaged by Demetrius, *On Style* 167, Plutarch, *Sympotic Questions* 622c, 711d, and performances of the *Anacreontea* and Sappho by boys and girls documented by Aulus Gellius, *Attic Nights* 19.9.3–4 (test. 53).

[41] Athenaeus, *Scholars at Dinner* 11.463e, 15.690e.

[42] Above, p. 304 with n. 8. For more detailed discussion of Longus' Sappho, see E. Bowie 2019.

[43] Above, pp. 303–4.

[44] Posidippus 122.8 A–B (test. 15, cited by Athenaeus, *Scholars at Dinner* 13.596c), ἔcτ' ἂν ἴηι Νείλου ναῦc ἔφ' ἁλὸc πελάγη.

the tokens found with the exposed Daphnis include a purple χλαμύδιον: the word is a diminutive of χλαμύς, which is no simple cloak (χλαῖνα), but a higher-status garment worn by military men and ephebes.[45] Here in a Mytilenean context Longus may gesture to the view (quoted, as we have seen, by Pollux 10.124 = fr. 54) that the word χλαμύς was first used by Sappho, precisely of the purple garment worn by Eros.

The next intertext is in the plot development that Eros engineers (1.11.1), and is with the first poem in Sappho Book 1. At 1.12.1 Daphnis pursues an aggressive goat that itself pursues another – 'he began to pursue the pursuer', a play on words that could trigger comparison and contrast with the situation where pursuers most often end up pursued, erotic pursuit, particularly Sappho fr. 1.21, 'for even if she flees, soon she will pursue'. There follows a cluster of intertexts deployed when Longus chooses to present his female lead Chloe (and not, perhaps significantly, Daphnis, who must wait until 1.17.2–4) pondering her symptoms of desire. 'Her heart ached' (ἄςη δὲ αὐτῆς εἶχε τὴν ψυχήν, 1.13.5) heads a sequence of canonical love symptoms drawn from poetry and from earlier novels. The word ἄςη is found first in Sappho, fr. 1.3, perhaps also fr. 96.17, then Euripides, *Medea* 245. Although found in medical writing, its rarity, and echoes of fr. 31 elsewhere in this passage, suggest that Longus draws directly on Sappho. So too the phrase 'her eyes kept wandering' dilutes Sappho's 'I see nothing' (fr. 31.11); her neglect of commitments (1.13.6, cf. 1.17.4) may recall the girl whose domination by desire prevents her working at the loom (fr. 102). Chloe's pallor (ὠχρία, 1.13.6) goes back to Sappho's 'I am paler than grass' (fr. 31.14–15) and although the fire of love – 'I burn' (1.14.1) – is found in many genres, for Longus the trope surely began with Sappho's 'and at once a delicate fire spread beneath my skin' (fr. 31.9–10), even if καίομαι ('I burn') in the mouth of a shepherdess also evokes Polyphemus' καιόμενος ... ἀνεχοίμαν ('may I put up with being burned', Theocritus 11.52).

Longus' next evocation of Sappho is indirect. Competing with Daphnis, the cow-herd Dorcon claims to be 'white like milk' (1.16.1; so too Eros at 2.4.1), and shortly Daphnis perceives for the first time that Chloe is 'whiter than milk' (1.17.3). This comparison, wholly appropriate to herdsmen, comes in the first instance from Theocritus 11.20: Polyphemus, punning, praises Galatea as 'whiter than cheese to behold'.[46]

---

[45] Cf. LSJ⁹ s.v. 1 and its presence alongside a sword among actors' props at Achilles Tatius 3.20.6.
[46] E. Bowie 2013: 184–5.

But Gregory of Corinth refers to 'Anacreon's and Sappho's phrases, like "whiter than milk, softer than water, ... more delicate than roses"'.[47] Longus' recurrent use of Sappho makes her a likelier intertext than Anacreon for 1.16.1 and for the reworking of the comparison for Chloe's face, 'truly whiter even than goats' milk' (1.17.3), as too for the description of her 'lips' as 'more delicate than roses' (1.18.1).

Daphnis' symptoms of *erôs* replicate Chloe's in their evocations of Sappho fr. 31. 'He felt cold and tried to restrain his pounding heart' (1.17.2: both symptoms recur in Philetas' tale, 2.7.5) recalls 'and (?cold?) sweat ran down me' (fr. 31.13), and 'set my heart aflutter in my breast' (fr. 31.6) – again recalled by Longus' 'my heart is leaping about' (1.18.1). That his 'face was paler than summer grass' (1.17.4) closely echoes fr. 31.14, 'paler than grass' (cf. Chloe at 1.13.6), with elegant amplification. The echo may be recalled at 4.31.1 by 'going pale' (χλωριῶντα, a rare verb).

Daphnis' contrast between the anguished lover and the outside world (not drawn earlier by Chloe) in 'how the lambs gambol, and I just sit' (οἶον σκιρτῶσιν οἱ ἔριφοι, κἀγὼ κάθημαι, 1.18.2) may recall the song 'the moon has set, and the Pleiades, and it is midnight, and the season passes, but I sleep alone' (fr. 168B = Lyr. adesp. fr. 976 *PMG*). His worry that Dorcon may seem εὐμορφότερος, 'more handsome' (1.18.2), using the comparative as Longus does again at 4.32.1, makes Sappho's use of the comparative the likeliest source: 'Mnasidica is more beautiful than tender Gyrinno' (εὐμορφοτέρα Μνασιδίκα τὰς ἀπάλας Γυρίννως, fr. 82(a)).

At 1.22.1–2 the couple's sheep and goats are thrown into confusion by Dorcon's wolf trick. Longus' term is πτοηθεῖσαι, a word first in Sappho (frr. 22.14, 31.6) but well enough attested for evocation of Sappho to be uncertain. At 2.2.6 the narrator observes that for their piety towards the Nymphs the couple 'for this later received rewards from the gods'. The idea is not rare, but Longus' remark may reverse fr. 133(a) 'Andromeda has a fine reward ...' At 2.20.3 the Methymnaeans kidnap Chloe 'uttering many abusive remarks about the cult statues' (πολλὰ τῶν ἀγαλμάτων κατακερτομήσαντες) of the Nymphs to which she clings for protection. Here Longus evokes two passages in Herodotus: in one Cambyses mocks a cult statue (πολλὰ τῶι ἀγάλματι κατεγέλασε, Herodotus 3.37.2; cf. 9.116), but the other is when 'in a song' Sappho 'uttered many abusive

---

[47] Fr. 156: for the text, see p. 309.

remarks' about either her brother Charaxus or his mistress (πολλὰ κατεκερτόμησέ μιν, 2.135.6 = fr. 202; cf. 1.129.1).

Daphnis and Chloe 3.33.4–34.2 reworks two passages of Sappho's *hymenaea*, known to us from Demetrius and Syrianus, but to Longus more probably together and in the context of a single poem.[48] Fr. 105(a) compares a bride to an apple: 'as the sweet apple blushes on the topmost bough, top on the topmost, and the apple-pickers have forgotten it – no, they have not forgotten, but they could not reach it'. Fr. 105(c) compares her to a fragile flower 'like the hyacinth that shepherds in the mountains trample with their feet, and on the ground its bright red flower . . .' Longus writes:

> one apple was ripening, the topmost on the tree's very top, large and beautiful . . . The harvester was afraid to climb up, had neglected to bring it down; and perhaps the beautiful apple was being preserved for a shepherd who felt desire. When Daphnis saw this apple he rushed to climb up and harvest it . . . and succeeded in harvesting it, and brought it as a gift to Chloe, and made this speech to her in her anger: 'Maiden, the beautiful Seasons created this apple . . . I was not going to abandon it, so that it might fall to the ground and either a beast might trample as it grazed or a creeping animal poison it as it slithered or time waste it away.'

Longus takes his apple from fr. 105(a), but offers two explanations different from Sappho's one for its remaining unpicked – 'he was afraid . . . he neglected', then adds a third which transfers a shepherd from fr. 105(c) – though by qualifying him as 'desiring' (ἐρωτικός) he becomes the desiring Daphnis instead of Sappho's heedless hill-shepherds. Longus then reapplies fr. 105(c) to one of the fates from which Daphnis wishes to save the apple, trampling not by a shepherd but by a sheep.

Less direct interactions may also be suggested. For instance, the wording of 4.40.2, 'and when they were near the doors they sang', suggests that Longus imagines not the ὑμέναιος sung in procession but the ἐπιθαλάμιον sung at the bedroom door. This may partly be homage to Sappho. Although some of her wedding songs may have been *hymenaea* (ὑμέναια), and one fragment has the refrain ὑμήναον (fr. 111.2, 4), all citations refer to her wedding poems as *epithalamia* (ἐπιθαλάμια).[49] Furthermore, the comparison in 4.40.3, 'more even than owls', may

---

[48] E. Bowie 2013: 187–91.
[49] Frr. 103.17 (second-century papyrus), 113 (Dionysius of Halicarnassus), 116 (Servius Auctus).

rework part of a wedding poem of Sappho: 'But rouse yourself, and go to the unmarried youths of your age, [so that] we may see [less] sleep than the clear-voiced [bird]' (fr. 30.6–9).

Given prose-writers' admiration for and knowledge of Sappho, it is perhaps surprising that no fan fiction was created, like the *Anacreontea* modelled on Anacreon's sympotic poetry. The nearest we find are the fictitious Damophyle of Philostratus' *Apollonius* and the Aeolic dialect affected by Julia Balbilla, friend of Hadrian's wife Sabina, in her metrically inappropriate elegiac epigrams inscribed on the Memnon Colossus during the visit of Hadrian and his party in November AD 130.[50]

Christian Writing

Clement's extensive citation of Greek literature (albeit aided by anthologies) includes quoting Sappho once, condemning garlands as associated with pagan cult: 'Sappho garlands the Muses with the rose', and then citing fr. 55.2–3 ('for you have no share in the roses that come from Pieria'), whose fullest text we know from Stobaeus.[51] Clement also lists Sappho as one of few women distinguished as poets, a recognition very different from the hysterical Tatian, who characterises the Sappho sculpted by Silanion as a *hetaira* and calls her a 'female who was a sex-mad prostitute, and she sings of her own lewd behaviour'.[52]

Menander to Stobaeus

Like second-century sophistic figures, Menander in the third still knows his Sappho. He notes that most of her hymns are cletic, like Anacreon's,[53] and that she summons Aphrodite from different places, implying familiarity with several poems.[54] His prescriptions for wedding speeches suggest introducing the gods' love lives, drawing on the love poetry of Sappho as well as Homer and Hesiod.[55] What Menander thought of Sappho's poetry about her own desires we never discover.

---

[50] Philostratus, *Life of Apollonius* 1.30 (test. 21). See E. Bowie 1990: 61–3, Brennan 1998, Cirio 2011, Rosenmeyer 2018, TRIBULATO pp. 143, 145.

[51] *Paedagogus* 2.8.72.3 (I 201.21–3 Stählin).

[52] Clement, *Miscellanies* 4.19.122.4 (II 302.17–18 Stählin); Tatian, *Oration to the Greeks* 33.1, 2.

[53] Menander, *On Display Speeches* 333.8–10 (pp. 6–7 R–W).

[54] Menander, *On Display Speeches* 334.26–32 (pp. 8–11 R–W).

[55] Menander, *On Display Speeches* 402.15–20 (pp. 140–1 R–W).

By contrast, Himerius, perhaps picking up Maximus of Tyre, says (*Oration* 28.2 = test. 50) 'alone among women Sappho with her lyre felt desire for beautiful people, and for this reason, dedicating her entire poetry to Aphrodite and the Erotes, made a girl's beauty and charms the occasion for her songs'. Despite this explicit recognition of Sappho's own love life, Himerius, like Menander, has more interest in her wedding poetry, in its ecphrases of bride and groom, of their wedding ceremonies, and of relevant mythology. Thus in *Oration* 9, his *Epithalamium for Severus*, he says that other poets have left the rituals of Aphrodite to Sappho, who describes in detail the wedding *thalamos* or νυμφεῖον (9.4 = fr. 194), and goes on (9.16 = fr. 105(b)):

> Sappho's move was to compare the girl to an apple allowing only so much to those eager to pick it before it was ripe as not even to touch it with the tip of a finger, but to the man who was ready to harvest the apple in its season to preserve its charm in its prime.

Like Longus (3.33.4–34.2), Himerius here reworks fr. 105(a), and the presence of 'preserved'/'preserve' (ἐτήρησε/τηρῆσαι) in both may suggest that this idea too was in Sappho in some form.[56] Sappho reappears twice in *Oration* 46, which documents her depiction of Apollo Musagetes and comparison of a person praised in the oration (presumably a bridegroom) to the evening star.[57]

Himerius' coevals Libanius and Themistius, less wholly absorbed in literature, likewise show knowledge of Sappho. Libanius' reference to her prayer to Time (Χρόνος) to double the night's length presumably draws on an *epithalamium* (wedding song);[58] by contrast, Themistius' remark that Sappho's and Anacreon's praise of their love objects was legitimately excessive because both parties were private individuals relates to her own desires.[59] So too do Julian's citations from Sappho. He knows frr. 34 (the moon is silver, *Letter* 194 = p. 264.10–11 B–C) and 116 (*Letter* 183 = p. 242.20–1). *Letter* 183 (pp. 240.16–241.2), if indeed by Julian, is also our only source for the passionate lines 'You came, and I was longing for you, and you cooled my heart as it burned with longing' (fr. 48), as is *Letter* 193 (p. 263.5) for the phrase 'my darling' (fr. 163).

Such pagan passion was not right for John of Stobi's fifth-century anthology, which admitted only two anodyne citations: fr. 55 at 3.4.12

---

[56] Unless Himerius read Longus, making him perhaps his earliest documented reader.
[57] *Oration* 46.6 (fr. 208), 46.8 (fr. 104(b)); cf. 47.17.
[58] *Oration* 12.99 (fr. 197). He also links her with music and dance at *Oration* 64.87.
[59] *On Love* [*Oration* 13] 170d–171a (test. 52).

(under 'On senselessness'), earlier, as we have seen, quoted twice by Plutarch and once by Clement; and fr. 121 at 4.22.112 (under 'On marriage'), also in the paroemiographers. The fire of burning Sappho was flickering towards extinction.

Further Reading

The best guide to the imperial reception of Sappho's poetry is the collection of testimonia and fragments in Campbell's Loeb, with texts and translation of the authors who cite or refer to Sappho. Her reception in the imperial period is discussed by Brooten 1996: 29–36, and touched on by Most 1995 ≈ Greene 1996b: 11–35, Prins 1996, and P. Freeman 2016. For Plutarch's use of Sappho, see E. Bowie 2008b: 150–1. For Sappho in Aelius Aristides, see E. Bowie 2008a: 10; in Athenaeus, De Kreij 2016; in Philostratus' *Paintings* 2.1, Platt 2011: 1–7; and in his *Apollonius*, E. Bowie 2009: 58, 60–1.

CHAPTER 23

Sappho at Byzantium

Filippomaria Pontani

I wished to expound the whole heresy of the Bogomils, but 'modesty pre-vents me', as the beautiful Sappho [fr. 137.1–2] says somewhere, because I am a woman writer, and among the *porphyrogeniti* [i.e., those born in the Palace's Purple Chamber] I am the most honourable and the eldest of Alexius' scions. I would really like to write what comes to the ears of the many (although this is best covered in silence), in order to present the Bogomilian heresy in full; but I will pass it over instead, so as not to defile my tongue.

> Anna Komnene, *Alexiad* 15.9.1 (I 489.47–53 Reinsch–Kambylis)

A member of the imperial dynasty ruling the Eastern Roman Empire throughout the twelfth century, the historian Anna Komnene evokes a fragment of Sappho in one of the last paragraphs of her great work devoted to the reign of her father Alexios I Komnenos (1056–1118). This quotation can hardly be regarded as fortuitous, since it occurs in the con-text of Anna's self-definition as a woman writer, who wants to abstain from describing dangerous heresies and the gruesome punishments inflicted on their partisans – here, the burning alive of Basil the Physician (1118).[1]

Scholars find it difficult to argue that Anna ever displayed feminist stances in her writings, for all her positive characterisation of historical figures such as Anna Dalassene, Maria of Alania, Irene Doukaina, and even the Norman princess Sigelgaita.[2] In showing a high consideration for women in power, Anna conveys the idea that, despite their natural inclination, women should never give in to the uncontrolled expression of emotions (fear, sorrow, etc.), even in such extreme cases as her own. In *Alexiad* 14.7.4 (I 451.34 Reinsch–Kambylis) she quotes again 'Sappho's lyre' among a series of literary authorities who in her view would be

---

[1] Buckley 2014: 270–7.
[2] Gouma-Peterson 2000b, Reinsch 2000, and above all Hill 2000.

incapable of singing adequately of the evils she has had to endure since childhood.

The mention of Sappho fr. 137 in Book 15 derives from Aristotle's *Rhetoric*, where it serves as an illustration of the laudable reactions to base proposals or shameful words; in an ambiguous passage, Aristotle seems to imply that these lines were part of Alcaeus' inappropriate request to Sappho rather than of Sappho's reply, as Anna takes them to be.[3] In the broader context of the *Alexiad*, modesty (αἰδώc) is not only an issue of rhetoric, style, or subject matter, but has to do with personal behaviour and with the self-definition of a woman author. When confronted with shameful actions, normally performed by men,[4] Anna displays the same miraculous grace of modesty and sobriety that the Byzantines associated with the best-known woman author of antiquity, 'Sappho the fair' (Cαπφὼ ἡ καλή).[5]

A Standardised Presence

We can easily imagine that Sappho's quotation in Anna Komnene was meant to conjure up some partial parallelism between the historian and her illustrious predecessor; but this remains an exceptional case. The presence of Sappho in Byzantium, though far from isolated in Anna's century (probably the most promising age in terms of attempts to appropriate and explain classical poetry),[6] is sporadic and above all standardised, rarely going beyond the limits of a cliché. This is one of the arguments ruling out the possibility, entertained by several scholars in recent decades, that a book of Sappho's poetry may have circulated during the Greek Middle Ages.[7] If this had been the case, we would expect to have such evident testimonies of Sappho's reception as we encounter in the cases of Hipponax (extensively quoted in Tzetzes's commentaries and *Chiliades*)[8] and of Callimachus' *Aitia* and *Hecale*, whose fragments feature

[3] Alcaeus fr. 384; Aristotle, *Rhetoric* 1367a7–15. Stephanus of Alexandria's commentary on Aristotle (p. 280.30–2 Rabe[b]) attributes the quotation to Sappho, but most editors since Fulvius Ursinus have opted for Alcaeus: Nagy 2007: 219, Yatromanolakis 2007: 168–71.

[4] A similar reaction occurs in *Alexiad* 1.13.3 (I 44.4–5 Reinsch–Kambylis), when *aidôs* prevents Anna from recounting in detail the atrocities inflicted on the German envoys by the Pope's guard: Hill 2000: 57.

[5] This description, found in both Anna Komnene and in Eustathius (*Commentaries on Homer's Iliad* 1205.17 = IV 396.15 Van der Valk, on *Iliad* 20.232–5), is as old as Plato (*Phaedrus* 235c3).

[6] Kaldellis 2009, Pontani 2015: 366–70.

[7] Moravcsik 1964 = 1967: 408–13, Cataudella 1965, Garzya 1971 = 1974, Chrestides 1985, Canfora 1995: 136–7.

[8] Masson 1962: 42–52.

repeatedly in the letters and orations of Michael Choniates, Archbishop of Athens (died 1222).[9] Indeed, Sappho as a name – without specific textual reference – occurs frequently in the works of writers and intellectuals, including one who openly states and deplores the loss of her verse: 'since Sappho and her works, her lyre and her songs, fell prey to time, I shall show you other poems as examples'.[10]

There is no decisive proof that a copy of Sappho in minuscule script ever existed. The latest surviving fragments of the direct tradition, P.Berol. inv. 5006 and 9722, from parchment codices found in Egypt, are dated to the late sixth or early seventh century AD;[11] but we do not have a single fragment or folium, or any indirect evidence of a codex containing Sappho's poetry copied after the transition (known as 'transliteration', late eighth–early ninth century) from majuscule to minuscule handwriting. As for the indirect tradition, in a vast majority of cases the quotations of Sappho in Byzantine authors are certainly made at second hand: that is, they derive from intermediate sources still extant today.

The few exceptions can easily be explained away as slips of memory, as refashionings of second-hand quotations, or else – in the rare cases when the quotation seems to stand in a vacuum – as indebted to lost manuals, lexica, or anthologies.[12] In particular, the only substantial Sapphic fragment which we can certainly say was transmitted exclusively by a Byzantine author – the celebrated fr. 34 on the moon outshining the stars – belongs to a lost commentary on Homer from which the twelfth-century scholar Eustathius of Thessalonica concocted his own exegesis.[13]

For the sake of clarity, I shall here provide not a mere chronological list of the various Byzantine authors quoting Sappho,[14] but rather a typological categorisation of the occurrences of her name and fragments in selected Greek writings dated between AD 529 (the closing of the Neoplatonic school at Athens) and 1453 (the fall of Constantinople).

---

[9] Pontani 2011: 114–17.

[10] Isaac Tzetzes, *On the Metres of Pindar* p. 15.10–12 Drachmann (test. 61). Isaac also, however, regrets the loss of the metrical scholia to Pindar's *Olympian* 1, which are extant.

[11] FINGLASS ch. 17 pp. 232–3.

[12] The role of anthologies might have been important even in late antiquity, yet e.g. in the times of Himerius and Syrianus (fifth century AD) Sappho's text still circulated in its entirety, so it might be far-fetched to ascribe to anthologies such a pivotal role as Dale 2011a: 62–7 implies for the *Excerpts* by the fourth-century AD sophist Sopater (test. 32).

[13] Eustathius, *Commentaries on Homer's Iliad* 729.22–3 (II 637.14–16 Van der Valk, on *Iliad* 8.555); Erbse 1960: 423–4. The reconstruction is made possible by the comparison with the entry in Apollonius Sophista, *Lexicon Homericum* 161.20–6 Bekker³.

[14] Pontani 2001.

Typologies of Quotations

First, some references occur in lexicographical, grammatical, or paroemiographical texts, which tell us nothing about the circulation or reception of our author in Byzantine times; such works simply inherit these quotations or allusions from a pre-existing tradition. Lexicography obviously has the lion's share in this respect – above all, Hesychius, Photius, the *Suda*, and the *Etymologica*[15] – but Eustathius also occasionally invokes Sappho's authority for the attestation of a term: e.g. on κατάρης 'strong wind', from Porphyry's *Homeric Questions*.[16]

The dialectal peculiarities of Sappho's Aeolic are sometimes highlighted in Byzantine lexica, but play virtually no role in Gregory of Corinth's systematic work on Greek dialects.[17] Mentions of Sappho's metre occur where we would expect: in ancient and Byzantine commentaries to Hephaestion, and in the twelfth-century metricologists Trichas and Isaac Tzetzes (the latter's poem *On the Metres of Pindar* refers to 'Sappho the writer of songs', Cαπφοῦς τῆς ἀιςματογραφούςης, p. 14.25 Drachmann). Even in these erudite works, however, Sappho never receives a place of honour, and appears just as one authority amongst others.

Perhaps the most curious element in this domain is represented by the fanciful etymology of Sappho's name, perhaps an original fruit of the Byzantine fondness for this kind of game. The connection with cαφής, 'clear', and an unattested verb cάφω is apparently unknown to lexica and grammarians before the twelfth-century *Etymologicum magnum*: '"Sappho" from *saphô*, "clarify", or from *saphô*, "touch": "Sapho" from *saphô*, as "Klotho" from *klôthô*, and then by addition of a *p*, "Sappho". Or else from *saphês*, "clear"' (708.19–21 Gaisford). As customary in this genre, it is impossible to gauge the date of this etymology, but it bears interesting fruit in such a seminal text as John Tzetzes's *Prolegomena to Comedy* (pp. 24.37–25.49 Koster = test. 254g V.). Here the scholar embarks on an allegorical joke by personifying the four virtues of dramatic poetry in a quartet of feminine figures by the names of Sappho, Gorgo, Peitho, and Polymnia, each of whom is made to stand for a stylistic virtue: *saphêneia, gorgotês, pithanon, megaloprepeia* ('clarity, vigour, persuasion, and magniloquence', p. 25.61–4).

---

[15] For Byzantine lexicography, see Alpers 2001: 201–5; also Calame 1970.
[16] Eustathius, *Commentaries on Homer's Iliad* 603.35 (11 194.6–7 Van der Valk, on *Iliad* 5.738); Porphyry, *Homeric Questions* 1.41.20 Schrader.
[17] For Byzantine dialectal learning, and on the composition of Gregory's handbook, see Consani 1991: 55–71.

The name of Sappho often occurs in Byzantine writing as a generic antonomasia for poetic authority. Since antiquity, Sappho was known as the 'tenth Muse'.[18] John Malalas in the sixth century presents her as a contemporary of the mythical Athenian king Cecrops, and as 'the first woman known to have performed music' (πρώτη μουσικὴ ἐγνωρίζετο, 4.5 = p. 51.72 Thurn); six centuries later, George Kedrenos in his *Chronicle* picks up Malalas' account almost word for word, but changes one term and introduces Sappho as 'she who was proclaimed first among the Muses' (ἣ καὶ πρώτη Μουςῶν ἀνηγόρευτο, p. 145.14–15 Bekker[b]).

Lyric poetry did not especially inspire Byzantine authors and intellectuals; the only classical poet to survive in school curricula and teaching was Pindar, in his capacity as a writer of epinicians.[19] That Sappho was the object of teaching in schools, as one might argue from a passage of the eleventh-century polymath and historian Michael Psellos (*Encomium of His Mother*, p. 151.1870–4 Criscuolo), is an exaggeration. Psellos enumerates a series of authors whom he allegedly introduces to his pupils – Homer, Menander, Archilochus, Orpheus, Musaeus, the Sibyls, 'Sappho the singer of poems' (Cαπφὼ ἡ μουcοποιός; cf. Herodotus 2.135.1 = fr. 202), Theano, and the 'female Egyptian scholar' (Hypatia). This list is in itself implausible, and stereotypically looks back at similar catalogues compiled by late antique writers such as Themistius (e.g. *Funeral Oration for His Father* [*Oration* 20] 236c).

In this frame, it is perhaps surprising that in the whole of Byzantine literature we hardly find any echo of the negative images of Sappho occasionally attested in Christian writers since the age of Tatian (second century AD), who notoriously insisted on her lewdness and wantonness as opposed to the modesty and self-control of Christian women[20] – a character also implied, albeit in less negative terms, by Themistius, but contradicted e.g. by Hermias, who reads Sappho and Anacreon as respectively the feminine and the masculine principle of 'prudent love', cώφρων ἔρωc.[21]

---

[18] Plato, *Greek Anthology* 9.506 (test. 60); also Antipater of Sidon, *ibid.* 7.14 (test. 27), 9.66 (244–5 *HE*), Anonymous 9.571.7–8 (1210–1 *HE*).

[19] Canfora 1995: 126–37.

[20] Tatian, *Oration to the Greeks* 33.2, γύναιον πορνικὸν ἐρωτομανές, 'a nymphomaniac whore'. For the context, see Brooten 1996.

[21] Themistius, *On Love* [*Oration* 13] 170d–171a (test. 52); Hermias on Plato, *Phaedrus* 235b (p. 45.8–17 Lu–M).

Several Byzantine writers simply regard Sappho as one of the excellent poets of antiquity, inserting her in a canon of ancient authors allegedly surpassed by the hyperbolic eloquence of their addressees, especially in terms of sweetness, persuasion, rhythm, and grace (χάρις); none of these occurrences testifies to contact with her text. Michael Psellos resorts to Sappho twice in his panegyric orations, associating her once (1.158–60 Dennis) with Pindar, Orpheus, Homer, Anacreon, and then (4.235–8) with Pindar, Anacreon, Orpheus, and Meleager. In the twelfth century, Constantine Manasses mentions Sappho in association with Herodotus, Xenophon, and Anacreon in his oration for Michael Hagiotheodorites.[22] Anna Komnene 14.7.4 (1 451.33–5 Reinsch–Kambylis) celebrates Sappho together with Isocrates, Pindar, Polemo, and Homer. Manganeios Prodromos writes an encomium for Emperor Manuel I Komnenos, where Sappho appears together with the Muses, the rhetors, Calliope, and Hermes (*Carmen* 5.192), as well as a eulogy for Andronikos Komnenos' daughter Eudokia, presented as an 'Attic bee' on a par with Sappho and Calliope, and more eloquent than Demosthenes, Lysias, and Isocrates (49.162–5).[23] Finally, in the late thirteenth century, Manuel Holobolos's encomium for Michael Palaiologos (1 37.23 Treu) lists Sappho together with Orpheus and Thamyris as representatives of the 'sweet and calm' style (μειλίχιον . . . καὶ γαληνόν).

Two more passages evoke Sappho's excellence without framing her in a canon of poets: the standard expression 'Sapphic grace' (ἡ Σαπφικὴ χάρις, Demetrius, *On Style* 140, 148) appears in a letter of the twelfth-century rhetor Michael Italikos (18, p. 158.20 Gautier); and in the satirical dialogue *Timarion*, ascribed by some to the same Italikos, the eloquence of the Duke of Thessalonica (perhaps Andronikos Palaiologos) is praised as follows: 'A Sappho must have contrived his speech to be full of its persuasion, grace, and musical cadence.'[24]

Sappho's excellence can sometimes be grounded more specifically in her rhetorical skill, as e.g. in an anonymous Byzantine poem on rhetoric (III 648.5–6 *RG*), where Sappho figures together with Anacreon and

---

[22] p. 181.279–81 Horna; see Chrestides 1985: 10–11.

[23] I quote the poems of Manganeios Prodromos from their only manuscript witness, Marcianus graecus XI.22, respectively fol. 9v (for poem 5) and 60r (for poem 49): the numbering of the poems is that of Mioni 1973: 116–31. I am indebted to D. Yatromanolakis for pointing these out to me.

[24] *Timarion* 9 line 264 Romano, Σαπφώ δέ τις αὐτῷ τὴν ὁμιλίαν ἐτόρευε γέμουσαν πειθοῦς καὶ χαρίτων καὶ μουσικῆς ἐμμελείας, transl. B. Baldwin 1984: 48. See B. Baldwin 1984: 97 n. 79, against Garzya's idea that this quotation implies direct knowledge of Sappho's poems.

Theocritus as a model of 'simplicity' (ἀφέλεια). As we have seen (p. 321), the quotation of fr. 137 in Aristotle's *Rhetoric* impressed Anna Komnene; Gregory of Corinth, too, the same man who shows little attention to Sappho in his treatise on dialects, followed Aristotle in quoting fr. 201 as an example of *epenthymêsis* or 'additional corroborative argument'.[25]

On the other hand, the praise bestowed by Hermogenes (*On Ideas* 2.4) on Sappho fr. 118 (her invocation to her lyre) proved extremely influential in Byzantium, not only on commentators of Hermogenes himself,[26] but above all on twelfth-century rhetors: Niketas Magistros, in the very 'Hermogenian' *incipit* of his letter to Emperor Constantine VII Porphyrogenitus dated Easter 946 or 947, introduces Sappho's lines as an example of the stratagems used by pagan writers to charm their audiences, stratagems to be seen as wholly irrelevant when compared to the substantial salvific virtue of the evangelic message.[27] Michael Italikos quotes Sappho's lines at the outset of his high praise of the immortal deeds of the emperor.[28] When commenting on the proem of Homer's *Iliad*, Eustathius takes Sappho's lines – along with lines from Pindar, Aristophanes, Hesiod, Antimachus, and Stesichorus – as a model for all poetic proems.[29] The aforementioned Manganeios Prodromos evidently shared the same idea, since he opened his *Carmen* 1 to Manuel I Komnenos with an address to the χέλυς, an overt allusion to Sappho's fragment.[30]

In some Byzantine texts, Sappho's special title to fame consists in her excellence in the genre of *epithalamium* (wedding song). This association dates back to late antiquity,[31] and is codified in the section on the 'discourse on marriage' (λόγος περὶ γάμου) of Menander Rhetor's important manual;[32] it emerges at least twice in the twelfth century. First, in his speech for the consecration of Patriarch Michael II Oxites (1143), Italikos describes the addressee's mystical marriage with the Church as different

---

[25] Aristotle, *Rhetoric* 1398b28–9; Gregory, *On Hermogenes' Method of Forcefulness* 5 (vii/2 1153.17–20 RG).

[26] E.g. John of Sicily vi 397.1 RG. Also indebted to Hermogenes are Maximus Planudes (v 534.10–11 RG with the quotation of fr. 2.5–6) and Manuel Moschopoulos; see Nickau 1974.

[27] *Letter* 31.1–9, pp. 129–31 Westerink; Chrestides 1985: 4.

[28] *Oration* 43, p. 247.13–14 Gautier, which Garzya 1971: 3–4 = 1974: 3–4 takes as proof of the circulation of Sappho's poems; *contra* Pontani 2001: 238–9.

[29] Eustathius, *Commentaries on Homer's Iliad* 9.42 (i 16.6–8 Van der Valk, on *Iliad* 1.1).

[30] Chrestides 1985: 4–5. The poem (see above n. 23) can be read in E. Miller 1873.

[31] Choricius of Gaza, *Epithalamium for Zacharias* 19–20, Aristaenetus, *Erotic Letters* 1.10 (drawing on Philostratus, *Paintings* 2.1.3), Dale 2011a: 55–67.

[32] Menander, *On Display Speeches* 402.17–18 (pp. 140–1 R–W); Garzya 1971: 5 = 1974: 5.

from ordinary mundane marriages, inasmuch as it is not 'such as the poetess Sappho sings, weaving her songs with soft rhythms and licentious melodies, likening the bridegrooms to prize-winning horses and the brides to the softness of roses, making her voice more tuneful than the lyre'.[33] This comparative πακτίδος ἐμμελεστέρα (cf. fr. 156, from Demetrius, *On Style* 162) belongs to a set of hyperbolae that comes back in various shapes in several other twelfth-century texts,[34] and has otherwise been connected with Sappho's authorship: John Geometres (tenth century) ascribes to Sappho the expression 'more golden than gold' (χρυσοῦ χρυσότερον), while the crop of hyperbolic comparatives from Anacreon and Sappho cited as examples of 'base adulation' (αἰσχρὰ κολακεία) by Gregory of Corinth poses the problem of sorting out which expressions belong to which of the two authors.[35] Whatever solution we adopt, it is most likely that both Michael and Gregory (as well as the rhetors quoted by Chrestides in n. 34) were drawing on an anthology or rhetorical handbook.[36]

Secondly, when the historian Niketas Choniates celebrates an imperial marriage, he refers to passages from the *Psalms* and the *Song of Songs*, but then adds that 'if we must add to these melodies of ours some foreign ones, let Sappho the poet sing, holding a chorded lyre in her hands: "Rejoice, O bride, and may the bridegroom rejoice too"'.[37] The 'foreign' melodies are those of pagan writers, and the quotation of fr. 117 is taken from Hephaestion's *Handbook on Metres*, but Niketas is the only source to ascribe this line to Sappho.[38]

One passage seems to alter this picture: when Manganeios Prodromos celebrates the wedding of a daughter of Andronikos Komnenos, he insists that the ceremony was attended by a large number of Muses, by the Horae and the Charites:[39]

> ὅλαι συνεληλύθεισαν ὥσπερ ἐκ Πιερίας
> ὅλαι συνδεδραμήκεσαν ὥσπερ ἐν Ἑλικῶνι
> ὅλαι συνεμουσούργησαν τὸ νυμφικόν σοι μέλος
> μόνη Σαπφὼ σοφώνυμος οὐ συμπαρῆν ταῖς Μούσαις

---

[33] Michael Italikos, *Oration* 2, pp. 68.14–69.4 Gautier (= fr. 117A); translation from Dale 2011a: 66.

[34] Chrestides 1985: 8–9.

[35] John Geometres, *Oration* 5, p. 22.12 Littlewood; Gregory of Corinth, *On Hermogenes' Method of Forcefulness* 13 (VII/2 1236.10–15 *RG*).

[36] Browning 1960, Wirth 1963, Pontani 2001: 239–42.

[37] *Oration* 5 (p. 43.25–8 Van Dieten).

[38] Probably because he read not only Hephaestion but also the scholia to Aratus, *Phaenomena* 250: Benelli 2018.

[39] *Carmen* 52.107–13, from Marc. gr. XI.22, f. 64v (n. 23).

ἐνταῦθα γὰρ θρηνητικὴ cυνεῖρεν ἐλεγεῖα
cεβαcτοκρατορήcαντα θεὸν ὀδυρομένη
ἐc νήcουc μετοικήcαντα μακάρων ἀθανάτων.

all came together as if from Pieria,
all gathered as if on Helicon,
all fashioned together your nuptial song:
only Sappho with her wise name did not join the Muses,
for she was there in mourning, singing elegies,
crying for the divine *sebastokratôr*
who had departed to the isles of the blessed immortals.

Sappho is here not only a Muse (along with Erato, Melpomene, Polymnia, 'Stesichorus', and Calliope), but her name is falsely etymologised from *sophos* 'wise', and she fulfils in this ceremony the special task of mourning the recent loss of the *sebastokratôr* (perhaps Andronikos Komnenos himself, the father of the bride, who died in 1142?); this role she performs probably in view of her status as a mortal creature, rather than because Prodromos may have possessed some lost information on her alleged funerary elegies.[40]

Other features that contribute to Sappho's paradigmatic role are her sex and homeland. She is listed by Michael Psellos in the category of illustrious woman intellectuals (together with Eriphyle, Diotima, Aspasia, and Theano: *Speeches in Court* 1.1113–15 Dennis), and by Eustathius among other women poets such as Praxilla, Corinna, Erinna (all named by Antipater of Thessalonica), and Charixena (taken from Aristophanes).[41] Elsewhere Eustathius lists Sappho amongst the great offspring of Lesbos, together with Arion, Pittacus, and Alcaeus, drawing on Strabo to call her 'a remarkable sort of woman with whom no other woman could compete in poetry'.[42]

As late as 1407, in an oration on the death of the scholar and teacher Theodore Antiochites, the great Byzantine scholar John Chortasmenos

---

[40] Yatromanolakis 1999: 185–6 considers this a testimony to the view of Sappho's *elegeia* (inferred from *Suda* c 107 = test. 2) as threnodic songs: but this must remain uncertain, given the conventional tone of Manganeios' passage, and the unlikelihood that he had access to any lost source on the topic.

[41] Eustathius, *Commentaries on Homer's Iliad* 326.37–327.9 (I 509.11–31 Van der Valk, on *Iliad* 2.711–15) = Erinna test. 16b Neri, where see N.'s commentary; Antipater, *Greek Anthology* 9.26 (175–84 *GP*); Aristophanes, *Ecclesiazusae* 943.

[42] Eustathius, *Commentary on Dionysius the Periegete* 536 (II 323.5–9 *GGM*), θαυμαστόν τι ... γυναικὸc χρῆμα πρὸc ἣν οὐδεμία γυνὴ ἐνάμιλλοc εἰc ποίηcιν, Strabo 13.2.3 (test. 7); cf. Plutarch, *Life of Antony* 31.2.

extols the national pride of Constantinople at having given birth to the deceased man, and compares the pride of Mytilene at having reared Sappho – perhaps not a fortuitous choice if we remember that throughout Chortasmenos's funeral oration one of Antiochites's great merits consists in his displaying and exploiting his deep familiarity with pagan literature while refraining from using it to undermine the Christian faith.[43]

Finally, one might regard as implicit indicators of the special popularity of Sappho's name the few instances in which the latter is quoted by mistake. Leaving aside a note in Eustathius's *Iliad* commentary where the reference is to the main character of Antiphanes' comedy entitled *Sappho* rather than to the poet herself,[44] we may recall Eustathius's incorrect attribution of the fragment on the 'public good' (καλὸν δημόςιον, fr. 209) to Sappho (rather than, as modern scholars tend to believe, to the Pythagorean philosopher Theano) in a letter thanks to a slip of memory.[45] In the fourteenth century, Theodore Metochites ascribes to Sappho a line on the love bestowed by the Muses on the poets ('blessed . . . the one whom the Muses love');[46] while the intended source is Hesiod (*Theogony* 96–7), the Doric (rather than Aeolic) patina is best explained through a Pindaric contamination.[47]

The Byzantine author with the highest number of overt quotations of Sappho – not particularly numerous in comparison with other lyric poets figuring in his work, from Alcman to Alcaeus to Anacreon – is once again the commentator on Homer *par excellence*, Eustathius. As we have seen, he includes fr. 34 – left out by the extant ancient scholia – as a precious *comparandum* for the splendid astronomical simile in *Iliad* 8.555–9. When picking up passages of Sappho from the vast archipelago of Athenaeus' *Scholars at Dinner* (one of his favourite sources of learning), Eustathius focuses on two elements still associated with Lesbos, i.e. flowers (here erebinths)[48] and sympotic culture: in his *Odyssey* commentary he quotes fr. 141 in support of the idea that ambrosia has the same nature and consistency as wine, while in his *Iliad* commentary he refers to Ganymede by

---

[43] *Oration* 2, p. 146.104–8 Hunger.

[44] Eustathius, *Commentaries on Homer's Iliad* 632.8–10 (II 270.7–10 Van der Valk, on *Iliad* 6.169); Antiphanes fr. 194 *PCG*, from Athenaeus, *Scholars at Dinner* 10.450e–451b (test. 25).

[45] *Letter* 43 (p. 114.60 Kolovou); Reinsch 2006 (superseding Pontani 2001: 247–8).

[46] Theodore Metochites, *On Morals* 63 (p. 270.17–18 Polemis), ὄλβιος . . . ὃν Μοῖςαι φιλέουτι.

[47] Pindar, *Olympian* 2.27a; rather than with Theocritus 2.12, as maintained by Gigante 1977 (though he also mentions Hesiod).

[48] Eustathius, *Commentaries on Homer's Iliad* 948.45 (III 519.44–5 Van der Valk, on *Iliad* 13.589); fr. 143.

comparing the role of cup-bearers performed by Hermes and Larichus in Sappho's poetry.[49] The latter instance is of special interest, since it represents the first known attempt to allegorise Sappho's poetry: the function of Hermes as a cup-bearer should be taken, in Eustathius's view, as an allegory of the *logos* that must always preside over the rational and sober conduct of human banquets:

> Beautiful Sappho (Σαπφώ ἡ καλή) says that Hermes acted as a cup-bearer for the gods, thereby showing in mythical terms that symposia must proceed in a rational way and according to the same justice shown by Homeric Themis, who is present amongst the celestial banqueters.[50]

Free borrowings from Sappho's verse without the indication of her name are difficult to detect in Byzantine authors. They have been spotted in some twelfth-century novelists, although few of the examples are really compelling,[51] and even in some hagiographical texts, although in this case the derivation from Sappho is definitely not direct.[52] A more topical, undeclared borrowing occurs once again in Michael Italikos, in his letter to Nikephoros Bryennios;[53] Sappho's authorship is invoked by the fourteenth-century scholar Theodore Hyrtakenos, who describes the affection for an absent person with the proverbial expression τὸ ἐμὸν μέλημα ('my darling', fr. 163), borrowed from a letter of Julian the Apostate (193, p. 263.5 B–C). Further enquiries into the texts of Byzantine authors may yield a larger crop of references, though it remains doubtful whether any sure gain can be made in terms of new fragments of Sappho.

A Disappointing Absence

The textual presence of Sappho in Byzantium appears less prominent and substantial than a modern scholar might wish: our expectations are no doubt influenced by the concomitant success of Sappho and Byzantium

---

[49] Eustathius, *Commentaries on Homer's Odyssey* 1633.1–3 (1 347.16–18 Stallbaum, on *Odyssey* 9.359); *Commentaries on Homer's Iliad* 1205.17–20 (iv 396.15–20 Van der Valk, on *Iliad* 20.232–5), from Athenaeus, *Scholars at Dinner* 10.425d, with a fuller version of frr. 141, 203b V.

[50] He compares Homer, *Iliad* 20.4–6.

[51] See Cataudella 1965 for alleged allusions in Eustathios Makrembolites and Niketas Eugenianos; *contra* Pontani 2001: 237.

[52] Costanza 1980 rightly terms the 'moon among the stars' simile (frr. 96.6–9, fr. 34) a 'Sapphic motif' not requiring direct knowledge – a wise caution even when the same motif occurs in the novelists Makrembolites and Niketas Eugenianos (quoted by Garzya 1971: 3 = 1974: 3).

[53] Fr. 148, at *Oration* 16, p. 152.5–6 Gautier; see Chrestides 1985: 5–6. (Pseudo-Plutarch's *On Nobility* is a humanistic forgery, and should therefore disappear from the catalogue of sources of this fragment.)

in a specific moment of the European literary and artistic tradition, namely late nineteenth-century Decadentism. Baudelaire's *Lesbos* (1850) and Pierre Louÿs's *Les Chansons de Bilitis* (*The Songs of Bilitis*, 1894) fall in the same time span as Victorien Sardou's *Théodora* (1884) and Hugues Le Roux's *Les Amants byzantins* (*The Byzantine Lovers*, 1897), and emerge from the same fashion and taste; nor do we need to recall here the 'Byzantine' atmospheres of a painter as committed to Sappho as Gustave Moreau.[54] An overt intersection of these two worlds can be found in the 1902 novel *Sapphos Verse* by the German schoolteacher Karl Roth. In this 'Byzantine Novel' (as the subtitle reads), set in Thessalonica under the reign of Michael IV (1034–41), the protagonist, named Anthimos, is the town's prefect and a passionate reader of Sappho's verse. Pure fiction, alas.

Further Reading

While the issue of the circulation of Sappho's poems in the Greek Middle Ages has been debated (e.g. Moravcsik 1964 = 1967: 408–13, Garzya 1971 = 1974 versus Pontani 2001, Reinsch 2006), no comprehensive study has been produced on the extent and the rationale of the continuing influence of classical poets in Byzantium (N. Wilson 1996 and Pontani 2015 rather discuss Byzantine scholarship on ancient authors). Several studies investigate single poets, from Homer to Hesiod to Callimachus (Browning 1992, Cardin and Pontani 2017, Pontani 2011), but lyric poets, mostly no longer available in Byzantium (the exceptions are Pindar and Hipponax, for which see Irigoin 1952, Kambylis 1991, Lauritzen 2010, Masson 1962), have received no special attention.

---

[54] DeJean 1989a, Greene 1996b, Auzépy 2003, Lavagnini 2004. For Louÿs, see JOHNSON ch. 26 pp. 369–70.

CHAPTER 24

Early Modern Sappho in France and England

Stuart Gillespie

The several Sapphos that may be encountered in the early modern world can all be said to have their origins in antiquity, but that antiquity is much more often Roman than Greek. As all recent discussion has acknowledged, the (pseudo-?)Ovidian letter of Sappho to Phaon (*Heroides* 15), far more widely known than any of Sappho's own poetry, was for centuries central to Sappho's reputation and reception.[1] Beyond this, Ovid's more neutral words about her in the *Tristia* (2.365 = test. 49), and even Catullus' imitation of her in poem 51, had more influence on Renaissance readers than the allusions of Greek comic playwrights or the comments of Aristotle and Longinus, simply because the early modern dominance of Latin over Greek ensured they were much better known.[2] First-hand acquaintance with the surviving Greek verse we now deem to be Sappho's is not unheard of, and indeed, as we shall see, may be slightly more widespread than has been assumed. But what has been assumed is extremely limited, at least beyond the scholarly world.[3] This means that any discussion of the early modern period might easily confine itself to what have been called 'Sapphic legends'[4] rather than examine more direct responses to the surviving poems and fragments, which is to say responses to the only Sappho that was in any sense recoverable. This is a

---

[1] This epistle, normally printed outside the rest of the sequence in Renaissance editions before Heinsius placed it as Epistle 15 in his edition of 1629, has a quite different textual transmission history from the rest of the *Heroides*, and is not indisputably by Ovid: Tarrant 1981, Rosati 1996, Bessone 2003.

[2] But see below, pp. 335–7, for the revival of Longinus and renewed interest in his comments on Sappho following Boileau's translation of 1674.

[3] Space constraints do not permit treatment of Renaissance scholarship here, but for Sappho in humanist commentary, see J. Mueller 1993: 184–90, Bonnet 1981; for the early editions by Henri Estienne and Anne Dacier, see FINGLASS ch. 18. The name 'Estienne' is conventionally anglicised as 'Stephen' and latinised as 'Stephanus'; thus, 'Henri Estienne' and 'Henricus Stephanus' denote the same person.

[4] Reynolds 2000: 97.

temptation to which recent discussion has commonly given way, one effect being to reaffirm the centrality of the Ovidian epistle for early modern Sapphos, but in what follows it will be resisted, because more direct responses must take precedence here. For this period, it is also worth saying at the outset, 'the surviving poems and fragments' amount to very little more than the 'Hymn to Aphrodite' (fr. 1) and *Phainetai moi* (fr. 31), and the second is very much the focus of attention, one recent commentator going so far as to suggest with only a little exaggeration that the first 'passes almost unnoticed through the Renaissance'.[5]

There can be little question that France made the running in Renaissance receptions of Sappho.[6] Henri Estienne, the great sixteenth-century scholar–printer of Paris, was the first to print Sappho's verse as fully as it was available to the early modern era, in his second edition of the Greek lyric poets in 1566.[7] Madeleine de Scudéry, in *Les Femmes illustres* (1642; English translation 1681), which contains a fictional letter in which Sappho exhorts a young pupil to become a poet, was 'the first woman to try and reclaim Sappho as a model for women writers'.[8] And Nicolas Boileau's French Longinus in his celebrated version of 1674, including translation of and commentary on *Phainetai moi*, was enormously influential for constructions of Sappho in France and beyond, as was Anne Dacier's French-language edition of Sappho of 1681 (both discussed below). Sappho's early modern French history also exemplifies a well-recognised bifurcation of which the Ovidian epistle is a prime cause. The two different Sapphos to which this bifurcation led from ancient times onwards are typically described in the argument provided by Guy Morillon, secretary to Charles V and friend of Erasmus of Rotterdam, for the *Letter to Phaon* in his mid-sixteenth-century edition of Ovid's *Heroides*.[9] As Morillon has it, one of the Sapphos of the ancient world, the contemporary of Alcaeus and Pittacus, was on the authority of Aelian and of Suidas a celebrated poet and the inventor of the plectrum, but all her work is lost. The later Sappho of Lesbos, Morillon writes, although poetically gifted and praised by Plato as the tenth Muse, was an

---

[5] DeJean 1989a: 31.

[6] *Pace* Andreadis 1996, who explicitly takes issue with DeJean 1989a on the point.

[7] *Poetae Graeci principes heroici carminis*, second edition (Paris 1566). Estienne's father Robert had previously printed the 'Hymn to Aphrodite' in his edition of Dionysius of Halicarnassus (1547), and Henri had added it to an edition of Anacreon (1554), augmented by *Phainetai moi* in the second edition of 1556 (see further pp. 338–9 below and FINGLASS ch. 18 pp. 249–53).

[8] Stevenson 2015: 131.

[9] Morillon 1546: fols. 82v–83r.

incorrigibly lascivious *meretrix* ('whore'), as the Ovidian epistle portrays her, and one who, moreover, made love to girls. Clearly, both these Sapphos would have had their ideological uses, and the notion that both had existed at separate times proved long-lived. It is evident that women writers needed the first as a predecessor, while men used the second as a warning of the shameful fate which awaits would-be female artists.

And so it was that, as Lawrence Lipking puts it, 'Sappho surfaced again, in the Renaissance, in the form of a question: Is it possible to be a respectable woman and also a serious poet?' It was not only in France that, as Lipking goes on to explain, the twin figures of Sappho were convenient: 'by separating the creature of dubious legend from the shining Tenth Muse, Renaissance poets could satirize the one . . . and worship the other'.[10] Both stances will produce a 'Sappho', but how far do they help with the discovery of Sappho? Many early responses both French and English are doomed to superficiality or distortion for this reason, even when the respondents have direct knowledge of parts of the Sappho corpus, and even when what they apparently offer is respectful homage. The very first French translation of Sappho is Rémi Belleau's version of *Phainetai moi*, 'Nul me semble egaler mieux', based on Estienne's Greek text, in his *Odes d'Anacréon* published in 1556.[11] Belleau's translation is unusual for its time in owing nothing to Catullus, and in retaining instead of adjusting the genders of Sappho's erotic triangle in which female poet watches female being watched by male – the later Renaissance norm being to make the second figure neuter. But its overall effect is that it 'prettifies, softens, and generally weakens' the Greek poem.[12] And far from this being an aberration, Ronsard's version of the same poem, 'Je suis un demi-dieu', which appears almost immediately afterwards, is 'the perfect realization of the veering away from Sappho' initiated by Belleau: in Ronsard's hands *Phainetai moi* becomes a *carpe diem* ('seize the day') text in which the woman the poet desires will be immortalised in his verse if she is kind to him.[13] To follow the further history of this traffic between French poets of the later sixteenth century in versions of Sappho is to see that writing which at first glance appears to

[10] Lipking 1988a: 42, 43 ≈ 1988b: 71.
[11] Belleau 1556: 61–2 = Demerson *et al.* 1995–2003: 1 124–5. For Estienne's importance (in conjunction with other contemporary scholars and editors) in facilitating the Sappho-inspired work of Belleau and other members of the Pléiade, see Aulotte 1958, Morrison 1962.
[12] DeJean 1989a: 34.
[13] DeJean 1989a: 36. Ronsard's version was also first printed in 1556. For a modern text, see Céard *et al.* 1993–4: 1 228.

bring an exciting new poet into their literary world amounts to a form of male bonding: what they are responding to is each other's riffs on Sappho, all of which remain at a distinct distance from the Sapphic texts themselves.

A no less significant distance separates her female French admirers from Sappho. The part these admirable pioneers played in legitimising Sappho as a model for the woman poet is well understood, and was influential for French women writers. In a poem of 1555, Louise Labé (*c.*1524–66) describes her poetic vocation as a gift of Phoebus, who 'gave me the lyre that was accustomed to sing poetry of Lesbian love' ('m'a donné la lyre, qui les vers | Souloit chanter de l'amour Lesbienne'), but this 'Lesbian love' is defined simply as unhappy love, and it is Ovid's Sappho who primarily lies behind it.[14] Madeleine de Scudéry (1607–1701) rewrote Ovid's narrative in her *Lettres amoureuses de divers auteurs de ce temps* (1641) and again in *Les Femmes illustres ou Les Harangues héroïques* (1642). Through careful research she later achieved something more: in the final volume of her novel *Artamène ou Le Grand Cyrus* (1653) she produced the first well-informed portrait of the biographical figure of Sappho. Scudéry knew no Greek or Latin, and had her friends translate the ancient texts she needed. But whatever their exertions or hers, all sources lead inevitably to a 'fiction of Sappho' to match Labé's 'fiction of Sapphism'.[15]

There was, though, a later episode, towards the end of the seventeenth century, when the French literary world quite suddenly made contact with another Sappho. When Boileau relaunched Longinus as an aesthetician by translating the Greek treatise *Peri hypsous* (*On the Sublime*) under the title *Traité du sublime ou du marveilleux* in 1674,[16] he was naturally obliged to present a French version of *Phainetai moi*, with the comments of Longinus. Three years later it is the foundation for a key moment in one of the masterpieces of French classical theatre, Racine's *Phèdre*. Boileau's version of the ode sets out to restore Sappho's passion and sublimity, for which he professes great admiration. But it is no more than a step on the way, because Boileau, whose literary language does not extend to sensations such as Sappho's poem describes, tones down and makes 'tasteful' the ode's stark high style. His notes explain, for instance, that in

---

[14] Lesko Baker and Finch 2006: 152.
[15] DeJean 1989a: 103, 41, and (on Scudéry in particular) 96–110.
[16] Boileau's influential translation of Longinus was not the first version in a modern language, but it had far greater impact than its predecessors. A previous translation into English by John Hall of Durham (1652) is sometimes credited as containing the first English rendering of a Sappho poem (Lipking 1988a: 47–8).

the lines describing the alternation of emotions 'il y a dans le Grec, *une sueur froide*' ('there is in the Greek "a cold sweat"'), but he has suppressed the phrase because the word *sueur*, 'sweat', 'can never be pleasing, and leaves a disagreeable idea in the mind' ('ne peut jamais estre agreable, et laisse une vilaine idée à l'esprit'):[17]

> Un nuage confus se répand sur ma vûë.
> Je n'entens plus: je tombe en de douces langueurs;
> Et, pâle, sans haleine, interdite, éperduë,
> Un frisson me saisit, je tremble, je me meurs.

Boileau's early eighteenth-century English translators are a little free with the sense, but give a fair impression of the artificiality of this French verse, and, partly because of what we can easily discern today as its 'period' feel, of its distance from anything Sappho might have written:[18]

> A Mist of Pleasure o'er my Eyes is spread:
> I hear no more, and am to Reason dead.
> Pale, Breathless, Speechless, I Expiring lie:
> I Burn, I Freeze, I Tremble and I Die.

Nevertheless, Boileau successfully emphasises (as the commentary by Longinus had emphasised) the uncontrollable excessiveness of the emotion and the speed with which one symptom is succeeded by the next. *Phainetai moi* is quoted here in the *Peri hypsous* as an example of how (in the words of the early English version of Boileau's translation) 'when *Sapho* wou'd express the Furies of Love . . . she chooses those [incidents], which Denote most the Excess and Violence of Love, and connects them well together'. The effect is that 'we can't say she's seiz'd with one particular Passion, but that her Soul is the Rendezvous of all the Passions'.[19] It seems to have been this 'Rendezvous' which made such an impression on Boileau's friend Racine that three years later the lines are at the heart of Phèdre's *aveu* ('confession') of her forbidden love for her son-in-law Hippolyte to her servant Oenone. The popularity of Boileau's *Traité* meant that contemporaries were easily able to recognise Sappho's place here in Racine's play:[20]

---

[17] Boudhors 1966: 202; passage below cited from *ibid.* 68.
[18] Boileau-Despreaux 1711: 32.
[19] Boileau-Despreaux 1711: 31, 32.
[20] DeJean 1989a: 86, citing as one example the young Baron de Longepierre, who points out the similarities in the notes to his 1684 translation of Anacreon and Sappho. DeJean 1989a: 87–93 offers a reading of Racine's play as a response to Sappho's ode and, more centrally, to (Pseudo-?)Ovid's *Letter to Phaon* (*Heroides* 15).

Je le vis, je rougis, je pâlis à sa vue.
Un trouble s'éleva dans mon âme éperdue.
Mes yeux ne voyaient plus, je ne pouvais parler,
Je sentis tout mon corps et transir, et brûler.
Je reconnus Vénus, et ses feux redoutables,
D'un sang qu'elle poursuit tourments inévitables.

I saw, I blushed, turned pale at the sight. Confusion ruled my distracted soul. My eyes no longer saw, I could not speak, I felt my whole body seized with cold, then with fire. I recognised Venus, and her deadly flames, searing with torments the blood she hunts down. (*Phèdre* 1.3.273–8)[21]

In Phèdre's speech situating the passion of love between Venus and the sentient body, Sappho has at last played a striking creative part in early modern culture. Racine's lines present a tangle of feelings without simplification or conventionalisation, and 'the precision, the analytic detachment, with which Phèdre regards her own seizure' is of a piece with a quality in the ode itself which has often been considered its most remarkable feature: the 'mixture of uncontrolled feeling with supremely controlled expression'.[22]

* * *

If this is a high point in the fortunes of the early modern French Sappho, what of the English experience? For purposes of transition across the Channel we shall return to Boileau and then to Estienne. In the second edition of his *Traité du sublime* (1683) Boileau added a substantial set of 'remarks' penned by the contemporary scholar André Dacier (mostly by way of disagreement with Boileau's interpretations), the result, Dacier's preface explains, of the two men's discussions of Longinus. The learned Dacier family was more widely influential on Sappho's reception through the edition and French translation of Sappho made in the same years (and printed in 1681) by the woman soon to become André's wife, Anne Le Fèvre (1647?–1720). Her *Poésies d'Anacréon et de Sapho traduites de grec en françois* (*Poems of Anacreon and Sappho Translated from Greek into French*) made Sappho a supplement to Anacreon on Estienne's model, but also included a French 'life of Sappho' which defended her respectability. The oft-reprinted edition of Madame Dacier (as she became known) was one of the principal forms in which Sappho, and information about Sappho, became accessible beyond the Latin-reading scholarly

---

[21] Forestier 1999: 831; my translation.
[22] Lipking 1988b: 79.

world in France and in England.[23] Her account of Sappho was important
enough, too, to be vigorously rejected by Pierre Bayle in his *Dictionnaire
historique et critique*.[24]

For Henri Estienne we must move backwards in time, to what may be
an example of historical under-recognition of Sappho's place in early mod-
ern English poetry. It has usually been assumed that in the following lines
of Sir Philip Sidney's from a short poem in *The Countess of Pembroke's
Arcadia* (the 'old' *Arcadia*), written *c*.1578–80, Sidney is using Catullus'
poem 51 and not Sappho. But there are reasons to question this idea.

> My tong to this my roofe cleaves,
> My fancy amazde, my thoughtes dull'd,
> My harte doth ake, my life faints,
> My sowle beginnes to take leave.[25]

What can this passage from 'My muse what ails this ardour?' owe to
Catullus that it cannot owe to Sappho? The inarticulate tongue is com-
mon to all three poets, as is the final suggestion that death seems close.
Thus far either source might have been Sidney's inspiration, but Catullus'
poem was far better known. The rest of the symptoms on Sidney's list are
at a distance from both his predecessors: neither Sappho nor Catullus
mentions anything like 'fancy' or 'thoughts' because both focus on the
corporeal, nor do they say anything about an aching heart. But there is
other evidence about the background to Sidney's poem. One of his main
interests in this composition as well as its neighbours is metrical experi-
ment, and this poem is expressly introduced as using 'Anacreon's kind of
verses'.[26] As his editors normally note, the source of Sidney's knowledge
of such 'verses'[27] would have been the *Anacreontis Teij odae* first printed
by his friend Henri Estienne in 1554.[28] What is much less often pointed

---

[23] For the reception, reprinting, and influence of Dacier's Sappho in France and England, see
Farnham 1976: 70–83.

[24] Bayle 1697: II 1006–11; Lipking 1988a: 49 (~ 1998b: 74), Reynolds 2000: 101–2.

[25] 'My muse what ails this ardour?', lines 12–15, quoted from Ringler 1962: 66.

[26] Duncan-Jones 1994: 143.

[27] In the poem just quoted Sidney is imitating the most common metre in the *Anacreontea* as known
to the early moderns: the three-foot iambic with a supernumerary short syllable. As is normal in
English imitations of Greek and Latin metres, the alternation of long and short syllables can only
be suggested, because there are no conventional quantities for syllables in English verse, only
stressed and unstressed syllables.

[28] A few years before Sidney wrote the 'old' *Arcadia*, a 'Greek book, or rather booklet' was presented
to him by Estienne at Strasbourg in 1573 'as a pledge of our then new friendship', as Sidney put it
(Buxton 1954: 57). We do not know what book or booklet this was, but presumably a common
interest in Greek was being alluded to. For the relationship between Sidney and Estienne, see also
Osborn 1972: 52, 88–9.

out in this connection is that, as we have already seen, Estienne's editions of Anacreon also contained texts of Sappho – the 'Hymn to Aphrodite' in 1554, and *Phainetai moi* in the expanded edition of 1556. There is no need to assume Catullus is a more likely source for Sidney's poem, which may thus constitute the first direct imitation of a passage from Sappho in English verse.[29]

Sidney's *Arcadia* is one example of how contested early modern responses to Sappho have become among commentators of recent years. With Sidney this perhaps began when a footnote in an edition of the old *Arcadia* noted the 'appropriateness' of another poem it contains, sung by a male character while disguised as a woman, being in sapphics.[30] From here, some commentators have moved close to suggesting that the use of sapphics in modern English verse at large is code for 'female homosexuality', while failing to take account of the prominence of the metrical form in Latin poems far more widely known than any Greek lyric (in particular poems by Horace). These often ingenious arguments quickly become discussions of 'Sappho' rather than Sappho – discussions, that is, of early modern references to Sappho's mythologised reputation.[31]

Looking back at the place Sappho had held over the centuries in 'the English-reading world', H. T. Wharton took it for granted from his late Victorian perspective that the definitive moment had been in 1711. In the preface to the first edition of his popular pocket edition of *Sappho*, he observed:

> As a name, as a figure pre-eminent in literary history, she has indeed never been overlooked. But the English-reading world has come to think, and to be content with thinking, that no verse of hers survives save those two hymns which Addison, in the *Spectator*, has made famous – by his panegyric, not by Ambrose Philips' translation.[32]

In the remainder of this short survey the 150 years from Sidney to Addison will be considered, with heavy weighting towards the later figures to whom Wharton alludes.

---

[29] DeJean 1989a: 33, however, rightly stresses the importance of the mediation that Catullus must have provided for readers at large through Estienne's inclusion of poem 51 in his 1566 *Poetae Graeci* (above, n. 3), a move decisive enough to 'launch the poetess's modern career'.

[30] Duncan-Jones 1994: 373.

[31] One example apparent from its subtitle is Andreadis 1996. Another succeeds in steering so far wide of Sappho as to claim on two occasions that it was the 'Hymn to Aphrodite' (rather than *Phainetai moi*) that Sidney 'translated . . . into anacreontics' in the *Arcadia* (Crawford 2002: 980; see also 985).

[32] Wharton 1885: v.

For much of this period we must bear in mind that Greek is an acqui-
sition of the few; that English translations of Sappho, unlike, say, of
Homer, are slow to arrive (and, again unlike with Homer, not produced
by any poet of the first rank); and that Latin or French will very often
have been the medium through which anglophone readers encountered
the tiny corpus. Interest in 'Sappho' can certainly be found, far less
intense than in France, but issuing in, for instance, the first appearance of
an imagined figure of Sappho on the stage, in John Lyly's play *Sapho and
Phao* (1584). This play is, however, in prose. It is little and late when the
learned Ben Jonson composes what is probably the first piece of English
translation of a Sapphic fragment in his uncompleted drama of 1637, *The
Sad Shepherd* – 'the dear good angel of the Spring, | The nightingale'.[33]

As the seventeenth century goes on, and turns into the eighteenth,
with further miscellaneous responses and scattered discussion, it strikes
us that the couplets and rhyming stanzas of the English Augustan era
bespeak a poetics that inevitably excludes anything we might today rec-
ognise as authentic to Sappho. Her aural and emotional subtleties belong
to a very different kind of poetry from the parallelism and symmetry that
the English Augustans prize, and therefore, quite naturally, impose on
Sappho in their occasional translations and imitations. Not that these are
numerous enough to amount to a particulary noticeable phenomenon. In
his *Spectator* essays of 1711 Joseph Addison introduces Philips's versions of
frr. 1 and 31 as 'Pieces [which] have never been attempted before by any
of our Countrymen', which seems to have been true enough for the first,
though not (as noted earlier) for the second.[34]

By this date Addison was a leading English writer and man of letters,
his contemporary Philips a more intermittently successful associate.
Addison was certainly able to promote Philips's work by incorporating
these two (previously unprinted) translations in the 'Sappho numbers' of
his recently established but widely read daily, *The Spectator*.[35] Addison
was also selling Sappho, as the epitome of a particular set of poetic val-
ues. She was, he claims, a poet who 'followed Nature in all her Thoughts,

[33] Ben Jonson, *The Sad Shepherd* 2.6.86–7; Barton and Giddens 2012: 465. Jonson's play, a pastoral
plotted on the Robin Hood story, was begun in the year of his death, and its three completed acts
first published in the second edition of his posthumous *Works*, 1641.

[34] Addison is quoted here from D. Bond 1965: II 369, all quotations being taken from *Spectator* 223
or 229. A third *Spectator* paper involving Sappho more briefly is No. 233, which discusses the
ancient tradition of suicidal leaps from the Leucadian rock; all belong to the year 1711.

[35] *The Spectator*, one of the earliest genuine periodicals, appeared in 1711–12, initially authored by
Richard Steele as well as Addison. In No. 223 Addison identifies Philips clearly enough as the
author of the translations, if not directly by name.

without descending to those little Points, Conceits and Turns of Wit with which many of our Modern Lyricks are so miserably infected'.[36] One emphasis of his discussions is particularly worth noting as an implicit reason for presenting Philips's translations. Introducing Philips's 'An Hymn to *Venus*', Addison claims that 'if the Ladies have a mind to know the manner of Writing practised by the so much celebrated *Sappho*, they may here see it in its genuine and natural Beauty'.[37] Why 'the Ladies'? Simply because at this time publishers and authors knew that English translations of Greek and Latin classics were avidly read by women, who almost always lacked the necessary languages to consult the originals (as well as by men, who sometimes did not).

And what of Philips's two translations? They may not unfairly be described as 'faintly ridiculous'[38] or even, in the case of fr. 31, as incipient soft-core erotica,[39] but this is the wisdom of hindsight. They proved enormously popular and enormously durable: later eighteenth-century attempts at translations are indebted to them, and as for readers, Byron is still asking his public, tongue-in-cheek, generations later, 'is not Phillips' translation of it [fr. 31] in the mouths of all your women?'[40] One reason lies in an apparently very minor change. In fr. 31 Philips alters present tense to past:

> My Bosom glow'd; the subtle Flame
> Ran quick thro' all my vital Frame;
> O'er my dim Eyes a Darkness hung:
> My Ears with hollow Murmurs rung:[41]

At a stroke the narrative changes: these events are now being recalled in memory, and the poem now presents a woman haunted by a loss. It has become a poem of melancholy, in which the closing reference to 'dying' may even be understood literally, so that the poet's voice is speaking from beyond the grave. To an age about to become fixated on melancholy and graveyard poetry, this did no harm whatever to Sappho's reputation.

With both Philips and Addison this chapter may end, geographically speaking, where it began, for both writers have been shown to owe debts

---

[36] D. Bond 1965: II 366.

[37] D. Bond 1965: II 367.

[38] P. Jay and C. Lewis 1996: 19.

[39] Lipking 1988a: 51 ≈ 1998b: 81.

[40] Byron, 'Observations upon observations of the Revd. W. L. B. &c. &c. &c.', 25 March 1821 (Nicholson 1991: 178). 'In the mouths of' may refer to the possibilities Philips's fr. 31 offers for dramatic recitation, on which see Lipking 1988a: 51 ≈ 1988b: 81.

[41] D. Bond 1965: II 392 (roman substituted for italic font).

to French scholarship more extensive than they confess to. Addison, to be sure, twice acknowledges his use of Dacier in his discussion of the 'Hymn to Aphrodite'; it is to be suspected that he was also influenced by her in his remarks on Sappho's style, since both commend her for following nature rather than cultivating the features too much admired by moderns. But there is more: Addison's essays draw heavily on Bayle's Dictionary articles on 'Sappho' and 'Leucas', and as for Philips, Dacier's influence is palpable in his version of fr. 1, for which there was no other easily accessible translation in either French or English.[42] Even at this late date, the most influential of Sappho's English critics and translators show themselves far from independent of the French tradition in Sappho's reception.

Further Reading

DeJean 1989a was seminal, and much of its early modern material is still useful, especially as regards France. Lipking 1988a is a suggestive and nuanced *tour d'horizon* covering, despite its title, much of the ground to 1711; Lipking 1988b contains a reworked version.

---

[42] Thus Farnham 1976: 77, who provides detailed verbal evidence covering Philips's translation. For Addison's debts to Bayle, see D. Bond 1965: 365 n. 3, 366 nn. 1–2 on *Spectator* 223 (November 1711). This is not to suggest that either Philips or Addison failed to consult Greek texts as well.

CHAPTER 25

Early Modern and Modern German, Italian, and Spanish Sapphos

Cecilia Piantanida

The literary and cultural reception of Sappho since the sixteenth century tells a story of a poet travelling across countries, nations, and languages. If her early modern reception is mainly a French affair, from the late seventeenth century onwards the international circulation of works like Anne Le Fèvre's edition and life of Sappho (1681) brings the Lesbian poet across Europe to include first England and the Holy Roman Empire,[1] and by the last decades of the eighteenth century also Italy and Spain. Following the trace of Sappho's transnational reception from the eighteenth century to the present, the ancient poet emerges as the agent of a vast network that reflected and often shaped contemporary values and ideas.

This chapter will focus in particular on German, Italian, and Spanish receptions,[2] which remain comparatively less studied than the French and Anglo-American, but played a key role in the development of a sustained pan-European discourse on Sappho from the 1780s.

The Eighteenth Century

Sappho's allegedly promiscuous love life, made infamous by the popularisation of (Pseudo-?)Ovid, *Heroides* 15, spurred accusations of immorality that tainted her poetic status throughout the early modern period.[3] While her literary legacy never ceased to carry sexual connotations, at the end of the seventeenth century Sappho was rediscovered as the original voice of female passion and as a positive model of aesthetic pleasure.[4] But this came at a cost. Her legendary life was rewritten to emphasise the

---

[1] DeJean 1989a: 1–5.
[2] For her reception in France and England, see GILLESPIE.
[3] DeJean 1989a: 37–8, 69; for the Italian reception, see Chemello 2012b: 23.
[4] DeJean 1989a: 12–13, 57–8, 79.

destructive power of the connection between erotic excess and poetic genius and promote conservative values of feminine chastity.[5] Thus, throughout Europe between the 1700s and early 1800s, Sappho became a heterosexual woman torn by unrequited love.[6]

The international dissemination of the treatise *On the Sublime* ascribed to Longinus in the French translation of Nicolas Boileau (1674) helped sway the consensus in favour of Sappho as a lyric model.[7] In the treatise, Sappho's fr. 31 is given as one of the highest examples of the sublime in poetry. Following the heterosexualising shift, however, the eighteenth century started privileging fr. 1, which since its first publication in 1508 had been regarded as a heterosexual poem until Volger's 1810 edition.[8] German Hellenists were the only ones to concern themselves with the whole extant corpus and to make an effort to distinguish between Sappho's life and works.[9] In 1733 Johann Christian Wolf published a groundbreaking edition of Sappho's fragments in Greek and Latin;[10] the following year saw the first German translation, by Jacob Stählin, making twenty-nine fragments of Sappho available to those who did not have Greek, Latin, or French.

The French tradition remained highly influential. Hellenists there increasingly focused on Sappho's poems as evidence for the proliferating heterosexual fictions of her life, continuing the seventeenth-century practice of merely appending Sappho's fragments to scholarly editions of male poets, especially Anacreon, drawing on the myth of the two poets as lovers, and encouraging the readers to associate the poets' styles.[11] Following this practice, German 'Anacreonticism' emerged as a collaboration of three students of Halle University: Johann Wilhelm Ludwig Gleim, Johann Peter Uz, and Johann Nikolaus Götz. In 1746 Gleim published their anonmyous translation *Die Oden Anakreons in reimlosen Versen. Nebst einigen andern Gedichten* (*The Odes of Ancreon in Unrhymed Verses. In Addition to Some Other Poems*), including versions of Sappho frr. 1 and 31 (pp. 45–8). An anonymous revision, attributed to Götz, was issued in 1760 with a new section on Sappho; Götz incorporated the myth of their

---

[5] DeJean 1989a: 84–102, Michelakis 2009: 349.
[6] DeJean 1989a: 23, 37–8, 58–60, 70, Chemello 2012b: 24, Puggioni 2012: 35.
[7] Michelakis 2009: 348–9.
[8] For French translations, see DeJean 1989a: 122, 132–3; for Italian, Favaro 2015; for the textual tradition, see FINGLASS ch. 18.
[9] DeJean 1989a: 124–5.
[10] FINGLASS ch. 18 p. 253.
[11] DeJean 1989a: 121.

mutual love in his own poem, 'Lob des Anakreons und der Sappho' ('In praise of Anacreon and Sappho'),[12] which became the standard for later Anacreontic poetry, deemed the 'linguistic high point of the Enlightenment in Germany'.[13] The French influence emerges clearly in the posthumous collection of poetry by Benjamin Neukirch (1665–1729), edited in 1744 by the prominent critic Johann Christoph Gottsched (1700–66), whose programme of reform of German poetics broke new ground in the conceptualisation of imagination, feeling, and national character, placing Aristotelian and French neoclassical aesthetics among his key models.[14] The collection includes translations and rewritings of Sappho by Neukirch with commentaries by Gottsched, including references to Boileau and the Baron de Longepierre.[15]

In Italy and Spain the first editions were issued much later. In 1783 Francesco Saverio de' Rogati published the first Italian edition with translation and commentary, though including only frr. 1, 31, and 168B.[16] José Antonio Conde published the first Spanish translation to include more poems than frr. 1 and 31, in 1797. In both countries the fulcrum of Sapphic reception remained her legendary love life, which was suited to dramatic and novelistic recreations. The recurring elements were as follows: after a marriage and giving birth to a daughter, Sappho falls in love with the beautiful boatman Phaon who, however, refuses her. After several failed attempts to win her beloved's attentions, including following him to Sicily, the poet is overcome with grief and takes her own life, jumping off the Leucadian rock into the sea. More often than not, Sappho's lustful relationships with girls and other men, central to the Ovidian fiction, were omitted.[17]

The first Italian rewriting of Sappho's legend is the neoclassical tragedy in five acts by Maria Fortuna entitled *Saffo*, performed in Livorno on 21 and 26 November 1776 and published the same year.[18] Saffo is both a great poet and a virtuous, beautiful woman, and she has never loved anyone but Faone, who nevertheless abandons her for Dori. Betrayed and wronged, trapped in the conflict between passion and rationality, Saffo

[12] C. Baldwin 2004: 69.
[13] Rowland 2000: 15.
[14] Duncan 2000: 358. For German translations, see also Rüdiger 1934: 10–12.
[15] Gottsched 1744: 282–8.
[16] De' Rogati 1782–3: II 193–217; for De' Rogati, see Favaro 2015: 143–8. This combination was first found in H. Stephanus 1556: FINGLASS ch. 18 p. 252.
[17] FINGLASS AND KELLY pp. 1–3.
[18] Fortuna 1776 = Chemello 2012a: 45–128; Puggioni 2012.

eventually looks for the release of death. The association of love, suffering, and virtue emerging in Fortuna's fiction (and several others of this time) reflects a broader cultural interest in sensibility and love's effect on the body. As one of the first documents of its symptoms as a sickness, fr. 31 became the original source for the representations of the physical and psychological impact of *erôs*, but was sometimes viewed unfavourably as mundane or excessive.[19] Fortuna certainly had read the ode, but to salvage Sappho's virtue, the play makes no reference to her raw eroticism or homosexual relationships. In her introductory note, Fortuna presents a play 'che non offenda la modestia, e che risvegli l'altrui compassione' ('that will not offend modesty but awaken compassion').[20] So she adopts a toned-down version of the Ovidian tale championed in many eighteenth-century accounts, including Anne Le Fèvre's biography, one of Fortuna's reference texts.

Fortuna's interest in Sappho is the Italian expression of a wider European trend where women used her to affirm their position as writers, poets, or performers. Fortuna herself was named the 'Italian Sappho', and so was the Lucchese performer Teresa Bandettini (1763–1837), also known as Amarilli Etrusca.[21] In Prussia Anna Louisa Karsch (1722–91), who became known as 'the German Sappho', impersonated the ancient poet in her improvisations.[22] Not a performer, but a nun in the convent of Santa María of Cadiz in Spain, María Gertrudis Hore (1742–1801) exploited Sappho's authority as a female poet to glorify her own work and claim space for female voices.[23] As an icon of female independence and literary achievement, Sappho has played a crucial inspirational role.

After these first experiments, the Italian reception gained more impetus with Alessandro Verri's novel *Le avventure di Saffo poetessa di Mitilene* (*The Adventures of Sappho, Poet from Mytilene*, 1780),[24] a striking indictment of Enlightenment ideals, warning against the danger of a boundless pursuit of pleasure and the disrespect of traditional religion. An impressionable girl who read many books as a child but never wrote poetry, Verri's Saffo falls madly in love with Faone when she sees his oiled, muscular body at the games in Mytilene, instilled with passion by Aphrodite

---

[19] Mari 1988: 111–12.
[20] Fortuna 1776: iv = Chemello 2012a: 45.
[21] Bandella 2012.
[22] C. Baldwin 2004: 62.
[23] In her poem 'Bellas pescadoras' ('Beautiful fisherwomen'), published 1796: E. Lewis 2004: 70–1, Barrero Pérez 2005: 106–7.
[24] <Verri> 1780 = L. Martinelli 1975: 71–215 = Cottignoli 1991.

because she failed to perform a sacrifice. When Saffo asks for a solution to her uncontrolled passion, she is told to jump from the Leucadian rock: if Saffo has faith in the gods she will survive the fall and be forgiven; if not, she will die, putting an end to her torment. Within a moral order in which virtue and duty to the gods are the ruling values, Sappho is thus deprived of both her agency to love and the freedom to choose to take her own life.[25]

To support his 'virtuous' portrayal, Verri rejects the legend of Sappho as lover of men and women: 'Ma di queste obbrobriose notizie, io non ritrovai memoria nè fama in Mitilene' ('I found no memory or reputation in Mytilene of these abominable notions').[26] Like many scholars at the time, he advocated the existence of two Sapphos, one chaste, the other promiscuous.[27] Upholding values of feminine decorum and balance, Verri's account fits within the contemporary normalising attitudes towards Sappho's biography. Following Claude-Louis-Michel de Sacy's *Les Amours de Sapho et de Phaon* (*The Loves of Sappho and Phaon*, 1769), his patriarchal portrayal of Sappho is matched by a hypermasculine hero-like Phaon, praised for his beauty and strength.[28] Verri's novel was often published in one volume with Vincenzo Maria Imperiali's *La Faoniade* (*The Phaoniad*, 1780),[29] which also emphasised the role of Phaon in Sappho's legend. Using the cliché of the discovered manuscript, the author presents his book as a translation of a previously unknown epic poem on Faone by Saffo. The work comprises ten odes in Saffo's voice, singing of her love for the boatman, who is celebrated for his physical beauty, just like in Verri's fiction.

With its adventurous plot and tale of morality and physical fitness, Verri's novel had great success abroad. The first English translation, *The Adventures of Sappho, Poetess of Mitylene*, was followed by *Sappho. After a Greek Romance*, attributed to John Nott, in 1803, and in French by *Fêtes et courtisanes de la Grèce* (*Celebrations and Courtesans of Greece*), attributed to Pierre-Jean-Baptiste Chaussard, in 1801.[30] Countering Enlightenment ideals of individual autonomy and freedom, Verri's

---

[25] L. Martinelli 1975: 33.
[26] <Verri> 1780: 178 ≈ Cottignoli 1991: 166; my translation.
[27] <Verri> 1780: 178–9 = Cottignoli 1991: 167; cf. Cotrone 2015: 149–53. For the ancient sources of the dual Sappho, see KIVILO pp. 12, 17.
[28] DeJean 1989a: 169.
[29] Imperiali 1780 = Chemello 2012a: 147–92. For this work and its complex editorial history, see Favaro 2012.
[30] Anonymous (c) 1789, <Nott> 1803, <Chaussard> 1801: IV 216–374.

rewriting represented an antidote to the morally seditious Sappho of pre-revolutionary France.[31]

Sappho becomes a vehicle of Enlightenment and counter-Enlightenment ideas in Spain, too. Friar Benito Jerónimo Feijóo, a father of the Spanish *Ilustración*, included the story of Sappho's leap in his 'Disertación sobre el salto de Leucadia' ('Dissertation on the Leucadian leap'), an essay against 'superstitious legends'.[32] Sappho's love for Phaon takes a revolutionary turn in Nicasio Álvarez de Cienfuegos's play *Pítaco* (1799);[33] and it becomes a tale on the role and rights of women in the play *Safo* by María Rosa Gálvez de Cabrera (1768–1806).[34] After a short unsuccessful marriage, Gálvez separated from her husband and, refusing to follow the traditional roles assigned to eighteenth-century women, lived on her own means, through her writing,[35] repeatedly using the theme of excess to comment on the feminine condition. Gálvez's one-act play focuses on Sappho immediately before her leap. Safo prizes her freedom, embracing her desire for Faón, with whom she shared many nights of love.[36] Yet, if her passion speaks of freedom, moving away from chaste representations and anticipating the Romantic Sappho, the poet also represents feminine excess, enacting the reality of social expectations on women.[37] As Safo falls during the last scene of the play, she ultimately regrets her suicide as a 'superstitious mistake' that fails to erase the memory of her beloved.

The Nineteenth Century

In the 1800s Italian writers begin to engage more consistently with Sappho's texts. The novelist, poet, and intellectual Ugo Foscolo (1778–1827), exiled to London for his anti-Napoleonic ideas, translated fr. 31 three times (1794, 1816, and 1821–3), and fr. 168B twice (1794, 1798).[38] Eros is a pivotal element of Foscolo's interest in Sappho, as in his last translation of fr. 31, which describes an increasingly intense erotic passion, until the melodramatic climax of the last lines:

> E tutta molle d'un sudor di gelo,
> E smorta in viso come erba che langue,

---

[31] DeJean 1989a: 174.
[32] Feijóo 1740: 335–49; p. 344 on Sappho.
[33] Álvarez de Cienfuegos 1816: II 207–95.
[34] Galvez de Cabrera 1804: II 23–56; cf. Barrero Pérez 2005: 107–10.
[35] E. Lewis 2004: 97.
[36] E. Lewis 2004: 142–3.
[37] E. Lewis 2004: 145.
[38] Bézzola 1961: 277–8, 456–8, Petrocchi 1981.

Tremo e fremo di brividi, ed anelo
Tacita, esangue.

And soaked in a sweat of ice
My face lifeless as fading grass
I tremble and shake with shivers, and I long
Silent, pale.

'Da Saffo' ('From Sappho'), 1821–3, lines 13–16; Bézzola 1961: 458

Gone is the chaste and decorous Sappho of the previous century. Her love physiology advances as a central theme of nineteenth-century Sapphic fictions.

Eroticism is foundational also to the epistolary novel *Ultime lettere di Jacopo Ortis* (*The Last Letters of Jacopo Ortis*), translated into English, French, and German during his life.[39] Containing several autobiographical elements, the novel tells of Jacopo and Teresa, who cannot marry because, after Napoleon cedes Venice to Austria, Jacopo flees the city to seek political asylum; the frustrated love affair concludes with Jacopo's suicide.

Sappho's texts and legend become the blueprint of Jacopo's life. In a scene describing the erotic attraction between the protagonists, Jacopo looks at Teresa through her window and hears her singing fr. 168B, which he translated as a gift for her, alongside the two longer odes of Sappho (pp. 35–6). The setting moon of fr. 168B is a returning theme, an omen of Jacopo's tragic end, while the legend of Sappho and Phaon is mirrored in the unhappy love affair. In a plot that juxtaposes social conformity and individual emotions, Sappho's/Jacopo's suicide becomes a statement of personal autonomy, which, according to Foscolo, was meant to encourage the participation of 'the females and the mass of readers' in public affairs.[40]

The poet and scholar Giacomo Leopardi (1798–1837) wrote a poem entitled 'Ultimo canto di Saffo' ('Sappho's last song', 1822), which itself comments on the modern condition.[41] The poet takes on Saffo's persona and makes her tragedy his own. Tormented by her ugliness, Saffo is an outcast who cannot partake of the beauty of nature or the joys of requited love. Nothing can aid her pain, not even her poetry, and so she

---

[39] Foscolo wrote three versions of his novel, the first published in 1798, the second in 1802, and the last and definitive one in 1817; all three are now in Gambarin 1955.

[40] <Foscolo> 1818: 454 = Foligno 1958: 11 469. For Sappho in Foscolo, see Fogli 1996.

[41] Leopardi 1824: 5–10 = 1831: 81–4 = Rigoni 1987: 40–2; for the date, see Rigoni 1987: 682.

chooses to die. Afflicted by deformity himself, Leopardi felt a deep consonance with Saffo and her alleged ugliness,[42] which he turned into a profoundly existential tragedy. In Leopardi's poem, Saffo chooses death as an act of personal affirmation, of rejection of her destiny, like Werther, Ortis, and Corinne before her. As in Foscolo, Leopardi's Saffo is a heroine epitomising the modern condition of women and men in conflict with society and excluded by nature.

In his unpublished 'Premessa all'ultimo canto di Saffo' ('Introduction to . . .'), Leopardi cites (Pseudo-?)Ovid's *Heroides* 15 as a source of his poem, while in an 1825 bibliographical note he points at Madame de Staël's *Delphine* (1802) as the only famous literary precedent to his recreation of Sappho's tragedy, suggesting the originality of his own take on the story of the poet's suicide. However, Madame de Staël's Corinne must have been in Leopardi's mind, too.[43] The object of Sappho's love remains ambiguous. Enamoured with nature, she never mentions Phaon, or any female lover, emphasising the existential nature of her suffering. As he comments the previous year:

> Non sarebbe fischiato oggidì, non dico in Francia, ma in qualunque parte del mondo civile, un poeta, un romanziere ec. che togliesse per argomento la pederastia, o l'introducesse in qualunque modo; anzi chiunque in una scrittura alquanto nobile s'ardisse di pur nominarla senza perifrasi? Ora la più polita nazione del mondo, la Grecia . . ., scriveva elegantissime poesie su questo soggetto, donna a donna (Saffo), uomo a giovane (Anacreonte) . . . Tutti i sentimenti nobili che l'amore inspirava ai greci, tutto il sentimentale loro in amore, sia nel fatto sia negli scritti, non appartiene ad altro che alla pederastia, e negli scritti di donne (come nella famosa ode o framm. di Saffo φαίνεται ec.) all'amor di donna verso donna.

> Nowadays a poet, novelist, etc. would be jeered at, wouldn't they, not just in France but in any part of the civilized world, if they chose the subject of pederasty or introduced it in any way? Indeed, wouldn't anyone who was so bold as to name it otherwise than by a periphrasis in a text that had any claim to nobility? Now, the most refined nation in the world, Greece, . . . wrote very elegant poems on this subject, between woman and woman (Sappho), between a grown man and a youth (Anacreon) . . . All the noble feelings that love inspired in the Greeks, all their feeling regarding love, whether in practice or in texts, are simply about pederasty, and, in the

---

[42] Leopardi, *Zibaldone* 718–20, 2456–7, 3443–6 = Pacella 1991: I 458–9, II 1330–1, 1800–1, Muscetta 1959: 203–4. For this theme in Sappho's biographical traditions, see KIVILO p. 18; in modern literature, Edo 2014.

[43] Rigoni 1987: 681; Donati 1917: 173–4. Cf. Muscetta 1959: 203, Gigante 2002: 58, Lonardi 2005: 94.

writings of women (as in Sappho's famous ode, or fragment, φαίνεται), love of a woman for a woman. (Leopardi, *Zibaldone* 1840 (4 October 1821) = Pacella 1991: 1 1056–7 (transl. *ap.* Caesar and D'Intino 2013: 827))

This gives an insight into Leopardi's reticence and the contemporary discourse on Sappho's sexuality. Even though her homoeroticism appears established, it was not considered a suitable subject.

Several recreations of Sappho had appeared at the same time, none mentioning her homosexuality. Franz Grillparzer's *Sappho* (written in 1817, first performed in Germany 1818, in Italy in 1819)[44] focuses on reinstating Sappho's image as a great poet. She is represented as a superior character just because she writes verse. Phaon falls in love with her after seeing her reciting poetry at the Olympian games, where she defeated Anacreon and Alcaeus. Her suicide is framed as a way to gain poetic immortality through the renunciation of sexuality and a necessary gesture of atonement. Echoing previous Napoleonic fictions, Grillparzer unties Sappho from sexual scenarios to grant her space in the modern literary canon as a neoclassical model – an interpretation corroborated by contemporary German philology.

Between the 1770s and 1850s more than twenty editions and translations of Sappho were published in Germany.[45] Philology placed the study of texts and language at the centre of an intellectual system that established a genealogical link between ancient Greece and the present. Sappho thus became entangled with discourses on sexuality and nationalism.[46] After Volger's edition had openly admitted the possibility of Sappho's homosexuality, Friedrich Gottlieb Welcker aimed at restoring her reputation as a chaste woman.[47] Welcker admits that Sappho's poetry shows love for women, but argues that her feelings could never be sensual, since homosexual *erôs*, the highest form of attraction, is the prerogative of men, and women can feel desire only for the opposite sex. Stressing the importance of male homosexuality in the formation of Greek 'national character', Welcker built a long-standing Sapphic fiction that indirectly defended contemporary male homosexuality as foundational to the German nation. Asexual and chaste Sappho appears again in Karl Otfried Müller's *History of the Literature of Ancient Greece*, while

---

[44] Sorelli 1819, Rüdiger 1933: 126–32, Harrigan 1980, DeJean 1989a: 193–5.
[45] Reynolds 2000: 229.
[46] DeJean 1989b.
[47] Volger 1810, Welcker 1816, DeJean 1989a: 207–11, Most 1995: 25–8 ≈ Greene 1996b: 24–8.

Christian Friedrich Neue's edition illustrated Welcker's position by dis-
missing any homosexual reading.[48]

Women writers of Spanish romanticism told a rather different story.
Following de Staël's Sapphic heroines and drawing from Gálvez's appro-
priations, they used Sappho as a female model of emancipation in a
male-dominated literary landscape. De Staël's *Corinne ou l'Italie* (*Corinne,
or Italy*, 1807, first published in Spanish in 1818), promoted a female dis-
course around Sappho.[49] At the centre of her collection *Poesías* (*Poems*,
1843[1], 1852[2], 1872[3]), Carolina Coronado (1820–1911) placed a cycle of four
songs entitled 'Los cantos de Safo' ('The songs of Sappho') and a com-
panion piece, 'El salto de Léucades' ('The leap of Leucades').[50] As in
Corinne, Safo is sure of her poetic powers and enjoys reciprocated passion
for a male lover. Adopting Safo's persona, the lyrical voice can speak as a
woman of poetic authority, freely expressing her ambition and embracing
erotic passion, which was forbidden in normative discourse to middle-
class Spanish women, confined to their role of angels of the house.[51]
Unfortunately, when Faón chooses another less emancipated but more
beautiful woman, Safo is overwhelmed by suffering and loses her poetic
gift, eventually taking her own life. The comparison between the two
rivals poses the opposition between talent and beauty. Safo is physically
unattractive, but her talent counterbalances this deficiency, or so she
thinks until she discovers that Faón prefers beauty. Both de Staël and
Coronado build female subjectivity upon the need for male recognition.
This subjectivity, however, is annihilated when the woman is desired only
as an object and not as an active subject – that is, as a poet.[52] Standing
against a predominantly male literary scene, Sappho's self-obliteration
represents Coronado's rebellion against the suffocation of the female
voice. To form a female literary tradition with which to identify,
Coronado even wrote two daring articles, gathered under the title 'Los
genios gemelos: paralelo de Safo y Santa Teresa de Jesús' ('The twin geni-
uses: parallel between Sappho and St Teresa of Jesus), in which she com-
pared Sappho's intensity of spirit to that of St Teresa of Avila.[53]

Another female Romantic poet, Gertrudis Gómez de Avellaneda (1814–
73), who was born in Cuba but moved to Spain when she was 22, took

[48] Müller 1840: 172–80 ≈ 1841: 1 310–25, Neue 1827: 5–8.
[49] de Staël Holstein 1807, Olive 1818, Kirkpatrick 1989: 230–1.
[50] Valis 1991: 108–14.
[51] Kirkpatrick 1989: 229.
[52] Kirkpatrick 1989: 230–1.
[53] Coronado 1850 – Hafter 2001; see Kirkpatrick 1989: 81, Kaminsky 1993, Barrero Pérez 2004: 64–5.

Sappho as a female model. In her poem 'Despedida a la señora D.ª D. G. C. de V.' ('Farewell to Mrs —', 1843), Gómez de Avellaneda expresses resentment against a patriarchal literary culture that did not recognise Sappho's value.[54] Another text, 'A la célebre cantatriz Señora Ana de la Grange. En la representación de le ópera *Safo*, que la mereció coronas del público sevillano' ('To the famous singer Mrs Ana de la Grange. For the performance in the opera *Safo*, which earned her the laurels of the Sevillian public'), portrays Sappho as a victim of an unfaithful Phaon, and of the slanders of the people around her.[55]

While empowered and erotic portrayals coexisted with chaste and pure ones, early nineteenth-century Sapphic fictions were predominantly heterosexual. Instrumental in establishing a homosexual version of the Sapphic text, in 1843 the German philologist Theodor Bergk published the most complete edition before the advent of papyri, with 109 fragments. Because of a corruption, fr. 1.24 (where Sappho asks Aphrodite for help in winning her beloved's attentions) had for over three centuries been understood to refer to a male lover, often identified with Phaon. Bergk's emendation made explicit that Sappho's beloved is a woman, producing an unambiguously homoerotic lyric, and the conjecture was subsequently confirmed by manuscript evidence, eventually becoming the standard text of fr. 1.[56]

The philological model as an exploration of the roots of Western cultures reflected also on contemporary poetic rewritings of Sappho. Giovanni Pascoli (1855–1912), poet and Professor of Classics at the universities of Bologna, Messina, and Pisa and, in his last years, Professor of Italian Literature back in Bologna, began translating Sappho as a student, but his most striking rewriting is the poem 'Solon' (1895), which centres on Aelian's anecdote that the famous Athenian legislator Solon wanted to learn a song of Sappho before dying.[57] It contains two odes sung by an unnamed woman from Eresso, one of the ancient cities which claimed to be Sappho's birthplace. The first speaks of Sappho's suicide for love:

> Dileguare! e altro non voglio: voglio
> farmi chiarità che da lui si effonda.
> Scoglio estremo della gran luce, scoglio
>   su la grande onda,

---

[54] Gomez de Avellaneda 1869–71: 1 137–42.

[55] Gomez de Avellaneda 1869–71: 1 378–9; Barrero Pérez 2004: 69–71. For the Spanish reception of Sappho in the second half of the nineteenth century, see Barrero Pérez 2007.

[56] DeJean 1989a: 243–7, Paradiso 1993: 54, Williamson 2009: 359–60, FINGLASS ch. 18 pp. 253–5.

[57] Aelian cited by Stobaeus, *Florilegium* 3.29.58 (test. 10), Pascoli 1895 = 1904: 5–8, now in Nava 2008: 9–20. For Pascoli's early translations of Sappho, see Piantanida 2013.

dolce è da te scendere dove è pace:
scende il sole nell'infinito mare;
trema e scende la chiarità seguace
    crepuscolare.

To fade away . . . that's all I want: I want
to become the glow that is diffused from him.
Outermost rock, where rest the final rays of the sun,
    rock poised over the wave,

sweet the descent from you to where is peace.
The sun descends into the infinite sea;
the afterglow of the twilight glimmers,
    follows the sun's descent.

'Solon', lines 53–60, transl. Lunardi and Nugent 1979: 4, 6

Pascoli describes Sappho's leap through analogy: she wants to jump from the Leucadian rock to follow her sun, Phaon, and shine with him as the evening twilight. In a letter to his editor Adolfo De Bosis, Pascoli explains:

> Si fonda in vero su un'idea che credo tutta mia che o Sappho fosse persona mitica significando la chiarità crepuscolare (Σαπφώ = clara) o la poetessa così nomata scherzasse in certo modo sul suo nome. Certo Faone significa Sole e probabilmente Sole Occidente. Con quel canto io spiegherei come nelle poesie di Sappho potesse trovarsi l'accenno al salto di Leucade (Rupe Leucade è per me l'orizzonte, la linea che passa il sole tramontando, seguìto dalla sua amante, la Sappho, la chiarità crepuscolare).[58]

> [The passage] is based on an idea, which I believe to be entirely my own, that either Sappho was a mythical figure representing the glimmer of twilight (Σαπφώ = bright) or the poet called Sappho in some way played with her own name. Certainly Faone means Sun and probably Western Sun. With that song, I would explain how one could find the mention of the Leucadian Leap in Sappho's poems (according to me, the Leucadian Rock is the horizon, the line crossed by the sun as it sets, followed by his lover, Sappho, the glimmer of twilight). [My translation]

Fuelled by his archaeological interest in reconstructing the origins of humankind, Pascoli makes Sappho's legend into an aetiological myth of the alternation of day and night, powered by the vital forces of *erôs* and

---

[58] Giovanni Pascoli, letter to Adolfo De Bosis, 24 April 1895, now in Ghelli 2007: 48; cf. Nava 2008: 16–17. For 'Solon', see further Debenedetti 1979: 199–264, Citti 1996. For this false etymology of Sappho's name, see PONTANI p. 323.

thanatos (death). His theory was inspired by Max Müller's comparative linguistic studies.[59] Using the etymological roots of patronymics for ancient divinities, Müller identified the sun as the original element of every myth and religion.[60] Anchoring Sappho's and Phaon's names to the root of the Greek word for light, Pascoli's myth strove to give the archetypal lyric poet a foundational role in Western civilisation, a role for which, as Welcker and his tradition had amply demonstrated, a feminine heterosexual persona appeared much more suitable.

Pascoli's rewriting is also in line with the development of the Sappho tradition in Italy, where representations of a lesbian Sappho would not make an appearance until well into the 1900s. Yet it contrasts with the French and English receptions, where works such as the openly erotic and lesbian *Les Chansons de Bilitis* (*The Songs of Bilitis*, 1894) by Pierre Louÿs, published a year before Pascoli's 'Solon', were gaining attention.[61] Similarly, in Germany in 1896, under the pseudonym Theodore Ramien, Magnus Hirschfeld published his first work in defence of homosexuality, *Sappho und Sokrates, oder Wie erklärt sich die Liebe der Männer und Frauen zu Personen des eigenen Geschlechts?* (*Sappho and Socrates, or How Can One Explain the Love of Men and Women for Individuals of Their Own Sex?*), arguing that homosexuality was natural. Sappho was turning into the lesbian icon that characterised her in later decades.

The Twentieth Century

The uncovering and publication of new fragments of Sappho began in 1880, and continued into the twentieth and now twenty-first centuries,[62] but the novelty of the early discoveries had an enormous impact on the way readers conceived of Sappho's verse and her biography. By the 1920s Sappho's name evoked fragmentary poetry and homosexual eroticism, while her associations with Phaon were drifting into literary memory.[63]

The Bohemian-Austrian poet Rainer Maria Rilke (1875–1926) picked up a sense of the fragmentary and intense eroticism from Sappho's works, soon followed by the Imagist recreations of Ezra Pound, H.D., and Richard Aldington in London. Modernist Sappho was born. The three

---

[59] Nava 1984: 537, 2008: 16–17.
[60] Nava 1984: 537.
[61] For Louÿs, see JOHNSON ch. 26 pp. 369–70.
[62] FINGLASS ch. 17.
[63] Reynolds 2000: 289–97, 309–12.

poems of Rilke's *Neue Gedichte* (*New Poems*, 1907), 'Eranna an Sappho' ('Eranna to Sappho'), 'Sappho an Eranna', and 'Sappho an Alkaïos (Fragment)', emphasise the quality of the brief lyric fragment as a self-standing object,[64] while Sappho's deep understanding of love is the theme of section 68 of *Die Aufzeichnungen des Malte Laurids Brigge* (*The Notebooks of Malte Laurids Brigge*, 1910). The novel's main character, Malte, thinks of women as the true great lovers and views Sappho as the ultimate model of female passion.[65] Sappho is a misunderstood woman:

> Er kennt auf einmal dieses entschlossene Herz, das bereit war, die ganze Liebe zu leisten bis ans Ende. Es wundert ihn nicht, daß man es verkannte; daß man in dieser überaus künftigen Liebenden nur das Übermaß sah, nicht die neue Maßeinheit von Liebe und Herzleid.

> Suddenly he apprehended this resolute heart, which was prepared to achieve the whole of love, right to the very end. He isn't surprised that it has been misunderstood, that in this woman, whose manner of love was entirely of the future, people only saw excess, not the new measure for love and the sickness of the heart. (Rilke 1910: I 160, transl. Vilain 2016: 138)

Sappho here becomes the embodiment of true love and erotic passion, to the point that the object of her desire is less important than the nature and paradigmatic value of desire itself.

Sappho's eroticism and the iconic power of her figure as the first woman writer and a lesbian was also central for women intellectuals such as Natalie Barney, Renée Vivien, and Colette. Inspired by Louÿs's *Les Chansons de Bilitis*, as the 'Sapho 1900' group, they were trying to recreate a lesbian society at Barney's literary salon in Paris, regularly visited by the contemporary modernist elite, including Louÿs and Rilke themselves. Across France and the United Kingdom, between the 1900s and the 1930s Sappho became resolutely a homosexual icon.[66]

In Spain, a teenage Federico García Lorca (1898–1936) engaged with the homoeroticism of Sappho's verse in a dialogue between Plato and Sappho, included in 'El poema de la carne. Nostalgia olorosa y ensoñadora' ('The poem of the flesh. Fragrant and dreamy nostalgia', 1918).[67] Asked why she is crying, Safo confesses her desire and unrestrained passion for the Lesbian girls, who do not love her back. The dialogue,

[64] Rilke 1907: 4–6; Ryan 2001: 136.
[65] Schoolfield 2001: 178, 180–1; also Rüdiger 1933: 157–60.
[66] Reynolds 2000: 337, GOFF AND HARLOE.
[67] Published in García-Posada 1997: IV 691–5.

however, was never published during Lorca's lifetime. After the crucial role Sappho played in nineteenth-century Spanish literature, she falls out of the picture, like many other ancient classics, probably as a consequence of the removal of classical subjects from school curricula.[68]

Openly homoerotic accounts of Sappho coexisted with more conservative portrayals across Europe. In Germany the philologist Ulrich von Wilamowitz-Moellendorff (1848–1931) was the most influential defender of Sappho's reputation. Responding to Louÿs, he revived Welcker's theories of Sappho's chastity to defend her from the imputation of homosexuality,[69] and centred his argument on the portrayal of Sappho as a schoolmistress, interested in girls exclusively because she ran a school. Even though Denys Page attacked Wilamowitz's theory, the schoolmistress picture remained influential.[70]

Around the same time in Italy, theories that defined homosexuality as sexual inversion were filtering from Germany, including Richard von Krafft-Ebing's *Psychopathia Sexualis. Eine klinisch-forensische Studie* (*Sexual Psychopathy. A Clinical-Forensic Study*, 1886; Italian translation, 1889). Medical literature tended to make a distinction between 'healthy' and 'perverted' individuals, but it also inspired the development of pseudo-scientific erotic texts which, while still portraying female sexuality and lesbianism in problematic and often derogatory ways, openly challenged normative medical categories.[71] One such work, *L'eredità di Saffo* (*Sappho's Legacy*, 1908), was written by the Luganese journalist Nada Peretti, under the pseudonym of Fede (Faith).[72] The text is a confessional erotic novel that tells the suffering of Franz, as Gina, the 'pure' girl he thought to be his soulmate, is revealed to be corrupted by a 'moral deformity' and 'perverted passion', namely female homosexuality. These homophobic traits, however, are toned down by a certain voyeuristic pleasure present in the novel and the positive account Gina gives of her homosexual erotic encounters. Unsurprisingly, the book caused a scandal.[73]

Only in the 1920s did lesbianism gain a fully positive press in Italy, with the first lesbian-themed novels such as *Il passaggio* (*The Crossing*,

---

[68] Hernández Miguel 2008: 379.
[69] Wilamowitz 1896 = 1913: 63–78.
[70] Page 1955: 30–3, DeJean 1989a: 278–9, Parker 1993 ≈ Greene 1996b: 146–83, Reynolds 2000: 295, MUELLER pp. 42–3.
[71] Ross 2015: 120–9.
[72] Danna 2004: 123.
[73] Ross 2015: 129–34.

1919) by Sibilla Aleramo and texts such as *Lesbiche* (*Lesbians*, 1927) by the humorist Guido Stacchini. Stacchini's book, a partial translation of Louÿs, expresses adoration for lesbians as quintessential women, and takes Sappho as the first conscious rebel against the submission of women. But Fascism counterbalanced these progressive steps, denouncing women's social progress and the presence of lesbians in society as a sign of decadence.[74] Italian explorations now refocused on Sappho as a poetic archetype. Salvatore Quasimodo's *Lirici greci* (*Greek Lyricists*, 1940), still the most famous Italian anthology of translations of ancient Greek lyric poetry, contained several poems of Sappho and became the flagship work of Hermeticism, the most prominent literary movement in Fascist Italy. An introduction by the philosopher and literary critic Luciano Anceschi outlined the selection criteria based on Hermeticist principles. For Quasimodo and Anceschi, the ancient lyric fragment represented the purest form of poetry, manifestation of a metaphysical absolute. Revisiting Sappho was a way to get in touch with the purity of the original lyric fragments to create a new contemporary poetry.[75]

Quasimodo used relatively free translations, often combining different fragments to emphasise the theme of loneliness in Sappho's corpus, which reflected Leopardi's portrait of a Sappho excluded from the world. Quasimodo's 1953 essay 'Saffo' voices more extended reflections on the lonely poet's role.[76] The Fascist position on homosexuality meant that Sappho's biography was not central to her reception; but while the eroticism is toned down, Sappho's lyrics are never normalised in Quasimodo's anthology. Immensely popular, *Lirici* went through several re-editions, becoming a main vehicle of Italian reception of Sappho in the second half of the twentieth century.[77]

Following in Quasimodo's footsteps, a young Pier Paolo Pasolini translated four fragments of Sappho into Friulian dialect between 1945 and 1947,[78] while the loneliness and existential tragedy of Sappho is picked up in Cesare Pavese's 'Schiuma d'onda' ('Wave foam'), one of the prose dialogues in *Dialoghi con Leucò* (*Dialogues with Leucò*, 1947): having become, after her leap, a sea creature living a timeless existence, Saffo explains to the nymph Britomarti that she killed herself because she

---

[74] Danna 2004: 127–8.
[75] Anceschi 1940 = Quasimodo 2004: 308–9.
[76] Quasimodo 1960: 99–100.
[77] Lorenzini 2004.
[78] Condello 2007.

could not bear the violence intrinsic to desire and sex, the inescapable and all-encompassing longing that condemns people to solitude and desperation. But while desire is the source of torment, life without love is also unthinkable. Sappho's new existence in the sea is plagued by boredom: 'Ma tu lo senti questo tedio, quest'inquietudine marina?' ('But do you feel this boredom, this marine unrest?'). Pavese, who committed suicide in 1950, makes Sappho speak of his own anxieties, turning them into a paradigm of existence.[79]

After Sappho the fragment, the embodiment of liberated eroticism, the illicit lesbian, the chaste schoolmistress, and the lonely poet, by the end of the twentieth century Sappho finally gained the right to stand among many other literary female models as a woman poet who wrote homoerotic lyric. Late twentieth-century Sappho was fully conscious of the history of her reception, of all her names in different languages, the roles she played throughout the centuries. In Grytzko Mascioni's biographical novel *Saffo* (1981), Sappho expresses her desire for girls passionately and explicitly. In Christine Brückner's 1983 prose monologue 'Vergeßt den Namen des Eisvogels nicht' ('Don't forget the kingfisher's name'), included in her volume *Wenn du geredet hättest, Desdemona. Ungehaltene Reden ungehaltener Frauen* (*Desdemona – If You Had Only Spoken! Eleven Uncensored Speeches of Eleven Incensed Women*), Ovid comes back into the story through the back door. Sappho recounts in detail her love and sexual relationships with the girls in Lesbos, but in an unexpected turn of events, facing death and her old age, Sappho reclaims her heterosexual legend: 'I love young Phaon! To have him – I would have given all of you up; all of you; all my girls!' (Brückner 1992: 68 ≈ 1983: 60). The Catalan Carme Riera imagines a 'Fragment mai no escrit de Safo' ('A fragment never written by Sappho'), drawing attention to Sappho's troubled editorial history, as Diane Rayor and Anne Carson do in their translations, emphasising the gaps which define Sappho's fragmented oeuvre.[80] Never has the Sapphic tradition been more aware of itself, its normalising tendencies, and its problematic textual history than at the beginning of the twenty-first century. Sappho today speaks of disembodiment and absence. The same absence allows her to travel in time and space through the many voices that have tried to fill her blanks, granting her and themselves an existence. Sappho forces us to choose; any attempt to give her

---

[79] Pavese 1947: 63; cf. Gragnolati 2006: 69–75.
[80] Riera 1975: 5, Rayor 1991: 18–20, Carson 2002: x–xiii, Rayor cited by Rayor and Lardinois 2014: 19–22. For Riera, see Rodríguez 2000: 110–42; for Carson, see GOFF AND HARLOE.

shape stands as a cultural and a political statement, which ultimately speaks of one's own identity in the world.

Further Reading

Rüdiger 1933, 1934 are still relevant on the German context, the former focusing on the literary reception, the latter on translations. DeJean 1989a, 1989b deal extensively with the treatment of Sappho's biography in German philology of the nineteenth and early twentieth centuries, while Parker 1993 ≈ Greene 1996b: 146–83 explores the interpretation of Sappho as schoolmistress in modern scholarship up to the late twentieth century, including an analysis of German and Italian studies. The essays in Chemello 2012a, 2015 discuss key aspects of the Italian reception of Sappho from the sixteenth to the early twentieth century in literature, music, and visual arts. For the Spanish literary reception in the eighteenth and nineteenth centuries, see Barrero Pérez 2004, 2005, 2007.

CHAPTER 26

Eighteenth- and Nineteenth-Century Sapphos in France, England, and the United States

*Marguerite Johnson**

The Sappho of the Enlightenment and Victorian age was manifest in many forms to express multifarious needs. Her plasticity exerted a significant influence on the representations that emerged in the century that followed. The Sappho manufacturers of the eighteenth and nineteenth centuries demonstrated how appropriation and misappropriation of an ancient icon could suit almost any need. References to Sappho in poetry, satire, moral tracts, fine art, academia, medical texts, and pornography demonstrate her flexibility as a subject and provide information on contemporaneous aesthetic trends and ideals. These receptions also function as a societal magnifying glass, enlarging snapshots of life to reveal more than the wider discourse of these eras.

While Sappho was the subject of celebrated male poets and artists, she also appealed to those outside the canon. It is from these less familiar case studies that alternative but no less compelling histories emerge. An example of an unconventional, even unexpected nineteenth-century Sappho is the creation of the Sapphonian Society in 1892 at Illinois State Normal University. While perhaps outside expected academic enquiries into the reception of Sappho, scholarship on this women's literary society demonstrates the rhetorical strategy behind the group, as symbolised by its eponym. It sought to prepare female students to challenge the contemporary polemic of the 'woman peril in education' that allegedly posed a threat to the male dominance of scholarship.[1]

Suffragettes included Sappho in their historical collectives of important women, illustrated by her inclusion in Cicely Hamilton's *A Pageant of Great Women*, published at the end of the long nineteenth century in 1910.[2] Classicism also appeared in broader, more egalitarian contexts in the eighteenth and nineteenth centuries. Sarah Hale's *Ladies' Magazine*

---

* Thanks to my colleague Professor Michael Ewans for feedback on this chapter.
[1] Ostergaard 2013.
[2] Hamilton 1910: 29.

encouraged readers to perfect their style based on classical models, and in an edition from 1831, Hale 'showed a bust of the poet Sappho, and held her up as a model of "coeffure"'.[3]

This chapter contains some of the lesser-known manifestations of Sappho during the two centuries under discussion, including her use in medical and nascent sex psychology treatises, pornography, and both satirical and political pamphlets. There is also attention to her better-known manifestations, with discussions of such poets and personalities as Mary Robinson, Samuel Taylor Coleridge, and William Wordsworth. These poets form a linchpin for this treatment of Sappho in the eighteenth century, representing as they do a complex series of engagements with her that go beyond straightforward homage. Similarly, the intricacies of Sappho's presence in the poetry of Michael Field and the coterie of Renée Vivien and Natalie Barney form the cornerstone of the analysis of Sappho in the nineteenth century.

Genre was the most significant influence on the sexuality of the eighteenth century Sappho, with references to her predilection for women mostly confined to risqué satires, pornography, and medical treatises.[4] The characteristically heterosexual Sappho of the eighteenth century was not, however, without its problems and complexities. Sappho's heterosexuality usually entailed promiscuity, a penchant for younger men, and an exaggerated passionate disposition, with (Pseudo-?)Ovid's *Letter to Phaon*, poem 15 from the *Heroides*, the means by which artists and writers could fashion this particular Sappho. Indeed, there was much interest in the *Heroides* in the sixteenth and seventeenth centuries, not only as a means of deference to Ovid, but also as a medium to explore contemporary 'politics, love, loss, and ambition'.[5] In Alexander Pope's 'Sapho to Phaon' (1712), based on the *Letter to Phaon*, 'Sapho' emerges as the prototype of the Gothic heroine and, like (Pseudo-?)Ovid's Sappho, Pope's female lead rejects her poetic muse (lines 13–14) and her 'guilty love' of women (lines 17–18) for the sake of the ferryman.[6] This poem, while indicative of its gendered cultural and generic contexts, emphasises not only the motif of the excessive passions of women, but also the disempowerment that instigates women's extreme reactions. While unsuited to modern feminist

---

[3] Winterer 2007: 158.

[4] The anonymous pamphlet, *A Sapphick Epistle, From Jack Cavendish, to the Honourable and Most Beautiful Mrs D***** (*c.*1770s), addressed to the sculptor Anne Demer, publicises her reputation for same-sex attraction and intimacies.

[5] S. Wiseman 2008: 295; GILLESPIE.

[6] P. Rogers 1993: 40–6.

tastes,[7] the poem conveys the contested emotions or 'doubling' of the original, as well as the self-reflexive nature of Ovid's heroic women per se.[8]

Pope's passionate heterosexual Sappho was the foremost image of the poet throughout the Enlightenment, reflecting what Tim Hitchcock refers to as the 'naturalisation of heterosexuality'.[9] Mary Robinson continued the tradition in *Sappho and Phaon. In a Series of Legitimate Sonnets* (1796). Known as 'the English/British Sappho', Robinson 'performed' her epithet through literary creations and self-presentation to ensure she was the worthiest inheritor of the poet's legacy.[10] Perhaps, therefore, *Sappho and Phaon* was a strategy to demonstrate the legitimacy of the title, although Robinson's message 'To the Reader' defies this interpretation:

> The story of the *Lesbian Muse*, though not new to the classical reader, presented to my imagination such a lively example of the human mind, enlightened by the most exquisite talents, yet yielding to the destructive controul of ungovernable passions, that I felt an irresistible impulse to attempt the delineation of their progress; mingling with the glowing picture of her soul, such moral reflections, as may serve to excite that pity, which, while it proves the susceptibility of the heart, arms it against the danger of indulging too luxuriant fancy.[11]

Composed of forty-four sonnets, *Sappho and Phaon* replaces Pope's heroic couplets with Petrarchan rhyme, but contains several close verbal echoes.[12] Robinson utilises the legend not only to pay homage to Sappho, but also to explore the poetic philosophies of the Enlightenment, particularly sublime love. Robinson sets out to rewrite *Heroides* 15 and to demonstrate the theoretical premise that championed sensibility and emotion as hallmarks of poetry.[13] In dialogue with contemporary theories of

---

[7] Gonda and Beynon 2010: 4: 'Sappho's amorous progress here, from an inappropriate same-sex desire for "Lesbian dames" to the hysterical self-deprivations of female heterosexual passion, seems to map neatly onto post-Freudian accounts of lesbian desire as formative, yet fleeting, or if persistent, then pathological.'

[8] Lindheim 2003, Fulkerson 2005: 152–8.

[9] Hitchcock 1997: 6.

[10] D. Robinson 2011: 17, 38–9, 105. Well-known Restoration poets such as Katherine Philips (1632–64) and Anne Finch (1661–1720) were also recipients of the title. The epithet, however, was not always complimentary. Pope's references to Mary Wortley Montagu (1689–1762) testify to its potentially volatile nature; see *Satires of Dr. John Donne, Dean of St. Paul's, Versified* 2.3–6 and *Of the Characters of Women. An Epistle to a Lady* (*Moral Essays/Epistles to Several Persons* 2) 24–8 (P. Rogers 1993: 358, 351) and Rainbolt 1997, D. Robinson 2011: 115–17.

[11] M. Robinson 1796: 17.

[12] Feldman and D. Robinson 1999: 247–9.

[13] See McGann 1996: 94–116 for Robinson's sonnet sequence as a manifesto of Enlightenment poetic theory.

aestheticism, Robinson's *Sappho and Phaon* casts the Enlightenment alongside the best of ancient Greek culture, as symbolised by Sappho's poetry, communicating the imperative to align scientific endeavours with cultural acumen. Only then, implies Robinson, may a culture achieve an authentic return to Hellenic grandeur.

In addition to the sonnets and the 'Preface', Robinson's introductory essay ('Account of Sappho') sheds light on the nature of Sappho's established biography in the eighteenth century. Drawing on the *Suda*,[14] (Pseudo-?)Ovid's *Letter to Phaon*, and previous biographies based on the same, Robinson constructs a panegyric that presents Sappho as a heterosexual, mother, and genius. She acknowledges Jean-Jacques Barthélemy's *Voyage du jeune Anacharsis en Grèce, dans le milieu du quatrième siècle avant l'ère vulgaire* (*Travels of Anacharsis the Younger in Greece, during the Middle of the Fourth Century before the Christian Era*) as a source of inspiration and includes a quotation from the English translation of his novel:[15]

> But a certain facility in her manners, and warmth in her expressions, were but too well calculated to expose her to the hatred of some women of distinction, humbled by her superiority, and of some of her disciples who happened not to be the objects of her preference.

The *Voyage*, which serves as an allegory for the ideal republic, chronicles the imaginary travels of Anacharsis throughout the classical world and, according to Joan DeJean, presents 'the most influential fiction of Sappho in the entire French tradition'.[16] As the quotation from Robinson illustrates, Barthélemy depicts Sappho as a brilliant poet forced to depart Mytilene to avoid further persecution at the hands of jealous and disgruntled women. However, Barthélemy, a classical scholar, could not help but include notes to explain the historical background to his fiction. Accordingly, the note on Sappho's departure from Mytilene reads:[17]

> It is probable that Alcaeus engaged her in the conspiracy against Pittacus, and that she was banished to Mitylene at the same time with him and his partisans.

The contradiction between fact and fiction collides in the *Voyage* and, thereafter, Barthélemy's Sappho as political exile becomes part of her representation in revolutionary France.

---

[14] *Suda* c 107–8 (testt. 2–3).
[15] <Barthélemy> 1788: I 288 ≈ Barthélemy 1794: II 63.
[16] DeJean 1989a: 138.
[17] <Barthélemy> 1788: I 535 ≈ Barthélemy 1794: II 478.

Despite the influence of Barthélemy's Sappho, her association with revolution was referenced before him in the 1724 novel *L'Histoire et les amours de Sapho de Mytilène*, later (falsely) ascribed to the solider and writer Jean Du Castre d'Auvigny (1712–43).[18] Here Sappho is a promiscuous heterosexual who, in her widowhood, exercises a healthy appetite for young men. Unsurprisingly, overcome by her unrequited love of Phaon, she leaps to her death (again). The novel's politicised Sappho manifests in her connection with Alcée (i.e. Alcaeus), a relative of her father and her most ardent suitor. While Sappho remains directly removed from political intrigues, Alcée's meddling leads to his banishment from Mytilene, which inevitably leads to his return as a triumphant freedom fighter. Both Alcée and Barthélemy's Alcaeus live in a state marked by a political turmoil intended to reference the factions and dangers of unstable alliances in a France on the cusp of revolution.[19]

The intellectual, libertine women of the Enlightenment regularly sought to present themselves through association with Sappho. This may explain their imperative to promote the image of the poet as both heterosexual and promiscuous, coinciding as it did with their own sexuality and rebellion against traditional morality. Robinson went to great lengths to embrace an idealised, intellectual Sappho, which she may have intended to assist in the repair of her own reputation. Her affair with the Prince of Wales (later George IV) in 1779, the gossip of London, was satirised in numerous cartoons and resulted in the epithet 'Perdita'.[20] The title stuck for years and marked Robinson as a 'whore' (the euphemistic meaning of the name). Ironically, however, the power of an appellation, no matter how grotesque, seems to have struck a chord with Robinson, who adopted a series of titles for herself throughout the rest of her life. The name 'Sappho', originally bestowed upon her by the press in 1787,[21] was something Robinson cherished and, like the prima donna she was, performed to the best of her ability.

---

[18] Anonymous (a) 1724. D'Auvigny's authorship is accepted without comment by De Jean 1989a: 134–7.

[19] For the political theme in Sappho's biographical tradition, see M. Johnson 2007: 37–40 (referencing Parian Marble A36 Rotstein = test. 5), Page 1955: 224–5; *contra* Kirkwood 1974: 100–1, DeJean 1989a: 160, Williamson 1995: 72.

[20] The Prince first cast eyes on Robinson in the role of Perdita in Shakespeare's *The Winter's Tale*. For the representations of Robinson in art, satirical literature, and cartoons, see Mellor 2000.

[21] D. Robinson 2011: 81: 'Robinson's first published sonnet appeared in the *Oracle* on 29 July 1789 (1: 62). And in his editorial headnote, Bell himself makes the first association between Robinson/Laura Maria and Sappho – two years before the *Monthly Review* proclaimed Robinson "the English Sappho"'.

Robinson's alter ego, 'the English Sappho', demonstrated the effective-
ness of an intellectual woman's association with the poet during this era.
While credited with a poetic skill and, in the opinion of some, a certain
genius, Robinson's avatar was a form of public shorthand that advertised
her intellect at a time of endemic masculinity and casual misogyny.
Among her most ardent admirers was Samuel Taylor Coleridge. Almost a
generation younger than Robinson, Coleridge sought her out as both a
critic of his work and as a friend, never doubting her talent, and praising
her as 'a woman of undoubted Genius'.[22] He responded to Robinson's
identification with Sappho on many occasions; for example, her innova-
tions in the use of the nonce stanza and Sappho's own metrical inven-
tions were not lost on him.[23] The relationship between them thereby
exemplifies another element in the homage to Sappho of the eighteenth
century – the use of her name as a means of denoting intimacy, friend-
ship, and literary camaraderie.

Coleridge and Robinson enjoyed mutual poetic compliments in the
Morning Post, and their contributions to the print media eventually
involved a strange literary *ménage à trois* with an unsuspecting William
Wordsworth.[24] In 1800, Coleridge sent four of Wordsworth's poems to
the *Morning Post* for publication. Three echoed Robinson's own works,
particularly 'The Solitude of Binnorie', which prompted Coleridge to
attach a letter addressed to the editor, Daniel Stuart, to request acknowl-
edgement of Robinson's metrical influence on Wordsworth. The letter
ends with a reference to Sappho, which casts Robinson as the Sappho to
Wordsworth's Alcaeus:[25]

> This acknowledgement will not appear superfluous to those who have felt
> the bewitching effect of that absolutely original stanza in the original
> Poem, and who call to mind that the invention of a metre has so widely
> diffused the name of Sappho, and almost constitutes the present celebrity
> of Alcaeus.

To reiterate the message, the fourth poem sent by Coleridge was entitled
'Alcaeus to Sappho', in which he 'repackaged an uncharacteristically
erotic lyric by Wordsworth', intending a 'wink to Robinson'.[26] Coleridge
published the poem under his own name on 24 November 1800.

---

[22] Letter to Robert Southey, 25 January 1800; Griggs 1956–71: I 562.
[23] D. Robinson 2011: 221–3.
[24] Cross 2001.
[25] Erdman 1978: III 291.
[26] D. Robinson 2011: 186–7. Reynolds 2000: 154, 2003: 50 attributes the poem to Coleridge, and
     thereby links Alcaeus to Coleridge, not Wordsworth (see Cross 2001: 587–8: 'it was clearly written

While Sappho was usually heterosexual throughout the eighteenth century, and entered the nineteenth century the same, she continued to worry the medical profession. A Swiss physician of the Enlightenment, Samuel-Auguste André David Tissot, discussed Sapphism in relation to masturbation in the French revision and translation of a treatise first published in Latin, itself subsequently translated into English:[27]

> Besides masturbation, or manual pollution, there is another kind of pollution, which may be called *clitorical*, the known origin of which is to be traced so far back as the time of the second *Sappho*.
>
> *Lesbides infamem quae me fecistis amatae:*[28]
>
> and which was so much too common amongst the Roman women, at the time when all morality was lost, that it was more than once the subject for the epigrammatists and satirists of that age.
>
> *Lenonum ancillas posita Laufella corona*
> *Provocat, & tollit pendentis praemia coxae.*
> *Ipsa Medullina frictum crisantis adorat.*
> *Palmam inter dominas virtus natalibus aequat.*[29]
>
> Nature has been pleased to give to some women a semi-resemblance to man; this has, upon slight inquiry, given rise to the chimera, which has prevailed for some centuries, of hermaphrodites.

Tissot references the 'two Sapphos' of antiquity. He cites the *Letter to Phaon* ascribed to Ovid for the 'second Sappho', the lover of women (*Heroides* 15.201 = test. 19), and blames her for inventing 'clitorical pollution' ('souillure clitoridienne'). He thereby conflates lesbianism with female masturbation by implying that Sapphism is a possible consequence of auto-eroticism. Tissot then associates lesbianism with hermaphroditism, going on to discuss the existence of women with enlarged clitorides who attempt to perform the role of men.[30]

---

by Wordsworth as early as February 1799'). The poem is included in both the Princeton Coleridge (Mays 2001: 1/1 539–40) and in the Cornell Wordsworth (James Butler and Green 1992: 296).

[27] Tissot 1766: 45–6 ≈ 1760: 50. The passage is not found in the original Latin treatise (Tissot 1758: 177–264), which nevertheless does briefly reference Sappho at p. 203.

[28] (Pseudo-?)Ovid, *Heroides* 15.201 (test. 19): 'Lesbian women, whom I have loved to my reproach'.

[29] Juvenal, *Satires* 6.320–3: 'Laufella removes her garland and challenges pimps' girls, | and wins the prize for wriggling her hips. | Medullina herself admires the rubbing of the shimmying woman. | The prize is shared between the ladies, their skill matching their breeding.'

[30] For the fantasy of the macroclitoris of the lesbian in nascent sexology literature in the seventeenth century, see <Venette> 1687. For the fantasy in eighteenth-century pornography, see <Mirabeau> 1783.

Ironically, the medical Sappho complemented the pornographic one. The most notorious English pamphlet on lesbian Sappho was *The Sappho-an. An Heroic Poem, of Three Cantos. In the Ovidian Stile* . . . (1749), which cost a shilling (the average daily wage). Addressed to the 'Swains of Britannia's happy, gladsome isle', the poem is a warning about Sapphism:[31]

> Women in secret joys consume their prime;
> Some fav'rite *maid*, or handy young *coquette*,
> Steals the rich prize you vainly strive to get;
> Of them be cautious; but the artful *prude*
> Watch most, for she will thoughtless girls delude;

As Tissot quotes Ovid and Juvenal, the author of *The Sappho-an* also cites Ovid in this classical fantasy featuring the Olympians. The text is a pornographic aetiology on the origin of the dildo, the creation of which lies with Juno's fury at the gods' predilection for promiscuity. Not surprisingly, Sappho features in the story:[32]

> To close the scene, quite ripe for am'rous sport
> The *Lesbian*, tho' no goddess, fills the court:
> Man's solid bliss she to the full had try'd,
> Nor to the other sex her aid denied;
> Awful she rushes in and claims a part
> To add new vigour to the blunted dart;

The anonymous poet mentions Phaon but is more preoccupied with the lesbian Sappho, whom he depicts, like Tissot, as a woman in possession of a macroclitoris. Caroline Gonda points to the political tenor of the pamphlet, noting the significance of the subtitle: 'Found amongst the Papers of a Lady of Quality, a great Promoter of *Jaconitism*'.[33] When it comes to politics, Sappho's sexuality is paramount. As a heroine associated with revolution in Barthélemy and D'Auvigny, Sappho is a heterosexual; but when associated with negative allusions to the Stuarts, she is both a lesbian and a macroclitoride.[34]

---

[31] Anonymous (b) 1749: 9.

[32] Anonymous (b) 1749: 29.

[33] Gonda 2015: 110; see also Lanser 2014: 101–5. 'Jaconitism' is most likely a misspelling of 'Jacobitism', the belief that the exiled James II and his heirs were the rightful kings of England, Ireland, and Scotland.

[34] The inclusion of Sappho's name in politics was a form of both praise and criticism of prominent women, depending on the attributor's political persuasion. British-American author Susanna Rowson (1762–1824) was ridiculed by the English journalist William Cobbett, who referred to her as 'our American Sappho' (Porcupine 1795 = Cobbett 1836: 23), in response to her republicanism as well as her promotion of women's equality in *Slaves in Algiers; or, A Struggle for Freedom: a Play, interspersed with Songs, in Three Acts* (1793).

While the Enlightenment privileged a heterosexual Sappho in the arts, with notable exceptions in less celebrated genres, the nineteenth century witnessed 'a complicated representational history'.[35] Sappho remained fascinated with Phaon, but was also a lover of women once more. Versions of the abandoned Sappho and her tendency to leap off the Leucadian cliff continued,[36] but inevitably these became tiresome and clichéd, as exemplified by various parodies. From a series satirising the overuse of classical motifs, Honoré Daumier's lithograph 'La Mort de Sapho' ('The Death of Sapho', 1843) shows Cupid shoving a hag-like Sappho over the cliff.[37] Daumier's series influenced Charles Baudelaire's *L'École païenne* (*The Pagan School*, 1852),[38] which also mocked artists who depicted ancient icons, including 'the burning Sappho, that patron saint of hysterics'.[39] Despite his disdain for classical clichés, Baudelaire went on to write *Les Fleurs du mal* (*The Flowers of Evil*, 1857), a collection of a hundred poems that included three on Sapphism and Sappho: 'Lesbos', 'Femmes damnées: A la pâle clarté . . .' ('Women damned: In the pallid light . . .'), and 'Femmes damnées: Comme un bétail pensif . . .' ('Women damned: Like thoughtful cattle . . .').[40]

Making fun of Sappho appeared elsewhere and earlier, as illustrated by the anti-Jacobite satire, *The Sappho-an* (above), which titillated readers with the poet cast as a soft-porn star. Less prurient and more light-heartedly earnest is the Sappho of the anti-Jacobin play *Elephantasmagoria. Or, The Covent Garden Elephant's Entrance into Elysium* (1812). Once the sacredness of Sappho began to erode by the introduction of these satirical, salacious, and generally lowbrow productions, the pornographic Sappho made her entrance. Pierre Louÿs's *Les Chansons de Bilitis* (*The Songs of Bilitis*) is an example of soft-core pornography featuring Sappho and Sapphism. Published in 1894, *Les Chansons de Bilitis* was a literary hoax, with Louÿs claiming that the prose poetry was a translation of the work of a contemporary of Sappho called Bilitis, whose tomb had been recently excavated by a German archaeologist. The text, as Venuti observed, 'is remarkable for its demystification of dominant cultural values, not only the academic reception of classical Greek literature and of Sappho's poetry

---

[35] Gonda 2015: 110, referring to the long eighteenth century.

[36] Lanser 2014: 243 provides examples from the French tradition from 1810 to 1830.

[37] Plate 49 from the series 'Histoire Ancienne' in the magazine *Le Charivari*; accompanied by the lines 'Young ladies, you see where love leads us | Under our feet so dainty and small | The wretched chasm of an abyss | Into which we eventually fall.'

[38] DeJean 1989a: 353 n. 79; also Olmsted 2016: 131–2.

[39] Pichois 1975–6: II 44–9, at 46; transl. Olmsted 2016: 132.

[40] Baudelaire 1857: 187–97, M. Johnson 2007: 132–6. 'Lesbos' was first published as Baudelaire 1850.

in particular, but also concepts of authorship and historical scholarship that still prevail today'.[41] Again, pornography and medical texts intersect at the pathology of same-sex desire. Louÿs presents Bilitis as a precocious young masturbator who enjoys frottage with tree limbs. She eventually ends up as Sappho's lover, followed by a series of same-sex relations, then prostitution and, finally, miserable old (middle) age. Unlike Baudelaire's *Les Fleurs du mal*, six poems from which were censored, including the three Sapphic verses, Louÿs's collection remained untouched. This was most likely due to the fabricated scholarship that shaped the work and legitimated its initial separation from pornography.[42] In the visual arts, allusions to Sappho or Sapphism featured in the boudoir illustrations of Édouard-Henri Avril (Paul Avril). The engraving 'Les temps anciens, planchet XII' ('Ancient times, plate XII') depicts the poet draped over rocks, gently holding a rose-garlanded lyre, receiving cunnilingus. The image is from a 1906 French edition of *De figuris Veneris* by Friedrich Karl Forberg, an anthology of classical texts on erotic themes.

In the *fin de siècle*, lesbians actively claimed Sappho's voice as their own, as illustrated by Michael Field's collection of poems entitled *Long Ago*.[43] This work foreshadows *Les Chansons de Bilitis*; for while neither particularly erotic nor claiming to be a translation, *Long Ago* was a literary hoax of sorts. Published in 1889, it was the work of aunt and niece, Katharine Bradley and Edith Cooper respectively, who as lovers and poets composed together under the name of Michael Field. By recourse to Sappho and her lyrics, Michael Field could express same-sex desire through the safety net of art and history in poems such as 'Atthis, my darling, thou did'st stray' and 'Not Gello's self loves more than I'. *Long Ago* demonstrates the enduring ubiquity of classicism during the closing decades of the nineteenth century and, in relation to Sappho, the importance of new editions and translations of her work for artists. In the Preface, the poet(s) acknowledge the influence of the edition by Henry Thornton Wharton, published in 1885, which they further reference in the Greek epitaphs that accompany each poem. Wharton's Sappho marks an important moment in the history of her reception because it presented a Sappho free from judgemental emphasis on her sexuality. Its use of

---

[41] Venuti 1998: 34.

[42] For the response of the great classical scholar Ulrich von Wilamowitz-Moellendorff (1896 = 1913: 63–78), see Venuti 1998: 40–3.

[43] Field 1889. It met with generally positive reviews and its modest print run of one hundred copies sold out within a month (Donoghue 1998: 50). For Field, see further GOFF AND HARLOE pp. 393–4, VANITA p. 461.

literal translations, including the employment of the feminine pronoun, inadvertently permitted artists, poets, and writers to create a Sappho of their own making. This was particularly liberating for lesbian artists.[44]

Armed with Wharton's Sappho and determined to make classicism their own, women such as Bradley and Cooper paved the way for others to follow. American heiress Natalie Clifford Barney and Anglo-American heiress Renée Vivien ('later dubbed "Sapho 1900"')[45] did likewise. Vivien and Barney, however, approached Sappho in a more public and visceral way compared to Michael Field, inspired not only by Wharton's Sappho,[46] but also by *Les Chansons de Bilitis* – of which, Barney wrote in her memoir, *Aventures de l'esprit* (*Adventures of the Mind*):[47]

> By a strength of nature and art, the author of *Songs of Bilitis* shows us a succession of liaisons that are sufficiently captivating and complicated in themselves to require no alloys, something which does not happen without the presence of a certain purity.

Both women sought to recreate romanticised versions of Sappho-inspired communities. Barney first established a salon in her home at Neuilly and, later, one in her *pavillon* on rue Jacob, Paris. In 1904, both she and Vivien planned a poetry school in Mytilene, recorded in her autobiographical essay 'Renée Vivien' from *Souvenirs indiscrets* (*Indiscreet Memories*):[48]

> 'Why don't we start our longed for poetry school right here, where young women vibrating with poetry, youth and love would come to us like the poetesses of old, travelling from all parts of the world to be with Sappho?'

The idea of starting a school marks an interesting intersection with the standard reception of Sappho, popularised by Ulrich von Wilamowitz-Moellendorff, in which the notion of a 'school' with a 'teacher' was being constructed to deflect attention away from unpalatable truths about her same-sex relationships.[49] While it could be argued that Barney and Vivien were appropriating the determined heterosexualising scholarly discourse in a subversive way, they were more probably inspired by the notion of

---

[44] The poet H.D. (GOFF AND HARLOE pp. 394–7) also consulted Wharton's edition (Rohrbach 1996: 188 n. 9).

[45] Prettejohn 2008: 121.

[46] Barney gave Wharton's edition to Vivien as a gift (Fabre-Serris 2016: 79).

[47] Barney 1929: 22 ≈ 1992a: 33. For the long, intense friendship between Barney and Louÿs, see Engelking 2005.

[48] Barney 1960: 80 ≈ 1992b: 45. Although Vivien purchased a house in Mytilene, the poetry school never came to pass.

[49] MUELLER pp. 42–3, KURKE pp. 94–5, FERRARI pp. 107–8.

creating an all-female school from the perspective of championing women's education.

To engage authentically with Sappho's poetics, both women sought tuition in classical Greek,[50] and published literature inspired by, and in homage to, Sappho. Vivien's *Sapho. Traduction nouvelle avec le texte grec* (*Sappho. New Translation with the Greek Text*) was the first publication in France to make available almost the entire collection of Sappho's oeuvre.[51] For Vivien, the act of learning Greek – like the act of translating Sappho – was an exercise in sexual and gender politics, as Jacqueline Fabre-Serris comments: 'to translate Sappho was clearly a way of agitating for a kind of life that the latter symbolized, as a poetess loving women and surrounded by them'.[52] *Sapho*, a testimony to Vivien's scholarly and poetic intellect, in turn inspired Barney's creativity, as she recounts in *Souvenirs indiscrets*:[53]

> Thanks to your translation of Sappho and the work of these poetesses, I will write a play whose plot I have already worked out. It will destroy the myth of Phaon, for Sappho will die because she has been betrayed by the best-beloved of her friends, as is fitting.

After Vivien's death in 1909, Barney published *Actes et entr'actes*, which included *Equivoque*, the lesbian version of the Sappho and Phaon myth.[54]

Women in America, like their British and European sisters, embraced Sappho as an icon, and in an era where few role models were available, she remained a steadfast mentor of female artistic expression. Poet and editor Mary Hewitt composed 'Imitation of Sappho' in 1853, described by Paula Bennett as 'an excellent example of a nineteenth-century U.S. women's poem explicitly using the Sapphic conventions'.[55] As prefaced in the title, Hewitt resurrects *imitatio* as traditionally practised; here is no direct translation, no heavy-handed linguistic replication, but a response to the original that empowers the new.[56] Hewitt expresses female erotic desire in an almost unprecedented manner in American poetry to date,[57] as illustrated by her closing stanza:

---

[50] K. Jay 1992: iii, Fabre-Serris 2016: 94–5.
[51] Vivien 1903.
[52] Fabre-Serris 2016: 79.
[53] Barney 1960: 81 ≈ 1992b: 46.
[54] Barney 1910.
[55] Bennett 2003: 176. Hewitt composed two other 'Sappho' poems: 'The child of Fame' and 'Sappho to the Sibyl'.
[56] Prins 1996: 60–3 (~ 1999: 47–51), Watts 1977: 79–81.
[57] Watts 1977: 80 notes: 'Except for the poems of Frances Sargent Osgood, … there is no other poet at this time, male or female, who dared to approach woman's sexuality this explicitly.'

> If at thy glance my heart all strength forsaking,
> Pant in my breast as pants the frighted dove;
> If to think on thee ever, sleeping – waking –
> Oh, if this be to love thee, I do love!

An allusive engagement with Sappho also informed a poem by Emily Dickinson, published posthumously in 1896:[58]

> "Heaven" – is what I cannot reach!
> The Apple on the Tree –
> Provided it do hopeless – hang –
> That – "Heaven" is – to Me!
>
> The Color, on the cruising cloud –
> The interdicted Land –
> Behind the Hill – the House behind –
> There – Paradise – is found!
>
> Her teazing Purples – Afternoons –
> The credulous – decoy –
> Enamored – of the Conjuror –
> That spurned us – Yesterday!

This reference is to Sappho fr. 105(a)[59] and, like Hewitt's erudite *imitatio*, Dickinson's allusion attests to developments in women's appropriation of Sappho almost one hundred years after the death of Robinson. Bennett interprets the poem as an example of Dickinson's homoerotic writing, this one dedicated to her friend and sister-in-law, Susan Huntington Gilbert Dickinson, who lived in the house 'Behind the Hill' where 'Paradise – is found!'[60]

To pursue a reading of Dickinson's allusion to an essentially spectral Sappho, her *imitatio* may well have extended to replicating the fragmented condition of the poems. A note that came with a gift, for example, reads:[61]

> Sweet friends,
> I send
> a message by

---

[58] R. Franklin 1998: I 329 (§310).

[59] Grahn 1985: 96 first made the comparison. Dickinson's classical education at Amherst Academy, the availability of English translations of Sappho in the United States, and the likely appeal of Sappho would suggest her familiarity with the poet's work.

[60] Bennett 1990: 170–1 with 210–11 n. 22. See also Dickinson's letters to Susan in Hart and Smith 1998.

[61] T. Johnson 1958: III 878 (§995), *c.*1885, on which see Bennett 1992: 90–2 (with facsimile). See also T. Johnson 1958: III 881 (§1002), *c.*1885: 'Let me thank the little Cousin in flowers, which without lips, have language' (a possible reference to Sappho's Cleis in fr. 132).

> a Mouth that
> cannot speak –
> The Ecstasy
> to guess,
> Were a receipted
> Bliss
> If Grace couldTalk –
> With love –

This example of Dickinson's poem-notes demonstrates the choice of an appropriate structure to capture the fragmented condition of Sappho's works. The 'Mouth that I cannot speak', echoing fr. 31, further extends the conceit. Some of Barney's compositions, including her *pensées* or 'thoughts', have been defined as 'a kind of poetics of the fragment',[62] which may suggest that she too was inspired by the fragmented state of Sappho's oeuvre.

The receptions of Sappho and her oeuvre are artefacts no less insightful than the traditional sources of the historian. To delve into her appearances in all manner of materials is to document the artistic, philosophical, medical, sexual, and gender politics of the Enlightenment and Victorian ages. Perhaps her greatest legacy during the eighteenth and nineteenth centuries was the gift she unknowingly gave to women. With a long history of her own biographical persecution, censorship, and bastardisation, Sappho survived in fragments to inspire intellectual, creative, and sexually emancipated women. The battles to own Sappho during these centuries, contributing to the history of sexuality, and the sexuality of history, set the scene for more battles during the twentieth century that women, ultimately, won.

Further Reading

The topic of eighteenth- and nineteenth-century Sapphos is increasingly covered by scholars working in a variety of fields, including classical reception, comparative literature, women's studies, and cultural history. Some examples of the broad discipline coverages include McCormick 1997, Andreadis 2001, and Beynon and Gonda 2010.

---

[62] Elliott and Wallace 1992: 19.

CHAPTER 27

Sappho and Modern Greece

Dimitrios Kargiotis

What – rather than who – is Sappho? What's in a name and how is that constructed? Sappho's effect and significance in history are impressive when considered next to her surviving textual corpus, and the quest for the 'actual' Sappho has mythologised, refigured, or disfigured what she and her work may originally have meant. As a result, the meaning of 'Sappho' is inextricably linked to the stories of her reception, and to the creative appropriation of her verses by literary tradition; and her impact and significance for European and indeed world culture depend to a great degree on the transgressing sexuality she has come to represent.

In the context of Modern Greek literature, we need also to address issues pertaining to linguistic continuity and change, considering linguistic, literary, historical, and ideological questions; likewise, we have to tackle problems of understanding cultural and national belonging, of negotiating the heritage and the uses of the past, and of confronting the weight of tradition and inscribing the present into the historical continuum.

So the presence of Sappho in Modern Greek literature is a story of mediations.[1] This chapter focuses on specific instances, including translations into Modern Greek, the way her work or her persona have constituted poetic material for major Greek poets, as well as their broader literary and cultural meanings and significance, particularly in the domain of education.

* * *

Translation enables cultural contact and cultural transmission. This is all the more evident when it comes to intralingual translation, a particular case governed by its own dynamics and the apparent paradox that both the original and the translated text belong to the same language.[2] As

---

[1] Yatromanolakis 2003, Antonopoulos 2015, 2016.
[2] Kargiotis 2017: 15–26, 29–41.

older forms of that language become impenetrable for the modern user, translation is needed to permit full access to the original. Yet intralingual translation marks not simply a linguistic moment, but also an ideological one in its own historical and cultural context. This determines both the theoretical bases of the translation project and its practice, in the choices pertaining to language, literary form, and rhetoric.

Sappho has been translated by important Modern Greek authors (such as Thrasyvoulos Stavrou or Ilias Voutieridis), poets (such as Odysseus Elytis), and scholars (such as Daniel Jakob, Ioannis Kakridis, Ioannis Kazazis, or D. N. Maronitis), and many more. Among these, we shall first turn to the classicist and ethnologist Panayis Lekatsas (1911–70), who in 1938 provided the first authoritative, bilingual edition of Sappho for the Greek public. The extensive introduction discusses biographical data on Sappho, provides an overview of the history and tradition of the corpus, surveys the bibliography and editions, and discusses Sappho's metre. Next follows the ancient (original) and modern (translated) texts printed side by side, with a critical and interpretive apparatus.

Lekatsas does not bypass Sappho's sexual orientation, writing that

> any study and interpretation of her work is bound to remain incomplete and ungrounded if it does not define her personality and the quality of her feelings; feelings that constituted the occasion for such passion in her works and for her fascinating inspirations . . . Unfortunately, this issue has been confronted in its moral aspect, and the aim of criticism has been to justify rather than interpret.[3]

Lekatsas deplores the scholarly attempts of Welcker and Wilamowitz to undo Sappho's lesbian reputation:

> whoever approaches her work is persuaded that we are dealing with a female voice moved, more than anything, by female corporeal beauty; that the most intense feelings that moved her existence were lesbian loves; and that the motive of those feelings, with their passionate excitement, was nothing else than sexual instinct.[4]

By seeking an objective, unbiased reading of Sappho on a strong philological foundation, his work makes a major contribution to her reception in Modern Greek culture.

His translation of the Sapphic corpus, and texts associated with it, is pleasing and appealing both to specialists and the erudite reader. While

---

[3] Lekatsas 1938: 10.
[4] Lekatsas 1938: 14. See further Parker 1993 ≈ Greene 1996b: 146–83, MUELLER pp. 42–3, KURKE pp. 94–5, FERRARI pp. 107–8.

remaining close to the original, his version reads flawlessly in Modern Greek; Lekatsas composes in a fluid vernacular, avoiding both extreme forms of demoticism and katharevousa (an archaic form of Modern Greek). He neither sacrifices accuracy nor hesitates to take liberties when necessary, though he refrains from editorial intrusion in the case of fragmentary words or verses.

Lekatsas renders the poems into Modern Greek in three ways. For poems that are more or less complete, he uses a four-verse stanza: three verses that are usually iambic and containing eleven syllables followed by one in seven syllables. At times there is one additional syllable or one missing. For less complete poems, Lekatsas translates in iambic fifteen-syllable verse, and for those that are extremely fragmentary he translates into prose, aiming to provide a more general framework within which meaning can be created, rather than a word for word translation.

In the first two cases, the connection between the original and the translation carries a specific aesthetic ideology. Lekatsas's stanzas connect to the sapphic stanza on both a visual and (to some extent) a metrical level (given the qualitative difference of rhythm and metre between Ancient and Modern Greek, for which all vowels have the same value), while the iambic fifteen-syllable verse inscribes Sappho into the Greek vernacular tradition. The literary, cultural, and broadly ideological significance of this verse cannot be underestimated.[5] It is the metrical form in which much of Modern Greek poetry has been written from the Middle Ages until today, one inextricably associated with a tradition ranging from the oral poetry of demotic songs to erudite, high poetry. This long history has formed an aesthetic horizon of expectations, linking the Greek people and their identity, culture, and historical unity. So to translate Sappho in fifteen-syllable verse attests both an aesthetic choice and an ideological stance, as already in Christos Paraskevaidis's 1935 translation, and then throughout the twentieth century.

Another significant moment in this history is the translation of Sotiris Kakisis (1954–), the poet, essayist, journalist, and translator whose first translations of Sappho were published in 1978. Kakisis's poetic text occupies the main part of the book, with the translation facing the original. The poems are preceded by a short introduction and followed by basic bibliography as well as an index of correspondence between his

---

[5] For the origins, significance, and developments of the 'political' verse form, see Beaton 1996: 98–100.

translation and other editions. Kakisis justifies his fifteen-syllable unrhymed verse as follows:[6]

> I use metre. The fifteen-syllable verse remains alive; and when it operates at a simple register on the level of personal creation, then it becomes a more common rhythmical code. I think that Sappho transmits personal style or, sometimes, a more limited social range, without difficulty; so that this popular metre does not betray her poetry.

His rationale was not always accepted easily by classicists; indeed, Kakisis's translation of Alcaeus, finished simultaneously with that of Sappho but published first, met with such criticism that his publisher delayed Sappho, prompting him to say 'Let me assume poetic responsibility for this metre, this wavy, Panhellenic metre.'[7]

Ironically, Kakisis's Sappho was a great success, in part because his translations were set to music, leading to composers, producers, and interpreters including Manos Hadjidakis, Dionysis Savvopoulos, Spyros Vlassopoulos, Dimitris Papadimitriou, Aleka Kanellidou, and Eleftheria Arvanitaki becoming involved with Sappho. The painter Alekos Fassianos repeatedly depicted her on the covers of vinyl records and books. This complex net of mediation inscribed Sappho in the natural continuum of Greek cultural heritage. Recounting his experience of a concert where many of Sappho's poems were sung, Kakisis wrote:

> I admit I was moved . . . I was thinking that in a country that could itself be named Sappho, since Sappho's poetry expresses Greece so accurately, in a lyrical country, but a bloody country from the ancient years, still so many people ignore so much, usually the best we have to offer.[8]

Kakisis endeavours to attain totality against the fragmentary nature of the Sapphic corpus. He delves into a poetics of restitution, inventing connections, relating fragments, assembling words, and constructing an urtext of translation. He combines several verses belonging to different original poems into a single new text. Kakisis's attempt alludes to a Romantic project that fantasises completeness, but also renegotiates traditional notions of the 'original text' as well as established practices of the discipline of Classics. He is therefore a good example of how 'Sappho' is constructed in Modern Greek culture: translation is no longer limited to

---

[6] Kakisis 1978: 7.
[7] S. Kakisis, "Της Σαπφώς μου ιστορίες (1979–2014)", *Andro*, 5 August 2014 (www.andro.gr/emp-neusi/tis-sapfos-mou-istories-1979–2014/).
[8] *Ibid.*

textual correspondence but has its own poetics and politics; and Sappho, from being an ancient author who needs to be translated in order to be accessed widely, becomes material to be worked by the skilled poet.

Another telling example is the twentieth-century poet Odysseus Elytis (1911–96). Appearing on the Greek literary scene in the 1930s, and winning the Nobel Prize in 1979, Elytis published his Sappho in 1984.[9] The typographic layout of the book, with the original and translation side by side, leads the reader to consider it, initially, a translation of Sappho. Yet Elytis's purpose is broader;[10] already in the title, the project is named 'recomposition and rendition', and subsequently the poet exposes his method of work. Explaining that his 'attempt aimed elsewhere and not at the discipline of philology', he makes clear that he uses 'Sappho' as poetic rather than translation material. In this sense, instead of following a specific, established ordering of the poems, he 'proceeded with the arbitrary connection of the fragments with the ultimate goal of creating a new poetic unity'.[11] He did not 'fill the textual *lacunae*', and did not hesitate to change grammatical tenses, add connecting particles, and do all work necessary towards creating a poem.

The book's aesthetic also serves this goal. The font and ornamentation allude to ancient Greece but also, more subtly, to the Greek Orthodox aesthetic. No capital letters are used, punctuation is limited, and there is no line-by-line separation of verses; instead, they all form a single text and each is separated by a rosette (a 'jewel', as the poet calls it – a practice he follows also elsewhere in his work), which does not disturb textual continuity. The book is divided into seven sections, each of which has as its title a verse from Sappho in the original Greek, and is introduced by a painting, made by Elytis himself, whose theme is related to the title of the section. Paintings also separate other sections of the book, such as the introduction and notes. Eleven in total, these images are inscribed in a modernist, figurative aesthetic. In total, Elytis composed fifty-two poems, using 139 fragments out of 192.[12]

A carefully designed artefact, the book intimately converses with Sappho both aesthetically and ideologically. While Elytis's postface emphasises poetics, his introduction exposes the tenets and orientation of

---

[9] Elytis 1984. This work first came out in a voluminous, luxurious limited edition, followed shortly by a pocket-sized one.

[10] Loulakaki-Moore 2010: 231–69.

[11] Elytis 1984: 143. This is arguably in line with surrealist practices, according to Yatromanolakis 2003: 180–1, Loulakaki-Moore 2010: 232.

[12] Loulakaki-Moore 2010: 237.

his project. He describes his affinity with Sappho in terms of kinship: she is a 'distant cousin', sharing the same island, the 'same sense of the natural world', and having the same notions and words to work with: 'the sky and the sea, the sun and the moon, the plants and the girls, love'.[13] But besides the material, what also connects the two is a common world view – 'faith in poetry' – and the idea that writing leads to immortality.

For Elytis, Sappho represents the passage from epic to lyric mode, to the personal and subjective, while her work reveals a poetic self-consciousness directed towards posterity: μνάcεcθαί τινά φαμι καὶ ὔcτερον ἀμμέων ('but I claim there will be some who remember us when we are gone', fr. 147) is for him Sappho's critical intervention.[14] The few surviving poems recreate a transcendent poetic persona and universe. In this sense, Elytis's project is a recreation,[15] and in the end his Sappho stands on equal terms next to the rest of his poetry: it is more Elytis than Sappho.

* * *

If we turn away from the broader domain of translation towards specific poems, the famous fr. 31 serves as a telling example of Sappho's complex transmission. Preserved in the treatise *On the Sublime* by Pseudo-Longinus, this poem has enjoyed a particular place in her long trajectory in European literature.[16]

For Modern Greek literature one of the earliest examples of this trajectory is a poem by Dimitrios Gouzelis (1774–1843), a writer and intellectual from Zante. Of noble descent, and educated in Greek, Latin, Italian, and French, Gouzelis blends Sappho's poem in his work *Η κρίσις του Πάριδος: ποίημα μυθολογικόν, ερωτικόν και ηθικόν* (*The Judgment of Paris. A Mythological, Love and Moral Poem*), published in 1817. Gouzelis lived a tumultuous life; having special bonds with France and French culture (he served in the French army and was a proponent of the French Enlightenment), his contribution to Greek intellectual life was significant. His work *The Judgment of Paris*, a long (at almost four hundred pages) narrative poem in fifteen-syllable, rhyming couplets across seven odes, takes as its background the moment where Paris is called to choose the most beautiful among Hera, Athena, and Aphrodite.

---

[13] Elytis 1984: 9–10.
[14] Elytis 1984: 18.
[15] Against Elytis's endeavour, see Ramfos 1999.
[16] GILLESPIE.

In the fourth ode, where Oenone, the wife of Paris, describes in a monologue the travails of love, at the same time expressing her passion for him and denouncing his infidelities, Gouzelis incorporates his translation of fr. 31, without mentioning its origin; he does not translate directly from Sappho, but from the 1674 French translation of Longinus by Nicolas Boileau (1636–1711), a major proponent of the Ancients in the famous 'Querelle des Anciens et des Modernes' ('Quarrel of the Ancients and the Moderns').[17] Gouzelis knew Boileau and his 1674 work, as he must have also known Jean Racine's *Phèdre,* published three years later, in which the French dramaturge (1639–99) creatively appropriated Boileau in the third scene of the first act of his play, as a comparison between the two texts can show.[18] Both French texts are composed in the twelve-syllable alexandrine, whose aesthetic and ideological functions are comparable to those of Greek fifteen-syllable verse.

Whether Gouzelis knew Pseudo-Longinus, and by extension Sappho's poem, before Boileau and Racine, we cannot tell. Yet his effortless appropriation of the French tradition and its creative incorporation into the architectonics of his poem mark an important moment in the reception of Sappho for the literature of Modern Greece within the wider stream of European culture.

Not all receptions were so admiring. For instance, Eugenios Voulgaris (1716–1806), a major figure of the Modern Greek Enlightenment and prolific writer and translator, dismissed Sappho because of her sexuality. A member of the Orthodox clergy, he grouped her among immoral ancient Greek writers and suggested that the curious reader should turn instead to the study of Scripture and the works of the Church Fathers.[19] Another significant personality of the Greek Enlightenment, the writer, translator, clergyman, and cartographer Anthimos Gazis (1758–1828), held a similarly negative view: for him, Sappho's bad reputation was due to her polyamorous, bisexual life, which contrasts sharply with her beautiful poetry; he noted that many educated people attempted to cleanse her work of her despicable character, but that it is difficult to dissociate the person from the work.[20]

For his portrait of Sappho, Gazis seems to have consulted the work of philosopher, writer, and lexicographer Pierre Bayle (1647–1706), who in

---

[17] Antonopoulos 2015: 13–21.
[18] Gillespie pp. 335–7.
[19] Voulgaris 1801: ii 21.
[20] Gazis 1807: i 135–6.

his *Dictionnaire historique et critique*, first published in 1697, had sketched an ambivalent image of Sappho based on meticulous study of sources as well as the available scholarly research.[21] This ambivalence rested on a foundational conviction of the discipline of classics, viz. the moral superiority of our classical ancestors. The unchaste Sappho (Martial 10.35.15–18) has thus always constituted a challenge for classical philology. Voulgaris and Gazis followed a European tradition against Sappho initiated by Domizio Calderini (1446–78) and Giglio Gregorio Giraldi (1479–1552), who were among the first early modern critics of her sexual preferences.[22] Lesbian or bisexual Sappho could not fit into the canonical, moralistic, and often patriarchal view of classical scholarship, yet she could not be ignored or bypassed. Consequently, the only path was to neutralise the moral hazard that she represented. Indeed, much Greek scholarship until the late twentieth century followed the rehabilitation project initiated by Welcker.[23] That project highlighted aspects of Sappho's life and poetry that would presumably support her moral 'innocence' while downplaying incompatible elements; Sappho had to be desexualised, sterilised, and idealised, and her poetry absolved of its corporeal dimension. As late as 1983, Ioannis Kakridis (1901–92), a major classicist and prominent progressive intellectual, constructs a Sappho motivated by the friendly or affectionate bond that unites a teacher with her students, one governed by motherly rather than sensual feelings: 'Her passion was pure, very pure, against what the dirty imagination of posterity has constructed, and this is why she is not afraid to express it in all sincerity.'[24]

Certainly, a Romantic, often bucolic Sappho fits better into the ideological project that highlights the continuum of Greek cultural history and identity, one for which national belonging combines the classical and Christian traditions. In this sense, translations of lines 18–20 of the famous 'Hymn to Aphrodite' (fr. 1) in the study manuals used in secondary education are telling. The textbook used in the late 1970s and 1980s employed Panayis Lekatsas's translation, without mentioning that the editors had changed the original translation of the (gender-ambiguous) ancient pronoun τίνα from Lekatsas's ποια ('whom' in the feminine) to ποιον and ποιος ('whom' and 'who' in the masculine).[25] The textbook

[21] Bayle 1697: II 1006–11; Antonopoulos 2016: 83, GILLESPIE p. 338.
[22] Antonopoulos 2016: 75.
[23] Welcker 1816; MUELLER pp. 42–3.
[24] Kakridis 1983: 44.
[25] Spyropoulos, Roussos, and Tsakatikas 1979: 44.

used from the 1990s on, providing two translations (both by renowned classicists), is in a similar vein: Daniel Jakob's reads ποιο αγαπημένο πρόσωπο ('what beloved person'), while Ioannis Kakridis's maintains the feminine pronoun, which nonetheless loses its gender specification given the language register and his overall translation strategy.[26] Not much has changed from when educator Sappho Leontias (1832–1900), often called 'the teacher of the nation' for her role in women's education in the nineteenth century, was interpreting fr. 31 to show that 'Sappho depicts her beloved man as equal to gods'.[27] To attune to normalised perceptions of gender and sexuality and avoid creating discomfort for educational institutions and conservative society in general, Sappho had to be repackaged.

* * *

Modern European literature renegotiated Sappho in many ways, especially through new perceptions of sexuality and sexual mores.[28] An important constituent of this norm was Pierre Louÿs's *Les Chansons de Bilitis* (*The Songs of Bilitis*, 1894), which invented an elaborate supporting apparatus that aimed to free Sappho from the prejudices of classical scholarship.[29] Louÿs's work and the universe that it depicted were influential for many traditions, including the Greek. Already from the beginning of the nineteenth century, Egyptian Alexandria was a major Greek cultural centre. Its diaspora belonged to the political, financial, and social elite; cosmopolitan and liberal, the city rivalled Athens in terms of cultural activity. For example, the creation of the Hedonistic School of Alexandria, a cultural club of the collaborators of the influential review *Grammata*, brought together prominent intellectual figures who delved into literary, artistic, and (allegedly) sexual explorations in line with *fin-de-siècle* Europe.[30]

Grammata was created in 1911 with the secession of some collaborators from the reviews *Nea Zoi* and *Serapion*. It published original literature, criticism, and cultural commentary, both original and in translation, and had a particular interest in ideas that transcended traditional norms,

---

[26] Kazazis and Karamitrou 2001: 72–3.
[27] Leontias 1899: 59.
[28] GILLESPIE, PIANTANIDA, JOHNSON ch. 26.
[29] For Louÿs, see JOHNSON ch. 26 pp. 369–70. Recall Wilamowitz's vehement review of Louÿs's work (1896 = 1913: 63–78), dedicated to Welcker's memory, and published twenty-four years after his violent review of Nietzsche's *The Birth of Tragedy*.
[30] Rota 1994: 80–4; Zachariadis 1912: 427–8, especially 428: 'the simultaneous and spontaneous appearance of hedonism in new poets we take to be a sign of literary renaissance'.

including sexual ones. The review closely followed cultural directions in Europe, something evident from the first issue, which, after the initial manifesto and a poem by C. P. Cavafy, contains a translation of an extract from Francis Vielé-Griffin's *Sapho* ('A Leucate'), published months before in Paris.

This sets the tone, and Sappho is present, directly or indirectly, in almost every issue during the review's first years. Translations of Louÿs's *Chansons* began to appear in the second issue of the review. The sixth issue published a poem by Kostas Varnalis (1884–1974, a major poet, critic, translator, and literature teacher),[31] 'How Sappho's girls lamented when she fell in love with Alcaeus' ("Πώς εθρήνησαν για τη Σαπφώ τα κορίτσια της όταν αγάπησε τον Αλκαίο"), and in the following issue we read a positive account of a lecture and subsequent publication about Sappho by M. G. Michailidis, Professor at Robert College in Istanbul, which attempts to rescue her from the moralistic inaccuracies of classical scholarship and translates her poems into demotic Greek. In the twelfth issue (1912), we find I. N. Gryparis's poem 'Sappho', and in issue 21–4 (1914) Myrtiotissa, an important woman poet, publishes 'Lust' and 'Into my tower', two sensual poems of which the second has clear lesbian undertones.

Let us focus on two of these. Varnalis's poem fictionalises a scene in which a chorus of 'Sappho's girls' sing, bemoaning her departure after falling in love with Alcaeus. Written in eleven stanzas of four verses which allude metrically to Sappho, the poem is written in the first person plural. The collective subject recollects images indicating lesbian love: arguably the first time this happens in Modern Greek literature.[32] Varnalis had experimented with sapphic metre before, as had influential European poets such as D'Annunzio.[33] Kangelaris considers the 'roses' in Varnalis's poem a creative reversal of the apple in fr. 105,[34] and Antonopoulos hears an echo of fr. 130 in the description of erotic spasms in the fifth stanza.[35] But the poetic link that the poem establishes with Sappho can be discerned in its general conception. It reverses fr. 94: if the girl there unwillingly abandons Sappho and is reminded of the sensual world she leaves behind, here Sappho willingly abandons the girls and

---

[31] For his essays on classical authors, see Varnalis 1958.

[32] Antonopoulos 2013.

[33] D'Annunzio's 'A Enotrio Romano', which refers to Sappho and Alcaeus, appears in *Grammata* 25–7 (1915).

[34] Kangelaris 2017: 43–6.

[35] Antonopoulos 2014: 666.

with them also 'a new kingdom of Love, richer and surprising, hostile to the hearth, where ember perpetuates nature' (lines 17–21).

Varnalis's poem can be seen both as 'an unconventional condemnation of heterosexuality and of nature's characteristic of perpetuation', with Varnalis a daring pioneer who does not hesitate 'to denounce the traditional institution of family',[36] and as a response to Louÿs's poems previously published in *Grammata*: roses, veils, purple dye, fire, hair, chicks, breasts, legs, and the motif of non-reproduction are repeatedly present in Louÿs, and are also motifs of modernism elsewhere too. In other words, Varnalis connects with Europe and links transgressive sexuality with Sappho, affirming her both as a classical author to be rescued from moralising philology and the female figure of modernism *par excellence*, epitomising the new woman who transcends patriarchy by dissociating sexuality from reproduction and associating it with pleasure.

For the second example we turn to Myrtiotissa (1885–1968), a poet and actress who published two poems in the twenty-first issue of *Grammata*. In the first, entitled "Πόθος" ('Lust'), a female voice addresses a person (whether male or female), describing her own transformation from a shy woman who 'speaks love words with her sweet trembling voice' (lines 1–4) when one night Lust visits her and tells her of 'some secrets that make [her] tremble even now as [she] remembers them' (lines 7–8). That moment marks the woman's sexual awakening, after which she becomes self-conscious of her beauty, her body, and the passion she can arouse; she longs for pleasure, a pleasure so intense that it reaches death.

The second poem is titled "Στον πύργο μου" ('Into my tower'), 'the first lesbian poem of Modern Greek literature written by a woman'.[37] The female voice invites her 'sisters' to her tower so that they can all live together without pain. Though it is unclear what this pain is, it will be eased both psychologically and sensually: the women will be received with a kiss, and 'fresh, perfumed beds' (lines 15–16) will ensure them 'sweet sleep' (lines 19–20). The craftiest allusion to sexuality occurs in lines 10–13, where the girls, 'crowned with amaranth and ivy', will enter lovingly into the poetic voice's 'mute attic' (βουβό δώμα). This peculiar image and its unusual vocabulary are explained by the indirect link of a mental rhyme formed both acoustically and visually between the expressed 'attic' (δώμα) and the implied 'body' (σώμα): the girls are invited to enter the 'mute body' and fulfil sexual desire.

---

[36] Antonopoulos 2014: 661.
[37] Antonopoulos 2013: 33.

'Amaranth and ivy', the 'fresh beds', and the 'sweet sleep' allude to fr. 94, published a few years earlier, which mentions garlands and soft beds.[38] Its first Modern Greek translation appeared shortly thereafter, in 1909, by the writer and philosopher Nikos Kazantzakis (1883–1957). Under the pseudonym Petros Pseloreitis, Kazantzakis published his second novel, Σπασμένες ψυχές (*Broken Souls*) in the Athenian review *Noumas*.[39] One of the novel's main protagonists is an elderly classicist in love with antiquity, named Gorgias (having changed his name from George). In an episode where Chrysoula learns that Orestes has abandoned her and is devastated, Gorgias consoles her by reading to her a prose translation of fr. 94 in the demotic register of the novel.[40]

Myrtiotissa includes her two poems in her 1925 poetry book Κίτρινες φλόγες (*Yellow Flames*),[41] which has a preface by Kostis Palamas (1859–1943), an authoritative literary personality. Refuting two possible objections to Myrtiotissa's work, inadequately elaborated versification and a general pessimistic atmosphere, Palamas emphasises its hedonistic dimension; though it may appear strange, these 'daring songs, somehow unusual for us' constitute an enriching 'dowry' for Modern Greek poetry.[42] He interprets Myrtiotissa's perceived drawbacks as indications of a new poetics, seeing affinities with contemporary Spanish and French traditions. Yet he neutralises the female and often lesbian imprint of her writing by expressing an aesthetic ideology according to which 'the poet has neither gender, nor age'; 'just as love ennobles everything, and first and foremost carnal desire, so the verse disembodies everything, since it has a divine origin'.[43] Thus Myrtiotissa's world is de-gendered, disincarnated, and spiritualised. Indeed, Palamas calls her a 'Muse' and relates her to Marceline Desbordes-Valmore (1786–1859), 'a French Sappho'.[44] This tumultuous poet and actress was respected by major writers in nineteenth-century France, including Barbey d'Aurevilly, Baudelaire, Hugo, Sainte-Beuve, and Verlaine, who dedicates a chapter to her in his *Poètes maudits* (*Accursed Poets*); for Verlaine, she is 'the only woman of genius

---

[38] Antonopoulos 2013: 33.
[39] Beginning in issue 355, 30 August 1909, p. 2.
[40] *Noumas* 371, 20 December 1909, p. 2.
[41] Myrtiotissa 1925.
[42] Myrtiotissa 1925: 10.
[43] Myrtiotissa 1925: 9–10.
[44] Myrtiotissa 1925: 10, 11. He had done so previously in 1913, in a poem "Τρίπτυχο" dedicated to her (1965: 153).

and talent of this century and of all centuries, in the company of Sappho, perhaps, and of St Teresa'.[45]

This French link between Desbordes-Valmore and Sappho is transferred by Palamas into the Greek context, connecting Myrtiotissa with ancient Greek as well as European tradition. These three are women *poets*, a title which (in his view) eradicates their womanly essence. When Palamas claims that true poetry has no gender, he means that it is an affair of men. Indeed, both his poetry and his critical writings reproduce traditional, patriarchal views of the female as pronounced by Emmanuel Roidis, the authoritative critic of the end of the nineteenth century,[46] in which women can enjoy equal status to men only if they belong to the transcendental domain. Ignoring or perhaps hostile to the tradition of European feminism, Palamas instead subscribes to a Romantic imaginary of the Woman-Muse, of which he makes Myrtiotissa a part.

Palamas adheres to a pattern that idealises Sappho. He calls ninth-century Eastern Roman hymnographer Kassia the 'Sappho of Christianity',[47] and composes a liberal translation of her famous *Hymn* (Τροπάριον) into sapphic verse.[48] Sappho is often mentioned or alluded to in her quality as a 'Muse', usually with no corporeal substance, while sometimes her depiction oscillates between her earthly and transcendental nature. For instance, in the eightieth poem of Palamas's landmark work *Η ασάλευτη ζωή* (*The Inert Life*, 1904), the poetic voice exclaims 'I am the fiery invocation of the singer from Lesbos' (line 1).[49] This short poem describes a clash between an ascetic poetic ideal, represented in the figure of a monk and the 'ascetic hymn', and the voice of poetry, still burning slowly in the ashes and about to ignite again. Again, in the poem "Η γυναίκα μούσα" ('The woman muse') from *Περάσματα και χαιρετισμοί* (*Passages and Salutations*, 1931), Palamas sketches a dichotomy between the past and the contemporary Muse: if 'then' the woman was a submissive, soft, and quiet being, 'now' she has revolted and vindicates her share in the expression of desire. Yet she has not stopped being a Muse, as the examples of Ackermann, Desbordes-Valmore, De Noailles, and Browning show, none of whom can equal Sappho, the last stanza says.

---

[45] Verlaine 1888: 76.
[46] E. Roidis, "Αι γράφουσαι Ελληνίδες", *Akropolis*, 28 April 1896 = Angelou 1978: v 121–31.
[47] K. Palamas, "Συγγραφείς και Βιβλία: Βιργινίας Π. Ευαγγελίδου *Έπεα πτερόεντα*", *Hestia*, 1 April 1890.
[48] Palamas 1915.
[49] Palamas 1904; cf. the seventy-seventh poem as well.

The poem where Sappho more explicitly appears is "Νέα ωδή του παλιού Αλκαίου" ('New ode by the old Alcaeus'), included in *The Inert Life*. This long narrative poem (eighty-two lines, with epic and lyric overtones) rewrites Alcaeus' abandonment of his sword and shield during his flight from battle in the famous war between the Athenians and the Lesbians over Sigeum, a disputed town on the Hellespont.[50] Palamas's Alcaeus mentions Lesbos' associations with poetry through the myth of Orpheus' lyre. While the 'Thracian lyre' has 'echoed ardently the heartbeats of Sappho and Erinna' (lines 9–11), Alcaeus' own poetry differs in that he uses 'the same lyre with a heroic breath' (17–18). The contrast between love poetry (exemplified in Sappho) and war poetry (as exercised by Alcaeus) is described in the first part. The poet is a warrior and prefers to sing of war, despite love's temptations. These temptations are depicted in homosexual terms, in the figures of Lycus, a rose-crowned boy with black hair and eyes, and the gentle-smiling Muse Sappho, 'pure mother of queer shame' (24–8). The middle of the poem marks the beginning of a transformation. The poet's lust for life overcomes his combative nature; seeing the beauty of Lesbos, as well as admiring the beauty of Lycus and Sappho, the poet has an epiphany, abandons the battle, and leaves 'losing heart and like a traitor' (82).

Palamas uses the famous episode of Alcaeus' desertion in his poetic treatment of beauty and love as the two major causes for Alcaeus' behaviour. Lycus' double mention as a beautiful boy having black hair and eyes (26, 60) echoes Horace, *Odes* 1.32, a sapphic ode addressed to the lyre and making extensive reference to Alcaeus, and in which Lycus is mentioned next to Cupid in a similar way (*Lycum nigris oculis nigroque | crine decorum*, 11–12). Sappho is mentioned three times, at the beginning in connection with the lyre, and twice in tandem with Lycus. Lines 27–8 ('gentle-smiling Muse Sappho, pure mother of queer shame') as well as lines 65–8 ('I was staring at the Muse Sappho next to me, | violet-tressed, pure, gentle-smiling, | and my tongue . . . never hesitated | because of queer shame, like then') echo both lyric poets: they translate Alcaeus fr. 384 (ἰόπλοκ' ἄγνα μελλιχόμειδε Σάπφοι) and also make direct reference to Sappho fr. 137.1–2 (θέλω τί τ' εἴπην, ἀλλά με κωλύει | αἴδως) as well as fr. 137.3–6 (αἰ δ' ἦχες ἔσλων ἴμερον ἢ κάλων | καὶ μή τί τ' εἴπην γλῶσσ' ἐκύκα κάκον, | αἴδως †κέν σε† οὐκ ἦχεν ὄππατ', | ἀλλ' ἔλεγες περὶ τὦδικαίως).

50 THOMAS pp. 27–9.

In short, the Palamas epitomises the multiple, productive directions that 'Sappho' has signified over her long history: her verses provide an occasion for exploration of the limits of linguistic translation and of broader cultural transfer, as well as fruitful poetic material to be elaborated by artistic craft. Sappho is mythologised and fictionalised as an historical figure, linked to sensuality, sexuality, and transgression while retaining her centuries-old, idealised dimension of the Woman-Muse; and at the same time she carries the weight, significance and history of the discipline of Classics.

* * *

I have focused on specific examples that constitute noteworthy moments in Sappho's itinerary, but her presence is not limited to them. Extensive research could endeavour to trace both the extent and the depth of that reception, though such is probably an overambitious task, unrealisable in its complexity. 'Sappho' is a problem in itself and as such it is a good example of the dynamics of literary and cultural formation, evolution and change.

Further Reading

For the relationship of Elytis, Varnalis, and Dionysios Solomos with antiquity, see Jakob 2000, Zarogiannis 1988, Veloudis 1989, Tomadakis 1943. The fundamental study on Palamas is Dimaras 1947. For the role of biblical and liturgical language in Palamas, Sikelianos, and Elytis, see Hirst 2004. For the role of ancient myth in Modern Greek poetry, see Mackridge 1996. Women's literacy and role in nineteenth-century Greek culture is discussed by Rizaki 2007, the origins and development of the Greek feminist movement by Varika 2011; Avdela and Psarra 1985 provides an anthology of feminist writings from the first decades of the twentieth century. Yatromanolakis 2003 discusses Sappho in Solomos and Stratis Myrivilis, as well as Dimitrios Paparrigopoulos, Aristotelis Valaoritis, Dimitrios Vernardakis, Alexandros Rizos Rangavis, Angelos Sikelianos, and Zoi Karelli – all major literary figures of Modern Greece.

CHAPTER 28

Sappho in the Twentieth Century and Beyond
Anglophone Receptions

*Barbara Goff and Katherine Harloe**

In her study of Sappho in early modern England, Harriette Andreadis suggests that its literary, artistic, and scholarly traditions bequeathed to later periods three chief modes of representation. The ancient poet

> was portrayed as a mythologized figure who acts as the suicidal abandoned woman in the Ovidian tale of Sappho and Phaon; she was used as the first example of female poetic excellence, most often with a disclaimer of any sexuality (or what Abraham Cowley called 'ill manners'); and she was presented as an early exemplar of 'unnatural' or monstrous sexuality.[1]

As JOHNSON argues (ch. 26), it was during the nineteenth century that a specifically lesbian Sappho re-emerged with greater prominence. A further important shift occurred at the turn of the twentieth, as lesbian and feminist literary voices claimed Sappho with increasing confidence as one of their own, and scholarly knowledge of her poetry was increased by new papyrus finds, in turn stimulating new editions and translations that displaced Wharton's influential 1885 edition.[2] While certain trends continued into the twentieth, most notably the interest in a biographical or mythologising approach to Sappho's life, changing modes of poetic creation and criticism stimulated a new appreciation of the aesthetic qualities of Sappho's fragments and a joy in the challenges of translating them.

---

* We gratefully acknowledge access to a research bibliography on this topic compiled by Allie Pohler, a graduate of Classics from Grand Valley State University, Allendale, MI.
[1] Andreadis 1996: 106, citing Abraham Cowley's 'Upon Mrs. K. Philips her poems' from Philips 1667: sig. C1 stanza 4 ('They talk of Sappho, but, alas! the shame I Ill manners soil the lustre of her fame'); for further on Philips/Orinda, see Andreadis 2001: 55–83.
[2] See for example Cox 1924 and Haines 1926, both translations that include the Greek text and take into account newly published fragments. For Wharton's edition, see JOHNSON ch. 26 pp. 370–1.

Life and Legend

The Sappho that readers confront at the start of the twenty-first century, celebrated for her distinctively female voice, lesbian sexuality, and poetic excellence, owes a great deal to the women's movement of the 1960s and 70s and its impact both on classical scholarship (evident largely from the 1980s onwards) and broader literary and cultural receptions. Much of this chapter is accordingly devoted to exploration of this pivot. Yet even before this stage of the women's movement we can note salient differences from nineteenth-century preoccupations. Even the time-honoured genre of biographical reconstruction, which had sometimes yielded to the temptation to titillate, can offer a strong and serious Sappho who is not defined solely by desire, and certainly not by the hopeless desire for Phaon that had been a feature of much of the 'life and legend' tradition.[3] In *Sappho of Lesbos. A Psychological Reconstruction of Her Life* (1938), Margaret Goldsmith explicitly rejects the Phaon story, pointing out that it contradicts Sappho's other predilections and suggesting that it arose in connection with a different Sappho – the name being common on Lesbos, and the historians all being men. Goldsmith is candid about her invention of Sappho's life – 'as I myself am convinced that she must have lived it' (p. v) – and frequently terms the poems 'letters' in order to use them as sources for the 'facts' of Sappho's existence. She is clear that Sappho's society had no prejudice against erotic encounters among women (called here 'charming experiences', p. 121) and presents them without judgement; the greater freedom of Lesbos spared her Sappho the need to rebel against women's restricted lives, and positioned her instead to foster the talents of other young women poets.

Goldsmith was not a classicist, but a writer who developed other biographies of historically important women, like Christina of Sweden.[4] Two male philhellenes also offered versions of Sappho in what now appears as the run-up to second-wave feminism. In Lawrence Durrell's *Sappho. A Play in Verse* (1950), Sappho is a twentieth-century woman and politician more than a poet/singer or even a lover. No love for women appears in this play, and she is safely married, but in other ways Sappho is an unsettling figure. She has been helping to undermine the career of Pittacus, partly by impersonating an oracle; when she is exiled to Corinth her children remain behind as hostages, but this does not deter her from

---

[3] For the Phaon story, see FINGLASS AND KELLY pp. 1–3.
[4] Goldsmith 1933.

organising the Corinthians against Pittacus. She briefly takes Phaon as a lover, but he differs from the tradition, being a hermit and a philosopher. This play seems surprisingly feminist in its orientation, not in terms of women's desire, or even of women's voices, but because of Sappho's power and authority.[5]

Peter Green's *The Laughter of Aphrodite* (1965) offers a very different figure, who loves both women and men. Her midlife-crisis infatuation with Phaon is caused by a vengeful Aphrodite, but before this she has numerous erotic entanglements with women. As in Durrell's play, this Sappho is often called, by herself or others, hard and self-centred, without 'feminine' sensibility; she prizes her fame and values the work that achieved it. As with Durrell, Sappho is a political operator, caught up in the tensions of the social shifts from aristocracy to tyranny and from land to trade. Told in the first person, this Sappho narrative flaunts the narrator's unreliability and the vagaries of her self-construction. The novel is arguably proto-feminist in its focus on woman's agency, authorship, and prominence, even if Sappho remains a bit of an operator.

The medicalisation of the 'life and legend' touched on in JOHNSON ch. 26 was occasionally pursued in scholarly literature. It reached its apogee in Devereux's now notorious article (1970) on fr. 31 as an anxiety attack provoked by consciousness of 'inversion'. Yet one of Devereux's aims was to provide 'proof positive of her lesbianism', i.e. of Sappho's erotic attraction to women.[6] This has now become a standard reading rather than a source of anxiety. Denys Page had made a similar acknowledgement in his influential *Sappho and Alcaeus. An Introduction to the Study of Ancient Lesbian Poetry* (1955). In a chapter entitled 'The contents and character of Sappho's poetry', he noted 'The Hellenistic biographies recorded, and the scandal-mongers broadcast, the accusation that Sappho was γυναικεραστρία, that she was addicted to the perversion which the modern world names after her native island.' Though professing himself – sensibly – sceptical of the 'gossip' of ancient legend, Page conceded that 'If we read Sappho without prejudice, we observe that she is deeply moved by the physical graces of young women.' His conclusion is highly awkward: although he states that 'such was the nature of Sappho, not to be altered', he also declares vehemently that 'in all that remains of Sappho's poetry there is not a word which connects her or her companions'

[5] Durrell's play was adapted by Peggy Glanville-Hicks to form the libretto for her opera *Sappho*: JOHNSON ch. 29 p. 411.
[6] Devereux 1970: 17.

with those 'perverse practices' for which 'it is at least probable that Lesbos in her lifetime was notorious'.[7] If Page's discomfort with Sappho's homo-eroticism shows him a mind of his age, his recognition of the reality of female same-sex desire is noteworthy in a decade when lesbianism remained for the most part unacknowledged.

In recent years the 'life and legend' tradition has received an unexpected boost from *Sappho's Leap*, a novel by Erica Jong (2004). This version of Sappho has learned not only from the feminist debates of the later twentieth century, and from earlier 'biographies', but also from scholarly discussions, although its parentage also includes Hollywood and soap operas. Written by an iconic figure of the women's movement, this up-to-date Sappho has an energetic sexual career that includes several male and female partners. Her main motivations are passion for Alcaeus and love for her daughter, Cleis, and she travels through the known and unknown world in quest of them. The novel is picaresque, modelling itself on the *Odyssey*, and the gods have a starring role in that much of Sappho's activity results from a bet between Zeus and Aphrodite. Sappho journeys to the Amazons, the philosophers, the Centaurs, and Hades, as well as to Sicily and Egypt. She is an accomplished singer who revels in her public profile. She becomes a political leader who helps build a utopian society of equality between the sexes, and frequently meditates on the roles of the sexes, on power and freedom, and on the social role of poetry and storytelling. All the characters from Sappho's legends, and others from antiquity, are gathered within the novel's wide-angle lens, and it will come as no surprise that Sappho dismisses Phaon and leaps from the Leucadian rock into a friendly waiting boat. She is living with her lovers and family still, on an unnamed island, alongside descendants of Centaurs and Amazons. While this book had a mixed reception,[8] we might conclude that it assumes feminism to the extent of not needing it, and it acknowledges the complexity of Sappho's poetic legacy by celebrating self-invention.

Sappho, Modernism, and the Fragment

JOHNSON (ch. 26) has already discussed the intense interest in Sappho manifest in avant-garde circles around 1900, in particular in the output of 'Michael Field' (Katharine Bradley and Edith Cooper) and the Decadent 'Sapho 1900' circle around Natalie Barney and Renée Vivien. The latter

---

[7] Page 1955: 142–3, 143, 144.
[8] Reynolds 2004, Beard 2004.

couple's attempt to recreate an erotically intimate, exclusively female and woman-centred community in homage to the Lesbian poet testifies to the power of imaginative reconstructions of Sappho's cultural and social context, the indeterminacy of which presents a rich field for speculation and identification. An equally important, contemporaneous set of engagements is evident in the coterie of transatlantic poets that gave birth to the Imagism movement before World War I and included Amy Lowell, Hilda Doolittle, William Carlos Williams, Richard Aldington, and Ezra Pound. Sappho was an early shared enthusiasm of Pound and H.D. (the pen name of Hilda Doolittle), who were briefly engaged before Pound left the United States in 1908; once both settled in London and had met Aldington, Sapphic material appears in the work of all three.

Aldington, who could read Greek and would go on to translate poems in the *Greek Anthology* by Anyte of Tegea,[9] facilitated the engagement by Pound and H.D. with newly published papyrus fragments. One example is their rewritings of frr. 95–6, contained in a single papyrus (P.Berol. inv. 9722) first published in 1902. Aldington's 'To Atthis (after the manuscript of Sappho now in Berlin)', which Pound included in the scene-setting *Des Imagistes. An Anthology* (1914), is perhaps the least radical, consisting indeed of a free rendering, but one which completes damaged sections to produce a considerably less challenging version than the original. Aldington restores the poem's beginning and makes the Atthis addressed(?) in line 16 into the figure who 'far from me and dear Mnasidika, | Dwells in Sardis'.[10] This contrasts with Pound's Ἱμέρρω' ('I desire'), first published as 'O Atthis' in *Poetry* (1916a) and then the following year in the second edition of Pound's solo collection, *Lustra*:

> Thy soul
> Grown delicate with satieties,
> Atthis.
>   O Atthis,
> I long for thy lips.
>
> I long for thy narrow breasts,
> Thou restless, ungathered.

Yet more stripped down, and published alongside Ἱμέρρω', is Pound's 'Papyrus', which is a translation of a perfectly plausible interpretation of fr. 95.2–4 V.:

[9] Aldington 1915, Aldington and Storer 1919.
[10] R. Aldington *ap.* <Pound> 1914: 19.

> Spring ...
> Too long ...
> Gongula ...[11]

Both the title and the ellipses call attention to the fragile materiality of Sappho's texts, while the evocative power of a few taut phrases exemplifies the Imagist principles of 'saying what you mean in the fewest and clearest words' and 'presenting an image, or enough images of concrete things arranged to stir the reader'.[12]

Among this triad it is, however, H.D. who displays the most sustained fascination with Sappho's fragments.[13] As Gubar observes, 'Sappho's imagery – the storm-tossed rose, lily, and poppy; the wind-swept sea garden; the golden Aphrodite – dominates H.D.'s early poetry.'[14] It is apparent in the horticultural and littoral settings of 'Orchard' and 'Hermes of the Ways', the poems that launched Imagism, which are rich with Sapphic imagery of fruit ripening on the bough or vine and honeybees. These recur in H.D.'s collections of the 1920s, penned after she had visited Lesbos with her daughter by Aldington and her eventual companion and lover, the English writer Bryher (Annie Winifred Ellerman). The 1921 collection, *Hymen*, which in name as well as themes alludes to Sapphic *epithalamia* (wedding songs), includes an expansive reworking of fr. 146 ('Fragment 113'[15]). *Heliodora* (1924) adds free versions of four more ('Fragment Thirty-six', 'Fragment Forty', 'Fragment Forty-one', 'Fragment Sixty-eight')[16] and also engages with a range of other Greek poetry: the *Greek Anthology*, Euripides, and especially Homer. Although *Heliodora*'s 'Helen' is arguably Homeric in outlook, adopting a third-personal perspective akin to that of the Trojan elders at *Iliad* 3.153–60, it marks the beginnings of a fascination with Helen which was to persist in H.D.'s later output, such as *Helen in Egypt* (1961). The poem 'Telesila', named after another, substantially lost Greek female poet, begins with a contrast of 'war' and 'love' that recalls Sappho's famous fr. 16. This contrast is also implicit in 'The Islands', included in *Hymen*, which alongside those in *Heliodora* hints at H.D.'s use of Sappho to provide a woman-centred, lyric, and specifically archipelagic Greek voice to counterpose to the warlike masculinity of mainland literary traditions:

---

[11] Pound 1916b: 49. In Pound 1917: 55 the two poems are presented on the same page.
[12] Letter to Iris Barry, 27 July 1916 = Paige 1971: 90.
[13] Collecott 1999.
[14] Gubar 1984: 54 = Greene 1996b: 209.
[15] Titled '"Not Honey"' (*sic*) when published in *Hymen* (H.D. 1921: 33–4).
[16] H.D. follows the numbering in Wharton 1885, who in turn followed Bergk. For H.D.'s reworkings of Sapphic fragments, see Gregory 1997: 148–61.

What can love of land give to me
that you have not,
what can love of strife break in me
that you have not?

Though Sparta enter Athens,
Thebes wrack Sparta,
each changes as water,
salt, rising to wreak terror
and fall back.[17]

The Modernist engagement with Sappho would, belatedly, give rise to one of the most celebrated anglophone translations of the twentieth century. Mary Barnard (1909–2001) studied Greek alongside contemporary creative writing at Reed College, Oregon in the late 1920s and gained her entrée into the literary world through Pound; she would also maintain decades-long correspondences with William Carlos Williams, Marianne Moore, and other luminaries of American Modernism.[18] Her *Sappho. A New Translation* (1958) returns to Imagist principles of clarity and concision; Dudley Fitts, the scholar and translator who introduced the work, hailed it as

> Antipoetry . . . but it may be that antipoetry is what one needs, if it implies the discarding of gauds and ornamental tropes, the throwing overboard of the whole apparatus of factitious 'beauty' that has for so long attached itself to the name of Sappho of Lesbos.[19]

Barnard's free-verse renderings are indeed spare and condensed. In place of the four-line sapphic stanza she favours the tercet, and although her decisions to expand (or alternatively, cut) and combine fragments, and to supplement poems with titles, sometimes amount to domestications of ambiguous or otherwise difficult material, she revels in the suggestiveness of the fragment. Barnard was led back to Sappho by encountering her in Salvatore Quasimodo's 1940 Italian translation. Her reflections on this discovery point to identification with a literary foremother and a desire to liberate Sappho from the condescension of male critics, a desire also evident in H.D.'s posthumously published notes on Sappho:

> I found the Italian translations very beautiful and wanted to match them, if I could, in my own language. Most important of all, however, I found here in Sappho's Greek, as revealed to me now through the medium of the

---

[17] H.D. 1921: 28.
[18] Barnsley 2013, JOHNSON CH. 29 pp. 412–13.
[19] Fitts *ap*. M. Barnard 1958: x.

Italian, the style I had been groping toward, or perhaps merely hungering for, when I ceased to write poetry a number of years before. It was spare but musical, and had, besides, the sound of the speaking voice making a simple but emotionally loaded statement. It is never 'tinkling' as Bill Williams's friend A. P. characterized it. Neither is it 'strident' as Rexroth described it. It is resonant although unmistakably in the female register.[20]

Sappho in the Second Wave

An understanding of Sappho as a crucial literary foremother and an example of a mature and woman-centred poetic sensibility is thus implicit in the works of earlier twentieth-century figures such as H.D., Vivien, and Barney, and explicit in that of contemporaries such as Amy Lowell and Virginia Woolf.[21] The second half of the century witnessed still clearer attempts to harness the political potential of what Sappho might represent, enlisting her in the cause as a feminist foremother. *Sappho was a Right-On Woman* states the case:

> Sappho was an educated woman at a time when most women could not read or write, a political exile, a mother, and one of the finest poets who ever lived. When virtually all women apparently lived to serve the male hierarchy and died anonymously without leaving a trace of their uniqueness, she said her name would live through history, and it has. Today she would be called a Feminist.[22]

Sappho is claimed as a forebear of 'second-wave' feminism, the women's movement of the 1970s. It is no coincidence that she appears thus in a book subtitled *A Liberated View of Lesbianism*, because Sappho's associations with desire among women were as important for the movement as her associations with women's writing and independent voice. To some extent the connections between lesbianism and feminism were problematic for 1970s feminists, some seeing the struggle for lesbian rights as a distraction and others claiming lesbianism as the logical corollary of women's liberation. When it comes to Sappho's later twentieth-century reception, however, the line between 'lesbian' and 'feminist' is usefully blurred, and rarely a site of contest. Consequently, we shall not distinguish too strictly here between 'feminism' and 'lesbian feminism'.

---

[20] M. Barnard 1984: 281–2, H.D. 1982: 55–69. For Quasimodo's translation, see Piantanida p. 358.
[21] For Lowell, Woolf, and others, see Reynolds 2000.
[22] Abbott and Love 1972: 158.

Believing that 'the personal is the political' and 'sisterhood is power-ful', second-wave feminism moved beyond earlier insistence on educa-tion and the vote to value women's claims on culture at large. The movement fought for women's rights to control their own bodies, focus-ing on access to contraception and abortion, but also on women's sexual-ity, and alongside this went greater openness about lesbianism. Another strand of the women's movement was the rediscovery of women writers and artists of the past, a work of recovery which took off especially in the 1980s, as women moved into academia in larger numbers. Ideas about Sappho played various roles in the feminist movement, and femi-nist classical scholarship delved into the poetry with new questions. Because of the increasing presence of women both in creative and in aca-demic sectors, and collaborations across fields, the three activities of cre-ative writing, scholarship, and translation were increasingly intertwined.[23]

Some fleeting, evocative versions of Sappho may be found in writing usually acknowledged as feminist. Carolyn Kizer's 'Pro Femina' (1965) begins 'From Sappho to myself, consider the fate of women'; aspects of Sappho can be read within the various unsatisfactory models of the 'Independent Woman' that it canvasses.[24] Sylvia Plath's 'Lesbos' (1962) is 'Sapphic' chiefly in the difficulty of construing it.[25] It might be thought of as 'feminist' in its apparent rejection of domesticity, or 'anti-feminist' in its apparent anger at a female figure. Although there are at least two women and one man in the poem, it is rarely easy to see who speaks to whom, or to describe the relationships. The baby daughter is possibly 'schizophrenic' and 'mad', and the object of terrible threats; meanwhile 'the moon', which might have alluded to Sappho,

> Dragged its blood bag, sick
> Animal
> Up over the harbor lights.
> And then grew normal,
> Hard and apart and white.

As with much of Plath's work, feminist interpretation is only partly licensed by statements within the poems.

---

[23] See Carol Ann Duffy collaborating with Aaron Poochigian on his translation (2009), or the col-laboration of Diane Rayor and André Lardinois (2014).
[24] Kizer 2001: 113, 114.
[25] T. Hughes 1981: 227–30.

Lesbian feminists who draw on Sappho in this period emphasise her identity as a poet as well as her sexuality. 'Sappho's Reply' by Rita Mae Brown (1944–) insists on Sappho's poetic legacy:[26]

> My voice rings down through thousands of years
> To coil around your body and give you strength,
> You who have wept in direct sunlight,
> Who have hungered in invisible chains,
> Tremble to the cadence of my legacy:
> An army of lovers shall not fail.

This last line makes it probable, but not necessary, that the poem addresses lesbians. The poem does not distinguish strictly between women who identify as lesbian lovers and women who identify as excluded and disempowered.

Jeannette Winterson's use of Sappho also exemplifies this kind of cross-over. In the novel *Art and Lies. A Piece for Three Voices and a Bawd* (1994), Sappho's is one of three narrative voices, along with Handel and Picasso. Unlike the latter two, she is the 'real' Sappho, a poet of love between women. Her narrative voice is often sexualised and bawdy, but also angry, insistent both on her poetic prowess and on the efforts of men across the centuries to diminish or silence her. Her question 'WHAT HAVE YOU DONE WITH MY POEMS?' continues: 'It isn't surprising that so many of you have chosen to read between the lines when the lines themselves have become more mutilated than a Saturday night whore.'[27] Sappho's words become a talisman and weapon against the death and destruction that she sees all around her. Yet the narrative recognises the impulse to belittle her and her work:

> . . . were every line of hers still extant, biographers would not be con-
> cerned with her metre or her rhyme. There would be one burning ques-
> tion from out the burning book . . . What do Lesbians do in bed?[28]

Winterson dedicates *Art and Lies* to the scholar Margaret Reynolds, who in turn dedicates her *Sappho Companion* (2000) to Winterson; later, Winterson was the editor at Brilliance Books who first published Josephine Balmer's Sappho translation in 1984 (below, pp. 402–4). This is just one example of the interplay among feminists approaching Sappho from different directions.

---

[26] R. Brown 1971: 63.
[27] Winterson 1994: 51.
[28] Winterson 1994: 141. (The Greek of Sappho's poems does not rhyme, but translations often do.)

Feminist scholarship on Sappho, produced by both men and women, takes several forms. The work of Judy Grahn is perhaps representative of early feminist criticism, presenting Sappho's poetry as woman-centred, as lesbian, and as inaugurating a tradition of women's writing. Grahn's Sappho is the product of 'millenia, during which people were tribal and spiritual and their culture was based primarily in womanly powers'; Grahn regards her 'not as the "first woman poet" but as the last of that great era'. The world she inhabits, and sings, considers love among women 'of obvious social value and esteem', generating a female tradition that was not suppressed or hidden underground.[29] While the myth of matriarchy Grahn invokes has fallen out of scholarly favour, her point in positing this woman-centred and lesbian tradition is to place other poets in it, such as Emily Dickinson, Amy Lowell, H.D., Adrienne Rich, Audre Lorde, Olga Broumas, and Paula Gunn Allen. To state in a scholarly context that there could be, and had been, a tradition of women speaking and writing about women's emotions, including those directed towards other women, was at the time remarkably empowering.[30]

Sappho scholarship has since pursued a feminist direction in that it has largely rejected the 'priestess' or 'schoolmistress' of earlier years whose emotions for her 'charges' were chaste if passionate.[31] Sappho is now considered a woman poet whose themes included erotic desire for women, possibly younger women, most likely within an aristocratic circle whose bonds included those of love as well as friendship, song, and joint worship of Aphrodite. Male figures are noticeably absent, whereas the 'chorus' of women and/or girls is quite prominent. Sappho is thus read as a woman-centred poet, whose work highlights symbols of a specifically female eroticism such as flowers and fruits.[32] According to other commentators, the eroticism of her writing may have operated as a form of 'sensual consciousness-raising', which could strengthen the younger women against the demands of the patriarchy.[33] Whether or not the patriarchy operated on archaic Lesbos as we recognise it from later

---

[29] Grahn 1985: 3–11 (quotations from pp. 3, 5, 6).

[30] Another contemporary woman poet who has used Sappho in her work is Harryette Mullen (1953–). Her 1995 collection *Muse & Drudge* embeds parts of eleven Sappho fragments with blues songs and other modern works, drawing on translations from Rayor 1991. We thank Cambridge University Press's anonymous reader for drawing our attention to Mullen's work.

[31] Parker 1993 ≈ Greene 1996b: 146–83.

[32] Winkler 1981 = H. Foley 1981: 63–89 ≈ Winkler 1990: 162–87 ≈ Greene 1996a: 89–109.

[33] Hallett 1979 ≈ Greene 1996a: 125–42.

sources, and what in either case we can understand the social role of Sappho and her poetry to have been, remain difficult questions.[34]

The current scholarly landscape includes other relevant versions of Sappho. In some scholarship her poetry challenges Homer's, in that it suggests different ways of understanding the world; it may speak to a 'double consciousness' of women who operate within a female subculture as well as the dominant, male-centred culture.[35] It has also been suggested that her work challenges predominantly masculine traditions of erotic lyric, as represented by Alcaeus and Anacreon, and proposed further that the relations represented among women are not hierarchical but prize a mutuality and reciprocity allied to female biology.[36] In that the audience and collective summoned by the poetry seems to be largely female, questions arise as to whether it counts as 'public' or as 'private', or whether it confounds those terms altogether.[37] In numerous ways, then, Sappho's songs can be read as speaking to a 'women's tradition', and as valuing the 'difference' of the female. Yet Sappho has been cited as a sign of the absence or loss of women's tradition as much as of its enduring power.[38] One of the most frequently cited versions of Sappho from the second wave is the blank page in Monique Wittig and Sande Zieg's *Brouillon pour un dictionnaire des amantes* (translated as *Lesbian Peoples. Material for a Dictionary*), indicating how great is our loss of Sappho and the alternative tradition that she might have represented.[39] Yet, in Wittig's *Le Corps lesbien* (1973), translated as *The Lesbian Body* (1975), Sappho is an animating presence and a presiding spirit, ripe for invocation by women-identified women who wish to recover such a tradition.[40]

Recent creative writers offer a Sappho who combines feminist tenets with postmodern explorations. The version of fr. 31 by the Canadian poet and scholar Anne Carson (1950–) has a Sappho who herself inaugurates a tradition of loss, appearing before the TV cameras to intone not the much-loved lines on passion, but only the frustrating last moment of the fragment, which she renders (not a literal translation) 'Since I am a poor

---

[34] Skinner 1996, MUELLER, LARDINOIS.
[35] Winkler 1981 = H. Foley 1981: 63–89 ≈ Winkler 1990: 162–87 ≈ Greene 1996a: 89–109. For Sappho and Homer, see KELLY.
[36] Stehle Stigers 1981 = H. Foley 1981: 45–61, Greene 1994 = 1996a: 233–47, Williamson 1996.
[37] Snyder 1991, Lardinois 1996.
[38] Gubar 1984: 55 = Greene 1996b: 210.
[39] Wittig and Zeig 1976: 213 = 1979: 136.
[40] The term 'women-identified women' was developed by lesbian feminists of the 1970s to describe their identity and sexuality.

man'.[41] Her identity as a fiction is sealed not only by the announcement that she is male, but also by her 'smearing on her makeup' and the way in which the very words of her poetry evaporate – each stanza ends with a line in which the words from the Sappho poem are listed and dismissed. 'Laugh Breathe Look Speak Is disappears | . . . | Tongue Flesh Fire Eyes Sound disappears'. The English author Maureen Duffy (1933–) has recently produced *Songs for Sappho*, a poetry book of a love affair between two women which refracts Sapphic imagery through a modern relationship. Published as *Paper Wings*, an 'artists' book' by Liz Mathews (2014), the poems are each 'set to paper' in a way that draws attention both to their gorgeous sensuality and to the fragility of the physical medium, thus sounding the Sapphic notes of tradition and loss in a new way.

New Translations

As well as, and in relation to, these creative receptions, the later twentieth and twenty-first centuries have witnessed a proliferation of new translations. These register the increasing emancipation of women in contemporary culture, in that the lone voice of a woman poet from antiquity is repeatedly, and variously, perceived as important to new audiences. Women are also increasingly prominent as translators, testimony to their better access to education and to the levers of cultural power. In some cases, as with Anne Carson and Josephine Balmer, the translator is also a poet. Finally, translators from the 1980s onwards can be seen to engage with feminist-orientated scholarship on 'women in antiquity' emerging, often in the USA, from the 1970s, including foundational work by Mary Lefkowitz and Page duBois.

Sappho. Poems and Fragments by Josephine Balmer (1959–) was issued in 1984 by Brilliance Books, a lesbian and gay publisher, and proceeds from this milieu.[42] Balmer's introduction leaves the reader in no doubt that her project is one of feminist emancipation: starting from citation of what she condemns as faint or condescending appreciations by contemporary male scholars, she fulminates that they 'appear to praise Sappho's work but in fact deny the strength of her poetic imagination, denigrate the artistry and subtlety of her work and ignore the importance of inherited literary

---

[41] Carson 1997: 228.
[42] Balmer 1984 (revised edn, 1992); see Balmer 2013: 97 n. 73.
[43] Balmer 1992: 8, 21, citing the judgment of Bowra 1961: 187 that Sappho's verses have the 'air of reality, of being derived immediately and directly from Sappho's own experience', and Jenkyns's verdict on fr. 132 as 'charming but slight' (1982: 72). See further Lefkowitz 1973 ≈ Greene 1996a: 26–34.

and social convention'.[43] Contrary to such appraisals, Balmer sets out to make the case for Sappho's excellence and artistry – which, as she points out, was universally acknowledged in antiquity. Her introduction contributes to this by providing a historical discussion which locates Sappho's poetry within the political and social changes of archaic Lesbos, while also highlighting the engrained misogyny and fear of female sexuality evident in ancient sources that treat of women. By thus exposing and criticising the phobic and condescending attitudes of both ancient and modern commentators, Balmer aimed to clear the way for her own recovery of Sappho's lyric voice as one that is 'sensual and emotional rather than sexually explicit', which subverts masculine erotic conventions of domination and subordination in order to present love between women as 'mutual and equal . . . a rejection of male values and a response to the increasing devaluation of women and fear of their sexuality'.[44]

If Balmer's introduction deploys the tools of scholarly historicism in service of a feminist rereading which now appears in many ways a product of its time, her translation takes a different route to the same goal, one that uses considerably more artistic licence: working through the clues in ancient commentators to group the smaller fragments into longer strings that a modern, monolingual reader would more readily recognise as 'poetry'.[45] An example is her juxtaposition of two verses cited by Demetrius (fr. 156) with another from Athenaeus (fr. 167) to create a new and suggestive, fragmentary poem of praise:

> [Her voice was]
> > far sweeter than any flute . . .
> [her hair,]
> > more golden than gold . . .
> [and her skin,]
> > far whiter than an egg . . .[46]

Unlike Carson, whose translations follow the critical edition of Voigt, Balmer refuses to subordinate her own sense of the form and arrangement of Sappho's poems to that of a scholarly editor. Or one could argue that Carson is more concerned to foreground the incomplete nature of the transmitted corpus and the impossibility of such a 'piecing together the fragments' as Balmer attempts.[47] In a recent reflection on her practice,

---

[44] Balmer 1992: 15, 16.
[45] Balmer 2013: 95–7; also Balmer 1992: 29–30.
[46] Balmer 1992: 41; for discussion, see Balmer 2013: 95.
[47] Balmer 2013, title. For reflections on her approach and Carson's, see Balmer 2013: 80–3.

Balmer comments that 'it has to be owned that my own decisions on the ordering and grouping of the fragments . . . speak far more for my own interaction with the text than for Sappho's now impenetrable, unknowable authorial intent'.[48] Yet she is right to argue that similar choices confront not just every translator of Sappho, but even every editor.

Anne Carson's *If Not, Winter. Fragments of Sappho* (2002) is a defining version of the period, partly because although the primary audience is the general reading public, many of whom may be familiar with Carson's own poetry, a scholarly audience is also accommodated by Greek and English on facing pages and by helpful notes. Typography and layout are also significant, especially brackets representing 'the drama of trying to read a papyrus' whose tattered state resists legibility. Not all papyrological marks are retained, however, because that would itself render reading more difficult; the brackets are an 'aesthetic gesture toward the papyrological event'.[49] Although Carson's translations aim to reflect Sappho's syntax and word order, she allows herself more leeway with the fragments that come down through the lexicographical tradition; here she may have 'manipulated [a fragment's] spacing on the page, to restore a hint of musicality or suggest syntactic motion'.[50] Carson aligns herself with Walter Benjamin's principles of translation to catch 'the echo of the original',[51] and does not elaborate, as Barnard does, on the transmitted texts in the interests of intelligibility. Her translations eschew reconstruction and offer instead a poetry welcomed by readers as spare and elegant. Crucially, Carson pays no attention to the historical Sappho's sexuality or even feminism; this Sappho is primarily poet and musician.

New Fragments

The figure of Sappho as 'poet and musician', rather than shorthand for feminism, lesbianism, or both, has been moved to the forefront of scholarly discourse by the recent emphasis within scholarship on ancient lyric on 'song culture' and new understandings of orality.[52] Recent papyrus findings have brought further complexity. Scholarship in the wake of the publication of the 2004 fragments has included research into the variety of ways in which Sapphic song might be transmitted, as well as studies of

[48] Balmer 2013: 96.
[49] Carson 2002: xi.
[50] *Ibid.* xii.
[51] Benjamin *ap.* Carson 2002: xii.
[52] STEINER, KURKE, FERRARI.

the new poem's philosophical discourse and deployment of myth. Scholarship on the 2014 fragments has investigated topics such as the connections between Lesbos and Egypt and how these might shape family and wider politics,[53] and the relation between Sappho's songs and the iambic tradition of abusive verses.[54] New topics of debate thus include the prominence of family in Sappho's poetry, public ritual contexts for Sappho's performances, and speculation as to her songs' popularity within the male-dominated symposium scene.[55] The extensive investigations into the composition of the Hellenistic books including or devoted to the works of Sappho have expanded our knowledge of her songs' role in the developing literary culture of ancient Greece and its relation to oral poetics.[56] As the poetry of the early twentieth century was motivated by groundbreaking scholarly discoveries, so the 'New' and 'Newest' Sapphos of the early twenty-first century reverberate in scholarship, translation, and creative writing. The Sappho that emerges from these new fragments differs from the established figure of previous scholarly or creative discourses, but remains difficult to reconstruct.

The 2014 poems elicited a notable response from translators. The *Times Literary Supplement* commissioned translations from seven 'classicists-poets-translators'.[57] Almost all seven kept to the shape of the sapphic stanza, with three long lines followed by a shorter, and many kept eleven syllables in the longer lines and five in the short. Some experimented with rhyme or pararhyme. Almost all kept to a fairly neutral register of English vocabulary and syntax, and kept the Greek poem's references to Zeus and Hera. Carson's version was, as Dirk Obbink noted, very different, with the colour and excitement that he says he felt on finding the actual Sappho.[58] Carson diverges completely from her practice in *If Not, Winter*, abandoning Sapphic word order and syntax for snappy and insouciant verse informed by slang and idiom. A particularly provocative part of the poem runs

> and if some god blows you a kiss, peacocks sweep the room
> handing out coupons.

---

[53] Raaflaub 2016, THOMAS.
[54] Dale 2011a, E. Bowie 2016b, STEINER.
[55] E. Bowie 2016a, RÖSLER, STEINER, FERRARI.
[56] PRAUSCELLO; Nagy 2009, KELLY, SWIFT.
[57] *TLS* 5791 (28 March 2014) 22 (Richard Janko, Anne Carson, Peter McDonald, A. E. Stallings), 5796 (2 May 2014) 23 (Alistair Elliott, Andrew McNeillie, Rachel Hadas).
[58] Obbink 2016c: 208.

This very neatly combines elements of the 'traditional' Sappho – deities, erotic encounters, exotic luxury items – with an economic motif more in tune with the practical concerns foregrounded in the new poem. Its distance from the Greek can be measured by Obbink's own translation, made without literary ambition for his 'working text':[59]

> All of those whom the King of Olympus wishes
> a divinity as helper to now turn them
> from troubles, become happy
> and richly blessed.

Other translators have also responded to the new fragments. Although the poet John Daley had previously published a translation of Sappho in 2011, his scholarly collaborator Page duBois included his translation of the Brothers Poem in a 2015 book on Sappho, remarking that the intimate and informal poem presented a Sappho who had a greater sense of family, and loyalty to a greater number of gods, than in earlier representations.[60] Daley works with duBois to 'establish a field of possible English meanings of the Greek'; the translation's expressed aims are then to preserve the range of tones and registers in the Sappho corpus, while experimenting with word order and versions of Greek metre.[61] Such collaboration between a scholar and a poet seems to feature more regularly in the discipline of classics as the importance of classical reception is recognised more fully. The most up-to-date translation of all of Sappho, including the 2014 fragments, is by Diane Rayor, with an introduction by André Lardinois. The book thus presents a scholarly digest of much recent research alongside a complete translation.[62] Like Carson, Rayor does not reconstruct any poem, but presents fragments and single words surrounded by ellipses – she suggests that part of her task is to 'guide the reader over and through the ellipsis gaps and brackets'. Her aim is to combine accuracy and poetry, developing verse which respects the lyric origin by being pleasant in the mouth and to the ear. Intriguingly, she discusses some of the translation choices she made while stressing that she also wishes to allow the reader some options in interpretation.[63]

New translations thus consolidate the gains that the twentieth and early twenty-first century have made. Sappho is not bound by her

---

[59] Obbink 2016a: 33, 14.
[60] J. Daley and duBois 2011; duBois 2015: 151–3.
[61] duBois 2015: 145.
[62] Rayor and Lardinois 2014, Finglass 2015; Rayor reflects on her practice in Rayor 2016.
[63] Rayor cited by Rayor and Lardinois 2014: 20–1.

sexuality, nor even by her femininity, although these remain important. She inherits Greek poetic tradition, reworks it, and comments on political and economic concerns close to many in her society. She stands at the head of women's literary tradition. In many respects, then, we have the Sappho that we need.

Further Reading

Sappho's post-1900 reception is so diffuse as to make all accounts selective. Good starting points, which attempt an overview, are provided in Reynolds 2000, duBois 2015, and Greene 1996b. Balmer 2013 is a rich reflection on the long history of translation practice in relation not only to Sappho, but also to other classical poets.

CHAPTER 29

Sappho in Australia and New Zealand

Marguerite Johnson*

Sappho's Antipodean reincarnations are not as extensive as they are in Europe and the United States. Nevertheless, what is fascinating about Australasian Sapphos is their manifestations in several familiar forms. This survey examines the main tropes of the Sappho legacy in Australasia with attention to the different forms of reception and their reasons, from the early colonial period to the twenty-first century. From the ensconcement of her portrait in a settler's home in Tasmania in 1825, to other unexpected references in newspapers throughout the nineteenth century, to the *art érotique* of the twentieth-century bohemians, Sappho, like many other classical icons, has inscribed a sense of belonging among white Australasians – not always in relation to their new home, but to the motherland. Amid the turbulence of the convict years (1788–1868), to the Federation of Australia in 1901, through the two World Wars, followed by second-wave feminism, to the present, Sappho shape-shifts in step with the historical processes of establishing, altering, and challenging both national and personal identities.

The Australasian Sappho trope covers a period of almost two hundred years, from the 1820s on. One of the earliest references to Sappho is unusual, fleeting, with minimum context but not without historical relevance, taking the form of an advertisement on the front page of the *Tasmanian and Port Dalrymple Advertiser* on Wednesday 9 March 1825. The advertisement is for the auction of household items and utensils in Launceston, Tasmania, among which is a picture of Sappho. This somewhat unexpected item, amid pictures of the Holy Family, St Cecilia and a Parisian cityscape, combined with a dinner set and 'a very handsome tea set', speaks to the process of settler acclimatisation during the early decades of the British colonisation of Tasmania, which began in 1803, fifteen

---

* Thanks to my colleague Professor Michael Ewans for feedback on this chapter.

years after the First Fleet arrived at Botany Bay, New South Wales.[1] In the words of an English critic in 1898: 'Britain was accustomed to thinking of the Colony as a convenient place to send paintings to, not receive paintings from.'[2]

As is evident in the example above, the earliest recorded references to Sappho in Australasia are to be found in newspapers. These references provide information on the various forms Sappho took in Australasia in the early nineteenth century. In addition to the advertisement for the sale of a picture of Sappho, other references come in entries such as Letters to the Editor, or reception pieces in the form of poems and short stories – Australasian originals and ones reprinted from overseas sources.[3] Newspapers also reprinted translations of Sappho's works as well as stories from the United Kingdom on discoveries of fragments.[4]

In addition to reviews of performances that included Sapphic verses or, more usually, renditions of Sappho-inspired works,[5] newspapers also reported on routines of a more unusual nature. In Australia and New Zealand, Melbourne-based Pansy 'La Milo' Montague performed as various 'living statues' (*poses plastiques*)[6] during the early twentieth century, making her debut at the Melbourne Opera House in June 1905. In her unique music hall act, Pansy would strip, cover herself with white paint, place some modest drapery about her body and 'become' a classical statue. Pansy toured the Antipodes with her Sappho and other classical females in a spectacle once described by a theatre critic in the *Kalgoorlie Western Argus* of Tuesday 26 September 1905 as having 'created quite a

---

[1] The liking for home decor on classical themes continued in Australasia into the early twentieth century; see, for example, an advertisement for the sale of items belonging to one F. D. Clayton, Esq. of Christchurch, including a statue of Sappho (*Feilding Star*, 7 February 1913, p. 3).

[2] D. Edwards 1989: 3, quoted in 'Art Notes', *Australian Musical Times and Magazine of Art*, 2 June, 1898, p. 15. Edwards notes (p. 61 n. 7) that the context for the statement was Australia's first art exhibition in London.

[3] *The Monitor*, Friday 6 June 1826, p. 3 (references in a Letter to the Editor); *Sydney Gazette and New South Wales Advertiser*, Thursday 15 October 1829, p. 4 (reprint of a poem on Sappho by Croly *ap.* Dagley and Croly 1822: 19–20); C. H. Souter, 'Sappho', *The Register*, Saturday 24 June 1916, p. 4 (an original poem).

[4] *Glen Innes Examiner and General Advertiser*, Tuesday 28 June 1892, p. 2 (biography and a translation of fr. 55). New Zealand examples of discoveries include *Evening Post*, 18 July 1914, p. 15 (on the discovery of fr. 16) and *Feilding Star*, 6 May 1914, p. 4 (possibly the same poem). On 6 May 1914 some twenty New Zealand newspapers printed the same story.

[5] *South Australian Chronicle and Weekly Mail*, Saturday 13 April 1872, p. 7 (on a performance of Pacini's opera), *Evening Star*, 1900 (on a version of Alphonse Daudet's 1886 novel *Sappho*, whose French original was published 1884, in Western Australia), *Evening Post*, 16 September 1901, p. 4 (on another version in Wellington).

[6] Anae 2008.

sensation in Melbourne and Sydney' (p. 43). So popular were Pansy's *poses plastiques* that when she toured New Zealand, some two thousand people were said to have been turned away from a performance in Christchurch.[7] In Dunedin's *Evening Star*, Pansy's cavalcade of ancient beauties was reviewed accordingly:

> The curtain rose slowly, and one saw, set in the midst of a garden scene . . . a white marble pedestal . . . bathed in pale light and on this pedestal, this Milo, a white figure whose faultless pose and exquisite form dominated the imagination and led it captive away to the fabled time when this same Hebe, Goddess of Youth, now so splendidly reincarnated in flesh and blood, served nectar to the Gods on high Olympus. A pause, and in a softer, dimmer, light there stood revealed the sad Psyche, emblem forever of the human soul, purged and purified by suffering. Sappho followed and gave place to the very latest in statuary, 'The Brown Venus', beautifully contrived. Next, the chaste Diana, protectress of the young; and finally the 'Venus de Milo', that noblest of all representations of love and beauty. In this pose the incomparable beauty of limb and form of the Modern Milo stopped; self-revealed.[8]

Articles chronicling incidents in the colonies provide details of the mundane and eccentric as well as events of more historical significance. Inclusions of Sappho occur in the more unusual reports, including one from the *Sydney Herald* in 1832 in its column entitled 'Police Incidents'. Therein, one Elizabeth Cox was caught performing an unusual public improvisation and is later revealed – somewhat unexpectedly – to be knowledgeable on matters Sappho:

> Elizabeth Cox, the very essence of sentiment, was charged with performing sundry evolutions in the streets, which on the first blush of the affair, the constable took to be the Phyrric dance, but on closer enquiry into the matter, it was found to be the rum waltz, and in consequence, he took charge of her.
>
> Bench – You must go to the stocks unless you can pay five shillings.
>
> Elizabeth – I'd rather spring like Sappho from the Lucadia's rock, than submit to such an expense. 'Here, take the blunt.'[9]

The details of Elizabeth Cox's life are shadowy, and she remains known to us only through this report on public disorder and drunkenness. However, her reference to Sappho and the apocryphal story of her

---

[7] C. Daley 2003: 91.
[8] Anae 2008: 119.
[9] *Sydney Herald*, Monday 9 July 1932, p. 2. Spelling and punctuation as printed.

unrequited love for Phaon suggests, tantalisingly, that some settlers at the lower end of the social spectrum possessed knowledge of the poet, even if in idiomatic parlance.

It could be argued that Federation marked – symbolically, if not materially – a more solidified Australian confidence in its own artistic prowess.[10] This does not mean, however, that one of the bedrocks of its colonial foundations, classicism, was abandoned. On the contrary, the Classical Revivalism that especially characterised the visual arts remained a distinguishing feature of the Australian art scene of the pre-Federation decade to the 1900s and of the interwar period. In this context, artists of all media continued to draw on the personae and lyrics of Sappho to create new works, often on an ambitious scale.

Among the most celebrated, albeit historically neglected, is the opera by Melbourne-born Peggy Glanville-Hicks (1912–90), entitled *Sappho* (1963). Glanville-Hicks's inspiration, not only for her Sappho opera, but for other Greek-inspired works, developed during her extensive time in Athens (1950–76).[11] In 1959, Glanville-Hicks was the recipient of a Fulbright Research Fellowship and a Rockefeller Grant that funded her to engage in a comparative study of Greece's demotic music and the music of India. The research led to the opera *Nausicaa* (composed 1959–60, premiered 1961) with a libretto based on the novel *Homer's Daughter* (1955) by Robert Graves. Such was the success of *Nausicaa* that in 1963 Glanville-Hicks was commissioned by the Ford Foundation to compose an opera for the San Francisco Opera House, which resulted in *Sappho*, with libretto by Lawrence Durrell, based on his 1950 play, *Sappho*. Glanville-Hicks's main adaptation of Durrell's play was the change to the ending, which has Sappho and her husband, Kreon, in exile.[12] Maria Callas was to star in the production, but the company rejected the score and it was never performed in its entirety until 2012.[13]

The most pervasive reception of the ideal of Sappho as a female artistic genius in the Antipodes is in its poetry, particularly the poetry of women. As Glanville-Hicks found a voice in the process of constructing her operatic homage to Sappho, poets like Ruth Gilbert (1917–2016) were also inspired by her. Noted Australasian women poets of the early twentieth

---

[10] New Zealand did not have a Federation process, nor did it formally endorse Australian Federation. The closest New Zealand equivalent to Federation was the ratification of Dominion status in 1907.

[11] V. Rogers 2009: 225–6.

[12] For Durrell's play, see GOFF AND HARLOE pp. 391–2.

[13] V. Rogers 2009: 227–8. The opera was publicly recorded in 2012, conducted by Jennifer Condon.

century, understandably empowered by the success of the suffrage move-
ment in both New Zealand and Australia,[14] were often supporters of
women's rights. There is thus an interpretive thread between their
Sappho-inspired poetry and a sense of self as newly enfranchised mem-
bers of a traditionally male-dominated artistic space.

Ruth Gilbert published the collection entitled *Complete Sappho Poems
of Ruth Gilbert* in 1998.[15] Long drawn to the poet and her oeuvre,
Gilbert's collection was in response to learning Greek at the age of 75.[16]
Prior to this, Gilbert had been a foremost figure in New Zealand literary
circles, having published widely in newspapers, magazines, anthologies,
and individual collections both nationally and internationally from 1941.
Despite her publishing success and several notable literary awards,
Gilbert was regarded with ambivalence if not hostility by some of the
leading men of New Zealand's literati during the 1950s and 1960s, par-
ticularly by the poets James K. Baxter and Louis Johnson, and her collec-
tions were regularly criticised by male reviewers. For example, in response
to a passive aggressive review of Gilbert's collection *The Sunlit Hour* by
Johnson in the magazine *Numbers*, New Zealand songwriter Willow
Macky wrote a letter of protest:

> Most women, if they wish for success, will try to conform, monkey-like,
> to the masculine pattern; others, by remaining true to their feminine
> insight, risk opposition and failure in male-dominated fields.[17]

Macky's letter attests to New Zealand's male-dominated literary enclave
prior to the 1960s and the rise of second-wave feminism in the 1970s.
Macky refers to women writers and the impetus to model their artistic
voices on 'the masculine pattern' or risk critical failure. In this sense, seek-
ing out predecessors like Sappho to explore female voices and concerns in
artistic contexts makes both political and artistic sense.

Gilbert became close to Mary Barnard (1909–2001), an American poet
well known for her translation of Sappho. This friendship, late in
Barnard's life, may have been an additional impetus to Gilbert to explore
the intricacies of Aeolic Greek so she could read Sappho in the original.

---

[14] New Zealand was the first self-governing country to grant women the vote (1893) and the
Australian Commonwealth did so in 1902 (although South Australia enfranchised women in 1894
and Western Australia followed in 1899). Aboriginal Australians were not given the right to vote
until 1962.
[15] Before this, Gilbert published *Gongyla Remembers. Poems* (1994).
[16] Wright 1998.
[17] L. Johnson 1957a, Macky 1957: 26; Johnson issued a reply in the same volume (L. Johnson 1957b).

Barnard's use of Sappho in her own poetry, both before and after her 1958 translation, which included reworkings of lines and fragments and experimentation with a Sapphic voice,[18] were clearly an influence on Gilbert. Like Barnard, for example, Gilbert's 'Sappho' poems reveal an authentic knowledge of the original poetry, which is then referenced in both overt and subtle new works. Gilbert's debt to Barnard's artistic championing of Sappho in both poetry and, in this instance, translation is evident in 'Sappho to one of her translators':[19]

> By Zeus and Aphrodite!
> When you pass
> You tread my poems underfoot
> Like grass;
> Distort my meaning; trample
> Text and truth apart:
> Watch where you walk –
> That papyrus is my heart.

The poem reveals much about Gilbert's approach to Sappho: there is the possible albeit indirect homage to one of her most venerated translators – Barnard – via a dismissal of some of the poet's less skilled interpreters; the intertextuality that references fr. 105(c); and the inclusion of familiar Sapphic topoi (the gods, nature).[20] That Gilbert's long fascination with Sappho clearly continued into her later years is evident in her reworking of the 'New Sappho':

> 'Untitled (August, 2005)'
> Children, guard well the Muses' precious gifts
> And doubly well the loved, the clear-voiced lyre
> For age has found me, and grown old, I tire.
> And this I mourn, but being human
> Such is the fate of man and woman.
> Is it not told how Dawn the rosy-armed
> Loving Tithonus, handsome then and young,
> Carried him where the eternal songs are sung
> Exchanging darkness for a world of light
> And how, youth's morning tuned too soon to night
> She saw him grey and old; lost to both love and life:
> A mortal husband wedded to an immortal wife.

---

[18] Barnsley 2013. For Barnard, see also GOFF AND HARLOE pp. 396–7.
[19] Gilbert 1998, reprinted in *Broadsheet. New New Zealand Poetry* 4 (2009) 23.
[20] There is a possible reference to Yeats's 'Aedh Wishes for the Cloths of Heaven', lines 7–8: 'I have spread my dreams under your feet; | Tread softly because you tread on my dreams' (Yeats 1899: 60).

Gilbert evokes the emotional essence and the subject matter of the original without producing a translation. Publishing the poem at the age of 86 and having had to compose it in at least her eighty-fifth year, Gilbert may have been drawn to the poem's topic of ageing as well as its very public, celebratory discovery.

Australian poet Gwen Harwood (1920–95) was also inspired by Sappho. Born in Brisbane and regarded as one of the country's foremost poets, Harwood wrote one of her most famous works, 'Burning Sappho', under the pseudonym Miriam Stone:[21]

> The clothes are washed, the house is clean.
> I find my pen and start to write.
> Something like hatred forks between
> my child and me. She kicks her good
> new well-selected toys with spite
> around the room, and whines for food.
> Inside my smile a monster grins
> and sticks her image through with pins.
>
> The child is fed, and sleeps. The dishes
> are washed, the clothes are ironed and aired.
> I take my pen. A kind friend wishes
> to gossip while she darns her socks.
> Scandal and pregnancies are shared.
> The child wakes, and the Rector knocks.
> Invisible inside their placid
> hostess, a fiend pours prussic acid.
>
> Night now. Orion first begins
> to show. Day's trivial angers cease.
> All is required, until one wins,
> at last, this hour. I start to write.
> My husband calls, rich in peace,
> to bed. Now deathless verse, good night.
> In my warm thighs a fleshless devil
> chops him to bits with hell-cold evil.
>
> All's quiet at last: the world, the flesh,
> the devils burning in my brain.
> Some air of morning stirs afresh
> my shaping element. The mind
> with images of love and pain

---

[21] <Harwood> 1962 = Kratzmann and Wallace-Crabbe 2009: 27. For Harwood's pseudonyms, including Miriam Stone (her only female pseudonym), see Atherton 2006.

> grapples down gulfs of sleep. I'll find
> my truth, my poem, and grasp it yet.
> 'The moon is gone, the Pleiads set . . . '

While Gilbert's reception of Sappho is overt, Harwood's is more limited.[22] While Gilbert's homage to Sappho may have been in response to reclaiming a female voice in an environment of male antagonism – as was Harwood's – 'Burning Sappho' burns with a far more intense female protest.[23] The work rails against the patriarchy in a feminist environment on the brink of its second wave. Characterised by its vehement opposition to male harassment and violence, and the restraints of gender essentialism with its privileging of motherhood above emancipation, second-wave feminism contextualises Harwood's poetic outburst of frustration and protest. Through the image of Sappho, referenced however fleetingly, Harwood screams out at the injustices of traditional marriage and motherhood as the enemies of woman's expression of creative genius.

Harwood also expressed a homage of sorts to Sappho in her personal mementos called 'Sappho Cards'. Harwood made these greeting tokens by cutting out pictures, often sourced from Victorian and Edwardian books and magazines, pasting them on to cardboard, always writing the words 'A Sappho Card' on the front, and then inserting an absurd speech bubble to accompany the illustration.[24] Often feminist in intent, the cards comment ironically on women's liberation from the confines of motherhood and domesticity, or satirise masculinity's acts of derring-do.[25]

Renowned feminist, poet and dramatist Dorothy Hewett (1923–2002) also found Sappho a source of inspiration. In several of her most applauded poems, Hewett regularly returns to Sappho as an icon of the female sublime, both in a creative and visceral sense. Sappho and other classical themes, evident in the sequence entitled *The Labyrinth* (Grono 1995), occupy a particularly powerful presence in Hewett's collection

---

[22] Line 32 references fr. 168B; the title references Byron, *Don Juan* 3.690, published 1821 (McGann 1980–93: v 188) (itself an allusion to fr. 48).

[23] Harwood's use of male pseudonyms, which began in 1959, constituted 'a guerrilla war on incompetent literary editors . . . As she had suspected, poems by "Walter Lehmann" and "Francis Geyer" were more readily accepted than those from Mrs Harwood of Hobart' (Sheridan 2007: 140).

[24] Pierce 2016: 16. See also Fryer Library UQFL45 Gwen Harwood Papers, box 23, folder 2, which contains *Cassells Weekly* from the 1920s, gifted to Harwood from her grandmother and a major source of images for the 'Sappho Cards'.

[25] Even the Harwood family yacht was named 'Sappho'. See also Fryer Library UQFL45 Gwen Harwood Papers, box 15, photographs (§48).

Greenhouse (1979). In 'For Sappho', Hewett pays homage not only to Sappho, but also to Harwood:[26]

> Last landstop on the searoad to Antarctica,
> Sappho and I once walked there gathering shells
> talking of love, our faltering bodies, burning senses,
> and now when I remember her, remember
>   that saltrunning melancholy sea ...
>
> two gallant boys, Prisoners of Zenda,
> we steered her yellow pick-up truck past
>   Harmony windmills,
> Hobart, beach motels, McAuley's gentled agony
> containing the willow-crested streams,
> Baby and Demon copulating, telling fragments
> of cantos on the autumnal air.
> The punt to Bruny beaches in the midst,
> in that calm house, a goosegirl in her denims,
> you give us grace to try for Launceston.
> We drive at midnight, the sky is close to us,
> the black sea roams in love in the libraries
> at the University   suitably luminous in Oyster Cove
> calling the geese   pulling the mullet in
> reading to each other   the wild and secret
>   messages we send to be decoded ...
> *The Derwent vanishes*   *The Poet's Corner*
> *convenes at the Bluebird Cafe*   *The Golem grows*
> *inside its incubator*   *Merlin is dead*
> *the seas ice over.*

The poem celebrates the time Hewett and Harwood spent together in Hobart, Harwood's home, in 1977. Harwood becomes Hewett's Sappho in this poem of friendship and love, with Hewett directly referencing her in 'Baby and Demon' (line 11) from the latter's 'Night thoughts: baby and demon'.[27]

From New Zealand, two male poets have also produced Sappho-inspired collections as well as individual poems.[28] The poet, publisher, and letterpress printer Alan Loney (1940–) has long been preoccupied

---

[26] Harwood is a dedicatee of *Greenhouse*.

[27] Priest 2014 (which also discusses Harwood's poems about and for Hewett).

[28] See also Trundle 2017: 322–3 on the 'one New Zealand-authored poem' in *The Anzac Book*. Entitled 'The true story of Sappho's death', and parodying Byron's famous poem 'The isles of Greece', it is attributed to a bomb-thrower of the New Zealand infantry brigade with the initials M. R. who had deciphered 'with much labour a very old tablet dug up in the trenches'.

with Sappho's works, and pays tribute to her genius in the monumental poem 'Testament: tenth muse'.[29] The poem begins with a quotation from Anne Carson's translation of fragments 151–2,[30] and continues in characteristic Loney style, described by Michael Morrissey as notable for its 'fragmentary, oddly cut lines, particular word abbreviations . . . and quotes'.[31] Arguably, among the most 'Sapphic' lines is an evocation of the poet, which also continues a main theme of the poem; namely, memory, its fragility, and the fragility of preserving it, be it on parchment, paper or vellum:

> who is tenth following the nine
>   sap springs ho there's something
> to sing about   arch your logos
>   over that and see what crumbles
> under you lifted in whatever honor
>   of ears and eyes opened never
> to close again   one and many as is
>   where is   vowels lost over time
> and space   digging even these verbs
>   into clay will not preserve them
> wind-blown leaves scuttling
>   thruout the house

The allusions to Sappho take the form of the references to the tenth Muse following the ninth, and the abbreviated 'sap' who 'springs' to the delight of the narrator, who exclaims 'ho'. Once she has sprung forth, the challenge for the enthusiast is to apply 'logos' to decipher what can be salvaged from her fragments and what still 'crumbles'. Her vowels have been lost over time and space. The verbs are also lost, despite having been dug into clay. Her fragments take on the form of leaves, blowing throughout the narrator's house; and, having experienced them, one's ears and eyes will be opened, never to close again, which returns us to the opening quotation from Carson's translation:

> and on the eyes
>   black sleep of night
> mingled with
>   all sorts of colors
>   *Sappho frr. 151–152 Anne Carson*[32]

---

[29] Loney 2009 (published without line numbers), reprinted here courtesy of Alan Loney.
[30] Carson 2002: 304–7.
[31] Morrissey 1996: 215. Loney has since situated the poem as part of a larger work, *Next to Nothing. Melbourne 2009–2016* (2018).
[32] Carson 2002: 304–7 reads 'kinds', not 'sorts', and there is no new line after 'with'.

As a letterpress printer with a practical and scholarly expertise in the
materiality of the book, and as a poet who has historically encountered
Sappho through translations (who writes of 'the last unparaphraseable
chunk of language'), Loney also creates images of approaching the frac-
tured lines of Sappho's Aeolic Greek:[33]

> on the horizon a single wing-shaped
>   cloud   compiling the uncompilable
> catalog of the dead   each time
>   you open the book it becomes
> unhinged   poetry in ruins ready
>   to fire up again   at that heat
> type will melt before it can
>   be printed   for an hour no birds
> were heard in the garden   listen as if
>   you were several thousand years old
> build things so as to think about them
>   what kind of levy on the world
> are we

A contemporary of Loney's, the New Zealand classicist, translator, and
poet Edward Jenner (1946–) published *Sappho Triptych* in 2007, a collec-
tion that reinforces his scholarly and artistic engagement with fragmen-
tary voices, rather than the metanarratives of the established canon.[34] His
reception of Sappho moves between gentle interpretations (not transla-
tions)[35] to more introspective contemplations of our place within big and
small universes. In the observational poems that deal with the smaller
things in life, Jenner replicates the fragmentary condition of Sappho's
work in poems on the fragments of individual actions:

> It is the colour of the petals of *Plumeria natalensis* we picked in the botani-
> cal gardens and carefully pressed between the pages of the novel we
> returned to the municipal library long before it was even due.[36]

On the poems more discernibly Sapphic in nature, Jenner recalls inci-
dents of digging up Sappho:

---

[33] Loney has been teaching himself Greek, mainly to read Sappho, Archilochus, and the Presocratics,
which he first read in the mid-1960s in the English translations of K. Freeman (personal commu-
nication, 19 December 2018; see K. Freeman 1947, 1948).

[34] Jenner has also published poems based on Ibycus (1997). *The Love Songs of Ibykos*, introduced and
translated by Jenner, with drawings by John Reynolds, was produced by his fellow New Zealander
Loney (P. Hughes 2001).

[35] Like Gilbert and Loney, Jenner has been influenced by Barnard's translations of Sappho.

[36] Jenner 2007: 6.

The texture of a dry and friable fragment of papyrus newly unearthed in the sand of an ancient rubbish dump at Oxyrhynchus on the Nile; a tattered and perforated fragment which looks a little like the first draft of a work in progress by a particularly fastidious poet who valued the pumice as much as she valued her pen and ink.[37]

In a similar historical vein, Jenner creates a poetic biography of Sappho, piecing the fragments of her life together from both the testimonia and her own words:

The colour Sappho turns when she turns 'paler than dry grass', her ears 'hum', her forehead 'drips with sweat' and a mist veils her eyes – 'at such times / death isn't far from me', Sappho of Lesbos who was small and dark and sang of a girl whose hair seemed to have been spun out of filaments of sunlight.[38]

In the visual arts, Sappho has been a source of inspiration for artists and sculptors. Bertram Mackennal (1863–1931) was an Australian sculptor who eventually received international accolades, including royal patronage in Britain; his bronze statuette 'Sappho' (1909) depicts a seated woman with head and arms on drawn-up knees.[39] Another Sappho piece, 'Sappho (possibly Reflections)' (*c.*1921), is a bronze on a marble base. While both bear the same title, neither suggests any tangible reference to the poet; rather, showing the influence of several European styles – Symbolist, Art Nouveau, New Classicism – Mackennal's sculptures are decorative and sophisticated but somewhat generic in their representation of a specific historical woman. As David J. Getsy comments, '*Sappho* 1909 … could equally have been called "Reverie" or "Meditation" or "Thinking while the billy boils". There is little sense of the lesbian poet of ancient times.'[40] Both works contrast with his powerful sculpture, 'Circe', one of Mackennal's most commanding femme fatales who stands intimidatingly, arms outstretched, poised to transform Odysseus' men into swine.[41]

The Classical Revivalism that characterised Mackennal's work was a distinguishing feature of Australian art of his era.[42] This style was

---

[37] Jenner 2007: 7.
[38] Jenner 2007: 7.
[39] Art Gallery of New South Wales, Sydney; marble version shown at the 1909 Royal Academy exhibition.
[40] Getsy 2007: 207 n. 44.
[41] Life-size bronze statue (1893), National Gallery of Victoria, Melbourne; statuette (*c.*1902–4), Art Gallery of New South Wales, Sydney.
[42] D. Edwards 1989: 1.

profoundly influential on the Australian artistic and literary polymath
Norman Lindsay (1879–1969), who, as part of the challenge to moder-
nity, dedicated his artistic and publishing pursuits to Classical
Revivalism, sometimes combined with Australian themes that were
sourced from his interest in Vitalist philosophy, to communicate his
vision of the country as new Arcadia.[43] As Tsokhas writes of Lindsay's
approach:[44]

> It was a rejection of life as embodied in the heritage of the ancient Greeks,
> the Renaissance and the nude. He contrasted modernist currents with his
> own philosophy of art, which had at its centre the individual as creator
> and the classical tradition set apart from its sociohistorical environment.

Lindsay's artwork was imbued with his interpretation of antiquity as
comprised of bucolic sexual libertines, and he, his brothers, and his son
Jack Lindsay (1900–90) were the self-appointed high priests of what they
championed as the Golden Age of the Australian avant-garde. Jack
Lindsay and Percy Reginald Stephenson (1901–65) were the driving force
behind Australia's first private press in the tradition of the Arts and Crafts
movement, The Fanfrolico Press, which was established in Sydney, then
based in Bloomsbury during the 1920s and 1930s.[45] The press enabled
them to publish the classics and works considered risqué by the standards
of the time (sometimes including certain classical authors, such as
Aristophanes and Petronius).[46] In 1928, The Fanfrolico Press produced a
limited edition of seventy copies of *A Homage to Sappho Made by Norman
and Jack Lindsay*, which showcases not only the poet's work but the
extravagant and erotic artwork of Norman, in the form of fifteen etch-
ings. What was extraordinary for the time was the explicit nature of
Norman Lindsay's etchings, which portrayed lesbian couples in an erotic
and yet unabashed style. While Lindsay had a reputation for upsetting
the Australian art scene with controversial subject matter, some of which
was censored, this publication was the only outstanding financial success
of The Fanfrolico Press.

Sappho has continued to influence artists of the twenty-first century,
including the playwright, director, actor, and academic Jane Montgomery

---

[43] D. Edwards 1989: 1.
[44] Tsokhas 1996: 220.
[45] Arnold 2009.
[46] Jack Lindsay was one of the most active and successful translators of classical texts in Australia in
the first half of the twentieth century. His choice of Greek and Latin authors was predicated on
their supposedly controversial content, which provided a preferred choice of inspiration for
Norman's illustrations.

Griffiths, who has had an extensive career as a practice-based scholar of classical reception studies. Her groundbreaking feminist play *Sappho . . . in 9 Fragments* (ellipsis original) is a tripartite-voiced one-woman production, which premiered in 2010 at the Malthouse Theatre, Melbourne. Like many Australasian Sapphos, Griffiths's Sapphos (there are two in the play) are not geographically or nationally fixed but rather, as Sarah Mullan writes, 'transcultural, transhistorical figure<s>'.[47]

Griffiths explores Sappho's biography and poetry – traditionally owned by men – through a 'historical' Sappho and a 'modern' Sappho, both of whom are introduced, navigated, mediated and developed through the voice of Atthis. The 'historical' Sappho is a witty and astute narrator of her own creation, while the 'modern' Sappho is a puffed-up stage diva who toys with an eager, lovelorn (and very minor) actor, Atthis. Trapped between two mighty egos, and yet refusing to be sidelined, Griffiths's Atthis tells us her own story, speaking as a star-struck protégée, the recipient of a brutal, modern-day erotic pedagogy:[48]

> Atthis had a story too. I am only a mediocre talent. She is the one with the genius: the ability to sing the songs – she has the voice . . . But I have a story too – and there can be no Sappho without an Atthis . . .

As noted above, Griffiths's play has an insightful universality, while remaining true to its authentic feminist and lesbian voice. Her decision to give a voice to Atthis, Sappho's original voiceless young woman, is part of the power of the play, and achieves Griffiths's aim that 'Atthis would become that everybody/nobody who has ever lost herself in the quagmire of longing; as empty and interchangeable with all the other victims of love'.[49]

Sappho's voice, the power of her voice, the singularity and omnipotence of her voice, dominated the writing process of *Sappho . . . in 9 Fragments*, or rather its writer, who describes the poet as 'the conspicuous manipulator of the entire process of creation', using the voice of the playwright 'to fill in her gaps'.[50] Artists, poets, playwrights, musicians, and scholars have, like Griffiths, explored the universality of poets such as Sappho, regularly charting the ways and means by which she speaks to us in whatever historical context we occupy. Griffiths, like many of the

---

[47] Mullan 2016: 245.
[48] Griffiths 2010: 5 (ellipses original).
[49] Griffiths 2010: xxv.
[50] Griffiths 2010: xvi.

Australasian practitioners discussed in this chapter, underlines the theme of universality inherent in the icon that is Sappho, and the intense power of what remains of her voice, reminding us that Sappho occupies 'our' world – in whatever 'our' world we occupy at any given time and place.

Further Reading

The topic of Sappho in Australasia per se has not been addressed by scholars and is still in need of research. For examples of classical reception in Australia and New Zealand, see the edited collections Burton *et al.* 2017, Johnson 2019.

CHAPTER 30

Sappho in Latin America

Robert de Brose[*]

Mapping Sappho's reception in Latin America is a challenge comparable to the size, population, and diversity of the region. It must be understood within the larger picture of the region's own classical tradition, which, although being a continuation of the European, developed a life of its own. Yet, as Andrew Laird writes:

> The classical tradition is often regarded as a monument that can stand only awkwardly on American soil, simply because European imperialism and elitism first put it there. But Greek and Roman antiquity has perfused the culture and imagination of Latin America.[1]

Indeed, if Laird's two criteria for establishing the existence of a classical tradition – that is, how far Latin has been kept alive, and the extent to which aspects of Greco-Roman antiquity were spontaneously incorporated into and transmuted by mainstream culture – then 'for the greater part of Latin America's modern history, both criteria are fully satisfied'.[2]

This rich and complex reception has only just begun to be addressed. The classical tradition is closely linked to the region's colonial past and the decolonisation processes that ensued in the nineteenth century; several other factors, such as the ethnic diversity of its society, its independence movements, and the educational influence of the Catholic Church (including in the teaching of classical languages), all have a bearing on the theme.[3]

[*] I am grateful to the editors for their suggestions and many improvements to this text. I would also like to thank the following friends and colleagues who helped me track information contained in this chapter: my student Willamy Fernandes, Leonardo B. Antunes, Jacyntho Lins Brandão, Teresa Virgínia Ribeiro Barbosa, Guilherme Gontijo Flores, and Bruno V. G. Vieira. Translations from Spanish and Portuguese are mine, except when stated otherwise; English translations from Sappho are from Campbell. 'Latin America', a concept first found in the nineteenth century, in this chapter is (anachronistically, but conveniently) used to denote South and Central America from the sixteenth century on.

[1] Laird 2007: 227.
[2] Laird 2007: 232.
[3] Laird 2007, Boccheti 2010, Taboada 2014.

Whereas the first printed texts of Sappho started to circulate in Europe around the sixteenth century,[4] the first Spanish translation (of frr. 1, 31) by Ignacio de Luzán (1702–54) appeared only in 1770,[5] and in Portuguese almost a century later, with two indirect 'translations' by J. B. Almeida-Garrett (1799–1854) of frr. 50, 81, and 94: 'Beleza e bondade' ('Beauty and goodness') and 'O sacrifício' ('The sacrifice') in his volume *Flores sem fruto* (*Flowers without Fruit*).[6] These translations stimulated Latin American poets to mention Sappho in their poetry.

In these early stages of Sappho's reception, Sappho was seen mainly through men's eyes,[7] since women were excluded from receiving a formal education (let alone from producing literature).[8] This male reception normally found itself at odds with her strong feminine lyrical voice and role as an active female lover, and subsequent discomfort gave rise to several attempts to explain away disturbing elements in her poetry, like the comparison traced by Cuban writer José Martí (1853–95) between Walt Whitman and Sappho, when he tries to reconcile the genius of the former with the reality of his homoeroticism:

> But what can express the scope of his vast and most passionate love? With a fire like Sappho's this man loves the world. To him the world seems like a giant bed. And the bed to him, an altar . . . One of the sources of this originality is the Herculean force with which he overpowers ideas, as if to violate them, only to give them a kiss with the passion of a saint. Another is the material, brutal, carnal way with which he expresses the most delicate images. His language seems lewd only to those incapable of understanding his greatness; there have been some imbeciles who – when he celebrates the love of friends in *Calamus* with the most ardent images of human language – think they are seeing, with the affectation of indecent schoolboys, a return to those vile desires of Virgil for Cebetes and of Horace for Gyges and Lyciscus.[9]

Therefore, and in keeping with other ancient and modern receptions of Sappho, her voice was frequently appropriated by a male readership to

---

[4] FINGLASS ch. 18, GILLESPIE.
[5] de Luzán 1770; see Sanz Morales 2008: 71.
[6] Almeida-Garrett 1845: 34–6; Ramalho 1965–6.
[7] For overviews of literature in Latin America from discovery to the end of Modernism, see Fernández Moreno 1972, González Echevarría and Pupo-Walker 1996, and (focusing on Brazil) Bosi 2015.
[8] With rare exceptions, such as that of the 'Tenth Muse', Sor Juana Inés de La Cruz (1648–95) in New Spain, and Mercedes Matamoros in Cuba (below, p. 434).
[9] Jiménez 2004: 133. Compare the analysis by Pseudo-Longinus, *On the Sublime* 10.1–3 of Sappho fr. 31.

serve primarily as a model for romantic emulation. In the early translations, her fictional lives are used to make those undesirable parts of Sappho's poetry conform to the horizon of expectations of her Christian, male audience. A common strategy in the face of homoerotic poems such as fr. 31 was to attribute her voice to a male lover, Phaon;[10] another was to ascribe to Sappho a more than human role – priestess, tenth Muse, genius, rebel; or else roles felt to be more suited to women – teacher, sister, mother. The Romantics in Latin America (including Gonçalves Dias, Castro Alvez, Herrera y Reissig, and Guido y Spano, all discussed below) would combine, as Glenn Most remarks for their European peers, the many conflicting features into one single fictional persona without any fear of contradiction.[11] In this respect, Herrera y Reissig's 'Prólogo a "Palideces y púrpuras"' ('Prologue to "Palenesses and purples"', 1905)[12] is paradigmatic:

> All poets have a symbol. Genius is emblematised in a liturgical form out of their inner nature: goddess, object, monster, animal. Within the quarters of their meanings, a myth dreams, sings, moves, recalls, foretells, raves, howls, amuses, sins, spits, corrodes, repulses, commits suicide, poisons, fumes, sloshes, writhes, explodes, horrifies, causes a shiver. All the verbs. All the Virtues. All the Sins.
>
> …
> Cicadas for Theocritus.
> Bees for Anacreon.
> …
> Pindar is a lion.
> Vultures for Aeschylus.
> … Sirens to Sappho.**
> Virgil is a lamb.
>
>   **Sappho is also a man.

By the second half of the nineteenth century, when women writers start to appear, Sappho is frequently used by male writers as a frame in which to value – not always positively – women's poetical output and status, while women in their turn used her to pursue and shape their own voices. From the twentieth century on, when there was a 'return to Greece' throughout Latin America,[13] and translations and studies of

---

[10] Finglass and Kelly pp. 1–3.
[11] Most 1995 ≈ Greene 1996b: 11–35.
[12] Estévez 1998: 602.
[13] González de Tobía 2005: 123.

Sappho's poetry began to appear more frequently,[14] the many fictional or idealised Sapphos started to give way to a more autobiographical persona. Then, from the sixties onwards, the feminist and LGBTQ movements appropriated her figure and poetry to produce a rich reception.[15]

Since the male and female receptions of Sappho differ in these respects, and because they happened at different times and started to overlap only at later stages in her reception, they are treated separately in this chapter. This does not deny their interrelationship; on the contrary, the male reception of Sappho has to some extent shaped the female, while trying to use Sappho and the fictions created around her to frame the reception of female poetry in general. For this reason, in the female reception of Sappho, there is sometimes a movement away from, and even a rejection of, the figure herself. In these cases, her reception manifests itself as the female pursuit of its own voice.

Sappho through Men's Eyes

Sappho was a common theme among neoclassical and Romantic poets. The Argentinian poet Esteban de Luca (1786–1824), for example, inserted an indirect quotation from fr. 31 in his ode 'A la señorita Joaquina Izquierdo' ('To the lady Joaquina Izquierdo'):[16]

> Un fuego más sublime
> Su honesto pecho anima
> Que á Safo cuando á Vénus
> Sus himnos repetía …

> A subtler fire
> Animates her chaste bosom
> Than that of Sappho when
> Singing her hymns to Venus …

---

[14] See González de Tobía 2005 for Spanish America, Duarte 2016 for Brazil. Until the nineteenth century, Greek literature was read mostly through Latin translations. Moreover, whereas the printing of books had always been allowed in the Spanish colonies, it was forbidden in Brazil until 1808; and while the first universities were founded by the Spanish shortly after colonisation in Santo Domingo (1538), Lima, and Mexico (both 1551), in Brazil they were founded only in the first half of the twentieth century, in Rio de Janeiro (1920), São Paulo (1934), and Brasília (1961).

[15] Although feminist attitudes and movements have obviously existed since colonisation, it was not until the twentieth century, with the Cuban Revolution (1959), and then, more intensely, from the seventies onwards, that feminism started to take an ideological, political, and organised form in Latin America, a form very different from its European and North American counterparts: Molyneux 2001, Guy 2011. For gender and sexuality studies in Latin America, see Balderston and Guy 1997, and Mogrovejo 2015 for its lesbian movement more generally.

[16] de Luca 1889. Throughout I preserve the original spelling.

The Brazilian neoclassical poet Basílio da Gama (1740–95) would speak of a 'tender Sappho ornate of a thousand flowers', who 'mixes the amorous myrtle to the winning laurels'.[17] The relatively unknown poet (and former governor of Macau) Lucas José de Alvarenga (or D'Alvarenga, 1768–1831) not only produced translations of Sappho fr. 31 from versions to which he had access while in Europe, but also imitated it in one of his *Improvisos*:[18]

> Sinto, que electrico fogo
>   Nos abaraza o Coração;
> …
>
> Só de pintar os seus mimos
>   Na minha imaginação;
>   Temo, emudeço, e me falta
>   A mesma respiraçam.
>
> I feel like an electrical fire
>   Scorches my heart
> …
>
> Just by picturing her grace
>   In my imagination; I fear
>   I tremble and go dumb
>   And lose my breath.

Tomás Antônio Gonzaga (1744–1810), another Brazilian poet and one of the alleged conspirators in the so-called 'Minas Conspiracy' which sought independence from Portugal, took inspiration in Sappho's fictional life to portray himself as Phaon in Part III Lyra VII of his most celebrated poem, *Marília de Dirceo* (*Dirceo's Marília*), while comparing Marília to Sappho: 'Não corres como Sapho sem ventura | Em seguimento de hum cruel ingrato, | Que não cede aos encantos da ternura' ('Thou runnest not, like unhappy Sappho, | After an ungrateful cruel lover | Who does not yield to thy beauty').[19] He also adapts Sappho fr. 31 in the second strophe of Part I Lyra IV:[20]

> Mal vi teu rosto,
> O sangue gelou-se,

---

[17] Teixeira 1996: 261 (poem dated 1772).

[18] Alvarenga 1830: 35–6; Oliveira 2017.

[19] Gonzaga 1802: 89. 'Dirceu' (or 'Dirceo' in the old spelling) was the poet's pen name, since, after being arrested and exiled to Mozambique, he had to hide behind a pseudonym, frequently authoring his books with only his initials. Marília was probably Maria Doroteia Joaquina de Seixas Brandão (1767–1853), co-conspirator in the Minas plot against the Portuguese Crown, and the poet's beloved.

[20] Gonzaga 1792: 15.

A lingoa prendeo-se,
Tremi, e mudou-se,
Das faces a côr.
  Marília, escuta
  Hum triste Pastor.

Soon as I saw thy face,
Then my blood did freeze,
And my tongue was tied,
I trembled, and the colour
Drained from my face.
  Marília, listen
  To a sad herder.

The Argentinian Romantic poet Carlos Guido y Spano (1827–1918), who had already translated an article on Greek women from an allegedly English source and some fragments therein cited,[21] also published translations from some Greek poets in his book of poetry *Hojas al viento. Libro lírico* (*Leaves in the Wind. Book of Lyrics*), among which three come from Sappho.[22] According to a note this was the first time the 'Hymn to Aphrodite' had been translated into Spanish (although probably not directly from the original Greek):

> We do not think that either this or the Greek poems that follow it, except for Sappho's ode 'To a Beloved Woman', have ever been translated into Castilian. In this case, the honour would fall to us of being the first to translate into our language these precious jewels of the ancient muse.[23]

However, he tells us, fr. 31 had already received five translations by others.[24] In a note to his version of the poem, he feels obliged – much like Martí (above) – to agree with the opinion of his French source, Amédée de Cesena's *Les Belles Pécheresses* (*The Beautiful Sinners*), that Sappho, instead of speaking herself, is here giving voice to Phaon, 'una ficcion muy frecuente' ('a very common fiction').[25]

    Fr. 31 also exerted its allure on the Ultra-Romantic Brazilian poet Álvares de Azevedo (1831–52), who, in his posthumous 'Poema do frade'

---

[21] Guido y Spano 1868. I was not able to identify his source, identified only as 'Revista Británica' ('British Magazine').

[22] Frr. 1, 31, 104(a–b); Guido y Spano 1871: 161–2, 164–6.

[23] Guido y Spano 1871: notas II.

[24] Guido y Spano 1868: 418 = 1871: notas II. There is a Latin American one too, unknown to him and until recently forgotten, by an unidentified Y. B. published in the 4 April 1815 issue of *El Diario de México*; González Delgado 2012.

[25] Guido y Spano 1871: notas II–III; de Cesena 1865: 8–9.

('Poem of the friar'),[26] speaks of his suffering upon watching his beloved's death, using language reminiscent of Sappho: 'Descreve minha dôr, minha agonia, | Meu intimo soffrer quando eu te via – | Como Sapho – morrer tomando um banho' ('Describe my pain, my agony, | My inner suffering when I saw you – | Like Sappho – die during a bath'). Brazilian abolitionist and poet Antônio Frederico de Castro Alves (1847–71) perpetuated the image of a rebellious, inspired Sappho in his poem 'Tríplice diadema' ('Triple diadem'),[27] calling her a 'burning, mystical' genius, whereas Antônio Gonçalves Dias (1823–64) would choose instead the image of a 'Christian' Sappho in his poem 'A uma poetiza' ('To a poetess'), dated from 1852[28] and addressed to his beloved Adélia Fonseca (1827–1920): 'Alli, Sapho christã, virgem formosa, | A vida aos sons da lyra dulcifica' ('There, Christian Sappho, beautiful virgin, | Makes life sweet by the sound of her lyre').

The fictional Sappho of the nineteenth century influenced the Symbolist poetry of Uruguayan poet Julio Herrera y Reissig (1875–1910), who called her 'mi hermana' ('my sister').[29] Unsurprisingly, in his poetry Sappho is depicted as a Romantic poetic genius driven to suicide by love, which led him to compare her to Ophelia, Romeo and Juliet, Werther, Petronius, and even Judas.[30] Such idealisation, however, did not prevent him from writing a clearly erotic poem titled 'El baño' ('The bath', 1907),[31] where he depicts Sappho and two other fictitious girls who go bathing in a mountain lake under the voyeuristic eyes of three young male characters hidden in the bushes. After gazing at the naked girls surrounded by the 'waves, | That writhe with sensual and masculine spasms', they flee from them through the woods as if scared. This poem is almost a metaphor for male attitudes of the epoch towards Sappho, women, and women's sexuality in general.

In the twentieth century, the recently rediscovered journalist, translator, and poet Mario Faustino (1930–62) took inspiration from Sappho fr. 168B to compose 'Ego de mona kateudo',[32] in which the absence of the beloved keeps the lyrical voice awake in the small hours of the morning,

[26] Azevedo 1862: III 155–248, at 194.
[27] Posthumously published in Gomes 1960: 426.
[28] Dias 1857: 279.
[29] E. Palmieri 1998: 1041.
[30] 'Las pascuas del tiempo' ('Timely feast days', 1901) and 'Nivosa' ('Snowy', 1900); Estévez 1998: 300, 340.
[31] Estévez 1998: 49.
[32] Faustino 1955: 80, a transliteration of fr. 168B.4, ἔγω δὲ μόνα κατεύδω, 'But I sleep alone'.

longing and burning with love.[33] While 'Sapphic' in its entirety, the last four verses are almost a free interpretation of Sappho's poem:

> Amor, amor, enquanto luzes, puro,
> Dormido e claro, eu velo em vasto escuro,
> Ouvindo as asas roucas de outro dia
> Cantar sem despertar minha alegria.

> Love, Love whereas you shine pure and stark,
> Asleep and rested, here I lie awake in deep dark,
> Listening to the hoarse wings of another day
> Beat and sing without taking my pain away.

Around the same time in Nicaragua, Salomón de la Selva (1893–1959), one of the greatest poets of his era and a World War I combatant, composed a dissonant and nihilistic 'Oda a Safo' ('Ode to Sappho') in his *El soldado desconocido* (*The Unknown Soldier*):[34]

> La humanidad, ¡alás! no huele a rosas.
> ¿Y dónde encontrar la belleza, Dios mío,
> si todo es podredumbre
> y dolor y miseria?
> ¡Oh Safo, ¿tus rosas dónde se abren?
> ¡No es en el lodo humano
> en donde alargan sus raíces!
> …
> ¡Oh Safo, ¿será cierto
> que Faón no te quiso
> porque tenías caspa?…
> …
> ¿En dónde, Safo hermana,
> está el Jardín de Pieria?
> …
> Busqué el Jardín de Pieria
> toda mi vida, en vano.
> Aquí puedo decirlo.
> Y de ti, Safo, ¿es cierto
> que Faón no te quiso?
> ¿Y qué te valió entonces
> haber cortado rosas?
> …
> Faón será mi amigo,
> y el Hipólito de Eurípides.

---

[33] For the reception of this poem in modern Hebrew literature, see JACOBS pp. 444–56.
[34] de la Selva 1922: 103–9.

Que el amor, adivino,
debe ser cosa
sudorosa y hedionda.
Que todo es podredumbre
y dolor y miseria.
Aquí puedo gritarlo.
¡Oh Safo, hermana mía,
recoge tú mi grito!

Humanity, alas, does not smell like roses.
Where is beauty to be found, my God,
if all is just a rotting dump
and pain and misery?
O Sappho, where do your roses bloom?
It is not in the human mud
that they spread their roots!
…
O Sappho, is it true
that Phaon did not want you
because you had dandruff?
…
Where, Sappho, sister mine,
is the garden of Pieria?
…
I have sought the garden of Pieria
all my life, in vain.
Here I can say it.
And you, Sappho, is it true
that Phaon did not want you?
And what was it worth then
to have pruned your roses?
…
Phaon will be my friend,
and Euripides' Hippolytus.
For love, I suspect,
must be something
ugly and sweaty.
For all is a rotten dump
and pain and misery.
Here I can scream it.
O Sappho, sister mine,
receive you my scream!

The conflation of idealised images of poetry and beauty here, represented by Sappho and the idyllic setting of her life which was dominant in nineteenth-century critics and poets and was promoted by classical humanism, clashes with the reality of the post-war period, experienced first-hand by the poet, in which (in the poet's view) technology plunged the world into chaos. The feeling is similar to the disillusionment in T. S. Eliot's *The Waste Land*, also published in 1922.

The fragmentary nature of Sappho's poetry appealed to the poets of the Concrete movement, which emphasises visual over verbal semiosis in poetic texts – especially Haroldo de Campos (1929–2003) and Décio Pignatari (1927–2012), both of whom produced translations of Sappho, collected in their own books of poetry or in translation anthologies. Haroldo's appropriations create new meanings and associations, inserting snippets of Sappho's poems in his own and thereby recontextualising them. An example can be seen in his 'Grécia tropigal / Paráfone de Alkaios' ('Tropigal Greece / Paraphrase of Alcaeus'), where he traces a parallel between Sappho and the Brazilian pop singer Gal Costa (1945–) through Alcaeus fr. 384 ἰόπλοκ' ἄγνα μελλιχόμειδε Cάπφοι ('violet-haired, holy, sweetly-smiling Sappho'):[35]

ó		
coroada	ἰόπλοκ'	antílope
de violetas	ióplok	
sorriso-mel	ἄγνα	alga
	ágna	
sagrada	μελλιχόμειδε	melicanora
	mellikhómeide	
Safo	Cάπφοι	gal
	Sápphoi	
oh		
crowned	ἰόπλοκα'	antelope
with violets	ióploka'	
sacred	ἄγνα	algae
	ágna	
honey-smiling	μελλικόμειδε	mellicanorous
	mellikhómeide	
Safo	Cάπφοι	gal
	Sápphoi	

In another fragment of his masterpiece *Galáxias* (*Galaxies*),[36] Haroldo inserts a quotation of fr. 44A.5, ἄϊ πάρθενος ἔccομαι ('I shall be forever a

---

[35] de Campos 1985: 74; 'tropigal Greece' is a pun on the name of Gal Costa, an exponent of the musical movement known as 'Tropicalismo'.
[36] de Campos 2004: 24.

virgin', stated by the goddess Artemis), giving it new meaning in a passage about the Statue of Liberty:

> a Liberdade tem uma cor verde verdeverdoso um ectoplasma verde fluoresce
> do cobre iluminado pois falo da estátua olhos de cobre esbugalhado
> da estátua que assoma agora quase para dentro do barco giganta de coroa
> estelar lampadifária *ai párthenos éssomai* ficarei para sempre virgem.

> Liberty has a greenishgreener green colour a green ectoplasm fluoresces
> from the illuminated copper for I speak of the copper statue of the bulging
> eyes
> of the statue that now almost steps into the ship crowned giantess
> lampadipharous star *ai párthenos éssomai* I shall remain forever virgin.

Pignatari also composed an ode to Sappho,[37] in which the allusions to her style, themes, and economical diction are conjoined with the fragmentary layout of her modern editions:

PARA SAFO

de bruços
o vento
se rala
no milharal
do plátano
ao quarto
minguante

tão só

TO SAPPHO

belly down
the wind
rubs against
the cornfield
from sycamore
to waning
moon

so lonely.

Sappho and Latin American Women Poets

Reception of Sappho by women writers has been characterised by a tension between conforming with and departing from her male readings. The few women writers of the nineteenth century had, however, almost

---

[37] Pignatari 2004: 304 (first published in the newspaper *Suplemento de Minas Gerais* (Belo Horizonte) in February 1998).

no other choice than to accept that male reading or submit to the place ascribed to them in it. The first case is well illustrated by Cuban poet and translator Mercedes Matamoros (1851–1906), who adhered to the current narrative of a Sappho madly in love with Phaon in a series of twenty sonnets entitled 'El último amor de Safo' ('Sappho's last love'),[38] in which she assumes Sappho's voice, addresses Phaon and narrates the whole affair, from the moment when they met to the jump from Leucas. Although the poems may not appeal to a modern audience for their flamboyant tone and neoclassical allusions (which mix Greek and Roman images in telling the story),[39] the fact that she spoke in the first person about unrequited love is remarkable. That she seemed to be a woman ahead of her time, and conscious of the limitations imposed on her by society, is indicated in a letter to the poet Manuel Serafín Pichardo (1865–1936):

> Aunque la mujer permanezca fiel a la consigna de la hipocresía que el hombre le ha impuesto, acude siempre a leer en secreto lo prohibido. Yo me he lanzado a escribir cada día con mayor libertad porque creo, como Milton, que lo impúdico es el pudor.

> Even though woman remains faithful to the commandment of hypocrisy that men have imposed, she secretly seeks to read what has been forbidden. I have come to write more freely each day because I believe, like Milton, that what is indecent is decency itself.[40]

This male-driven framing can also be seen in the case of the Uruguayan poet Juana de Ibarbourou (1892–1979), also known as Juana de América, to whom the role of an idealised Sappho was granted by the authority of Miguel de Unamuno (1864–1936), the Spanish writer, philosopher, and Professor of Greek literature at the University of Salamanca. In a letter thanking her for having sent him an exemplar of her debut book of poems, *Las lenguas de diamante* (*The Diamond Tongues*), he tells her, in a typically chauvinistic tone, that he read it[41]

> first with distrust and then with increasing interest and pleasure . . . My distrust for poetry written by women is an old one. The poetic breeze of a Sappho, who chastely undresses her soul – which is harder than

---

[38] Matamoros 1902 = Palacios 2012.
[39] The rival is either Cloé (Part V) or a Roman Mirene (VIII); the agent of love, Cupido, and the wine that Sappho gives Phaon in an 'orgy' is from Cyprus (VII). Sappho invokes the Furies of Avernus (IX) against Phaon if he leaves her, and is worried about the 'impure fire of a late passion ('el fuego impuro de pasión temprana') which he arouses in Glaucus and Antenor (VIII).
[40] Quoted as an epigraph to Matamoros 1902 = Palacios 2012: 5.
[41] Letter dated 18 September 1919, in Fischer 2008: 33–5.

undressing one's body – in her poems, has disappeared almost with [the beginning of] Christianity . . . This is the reason why I was so pleasantly surprised by the most chaste spiritual nakedness of your poems, so fresh and passionate at the same time . . . I reread your book, this time out loud, to a blind friend who is also a poet . . . and it was him, in the end, who suggested to me – to me, a teacher of Greek literature! – the similarity to Sappho; to the historical Sappho, of course, not the one from legend.

More recently, the Uruguayan poet Cristina Peri Rossi (1941–) has produced homoerotic poetry classified as 'Sapphic' in style.[42] Her 1971 book *Evohé. Poemas eróticos* (*Evohe. Erotic Poems*), which gives a male voice to the lyric I, has aroused controversy for its explicitness, and quotes Sappho fr. 130 as its first epigraph.[43] Sappho's poetry and her fictitious persona also helped to frame the output and critical reception of two of the most important Argentinian poets, Alfonsina Storni (1892–1938) and Alejandra Pizarnik (1936–72).

Much like Sappho, Storni achieved by antonomasia the ambivalent status of 'the Poetess' ('la Poetisa') in Argentinian letters on account of her distinctly feminine lyrical voice, despite Jorge Luis Borges's judgement that her poetry was obscure and a 'chillonería de comadrita' ('gossipy shrillness').[44] Both in 'Carta lírica a otra mujer' ('Lyrical letter to another woman') and in the sonnet 'Esclava' ('Slave'), her poetry verges on a homoeroticism that some critics have found troubling. In 'Carta lírica' the echoes of Sappho's fr. 31 and other fragments surface in verses like 'I do not know your name. I have never seen | your face: I imagine you fair, | delicate as young buds, | small and sweet and . . . somehow, I don't know . . . divine' or 'Let his lips wander | over your hands . . . | And maybe, someday, . . . | I will humbly come up beside you | and quietly, whispering, | ask to hold your hands for just a moment, | so that I can kiss them, I, as he kisses them'.[45] Whereas here she contents herself in merely kissing the hands of the woman who married her beloved, in 'Esclava' she longs for more: at the end of the poem, she says 'cuando la besas tú, beso su boca' ('when you kiss her, I kiss her mouth'), which led Roberto Giusti to remark that 'De ahí, a cantar como Safo en la oda inmortal: "Semejante a un dios me parece el hombre que está sentando

---

[42] duBois 2017: 34–5.

[43] 'Otra vez Eros que desata los miembros me tortura, dulce y amargo, monstruo invencible' ("Ερος δηὖτέ μ' ὀ λυσιμέλης δόνει, | γλυκύπικρον ἀμάχανον ὄρπετον, 'Once again limb-loosening Love makes me tremble, the bitter-sweet, irresistible creature').

[44] J. Borges 1925: 51 = 1997: 231; cf. Genovese 1998: 55.

[45] Translated by Dana Stangel in Tapscott 1996: 107–10; in the first quotation, '. . .' is original to the poem and its translation; in the second, it represents text not quoted here.

ante tí . . .", no hay más que un paso' ('Here, she is just one step away from singing like Sappho in her immortal ode "He seems as fortunate as the gods to me who sits there opposite you"').[46]

Storni committed suicide by jumping from a breakwater at La Perla beach in Mar del Plata, which led Roberto Giusti to associate her with Sappho when he commemorated her in the literary magazine *Nosotros*: 'No puede substraerme en este momento al recuerdo de que a Safo la tradición la hizo fea y suicida' ('In a moment like this, I cannot help but remember that tradition has made Sappho ugly and suicidal').[47] Commenting on Giusti, Genovese remarks: 'One fact, the suicide that closes the life of both poets, becomes, too frequently, a reason for the reading of their work. As if a dangerous rarity, that of poetry, were a lethal poison to women.'[48]

The work of Alejandra Pizarnik (1936–72) 'explores eroticism, ecstasy, and depression, and her verses echo some of Sappho's themes, her forms of same-sex desire, and the fragmentary form in which we must read her poems'.[49] Sappho's influence becomes evident when one of her prose pieces of Borgesian inspiration, the *Índice ingenuo (o no)* (*Naïve – or not – Summary*), dedicates the imagined story 'a Safo y a Baffo' ('to Sappho and to Baffo').[50] Molloy rightly notices that Pizarnik is here 'performing an act of literary vandalism, both honoring and defacing the sapphic monument (and the complex narratives it stands for), calling attention to the lady as she literally draws a mustache ("Baffo" is "whiskers" in Italian) on her face'.[51] As with Storni, her suicide brought her into closer association with Sappho; commenting on the association between Sappho fr. 94.1[52] and Pizarnik's poem 'Lovers', David Damrosch says that 'Such damaged lines [i.e. Sappho's] inspired Pizarnik in the years before her suicide at age thirty-six to compose deliberately broken verses.'[53]

A rejection and distancing from the figure of Sappho is also present in 'Meditación en el umbral' ('Meditation at the threshold')[54] by the Mexican poet Rosario Castellanos (1925–74):

---

[46] Giusti 1938: 378.
[47] Giusti 1938: 397.
[48] Genovese 1998: 54 (my translation).
[49] duBois 2017: 33.
[50] Becciu 2002: 90.
[51] Molloy 1997: 250.
[52] τεθνάκην δ' ἀδόλως θέλω ('and honestly, I wish I were dead').
[53] Damrosch 2009a: 198.
[54] Castellanos 1972: 326.

Debe haber otro modo que no se llame Safo
ni Mesalina ni María Egipciaca
ni Magdalena ni Clemencia Isaura.

Otro modo de ser humano y libre.

Otro modo de ser.

There must be another way not called Sappho
or Messalina or Mary of Egypt
or Magdalen or Clémence Isaure.

Another way of being human and free.

Another way of being.

The Cuban poet Mercedes Cortázar (1940–) distances herself from
Sappho's aesthetics when, in her poem 'Las tribulaciones'
('Tribulations'),[55] she establishes a dialogue with fr. 16 to discard romantic
love by means of *praeteritio*, a figure of thought by which attention is
drawn to something only to dismiss it in favour of another:

y no digo como Safo que lo más grande de la tierra
es aquello que se ama
sino el niño que extiende sus brazos escuálidos
en algún lugar de la India
el boliviano que reduce cabezas humanas
por quince dólares
el negro del sur
que sirve de pira en los atardeceres

And I do not say like Sappho that the greatest thing on Earth
is whatsoever one loves
but the little child stretching out its squalid arms
somewhere in India
the Bolivian who shrinks human heads
for fifteen dollars
the black man from the South
who serves as a bonfire in the afternoons

In Brazil, the association of women poets with Sappho does not seem to
have been common, perhaps because of its comparative scarcity of
women in literature before the beginning of the twentieth century. As the
poet, translator, and literary critic Ana Cristina César (1952–83) remarked:

Women always added to the readership of literature, but rarely to the
ranks of literary contributors. Besides, in Brazil women writers can be
counted on the fingers of one hand, and when one thinks of poetry,

[55] Cabezas Miranda 2012: 137.

Cecília Meireles [1901–64] is the first name to come up. And precisely because hers is the first name to come up, she delimits the place from where women start to see themselves in poetry.[56]

By this César does not imply, of course, that there were no women poets before Meireles. Her point is that those earlier writers, by not conforming to men's expectations of how women should write, were excluded from the canon and nowadays have fallen out of memory. One case in point is Ana Eurídice Eufrosina de Barandas (1806–56), who, besides producing a tale named *A queda de Safo* (*Sappho's Leap*), also wrote the poetry book *O ramalhete ou Flores escolhidas no jardim da imaginação* (*The Bouquet, or Flowers Plucked in the Garden of Imagination*),[57] which is inspired by the lyrics of Sappho and other Greek poets.

Translations of Sappho in Latin America

The task of tracking Sappho's translations in Latin America is complicated. The language barrier renders the commercial circulation of translations between Brazil and its neighbours almost non-existent.[58] The region's huge extent makes visits to libraries difficult and expensive, and online catalogues are still largely unreliable. There is also no systematic history of the reception and translation of the classics in Latin America,[59] and a culture of review of translations is still wanting. Translators show little awareness, if not disregard, for the work of their predecessors and rarely reference each other. Finally, the very academic status of translation is precarious, and the task itself still provokes ambivalent feelings in the very people who are the main source of the endeavour, professors and graduate students: while indispensable for the survival of the classics, it is sometimes looked down as a minor task unworthy of serious study.

There are more Brazilian translations of Sappho than in any other individual country of Latin America, thanks to recent investment in Brazilian universities, which led to a boom in the study of classical Greek and Roman antiquity. Furthermore, while translations of Greek lyric made in Spain are readily accessible in Hispanic America, the same does not happen in Brazil, simply because there are not as many translations

---

[56] César 1999: 227 (essay originally published 1979).
[57] de Barandas 1845.
[58] Spanish speakers have more difficulty understanding Portuguese than vice versa: Jensen 1989.
[59] Duarte 2016.

of Greek lyric and Sappho produced in Portugal, so the demand for translations made in Brazil is naturally higher.[60]

In Argentina, the most recent translation of Sappho is by Pablo Ingberg (2003). The latest translations of Sappho in Chile include another by Ingberg (1997), and a version by the poet Soledad Fariña titled *Ahora, mientras danzamos* (*Now, While We Dance*, 2012), an indirect poetic translation from the English of Mary Barnard.[61] In Bolivia, there is the translation by Gary Daher (2005), and in Colombia, the one by Rosa Angela Bonilla Malaver (2008). In Mexico, Carlos Montemayor published all the fragments available in the 1980s (1986); the latest translation is the 2012 bilingual edition of Mauricio López Noriega. Translations of Sappho have also appeared in anthologies.[62]

In Brazil, since the groundbreaking contributions of Décio Pignatari (1996) and Haroldo de Campos (1985, 1998), most translations of Sappho have been carried out by academics for the use of undergraduates. The first extensive translation of Sappho was made in 1942 by a Professor of Literary Theory at the University of São Paulo, Jamil Almansur Haddad, who published *Safo lírica* (*Lyrical Sappho*), an indirect translation from the French. Forty-five years later, Alvaro A. Antunes published *Safo. Tudo que restou* (*Sappho. All That Remains*), the first complete translation of all the available fragments. Then in 1991 came Joaquim Brasil Fontes's *Eros, tecelão de mitos. A poesia de Safo de Lesbos* (*Eros, Weaver of Myths. The Poetry of Sappho of Lesbos*), which contains a critical study of the poet, her receptions in antiquity, and a bilingual translation of all of Sappho's then extant poetry; in 2003 he gathered the translated poems from that book into a bilingual volume. In 2009, Jaa Torrano published a small book called *Safo de Lesbos. Três poemas* (*Sappho of Lesbos. Three Poems*), containing the famous frr. 1, 16, and 31, and two years later appeared Giuliana Ragusa's *Safo de Lesbos. Hino a Afrodite e outros poemas* (*Sappho of Lesbos. Hymn to Aphrodite and Other Poems*). Guilherme Gontijo Flores published in 2017 the most comprehensive and up-to-date bilingual translation. Sappho has also appeared in anthologies by Péricles Eugênio da Silva Ramos (1964), Paulo Martins (2010), Giuliana Ragusa (2013), and Trajano Vieira (2017).

---

[60] de Vasconcellos 2011. Almost the only Portuguese anthology of Greek lyric used in Brazil is Lourenço 2006.
[61] M. Barnard 1958; Goff and Harloe pp. 396–7.
[62] de Esclasans *et al.* 1954, Torres 1970, Nuño 1988, Cataldo 2017.

Further Reading

Ragusa 2005 explores the representations of Sappho in antiquity and compares them to the descriptions of the goddess Aphrodite in her poems. On translation, orality, and the feminine in Sappho, Flores 2017, in the introduction to his translation, 'Safo de Lesbos: corpo, corpos, *corpus*' ('Sappho of Lesbos: body, bodies, body of work', pp. 7–22), frames the translation of Sappho's fragments by taking advantage of their modern and contemporary reception. For the history of the translation of the classics in Brazil, see Duarte 2016; for contemporary trends in the translation of Greek poetry, see Oliva Neto 2015, a special issue of the journal *Cadernos de literatura em tradução*. For the broader topic of classics in Hispanic America, see the collection Maquieira and Fernández 2012 (the most geographically comprehensive), González de Tobía 2001 ≈ 2005, 2008, Laird 2007, Taboada 2014. For classical scholarship in Spain and Hispanic Latin America until the sixties, see Demetrius 1965.

CHAPTER 31

Sappho in Hebrew Literature

Adriana X. Jacobs[*]

For the better part of the last century, the most substantial collection of Sappho's poetry in Hebrew translation was to be found in Margot Klausner's historical novel *Sapfo mi-lesbos* (*Sappho from Lesbos*).[1] Better known today as one of the founders of Israeli theatre and cinema, the German-born Klausner (1905–75) originally wrote the novel in German under the title *Sappho von Lesbos* and published it in 1945 in Buenos Aires.[2] Klausner's story is speculative, one of many fictionalised reconstructions of the life of Sappho that circulated in the early twentieth century, but the novel serves fundamentally as a vehicle for Sappho's poetry. Almost every page contains poetic text in a variety of contexts, ranging from dialogue to exposition. When the novel came out the following year in Eliezer Lubrani's Hebrew translation, the task of translating the poetry was undertaken by the highly regarded poet, playwright, and translator Aharon Kaminka (1866–1950). Indeed, the poems, which is to say the translations, occupied such a prominent place in the novel that the Hebrew jacket description acknowledged that poetry and prose formed a single tapestry, 'with the poems interwoven throughout'.[3]

Kaminka's translations serve as a point of departure for this critical overview of modern Hebrew translations of Sappho. Until the late nineteenth century, Hebrew translators had focused on Greek historical and philosophical texts, so Kaminka's scholarship on and translations of classical Greek literature, which began to appear in the 1880s, not only broke new ground, but also coincided with a transformative period for European Jewish culture in general and Hebrew literature in particular.[4] In what follows, I contextualise Kaminka's translations of Sappho in late

---

[*] I am grateful to Ronen Sonis for his comments on this chapter.
[1] Klausner 1946.
[2] Klausner 1945. A Spanish translation by Greta Mayena came out in 1946.
[3] Klausner 1946, front jacket copy.
[4] For Hebrew translations of Greek literature, see Shpan 1953.

nineteenth-century developments in modern Hebrew literature and in particular its Hellenic turn, which introduced a variety of new themes and subjects to this literature in a period of rapid vernacularisation.[5] I also highlight how Hebrew translations of Sappho evince key developments in modern Hebrew literature and acknowledge, in their continuous retranslation, the shifts and swerves that have shaped Hebrew literature's gender and cultural politics.[6]

Kaminka's biography reflects the rapid changes that European Jewish cultures underwent in the late nineteenth century, and the direct effect these would have on the subsequent development, publication, and circulation of modern Hebrew literature. Born in 1866 in Berdichev in the Russian Empire (today Ukraine), Kaminka received a comprehensive private education at home, which included secular subjects. At the age of fourteen, he moved to Berlin to pursue rabbinical training, which he complemented with university coursework in Berlin (and later Hamburg and Riga). In this period, he most likely undertook serious study of ancient Greek. Kaminka's translations of Greek literature, and Sappho in particular, first appear in the wake of the *Haskala*, or Jewish Enlightenment, a multifaceted intellectual movement that began in Germany in the late eighteenth century with a focus on Jewish emancipation. For the early *maskilim* (those affiliated with the *Haskala* movement), the modernisation of Jewish culture was vital to emancipation, and this included an investment in developing a vernacular, secular Hebrew literature.[7] Throughout the *Haskala*, but particularly in the nineteenth century, Hebrew writers turned to literary translation as a source of creative inspiration for their own writing and as part of a commitment to a literary output in Hebrew that could stand alongside other European languages.[8] The *Haskala*'s movements from Western to Central and Eastern Europe chart key developments in Hebrew literature and literary translation. Early modern Hebrew translations, for example, generally drew from and were mediated by the languages in which *maskilim* were most proficient, typically German.[9] With regard to Greek, a few exceptions notwithstanding, Hebrew translations that worked directly with the Greek began to appear with greater frequency in the 1860s than in the

---

[5] Silberschlag 1977, G. Levin 1985.
[6] Jacobs 2015.
[7] Pelli 1979, 2010, Litvak 2012.
[8] Jacobs 2018.
[9] Kahn 2017: 1–2.

earlier decades of the *Haskala*.[10] *Maskilim* who pursued university studies in German universities would have had the opportunity to combine a study of classical languages with German classical scholarship, training that encouraged translators like Kaminka to work directly with the Greek.

In 1887, Kaminka's essay 'Introduction to Greek poetry' appeared in the almanac *Keneset Yisra'el* (*The Assembly of Israel*), edited by Saul Pinchas Rabinowitz (1845–1910).[11] The journal was affiliated with the proto-Zionist movement *Hibat Tsiyon* (*Love of Zion*) and continued the late *Haskala*'s investment in secular Hebrew scholarship. When 'Introduction to Greek poetry' was published, the circulation of modern Hebrew literature in the Jewish diaspora was still limited primarily to highly educated men. And as his prefatory remarks make clear, Kaminka could not draw on much pre-existing Hebrew scholarship on Greek literature, so his essay contributed to creating, in Hebrew, a scholarly vocabulary for and discourse on this subject.

Although the essay serves as a preface to Kaminka's Hebrew translation of the twenty-first book of the *Iliad*, which also appears in this issue, his discussion of the characteristics of Greek poetry also includes observations about the particular issues that arise in the linguistic and cultural translation between Greek and Hebrew. Kaminka notes, rather sweepingly, that difficulties in translating between the two come down to fundamental differences in 'form and content'.[12] For one, the polytheism of the ancient Greeks shaped a distinct way of understanding and writing about the natural world and its phenomena. 'When the Greeks look at the afternoon sun in the sky', Kaminka notes, 'they don't say "the-God-I-am-not-able-to-name said *let there be light*" but rather "the sun god (Helios) is riding his horse across the sky".'[13] So that the Hebrew reader can appreciate the ancient Greek world view, Kaminka offers an overview of Greek mythology, providing Hebrew transliterations for the names of Greek deities but also signalling where there may be an appropriate Hebrew equivalent. To highlight the specific linguistic and rhetorical features of the *Iliad*, he also translates examples from a wide range of Greek literature. 'It is understood', Kaminka writes,

---

[10] There were exceptions; for example, Josef Flesch (1781–1839) independently studied Greek and translated the writings of Philo into Hebrew (cf. M. Miller 2011: 89–90).
[11] Kaminka 1887.
[12] Kaminka 1887: 129.
[13] Kaminka 1887: 132.

[that] all myths and legends always bear the mark of the time in which they fully developed and take on an enduring literary form, and therefore are like a polished mirror [reflecting] the will, spirit, and faith of the people at different points in their history.[14]

In keeping with this principle, Kaminka assiduously contextualises the life and work of each Greek author that his introduction addresses.

In this work, Sappho fr. 168B appears as part of a discussion on the literature of Lesbos, and its inclusion likely marks the first appearance of her poetry in Hebrew translation.[15] But the principle that Kaminka applies to literature – that it is a reflection of its time and place – also applies to translation, as he shows. As far as his translations are concerned, Kaminka states that he has elected to forgo the Aeolian metre (*metrum*) of the original in favour of rhymes cast 'in the spirit of the new era' (*ba-ru'ach ha-'et ha-chadasha*), and specifically to the spirit of Hebrew 'revival' (*techiya*).[16] To elaborate Kaminka's theory and praxis of translation with respect to fr. 168B, I have provided Campbell's Greek text, Diane Rayor's English translation, Kaminka's Hebrew translation, a Romanisation of the Hebrew, and my own, more or less literal, English rendering of Kaminka's translation:

δέδυκε μὲν ἀ σελάννα
καὶ Πληΐαδες· μέσαι δὲ
νύκτες, παρὰ δ' ἔρχετ' ὤρα,
ἔγω δὲ μόνα κατεύδω.

The Moon and Pleiades have set –
half the night is gone.
Time passes.
I sleep alone.[17]

הַיָּרֵחַ וְהַפְּלֵיָאדִים

סָפוּ! וַחֲצוֹת לַיְלָה בָּאִי!

כֹּה רְגָעִים וְשָׁעוֹת נָדִים—

וַאֲנִי אֲהָהּ, לְבַדִּי אֲנִי!‏[18]

Ha-yare'ach ve-ha-pleyadim
Safu! Va-chatsot layla ba-i!

---

[14] Kaminka 1887: 130.
[15] Kaminka 1887: 143–4.
[16] Kaminka 1887: 143. Kaminka's *metrum* derives through Latin from the Greek *metron*. The term *mishkal* (weight, measure) later replaced *metrum*.
[17] Rayor cited by Rayor and Lardinois 2014: 85.

Ko rega'im ve-sha'ot nadim –
Va-ani a-ha, levadi ani!

The moon and the Pleiades
[were] swept away! And [it is] midnight on the island!
Thus, moments and hours wander –
And I, oh, I am alone!

Kaminka's version bears the characteristics of nineteenth-century Hebrew translation, particularly in its prioritisation of prosody over content. He employs an ABAB rhyme, common to the Hebrew quatrain, and while Hebrew poetry of this period had not yet fully adopted accentual-syllabic metre, his poem scans according to the Ashkenazic (Northern, Central, and Eastern European Jewish) pronunciation of Hebrew that Kaminka would have employed at the time, resulting in a preponderance of amphibrachs.[19] The liberal use of exclamation marks to heighten dramatic and emotional effect, a recurrent feature of Hebrew poetry in this period, could be traced back to the influence of German romanticism on the *Haskala*. His insistence on rhyme and a consistent syllabic count, however, results in the addition of language and imagery that are not present in the Greek, notably the island (*i*) in the second line. Alienation was a recurrent theme in the poetry of the *Haskala*; combined with the final line of the translation, to which I turn next, this image of the island has the effect of turning Sappho into a late *maskilic* Hebrew poet.

For a scholar of Hebrew literature, Kaminka's translation of the final line – *Va-ani a-ha, levadi ani!* – invites comparisons to the poem 'Levadi' ('Alone') by Chaim Nachman Bialik (1873–1934), with whom Kaminka was later acquainted.[20] Bialik's poem was written many years later, in 1902, but it describes the cultural and spiritual crossroads that *fin-de-siècle* Hebrew writers like Kaminka and Bialik straddled, between the world of Jewish tradition and study and a commitment to a vernacular, secular (and soon, politically Zionist) Hebrew culture. In his translation, Kaminka reworks Sappho's final line (ἔγω δὲ μόνα κατεύδω, 'but I sleep

---

[18] Kaminka 1887: 144. All translations from the Hebrew are mine unless otherwise noted.

[19] Kaminka 1887: 136, Harshav 2014: 127. Dactylic rhythm was not a common feature of Sappho's poetry (KELLY pp. 56–7, BATTEZZATO p. 125) and certainly is not utilised in this fragment. Kaminka's dactylic-amphibrachic metre therefore departs significantly from the Greek, and in a way that further Hebraises Sappho. This metre, as Harshav has noted, follows the Ashkenazic pronunciation, which places the stress on the penultimate syllable. In later Hebrew translations of Sappho, iambs are more prominent, in keeping with the Sephardic pronunciation, where the stress typically falls on the final syllable.

[20] Bialik 1950: 33.

alone') with the repetition of *ani* ('I') and the addition of an exclamation mark, and in so doing further emphasises and dramatises the solitude of the speaker. Additionally, by rhyming *i* ('island') and *ani*, and internally rhyming *i* and *levadi* ('alone'), Kaminka underscores a state of displacement that Bialik's poem also acknowledges; indeed, Hebrew poetry in the Jewish diaspora of this period had begun to address the tension between place and identity with greater urgency. While I am less invested here in claiming Kaminka's translation as a potential source of Bialik's poem, acknowledging a relation between these texts highlights how tropes of displacement and alienation were circulating in Hebrew original writing and in the literary translations of the late nineteenth century, in the texts and authors that Hebrew writers were choosing to translate.

By the time Klausner's novel appeared in its Hebrew translation, the institutions that had supported Hebrew literature and translation in the Jewish diaspora had either closed definitively or relocated to Mandatory Palestine.[21] Hebrew literature, including translation, was now a fundamental agent of the Jewish nation-building project in Palestine. Following 1887, no further translations of Sappho by Kaminka appeared until he published versions of fr. 20 and part of fr. 96 in the Tel Aviv-based journal *Gazit* in 1944.[22] The publication of Klausner's novel thereby gave the Hebrew-reading public the most expansive compilation of Sappho's poetry in Hebrew translation to date, and by providing a platform for Kaminka, also served as a site of textual encounter for modern Hebrew literatures of the nineteenth and twentieth centuries.[23] Critics of the novel praised the poems in particular, but the growing popularity of twentieth-century Hebrew theatre, an area where Klausner was active, also created a demand for translations from classical Greek and an audience receptive to these works.[24] The novel was, as Klausner correctly estimated, a 'bestseller'.[25]

Klausner reportedly wrote the novel in German while living in Palestine, and even before it appeared in Hebrew translation, public lectures by Klausner and others on the subject of Sappho were reported in

---

[21] Patterson 1985.

[22] Kaminka 1944: 31.

[23] The first stand-alone publication of Sappho's poetry in Hebrew translation did not appear until Bronowski 1978.

[24] Bin-Gorion 1946.

[25] T. Maroz, 'Ha-medi'um' ['The medium'], *Musaf Ha-aretz*, 29 October 1977: 12–13, 34–5, at 13.

the Hebrew press.[26] Though Klausner never made any pretensions that the novel was anything more than imaginative speculation, during her university years in Berlin she had studied Greek drama with, among others, the great philologist Ulrich von Wilamowitz-Moellendorff; it is possible that she could translate the poems directly or at least consult the Greek originals.[27] In an afterword to the German edition, she credits Wilamowitz 1913 and Edmonds 1922a as primary sources for the poetry and other citations from Greek literature that the novel contains.[28] But locating the source of Kaminka's translations is more complicated. Edmonds's collection would have been available by 1944, but in 1887, it is more likely that he consulted German studies and editions of Sappho. In keeping with the nineteenth-century convention for translating Sappho, both the German and Hebrew translations reconstruct her poetry by supplementing the fragments, but their placement in the novel also has a restorative function, since many poems appear in dialogue or are embedded in a description in ways that contextualise the poetry.

In the opening scene of *Sapfo mi-lesbos*, Glaukis, Sappho's fictional and faithful servant, finds her wandering on the rooftop of her house, a habit that preoccupies the servant, since for some time Sappho has been unable to write. But tonight, Sappho tells her, Apollo 'indeed came . . . but he was silent so I spoke'.[29] The words that Sappho 'speaks' constitute fr. 168B.[30] Below, I translate part of this scene into English to illustrate how Klausner integrates Sappho's verse into the plot of the novel:

'And what did you say to him, my lady?'

Sappho's face shone. Her bent, slouching figure straightened up in an instant and she stood there with that wonderful glow that Glaukis had always admired. Steady was Sappho's voice as it rose before the night:

שׁוֹקְעִים יָרֵחַ וְכִימָה,

חֲצוֹת הַלַּיְל עָבָרָה,

---

[26] For example, on 11 April 1941, a talk on 'Sappho the poet and teacher' by Moshe (Max) Schwabe was advertised in the Hebrew press as part of Habima's youth outreach programme. A former student of Wilamowitz, Schwabe was among the founders of the Department of Classical Studies of the Hebrew University of Jerusalem.

[27] Klausner 1954: front jacket copy.

[28] Klausner 1945: 213.

[29] Klausner 1945: 12 ≈ 1946: 6. Glaukis appears to be Klausner's invention.

[30] The attribution to Sappho has been debated; English and Hebrew translations of Sappho continue to include it (e.g. Carson 2002, Bouzaglo 2009, Rayor and Lardinois 2014).

שָׁעָה עַל שָׁעָה חוֹלֶפֶת,

לְבַדִי עַל יְצוּעִי אַךְ אָנִי.

Shok'im yare' ach ve-khima,
chatsot ha-layl 'avara,
sha'a 'al sha'a cholefet,
levadi 'al yetsu'i akh ani

The moon and Pleiades (*kima*) set,
midnight has gone,
hour after hour passes by,
but I am alone on my bed.[31]

And once the echo of her poetry had quieted down, so did Sappho's sorrow fade.[32]

What is remarkable about this poem, and its translation into Hebrew, is how it compares to the version that Kaminka published back in 1887. A few differences stand out. For one, in this version, Kaminka has replaced his earlier Hebrew transliteration of Pleiades – *pleyadim* – with *kima* ('heap, cluster'), a word arguably of Syriac provenance, which can be traced back to the books of Amos and Job in the Hebrew Bible. The substitution of *kima* for *pleyadim* could be understood both in poetic and ideological terms. In Mandatory Palestine, and later Israel, Hebrew language politics exerted pressure to minimise the use of *lo'azit* (foreign language/loan words) in favour of words that were Hebraic in origin. But while this may explain the presence of *kima*, it is also clear that in the 1887 version, pressure to rhyme this line with the third (according to the conventions of maskilic translation) resulted in the use of the masculine plural *-im*, instead of the feminine plural *-ot*, the more common suffix in the Hebrew transliteration of the Greek. In this respect, given that the Pleiades were, by some accounts, named after the seven daughters of the nymph Pleione, the Hebrew *kima*, a feminine word, could be construed as a more faithful translation that nonetheless conforms to a Hebraising translation strategy. By way of further example, the translation of the fourth line now includes the addition of *yetsu'i* ('my bed', 'chamber'). Like *kima*, *yetsu'i* also traces back to the Book of Job, where Job laments, 'in the darkness I have made my bed' (*ba-choshekh ripadti yetsu'i*, 17.13).

---

[31] 'Der Mond is untergegangen und die Plejaden. Es ist | schon mitten in der Nacht, die Stunde eilt vorbei. | Ich aber ruhe allein' (Klausner 1945: 12).

[32] Klausner 1946: 6.

While Kaminka's 1887 translation relies on prosody to shape the translation into a Hebrew poem, his 1946 version accomplishes this Hebraisation through additional strategies of domestication, for example, through a more explicit Jewish intertextuality, as in the example described above. The effect is a poem that situates Sappho's lyric in a more explicitly Jewish context, turning her woes into Jewish sorrows. Additionally, Kaminka's 1946 translation does not rhyme, as it did in 1887, and this is the case for most of the poems in the novel: another way in which the later translation distinguishes itself from *maskilic* poetic conventions. Not to mention that by 1946 these poems would have been read in the Sephardic (Southern/South-eastern European and North African) pronunciation, which had replaced the now 'diasporic' Ashkenazic pronunciation of modern Hebrew – that is, Kaminka's nineteenth-century Hebrew. The iambs and anapaests in the 1946 translation are an indication of how the Sephardic pronunciation, where stress tends to fall on the final syllable, had shaped modern Hebrew rhythms and metre. The changes that Kaminka applies to the 1946 translation of fr. 168B also involve punctuation. Instead of the dramatic dashes and exclamation marks in the 1887 translation, Kaminka opts instead for end-line commas, allowing for pauses that complement the novel's description of Sappho's recitation of the lyric. In other words, in addition to the cultural and ideological shifts described above, differences between the two translations can be attributed to the different contexts in which they appear.

In his review of the Hebrew translation of the novel, Michael Levin found the frequent exegetical *intermetsot* (interludes) of the poetry to be plodding, slowing down an otherwise engaging story of an ageing female poet's romance with a younger man. Nevertheless, he cited fr. 168B as an example of how Klausner makes the world of Sappho come alive. He further explains that this poem portends the doomed love affair that preoccupies the novel: 'The sunrise is only for those whose hearts Aphrodite has come down to lead.'[33] Indeed, fr. 168B is one of several Sapphic lyrics that has proven popular for translators over the centuries.[34] These retranslations illustrate a range of approaches to rendering classical Greek in Hebrew, but as a short lyric it also applies pressure on translators to

[33] M. Levin 1946: 2.
[34] D. Clay 2011. Fr. 1 has proven popular as well with Hebrew translators; in the Hebrew translation of Klausner's novel, the only version of Sappho's poems not by Kaminka is Benzion Benshalom's translation of fr. 1 (Klausner 1946: 44–5; Benshalom's translation first appeared in 1934 in the journal *Gazit*).

distinguish their productions from previous efforts. If we follow the thread of fr. 168B in Hebrew, we encounter new variations by (among others) Yoram Bronowski (1978), Aharon Shabtai (1992), Amir Or (1993), and Shimon Bouzaglo (2009). By the 1970s, Classics was a thriving discipline in Israel, which encouraged the translation of classical texts into Hebrew. With respect to the four translators mentioned here, Bronowski studied Classics as an undergraduate at Tel Aviv University, and Shabtai, Or, and Bouzaglo received their training at the Hebrew University of Jerusalem. This thread underscores the appeal of translation to Hebrew poet–translators (Bronowski being the exception), as well as the fact that most, if not all, of Sappho's Hebrew translators have been men.[35]

In the anglophone context, Sappho became a feminist and gay paragon for twentieth-century women poets, and retranslations of her work by translators like Mary Barnard and Anne Carson have been highly praised.[36] But in Hebrew, Sappho's translation and circulation has relied almost exclusively on the work of male poets and translators,[37] and their intervention has complicated matters with respect to gender and sexuality in Sappho's poetry.[38] In his 1937 translation of fr. 1, Shlomo Dyckman has Aphrodite refer to Sappho's lover or romantic interest as a man, an example of 'straightening' Sappho through heteronormative translation strategies.[39] Kaminka sidesteps the issue of sexuality by avoiding any specific references to the speaker's gender. But in many other, more contemporary cases (some highlighted below), male Hebrew translators have remained faithful to the gender markers in the original text, suggesting a practice of queer translation.[40]

Placing various Hebrew translations of fr. 168B side by side, beginning with the following version by Bronowski, reveals distinct understandings of the Sapphic lyric and a wide range of translation choices and strategies.

---

[35] In the 1940s, the American Hebrew poet Annabelle Farmelant studied Classics with the Hebraist Eisig Silberschlag at Hebrew College (Boston, MA) and later included two lines of Sappho fr. 105(a) in her poem 'The Unwed Maiden' ('Ha-'alma she-lo hitchatna'), quite possibly her own translation (Jacobs 2015: 165–8).

[36] GOFF AND HARLOE pp. 396–7, 401–6.

[37] E.g. Benshalom (1907–68), Shlomo Dyckman (1917–65), Aviv Ekrony (1935–: Ekrony 1971) and Yehuda Liebes (1947–: Liebes 2011).

[38] In the early twentieth century, Hebrew women poets focused their attention on a radical revision of the Jewish textual tradition that involved, in part, reclaiming biblical figures like Miriam and Deborah as models for a feminist Hebrew poetry: Zierler 2004.

[39] Dyckman 1937: 9.

[40] Editors Dory Manor and Ronen Sonis raise this issue in their introduction to *Niflata*, an anthology of LGBTQ poetry which includes Shabtai's translations of Sappho (2015: 16).

Some of these relate to gender, but others coincide with developments in late twentieth-century modern Hebrew poetry, specifically with respect to form.

עָלָה הַיָּרֵחַ

וְכוֹכְבֵי-הַכִּימָה, חֲצוֹת

לַיְלָה, הַ שָּׁעָה עוֹבֶרֶת לְאִטָּהּ

וַאֲנִי נָחָה לְבַדִּי.[41]

'Ala ha-yare'ach
ve-khokhvei-ha-kima, chatsot
layla, ha-sha'a 'overet le-ita
va-ani nacha levadi

The moon rose
and the stars of the Pleiades (*kima*), mid-
night, the hour passes slowly
and I rest alone.[42]

Bronowski was also a translator of Modern Greek, Cavafy in particular, and was invested in highlighting points of linguistic and cultural contact between Greek and Hebrew.[43] As the translation above shows, he is faithful to the syntactical arrangement of the Greek text, but also far more colloquial than previous Hebrew translators, a characteristic praised by Shabtai in his review.[44] Notable features include Bronowski's insistence that the moon is rising (*'ala*) and not setting, his rendering of the Pleiades as *kokhvei ha-kima* ('the stars of *Kima*'), and the preservation of the feminine speaker in the final line of the poem (marked by the feminine singular *nacha*, 'I rest'). In keeping with trends in modern Hebrew poetry in the 1970s, his translations favour minimalism and eschew metre for free verse. Compare this with Shabtai's 1992 translation:

כְּבָר שָׁקְעָה הַלְּבָנָה,

גַּם הַפְּלֵיאָדִים, חֲצוֹת

הַלַּיְלָה. זְמַנִּי חוֹלֵף לוֹ,

וַאֲנִי יְשֵׁנָה לְבַדִּי.[45]

---

[41] Bronowski 1978: 94.

[42] The Hebrew *chatsot layla*, midnight, combines the words meaning 'middle/half' and 'night'. Shabtai's enjambment in lines 2 and 3 is common to Hebrew, and while 'mid/night' is a contrived solution, I retain this enjambment in the English as an approximation of the Hebrew.

[43] Goldwyn 2016.

[44] Shabtai 1978: 16.

Kevar shak'a ha-levana
gam ha-pleyadim, chatsot
ha-layla. Zmani cholef lo,
va-ani yeshana levadi.

Already the Moon (*levana*) has set,
also the Pleiades (*pleyadim*), mid-
night. My time passes by
and I am sleeping alone.

Shabtai is one of the foremost contemporary translators of the Greek classics into Hebrew, and his translations of Sappho, including this poem, appeared as an addendum to his version of Euripides' *Hippolytus*. Though not the case for this poem, Shabtai's translations of Sappho generally acknowledge 'the papyrological event' through the use of brackets and ellipses.[46] Like Bronowski, Shabtai's translation of fr. 168B observes the line breaks in the original Greek lyric, but he also keeps to a more consistent form and metre (trochaic tetrameter) than previous Hebrew translators.

Furthermore, Shabtai's lexical choices suggest an attempt to retain echoes of the Greek, for instance, in the translation of the Greek *selanna* as *levana* (feminine, 'moon'), instead of the masculine *yare'ach* that most other Hebrew translations employ. *Levana* is a poetic variant that traces back to the Hebrew Bible; but the Jewish calendar is also lunar, and in the rabbinic period, the practice developed of offering a blessing for the new moon, *kiddush levana*. In the Talmudic tractate *Sanhedrin*, it is written that 'whoever pronounces the benediction over the new moon in its due time welcomes, as it were, the presence of the *Shechina* ["feminine divine presence"]'.[47] Jewish law specifically prohibits *'avodat kokhavim* ('worship of the stars'), and therefore rabbinic commentary on this practice carefully distinguishes it from forms of idolatry.[48] In Klausner's novel, in the scene where fr. 168B first appears, Sappho claims that a nocturnal encounter with Apollo has reactivated her creative powers. In this respect, Shabtai's translation of *selanna* as *levana* both acknowledges, as does the

---

[45] Shabtai 1992: 14.
[46] Carson 2002: xi. See, for example, Shabtai's translation of fr. 94. Shabtai 1992: 29. In the early 1970s, the periodical *Davar* published translations by Bronowski and Jonah Arouetty that strategically employed ellipses and line breaks to recreate the experience of the fragment; cf. Arouetty 1972: 22, 1973: 21, Bronowski 1974: 20.
[47] Shachter and Freedman 1948: 42a.
[48] Russell and Weinberg 1983: 70–2.

practice of *kiddush levana*, a divine source of renewal that is explicitly feminine, and also provocatively narrows the cultural gap between Hebrew and Greek.

Amir Or's 1993 translation opts for the masculine *sahar*, a half or crescent moon, a post-biblical term that shares a root with *sohar*, prison. This choice preserves a syllabic balance between the first and third line, the latter performing double duty as part of a final rhyming couplet (*cholefet/ shokhevet*). Or's prosody and his attention to cadence result in a translation that evokes the form of the lullaby, but the caesura in the second line and the long dash at the end of the third create dramatic disruptions that recall Kaminka's 1887 translation:

כְּבָר שָׁקַע הַסַּהַר

גַּם כִּימָה; חֲצוֹת

לַיְלָה, שָׁעָה חוֹלֶפֶת–

וַאֲנִי לְבַדִּי שׁוֹכֶבֶת. 49

Kevar shak‘a ha-sahar
gam kima; chatsot
layla, sha‘a cholefet –
va-ani levadi shokhevet.

Already the crescent moon (*sahar*) has set
also the Pleiades (*kima*); mid-
night, an hour is passing –
and I alone am lying [down].

As in the translations by Bronowski and Kaminka (1946), Or's *sha‘a* ('hour') explicitly marks time as feminine, suggesting a close relation between passing time and the alienated speaker, who is also marked as feminine in all three of these Hebrew translations and in the original Greek.

Shimon Bouzaglo's translations of Sappho are the most recent, and reviews of his collection *Mishehi, ani omeret, tizkor otanu* (*Someone, I Say, Will Remember Us*) praise in particular the context he provides for each fragment, which 'sometimes read like true adventure tales'.[50] As is evident in his translation of fr. 168B, Bouzaglo favours strategies, like colloquialism, that contemporise the ancient text:

---

49 Or 1993: 50.
50 Schweitzer 2010.

הֵגִיחַ יָרֵחַ וְעִמּוֹ הַפְּלֵיָאדוֹת;

חֲצוֹת הַלֵּיל,

הַזְּמַן עוֹבֵר,

אֲנִי שׁוֹכֶבֶת לְבַדִּי.[51]

Hegi'ach yare'ach ve-'imo ha-pleyadot;
chatsot ha-leyl,
ha-zman 'over,
ani shokhevet levadi.

The moon burst out (*hegi'ach*) and with [him] the Pleiades (*pleyadot*);
Midnight,
Time passes,
I am lying alone.

Like Kaminka 1887, Bouzaglo dispenses with the enjambment in line 1 and also places the references to midnight and passing time in separate lines. On the other hand, like Rayor, the language he employs is more laconic, his four-syllable lines recalling the poet and literary critic John Addington Symonds's late nineteenth-century English translation ('It is midnight | And time slips by').[52] But where he firmly puts his own stamp on the poem is in the opening word, where the Hebrew *hegi'ach*, break or burst out, renders this regular occurrence as a sudden, forceful event. Like Bronowski, he retains the syntax of the Greek but reverses the meaning of δέδυκε, so that the moon is emerging, not setting, in the Hebrew. But while other translators have rendered Sappho's feminine *selanna* as the masculine *yare'ach*, Bouzaglo's *hegi'ach* spotlights a sexual power dynamic, whereby the feminine *Pleyadot* are made visible by the power of the male *yare'ach*.

In all of these translations, certain lexical choices remain constant from the nineteenth century to the twenty-first. For example, while expressions for 'moon' and 'Pleiades' may change, the translation of 'midnight' remains more or less unaltered. This point of similarity may reveal an area where Hebrew proves less flexible or varied. The translation of 'alone' as *levadi* is also consistent throughout the twentieth century, acquiring over time a meaningful intertextual relation to Bialik's poem 'Levadi'. Negotiations with form and gender shift according to

[51] Bouzaglo 2009: 136.
[52] Symonds in Wharton 1885: 94; for Symonds, see MUELLER p. 47.

developments in modern Hebrew vernacularisation and the cultural discourse on gender and sexuality respectively.

Prins has described the task of reading Sappho as 'a form of riddling', a formulation that extends as well to the translation of what remains of her poems.[53] Such a riddle can be found in the form of another Hebrew translation of fr. 168B, which appeared in the 1968 collection *Lu'ach ha-ohavim* (*A Calendar for Lovers*), edited by the poet Leah Goldberg. Sappho's poem appears in the section 'Heshvan', the Jewish month that usually coincides with October and November:

שָׁקַע הַיָּרֵחַ וְחָוְרוּ

הַכּוֹכָבִים בַּחֲצוֹת הַלָּיְלָה.

חוֹלְפִים עֲלוּמַי וַאֲנִי

לְבַדִּי אֶשְׁכַּב עַל יְצוּעִי.[54]

Shak'a ha-yare' ach ve-chavru
ha-kokhavim ba-chatsot ha-layla.
Cholfim 'alumai va-ani
levadi eshkav 'al yetsu'i.

The moon set and they dimmed,
the stars at midnight.
My youth passes by and I
alone on my bed will lie.

The poem continues for an additional two stanzas, combining this fragment with frr. 47, 130, and 146. This restoration is unique to the Hebrew translation history of Sappho, but the translator responsible for it remains elusive, identified only as 'S. K.', initials that do not correspond to any known Hebrew translator. And while several male translators of Sappho have retained the female speaker, this translation pointedly employs the genderless future tense in the last line. The adjacent page features a sketch of a woman lying in bed and looking out of a window towards a cluster of stars.[55] This may be a clue, given the recurrence of the woman at a window in a number of Goldberg's own poems. Or this may constitute a typographical error, given the similarity between the Hebrew samekh (ס) and mem (מ), in which case the translator could be 'M. K.',

---

[53] Prins 1999: 25.
[54] Goldberg 1968: 85.
[55] The image is by the artist Arie Navon (1909–96); Goldberg 1968: 84.

possibly Margot Klausner herself, who was acquainted with Goldberg.[56] But whether or not Goldberg or Klausner is the translator of this version of fr. 168B, which would make one of them the first woman to translate Sappho into Hebrew, must remain a riddle for future readers, and translators, of Sappho to decipher.

Further Reading

See DeJean 1989a and Prins 1999 for rewritings and fictionalisations of Sappho. Though critical of Klausner's novel, Silberschlag 1977 offers a cogent overview of Hellenic influences on modern Hebrew literature. Close readings of fr. 168B in Reiner and Kovacs 1993 and in D. Clay 2011 address lingering questions of authorship, as well as the text's reference to astronomy and celestial phenomena.

---

[56] Giddon Ticotsky, who has edited several works by Leah Goldberg, shared this speculation in a personal communication.

CHAPTER 32

Sappho in India

Ruth Vanita

As violets fair, O chaste sweet-smiling Sappho

transl. Beram Saklatvala[1]

Violet.

I were the colour of Things (if hue they had)
    That are hard to name.
Of curious, twisted thoughts that men call 'mad'
    Or oftener 'shame'.

Laurence Hope
(Adela 'Violet' Florence Nicolson),
'Song of the colours: by Taj Mahomed'[2]

Sappho's poems came to India in the late eighteenth century. Sir William
Jones (1746–94), whose main life work was in and on India, as philolo-
gist, scholar, translator, and poet, translated fr. 1 into Latin sapphics,[3]
compared Asian poets' immersion in natural beauty with that of
Sappho,[4] and accepted the idea that 'a Greek Emperor' at Constantinople
had Sappho's poems publicly burnt, together with those of Menander
and Alcaeus.[5] Other British poets in India also referred to Sappho in their
verse, for example, Anna Maria (born c.1770).[6] The first Indian poet to
write in English, Henry Derozio (1809–31), took Byron's view of 'burning
Sappho' as a poet of unrequited love,[7] a view that persisted in India for

---

[1] Alcaeus fr. 384, which Saklatvala 1968: 114, like many editors, combines with Sappho fr. 137.
[2] Hope 1902: 140.
[3] Jones 1777: 152–3 = 1807: VI 403 = 1808: I 119–20. The poem is entitled 'Ad eandem' ('To the same'
– i.e. Venus, addressee of the preceding poem), and begins 'Perfido ridens Erycina vultu' ('Erycina
[Venus/Aphrodite], smiling with treacherous expression').
[4] Jones 1772: 176–7 = 1777: 166–7 = 1808: II 141–2 = R. Beck 2009: 75–6.
[5] Jones 1773: unpaginated Preface (signature b7.i) = 1807: XII 343–4.
[6] See Gibson 2011b: 52–3 for this figure, sometimes identified with Anna Maria Jones, wife of Sir
William. She invokes Sappho and the story of Phaon at verse 28 in the poem 'Ode' (subtitled 'to
Della Crusca') as printed in Gibson 2011b: 54–5 (originally written and published in 1793).
[7] *Don Juan* 3.690, published 1821 (McGann 1980–93: V 188); Gibson 2011a: 81.

over a century. In his 1827 sonnet 'Sappho', Derozio quotes a line from Byron's *Don Juan*, and writes:[8]

> Her love was like the raging of a storm,
>   Sweeping all things before it; and her song
> Was like her soul of passion

Although Sappho as lover of women appeared in English as early as John Donne's 'Sappho to Philaenis' (1633), and also in seventeenth- and eighteenth-century English translations,[9] the idea of her as a poet of heterosexual passion, supported by the story of her suicide for Phaon, was accepted as fact in India until the twentieth century.[10]

Throughout the nineteenth century, Sappho was perceived in India as the greatest European woman poet. Her name was used to praise ancient and medieval Indian women poets; thus, the ninth-century Tamil poet Avvaiyar was termed the 'Sappho of Southern India',[11] and the eighth-century love poet Vidya the 'Sappho of India'.[12]

Once Indian women started writing English poetry, Sappho's name was more often associated with them. Of Toru Dutt (1856–77), the first Indian woman to publish poetry in English, E. J. Thompson wrote, 'Toru Dutt remains one of the most astonishing women that ever lived, a woman whose place is with Sappho and Emily Brontë, fiery and unconquerable of soul as they'.[13] Another critic wrote of Sarojini Naidu (1879–1949), 'perhaps even the mind of a Sappho, reborn in a Sarojini Naidu, must pass through Lethe'.[14]

Decades later, Kamala Das (1934–2009) was frequently compared to Sappho, but this comparison was more specific.[15] Das was a confessional poet and fiction-writer in English and Malayalam whose main theme was love. In her controversial 1976 memoir, *My Story*, she described her polyamorous and bisexual feelings.[16] In 1988 she published *Chandana Marangal*, translated into English as *The Sandal Trees and Other Stories*,[17] perhaps the most searing lesbian love story by an Indian woman.

---

[8] Rosinka Chaudhuri 2008: 164.
[9] Vanita 1996: 41–50, R. Robbins 2013: 929–33.
[10] For the Phaon story, see FINGLASS AND KELLY pp. 1–3.
[11] Caldwell 1878: 722; cf. Zvelebil 1974: 125 ('Tamil Sappho').
[12] Schelling 1994.
[13] Thompson 1921: 344. Toru herself follows Plato in calling Sappho 'beautiful': H. Das 1921: 244.
[14] Crippen 1914: 163.
[15] Dwivedi 1983: 32, 54, 117.
[16] George 2000.
[17] V. Harris and Mohamed Ummer 1995.

Sappho came to Das through a mediating literary ancestor – Adela 'Violet' Nicolson (1865–1904), an Englishwoman who lived and died in India, writing under the pen name Laurence Hope, and who in her time was repeatedly compared to Sappho. Das mentions Hope,[18] and Das's biographer quotes her as saying: 'Poet Laurence Hope had many lovers, including a lowly boatman . . . She wrote *The Garden of Kama*, erotic poems of flesh, blood, bangles, and charm bracelets. That is the poet I could identify with.'[19] Hope's rumoured Indian boatman lover recalls Sappho's invented boatman lover, Phaon.

Hope's claim to being an Indian Sappho is grounded in more than a rumour. In her three volumes, about half the poems are in the voices of Indian characters, mostly men. Most of her poems are about passionate love, and are cast in an I–You mode that conceals the speaker's gender while often revealing that of the beloved, which is usually but not always female. Typical is her most famous poem, 'Kashmiri Song' ('Pale hands I loved beside the Shalimar'), which became popular in Europe between the wars, and still appears in numerous works, from Vikram Seth to Mary Higgins Clark.[20]

Unlike Sappho's poems, Hope's generally celebrate clandestine love. In 'From behind the lattice' in her posthumously published *Last Poems*, the ungendered speaker addresses a white woman with 'red-gold hair':

> My great desire (ah, whisper low)
> To plant on thy forbidden snow
> The rosebud of a kiss.[21]

In 'Oh, Unforgotten and Only Lover', the speaker remembers a night spent with the only woman s/he ever loved, confesses to unworthy loves since, and knows that the unforgotten lover considered their night together not just 'a sin' but 'a crime'.[22] The speaker debates ideas of sin and love, in a manner reminiscent of Lord Alfred Douglas's 1892 poem, 'Two Loves'. Douglas uses the word 'shame' for homosexual love:[23]

> He [homosexual love] said, 'My name is Love.'
> Then straight the first [heterosexual love] did turn himself to me,

---

[18] K. Das 1978: 142 (towards end of ch. 37).
[19] Weisbord 2010: 194.
[20] Hope 1902: 93; Gibson 2011b: 321–5, Seth 1993: 57, Clark 2008 (title and, on p. ix, epigraph both come from the poem).
[21] Hope 1905: 48.
[22] Hope 1905: 88.
[23] Douglas 1896: 110.

And cried, 'He lieth, for his name is Shame'
…
Then sighing said the other, 'Have thy will,
I am the Love that dare not speak its name.'

Douglas's 1894 sonnet, 'In Praise of Shame' concludes, 'Whereat I said this song, "Of all sweet passions Shame is loveliest."'[24] The word was a euphemism for homosexual love by the time Hope's speaker declares:

And not for the highest virtues in Heaven,
   The utmost grace that the soul can name,
Would I resign what the sin has brought me,
   Which I hold glory and thou – thy shame.[25]

In the dedication of this volume to her deceased husband, Adela Nicolson confessed having indulged in 'lighter love' and concluded: 'Useless my love – as vain as this regret | That pours my hopeless life across thy grave.'[26] Two months later, having prepared the book for publication, Nicolson, then thirty-nine, committed suicide.

Nicolson had moved to India at the age of twenty-four, with her forty-six-year-old husband. Other British residents in India considered them eccentric because of their closeness to Indians and Indian ways of life. He taught her Urdu and both wore Indian dress; she also dressed as a Pathan boy to travel with him.[27] After he retired, they visited England briefly and met the literati, including Thomas Hardy, but then returned and settled in Kerala, Kamala Das's home state.

Reviewers of *The Garden of Kama* (1901) doubted that Hope's poems were translations of Indian lyrics as they purported to be, and one noted: 'It is now an open secret that "Laurence Hope" is the pen-name of Mrs. Malcolm Nicolson.'[28] Following Nicolson's suicide, R. Garnett reviewed her posthumous volume, praising its 'consuming intensity of passion, recalling the strains of Sappho', and added that 'India and "Laurence Hope" were made for each other'.[29] In an obituary in the *Athenaeum*, Thomas Hardy praised the 'tropical luxuriance and Sapphic fervour' of her poems.[30] It was widely rumoured that she had briefly eloped with

[24] Douglas 1896: 22.
[25] Hope 1905: 89.
[26] Hope 1905: unpaginated prefatory material.
[27] MacMillan 1988: 206–7.
[28] 'Hindoo love poems', *The Academy and Literature* 62/1558 (15 March 1902), 263.
[29] Garnett 1905.
[30] Millgate 2001: 212.

composer Amy Woodforde-Finden (married to an officer in Nicolson's husband's regiment in India), who set 'Kashmiri Song' to music.[31]

As with Sappho, whether or not Nicolson herself experienced lesbian love is less important than the fact that she wrote about it, among many other forbidden types of eroticism, such as male–male love, interracial love, polyamory, and sadomasochism.[32] The clinching evidence is textual, in the little-noticed 'Song of the Colours: by Taj Mahomed' (1901). Six colours speak, and 'Violet' says:

> I were the colour of Things (if hue they had)
>> That are hard to name.
> Of curious, twisted thoughts that men call 'mad'
>> Or oftener 'shame'.
> Of that delicate vice, that is hardly vice,
>> So reticent, rare,
> Ethereal, as the scent of buds and spice,
>> In this Eastern air.[33]

Nicolson's husband and friends called her by the pet name Violet. At the *fin de siècle*, violets were symbols of homosexual, especially lesbian, amours, as in Michael Field's transcreations of Sappho in *Long Ago*: 'Theirs was the violet-weaving bliss, | And theirs the white, wreathed brow to kiss';[34] this symbolism persisted into the late twentieth century.[35]

Given the code meanings of the words 'shame' and 'violet', it is hardly surprising that other homosexual writers were drawn to Hope's poems. In 1946, Somerset Maugham, himself homosexual and associated with India, published 'The Colonel's Lady', based on the lives of the Nicolsons, with whom he was acquainted.[36] In this story, a pompous man discovers that his wife's acclaimed book of poems published under her maiden name recounts her affair with a younger man. Maugham deploys literary allusion to hint that this may stand in for a same-sex relationship. An admiring critic remarks, 'You know, now and then, as I read

---

[31] Castle 2003: 614–15.

[32] 'To Aziz: song of Mahomed Akram' (Hope 1903: 1), 'Devotion of Aziz to Mir Khan' (1903: 100–7), 'Lalila, to the Ferengi lover' (1902: 142–3), 'On the city wall' (1902: 144–5), 'Afridi love' (1902: 45–7), 'Yasmini' (1902: 48–51).

[33] Hope 1902: 140.

[34] Field 1889: 3; JOHNSON ch. 26 pp. 370–1, GOFF AND HARLOE pp. 393–4.

[35] Bergman 2004.

[36] Maugham travelled to India in 1938 and based several of his writings on his experiences, including his 1944 novel *The Razor's Edge* (the title of which is taken from the *Katha Upanishad*) and his 1958 essay 'The Saint', which is about Sri Ramana Maharishi, whose *ashram* (hermitage) in India he had visited.

and re-read those heart-rending pages I thought of Sappho', and a book-seller compares it to Housman's *A Shropshire Lad*.[37] Fifty years later, in his 1997 *ghazal* (Persian or Urdu poem with a very specific metrical and rhyme scheme) 'Tonight', Agha Shahid Ali (1949–2001), a gay poet of Indian origin, uses as an epigraph the first line of Hope's 'Kashmiri Song' and quotes a phrase from its second verse.[38]

Hope inaugurates the connotation that would increasingly accrue to Sappho in twentieth-century India – that of homosexuality in general and lesbianism in particular. Both in literary debates and in popular fiction, Sappho becomes a site for writers to discuss lesbianism. As early as 1936, the Urdu poet Raghupati Sahay (1896–1982), whose pen name was Firaq Gorakhpuri and whose homosexuality, although he never stated it, was an open secret, defended homoeroticism in the Urdu *ghazal* by listing ten great writers, among whom he included two women:[39]

> Sir, are you aware of Shakespeare's Sonnets and their motives? Do you know of Walt Whitman and his poem 'To a Boy'? Have you heard Sappho's name? Do you know the meaning of Lesbianism? Do you know of the refined and pure book called *The Well of Loneliness*?

In 1945, conversely, in woman writer Bani Ray's Bengali story, 'Sappho', the woman narrator is disgusted by Mondira, a spinster described as 'manly' and 'masculine'.[40] A beautiful young man sets out to seduce Mondira and then rejects her, whereupon she commits suicide. The narrator frequently apostrophises Sappho as the first and unequalled woman poet of passion, 'the dark eyed luscious Greek beauty who had breasts hard as ivory, thighs like silver, toes bright as gold, eyes shining like blue sapphire', who 'stood against nature' by making love to a woman, and on whom nature avenged herself.[41] The story ends: 'The glamourous woman poet in the glowing background of Lesbos and this girl without wealth or beauty – there was nothing to link them together, yet both were destined for an identical end.'[42] Twenty years later, Rajkamal Chaudhuri in his homophobic Hindi novel *Machhli mari hu'i* (*Dead Fish*) compares his

[37] Maugham 1947: 12, 16.
[38] Ali 2003: 82–3.
[39] Kidwai 2000: 265.
[40] Ray 1977: 34.
[41] Ray 1977: 33.
[42] Ray 1977: 42.

bisexual heroine to Sappho.[43] All the other writers on homosexuality that Chaudhuri cites are modern.[44]

Two mid-century Urdu poets engage with Sappho in a more nuanced manner. Though they try to explain away her love poems to women, they use terms and categories from eighteenth-century Urdu lesbian-themed poetry to frame female–female desire. Indian poetry by both men and women has a long tradition of bridal mysticism, with female speakers addressing male divinities. However, the late eighteenth-century Lucknow poets Sa'adat Yar Khan, pen name Rangin ('Colourful') (1755–1835), and Insha Allah Khan, pen name Insha ('Elegant Style') (1756–1817) invented a type of non-mystical Urdu poetry in which female speakers, usually addressing other women, discussed their everyday lives and loves, especially love between women. This type of poetry, known as *rekhtī* (henceforth *rekhti*), became the rage for a while but, after the defeat of the 1857 revolt, was labelled obscene and excised from the canon.[45]

Urdu poets, however, continued to read it. Between 1936 and 1941, the eminent modernist and bohemian Urdu poet Mohammad Sana'ullah Dar, pen name Miraji (1912–49), wrote a series of essays on world poets, in a literary magazine published from Lahore (then in pre-Partition India). Among them was 'Maghrib ki Sabse Bari Sha'ira: Sappho' ('The greatest woman poet of the west: Sappho'). The essay is devoted to narrating Sappho's life, stating as facts many legends, including those of her marriage and suicide. He speculates that had Lesbos not been at war during Sappho's youth she might not have spent as much time in the company of '*humjins* companions', and her verse might not have focused on the theme that caused it to be burnt later.[46] *Humjins*, a created compound (from *hum*, meaning 'we' or 'shared' and *jins,* meaning 'body'), is still used as a translation of 'homosexual'.

Miraji draws on Indic lexicons, writing that the ancient Greeks considered Sappho a daughter of Eros and Aphrodite, and glossing these names in parentheses as Kamadeva and Rati (the Hindu god of love or desire and his wife, whose name means 'erotic pleasure'). He notes that Sappho uses a term for her female companions which later came to mean *tawaif* (the north Indian word for 'courtesan'), but it did not have this meaning

43 Rajkamal Chaudhuri 1966: 115.
44 Rajkamal Chaudhuri 1966: 122.
45 Vanita 2012.
46 Miraji 2009: 232.

in her time. Nor, he continues, should we consider this term as similar to
zanakhi or *dogana*.[47] These two words, drawn from nineteenth-century
Urdu glossaries, occur frequently in *rekhti* poetry, referring to a woman's
female lover. *Zanakhi* comes from *zanakh* ('wishbone'), because women
formed couples by breaking a wishbone together, while *dogana*, from *do*
('two'), refers to twinned fruits and by extension to a woman's intimate
companion, who is her second self. Both words also referred to sexual
intercourse between women.[48]

Miraji states that Sappho's term for her companions had the meaning
that *saheli* (a woman's female friend) or *dupatta badal bahen* ('sisters by
exchanging veils') now has. The latter term refers to north Indian wom-
en's practice of exchanging items of dress to declare themselves sisters;
men exchanged turbans to become brothers.[49] Miraji seems unaware that
female lovers in *rekhti* also perform this ritual. Insisting that Sappho's
relations with women were neither sexual nor pedagogic, he writes that
she gathered around her young women who were informal and intimate
with one another.[50] He terms the young women *humdum* and *humraaz*.
Humdum, literally 'those who breathe together', refers to close compan-
ions, and is used in both friendly and romantic contexts; *humraaz* means
'those who share secrets'. Translating Sappho's verses about virginity into
Urdu, Miraji speculates that she had suffered some harm of which she
could not speak, and that purity was very dear to her, which is why she
could not surrender her body or soul to any man, but the untouched
bodies and souls of unmarried girls were pleasing to her.[51]

He proceeds to say that Sappho developed romantic feelings for several
girls, especially Atthis, which 'may upset the narrow-minded',[52] and that
although he has no argument in favour of such love, we should expand
the circuit of our thoughts to view these events sympathetically.
Suggesting that love poems to Atthis may have caused Sappho's works to
be destroyed, he asks,

> now when a few fragments remain to us, can we say that the world has
> benefited from the destruction of these gems? Rather, we would say that a
> few narrow-minded people deprived posterity of beautiful poems. For

---

[47] Miraji 2009: 238.
[48] Vanita 2005: 184–8.
[49] Vanita 2012: 118, 139, 246–7.
[50] For the European scholarly background to this conception of Sappho, see GOFF AND HARLOE.
[51] Miraji 2009: 237.
[52] Miraji 2009: 239.

beauty does not arise from rules or norms. Rules and norms change, they are born and die every day. But beauty is not an everyday matter.[53]

Miraji's Sappho is constructed on the *Well of Loneliness* model, and her suicide for Phaon is the outcome of lifelong anguish. He translates a few poems, but omits fr. 1, and adds three lines to fr. 31 to end it thus:[54]

> But alas, this is not in my fate
> It's written in my fate that I sit here, sorrowing
> Life does not release me from sorrow
> Even death seems not far from me.[55]

This construction derives from the typical male lover in the Urdu love poem (*ghazal*), who yearns and pines but rarely enjoys fulfilment. Women lovers in *rekhti* form couples and are often happy, but having rejected them as analogues for Sappho, Miraji casts her as a great poet and therefore necessarily sorrowful. He himself took his pen name from his beloved, Mira Sen, a Hindu girl who did not return his feelings, and modelled himself partly on medieval woman mystic Mirabai, whose songs express a largely unfulfilled yearning for union with Krishna.[56] He draws an implicit parallel between the conventions of Urdu and ancient Greek poetry, pointing out that poems in Sappho's era were composed not for the solitary reader but to be sung or recited to a group of listeners.[57]

The next Urdu commentator was Abdul Aziz Khalid (1927–2010), a poet of Indian origin who moved to Pakistan at Partition. An erudite scholar who knew many languages including Hindi, Sanskrit, Arabic, and Persian, he was a poet and translator, who translated the *Mahabharata* into Urdu. In his translation of Sappho, *Sarood-e Rafta* (*Lost Lyrics*), he adopts an eclectic style, sometimes heavily Persianised and Arabicised, and at other times colloquial, also using Hindi and Sanskrit words.[58] It is unclear whether he translated from Greek or from English, because he makes some errors, translating *Dika* as *Disa*, possibly

---

[53] Miraji 2009: 239.
[54] Miraji 2009: 241.
[55] All translations from Urdu are my own.
[56] Patel 2002: 241–54.
[57] Miraji 2009: 227–8.
[58] Urdu and Hindi are the same language grammatically and syntactically, sharing most of their everyday vocabulary, and are not distinguishable as spoken languages. However, they are written in different scripts; also, Urdu literature tends to have more Persian and Arabic words in its vocabulary and Hindi more Sanskrit words. Some Urdu poets use more Arabic and Persian words than do others, just as some Hindi poets use more Sanskrit words than do others.

from English *Dica*, which was often used in nineteenth- and early twentieth-century translations, and continued to be used much later too.[59]

He chooses as epigraph a famous phrase from the poet Ghalib, *Zikr us parivash ka* ('Speaking of that fairy-faced one'), which is often used in a complimentary way by Urdu biographers; Abdul Salaam Khurshid used it as the title of an essay about Khalid himself. Opening with a string of quotations about Sappho, from Plato to Byron and Miraji, Khalid's introduction terms her the greatest of all women poets, and says that the ancient Greeks admired the beauty of her work as much as they did Helen's physical beauty.[60] He too uses the word *tawaif* for 'courtesan'.

Khalid follows Miraji in arguing that Sappho's relationships with her female friends (*saheli*) and disciples (*shagird*) was innocent (*masoom*) and in keeping with the spirit of Greek religion. He claims that the word *hetaira*, used by Sappho for her companions, later became associated with homosexuality, as a result of which Sappho's name was tarnished, people tried to show that she was a voluptuary, and colourful, pleasurable (*rangin'o laziz*) stories were told about her.[61]

The words that Khalid uses for homosexuality have specific connotations in Urdu. One, *shahidbazi*, refers to male pursuit of sweethearts, generally beautiful male youth, and the other, *s'atari*, refers to women who love women, and also to dildoes. Departing from Miraji, Khalid states that there were two Sapphos, putting this forward not as a theory but as fact.[62] He says the other Sappho was a *deredaar tawaif* ('high-class courtesan') and a *kasbi* ('prostitute') who also wrote poetry and who threw herself from the Leucadian rock for love of Phaon.

Following a strategy employed by nineteenth- and early twentieth-century English translators, such as Michael Field (p. 461 above), Khalid adds many lines to the fragments, but does not indicate which are his additions and which translations. He uses an inordinate number of exclamation marks, one in almost every poem; virtually all the smaller fragments become one-liners with exclamation marks. Many of his translations are replete with Arabic and Persian words, but he also uses the Hindi term *deviyon* for both goddesses and women, in accordance with modern Hindu practice, and draws on Sanskritic phraseology, as in

---

[59] Field 1889: 20–1, Carman 1904: 14, Way 1920: 15–16, M. Barnard 1958: 19.
[60] Khalid 1959: 9.
[61] Khalid 1959: 12.
[62] For this story, see KIVILO pp. 12, 17, COO pp. 275–6, JOHNSON ch. 26 p. 367.

Mrig naini hans roopi goriyon! ('Doe-eyed, swan-like fair ones!', fr. 41).
His addition of Urdu tropes often dilutes a poem's power, as in fr. 1:[63]

> Don't be sorrowful, don't weep,
> The fairy will descend into the glass, the idol will speak,
> Willingly or not, she will love you
> Where's the beloved (*mashuq*) who has not turned lover (*ashiq*)?
> She'll beat her head to your verses for hours
> Your melodies will run through her veins . . .

Likewise, he ends fr. 31 with an odd, tacked-on couplet:[64]

> Ae naubahaar-e naaz, rahe tu sadaa suhaag!
> Us mast ko tu laghzish-e mastaanaa le chali!
>
> Oh delicacy of the spring, may you remain ever happily wedded!
> You lead that drunken one down a pleasurable slippery slope!

In this invented couplet that has nothing to do with Sappho's fragment,
Persian words like *laghzish* combine strangely with *suhaag*, the Hindu
word for a married woman's status, and the idea of marriage combines
equally strangely with that of her seducing a man intoxicated with desire.

His translations of the shorter fragments escape the verbosity of the
longer ones. Thus he turns fr. 143 into a couplet:[65]

> Kinaar-e darya chane ke paudhe
> Ajab bahaaren dikha rahe hain!
>
> Chickpea plants on the seashore
> Display a rare splendour!

Occasionally, his expansions are charming, as in this *rekhti*-like translation of fr. 81, which adds details and puns, altering the meaning:[66]

> Lekin sundar, sudaul Disa!
> Kya saunf ke taaze konpalon se
> Apni zulfon ko baandhti ho
> Mehndi lagi naazuk ungliyon se?
> Is baat ko jaan-e man na bhoolo
> Karti hain shaguftagi ki pariyaan
> Pyaar un se jo phool daaliyaan hon
> Jin ke joode hon soone soone
> Rahti hain voh door door un se!

---

[63] Khalid 1959: 22.
[64] Khalid 1959: 24.
[65] Khalid 1959: 65.
[66] Khalid 1959: 38.

But beautiful, well-shaped Disa!
Why do you, with delicate, henna-stained fingers,
Bind your tresses with fresh fennel buds?
Don't forget, my life, that the fairies of blossoming
Love those who wear flowers.[67]
They stay far from those
Whose knotted hair is bare!

Khalid was a modernist poet, and most of his translations are in free verse, but he employs some internal rhymes and catchphrases from Hindi verse, as in fr. 48 (which he expands to thirteen lines): *Ae mohini murat! Ae sundar surat!* ('Oh enchanting one! Oh beautiful face!'),[68] and fr. 96, which he transcreates in rhyming quatrains.[69]

Later in the century, several Indian writers in English interpret Sappho variously. Keki N. Daruwalla (1937–) uses sapphic stanzas in his four 'Sappho Poems', sometimes with unintended comic results, as in his 'Sappho to Aphrodite':[70]

Bring back Gongyla to my side!
May she once more become my bride!
May she, her lyre and her fire
beside me purr!

Marxist writer K. Satchidanandan (1946–), in his 'Burnt Poems', which were originally in Malayalam and translated by him into English, claims not only that girls' love poems worldwide seldom escape being burnt but also that women mystics, Hindu and Christian, hid their sexual desires under 'the veil of piety' to escape fire. Oddly inverting the history of Sappho's reception in the West, he concludes: 'Of course, Sappho: | she was saved only as | her love poems were | addressed to women'.[71]

Equally oddly, Indian English poet and critic Rukmini Bhaya Nair (1952–), positing a 'feminine sexuality' which 'rejects strong heterosexual boundaries',[72] and claiming that Sappho's poetry survives '*only* in fragments because it posed such a threat within her culture',[73] suggests that

---

[67] There is a pun here: *daaliyaan hon* could be a *rekhti*-type dialect verb, 'those who wear flowers', or the plural noun *daaliyan*, 'those who are flowering branches'.

[68] Khalid 1959: 39.

[69] Khalid 1959: 56–7.

[70] Daruwalla 2006: 8–9.

[71] Alexander 2018: 281–2.

[72] Nair 2002: 202.

[73] Nair 2002: 211 (his italics).

postcolonial women writers should develop 'a sexual poetics that embraces a sensibility that I call, after Sappho, a "hermaphrodite aware- ness"'.[74] Though her poem 'Love', a meditation on the nature of love, is entirely about heterosexual emotion,[75] in 'Hermaphrodite Longings', a *hijra* who tries to rob her on the street reminds her of Sappho:[76]

> Sappho knew well
>
> That scored, transvestite passage
> That politic mixing
> Of the sexes
>
> …
>
> It was your face I saw
> In the mutilated body, in the coarse
> Horsewhip tactics of that hijra …
>
> …
>
> I had to face
>
> Your terrible longing, Sappho

Though Sappho's poetry has nothing to do with transvestism or transgendering, this rewriting of her is in tune with a common modern Indian tendency to conflate same-sex desire with androgyny and transgender, based on the assumption that same-sex desire is an inversion of cross-sex desire and must therefore arise from a desire to change sex.

More interestingly, Sujata Bhatt (1956–) intersperses lines from Sappho in her 'Reading Sappho, I am reminded of Chickpeas',[77] to recall her mother as a sweet-voiced young woman, finding many uses for chickpeas (which take various forms in Indian cuisine), wearing silk garments and flowers in her hair, and later, on her deathbed, telling her daughter not to cry.

India's first lesbian writers claimed Sappho too. In the poem 'Mitylene in Bombay' published in 1986 by Inez Vere Dullas (1914–94), Sappho's songs are sung 'by voices new, in tropic clime';[78] Gillian Hanscombe and Suniti Namjoshi quote Sappho in the title of a 1991 essay about lesbian sensibility in lyric poetry;[79] and in 1999 six women in Calcutta founded an organisation, Sappho for Equality (www.sapphokolkata.in), whose website bears the legend 'you may forget, but let me tell you this: I

---

[74] Nair 2002: 201.
[75] Nair 1999: 120–5.
[76] Nair 1999: 132–7 (quoted passsage from pp. 133–4).
[77] Bhatt 2015: 39–40.
[78] Printed in Vanita and Kidwai 2000: 347.
[79] Hanscombe and Namjoshi 1991.

someone in some future time will think of us'. From 1998, when the film *Fire* launched the first public debate in India about lesbianism, journalists have used 'Sappho' as a signifier.[80]

Indian classicists in England and in India developed a special relationship with Sappho. Poet and philosopher Sri Aurobindo (1872–1950) 'waxed enthusiastic over Sappho' when studying at Cambridge;[81] as K. D. Sethna (aka Amal Kiran) points out, Aurobindo wrote in sapphic stanzas a mystical poem, 'Descent', about being possessed by God and experiencing the oneness of the universe, which in some ways recalls Sappho's poems about the descent of Aphrodite and Eros to earth.[82]

Beram Saklatvala, aka Henry Marsh (1911–76), poet and historian, belonged to an eminent Indian Parsi family which migrated to England. In the introduction to his *Sappho of Lesbos* (1968), Saklatvala ably assesses the poet, her reception, and unproven stories about her, such as that of her suicide. He points out a fact that commentators rarely notice after Greece's unquestioned absorption into Europe: that 'her birthplace was in fact in Asia Minor' because Lesbos was 'an outpost of Greece in Asia', and part of the Persian Empire about a century after her birth.[83] Quoting Maximus of Tyre's comparison of Sappho's loves to Socrates', Saklatvala dismisses modern attempts to explain away her love for women, but reads this love as colouring 'all her poems' with sorrow, 'with the sense of passion denied and of desire unfulfilled', while her poems about marriage 'are full of passion and of joys remembered'.[84]

He translates many of the poems into accomplished sapphic stanzas. With those fragments wherein words have survived only on one side, either right or left, he employs the ingenious method of italicising Sappho's words and completing them with his own. This method is the opposite of that employed by translators like Anne Carson, but the results are often surprisingly satisfying, even beautiful, as in fr. 63:[85]

> Dream, in the dark night, *here in my silent room,*
> You come when sleep *like to a god descends;*
> Sweet god of power, from pain *he sets me free,*
> To separate the power *of love from sorrow.*

---

[80] R. Martins, 'Sappho comes out of the closet', *Telegraph*, 3 December 2006: 1; 'Sappho out of the Indian closet', *Hindustan Times*, 15 November 2006: 4.

[81] Sethna 1998: 51.

[82] Sethna 1998: 52–4.

[83] Saklatvala 1968: 3.

[84] Maximus of Tyre, *Oration* 18.9 (test. 20); Saklatvala 1968: 9, 10, 11, 14.

[85] Saklatvala 1968: 100.

And yet I hope not to be joined *in this*.
Nothing from all the gods *can give me pleasure*
For, being not *with you now, the dream is false*.
All the sweet joys of love *cannot console me!*
Would it might happen to me *that you came*
In the real night, to give me for my love,
Not the dark dreams of night, but your true presence!

There is an early connection between the matrix of Sappho's songs and the earliest Indian songs: her poetry 'is rhizomically connected to Vedic hymns to the goddess of the dawn, and to the verse forms of the earliest Indian epics'.[86] *Rigveda* 1.81.5, 'None like thee, Indra, has ever been born or will be' has been compared in this regard with fr. 56.[87]

Perhaps for this reason, one of the most successful translations is Sisir Kumar Das's out-of-print translation into Bengali.[88] Bengali is a daughter of Sanskrit, and Sanskrit a sister of Greek; Das's use of a Sanskritic Bengali vocabulary produces fine effects. An eminent scholar of comparative literature, Das translates ninety ancient Greek poems, eighteen by Sappho. He selects those of Sappho's fragments that lend themselves to translation as complete-sounding poems, translating some in free verse and some in metrical forms, four in an approximation of the sapphic stanza. His translations of frr. 1 and 31 are particularly successful.

Das's translations stay close to the originals; he uses English words like 'violet' and 'hyacinth' when there are no Indian equivalents. In his extensive endnotes, Das presents legends about and debates around Sappho. He uses *shohocharini* for female companion, a word that conveys the sense of living and walking together. He notes that Sappho was later accused of being *shomokami* (one who desires the same sex) but remarks that most ancient Greek love poems are *shomokami*.[89]

In fr. 96, which he translates in three-line stanzas, simple equivalents for 'moon' (*chaand*) and 'rose-fingered' (*golaap aangul*) combine with the Indic *jholmol* ('sparkling, twinkling') and *godhuli* ('cow-dust', the golden haze produced by returning cattle at dusk) to create felicitous visual and sound effects:

---

[86] duBois 2010: 57.
[87] West 2007: 104.
[88] Many thanks to the author's wife and his daughter-in-law, Shampa Roy, for sending me scans of the book, and to Abhishek Chatterjee and Srijeet Mukherjee for reading the poems aloud to me and checking my translations.
[89] S. Das 1989: 57.

Ekhon she'i lidiyaar mohilaa shobhaay
Roopey jholmol korey, jaimon aakashey
Golaap aangul chaand daikhadiley godhuleer sheshe.[90]

Now she, in the company of Lydian women,
Sparkles in beauty, as in the sky
The rose-fingered moon emerges as twilight ends.

In fr. 94, he employs three-line stanzas with two shorter lines followed by
a longer one, as in the original, and fills out the last stanza, as do many
English translators. Translators into Indian languages can draw on Hindu
equivalents for the Greek gods, goddesses, altars, and worship rituals:

She'i ghoore ghoore phira, debotaar poojaar beditey
She'i bonobhoomi, she'i paakheeder abishraam daak
Nirjoney dujoney.[91]

That same encircling the gods' altar to offer puja,
That same forest, those same incessant bird calls
We both, alone together.

It would appear, now that transnational scholarship is spreading its
wings, that 'in the future' there will be many more in India who will
'remember' Sappho and her 'immortal daughters, [her] songs'.[92]

Further Reading

For more on the reception of classical literature in India, see Vasunia
2013, although he does not mention Sappho. The thirty-six volume
Complete Works of Sri Aurobindo, now available online (www.sriaurob-
indoashram.org/sriaurobindo/writings.php), will repay further study, as
he both commented on and imitated many classical authors.

---

[90] S. Das 1989: 16.
[91] S. Das 1989: 16.
[92] Fr. 147; Dioscorides, *Greek Anthology* 7.407.9–10 (test. 58).

CHAPTER 33

Sappho in China and Japan

Jingling Chen

The Isles of Greece, The Isles of Greece,
Where burning Sappho loved and sung.

Lord Byron might not have expected that his reference to Sappho, from a poem on modern Greece then under Turkish rule, would bring the ancient Greek poet to modern China – and East Asia – in a most distinguished fashion.[1] For more than a millennium, the East Asian cultural sphere was dominated, politically and culturally, by the Chinese. But from the second half of the nineteenth century, Western imperial incursions transformed the power dynamic in the area. In less than a few decades, the Chinese found themselves outmatched not only by the West, but also by Japan, their traditionally subordinate neighbour, after China's defeat in the First Sino-Japanese War (1894–5). It was in this moment that Sappho made her debut, through Byron's song, in China's literary imagination.

Byron's verses appeared in a 1902 political novel *The Future of New China*.[2] The author, Liang Qichao (1873–1929), had been a leader in the brief 1898 Hundred Days' Reform – an effort on the part of intellectuals to revive China in the aftermath of the war. After the failure of the reform, Liang went into exile in Japan, where he continued to encourage his countrymen to embrace nationalism, this time through writing. A man of letters at heart, Liang considered nothing more powerful than the appeal of fiction to the emotions. He borrowed Byron's sharp contrast between Greece's glorious past and colonised present to alert his readers to China's similar situation, as an ancient civilisation suffering degeneration. And his readers would, like his protagonists, find particularly moving Byron's outcry that 'A land of slaves shall ne'er be mine'.[3] 'The Isles of

---

[1] *Don Juan* 3.689–90, published 1821 (McGann 1980–93: v 188).

[2] Originally serialised in the Yokohama magazine *New Fiction* (*Xin xiaoshuo*) in 1902, the novel was published as Liang Qichao 1936, where Byron's poem appears at pp. 44–5 (along with a few lines from *The Giaour*, pp. 42–3).

[3] *Don Juan* 3.783 (McGann 1980–93: v 192); Liang Qichao 1936: 46.

Greece', which circulated under the Classical Chinese name 'Ai Xila' ('Lamenting Greece'), would become one of the most famous Western poems in China, available in various translations.[4]

For Chinese intellectuals at the turn of the twentieth century, 'Lamenting Greece' was a substitute for lamenting China. Distressed by the dismal reality, they shed tears for a foreign country in whose story they saw that of their own. Sappho, however, standing at the beginning of Byron's poem, presents a counterpoint to the tragedy of modern Greece. She represents Greece's ancient splendour, which intellectuals could use as a symbol of the glories of Chinese civilisation. The Chinese were of course not the only people fascinated by Byron's poems about modern Greece. Particularly because he met his demise in Greece, Byron had a sweeping influence over Westerners' ambivalent attitude towards the nation, a nation they saw both as the origin of their civilisation and a laggard country which they helped to liberate. Such feelings prompted Victor Hugo to coin the term *Grèce de Byron* in contrast to *Grèce d'Homère* ('Byron's Greece' to 'Homer's Greece'), *notre soeur* to *notre mère* ('our sister' to 'our mother').[5] But when China too fell under Byron's spell, *Grèce d'Homère* became *Grèce de Sappho*, since Sappho was evoked at the beginning of a poem that played a role in establishing modern China's nationalist discourse.

Grèce de Sappho would be verified by the remarkable attention given to Sappho in China in the decades to come. She was the first ancient Greek author introduced in detail by Zhou Zuoren (1885–1967), the most prominent translator and scholar of Greek literature in modern China, in 1914, two years before he wrote about Homer.[6] Three decades later, Zhou would again write a book, entitled *The Greek Poetess Sappho*, a combination of his own comments and the translated excerpts from Arthur Weigall's *Sappho of Lesbos. Her Life and Times*.[7] Published in 1951, Zhou's book was the first in China that focused on a single Greek poet or writer; it also provides a relatively complete collection of the extant poetry of Sappho. In China's Republican era (1912–49), some of those poems were

---

[4] It was given the title 'Ai Xila' in 1905 by Ma Junwu (1881–1940), a prominent educator and revolutionary; the poem can be found in Ma Junwu 1991: 438–45. Other important early translations include a collaboration between Zhang Binglin (aka Zhang Taiyan, 1868–1936), a leading figure in Chinese philology and the nationalist revolution, and Su Manshu (1840–1918), a Buddhist monk and important translator of European Romantic literature; and a 1914 translation by Hu Shih (1891–1962), a founding father of modern Chinese literature.
[5] Victor Hugo, 'Navarin', 1827. For Byron's influence on Hugo's poem, see Roessel 2002: 42–71.
[6] Zhou Zuoren, 'Sappho, The Greek Poetess' ('Xila nüshiren') in 2009: 1 308, 337–9.
[7] Zhou Xiashou (Zhou Zuoren) 1951; Weigall 1932.

already translated, both directly from Greek and from translations in modern Western languages, by various writers and poets, including Zhou himself. Some of her most famous poems were translated into Chinese multiple times.

Sappho continued to be translated during the Maoist era, though the translations generally remained unpublished.[8] As the socialist revolution ebbed by the late 1970s, the passion for Sappho returned. The poet Luo Luo (1927–98) produced a phenomenal rendition of Sappho in 1986, based on Mary Barnard's English translation.[9] Luo Luo's translations of Sappho were published as a stand-alone, single-author volume, an honour enjoyed by only a handful of Western poets in 1980s China. Finally, at the turn of the new century, Xiaofei Tian (1971–), Professor of Chinese Literature at Harvard University and a poet in her own right, published a book entitled *Sappho. The Making of a Literary Tradition*.[10] This edition of Sappho's poetry includes an extensive introduction, detailed commentaries on the Sapphic poems and their Chinese translations, supplementary materials from the reception history of Sappho in the West, and, as a coda, Tian's own poem dedicated to Sappho. The Chinese poet thus strives to integrate the Chinese reception into the Sapphic tradition from the Greek archaic period on. Unlike Zhou's book, which was received lukewarmly by Chinese readers, Tian's volume became a bestseller.

Across the East China Sea, when a few of Sappho's poems were translated into Chinese in the early twentieth century, there was already a Japanese edition of Sappho available. In 1923, a young writer, Ozeki Iwaji (1896–1980), published a book entitled *Selected Famous Poems of Sappho* in Tokyo.[11] Next year, another Tokyo press republished the same book with a different title, *Poems of Romantic Love*.[12] Both Ozeki's books contain thirty-five poems by Sappho, including some of her most famous songs, such as frr. 1 (under the title 'Hymn to Aphrodite') and 31 ('Hymn to the Lover'). In *Poems of Romantic Love*, he also adds an epilogue to introduce Sappho's life and her poetry.[13]

---

[8] For example, Yang Xianyi (1915–2009), an important translator of Greek and Roman literature, translated nine poems of Sappho during the 1950s and 60s, but they were not published until decades afterwards (Yang Xianyi 1995: 332–6). For Chinese translations of Sappho in the twentieth century, see also Liu Qun 2012.

[9] Luo Luo 1989.

[10] Tian 2003.

[11] Ozeki Iwaji 1923.

[12] Ozeki Iwaji 1924.

[13] 'On Sappho' ('Saffuo nitsuite', Ozeki Iawji 1924: 89–98).

Ozeki notes at the end of the epilogue that he bases his translations on various English renditions. But fr. 104(a), two lines in the original Greek, becomes a ten-line poem, the short lines in Ozeki's translations reflecting his own style.[14] The introductory epilogue also contains obvious errors: for example, Sappho is considered the ninth Muse rather than the tenth.[15] Ozeki's renditions did not remain popular; he would be remembered largely as an author and critic of children's literature. In the late 1980s, when Kutsukake Yoshihiko (1941–), author of a currently popular translation of Sappho, recounted the history of Sappho's reception in Japan, he omitted Ozeki's books. Kutsukake mentions a literary rendition of twelve Sapphic poems by Hinatsu Kōnosuke (1890–1971), a Romantic poet, who translated from the Canadian poet Bliss Carman's 1904 literary rendition *Sappho. One Hundred Lyrics.* Kutsukake particularly pays homage to Kure Shigeichi (1897–1977), a prominent scholar and translator of the classics. Twenty-five poems in Kure's anthology of Greek and Roman lyrics are under Sappho's name.[16] The publication of Ozeki's translation twice in two years, however, reveals the popularity Sappho already enjoyed before the Showa period (1926–89).

Indeed, Sappho would not have been an unfamiliar name for Ozeki's generation. He uses the same transliteration for her name as that deployed by Ueda Bin (1874–1916), a famous critic and poet of the Meiji and early Taishō periods, to whom Kutsukake also pays his respect. In 1895 Ueda wrote a long essay on Greek literature and philosophy from Homer to the Roman Empire: a history, according to Ueda, threaded by a love for what is beautiful and joyful, nourished in Greece's sunny land and warm weather. The essay discusses Sappho, whose 'fragrance remains radiating' (餘香薫る), and renders her name into the katakana サッフォ ('Saffuo').[17] A year later, Ueda published another long journal article, this time dedicated entirely to Sappho, presenting her as a representative of Greek literature and art, and passionately praising her poetry and defending her character. Such stories as her problematic relation with her pupils and her suicide for Phaon, he points out, are merely the baseless conjecture or even malicious inventions of later literature. So is the rumour of

---

[14] 'Evening' ('Yūgure', Ozeki Iawji 1924: 33–4).

[15] 'On Sappho' (Ozeki Iawji 1924: 93).

[16] Kutsukake Yoshihiko 1988 (five editions were published between 1988 and 2006), Hinatsu Kōnosuke 1937: 78–101, Kure Shigeichi 1948. For Kure Shigeichi, see Taida 2015.

[17] Ueda Bin 1895, collected in Ueda Bin 1901; paragraph on Sappho at p. 12. Ueda's transliteration is one of a few variations in Japanese.

her ugly appearance. How could Sappho from Lesbos, famous for her pretty girls, not be pretty?[18]

Ueda quotes six Sapphic verses in his own Japanese translations (frr. 104(a), 105(a), 105(b), 132, 136, 137). The evening song (fr. 104(a)) first made its way into a 1922 posthumously published extension to his most famous work, *Sounds of the Ocean Tides,* a 1905 publication that collects his translations of European poems from Dante to French Symbolism.[19] When expanded in 1927, this edition of Ueda's collected poems also included frr. 105 and 137. From then on, the three poems would continue to appear together in *The Extended Sounds of the Ocean Tides* in varied editions of his works.[20] In the late Meiji period (1868–1912), Ueda became famous young and died young. *Sounds of the Ocean Tides,* particularly in its later circulation, would continue to win the hearts of Japanese young men and women. His renditions, along with his introductions to Sappho, would contribute to her imaginary in Japan's literary life. I will return to his work after taking a closer look at the Chinese and Japanese translations and their contexts.

In his 1914 introduction to Sappho, Zhou Zuoren includes translations of five short Sapphic poems into Classical Chinese (frr. 2.5–8, 47, 105(a), 168B, and a combination of frr. 154 and Lesb. inc. auct. 16).[21] In another introduction by Zhou in 1923, he translates a partially overlapping series (frr. 47, 130, 104(a), 105(a), 168B, as well as the Pelagon epigram) into modern Chinese, in free verse.[22] The language change is significant. In the nine-year gap between the two introductions, Zhou became a leading figure in China's New Literary Movement, whose agenda was to sweep away the ossified classical tradition and replace archaic Classical Chinese with a new literary language – a vernacular tinted with Latinised syntax. Zhou's two translations of Sappho epitomised the swift transformation of Chinese literature and language in less than a decade.

---

[18] Ueda Bin 1896: 1–10 = 1901: 261–80; KIVILO p. 18.

[19] Ueda Bin 1922: 212.

[20] Ueda Bin 1927a: 265–7. As the editor notes (p. 751), there are different opinions about whether these poems should be included in his collected works, standing on their own. Another 1927 edition of his collected poems includes only frr. 104(a) and 105(a) (Ueda Bin 1927b: 82). The 1929 edition of *The Complete Works* includes none of them. But the popular editions of his works published in the next decades, including the 1978 revised edition of *The Complete Works,* all have these three poems.

[21] Zhou Zuoren 2009: I 337–9; the translation was based on Wharton 1885: 95, which includes a translation by Moreton J. Walhouse of those two fragments combined.

[22] Zhou Zuoren 2009: III 176–8, 'Short poems of Greece' ('Xila de xiaoshi').

With both translations, despite the change in language, Zhou shares with Ueda a preference for Sappho's short poems. Admittedly, Ueda's renditions were originally citations in his essays, and citations are short as a rule. Zhou may have been under Ueda's influence; he himself once acknowledged his indebtedness to the Japanese writer.[23] But short poems seem to be favoured by the early translators, poets in particular, in Japan.[24] One reason for this was the difficulty presented by the language barrier; this was Zhou's explanation when he finally brought forth a translation of fr. 31 in 1927.[25] But particularly for translators who based their works on modern European writers' renditions, difficulty cannot fully account for this preference, as they frequently translated and wrote much longer poetry. Zhou, for example, translated Theocritus from Andrew Lang's English translation in the 1910s and from Greek in the 1920s.

Reading Zhou's 1914 series, however, one notes a transcultural similarity between the selected Sapphic poems and classical Chinese poetry that might explain the preference for the short poems. It is hard to tell that Zhou's translations, dressed as they are in a highly formulaic, poetic Chinese, are Hellenic in origin. Sappho's poetic style, as rendered by Zhou, would have been readily familiar to his Chinese audience. In the popular fr. 105(a), for instance, an image of a neglected apple on the tree would easily remind an educated Chinese of some love poems in *The Book of Songs*, China's first collection of poetry, supposedly edited by Confucius in the fifth century BC. The word *gantang*, which Zhou uses to translate γλυκύμαλον in both his 1916 and 1923 versions, is the title of a poem in *Songs*. Fr. 168B also echoes another image from classical Chinese literature: the sleepless poet on a moonlit night, as in (to take just one example) 'The bright moon lightens my bed in pure whiteness | When the Milky Way flows to the west in the endless night', from 'The Song of Yan Land' ('Yan'ge xing') by Cao Pi (*c*.187–226).

---

[23] Zhou Zuoren 2009: VI 565, 'Remembering Mr Yosano' ('Yuxieye xiansheng jinian', 1935).

[24] Hinatsu's selections are mostly short. The two long poems translated by Ozeki are frr. 1 and 31, beside the so-called 'Song of the rose', a relatively long poem quoted by Achilles Tatius (2.1). Among Chinese translators, both Xu Zhimo (1897–1931) and Zhu Xiang (1904–33) translated frr. 105(a) and 105(b), though Zhu translated fr. 1 too. Xiaofei Tian also mentioned the translation of fr. 114 by Fei Bai (1920–72).

[25] Zhou Zuoren 2009: V 165–7 ('Sappho's "To my love"', 'Sapufu de zengsuohuan').

Ueda's descriptions of Sappho suggest that he also saw an affinity between Sappho and indigenous poetries. To describe the beauty of her poetry, Ueda repeatedly employs a series of adjective combinations of such kanji as serene (幽), graceful (婉), beautiful (美), elegant (雅), and pure (清). These terms were originally used in classical Chinese literary criticism to suggest a feminine style composed in emotion and balanced in syntax. Ueda praises Sappho's ebullient, exuberant feelings (奔放華麗 の情緒) which flow over her poetry;[26] yet he seems inclined to tame her poetry by including it within the classical category of the feminine, elegant style. These short, sophisticated poems by Sappho are thereby assimilated to traditional short verses at home, making them more easily accepted by readers who had grown up in the traditional poetic world of Japan – and of China.

Neither Zhou nor Ueda was aesthetically conservative; both were innovative figures in their rapidly changing times. Ueda was a pioneer of Japanese poetic modernity and, in particular, Symbolist poetry. His introduction to Sappho starts with an epigraph of verses from the 'Sapphics' by the English poet Algernon Charles Swinburne (1837–1909), placing her in a modern context from the start.[27] Zhou also mentions Swinburne in his essays on Sappho.[28] As Zhou sees it (agreeing with Ueda), Sappho of sunny Lesbos, filled with a love for worldly life, represents Greek literature at its best and should be considered a model for the modern Chinese literature that he and his comrades are striving to make. Particularly in his 1923 retranslation, Zhou enlists Sappho to help construct the New Literature. As writers and intellectuals, Ueda and Zhou (among others) received, reformed, and repurposed Sappho for the future of their national literatures; nevertheless, she also evoked the past of those literatures. As a result, the figure of Sappho brings into question the alleged abrupt discontinuity between the pre-modern and modern tradition.

The late 1920s also witnessed a coming of age for modern Chinese poetry – completely different from classical poetry in form, content, and spirit – as the first generation of young poets raised after the advent of the New Literature began to write. One of these poets had a life-changing encounter with Sappho:

---

[26] Ueda Bin 1901: 269.
[27] Swinburne 1866: 235–8 = McGann and Sligh 2004: 134–6.
[28] Zhou Zuoren 2009: I 339, V 166.

Before heading for Europe, I was gifted with *Goddess* and *Winter Night*. I felt the rising of a new energy, but was unsatisfied with them for being unrefined and undisciplined. After coming ashore in Naples, a fresco in the museum stunned me with the divine charm of the Greek poet Sappho. I managed to find a copy of her poetry in English translation. *In her metre, I wondered at the similarity of the forms to those of Chinese regulated poetry . . . I then harboured a desire to create a new metre. I wrote a dozen poems borrowing Sapphic metre at that time . . .* (Shao Xunmei, 'Preface to the Twenty-five Poems' ('Shi ershiwushou zixu'), 1936)[29]

This poet, Shao Xunmei (1906–68), the most passionate admirer of Sappho in modern China, would become the Chinese flagbearer for poetry of decadence and 'art for art's sake'. His story probably best illuminates the way in which Sappho's presence mediated between China's literary classicism and modernism. A modernist from the outset, Shao started his poetic career by imitating Sappho, who reminded him of classical Chinese poetry. Even though he read Sappho only in English, he sought to adopt Sappho's metre. According to Shao, it was actually a Cambridge poet and classicist, J. M. Edmonds (1875–1958), editor of Sappho, who pointed out to him the similarity between her work and classical Chinese poetry.[30] In Liang Qichao's nationalist discourse, Sappho appears to remind his audience of the contrast between the splendid national pasts and current predicaments of both Greece and China. In Shao's work, Sappho's presence once again opens a space for the old legacy to contribute to the formation of the modern tradition. She prompted Chinese poets, writers, and intellectuals to imagine the relationship between the past and the present in literature and culture in a more sophisticated way.

Shao's imitation of Aeolic metre threaded Sappho into the fabric of modern Chinese poetry. His relationship with Sappho, however, expresses an emotional need far beyond translation and introduction. The passage quoted above is from the preface to his selected poems of his youthful years. The poet presents his work to the world by first telling the story of a young man, primed for a literary career, who by chance falls in love with an image of an ancient female poet. She then becomes his beloved Muse, at a time when he is struggling to find his own voice – in other words, to become a poet himself.

---

[29] Italics mine; see Shao Xunmei 2006: 367. *Goddess* (*Nüshen*) by Guo Moruo (1892–1978), published in 1921, was the first collection of modern Chinese poetry. *Winter Night* (*Dongye*) by Yu Pingbo (1900–90) was published in 1922.

[30] Shao Xunmei 2012a: 99; Edmonds 1922a, on which see FINGLASS ch. 18 p. 256.

Shao thus joined other poets across the world and across time in writing 'fictions of Sappho', a term coined by the literary historian Joan DeJean to address the continual rediscoveries of Sappho – the woman and her poetry – throughout French history.[31] The fresco in the Archaeological Museum of Naples that stunned Shao was recovered from Pompeii, and there is no reason to think that it represents Sappho.[32] Rather than attempt the quixotic task of recovering the historical truth about Sappho, DeJean's term 'fictions' instead highlights the intriguing role imposed on Sappho as each generation of writers, translators, and commentators claimed to rediscover her. Since each rediscovery is a recreation shaped by the mentality of both the creators and their time, it reveals, in DeJean's words, 'at least in part, a projection of the critic's/ writer's desire onto the corpus, the fictive body, of the original woman writer'.[33] As an object of male literary desire, Sappho rediscovered becomes a medium to fulfil 'a male rite of authorial passage' that leads to literary maturity.[34] DeJean's argument maps on to the case of Shao Xunmei particularly well. After his encounter with 'Sappho' in Naples, Shao went on to study at the University of Cambridge, where he got to know Edmonds. He eventually returned to Shanghai, where he achieved his fame as a poet. Throughout this period in his life, he always kept a picture of the 'Sappho' fresco in his study. His first encounter with the Sappho image was an epiphanic manifestation of both his ambition and desire. In the poem dedicated to Sappho, he writes:

> 你坐着你底金鸾车而来吧，
> 来唱你和宇宙同存的赞歌

> Thou arrivest with Thy golden carriage,
> Singing the hymn for Thy coexistence with the cosmos.

Just as Sappho summons Aphrodite, Shao summons Sappho; she takes Aphrodite's place as his patron goddess. Yet, towards the end of the poem, her position changes:

> 海水像海鸥般地向你飞来，
> 一个个漩涡都对你做眉眼。
> 你仍坐着不响只是不响吗？
> 咳我底莎茀[35]

---

[31] DeJean 1989a.
[32] Naples, Museo archeologico nazionale, inv. 9084.
[33] DeJean 1989a: 3.
[34] DeJean 1989a: 6.
[35] Shao Xunmei, 'Sappho' ('Shafu'), written 1925; Shao Xunmei 2012b: 89–91.

> Waves fly to Thee like white seagulls,
> Eddies are the ocean's coquettish smiles to Thee.
> Art Thou going to sit quietly, still so quietly?
> Oh my Sappho!

In this stanza, which itself imitates the sapphic stanza, the quiet Sappho recalls an ungratified 'her' in fr. 1, whose heart Sappho wishes to win when she calls on Aphrodite to help her. But in Shao's poem, the singing Sappho becomes the silent 'her', whom the male poet calls 'my Sappho'.

Furthermore, by engaging with Sappho, Shao finds himself in the company of many illustrious poets throughout European literary history, 'from Swinburne to the Pre-Raphaelite Brotherhood, who in turn lead me to the French poets Baudelaire and Verlaine'.[36] These were all influential poets for Shao. The list also includes Catullus, whose poems Shao admires and translates.[37] DeJean observes that fictions of Sappho in French literature are usually collectively made by 'a cluster of closely connected, aspiring men of letters'.[38] By contrast, Shao's actual friends responded lukewarmly to his passion for Sappho. Yet, by evoking her, he forged a connection with this transnational tradition of young poets throughout history.

But Shao Xunmei did receive a strong echo at home six decades later, from the new generation of poets in the post-Mao era. Haizi (1964–89), to this day an iconic poet in Chinese youth culture, writes in his 'To Sappho':

> 美丽如同花园的女诗人们
> 互相热爱 坐在谷仓中
> 用一只嘴唇摘取另一只嘴唇

> Beautiful are the poetesses like the garden
> Loving each other, sitting in the barn
> One lip plucks another's lip

Such a kiss of Sappho, the poet desires to seize from her female companion:

> 谷色中的嘤嘤之声
> 萨福萨福
> 亲我一下[39]

---

[36] Shao Xunmei 2006: 368 ('Preface to the twenty-five poems').
[37] Shao Xunmei 2006: 75–80 ('Catullus' love poems').
[38] DeJean 1989a: 6.
[39] Haizi, 'To Sappho' ('Gei Safu'), written 1983–6; taken from 2009: 163–4.

The humming in the barn
Sappho, Sappho
Give me a kiss

The kiss passed between the female poets finally calls attention to female same-sex love, an aspect of the Sapphic tradition long repressed in China. Zhou Zuoren, Shao Xunmei, and Luo Luo all sought to shield Sappho from this association, dismissing it as rumour or slander. Xiaofei Tian's study was the first in Chinese to discuss how male desire suffocated the female love and voice throughout the Sapphic tradition.[40] As we have seen with regard to the early Japanese reception, Ueda also argued that Sappho was a noble woman who kindly taught female pupils, and that later it was the Athenian comedians and Christian fathers who, for their different purposes, made up the story of her same-sex love.[41] But in the 1920s, a female novelist would use Ueda's translation of fr. 104(a) to shelter a love between two women.

In 1923 in the magazine *Girls' Pictorial*, a young woman Yoshiya Nobuko (1896–1973) serialised a novel entitled *Yellow Rose*, a romance with a sad ending between two young women:[42] a student of a girls' high school and her teacher, a recent graduate from a women's college, become close, and anticipate a future of studying abroad together in America, when the student's family suddenly pushes her to get married immediately after her upcoming graduation. This sentimental and subtle work about girls is typical of Japan's *shojo* (girl) culture. The writer Yoshiya was also a young woman at the time of writing, a reader-turned-contributor to the magazine dedicated to young female readers. As one of the most commercially successful writers in modern Japan, her career itself provided a powerful testimony to the popularity of Japanese girl culture, which had its foundation in the rise of girls' schools in the early twentieth century, and which continued to exist after co-education became the mainstream. Yoshiya's adolescent readers would have identified with the emotional attachment between her protagonists. In Yoshiya's novel, only the emotional bond is made explicit, and it is debatable whether same-sex relationships in Japan's girl schools were actually sexual or simply platonic.[43] Whatever the nature of the relationship is, Yoshiya's novel

---

[40] Tian 2003: 36–40.
[41] Ueda Bin 1901: 269.
[42] Translated as Frederick 2016. Sarah Frederick notes the relationship of Yoshiya's story to Ueda's translation, as well as to Takayama Chogyū's essay 'Records of my sleeves'; my section about these writers owes much to her insight.
[43] Pflugfelder 2005.

provides a space for female voices to be heard, in which Sappho's poetry plays a crucial role.

At their happiest moment, just before the unexpected separation, the young teacher, Miss Katsuragi, tells her student, Reiko, of Sappho:

> She's really unparalleled in the world. I love her beautiful and pure passion! Singing the pure moonlight at dusk, her poem of just three lines, is all that has been translated into Japanese, by the pen of Dr. Ueda Bin. We should show so much more appreciation and love for this woman poet.[44]

This is a moment of fantasy, as Reiko will eventually be compelled to marry. But Katsuragi seeks an alternative road, and uses Sappho as a prototype. The first edition of Ueda's collected poems, which includes only fr. 104(a) of all his translations of Sappho, was published one year before Yoshiya's writing of the novel. Katsuragi – and Yoshiya behind her – seems unaware of Ueda's other translations. But she must know the tradition of an unusually strong bond between Sappho and her pupils. It is because of her pupil's betrayal, Katsuragi laments, that Sappho jumps from the White Rock. The absence of the other poems, particularly fr. 105(a), one of the most famous Sapphic lyrics, therefore works nicely with Katsuragi's motivation for discussing Sappho with Reiko. The metaphor Sappho uses in that poem of a sweet apple waiting to be picked suggests cross-culturally a maiden waiting for her marriage. Katsuragi presents a discourse to articulate the relationship between two women, leaving no space for her pupil to read Sappho into a traditional society.

In *Yellow Rose*, the immediate reason that Katsuragi brings up Sappho is because the teacher and the student are on a beach, envisioning a trip to Shimizu, a coastal town facing the Pacific that is home to the grave of Takayama Chogyū (1871–1902). Remembered for both his nationalist writings on aesthetics and highly ornamented essays on individual life, Takayama was a famous Meiji figure. References to him were part of the curricula for young women as early as in the 1910s.[45] His famous essay 'Records of my sleeves' includes a passage about Sappho,[46] a passage that Katsuragi claims to remember from her school days and recites almost word for word to her dear Reiko. In that passage, as pointed out by the

---

[44] *Yellow Rose*, chapter 3, 'Sappho's pledge.'
[45] *Yellow Rose*, note 45.
[46] Takayama Chogyū, 'Records of my sleeves' ('Waga sode no ki'), written in 1897, published in Takayama Chogyū 1915: 2–19; the passage recited by Katsuragi is on pp. 10–11.

novel's English translator Frederick, Takayama and his friend are sitting facing the sea, just like Katsuragi and Reiko.[47]

The subject of Takayama's essay is a depressed young man suffering from lung ailments, who seeks healing not only from the fresh air in a small seaside town, but also from Sappho's poetry and, particularly, from the story of her tragic ending with Phaon. He brings a volume of Sappho to go to the seashore to read with a friend who has come down to visit him. He laments Sappho's romantic misadventure, and feels more sympathy for her as a human, in a transient world in which she finds no understanding. Her suicide, Takayama sighs, is prompted by such solitude. This pity is obviously directed towards the writer himself. Reading Sappho on the seashore, he wonders if she jumped into the sea from a cliff that was just like the one where he now sits. In this way, before Yoshiya has her protagonists moved by Sappho's suicide, Takayama has already bonded the poet's early death, jumping from the White Rock, with his own fate. He has his friend at his side. But his illness, possibly fatal back in the nineteenth century, overshadows his future and changes his view of the world. The reclusive life of convalescence also intensifies his feeling of isolation.

In Takayama's narrative, the ancient island poet becomes a mirror for a young writer from another island country. In that same period around the turn of the twentieth century, when Sappho became associated with the Chinese people's melancholia for their country, seen as both an ancient mother for a wounded civilisation and a sister for a modern China struggling for a future, a young Japanese writer projected another kind of melancholia on to Sappho's life, based on the similarity of the natural environments of Japan and Lesbos. This projection sadly became reality when Takayama died of lung disease only a few years later, amplifying the power of his invocation of Sappho and her early death. Two decades later, Yoshiya's characters turn to Takayama's Sapphic imagery, as well as Ueda's translation, in order to pursue their own path. Inspired by Takayama and his Sappho, they spend a beautiful summer together in Okitsu of Shimizu, on the seashore, a few miles from Takayama's grave, fantasising about a shared future that will never happen. But Takayama and his essay would continue to influence Japanese young women into the 1930s, when some sections of 'Records of my sleeves', as well as a memorial essay dedicated to him, were included in textbooks for girls.[48]

---

[47] *Yellow Rose*, note 45.
[48] *Ibid.* The essay 'Remembering Takayama Chogyū' ('Takayama Chogyū shi wo omofu') by Chikamatsu Shūkō (1876–1944) also appeared in Volume 8 of the same textbook series for girls, testifying to the popularity of Takayama during that period (Chikamatsu Shūkō 1924).

Thus Sappho's figure on the island of Lesbos and on the White Rock overseeing the ocean is layered over with Takayama's reading of her poetry on Japan's seashore, and with the seaside discussion of Yoshiya's protagonists.[49] Sappho and her poetry arrived in Japan (as it had in China) gradually through a dialogue with the national tradition, with a transforming society, and with a people who stood on the threshold between the past and the present. The story of Takayama, Ueda, and Yoshiya, among others, sketches how this Sapphic tradition was first planted in the soil of these foreign islands. To tweak Lord Byron's famous verses:

> The isles of Japan, the isles of Japan
> Where burning Sappho is loved and sung.

---

[49] Compare how Natsume Sōseki (1867–1916) refers to Sappho jumping from the cliff in his 1908 Bildungsroman *Sanshirō* (Natsume Sōseki 1966: 165).

Bibliography

Aaron, J., and Walby, S. 1991 (eds.). *Out of the Margins. Women's Studies in the Nineties*. London, New York, Philadelphia.

Abbott, S., and Love, B. 1972. *Sappho was a Right-On Woman. A Liberated View of Lesbianism*. New York.

Abramson, G., and Parfitt, T. 1985 (eds.). *The Great Transition. The Recovery of the Lost Centers of Modern Hebrew Literature*. Totowa, NJ.

Acosta-Hughes, B. 2010. *Arion's Lyre. Archaic Lyric into Hellenistic Poetry*. Princeton and Oxford.

Acosta-Hughes, B., and Barbantani, S. 2007. 'Inscribing lyric', in Bing and Bruss 2007 (eds.), 429–57.

Acosta-Hughes, B., Lehnus, L., and Stephens, S. 2011 (eds.). *Brill's Companion to Callimachus*. Leiden and Boston.

Adams, J. N., and Mayer, R. G. 1999 (eds.). *Aspects of the Language of Latin Poetry*. Proceedings of the British Academy 93. Oxford and New York.

Agócs, P., Carey, C., and Rawles, R. 2012 (eds.). *Reading the Victory Ode*. Cambridge.

Ahmed, S. 2006. *Queer Phenomenology. Orientations, Objects, Others*. Durham, NC and London.

Aldington, R. 1915. *The Poems of Anyte of Tegea*. London.

Aldington, R., and Storer, E. 1919. *The Poems of Anyte of Tegea. Translated by Richard Aldington. Poems and Fragments of Sappho. Translated by Edward Storer*. The Poets' Translation Series Second Set 2. London.

Aleramo, S. 1919. *Il passaggio*. Milan.

Alexander, M. 2018. *Name Me a Word. Indian Writers Reflect on Writing*. New Haven and London.

Alexandrou, M., Carey, C., and D'Alessio, G. B. 2021 (eds.). *Song Regained. Working with Greek Poetic Fragments*. Sozomena 20. Berlin and Boston.

Alfonsi, L. 1950. 'Lesbia', *American Journal of Philology* 71: 59–66.

Ali, A. S. 2003. *Call Me Ishmael Tonight. A Book of Ghazals*. New York and London.

Almeida-Garrett, J. B. de 1845. *Flores sem fructo*. Obras de J. B. de A. Garrett 6. Lisbon.

Aloni, A. 1997. *Saffo. Frammenti*. Florence.

    1998. *Cantare glorie di eroi. Comunicazione e performance poetica nella Grecia arcaica*. Gli Alambicchi 19. Turin.

Alpers, K. 2001. 'Lexikographie. Griechische Antike. Byzanz. Lateinische Antike', in Ueding 2001 (ed.), 194–210.

Alvarenga, L. J. de 1830. *Poezias*. Rio de Janeiro.

Álvarez de Cienfuegos, N. 1816. *Obras poeticas de Don Nicasio Alvarez de Cienfuegos*, 2 vols. Madrid.

Amato, E., Bost-Pouderon, C., Grandjean, T., Thévenet, L., and Ventrella, G. 2016 (eds.). *Dion de Pruse: l'homme, son oeuvre et sa postérité. Actes du colloque international de Nantes (21–23 mai 2015)*. Spudasmata 169. Hildesheim, Zurich, New York.

Anae, N. 2008. '*Poses plastiques*: the art and style of "statuary" in Victorian visual theatre', *Australasian Drama Studies* 52: 112–30.

Anceschi, L. 1940. 'Introduzione', in Quasimodo 1940, 7–28. [= Quasimodo 2004: 305–19]

Andersen, Ø., and Haug, D. T. T. 2012 (eds.). *Relative Chronology in Early Greek Epic Poetry*. Cambridge.

Anderson, M. J. 1997. *The Fall of Troy in Early Greek Poetry and Art*. Oxford.

Andreadis, H. 1996. 'Sappho in early-modern England: a study in sexual reputation', in Greene 1996b (ed.), 105–21.

2001. *Sappho in Early Modern England. Female Same-Sex Literary Erotics 1550–1714*. Chicago and London.

Andrews, N. E. 1996. 'Narrative and allusion in Theocritus, Idyll 2', in Harder *et al.* 1996 (eds.), 21–53.

Andrisano, A. M. 2001. 'Iambic motifs in Alcaeus' lyrics', in Cavarzere *et al.* 2001 (eds.), 41–63.

Angelou, A. 1978 (ed.). *Εμμανουήλ Ροΐδης. Άπαντα*, 5 vols. Athens.

Anonymous (a) 1724. *L'Histoire et les amours de Sapho de Mytilène. Avec une lettre qui contient des reflexions sur les accusations formées contre ses moeurs*. Paris.

Anonymous (b) 1749. *The Sappho-an. An Heroic Poem, of Three Cantos. In the Ovidian Stile, Describing the Pleasures which the Fair Sex Enjoy with Each Other. According to the Modern and Most Polite Taste. Found Amongst the Papers of a Lady of Quality, a Great Promoter of Jaconitism*. London.

Anonymous (c) 1789. *The Adventures of Sappho, Poetess of Mitylene. Translation from the Greek Original, Newly Discovered*, 2 vols. London.

Antonopoulos. P. 2013. "Από τη Μαριέττα Μπέτσου στη Ρίτα Μπούμη. Η Σαπφώ, η λεσβιακή λογοτεχνία και ο φεμινισμός στην Ελλάδα από τα τέλη του 19ου αιώνα μέχρι το Μεσοπόλεμο", in Vassiliadou *et al.* 2013 (eds.), 245–84.

2014. "Η Σαπφώ και ο λεσβιακός ερωτισμός στο πρώιμο έργο του Κώστα Βάρναλη", in *Πρακτικά 7ου Συνεδρίου Μεταπτυχιακών Φοιτητών & Υποψηφίων Διδακτόρων του Τμήματος Φιλολογίας του Εθνικού και Καποδιστριακού Πανεπιστημίου Αθηνών, 16–18 Μαΐου 2013*, vol. 2. Athens: 658–69.

2015. 'Ο Δημήτριος Γουζέλης και το απόσπασμα 31 της Σαπφώς: μεταφράζοντας την απόδοση του Nicolas Boileau', in Tabaki and Sechopoulou 2015 (eds.), 13–21.

2016. "Η καταδίκη της Σαπφώς από τον Ευγένιο Βούλγαρη και τον Άνθιμο Γαζή", in Tabaki and Polykandrioti 2016 (eds.), ΙΙ 73–86.

Antunes, A. A. 1987. *Safo. Tudo que restou*. Além Paraíba.

Arnold, J. 2009. *The Fanfrolico Press. Satyrs, Fauns and Fine Books*. Pinner.

Arouetty, J. 1972. 'Tirgumei shira: Sapfo' ['Poetry in translation: Sappho'], *Davar* (11 February): 22.

1973. 'Be-emet, ani rotsa lamut' ['Truly, I want to die'], *Davar* (19 January): 21.

Ascheri, P. 2011. 'The Greek origins of the Romans and the Roman origins of Homer in the Homeric scholia and in *POxy*. 3710', in Montanari and Pagani 2011 (eds.), 65–86.

Athanassaki, L., and Bowie, E. 2011 (eds.). *Archaic and Classical Choral Song. Performance, Politics and Dissemination*. Trends in Classics Supplement 10. Berlin and Boston.

Atherton, C. L. 2006. *'Flashing Eyes and Floating Hair'. A Reading of Gwen Harwood's Pseudonymous Poetry*. Melbourne.

Aulotte, R. 1958. 'Sur quelques traductions d'une ode de Sappho au XVIᵉ siècle', *Bulletin de l'Association Guillaume Budé: Lettres d'humanité* 17: 107–22.

Austin, C., and Olson, S. D. 2004. *Aristophanes. Thesmophoriazusae*. Oxford.

Auzépy, M.-F. 2003 (ed.). *Byzance en Europe*. Saint-Denis.

Avdela, E., and Psarra, A. 1985 (eds.). *Ο φεμινισμός στην Ελλάδα του Μεσοπολέμου. Μία ανθολογία*. Athens.

Azevedo, M. A. A. de 1862. *Obras*, 3 vols. Rio de Janeiro.

Bachmann, C. 2015. *Wenn man die Welt als Gemälde betrachtet. Studien zu den Eikones Philostrats des Älteren*. Heidelberg.

Bachvarova, M. R. 2007. 'Oath and allusion in Alcaeus fr. 129', in Sommerstein and Fletcher 2007 (eds.), 179–88.

Bagordo, A. 2009. *Sappho. Gedichte. Griechisch-deutsch*. Düsseldorf.

Bakhtin, M. M. 1986. *Speech Genres and Other Late Essays*, transl. V. M. McGee, ed. C. Emerson and M. Holquist. University of Texas Press Slavic Series 8. Austin.

Bakker, E. J. 2010 (ed.). *A Companion to the Ancient Greek Language*. Malden, MA, Oxford, Chichester.

2017 (ed.). *Authorship and Greek Song. Authority, Authenticity, and Performance*. Mnemosyne Supplement 402. Studies in Archaic and Classical Greek Song 3. Leiden and Boston.

Bakogianni, A., and Hope, V. M. 2015 (eds.). *War as Spectacle. Ancient and Modern Perspectives on the Display of Armed Conflict*. London and New York.

Balderston, D., and Guy, D. J. 1997 (eds.). *Sex and Sexuality in Latin America*. New York and London.

Baldwin, B. 1984. *Timarion*. Detroit.

Baldwin, C. 2004. 'Anna Louisa Karsch as Sappho', *Women in German Yearbook* 20: 62–97.

Balmer, J. 1984. *Sappho. Poems and Fragments*. London.

1992. *Sappho. Poems and Fragments.*[2] Newcastle upon Tyne.

2013. *Piecing Together the Fragments. Translating Classical Verse, Creating Contemporary Poetry.* Oxford.

Bandella, M. 2012. "'L'aspro senso del martir": La Saffo di Teresa Bandettini', in Chemello 2012a (ed.), 259–71.

Bär, S. 2016. "'Ceci n'est pas un fragment": identity, intertextuality and fictionality in Sappho's "Brothers Poem"', *Symbolae Osloenses* 90: 8–54.

Barandas, A. E. E. de 1845. *O ramalhete, ou Flores escolhidas no jardim da imaginação.* Porto Alegre.

Barbantani, S. 2010. *Three Burials (Ibycus, Stesichorus, Simonides). Facts and Fiction about Lyric Poets in Magna Graecia in the Epigrams of the Greek Anthology.* Hellenica 38. Alessandria.

Barber, C., and Jenkins, D. 2009 (eds.). *Medieval Greek Commentaries on the Nicomachean Ethics.* Studien und Texte zur Geistesgeschichte des Mittelalters 101. Leiden and Boston.

Barchiesi, A. 2009. 'Lyric in Rome', in Budelmann 2009 (ed.), 319–35.

Barker, A. 1984. *Greek Musical Writings. Volume 1. The Musician and His Art.* Cambridge.

1989. *Greek Musical Writings. Volume 2. Harmonic and Acoustic Theory.* Cambridge.

1995. '*Heterophonia* and *poikilia*: accompaniments to Greek melody', in Gentili and Perusino 1995 (eds.), 41–60.

Barnard, F. A. P., and Guyot, A. 1878 (eds.). *Johnson's New Universal Cyclopedia. A Scientific and Popular Treasury of Useful Knowledge. Volume IV.* New York.

Barnard, M. 1958. *Sappho. A New Translation.* Berkeley and Los Angeles.

1984. *Assault on Mount Helicon. A Literary Memoir.* Berkeley, Los Angeles, London.

Barner, W. 1967. *Neuere Alkaios-Papyri aus Oxyrhynchos.* Spudasmata 14. Hildesheim.

Barney, N. C. 1910. *Actes et entr'actes.* Paris.

1929. *Aventures de l'esprit.* Paris.

1960. *Souvenirs indiscrets.* Paris.

1992a. *Adventures of the Mind*, transl. J. S. Gatton. New York and London.

1992b. *A Perilous Advantage. The Best of Natalie Clifford Barney*, ed. and transl. A. Livia. Norwich, VT.

Barnsley, S. 2013. *Mary Barnard, American Imagist.* Albany.

Barrero Pérez, Ó. 2004. 'Imágenes de Safo en la literatura española (II). El Romanticismo', *Cuadernos de ilustración y romanticismo* 12: 61–75.

2005. 'Imágenes de Safo en la literatura española (I). El siglo XVIII', *Dieciocho* 28.2: 101–17.

2007. 'Imágenes de Safo en la literatura española (III). La segunda mitad del siglo XIX', *Dicenda. Cuadernos de filología hispánica* 25: 5–14.

<Barthélemy, J.-J.> 1788. *Voyage du jeune Anacharsis en Grèce, dans le milieu du quatrième siècle avant l'ère vulgaire*, 4 vols. Paris.

Barthélemy, <J.-J.> 1794. *Travels of Anacharsis the Younger in Greece, during the Middle of the Fourth Century Before the Christian Era²*, 7 vols., <transl. W. Beaumont.> London. [1st edn 1790–1]

Barton, A., and Giddens, E. 2012. '*The Sad Shepherd, or a Tale of Robin Hood* (printed 1641)', in Bevington *et al.* 2012 (eds.), VII 417–80.

Bastianini, G. 2008. '1470. Prosa su Saffo, fr. 31 Voigt', *Papiri Greci e Latini* 15: 41–2.

Bastianini, G., and Casanova, A. 2007 (eds.). *I papiri di Saffo e di Alceo. Atti del convegno internazionale di studi, Firenze, 8–9 giugno 2006*. Studi e Testi di Papirologia 9. Florence.

Bastianini, G., Haslam, M., Maehler, H., Montanari, F., and Römer, C. 2004 (eds.). *Commentaria et lexica Graeca in papyris reperta. Pars I. Commentaria et lexica in auctores. Vol. 1. Aeschines–Bacchylides. Fasc. 1. Aeschines–Alcaeus.* Munich and Leipzig.

Battezzato, L. 2003. 'Song, performance, and text in the New Posidippus', *Zeitschrift für Papyrologie und Epigraphik* 145: 31–43.

2008. *Linguistica e retorica della tragedia greca*. Sussidi Eruditi 78. Rome.

2009. 'Metre and music', in Budelmann 2009 (ed.), 130–46.

2018. 'The structure of Sappho's books: metre, page layout, and the Hellenistic and Roman poetry book', *Zeitschrift für Papyrologie und Epigraphik* 208: 1–24.

Baudelaire, C. 1850. 'Lesbos', in Lemer 1850: 469–72. [1857: 187–90]

1857. *Les Fleurs du mal*. Paris.

Bayle, P. 1697. *Dictionnaire historique et critique*. Rotterdam.

Beard, M. 2004. '*Sappho's Leap* by Erica Jong' (review of Jong 2004). *The Independent*, 20 August.

Beaton, R. 1996. *The Medieval Greek Romance²*. London and New York. [1st edn Cambridge 1989]

Becciu, A. 2002. *Alejandra Pizarnik. Prosa completa*. Barcelona.

Bechtel, F. 1921. *Die griechischen Dialekte. Erster Band. Der Lesbische, Thessalische, Böotische, Arkadische und Kyprische Dialekt*. Berlin.

Bechtel, F., Kern, O., Praechter, K., Robert, C., Stern, E. von, and Wilcken, U. 1913a. '3. Sappho', in Bechtel *et al.* 1913b: 182–4.

1913b. *Dikaiomata. Auszüge aus alexandrinischen Gesetzen und Verordnungen in einem Papyrus des Philologischen Seminars der Universität Halle Pap. Hal. 1. Mit einem Anhang weiterer Papyri derselben Sammlung*. Berlin.

Beck, M. 2014 (ed.). *A Companion to Plutarch*. Malden, MA, Oxford, Chichester.

Beck, R. 2009. *Sir William Jones. Poems, Consisting Chiefly of Translations from the Asiatick Tongues*. Augsburg.

Becker, A. 2010. 'Listening to lyric: accent and ictus in the Latin sapphic stanza', *Classical World* 103: 159–82.

Beecroft, A. 2010. *Authorship and Cultural Identity in Early Greece and China. Patterns of Literary Circulation*. Cambridge and New York.

Belleau, R. 1556. *Les Odes d'Anacreon Teien, traduites de Grec en Francois, par Remi Belleau de Nogent au Perche, ensemble quelques petites hymnes de son inuention.* Paris.

Belloni, L., Milsnese, G., and Porro, A. 1995 (eds.), *Studia classica Iohanni Tarditi oblata*, 2 vols. Biblioteca di Aevum antiquum 7. Milan.

Benelli, L. 2017. *Sapphostudien zu ausgewählten Fragmenten*, 2 vols. Papyrologica Coloniensia 39. Leiden and Boston.

    2018. 'Sapph. fr. 117 V. A neglected testimony (schol. vet. in Arat. *Phaen.* 250)', *Seminari Romani di Cultura Greca* ns 7: 47–62.

Benner, A. B., and Fobes, F. H. 1949. *The Letters of Alciphron, Aelian and Philostratus.* London and Cambridge, MA.

Bennett, P. B. 1990. *Emily Dickinson. Woman Poet.* New York etc.

    1992. '"By a mouth that cannot speak": spectral presence in Emily Dickinson's letters', *The Emily Dickinson Journal* 1: 76–99.

    2003. *Poets in the Public Sphere. The Emancipatory Project of American Women's Poetry, 1800–1900.* Princeton and Oxford.

Bergk, T. 1835. 'De aliquot fragmentis Sapphonis et Alcaei', *Rheinisches Museum* 3: 209–31.

    1843. *Poetae lyrici Graeci.* Leipzig.

    1853. *Poetae lyrici Graeci. Editio altera auctior et emendatior.* Leipzig and London.

    1867. *Poetae lyrici Graeci. Tertiis curis recensuit T. B. Pars* iii *poetas melicos continens.* Leipzig.

    1882. *Poetae lyrici Graeci. Editionis quartae vol.* iii *poetas melicos continens.* Leipzig.

Bergman, D. 2004. *The Violet Hour. The Violet Quill and the Making of Gay Culture.* New York.

Bergson, L. 1967. 'Zum periphrastischen χρῆμα', *Eranos* 65: 79–117.

Bernand, A., and Bernand, É. 1960. *Les Inscriptions grecques et latines du Colosse de Memnon.* Institut français d'archéologie orientale, Bibliothèque d'étude 31. <Cairo>.

Bernsdorff, H. 2004. 'Schwermut des Alters im neuen Kölner Sappho-Papyrus', *Zeitschrift für Papyrologie und Epigraphik* 150: 27–35.

Bessone, F. 2003. 'Saffo, la lirica, l'elegia: su Ovidio, *Heroides* 15', *Materiali e Discussioni per l'Analisi dei Testi Classici* 51: 209–43.

Bettarini, L. 2005. 'Note linguistiche alla nuova Saffo', *Zeitschrift für Papyrologie und Epigraphik* 154: 33–9.

Bevington, D., Butler, M., and Donaldson, I. 2012 (eds.). *The Cambridge Edition of the Works of Ben Jonson*, 7 vols. Cambridge.

Beynon, J. C., and Gonda, C. (eds.). 2010. *Lesbian Dames. Sapphism in the Long Eighteenth Century.* Farnham and Burlington, VT.

Bézzola, G. 1961. *Ugo Foscolo. Tragedie e poesie minori.* Edizione Nazionale delle Opere di Ugo Foscolo 2. Florence.

Bhatt, S. 2015. *Poppies in Translation.* Manchester.

Bialik, C. N. 1950. *Kol kitvei Ch. N. Bialik [Complete Works of Ch. N. Bialik]*. Tel Aviv.

Bierl, A. 2016a. '"All you need is love": some thoughts on the structure, texture, and meaning of the Brothers Song as well as on its relation to the Kypris Song (P. Sapph. Obbink)', in Bierl and Lardinois 2016 (eds.), 302–36.

   2016b. 'Sappho as Aphrodite's singer, poet, and hero(ine): the reconstruction of the context and sense of the Kypris song', in Bierl and Lardinois 2016 (eds.), 339–52.

   2016c. 'Visualizing the Cologne Sappho: mental imagery through chorality, the sun, and Orpheus', in Cazzato and Lardinois 2016 (eds.), 307–42.

Bierl, A., and Lardinois, A. 2016 (eds.). *The Newest Sappho. P. Sapph. Obbink and P. GC inv. 105, frs. 1–4*. Mnemosyne Supplement 392. Studies in Archaic and Classical Greek Song 2. Leiden and Boston.

Bierl, A., Lämmle, R., and Wesselmann, K. 2007 (eds.). *Literatur und Religion. Wege zu einer mythisch-rituellen Poetik bei den Griechen*, 2 vols. MythosEikonPoiesis 1/1–2. Berlin and New York.

Bing, P. 2018. 'Tombs of poets' minor characters', in Goldschmidt and Graziosi 2018 (eds.), 147–70.

Bing, P., and Bruss, J. S. 2007 (eds.). *Brill's Companion to Hellenistic Epigram*. Leiden and Boston.

Bin-Gorion, E. 1946. 'Im kri'a rishona: *Sapfo mi-lesbos*' ['At first reading: *Sappho of Lesbos*'], *Davar* (date unknown): 4.

Blass, F. 1880a. 'Fragmente griechischer Handschriften im Königl. ägyptischen Museum zu Berlin', *Zeitschrift für Ägyptische Sprache und Altertumskunde* 18: 34–40.

   1880b. 'Neue Fragmente des Euripides und andrer griechischer Dichter', *Rheinisches Museum* NS 35: 74–93, 278–97.

Blomfield, C. J. 1814. 'Sapphonis fragmenta', *Museum Criticum* 1: 1–31.

Blondell, R. 2010. 'Refractions of Homer's Helen in archaic lyric', *American Journal of Philology* 131: 349–91.

   2013. *Helen of Troy. Beauty, Myth, Devastation*. Oxford and New York.

Blondell, R., and Ormand, K. 2015a. 'One hundred and twenty-five years of homosexuality', in Blondell and Ormand 2015b (eds.), 1–22.

   2015b (eds.). *Ancient Sex. New Essays*. Columbus, OH.

Blümel, W. 1982. *Die aiolischen Dialekte. Phonologie und Morphologie der inschriftlichen Texte aus generativer Sicht*. Ergänzungshefte zur Zeitschrift für vergleichende Sprachforschung 30. Göttingen.

Boardman, J. 1999. *The Greeks Overseas. Their Early Colonies and Trade*⁴. London. [1st edn 1964]

Bocchetti, C. 2010 (ed.). *La influencia clásica en América Latina*. Bogotá.

Boedeker, D. D. 1979. 'Sappho and Acheron', in Bowersock *et al.* 1979 (eds.), 40–52.

   2016. 'Hera and the return of Charaxos', in Bierl and Lardinois 2016 (eds.), 188–207.

Boehringer, S. 2007. *L'Homosexualité féminine dans l'Antiquité grecque et romaine.* Collection d'études anciennes publié sous le patronage de l'Association Guillaume Budé 135. Paris.

2013. '"Je suis Tithon, je suis Aurore": performance et érotisme dans le "nouveau" fr. 58 de Sappho', *Quaderni Urbinati di Cultura Classica* NS 133: 23–44.

2014. 'Female homoeroticism', in Hubbard 2014b (ed.), 150–63 ~ 154–67.

Boehringer, S., and Calame, C. 2016. 'Sappho and Kypris: "the vertigo of love" (P. Sapph. Obbink 21–29; P. Oxy. 1231, fr. 16)', in Bierl and Lardinois 2016 (eds.), 353–67.

<Boileau-Despreaux, N.> 1674. *Oeuvres diverses du Sieur D*** avec le traité du sublime ou du marveilleux dans les discours. Traduit du Grec de Longin.* Paris.

1711. *The Works of Monsr. Boileau Despreaux. Volume II.* London.

Bond, D. F. 1965 (ed.). *The Spectator,* 5 vols. Oxford.

Bond, G. W. 1981. *Euripides. Heracles.* Oxford.

Bonnet, M.-J. 1981. *Un Choix sans équivoque. Recherches historiques sur les relations amoureuses entre les femmes XVIe–XXe siècle.* Paris.

Bordo, S., Alcade, M. C., and Rosenman, E. 2015 (eds.). *Provocations. A Transnational Reader in the History of Feminist Thought.* Oakland, CA.

Borges, C., and Sampson, C. M. 2012. *New Literary Papyri from the Michigan Collection. Mythographic Lyric and a Catalogue of Poetic First Lines.* Ann Arbor.

Borges, J. L. 1925. 'Nydia Lamarque: *Telarañas*', *Proa* 2.14: 50–1. [= 1997: 231–2] 1997. *Textos recobrados, 1919–1929.* Buenos Aires.

Bornmann, F. 1992. 'Kleine Gemeinsamkeiten bei Nietzsche und Wilamowitz', *Zeitschrift für Papyrologie und Epigraphik* 91: 18–19.

Bosi, A. 2015. *História concisa da literatura Brasileira,* 50th impression. São Paulo. [1st impression 1970]

Boudhors, C.-H. 1966. *Nicolas Boileau-Despréaux. Dissertation sur la Joconde. Arrest Burlesque. Traité du Sublime^2.* Paris. [1st edn 1942]

Bouzaglo, S. 2009. *Mishehi, ani omeret, tizkor otanu [Someone, I Say, Will Remember Us].* Jerusalem.

Bowersock, G. W., Burkert, W., and Putnam, M. C. J. 1979 (eds.). *Arktouros. Hellenic Studies presented to Bernard M. W. Knox on the Occasion of his 65th Birthday.* Berlin and New York.

Bowie, A. M. 1981. *The Poetic Dialect of Sappho and Alcaeus.* Salem, NH.

Bowie, E. L. 1990. 'Greek poetry in the Antonine Age', in Russell 1990 (ed.), 53–90.

1993. 'Lies, fiction and slander in early Greek poetry', in Gill and Wiseman 1993 (eds.), 1–37.

2008a. 'Aristides and early Greek lyric, elegiac and iambic poetry', in W. Harris and Holmes 2008 (eds.), 9–29.

2008b. 'Plutarch's habits of citation: aspects of difference', in Nikolaidis 2008 (ed.), 143–57.

2009. 'Quotation of earlier texts in Τὰ ἐc τὸν Τυανέα Ἀπολλώνιον', in Demoen and Praet 2009 (eds.), 57–73.

2010. 'The Trojan War's reception in early Greek lyric, iambic and elegiac poetry', in Foxhall *et al.* 2010 (eds.), 57–87.

2013. 'Caging grasshoppers: Longus' materials for weaving "reality"', in Paschalis and Panayotakis 2013 (eds.), 179–97.

2014. 'Poetry and education', in M. Beck 2014 (ed.), 177–90.

2016a. 'How did Sappho's songs get into the male sympotic repertoire?', in Bierl and Lardinois 2016 (eds.), 148–64.

2016b. 'Literary criticism of archaic lyric, elegiac and iambic poetry in Dio of Prusa', in Amato *et al.* 2016 (eds.), 365–72.

2019. *Longus. Daphnis and Chloe.* Cambridge.

Bowman, L. 1998. 'Nossis, Sappho and Hellenistic poetry', *Ramus* 27: 39–59.

2004. 'The "women's tradition" in Greek poetry', *Phoenix* 58: 1–27.

Bowra, C. M. 1961. *Greek Lyric Poetry. From Alcman to Simonides²*. Oxford. [1st edn 1936]

Brasil Fontes, J. 1991. *Eros, tecelão de mitos. A poesia de Safo de Lesbos.* São Paulo.

2003. *Safo de Lesbos. Poemas e fragmentos.* São Paulo.

Bremer, J. M. 1975. 'The meadow of love and two passages in Euripides' *Hippolytus*', *Mnemosyne* 4th ser. 28: 268–80.

Bremmer, J. 1989 (ed.). *From Sappho to de Sade. Moments in the History of Sexuality.* London and New York.

Brennan, T. C. 1998. 'The poets Julia Balbilla and Damo at the Colossus of Memnon', *Classical World* 91: 215–34.

Bresson, A. 1983. 'La dynamique des cités de Lesbos', *Université de Bordeaux III Centre G. Radet Cahiers* 3. [= 2000: 101–8]

2000. *La Cité marchande.* Scripta Antiqua 2. Bordeaux.

Brink, C. O. 1971. *Horace on Poetry. Volume II. The 'Ars Poetica'.* Cambridge.

Brock, R., and Hodkinson, S. 2000 (eds.). *Alternatives to Athens. Varieties of Political Organization and Community in Ancient Greece.* Oxford.

Broger, A. 1996. *Das Epitheton bei Sappho und Alkaios. Eine sprachwissenschaftliche Untersuchung.* Innsbrucker Beiträge zur Sprachwissenschaft 88. Innsbruck.

Bronowski, Y. 1974. 'El Afroditei' ['To Aphrodite'], *Davar* (17 May): 20.

1978. *Sapfo. Shirim [Sappho. Poems].* Tel Aviv.

Brooten, B. J. 1996. *Love between Women. Early Christian Responses to Female Homoeroticism.* Chicago and London.

Brown, C. G. 1989. 'Anactoria and the Χαρίτων ἀμαρύγματα: Sappho fr. 16, 18 Voigt', *Quaderni Urbinati di Cultura Classica* NS 32: 7–15.

2011. 'To the ends of the earth: Sappho on Tithonus', *Zeitschrift für Papyrologie und Epigraphik* 178: 21–5.

Brown, R. M. 1971. *The Hand That Cradles the Rock.* New York.

Browning, R. 1960. 'An unnoticed fragment of Sappho?', *Classical Review* NS 10: 192–3.

1992. 'The Byzantines and Homer', in Lamberton and Keaney 1992 (eds.), 134–48.

Brückner, C. 1983. *Wenn du geredet hättest, Desdemona. Ungehaltene Reden ungehaltener Frauen.* Hamburg.

1992. *Desdemona – If You Had Only Spoken! Eleven Uncensored Speeches of Eleven Incensed Women*, transl. E. Bron. London.

Buchholz, H.-G. 1975. *Methymna. Archäologische Beiträge zur Topographie und Geschichte von Nordlesbos*. Mainz.

Buck, C. D. 1955. *The Greek Dialects. Grammar, Selected Inscriptions, Glossary*. Chicago.

Buckley, P. 2014. *The Alexiad of Anna Komnene. Artistic Strategy in the Making of a Myth*. Cambridge.

Budelmann, F. 2009 (ed.). *The Cambridge Companion to Greek Lyric*. Cambridge. 2018. *Greek Lyric. A Selection*. Cambridge.

Budelmann, F., and Phillips, T. 2018 (eds.). *Textual Events. Performance and the Lyric in Early Greece*. Oxford.

Burgess, J. S. 2001. *The Tradition of the Trojan War in Homer and the Epic Cycle*. Baltimore and London.

2012. 'Intertextuality without text in early Greek epic', in Andersen and Haug 2012 (eds.), 168–83.

Burkert, W. 1985. *Greek Religion*, transl. J. Raffan. Cambridge, MA.

Burnett, A. P. 1983. *Three Archaic Poets. Archilochus, Alcaeus, Sappho*. London.

Burris, S. P. 2017. 'A new join for Sappho's "Kypris poem": P.GC. inv. 105 fr. 4 and P.Sapph.Obbink', *Zeitschrift für Papyrologie und Epigraphik* 201: 12–14.

Burris, S., Fish, J., and Obbink, D. 2014. 'New fragments of Book 1 of Sappho', *Zeitschrift für Papyrologie und Epigraphik* 189: 1–28.

Burton, D., Perris, S., and Tatum, J. 2017 (eds.). *Athens to Aotearoa. Greece and Rome in New Zealand Literature and Society*. Wellington.

Burton, J. 1998. 'Women's commensality in the ancient Greek world', *Greece & Rome* 2nd ser. 45: 143–65.

Burzacchini, G. 1976. 'Alc. 130b Voigt ~ Hor. *Carm.* I 22', *Quaderni Urbinati di Cultura Classica* 22: 39–58.

Butler, James, and Green, K. 1992 (eds.). *William Wordsworth. Lyrical Ballads, and Other Poems, 1797–1800*. Ithaca, NY and London.

Butler, Judith 1997. *Excitable Speech. A Politics of the Performative*. New York and London.

Buxton, J. 1954. *Sir Philip Sidney and the English Renaissance*. London and New York.

Cabezas Miranda, J. 2012. *Proyectos poéticos en Cuba (1959–2000). Algunos cambios formales y temáticos*. San Vicente del Raspeig.

Caciagli, S. 2009. 'Sapph. fr. 27 V.: l'unita del pubblico Saffico', *Quaderni Urbinati di Cultura Classica* NS 91: 63–80.

2010. 'Il *temenos* di *Messon*: uno stesso contesto per Saffo e Alceo', *Lexis* 28: 227–56.

2011. *Poeti e società. Comunicazione poetica e formazioni sociali nella Lesbo del VII/VI secolo a.C.* Supplementi di Lexis 64. Amsterdam.

2016. 'Sappho fragment 17: wishing Charaxos a safe trip?', in Bierl and Lardinois 2016 (eds.), 424–48.

Caesar, M., and D'Intino, F. 2013 (eds.). *Giacomo Leopardi. Zibaldone: The Notebooks of Leopardi.* London.

Cairns, D., and Scodel, R. 2014 (eds.). *Defining Greek Narrative.* Edinburgh Leventis Studies 7. Edinburgh.

Cairns, F. 1977 (ed.). *Papers of the Liverpool Latin Seminar 1976. Classical Latin Poetry / Medieval Latin Poetry / Greek Poetry.* ARCA Classical and Medieval Texts, Papers and Monographs 2. Liverpool.

  1983 (ed.). *Papers of the Liverpool Latin Seminar Fourth Volume.* ARCA Classical and Medieval Texts, Papers and Monographs 11. Liverpool.

  1989. *Virgil's Augustan Epic.* Cambridge.

Calame, C. 1970. *Etymologicum genuinum. Les citations de poètes lyriques.* Filologia e Critica 5. Rome.

  1977. *Les Choeurs de jeunes filles en Grèce archaïque,* 2 vols. Filologia e Critica 20. Rome.

  1996. 'Sappho's group: an initiation into womanhood', in Greene 1996a (ed.), 113–24. [≈ 2001: 210–14, 231–3, 249–52 ≈ 1977: 1 367–72, 400–4, 427–32]

  1999. *The Poetics of Eros in Ancient Greece,* transl. J. Lloyd. Princeton.

  2001. *Choruses of Young Women in Ancient Greece. Their Morphology, Religious Role, and Social Function*[2], transl. D. Collins and J. Orion. Lanham, MD and London. [Translation of 1977 volume one; revision of translation first published 1997]

  2005a. *Masks of Authority. Fiction and Pragmatics in Ancient Greek Poetics.* Ithaca, NY and London.

  2005b. 'Une poétique de la mémoire: espace et temps chez Sappho', in Kolde et al. 2005 (eds.), 53–67.

  2009. 'Referential fiction and poetic ritual: towards a pragmatics of myth (Sappho 17 and Bacchylides 13)', *Trends in Classics* 1: 1–17.

Caldeira, I., Capinha, G., and Matos, J. 2017 (eds.). *The Edge of One of Many Circles. Homenagem a Irene Ramalho Santos,* 2 vols. Coimbra.

Calder, W. M. III 1986. 'F. G. Welcker's *Sapphobild* and its reception in Wilamowitz', in Calder et al. 1986 (eds.), 131–56.

Calder, W. M. III, Köhnken, A., Kullmann, W., and Pflug, G. 1986 (eds.). *Friedrich Gottlieb Welcker. Werk und Wirkung. Vorträge, gehalten auf der Welcker-Tagung in der Werner-Reimers-Stiftung in Bad Homburg vom 5.–7. November 1984 (I) und zur Eröffnung der Ausstellung 'Friedrich Gottlieb Welcker (1784–1868): Philologe, Archäologe und Oberbibliothekar in Bonn' in der Universitätsbibliothek Bonn am 5. November 1984 (II).* Hermes Einzelschriften 49. Stuttgart.

Caldwell, R. C. 1878. 'Tamil, its language and literature', in F. Barnard and Guyot 1878 (eds.), 720–2.

Cambiano, G., Canfora, L., and Lanza, D. 1995 (eds.). *Lo spazio letterario della Grecia antica. Volume II. La ricezione e l'attualizzazione del testo.* Rome.

Cameron, A. 1939. 'Sappho's prayer to Aphrodite', *Harvard Theological Review* 32: 1–17.

Campbell, A., and Farrier, S. 2016 (eds.). *Queer Dramaturgies. International Perspectives on Where Performance Leads Queer.* Basingstoke and New York.

Campbell, D. A. 1983. *The Golden Lyre. The Themes of the Greek Lyric Poets.* London.

Campos, H. de 1985. *A educação dos cinco sentidos. Poemas.* São Paulo.
1998. *Crisantempo. No espaço curvo nasce um.* Signos 24. São Paulo.
2004. *Galáxias².* São Paulo. [1st edn 1984]

Canfora, L. 1995. 'Libri e biblioteche', in Cambiano *et al.* 1995 (eds.), 11–93.

Capra, A. 2014. *Plato's Four Muses. The Phaedrus and the Poetics of Philosophy.* Hellenic Studies 67. Cambridge, MA and London.
2019. 'Lyric oblivion: when Sappho taught Socrates how to forget', in Castagnoli and Ceccarelli 2019 (eds.), 179–94.

Cardin, M., and Pontani, F. 2017. 'Hesiod's fragments in Byzantium', in Tsagalis 2017 (ed.), 245–87.

Carey, C. 1986. 'Archilochus and Lycambes', *Classical Quarterly* NS 36: 60–7.
2016. 'Mapping *iambos*: mining the minor talents', in Swift and Carey 2016 (eds.), 122–39.

Carman, B. 1904. *Sappho. One Hundred Lyrics.* Boston.

Carson, A. [= Giacomelli, A., *q.v.*]
1986. *Eros the Bittersweet. An Essay.* Princeton.
1990. '"Just for the thrill": sycophantizing Aristotle's *Poetics*', *Arion* 3rd series 1.1: 142–54.
1996. 'The justice of Aphrodite in Sappho 1', in Greene 1996a (ed.), 226–32. [= Giacomelli 1980]
1997. 'Sappho shock', in Prins and Shreiber 1997 (eds.), 223–9.
2002. *If Not, Winter. Fragments of Sappho.* New York.

Casanova, A. 2007. 'Cent'anni e più di papiri per i poeti di Lesbo', in Bastianini and Casanova 2007 (eds.), 1–15.

Cassio, A. C. 1986. 'Continuità e riprese arcaizzanti nell'uso epigrafico dei dialetti greci: il caso dell'eolico d'Asia', *AION. Annali del Dipartimento di studi del mondo classico e del Mediterraneo antico. Sezione linguistica* 8: 131–46.
1993. 'Parlate locali, dialetti delle stirpi e fonti letterarie nei grammatici greci', in Crespo *et al.* 1993 (eds.), 73–90.
2007. 'Alcman's text, spoken Laconian, and Greek study of Greek dialects', in Hajnal 2007 (ed.), 29–45.
2016 (ed.). *Storia delle lingue letterarie greche².* Florence. [1st edn 2008]

Castagnoli, L., and Ceccarelli, P. 2019 (eds.). *Greek Memories. Theories and Practices.* Cambridge.

Castellanos, R. 1972. *Poesía no eres tú. Obra poética: 1948–1971.* Mexico City.

Castle, T. 2003 (ed.). *The Literature of Lesbianism. A Historical Anthology from Ariosto to Stonewall.* New York.

Cataldo, H. G. 2017. *Poesía lírica griega arcaica. Antología de fragmentos de Arquíloco a Simónides.* Santiago.

Cataudella, Q. 1965. 'Saffo e i Bizantini', *Revue des Études Grecques* 78: 66–9.

Cavallo, G. 2004 (ed.). *Lo spazio letterario del Medioevo. 3. Le culture circostanti. Volume I. La cultura bizantina.* Rome.

Cavarzere, A., Aloni, A., and Barchiesi, A. 2001 (eds.). *Iambic Ideas. Essays on a Poetic Tradition from Archaic Greece to the Late Roman Empire.* Lanham, MD, Boulder, CO, New York, Oxford.

Cazzato, V. 2016. 'Symposia *en plein air* in Alcaeus and others', in Cazzato and Lardinois 2016 (eds.), 184–206.

Cazzato, V., and Lardinois, A. 2016 (eds.). *The Look of Lyric. Greek Song and the Visual.* Mnemosyne Supplement 391. Studies in Archaic and Classical Greek Song 1. Leiden and Boston.

Cazzato, V., Obbink, D., and Prodi, E. E. 2016 (eds.). *The Cup of Song. Studies on Poetry and the Symposion.* Oxford.

Céard, M., Ménager, D., and Simonin, M. 1993–4. *Ronsard. Œuvres complètes*, 2 vols. No place of publication.

Ceccarelli, P. 2013. *Ancient Greek Letter Writing. A Cultural History (600 BC–150 BC).* Oxford.

César, A. C. 1999. *Crítica e tradução.* São Paulo.

Cesena, A. de 1865. *Les Belles Pécheresses.* Paris.

Cestaro, G. P. 2004 (ed.). *Queer Italia. Same-Sex Desire in Italian Literature and Film.* New York and Basingstoke.

Chatterjee, E. 1977 (ed., transl.). *An Anthology of Modern Bengali Short Stories.* Calcutta.

Chaudhuri, Rajkamal. 1966. *Machhli mari hu'i [Dead Fish].* New Delhi.

Chaudhuri, Rosinka. 2008. *Derozio, Poet of India. The Definitive Edition.* New Delhi.

<Chaussard, P.-J.-B.> 1801. *Fêtes et courtisanes de la Grèce. Supplément aux Voyages d'Anacharsis et d'Antenor*, 4 vols. Paris.

Chemello, A. 2012a (ed.). *Saffo tra poesia e leggenda. Fortuna di un personaggio nei secoli XVII e XIX.* Il Testo e le Forme 5. Padua.

  2012b. 'Saffo: intersezioni e contaminazioni di una *fabula* dal XVI al XIX secolo', in Chemello 2012a (ed.), 9–28.

  2015 (ed.). *Saffo. Riscritture e interpretazioni dal XVI al XX secolo.* Humanitas 22. Padua.

Chen, M. Y. 2012. *Animacies. Biopolitics, Racial Mattering, and Queer Affect.* Durham, NC and London.

Cheney, P., and Hardie, P. 2015 (eds.). *The Oxford History of Classical Reception in English Literature. Volume 2 (1558–1660).* Oxford.

Chikamatsu Shūkō. 1924. 'Takayama Chogyū shi wo omofu' ['Remembering Takayama Chogyū'], in *Shinsei joshi kokugo-dokuhon kyōjusankōsho [Teacher's Guide to the New Textbooks of the National Language and Literature for Women]* 8: 62–70.

Chrestides, D. A. 1985. 'Σαπφικά', *Ἑλληνικά* 36: 3–11.

Christian, T. 2015. *Gebildete Steine. Zur Rezeption literarischer Techniken in den Versinschriften seit dem Hellenismus.* Hypomnemata 197. Göttingen.

Cingano, E. 2005. 'A catalogue within a catalogue: Helen's suitors in the Hesiodic *Catalogue of Women*', in Hunter 2005 (ed.), 118–52.

Cirio, A.M. 2011. *Gli epigrammi di Giulia Balbilla (ricordi di una dama di corte) e altri testi al femminile sul colosso di Memnone*. Satura: Testi e Studi di Letteratura Antica 9. Lecce.

Citti, V. 1996. '"Solon" e la ricezione dell'antico', *Rivista Pascoliana* 8: 63–80.

Clark, M. H. 2008. *Where Are You Now?* London, New York, Sydney, Toronto.

Clay, D. 2011. 'Sappho, Selanna, and the poetry of the night', *Giornale Italiano di Filologia* NS 2: 3–11.

Clay, J. S. 1993. 'Sappho 55: going, going, gone', *Electronic Antiquity* 1.1.

Coarelli, F. 1972. 'Il complesso pompeiano del Campo Marzio e la sua decorazione scultorea', *Atti della Pontificia Accademia Romana di Archeologia (Rendiconti)* 3rd ser. 44: 99–122.

Cobbett, W. 1836. *Beauties of Cobbett*. London.

Coleman, K. M. 1988. *Statius. Silvae IV*. Oxford.

Coleman, P., Lewis, J., and Kowalik, J. 2000 (eds.). *Representations of the Self from the Renaissance to Romanticism*. Cambridge.

Collecott, D. 1999. *H.D. and Sapphic Modernism, 1910–1950*. Cambridge.

Colvin, S. 2007. *A Historical Greek Reader. Mycenaean to the Koiné*. Oxford.

Conde, J. A. 1797. *Poesias de Saffo, Meleagro y Museo*. Madrid.

Condello, F. 2007. 'Pasolini traduttore di Saffo: note di lettura', *Testo a Fronte* 37: 23–40.

Consani, C. 1991. Διάλεκτος. *Contributo alla storia del concetto di 'dialetto'*. Testi Linguistici 18. Pisa.

Contiades-Tsitsoni, E. 1990. *Hymenaios und Epithalamion. Das Hochzeitslied in der frühgriechischen Lyrik*. Beiträge zur Altertumskunde 16. Stuttgart.

Coronado, C. 1843. *Poesías*. Madrid. [2nd edn 1852, 3rd edn 1872]
   1850. 'Los genios gemelos. Primer paralelo. Safo y Santa Teresa de Jesús', *Semanario Pintoresco Español* 24 March: 89–94, 23 June: 193–5.

Costanza, S. 1950. *Risonanze dell'ode di Saffo Fainetai moi kēnos da Pindaro a Catullo e Orazio*. Messina and Florence.
   1980. 'Un motivo saffico in Teodoro Besto e in Simeone Metafraste (Saffo, fr. 96 V., 6–9; Teodoro, BHG³, 624,4; Simeone BHG³, 620,4)', *Orpheus. Rivista di umanità classica e cristiana* NS 1: 106–14.

Cotrone, R. 2015. 'La "Saffo" Verriana: trascrizione e rivisitazione di un mito', in Chemello 2015 (ed.), 149–60.

Cottignoli, A. 1991. *Alessandro Verri. Le avventure di Saffo poetessa di Mitilene*. Omikron 37. Rome.

Courtney, E. 1993. *The Fragmentary Latin Poets*. Oxford.

Cox, E. M. 1924. *The Poems of Sappho*. London and New York.

Crawford, J. 2002. 'Sidney's Sapphics and the role of interpretive communities', *English Literary History* 69: 979–1007.

Crespo, E., García Ramón, J. L., and Striano, A. 1993 (eds.). *Dialectologica Graeca. Actas del II Coloquio Internacional de Dialectología Griega (Miraflores de la Sierra [Madrid], 19–21 de junio de 1991)*. Madrid.

Cribiore, R. 2001. *Gymnastics of the Mind. Greek Education in Hellenistic and Roman Egypt*. Princeton and Oxford.

Crippen, L. 1914. *Clay and Fire*. London.

Cross, A. J. 2001. 'From *Lyrical Ballads* to *Lyrical Tales*: Mary Robinson's reputation and the problem of literary debt', *Studies in Romanticism* 40: 571–605.

Cucchiarelli, A. 1999. 'Hor. Epist. 1, 19, 28: *pede mascula Sappho*', *Hermes* 127: 328–44.

Culler, J. 2015. *Theory of the Lyric*. Cambridge, MA and London.

Currie, B. 2015. '*Cypria*', in Fantuzzi and Tsagalis 2015 (eds.), 281–305.

Dagley, R., and Croly, G. 1822. *Gems, Principally from the Antique*. London.

Daher, G. 2005. *Safo y Catulo. Poesía amorosa de la antigüedad*. <Santa Cruz de la Sierra.>

Dale, A. 2011a. 'Sapphica', *Harvard Studies in Classical Philology* 106: 47–74.

2011b. 'Alcaeus on the career of Myrsilos: Greeks, Lydians and Luwians at the east Aegean–west Anatolian interface', *Journal of Hellenic Studies* 131: 15–24.

2015. 'The Green Papyrus of Sappho (*P.GC* inv. 105) and the order of poems in the Alexandrian edition', *Zeitschrift für Papyrologie und Epigraphik* 196: 17–30.

D'Alessio, G. B. 2018. 'Fiction and pragmatics in ancient Greek lyric: the case of Sappho', in Budelmann and Phillips 2018 (eds.), 31–62.

2019. 'Textual notes on the "Newest" Sappho (on Sappho, fragments 5, 9, 17 V., and the Kypris Poem)', *Zeitschrift für Papyrologie und Epigraphik* 211: 18–31.

2021. 'Physical lay-out, material damages and reconstruction of fragmentary texts: two case studies from lyric poetry', in Alexandrou *et al.* 2021 (eds.).

Daley, C. 2003. *Leisure and Pleasure. Reshaping and Revealing the New Zealand Body 1900–1960*. Auckland.

Daley, J., and duBois, P. 2011. *Poetry of Sappho*. San Francisco.

Dally, O., Hölscher, T., Muth, S., and Schneider, R. M. 2014 (eds.). *Medien der Geschichte. Antikes Griechenland und Rom*. Berlin and Boston.

Damrosch, D. 2009a. 'Major cultures and minor literatures', in Damrosch 2009b (ed.), 193–204.

2009b (ed.). *Teaching World Literature*. New York.

Danek, G. 2015. '*Nostoi*', in Fantuzzi and Tsagalis 2015 (eds.), 355–79.

D'Angour, A. 2006. 'The New Music: so what's new?', in Goldhill and Osborne 2006 (eds.), 264–83.

Danna, D. 2004. 'Beauty and the beast: lesbians in literature and sexual science from the nineteenth to the twentieth centuries', in Cestaro 2004 (ed.), 117–32.

Daruwalla, K. N. 2006. *Collected Poems 1970–2005*. New Delhi.

Das, H. 1921. *Life and Letters of Toru Dutt*. Oxford.

Das, K. 1978. *My Story*. London, Melbourne, New York. [Original printing New Delhi 1976.]

1988. *Chandana Marangal*. Kottayam.

Das, S. K. 1989. *Bohu Yuger Opaar Hote. Nirbachita Kobita [From the Farther Shore of Time. Selected Poems]*. Kolkata.

Daudet, A. 1884. *Sapho. Mœurs parisiennes*. Paris.

1886. *Sappho*. London.

Davidson, J. 2007. *The Greeks and Greek Love. A Radical Reappraisal of Homosexuality in Ancient Greece.* London.

Davies, M., and Finglass, P. J. 2014. *Stesichorus. The Poems.* Cambridge Classical Texts and Commentaries 54. Cambridge.

Davis, G. 1991. *Polyhymnia. The Rhetoric of Horatian Lyric Discourse.* Berkeley, Los Angeles, Oxford.

Debenedetti, G. 1979. *Pascoli: la rivoluzione inconsapevole. Quaderni inediti.* Milan.

DeJean, J. 1989a. *Fictions of Sappho 1546–1937.* Chicago and London.

1989b. 'Sex and philology: Sappho and the rise of German nationalism', *Representations* 27: 148–71.

Demerson, G., *et al.* 1995–2003. *Remi Belleau. Œuvres poétiques,* 6 vols. Textes de la Renaissance 5, 21, 41, 47, 65, 78. Paris.

Demetrius, J. K. 1965. *Greek Scholarship in Spain and Latin America.* Chicago.

Demoen, K., and Praet, D. 2009 (eds.). *Theios Sophistes. Essays on Flavius Philostratus' Vita Apollonii.* Mnemosyne Supplement 305. Leiden and Boston.

Derda, T., Łajtar, A., and Urbanik, J. 2016 (eds.). *Proceedings of the 27th International Conference of Papyrology,* 3 vols. The Journal of Juristic Papyrology Supplement 28. Warsaw.

Derda, T., Hilder, J., and Kwapisz, J. 2017 (eds.). *Fragments, Holes, and Wholes. Reconstructing the Ancient World in Theory and Practice.* The Journal of Juristic Papyrology Supplement 30. Warsaw.

De' Rogati, F. S. 1782–3. *Le odi di Anacreonte e di Saffo, recate in versi italiani,* 2 vols. Colle.

Destrée, P., and Herrmann, F.-G. 2011 (eds.). *Plato and the Poets.* Leiden and Boston.

Destrée, P., and Murray, P. 2015 (eds.). *A Companion to Ancient Aesthetics.* Malden, MA, Oxford, Chichester.

Detienne, M. 1994. *The Gardens of Adonis. Spices in Greek Mythology,* transl. J. Lloyd. Princeton.

2007. *Les Jardins d'Adonis. La Mythologie des parfums et des aromates en Grèce³.* Paris. [1st edn 1972]

Devereux, G. 1970. 'The nature of Sappho's seizure in fr. 31 LP as evidence of her inversion', *Classical Quarterly* NS 20: 17–31.

Dias, A. G. 1857. *Cantos. Collecção de poezias. Segunda edicção.* Leipzig.

Di Benedetto, V. 1982. 'Sulla biografia di Saffo', *Studi Classici e Orientali* 32: 217–30.

1987. 'Introduzione', in Di Benedetto and F. Ferrari 1987: 5–78.

2005. 'La nuova Saffo e dintorni', *Zeitschrift für Papyrologie und Epigraphik* 153: 7–20. [= 2007: II 925–46]

2007. *Il richiamo del testo. Contributi di filologia e letteratura.* Anthropoi. Biblioteca di Scienza dell'Antichità 1–4. Pisa.

Di Benedetto, V., and Ferrari, F. 1987. *Saffo. Poesie.* Milan.

Diehl, E. 1908. *Supplementum lyricum. Neue Bruchstücke von Archilochus Alcaeus Sappho Corinna Pindar Bacchylides.* Kleine Texte für theologische und philologische Vorlesungen und Übungen 33–4. Bonn. [2nd edn 1910, 3rd edn 1917]

Dijkstra, J., Kroesen, J., and Kuiper, Y. 2010 (eds.). *Myths, Martyrs, and Modernity. Studies in the History of Religions in Honour of Jan N. Bremmer.* Numen Book Series Studies in the History of Religions 127. Leiden and Boston.

Diller, H. 1962/3. 'Möglichkeiten subjektiver Aussage in den frühen griechischen Lyrik', Ἐπιστημονικὴ Ἐπετηρὶς τῆς φιλοσοφικῆς Σχολῆς τοῦ Πανεπιτημίου Ἀθηνῶν 13: 558–66. [= 1971: 64–72]

1971. *Kleine Schriften zur antiken Literatur*, ed. H.-J. Newiger and H. Seyffert. Munich.

Dimaras, K. T. 1947. Κωστῆς Παλαμάς. Η πορεία του προς την τέχνη. Athens.

Donati, A. 1917. *Giacomo Leopardi. Canti.* Bari.

Donoghue, E. 1998. *We Are Michael Field.* Bath and New York.

Dougherty, C., and Kurke, L. 1993 (eds.). *Cultural Poetics in Archaic Greece. Cult, Performance, Politics.* Cambridge.

Douglas, Lord A. 1896. *Poems – Poèmes.* Paris.

Doukas, D. 1508. *Rhetores in hoc volumine habentur hi. Aphthonii Sophistae progymnasmata . . .* Venice.

Dover, K. J. 1978. *Greek Homosexuality.* London.

Duarte, A. da S. 2016. 'Por uma história da tradução dos clássicos greco-latinos no Brasil', *Translatio* 12: 43–62.

Dubischar, M. 2015. 'Typology of philological writings', in Montanari *et al.* 2015 (eds.), II 545–99.

duBois, P. 1978. 'Sappho and Helen', *Arethusa* II: 89–99. [= Greene 1996a: 79–88]

1985. 'Phallocentrism and its subversion in Plato's *Phaedrus*', *Arethusa* 18: 91–103.

1992. 'Eros and the woman', *Ramus* 21: 97–116.

1995. *Sappho is Burning.* Chicago and London.

2010. *Out of Athens. The New Ancient Greeks.* Cambridge, MA and London.

2015. *Sappho.* London and New York.

2017. 'Transatlantic Sapphos', in Caldeira *et al.* 2017 (eds.), II 27–35.

Duncan, B. 2000. 'Johann Christoph Gottsched 1700–1766', in Konzett 2000 (ed.), I 357–9.

Duncan-Jones, K. 1994. *Sir Philip Sidney. The Countess of Pembroke's Arcadia (The Old Arcadia).* Oxford.

Durrell, L. 1950. *Sappho. A Play in Verse.* London.

Dwivedi, A. N. 2000. *Kamala Das and Her Poetry. Second Revised and Enlarged Edition.* New Delhi. [1st edn 1983]

Dyckman, S. 1937. 'El Afroditei' ['To Aphrodite'], *Davar* (16 April): 9.

Edmonds, J. M. 1922a. *Lyra Graeca. Being the Remains of All the Greek Lyric Poets from Eumelus to Timotheus Excepting Pindar. Volume I Including Terpander Alcman Sappho and Alcaeus.* London and New York.

1922b. 'Sappho's book as depicted on an Attic vase', *Classical Quarterly* 16: 1–14.

Edmunds, L. 2006. 'The New Sappho: ἔφαντο (9)', *Zeitschrift für Papyrologie und Epigraphik* 156: 23–6.

Edo, M. 2014. 'La fealdad de Safo en la literatura moderna: historia de un eufemismo', *Lexis* 32: 398–410.

Edwards, D. 1989. *Stampede of the Lower Gods. Classical Mythology in Australian Art 1890s–1930s. Art Gallery of New South Wales 19th October–26th November 1989.* Sydney.

2007 (ed.). *Bertram Mackennal. The Fifth Balnaves Foundation Sculpture Project.* Sydney.

Edwards, M. J. 1991. 'A quotation of Sappho in Juvenal *Satire 6*', *Phoenix* 45: 255–7.

Eidinow, E., and Maurizio, L. 2020 (eds.). *Narratives of Time and Gender in Antiquity.* Abingdon and New York.

Ekrony, A. 1971. *Shirim ve-shurot shel Sapfo mi-lesbos [Poems and Fragments by Sappho of Lesbos].* Tel Aviv.

Elliott, B., and Wallace, J.-A. 1992. 'Fleurs du mal or second-hand roses?: Natalie Barney, Romaine Brooks, and the "originality of the avant-garde"', *Feminist Review* 40: 6–30.

Ellis-Evans, A. 2019. *The Kingdom of Priam. Lesbos and the Troad between Anatolia and the Aegean.* Oxford.

Elytis, O. 1984. Σαπφώ. Ανασύνθεση και απόδοση. <Athens.>

Engelking, T. L. 2005. 'Translating the lesbian writer: Pierre Louÿs, Natalie Barney, and "Girls of the Future Society"', *South Central Review* 22: 62–77.

Erbse, H. 1960. *Beiträge zur Überlieferung der Iliasscholien.* Zetemata 24. Munich.

Erdman, D. V. 1978. *The Collected Works of Samuel Taylor Coleridge. Essays on His Times in The Morning Post and The Courier*, 3 vols. Bollinger Series 75. London and Princeton.

Esclasans, A. de, Montes de Oca, I., Vega, A. L. de la, and Soms y Castelín, E. 1954. *Bucólicos y líricos griegos.* Buenos Aires.

Estévez, A. 1998. *Julio Herrera y Reissig. Poesía completa y prosas.* Colección Archivos 32. Madrid.

E<strada>, J. M. 1889 (ed.). *Lira Argentina. Recopilación de poesías selectas de poetas argentinos.* Buenos Aires.

Fabre-Serris, J. 2016. 'Anne Dacier (1681), Renée Vivien (1903) or what does it mean for a woman to translate Sappho?', in Wyles and Hall 2016 (eds.), 78–102.

Fairweather, J. A. 1974. 'Fiction in the biographies of ancient writers', *Ancient Society* 5: 231–75.

1983. 'Traditional narrative, inference and truth in the *Lives* of Greek poets', in F. Cairns 1983 (ed.), 315–69.

Fanfani, G., Harlow, M., and Nosch, M.-L. 2016 (eds.). *Spinning Fates and the Song of the Loom. The Use of Textiles, Clothing and Cloth Production as Metaphor, Symbol and Narrative Device in Greek and Latin Literature.* Ancient Textiles Series 24. Oxford and Philadelphia.

Fantalkin, A., and Lytle, E. 2016. 'Alcaeus and Antimenidas: resassessing the evidence for Greek mercenaries in the Neo-Babylonian army', *Klio* 98: 90–117.

Fantuzzi, M. 1995. 'Levio, Saffo e la grazia delle fanciulle lidie (Laev. fr. 18)', in Belloni *et al.* 1995 (eds.), 1 341–7.

Fantuzzi, M., and Hunter, R. 2004. *Tradition and Innovation in Hellenistic Poetry.* Cambridge.

Fantuzzi, M., and Pretagostini, R. 1995–6 (eds.). *Struttura e storia dell'esametro greco*, 2 vols. Studi di Metrica Classica 10. Rome.

Fantuzzi, M., and Tsagalis, C. 2015 (eds.). *The Greek Epic Cycle and Its Ancient Reception. A Companion.* Cambridge.

Faraone, C. A. 1999. *Ancient Greek Love Magic.* Cambridge, MA and London.

Fariña, S. 2012. *Ahora, mientras danzamos. Poemas de Safo.* Santiago.

Farnham, F. 1976. *Madame Dacier. Scholar and Humanist.* Monterey, CA.

Fassino, M., and Prauscello, L. 2001. 'Memoria ritmica e memoria poetica: Saffo e Alceo in Teocrito Idilli 28–30 tra ἀρχαιολογία metrica e innovazione alessandrina', *Materiali e Discussioni per l'Analisi dei Testi Classici* 46: 9–37.

Faulkner, A. 2008. *The Homeric Hymn to Aphrodite.* Oxford.

Faustino, M. 1955. *O homem e sua hora e outros poemas.* Rio de Janeiro.

Favaro, F. 2012. 'I canti d'amore (e di morte) di una Saffo del Settecento', in Chemello 2012a (ed.), 131–45.

2015. 'Per uno "stil soave e raro": traduttori (e traduzioni) di Saffo tra XVII e XIX secolo', in Chemello 2015 (ed.), 135–48.

Fede. 1908. *L'eredità di Saffo.* Rome.

Feeney, D. 1993. 'Horace and the Greek lyric poets', in Rudd 1993 (ed.), 41–63.

Feijóo, B. J. 1740. *Supplemento de el theatro critico, o adiciones, y correcciones a muchos de los assumptos que se tratan en los ocho Tomos de el dicho Theatro. Tomo nono.* Madrid.

Feldman, P. R., and Robinson, D. 1999. *A Century of Sonnets. The Romantic-Era Revival 1750–1850.* New York and Oxford.

Felson, N. 2004. 'Introduction', *Arethusa* 37: 253–66.

Fernández Moreno, C. 1972. *América Latina en su literatura.* Mexico City and Paris.

Ferrari, F. 1987. *Sappho. Poesie.* Milan.

2000. 'Due note al testo del fr. 2 di Saffo', *Analecta Papyrologica* 12: 37–44.

2003. 'Il pubblico di Saffo', *Studi Italiani di Filologia Classica* 4th ser. 1: 42–89.

2007. *Una mitra per Kleis. Saffo e il suo pubblico.* Biblioetca di Materiali e discussioni per l'analisi dei testi classici 19. Pisa.

2010. *Sappho's Gift. The Poet and Her Community*, transl. B. Acosta-Hughes and L. Prauscello. Ann Arbor. [Translation of F. Ferrari 2007]

2011. 'Da Kato Simi a Mitilene: ancora sull'ode dell'ostrakon fiorentino (Sapph. fr. 2 Voigt)', *La Parola del Passato* 66: 442–63.

2014. 'Saffo e i suoi fratelli e altri brani del primo libro', *Zeitschrift für Papyrologie und Epigraphik* 192: 1–19. [English translation by C. Meccariello: 'Sappho and her brothers, and other passages from the first book', www.papyrology.ox.ac.uk/Fragments/Translation.Ferrari.i.15.pdf]

Ferrari, G. 2002. *Figures of Speech. Men and Maidens in Ancient Greece.* Chicago and London.

Ferrari, G. R. F. 1987. *Listening to the Cicadas. A Study of Plato's Phaedrus.* Cambridge.

Ferrero, L., *et al.* 1963 (eds.). *Miscellanea di studi alessandrini in memoria di Augusto Rostagni.* Turin.

Field, M. 1889. *Long Ago.* London.

Finglass, P. J. 2014. 'Introduction', in Davies and Finglass 2014: 1–91.

  2015. Review of Rayor and Lardinois 2014, *Bryn Mawr Classical Review* 2015.05.30.

  2017. 'Dancing with Stesichorus', in Gianvittorio 2017 (ed.), 67–89.

  2018. *Sophocles. Oedipus the King.* Cambridge Classical Texts and Commentaries 57. Cambridge.

Finglass, P. J., and Kelly, A. 2015a (eds.). *Stesichorus in Context.* Cambridge.

  2015b. 'The state of Stesichorean studies', in Finglass and Kelly 2015a (eds.), 1–17.

Finkelberg, M. 2011 (ed.). *The Homer Encyclopedia*, 3 vols. Malden MA, Oxford, Chichester.

  2018. 'Lesbian and mainland Greece', in Giannakis *et al.* 2018 (eds.), 447–56.

Fischer, D. 2008. *Al encuentro de las tres Marías. Juana de Ibarbourou más allá del mito.* Montevideo.

Fitzgerald, W. 1995. *Catullan Provocations. Lyric Poetry and the Drama of Position.* Classics and Contemporary Thought 1. Berkeley, Los Angeles, London.

Flores, G. G. 2017. *Safo. Fragmentos completos.* São Paulo.

Fogli, G. 1996. 'La "canzoncina di Saffo" ed il tramonto della luna nelle *Ultime lettere di Jacopo Ortis*', *Strumenti Critici* NS 11: 431–48.

Foley, H. P. 1981 (ed.). *Reflections of Women in Antiquity.* New York, London, Paris.

  1994. *The Homeric Hymn to Demeter. Translation, Commentary, and Interpretive Essays.* Princeton.

  1998. '"The mother of the argument": *eros* and the body in Sappho and Plato's *Phaedrus*', in Wyke 1998 (ed.), 39–70.

Foley, J. M. 1991. *Immanent Art. From Structure to Meaning in Traditional Oral Epic.* Bloomington, IN and Indianapolis.

Foligno, C. 1958. *Ugo Foscolo. Saggi di letteratura italiana*, 2 vols. Edizione Nazionale delle Opere di Ugo Foscolo 11. Florence.

Forberg, F. K. 1906. *Manuel d'érotologie classique (De figuris Veneris).* Paris. [First published 1824]

Ford, A. L. 2006. 'The genre of genres: paeans and *paian* in early Greek poetry', *Poetica. Zeitschrift für Sprach- und Literaturwissenschaft* 38: 277–95.

  2010. '"A song to match my song": lyric doubling in Euripides' *Helen*', in Mitsis and Tsagalis 2010 (eds.), 283–302.

Ford, B. B., and Kopff, E. C. 1976. 'Sappho fr. 31.9: a defense of the hiatus', *Glotta* 54: 52–6.

Forestier, G. 1999. *Racine. Oeuvres complètes.* 1. *Théâtre – poésie.* Paris.

Forsyth, N. 1979. 'The allurement scene: a typical pattern in Greek oral epic', *Classical Antiquity* 12: 107–20.

Fortenbaugh, W. W. 1966. 'Plato *Phaedrus* 235C3', *Classical Philology* 61: 108–9.

Fortuna, M. 1776. *Saffo. Tragedia.* Livorno. [= Chemello 2012a (ed.), 45–128]

<Foscolo, U.> 1817. *Ultime lettere di Jacopo Ortis.* 2 vols. London. [Earlier versions published 1798, 1802]

    1818. 'Essay on the present literature of Italy', in Hobhouse 1818: 345–484. [= Foligno 1958: ɪɪ 399–490]

Foster, M., Kurke, L., and Weiss, N. 2020 (eds.). *Genre in Archaic and Classical Greek Poetry. Theories and Models.* Mnemosyne Supplement 428. Studies in Archaic and Classical Greek Song 4. Leiden and Boston.

Foucault, M. 1976–2018. *Histoire de la sexualité,* 4 vols. Paris.

    1978–86. *The History of Sexuality,* 3 vols. New York.

Fowler, D. 1994. 'Postmodernism, romanticism, and classical closure', in De Jong and Sullivan 1994 (eds.), 231–56. [= 2000: 5–33]

    2000. *Roman Constructions. Readings in Postmodern Latin.* Oxford.

Fowler, R. L. 1987. *The Nature of Early Greek Lyric. Preliminary Studies.* Phoenix Supplement 21. Toronto.

Foxhall, L., Gehrke, H.-J., and Luraghi, N. 2010 (eds.). *Intentional History. Spinning Time in Ancient Greece.* Stuttgart.

Fränkel, H. 1968. *Wege und Formen frühgriechischen Denkens. Literarische und philosophiegeschichtliche Studien*[3], ed. F. Tietze. Munich. [1st edn 1955]

    1969. *Dichtung und Philosophie des frühen Griechentums. Eine Geschichte der griechischen Epik, Lyrik und Prosa bis zur Mitte des fünften Jahrhunderts*[3]. Munich. [1st edn 1951]

    1975. *Early Greek Poetry and Philosophy. A History of Greek Epic, Lyric, and Prose to the Middle of the Fifth Century,* transl. M. Hadas and J. Willis. Oxford.

    1995–6. 'L'esametro di Omero e di Callimaco', in Fantuzzi and Pretagostini 1995–6 (eds.), ɪɪ 173–248.

Franklin, J. C. 2002. 'Diatonic music in Greece: a reassessment of its antiquity', *Mnemosyne* 4th ser. 55: 669–702.

    2015. *Kinyras. The Divine Lyre.* Hellenic Studies 70. Cambridge, MA and London.

Franklin, R. W. 1998. *The Poems of Emily Dickinson. Variorum Edition,* 3 vols. Cambridge, MA and London.

Frederick, S. 2016. *Yoshiya Nobuko's Yellow Rose.* Los Angeles and Tokyo.

Freeman, K. 1947. *The Greek Way. An Anthology. Translations from Verse and Prose.* London.

    1948. *Ancilla to the Pre-Socratic Philosophers. A Complete Translation of the Fragments in Diels, Fragmente der Vorsokratiker.* Oxford.

Freeman, P. 2016. *Searching for Sappho. The Lost Songs and World of the First Woman Poet.* New York and London.

Fulkerson, L. 2005. *The Ovidian Heroine as Author. Reading, Writing, and Community in the Heroides.* Cambridge.

Funghi, M. S., and Messeri Savorelli, G. 1992. 'Lo "scriba di Pindaro" e le biblioteche di Ossirinco', *Studi Classici e Orientali* 42: 43–62.

Furley, W. D. 2000. '"Fearless, bloodless . . . like the gods": Sappho 31 and the rhetoric of "godlike"', *Classical Quarterly* NS 50: 7–15.

Furley, W. D., and Bremer, J. M. 2001. *Greek Hymns. Selected Cult Songs from the Archaic to the Hellenistic Period*, 2 vols. Studien und Texte zu Antike und Christentum 9–10. Tübingen.

Gabba, E. 1963. 'Il latino come dialetto greco', in Ferrero *et al.* 1963 (eds.), 188–94. [= 2000: 159–64]

2000. *Roma arcaica. Storia e storiografia.* Storia e Letteratura 205. Rome.

Gagné, R. 2013. 'Dancing letters: the *Alphabetic Tragedy* of Kallias', in Gagné and Hopman 2013 (eds.), 297–316.

Gagné, R., and Hopman, M. G. 2013 (eds.), *Choral Mediations in Greek Tragedy.* Cambridge.

Gallavotti, C. 1948. *La lingua dei poeti eolici. Con appendice metrica.* Μουσικαὶ διάλεκτοι 3. Bari and Naples.

1961. '40. Ode di Saffo', *Papiri della Università degli Studi di Milano P. Mil. Vogliano* 2: 17–21.

Galvez de Cabrera, M. R. 1804. *Obras poéticas*, 3 vols. Madrid. [*sic*, no accent on a of 'Gálvez']

Gambarin, G. 1955. *Ugo Foscolo. Ultime lettere di Jacopo Ortis.* Edizione Nazionale delle Opere di Ugo Foscolo 4. Florence.

Gantz, T. 1993. *Early Greek Myth. A Guide to Literary and Artistic Sources.* Baltimore and London.

García-Posada, M. 1997. *Federico García Lorca. Obras completas*, 4 vols. Barcelona.

García Teijeiro, M. 1993. 'Vestigios de acentuación dialectal en textos dóricos y eólicos', in Crespo *et al.* 1993 (eds.), 147–65.

Garnett, R. 1905. 'Indian love', *The Bookman* 28.168 (September): 206.

Garzya, A. 1971. 'Per la fortuna di Saffo a Bisanzio', *Jahrbuch der Österreichischen Byzantinistik* 20: 1–5. [= 1974: ch. 15]

1974. *Storia e interpretazione di testi bizantini. Saggi e ricerche.* London.

Gazis, A. 1807. Βιβλιοθήκης Ἑλληνικῆς βιβλία δύο. Περιέχοντα κατὰ χρονικὴν πρόοδον τὰς περὶ τῶν ἐξόχων Ἑλλήνων Συγγραφέων βεβαιωτέρας εἰδήσεις, 2 vols. Venice.

Gennep, A. van 1909. *Les Rites de passage. Étude systématique des rites de la porte et du seuil, de l'hospitalité, de l'adoption, de la grossesse et de l'accouchement, de la naissance, de l'enfance, de la puberté, de l'initiation, de l'ordination, du couronnement des fiançailles et du mariage, des funérailles, des saisons, etc.* Paris.

Genovese, A. 1998. *La doble voz. Poetas argentinas contemporáneas.* Biblioteca de Las Mujeres 7. Buenos Aires.

Gentili, B. 1984. *Poesia e pubblico nella Grecia antica. Da Omero al V secolo.* Rome and Bari.

1988. *Poetry and Its Public in Ancient Greece. From Homer to the Fifth Century*, transl. with an introduction by A. T. Cole. Baltimore and London.

Gentili, B., and Lomiento, L. 2003. *Metrica e ritmica. Storia delle forme poetiche nella Grecia antica.* Milan.

Gentili, B., and Perusino, F. 1995 (eds.), *Mousike. Metrica ritmica e musica greca in memoria di Giovanni Comotti.* Pisa and Rome.

Georgakopoulou, A., and Silk, M. 2009 (eds.). *Standard Languages and Language Standards. Greek, Past and Present.* Centre for Hellenic Studies King's College London Publications 12. Farnham and Burlington, VT.

George, R. M. 2000. 'Calling Kamala Das queer: rereading *My Story*', *Feminist Studies* 26: 731–63.

Getsy, D. J. 2007. '"Her invitation and her contempt": Bertram Mackennal and the sculptural femme fatale in the 1890s', in D. Edwards 2007 (ed.), 97–103, 206–7.

Ghelli, M. L. 2007. 'Carteggio Pascoli – De Bosis', in Ghelli and Cevolani 2007: 1–157.

Ghelli, M. L., and Cevolani, C. 2007. *Carteggio Pascoli – De Bosis. Carteggio Pascoli – Bianchi.* Edizione Nazionale delle Opere di Giovanni Pascoli Carteggi 1. Bologna.

Giacomelli, A. [= Carson, A., *q.v.*]
  1980. 'The justice of Aphrodite in Sappho 1', *Transactions of the American Philological Association* 110: 135–42. [= Carson 1996]

Giannakis, G. K., Crespo, E., and Filos, P. 2018 (eds.). *Studies in Ancient Greek Dialects. From Central Greece to the Black Sea.* Trends in Classics Supplement 49. Berlin and Boston.

Giannini, P. 2010. 'Tre noterelle sulla colometria antica', *Quaderni Urbinati di Cultura Classica* NS 94: 17–24.

Gianvittorio, L. 2017 (ed.). *Choreutika. Performing and Theorizing Dance in Ancient Greece.* Biblioteca di Quaderni Urbinati di Cultura Classica 13. Pisa and Rome.

Gibson, M. E. 2011a. *Indian Angles. English Verse in Colonial India from Jones to Tagore.* Athens, OH.
  2011b. *Anglophone Poetry in Colonial India, 1780–1913. A Critical Anthology.* Athens, OH.

Gigante, M. 1977. 'Anecdoton pseudosapphicum', *Rivista di Cultura Classica e Medioevale* 19: 421.
  2002. *Leopardi e l'antico.* Naples.

Gilbert, R. 1994. *Gongyla Remembers. Poems.* Wellington.
  1998. *Complete Sappho Poems of Ruth Gilbert.* Wellington.

Gilhuly, K. 2015. 'Lesbians are not from Lesbos', in Blondell and Ormand 2015b (eds.), 143–76. [≈ 2018: 92–116]
  2018. *Erotic Geographies in Ancient Greek Literature and Culture.* Abingdon and New York.

Gill, C., and Wiseman, T. P. 1993 (eds.). *Lies and Fiction in the Ancient World.* Exeter.

Giusti, R. F. 1938. 'Alfonsina Storni', *Nosotros* 32 (segunda época 3): 372–97.

<Gleim, J. W. L.> 1746. *Die Oden Anakreons in reimlosen Versen. Nebst einigen andern Gedichten.* Frankfurt and Leipzig.

Goldberg, L. 1968. *Lu'ach ha-ohavim. Leket shirei ahava mi-shirat yisra'el ve-'amim [A Calendar for Lovers. An International Anthology of Love Poetry].* Tel Aviv.

Goldhill, S. 2006. 'The touch of Sappho', in Martindale and Thomas 2006 (eds.), 250–73. [≈ 2011: 65–83]
  2011. *Victorian Culture and Classical Antiquity. Art, Opera, Fiction, and the Proclamation of Modernity.* Princeton and Oxford.

Goldhill, S., and Osborne, R. 2006 (eds.). *Rethinking Revolutions through Ancient Greece*. Cambridge.

Goldschmidt, N., and Graziosi, B. 2018 (eds.). *Tombs of the Ancient Poets. Between Literary Reception and Material Culture*. Oxford.

Goldsmith, M. 1933. *Christina of Sweden. A Psychological Biography*. London.

1938. *Sappho of Lesbos. A Psychological Reconstruction of Her Life*. London.

Goldwyn, A. 2016. '"The virtue of Hellenism": Yoram Bronowski's Hebrew translations of Constantine Cavafy and Israel's Mediterranean identity', *Journal of Mediterranean Studies* 25: 137–53.

Gomes, E. 1960. *Castro Alves. Obra completa*. Rio de Janeiro.

Gomez de Avellaneda, G. 1869–71. *Obras literarias. Coleccion completa*, 5 vols. Madrid.

Gonda, C. 2015. 'Writing lesbian desire in the long eighteenth century', in Med 2015 (ed.), 107–21.

Gonda, C., and Beynon, J. C. 2010. 'Introduction', in Beynon and Gonda 2010: 1–7.

Gonzaga, T. A. 1792. *Marília de Dirceo*. Lisbon.

1802. *Marília de Dirceo. Terceira Parte*. Lisbon.

González Delgado, R. 2012. 'Una traducción desconocida de Safo de 1815', in González González 2012 (ed.), 75–103.

González de Tobía, A. M. 2001. 'Lateinamerika', *Der neue Pauly. Enzyklopädie der Antike. Rezeptions- und Wissenschaftsgeschichte* 15.1: 20–47. [Surname misspelt as 'Gonzáles' in publication]

2005. 'Tradición clásica en Iberoamérica', *Synthesis* 12: 113–29.

2008. 'Latin America', *Brill's New Pauly. Encyclopedia of the Ancient World. Classical Tradition* 3: 112–41. [Surname misspelt as 'Gonzáles' in publication]

González Echevarría, R., and Pupo-Walker, E. 1996 (eds.). *The Cambridge History of Latin American Literature*, 3 vols. Cambridge.

González González, M. 2012 (ed.). *Mujeres de la Antigüedad. Texto e imagen. Homenaje a Mª Ángeles Durán López*. Málaga.

Goold, G. P. 1983. *Catullus*. London.

1995. *Chariton. Callirhoe*. Loeb Classical Library 481. Cambridge, MA and London.

Gordon, P. 1997. 'The lover's voice in *Heroides* 15: or, why is Sappho a man?', in Hallett and Skinner 1997 (eds.), 274–91.

Gostoli, A. 1990. *Terpandro*. Lyricorum Graecorum quae exstant 8. Rome.

Gottsched, J. C. 1744. *Herrn Benjamin Neukirchs, weiland Marggräfl. Brandenburg-Anspachischen Hofraths, auserlesene Gedichte aus verschiedenen poetischen Schriften gesammlet und mit einer Vorrede von dem Leben des Dichters begleitet von Joh. Christoph Gottscheden*. Regensburg.

<Götz, J. N.> 1760. *Die Gedichte Anakreons und der Sappho Oden aus dem Griechischen übersezt, und mit Anmerkungen begleitet*. Karlsruhe.

Gouma-Peterson, T. 2000a (ed.). *Anna Komnene and Her Times*. Garland Medieval Casebooks 29. Garland Reference Library of the Humanities 2201. New York and London.

2000b. 'Gender and power: passages to the maternal in Anna Komnene's *Alexiad*', in Gouma-Peterson 2000a (ed.), 107–24.

Gouzelis, D. 1817. *Η κρίσις του Πάριδος. Ποίημα μυθολογικόν, ερωτικόν και ηθικόν.* Trieste.

Gragnolati, M. 2006. 'Lo scrittore, l'amore e la morte. Per una lettura leopardiana dei *Dialoghi con Leucò*', *Testo. Studi di Teoria e Storia della Letteratura e della Critica* 52: 59–75.

Grahn, J. 1985. *The Highest Apple. Sappho and the Lesbian Poetic Tradition.* San Francisco.

Gram, L. M. 2019. '*Odi et amo*: on Lesbia's name in Catullus', in Thorsen and Harrison 2019 (eds.), 95–117.

Granarolo, J. 1971. *D'Ennius à Catulle. Recherches sur les antécédents romains de la 'poésie nouvelle'.* Paris.

Grand-Clément, A. 2015. '*Poikilia*', in Destrée and Murray 2015 (eds.), 406–21.

Graziosi, B., and Haubold, J. 2009. 'Greek lyric and early Greek literary history', in Budelmann 2009 (ed.), 95–113.

Green, P. 1965. *The Laughter of Aphrodite.* London.

Greene, E. 1994. 'Apostrophe and women's erotics in the poetry of Sappho', *Transactions of the American Philological Asssociation* 124: 41–56. [= 1996a (ed.), 233–47]

1996a (ed.). *Reading Sappho. Contemporary Approaches.* Classics and Contemporary Thought 2. Berkeley, Los Angeles, London.

1996b (ed.). *Re-reading Sappho. Reception and Transmission.* Classics and Contemporary Thought 3. Berkeley, Los Angeles, London.

1996c. 'Introduction', in Greene 1996a (ed.), 1–8.

1996d. 'Introduction', in Greene 1996b (ed.), 1–9.

1996e. 'Sappho, Foucault, and women's erotics', *Arethusa* 29: 1–14.

2005 (ed.). *Women Poets in Ancient Greece and Rome.* Norman, OK.

2009. 'Sappho 58: philosophical reflections on death and aging', in Greene and Skinner 2009 (eds.), 147–61.

2011. 'Catullus and Sappho', in Skinner 2011 (ed.), 131–50.

Greene, E., and Skinner, M. 2009 (eds.). *The New Sappho on Old Age. Textual and Philosophical Issues.* Hellenic Studies 38. Cambridge, MA and London.

Gregory, E. 1997. *H.D. and Hellenism. Classic Lines.* Cambridge Studies in American Literature and Culture III. Cambridge.

Grenfell, B. P., and Hunt, A. S. 1898. 'VII. Sappho', *The Oxyrhynchus Papyri* 1: 10–13.

1903. '421–434. Poetical fragments', *The Oxyrhynchus Papyri* 1: 67–76.

1914a. '1231. Sappho, book i', *The Oxyrhynchus Papyri* 10: 20–43.

1914b. '1232. Sappho, book ii', *The Oxyrhynchus Papyri* 10: 44–50.

1922. '1787. Sappho, book iv', *The Oxyrhynchus Papyri* 15: 26–46.

Griffiths, J. M. 2010. *Sappho . . . in 9 Fragments.* Strawberry Hills, NSW.

Griggs, E. L. 1956–71. *Collected Letters of Samuel Taylor Coleridge*, 6 vols. Oxford.

Gronewald, M. 1974. 'Fragmente aus einem Sapphokommentar: Pap. Colon. inv. 5860', *Zeitschrift für Papyrologie und Epigraphik* 14: 114–18.

Gronewald, M., and Daniel, R. W. 2004a. 'Einer neuer Sappho-Papyrus', *Zeitschrift für Papyrologie und Epigraphik* 147: 1–8.

2004b. 'Nachtrag zum neuen Sappho-Papyrus', *Zeitschrift für Papyrologie und Epigraphik* 149: 1–4.

2005. 'Lyrischer Text Sappho-Papyrus', *Zeitschrift für Papyrologie und Epigraphik* 154: 7–12.

2007a. '429. Sappho', *Kölner Papyri* 11: 1–11.

2007b. '430. Lyrischer Text Sappho-Papyrus', *Kölner Papyri* 11: 12–19.

Grono, W. 1995. *Dorothy Hewett. Collected Poems, 1940–1995*. South Fremantle, WA.

Gubar, S. 1984. 'Sapphistries', *Signs: Journal of Women in Culture and Society* 10: 43–62. [= Greene 1996b (ed.), 199–217]

Guido y Spano, C. 1868. 'Mujeres griegas. Artículo de la "Revista Británica"', *La Revista de Buenos Aires. Historia Americana, literatura, derecho y variedades* 17: 399–432.

1871. *Hojas al viento. Libro lírico*. Buenos Aires.

Gutzwiller, K. J. 1998. *Poetic Garlands. Hellenistic Epigrams in Context*. Berkeley, Los Angeles, London.

Guy, D. J. 2011. 'Gender and sexuality in Latin America', in Moya 2011 (ed.), 367–81.

Gyraldus, L. G. 1545. *Historiae poetarum tam graecorum quam latinorum dialogi decem, quibus scripta et vitae eorum sic exprimuntur, ut ea perdiscere cupientibus, minimum iam laboris esse queat*. Basel.

Habinek, T. 1996. 'Series Editor's foreword', in Greene 1996b (ed.), xi–xiii.

Haddad, J. A. 1942. *Safo lírica*. Serie clássica de cultura 22. São Paulo.

Hafter, M. Z. 2001. *Carolina Coronado. Jarilla: novella original. Los genios gemelos*. Colección clásicos extremeños 16. Badajoz.

Hagel, S. 1994–5. 'Zu den Konstituenten des griechischen Hexameters', *Wiener Studien* 107–8: 77–108.

2010. *Ancient Greek Music. A New Technical History*. Cambridge.

Hague, R. H. 1983. 'Ancient Greek wedding songs: the tradition of praise', *Journal of Folklore Research* 20: 131–43.

Haines, C. R. 1926. *Sappho. The Poems and Fragments*. London and New York.

Haizi. 2009. *Haizi shiquanji [Complete Poems of Haizi]*. Beijing.

Hajnal, I. 2007 (ed.). *Die altgriechischen Dialekte. Wesen und Werden. Akten des Kolloquiums Freie Universität Berlin 19.–22. September 2001*. Innsbrucker Beiträge zur Sprachwissenschaft 26. Innsbruck.

Hallett, J. P. 1979. 'Sappho and her social context: sense and sensuality', *Signs* 4: 447–64. [≈ Greene 1996a: 125–42]

1982. 'Beloved Cleïs', *Quaderni Urbinati di Cultura Classica* NS 10: 21–31.

2005. 'Catullan voices in *Heroides* 15: how Sappho became a man', *Dictynna* 2: 1–15.

Hallett, J. P., and Skinner, M. B. 1997 (eds.). *Roman Sexualities*. Princeton.

Halperin, D. M. 1990. *One Hundred Years of Homosexuality and Other Essays on Greek Love*. New York and London.

Hamilton, C. 1910. *A Pageant of Great Women*. London.

Hamm, E.-M. 1958. *Grammatik zu Sappho und Alkaios*². Abhandlungen der Deutschen Akademie der Wissenschaften zu Berlin Klasse für Sprachen, Literatur und Kunst Jahrgang 1951 nr. 2. Berlin. [1st edn 1957]

Hanscombe, G., and Namjoshi, S. 1991. '"Who wrongs you, Sappho?" – developing Lesbian sensibility in the writing of lyric poetry', in Aaron and Walby 1991 (eds.), 156–67.

Harder, M. A., Regtuit, R. F., and Wakker, G. C. 1996 (eds.). *Theocritus.* Hellenistica Groningana 2. Groningen.

Hardie, A. 2005. 'Sappho, the Muses, and life after death', *Zeitschrift für Papyrologie und Epigraphik* 154: 13–32.

Harrigan, R. K. 1980. 'Woman and artist: Grillparzer's Sappho revisited', *The German Quarterly* 54.3: 298–316.

Harris, V. C., and Mohamed Ummer, C. K. 1995. *Kamala Das. The Sandal Trees and Other Stories.* Hyderabad.

Harris, W. V., and Holmes, B. 2008 (eds.). *Aelius Aristides between Greece, Rome, and the Gods.* Columbia Studies in the Classical Tradition 33. Leiden and Boston.

Harrison, S. 2019. 'Shades of Sappho in Vergil', in Thorsen and Harrison 2019 (eds.), 137–49.

Harshav, B. 2014. *Three Thousand Years of Hebrew Versification. Essays in Comparative Prosody.* New Haven and London.

Hart, E. L., and Smith, M. N. 1998 (eds.). *Open Me Carefully. Emily Dickinson's Intimate Letters to Susan Huntington Dickinson.* Ashfield, MA.

<Harwood, G.> 1962. 'Burning Sappho', *The Bulletin*, 23 June: 51.

Haselswerdt, E. 2016. 'Re-queering Sappho', *Eidolon*, 8 August (https://eidolon. pub/re-queering-sappho-c6c05b6b9f0b).

Haslam, M. W. 1997. '4411. Old comedy', *The Oxyrhynchus Papyri* 64: 62–75.

Haß, P. 1998. *Der locus amoenus in der antiken Literatur. Zu Theorie und Geschichte eines literarischen Motivs.* Bamberg.

Haubold, J. 2000. *Homer's People. Epic Poetry and Social Formation.* Cambridge.

Hauser, E. 2016. 'In her own words: the semantics of female authorship in ancient Greece, from Sappho to Nossis', *Ramus* 45: 133–64.

H.D. 1921. *Hymen.* London.

    1924. *Heliodora and Other Poems.* London.

    1961. *Helen in Egypt.* New York.

    1982. *Notes on Thought and Vision and The Wise Sappho.* San Francisco.

Hedreen, G. 2016. *The Image of the Artist in Archaic and Classical Greece. Art, Poetry, and Subjectivity.* Cambridge and New York.

Heller, J. L. 1974 (ed.). *Serta Turyniana. Studies in Greek Literature and Palaeography in Honor of Alexander Turyn.* Urbana, IL, Chicago, London.

Hernández Miguel, L. A. 2008. *La tradición clásica. La transmisión de las literaturas griega y latina antiguas y su recepción en las vernáculas occidentales.* Madrid.

Hewett, D. 1979. *Greenhouse*. Sydney.

Heyworth, S. J. 2001. 'Catullian iambics, Catullian *iambi*', in Cavarzere *et al.* 2001 (eds.), 117–40.

Hill, B. 2000. 'Actions speak louder than words: Anna Komnene's attempted usurpation', in Gouma-Peterson 2000a (ed.), 45–62.

Hinatsu Kōnosuke. 1937. *Kaihyōshū [Surface of the Ocean]*. Tokyo.

Hirst, A. 2004. *God and the Poetic Ego. The Appropriation of Biblical and Liturgical Language in the Poetry of Palamas, Sikelianos and Elytis*. Byzantine and Neohellenic Studies 1. Oxford etc.

Hitchcock, T. 1997. *English Sexualities, 1700–1800*. Basingstoke and London.

Hobhouse, J. 1818. *Historical Illustrations of the Fourth Canto of Childe Harold: containing Dissertations on the Ruins of Rome; and an Essay on Italian Literature*. London.

Hodot, R. 1975. 'Le décret de Kymè en l'honneur de Labéon', *Zeitschrift für Papyrologie und Epigraphik* 19: 121–33.

    1990. *Le Dialecte éolien d'Asie. La Langue des inscriptions (VIIe s. a.C.–IVe s. p.C.)*. Éditions recherche sur les civilisations Mémoire 88. Paris.

    2018. 'Lesbian, in space, time, and its uses', in Giannakis *et al.* 2018 (eds.), 457–69.

Holmes, B. 2012. *Gender. Antiquity and Its Legacy*. London and New York.

Holzberg, N. 2000. 'Lesbia, the poet, and the two faces of Sappho: "womanufacture" in Catullus', *Proceedings of the Cambridge Philological Society* NS 46: 28–44.

Hooker, J. T. 1977. *The Language and Text of the Lesbian Poets*. Innsbrucker Beiträge zur Sprachwissenschaft 26. Innsbruck.

Hope, L. 1902. *The Garden of Kama and Other Love Lyrics from India*. London. [First impression 1901]

    1903. *Stars of the Desert*. London and New York.

    1905. *Last Poems. Translations from the Book of Indian Love*. New York and London.

Houston, G. W. 2014. *Inside Roman Libraries. Book Collections and Their Management in Antiquity*. Chapel Hill.

Howie, J. G. 1977. 'Sappho *fr.* 16 (LP): self-consolation and encomium', in F. Cairns 1977: 207–35. [= 2012: 102–25]

    2012. *Exemplum and Myth, Creation and Criticism. Papers on Early Greek Literature*. Collected Classical Papers 3. Prenton.

Hualde Pascual, P., and Sanz Morales, M. 2008 (eds.). *La literatura griega y su tradición*. Madrid.

Hubbard, T. K. 2014a. 'Peer homosexuality', in Hubbard 2014b (ed.), 128–49.

    2014b (ed.). *A Companion to Greek and Roman Sexualities*. Malden, MA, Oxford, Chichester.

Hughes, P. H. 2001. 'Alan Loney, Ted Jenner, and *The Love Songs of Ibykos*', *The Turnbull Library Record* 34: 99–110.

Hughes, T. 1981. *Sylvia Plath. Collected Poems*. London and Boston.

Hunt, A. S. 1927. '2076. Sappho, Book ii', *The Oxyrhynchus Papyri* 17: 26–30.

Hunter, R. L. 1989. *Apollonius of Rhodes. Argonautica Book III*. Cambridge.
1996. *Theocritus and the Archaeology of Greek Poetry*. Cambridge.
1999. *Theocritus. A Selection. Idylls 1, 3, 4, 6, 7, 10, 11 and 13*. Cambridge.
2005 (ed.). *The Hesiodic Catalogue of Women. Constructions and Reconstructions*. Cambridge.
2007. 'Sappho and Latin poetry', in Bastianini and Casanova 2007 (eds.), 213–25. [= Thorsen and Harrison 2019 (eds.), 151–63]
2014. '"Where do I begin?": an Odyssean narrative strategy and its afterlife', in D. Cairns and Scodel 2014 (eds.), 137–55.
2015a. *Apollonius of Rhodes. Argonautica Book IV*, Cambridge.
2015b. 'Sweet Stesichorus: Theocritus 18 and the *Helen* revisited', in Finglass and Kelly 2015a (eds.), 145–63.
2016. '"Palaephatus", Strabo, and the boundaries of myth', *Classical Philology* 111: 245–61.
2019. 'Notes on the ancient reception of Sappho', in Thorsen and Harrison 2019 (eds.), 45–59.
Hutchinson, G. O. 2001. *Greek Lyric Poetry. A Commentary on Selected Larger Pieces*. Oxford.
Imperiali, V. M. 1780. *La Faoniade. Inni e odi di Saffo tradotti dal greco in metro italiano da S.I.P.A.* Venice. [= Chemello 2012a (ed.), 147–92]
Ingberg, P. 1997. *Safo. Poesía lírica de la antigua Lesbos. Edición bilingüe.* Santiago.
2003. *Safo. Antología. Edición bilingüe.* Buenos Aires.
Irigoin, J. 1952. *Histoire du texte de Pindare.* Études et Commentaires 13. Paris.
1956. 'La structure des vers éoliens', *L'Antiquité Classique* 25: 5–19.
Irwin, E. 1998. 'Biography, fiction, and the Archilochean *ainos*', *Journal of Hellenic Studies* 118: 177–83.
Itsumi, K. 1982. 'The "choriambic dimeter" of Euripides', *Classical Quarterly* NS 32: 59–74.
1984. 'The glyconic in tragedy', *Classical Quarterly* NS 34: 66–82.
2009. *Pindaric Metre. The 'Other Half'.* Oxford and New York.
Jackson, V. 2005. *Dickinson's Misery. A Theory of Lyric Reading.* Princeton and Oxford.
Jackson, V., and Prins, Y. 2014 (eds.). *The Lyric Theory Reader. A Critical Anthology.* Baltimore.
Jacobs, A. X. 2015. 'Hebrew on a desert island: the case of Annabelle Farmelant', *Studies in American Jewish Literature* 34: 154–74.
2018. *Strange Cocktail. Translation and the Making of Modern Hebrew Poetry.* Ann Arbor.
Jakob, D. 2000. *Η αρχαιογνωσία του Οδυσσέα Ελύτη και άλλες νεοελληνικές δοκιμές.* Thessaloniki.
Janko, R. 2005. 'Sappho revisited', *Times Literary Supplement* 5360 (23 and 30 December): 19–20.
2017. 'Tithonus, Eos and the cicada in the *Homeric Hymn to Aphrodite* and Sappho fr. 58', in Tsagalis and Markantonatos 2017 (eds.), 267–92.

Jarratt, S. C. 2002. 'Sappho's memory', *Rhetoric Society Quarterly* 32: 11–43.

Jay, K. 1992. 'Introduction', in Barney 1992a: i–xiv.

Jay, P., and Lewis, C. 1996. *Sappho through English Poetry*. London.

Jenkyns, R. 1982. *Three Classical Poets. Sappho, Catullus and Juvenal.* London.

Jenner, E. 1997. *The Love-Songs of Ibykos. 22 Fragments*. Auckland.

　　2007. *Sappho Triptych*. Auckland.

Jensen, J. B. 1989. 'On the mutual intelligibility of Spanish and Portuguese', *Hispania* 72: 848–52.

Jiménez, J. O. 2004. *José Martí. Ensayos y crónicas*. Madrid.

Jocelyn, H. D. 1999. 'The arrangement and the language of Catullus' so-called *polymetra* with special reference to the sequence 10–11–12', in Adams and Mayer 1999 (eds.), 335–75.

Johnson, B. 1986. 'Apostrophe, animation, and abortion', *Diacritics* 16: 29–47.

　　2014. *A Life with Mary Shelley*. Stanford.

Johnson, L. 1957a. Review of R. Gilbert, *The Sunlit Hour. Poems*. London 1955, *Numbers. New Zealand Quarterly of New Writing* 6: 28–30.

　　1957b. 'Our critic replies', *Numbers. New Zealand Quarterly of New Writing* 7: 28–9.

Johnson, M. 2007. *Sappho*. London.

　　2012. 'The role of *eros* in improving the pupil, or what Socrates learned from Sappho', in M. Johnson and Tarrant 2012 (eds.), 7–29.

　　2019 (ed.). *Antipodean Antiquities. Classical Reception Down Under*. London.

Johnson, M., and Tarrant, H. 2012 (eds.). *Alcibiades and the Socratic Lover Educator*. London.

Johnson, T. H. 1958 (ed.). *The Letters of Emily Dickinson*, 3 vols. Cambridge, MA.

Johnson, W. A. 2004. *Bookrolls and Scribes in Oxyrhynchus*. Toronto, Buffalo, London.

Johnson, W. R. 1982. *The Idea of Lyric. Lyric Modes in Ancient and Modern Poetry*. Berkeley, Los Angeles, London.

Jones, W. 1772. *Poems, consisting chiefly of Translations from the Asiatick Languages. To which are added Two Essays: I. On the Poetry of the Eastern Nations. II. On the Arts, commonly called Imitative*. London. [= R. Beck 2009]

　　1773. *The History of the Life of Nader Shah, King of Persia*. London.

　　1777. *Poems, consisting chiefly of Translations from the Asiatick Languages. To which are added Two Essays: I. On the Poetry of the Eastern Nations. II. On the Arts, commonly called Imitative.*[2] London.

　　1807. *The Works of Sir William Jones. With the Life of the Author, by Lord Teignmouth*, 13 vols. London.

　　1808. *The Poetical Works of Sir William Jones*, 2 vols., ed. T. Park. London.

Jong, E. 2004. *Sappho's Leap. A Novel*. London.

Jong, I. J. F. de, and Sullivan, J. P. 1994 (eds.). *Modern Critical Theory and Classical Literature*. Mnemosyne Supplement 130. Leiden, New York, Cologne.

Jouanna, J. 1999. 'Le trône, les fleurs, le char et la puissance d'Aphrodite (Sappho 1, v. 1, 11, 19 et 22). Remarques sur le texte, sur les composés en –θρονος et sur les homérismes de Sappho', *Revue des Études Grecques* 112: 99–126.

Kahn, L. 2017. *The First Hebrew Shakespeare Translations. Isaac Edward Salkinson's Ithiel the Cushite of Venice and Ram and Jael. A Bilingual Edition and Commentary.* London.

Kakisis, S. 1978. Σαπφώ. Τα ποιήματα. Athens.

Kakridis, J. T. 1966. 'Zu Sappho 44 LP', *Wiener Studien* 79: 21–6.

1983. Έλα, Αφροδίτη, Ανθοστεφανωμένη. Athens.

Kaldellis, A. 2009. 'Classical scholarship in twelfth-century Byzantium', in Barber and Jenkins 2009 (eds.), 1–43.

2018. 'Myrsilos of Methymna (477)', *Brill's New Jacoby.*

Kallendorf, C. W. 2007 (ed.). *A Companion to the Classical Tradition.* Malden, MA, Oxford, Chichester.

Kambylis, A. 1991. *Eustathios über Pindars Epinikiendichtung. Ein Kapitel der klassischen Philologie in Byzanz.* Berichte aus den Sitzungen der Joachim Jungius-Gesellschaft der Wissenschaften E.V. 9/1. Hamburg.

Kaminka, A. 1887. 'Mavo le-shirat ha-yavanim' ['Introduction to Greek poetry'], *Keneset Yisra'el* 2: 127–60.

1944. 'Frr. 20 and 96', *Gazit* 6.5–6: 31.

Kaminsky, A. 1993. 'The construction of immortality: Sappho, Saint Theresa and Carolina Coronado', *Letras femeninas* 19: 1–13.

Kämmerer, T. R. 2011 (ed.). *Identities and Societies in the Ancient East-Mediterranean Regions. Comparative Approaches.* Acta Antiqua Mediterranea et Orientalia 1. Münster.

Kangelaris, N. I. 2017. "Σαπφώ fr. 105(a) LP – Βάρναλης. Πῶς ἐθρήνησαν γιὰ τὴ Σαπφὼ τὰ κορίτσια της ὅταν ἀγάπησε τὸν Ἀλκαῖο (στ. 26–9): Μια νέα ανάγνωση της διακειμενικής τους σχέσης", *Philologiki* 138: 43–6.

Kaplan, P. 2003. 'Cross-cultural contacts among mercenary communities in Saite and Persian Egypt', *Mediterranean Historical Review* 18: 1–31.

Kargiotis, D. 2017. Γεωγραφίες της μετάφρασης. Χώροι, κανόνες, ιδεολογίες. Athens.

Kazazis, I. N., and Karamitrou, A. 2001 (eds.). Ανθολόγιο αρχαϊκής λυρικής ποίησης. Athens.

Kelly, A. 2007. *A Referential Commentary and Lexicon to Iliad VIII.* Oxford.

2008. 'Performance and rivalry: Homer, Odysseus, and Hesiod', in Revermann and Wilson 2008 (eds.), 177–203.

2015a. 'Stesichorus' Homer', in Finglass and Kelly 2015a (eds.), 21–44.

2015b. '*Ilias parva*', in Fantuzzi and Tsagalis 2015 (eds.), 318–43.

Kenney, E. J. 2014. *Lucretius. De Rerum Natura Book III³.* Cambridge. [1st edn 1971]

Khalid, A. A. 1959. *Sarud-i raftah. Sappho [Lost Lyrics. Sappho].* Lahore.

Kidwai, S. 2000. '"Firaq" Gorakhpuri: poet vs. "critic" (Urdu)', in Vanita and Kidwai 2000 (eds.), 264–6.

Kirkpatrick, S. 1989. *Las Románticas. Women Writers and Subjectivity in Spain, 1835–1850*. Berkeley, Los Angeles, London.

Kirkwood, G. M. 1974. *Early Greek Monody. The History of a Poetic Type*. Cornell Studies in Classical Philology 37. Ithaca, NY and London.

Kitzbichler, J., and Stephan, U. C. A. (eds.) 2016. *Studien zur Praxis der Übersetzung antiker Literatur. Geschichte – Analysen – Kritik*. Transformationen der Antike 35. Berlin and Boston.

Kivilo, M. 2010. *Early Greek Poets' Lives. The Shaping of the Tradition*. Mnemosyne Supplement 322. Leiden and Boston.

　2011. 'The early biographical tradition of Homer', in Kämmerer 2011 (ed.), 85–104.

Kizer, C. 2001. *Cool, Calm and Collected. Poems 1960–2000*. Port Townsend, WA.

Klausner, M. 1945. *Sappho von Lesbos*. Buenos Aires.

　1946. *Sapfo mi-lesbos [Sappho of Lesbos]*. Mandatory Palestine.

　1954. *Mekorot ha-drama [On the Sources of Drama]*. Ramat Gan.

Klinck, A. L. 2005. '"Sleeping in the bosom of a tender companion": homoerotic attachments in Sappho', *Journal of Homosexuality* 49: 193–208.

　2008. 'Sappho's company of friends', *Hermes* 136: 15–29.

Kolde, A., Lukinovich, A., and Rey, A.-L. 2005 (eds.). Κορυφαίῳ ἀνδρί. *Mélanges offerts à André Hurst*. Recherches et Rencontres 22. Geneva.

Konstantakos, I. 2000. A Commentary on the Fragments of Eight Plays of Antiphanes. Diss. Cambridge.

　2004. 'Trial by riddle: the testing of the counsellor and the contest of kings in the legend of Amasis and Bias', *Classica et Mediaevalia* 55: 85–137.

Konzett, M. 2000 (ed.). *Encyclopedia of German Literature*, 2 vols. Chicago and London.

Krafft-Ebing, R. von. 1886. *Psychopathia Sexualis. Eine klinisch-forensische Studie*. Stuttgart.

　1889. *Le psicopatie sessuali con speciale considerazione alla inversione sessuale. Studio clinico-legale*, transl. E. Sterz and L. Waldhart. Turin.

Kramer, B. 1978a. '60. Sappho?', *Kölner Papyri* 2: 40.

　1978b. '61. Fragmente aus einem Sapphokommentar', *Kölner Papyri* 2: 40–4.

Kratzmann, G., and Wallace-Crabbe, C. 2009. *Gwen Harwood. Mappings of the Plane: New Selected Poems*. Manchester.

Kreij, M. de 2016. "Οὔκ ἐστι Σαπφοῦς τοῦτο τὸ ᾆσμα. Variants of Sappho's songs in Athenaeus' *Deipnosophistae*', *Journal of Hellenic Studies* 136: 59–72.

Kure Shigeichi. 1948. *Girishia, Rōma jojō shisen [Selected Lyrics of Greece and Rome]*. Tokyo.

Kurke, L. 1992. 'The politics of ἁβροσύνη in archaic Greece', *Classical Antiquity* 11: 91–120.

　1999. *Coins, Bodies, Games, and Gold. The Politics of Meaning in Archaic Greece*. Princeton.

　2016. 'Gendered spheres and mythic models in Sappho's Brothers Poem', in Bierl and Lardinois 2016 (eds.), 238–65.

Kutsukake Yoshihiko. 1988. *Saffō. Shi to shōgai [Sappho. Poetry and Life]*. Tokyo.

Ladianou, K. 2005. 'The poetics of *choreia*: imitation and dance in the *Anacreontea*', *Quaderni Urbinati di Cultura Classica* NS 80: 47–58.

La Genière, J. de 1997 (ed.). *Héra. Images, espaces, cultes. Actes du colloque international du Centre de Recherches Archéologiques de l'Université de Lille III et de l'Association P.R.A.C., Lille, 29–30 novembre 1993*. Collection du Centre Jean Bérard 15. Naples.

Laird, A. 2007. 'Latin America', in Kallendorf 2007 (ed.), 222–36.

Lamberton, R., and Keaney, J. J. 1992 (eds.). *Homer's Ancient Readers. The Hermeneutics of Greek Epic's Earliest Exegetes*. Princeton.

Lanata, G. 1966. 'Sul linguaggio amoroso di Saffo', *Quaderni Urbinati di Cultura Classica* 2: 63–79.

  1996. 'Sappho's amatory language', in Greene 1996a (ed.), 11–25.

Lanser, S. S. 2014. *The Sexuality of History. Modernity and the Sapphic, 1565–1830.* Chicago and London.

La Penna, A. 1963. *Orazio e l'ideologia del principato*. Saggi 332. Turin.

Lardinois, A. 1989. 'Lesbian Sappho and Sappho of Lesbos', in Bremmer 1989 (ed.), 15–35.

  1994. 'Subject and circumstance in Sappho's poetry', *Transactions of the American Philological Association* 124: 57–84.

  1996. 'Who sang Sappho's songs?', in Greene 1996a (ed.), 150–72.

  2001. 'Keening Sappho: female speech genres in Sappho's poetry', in Lardinois and McClure 2001 (eds.), 75–92. [= Rutherford 2019 (ed.), 286–308]

  2008. '"Someone, I say, will remember us": oral memory in Sappho's poetry', in Mackay 2008 (ed.), 79–96.

  2009. 'The new Sappho poem (*P.Köln* 21351 and 21376): key to the old fragments', in Greene and Skinner 2009 (eds.), 41–57.

  2010. 'Lesbian Sappho revisited', in Dijkstra *et al.* 2010 (eds.), 13–30.

  2011. 'The *parrhesia* of young female choruses in ancient Greece', in Athanassaki and Bowie 2011 (eds.), 161–72.

  2016. 'Sappho's Brothers Song and the fictionality of early Greek lyric poetry', in Bierl and Lardinois 2016 (eds.), 167–87.

Lardinois, A., and McClure, L. 2001 (eds.). *Making Silence Speak. Women's Voices in Greek Literature and Society*. Princeton and Oxford.

Larmour, D. H. J., Miller, P. A., and Platter, C. 1998 (eds.). *Rethinking Sexuality. Foucault and Classical Antiquity*. Princeton.

Lasserre, F. 1974. 'Ornements érotiques dans la poésie lyrique archaïque', in Heller 1974 (ed.), 5–33.

  1989. *Sappho. Une Autre Lecture.* Προαγῶνες: Collezione di Studi e Testi 21. Padua.

Lauritzen, F. 2010. 'Students of Pindar and readers of Mitylenaios. Allusions in Christopher Mitylenaios 6 Kurtz', *Byzantion* 80: 188–96.

Lavagnini, R. 2004. 'Bisanzio nella letteratura del XIX e del XX secolo', in Cavallo 2004 (ed.), 729–64.

Lawler, L. B. 1948. 'On certain Homeric epithets', *Philological Quarterly* 27: 80–4.

Lebessi, A. 2009. 'The erotic goddess of the Syme sanctuary, Crete', *American Journal of Archaeology* 113: 521–45.

Lectius, J. 1614. *Poetae graeci veteres tragici, lyrici, comici, epigrammatarii, additis fragmentis exprobatis authoribus collectis, nunc primum Graece et Latine in unum redacti corpus.* Cologne.

Le Fèvre, <A.> 1681. *Les Poesies d'Anacreon et de Sapho, traduites de grec en françois, avec des remarques.* Paris.

Lefkowitz, M. R. 1963. 'Τὼ καὶ ἐγώ: the first person in Pindar', *Harvard Studies in Classical Philology* 67: 177–253. [≈ 1991: 1–71]

  1973. 'Critical stereotypes and the poetry of Sappho', *Greek, Roman, and Byzantine Studies* 14: 113–24. [≈ Greene 1996a: 26–34]

  1991. *First-Person Fictions. Pindar's Poetic 'I'.* Oxford.

  1995. 'The first person in Pindar reconsidered – again', *Bulletin of the Institute of Classical Studies* 40: 139–50.

  2012. *The Lives of the Greek Poets*[2]. London. [1st edn 1981]

Leitao, D. D. 2012. *The Pregnant Male as Myth and Metaphor in Classical Greek Literature.* Cambridge.

Lejeune, M. 1972. *Phonétique historique du mycénien et du grec ancien.* Tradition de l'Humanisme 9. Paris.

Lekatsas, P. G. 1938. *Σαπφούς άπαντα. Αρχαίον κείμενον, εισαγωγή, μετάφρασις, σχόλια.* Athens.

Lemer, J. 1850. *Les Poètes de l'amour. Recueil de vers français des XVe, XVIe, XVIIe, XVIIIe et XIXe siècles.* Paris.

Lentini, G. 2012. 'L'idillio 2 di Teocrito e il "genere" oaristys', *Materiali e Discussioni per l'Analisi dei Testi Classici* 68: 181–90.

Leontias, S. 1899. *Ο ανήρ και η γυνή.* Istanbul.

Leopardi, G. 1824. *Canzoni.* Bologna.

  1831. *Canti.* Florence.

Lesko Baker, D., and Finch, A. 2006. *Louise Labé. Complete Poetry and Prose. A Bilingual Edition.* Chicago and London.

Levin, G. 1985. 'What different things link up: Hellenism in contemporary Hebrew poetry', *Prooftexts. A Journal of Jewish Literary History* 5: 221–43.

Levin, M. 1946. 'Sapfo mi-lesbos', *Al ha-mishmar* (4 March): 2.

Lewis, E. F. 2004. *Women Writers in the Spanish Enlightenment. The Pursuit of Happiness.* Aldershot and Burlington, VT.

Leypold, C. 2008. *Bankettgebäude in griechischen Heiligtümern.* Wiesbaden.

Liang Qichao. 1936. 'Xin Zhongguo weilai ji' ['The future of new China'], in *Yinbingshi wenji [Drinking Ice. Monographic Edition]*, 89. Shanghai.

Liberman, G. 1999. *Alcée. Fragments*, 2 vols. Paris.

  2007. 'L'édition alexandrine de Sappho', in Bastianini and Casanova 2007 (eds.), 41–65.

  2016. 'Some thoughts on the symposiastic catena, *aisakos*, and *skolia*', in Cazzato and Lardinois 2016 (eds.), 42–62.

Lidov, J. B. 1993. 'The second stanza of Sappho 31: another look', *American Journal of Philology* 114: 503–35.

2002. 'Sappho, Herodotus, and the *hetaira*', *Classical Philology* 97: 203–37.

2004. 'Hera in Sappho, fr. 17 L-P, V – and *Aeneid* I?', *Mnemosyne* 4th ser. 57: 387–406.

2009. 'The meter and metrical style of the new poem', *ibid.* 103–17.

2012. Review of Silva Barris 2011. *Bryn Mawr Classical Review* 2012.12.18.

2016. 'Songs for sailors and lovers', in Bierl and Lardinois 2016 (eds.), 55–109.

Liebes, Y. 2011. *Menemosinei. Tirgumei shira 'atika [Mnemosyne. Translations of Ancient Poetry]*. Jerusalem.

Lindheim, S. H. 2003. *Mail and Female. Epistolary Narrative and Desire in Ovid's Heroides*. Madison.

Lindsay, N., and Lindsay, J. 1928. *A Homage to Sappho*. London.

Lipking, L. 1988a. 'Sappho descending: eighteenth-century styles in abandoned women', *Eighteenth-Century Life* NS 12.2: 40–57.

1988b. *Abandoned Women and Poetic Tradition*. Chicago and London.

Litvak, O. 2012. *Haskalah. The Romantic Movement in Judaism*. Key Words in Jewish Studies 3. New Brunswick, NJ and London.

Liu Qun. 2012. 'Guxila nüshiren Safu zai Zhongguo de yijie jiqi yingxiang' ['Introductions to and translations of Sappho in China and their influences'], *Zhongguo bijiao wenxue [Chinese Comparative Literature]* 89: 39–53.

Lloyd, A. B. 1975–88. *Herodotus. Book II*, 3 vols. Études préliminaires aux religions orientales dans l'empire Romain 43. Leiden, New York, Copenhagen, Cologne.

Lobel, E. 1922. Review of Edmonds 1922a, *Classical Review* 36: 120–1.

1923–5. 'Nine fragments of Alcaeus (*P.Oxy.* 1233)', *The Bodleian Quarterly Record* 4: 20–1.

1925. *ΣΑΠΦΟΥΣ ΜΕΛΗ. The Fragments of the Lyrical Poems of Sappho*. Oxford.

1941. '2166. Supplement to 1231, 1233, 1234, 1360, 1787, 1789, 2081c, d', *The Oxyrhynchus Papyri* 18: 38–46.

1951a. '2288. Sappho, book i 1', *The Oxyrhynchus Papyri* 21: 1–2.

1951b. '2289. Sappho, book i', *The Oxyrhynchus Papyri* 21: 2–6.

1951c. '2290. Sappho, book iv?', *The Oxyrhynchus Papyri* 21: 7–10.

1951d. '2291. Sappho?', *The Oxyrhynchus Papyri* 21: 10–14.

1951e. '2292. Commentary on Sappho', *The Oxyrhynchus Papyri* 21: 15.

1951f. '2293. Commentary on Sappho book iv?', *The Oxyrhynchus Papyri* 21: 16–23.

1951g. '2294. Bibliographical details about a book on Sappho', *The Oxyrhynchus Papyri* 21: 23–6.

1951h. '2308. Aeolic verses?', *The Oxyrhynchus Papyri* 21: 121.

1951i. 'Addenda', *The Oxyrhynchus Papyri* 21: 122–47.

1956a. '2357. Sappho', *The Oxyrhynchus Papyri* 23: 7–9.

1956b. '2378. Lyric verses in the Aeolic dialect', *The Oxyrhynchus Papyri* 23: 7–9.

1967. '2637. Commentary on choral lyric', *The Oxyrhynchus Papyri* 32: 138–59.

1972. '2878. Lyric verses in the Aeolic dialect?', *The Oxyrhynchus Papyri* 39: 1–8.

Lobel, E., and Page, D. L. 1952. 'A new fragment of Aeolic verse', *Classical Quarterly* NS 2: 1–3.

1955. *Poetarum Lesbiorum fragmenta*. Oxford. [Reprinted with addenda 1963]

Lomiento, L. 2013. Review of Silva Barris 2011. *Greek and Roman Musical Studies* 1: 258–9.

Lonardi, G. 2005. *L'oro di Omero. L'Iliade, Saffo: antichissimi di Leopardi*. Testi e Studi Leopardiani 7. Venice.

Loney, A. 2009. 'Testament: tenth muse', *Jacket* 37. (http://jacketmagazine .com/37/loney.shtml)

2018. *Next to Nothing. Melbourne 2009–2016*. Northfield, MN.

López Noriega, M. 2012. *Safo. Poemas y fragmentos*. Mexico City.

Loraux, N. 1993 (ed.). *Grecia al femminile*. Rome and Bari.

Lorenzini, N. 2004. 'Postfazione', in Quasimodo 2004 (ed.), 219–64.

Loscalzo, D. 2019. *Saffo, la hetaira*. Syncrisis 4. Pisa and Rome.

Loulakaki-Moore, I. 2010. *Seferis and Elytis as Translators*. Byzantine and Neohellenic Studies 4. Oxford etc.

Lourenço, F. 2006. *Poesia grega de Álcman a Teócrito*. Lisbon.

2011. *The Lyric Metres of Euripidean Drama*. Humanitas Supplementum 12. Coimbra.

Louÿs, P. 1894. *Les Chansons de Bilitis*. Paris.

Lowrie, M. 2009 (ed.). *Oxford Readings in Classical Studies. Horace: Odes and Epodes*. Oxford and New York.

Luca, E. de 1889. 'A la Señorita Joaquina Izquierdo', in E<strada> 1889 (ed.), 161–2.

Luciano, D., and Chen, M. Y. 2015. 'Introduction: has the queer ever been human?', *GLQ* 21: 183–207.

Lunardi, E., and Nugent, R. 1979. *Giovanni Pascoli. Convivial Poems. Part 1. Text and Translation*. Lake Erie College Studies 8. Painesville, OH.

Luo Luo. 1989. *Safu shuqing shiji [Lyrics of Sappho]*. Tianjin.

Luppino, A. 1950. 'Per l'interpretazione del nuovo Alceo', *La Parola del Passato* 5: 206–14.

Luraghi, N. 2006. 'Traders, pirates, warriors: the proto-history of Greek mercenary soldiers in the eastern Mediterranean', *Phoenix* 60: 21–47.

Luzán, I. de 1770. 'Las dos odas de Safo. Ineditas', in *Parnaso español. Coleccion de poesías escogidas de los mas célebres poetas castellanos. Tomo* IV (Madrid): 169–71.

Lyly, J. 1584. *Sapho and Phao*. London.

Ma Junwu. 1991. *Ma Junwu ji [Works of Ma Junwu]*. Wuchang.

Mace, S. T. 1993. 'Amour, encore! The development of δηὖτε in archaic lyric', *Greek, Roman, and Byzantine Studies* 34: 335–64.

Mackay, E. A. 2008 (ed.). *Orality, Literacy, Memory in the Ancient Greek and Roman World*. Mnemosyne Supplement 298. Orality and Literacy in Ancient Greece 7. Leiden and Boston.

Mackridge, P. 1996 (ed.). *Ancient Greek Myth in Modern Greek Poetry. Essays in Memory of C. A. Trypanis.* London and Portland, OR.

Macky, W. 1957. 'Controversy: the critic on the mat', *Numbers. New Zealand Quarterly of New Writing* 7: 26–8.

MacMillan, M. 1988. *Women of the Raj.* London.

Malaver, A. B. 2008. *La poesía de Safo. Estudio y traducción.* Bogotá.

Manfredi, M. 1965. 'Sull'ode 31 L.-P. di Saffo', in *Dai papiri della Società italiana. Omaggio all'XI Congresso Internazionale di Papirologia. Milano 2–8 settembre 1965*, 16–17. Florence.

Manor, D., and Sonis, R. 2015. *Niflata. Antologiya shel shira lahatabit [Thy Love to Me Was Wonderful. An Anthology of LGBT Poetry].* Tel Aviv.

Maquieira, H., and Fernández, C. N. (eds.). 2012. *Tradición y traducción clásicas en América Latina.* La Plata.

Mari, G. 1988. *Venere celeste e Venere terrestre. L'amore nella letteratura italiana del Settecento.* Il Vaglio: Studi e Documenti di Storia della Cultura Italiana 4. Modena.

Marquardt, P. A. 1982. 'Hesiod's ambiguous view of woman', *Classical Philology* 77: 283–91.

Marry, J. D. 1979. 'Sappho and the heroic ideal: ἔρωτος ἀρετή', *Arethusa* 12: 71–92.

Martin, R. P. 1993. 'The Seven Sages as performers of wisdom', in Dougherty and Kurke 1993 (eds.), 108–28.

  2001. 'Just like a woman: enigmas of the lyric voice', in Lardinois and McClure 2001 (eds.), 55–74.

  2016. 'Sappho, iambist: abusing the brother', in Bierl and Lardinois 2016 (eds.), 110–26.

Martindale, C. 2013. 'Reception – a new humanism? Receptivity, pedagogy, the transhistorical', *Classical Receptions Journal* 5: 169–83.

Martindale, C., and Thomas, R. F. 2006 (eds.). *Classics and the Uses of Reception.* Malden, MA, Oxford, Carlton, VIC.

Martinelli, L. 1975. *Alessandro Verri. I romanzi. Le avventure di Saffo poetessa di Mitilene. Le notti romane. La vita di Erostrato.* Classici Italiani Minori 2. Ravenna.

Martinelli, M. C. 1997. *Gli strumenti del poeta. Elementi di metrica greca.*² Bologna. [Corrected version of 1995 impression]

Martins, P. 2010. *Antologia de poetas gregos e latinos (monódica e coral, jâmbica, polímetra e elegíaca). 3ª Edição.* São Paulo.

Martyn, J. R. C. 1990. 'Sappho and Aphrodite', *Euphrosyne* ns 18: 201–12.

Mascioni, G. 1981. *Saffo.* Milan.

Mason, H. J. 2001. '*Lesbia oikodomia.* Aristotle, masonry, and the cities of Lesbos', *Mouseion* 3rd ser. 1: 31–53.

Masson, O. 1962. *Les Fragments du poète Hipponax.* Études et Commentaires 43. Paris.

Matamoros, M. 1902. *El último amor de Safo. Sonetos.* Havana.

Mathews, L. 2014. *Paper Wings. Songs for Sappho [on first page 55 Love Poems] by Maureen Duffy. Set to Paper by Liz Mathews.* London.

Maugham, W. S. 1947. *Creatures of Circumstance.* London and Toronto.

Mayer, R. 1983. 'Catullus' divorce', *Classical Quarterly* NS 33: 297–8.

Mays, J. C. C. 2001. *The Collected Works of Samuel Taylor Coleridge. Poetical Works*, 3 vols. Bollinger Series 75. <Princeton.>

Mazza, R. 2019. 'The Green fiasco in context', *Eidolon*, 8 November (https:// eidolon.pub/the-green-fiasco-in-context-f6f6d2c87329).

McCarthy, K. 2010. 'Lost and found voices: Propertius 3.6', *Helios* 37: 153–86.

 2013. 'Secrets and lies: Horace carm. 1.27 and Catullus 10', *Materiali e Discussioni per l'Analisi dei Testi Classici* 71: 45–74.

 2019. *I, the Poet: First-Person Form in Horace, Catullus, and Propertius.* Ithaca, NY and London.

McCormick, I. 1997 (ed.). *Secret Sexualities. A Sourcebook of 17th and 18th Century Writing.* London and New York.

McEvilley, T. 1971. 'Sappho, fragment ninety-four', *Phoenix* 25: 1–11. [≈ 2008: 48–64]

 1972. 'Sappho, fragment two', *Phoenix* 26: 323–33. [≈ 2008: 28–46]

 2008. *Sappho.* Putnam, CT.

McGann, J., and Sligh, C. L. 2004. *Algernon Charles Swinburne. Major Poems and Selected Prose.* New Haven and London.

McGann, J. J. 1980–93. *Lord Byron. The Complete Poetical Works*, 7 vols. Oxford.

 1996. *The Poetics of Sensibility. A Revolution in Literary Style.* Oxford.

Med, J. 2015 (ed.). *The Cambridge Companion to Lesbian Literature.* Cambridge.

Mellor, A. K. 2000. 'Mary Robinson and the scripts of female sexuality', in P. Coleman *et al.* 2000 (eds.), 230–59.

Merkelbach, R. 1957. 'Sappho und ihr Kreis', *Philologus* 101: 1–29. [= 1996: 87–114]

 1973. 'Verzeichnis von Gedichtanfaengen', *Zeitschrift für Papyrologie und Epigraphik* 12: 86.

 1974. 'Wartetext 11: Sappho?', *Zeitschrift für Papyrologie und Epigraphik* 13: 214.

 1996. *Hestia und Erigone. Vorträge und Aufsätze.* Stuttgart and Leipzig.

Metzger, E. A., and Metzger, M. M. 2001 (eds.). *A Companion to the Works of Rainer Maria Rilke.* Rochester, NY and Woodbridge.

Meyerhoff, D. 1984. *Traditioneller Stoff und individuelle Gestaltung. Untersuchungen zu Alkaios und Sappho.* Beiträge zur Altertumswissenschaft 3. Hildesheim, Zurich, New York.

Michelakis, P. 2009. 'Greek lyric from the Renaissance to the eighteenth century', in Budelmann 2009 (ed.), 336–51.

Miller, E. 1873. 'Poëmes historiques de Théodore Prodrome', *Revue Archéologique* NS 25: 251–5.

Miller, M. 2011. *Rabbis and Revolution. The Jews of Moravia in the Age of Emancipation.* Stanford.

Miller, P. A. 1994. *Lyric Texts and Lyric Consciousness. The Birth of a Genre from Archaic Greece to Augustan Rome.* London and New York.

Millgate, M. 2001 (ed.). *Thomas Hardy's Public Voice. The Essays, Speeches, and Miscellaneous Prose.* Oxford.

Mioni, E. 1973. *Bibliotheca Divi Marci Venetiarum. Codices Graeci manuscripti. Volumen III. Codices in classes nonam decimam undecimam inclusos et supplementa duo continens.* Rome.

<Mirabeau, H. G. Riqueti Comte de> 1783. *Erotika Biblion.* Rome[?].

Miraji. 2009. 'Maghrib ki Sab se Bari Sha'ira: Sappho' ['The greatest poetess of the western world'], in *Mashriq o Maghrib ke Naghme [Poems from East and West].* Lahore: 226–49.

Mitsis, P., and Tsagalis, C. 2010 (eds.). *Allusion, Authority, and Truth. Critical Perspectives on Greek Poetic and Rhetorical Praxis.* Trends in Classics Supplement 7. Berlin and New York.

Mogrovejo, N. 2015. 'The Latin American lesbian movement: its shaping and its search for autonomy', in Bordo *et al.* 2015 (eds.), 312–20.

Möller, A. 2000. *Naukratis. Trade in Archaic Greece.* Oxford and New York.

Molloy, S. 1997. 'From Sappho to Baffo: diverting the sexual in Alejandra Pizarnik', in Balderston and Guy 1997 (eds.), 250–8.

Molony, B., and Uno, K. 2005 (eds.). *Gendering Modern Japanese History.* Harvard East Asian Monographs 251. Cambridge, MA and London.

Molyneux, M. 2001. *Women's Movements in International Perspective. Latin America and Beyond.* Basingstoke and New York.

Montanari, F. 2015. '*Ekdosis.* A product of the ancient scholarship', in Montanari *et al.* 2015 (eds.), II 641–72.

Montanari, F., and Pagani, L. 2011 (eds.). *From Scholars to Scholia. Chapters in the History of Ancient Greek Scholarship.* Trends in Classics Supplement 9. Berlin and New York.

Montanari, F., Matthaios, S., and Rengakos, A. 2015 (eds.). *Brill's Companion to Ancient Greek Scholarship,* 2 vols. Leiden and Boston.

Montemayor, C. 1986. *Safo. Poemas.* Mexico City.

Moravcsik, G. 1964. 'Sapphos Fortleben in Byzanz', *Acta antiqua Academiae Scientiarum Hungaricae* 12: 473–9. [= 1967: 408–13]

1967. *Studia Byzantina.* Budapest.

Morgan, L. 2005. 'A yoke connecting baskets: *Odes* 3.14, Hercules, and Italian unity', *Classical Quarterly* NS 55: 190–203.

2010. *Musa pedestris. Metre and Meaning in Roman Verse.* Oxford.

2016. 'The reception of Sappho's Brothers Poem in Rome', in Bierl and Lardinois 2016 (eds.), 293–301.

Morillon, G. 1546. *Heroidum epistolae Pub. Ovidii Nasonis, et Auli Sabini responsiones, cum Guidonis Morilloni argumentis ac scholiis.* Venice.

Morpurgo Davies, A. 1976. 'The –εccι datives, Aeolic –cc–, and the Lesbian poets', in Morpurgo Davies and Meid 1976 (eds.), 181–97.

Morpurgo Davies, A., and Meid, W. 1976 (eds.). *Studies in Greek, Italic, and Indo-European Linguistics Offered to Leonard R. Palmer on the Occasion of His Seventieth Birthday, June 5, 1976.* Innsbrucker Beiträge zur Sprachwissenschaft 16. Innsbruck.

Morrison, M. 1962. 'Henri Estienne and Sappho', *Bibliothèque d'Humanisme et Renaissance* 24: 388–91.

Morrissey, M. 1996. 'Lyricism, language and history: New Zealand poetry in 1992', *Journal of New Zealand Literature* 14: 203–20.

Mosshammer, A. A. 1979. *The Chronicle of Eusebius and Greek Chronographic Tradition*. Lewisburg, PA and London.

Most, G. W. 1995. 'Reflecting Sappho', *Bulletin of the Institute of Classical Studies* 40: 15–38. [≈ Greene 1996b: 11–35]

Moya, J. C. 2011 (ed.). *The Oxford Handbook of Latin American History*. Oxford and New York.

Mueller, J. 1993. 'Troping Utopia: Donne's brief for lesbianism', in J. Turner 1993 (ed.), 182–207.

Mueller, M. 2016. 'Re-centering epic *nostos*: gender and genre in Sappho's Brothers Poem', *Arethusa* 49: 25–46.

Mullan, S. 2016. 'Queer anachronisms: reimagining lesbian history in performance', in Campbell and Farrier 2016 (eds.), 244–56.

Mullen, H. 1995. *Muse and Drudge*. Philadelphia.

Müller, K. O. 1840. *History of the Literature of Ancient Greece*, 2 vols. London.
  1841. *Geschichte der griechischen Litteratur bis auf das Zeitalter Alexanders*, 2 vols. Breslau.

Muretus, M. A. 1554. *Catullus et in eum commentarius*. Venice.

Muscetta, C. 1959. 'L'ultimo canto di Saffo', *La Rassegna della letteratura italiana* 7th ser. 63: 194–218.

Myrtiotissa. 1925. Κίτρινες φλόγες *[Yellow Flames]*. Alexandria.
  1965. Άπαντα, vol. II, Athens.

Nagy, G. 1973. 'Phaethon, Sappho's Phaon, and the White Rock of Leukas', *Harvard Studies in Classical Philology* 77: 137–77. [≈ 1990: 223–62 ≈ Greene 1996a: 35–57]
  1974. *Comparative Studies in Greek and Indic Meter*. Harvard Studies in Comparative Literature 33. Cambridge, MA.
  1990. *Greek Mythology and Poetics*. Ithaca, NY and London.
  2004. 'Transmission of archaic Greek sympotic songs: from Lesbos to Alexandria', *Critical Inquiry* 31: 26–48.
  2007. 'Did Sappho and Alcaeus ever meet? Symmetries of myth and ritual in performing the songs of ancient Lesbos', in Bierl *et al.* 2007 (eds.), 1 211–69.
  2009. 'The "New Sappho" reconsidered in the light of the Athenian reception of Sappho', in Greene and Skinner 2009 (eds.), 176–99.
  2010. *Homer the Preclassic*. Berkeley, Los Angeles, London.
  2016. 'A poetics of sisterly affect in the Brothers Song and in other songs of Sappho', in Bierl and Lardinois 2016 (eds.), 449–92.

Nagy, G., and Stavrakopoulou, A. 2003 (eds.). *Modern Greek Literature. Critical Essays*. New York and London.

Nair, R. B. 1999. *The Ayodhya Cantos. Poems*. New Delhi.

2002. *Lying on the Postcolonial Couch. The Idea of Indifference*. Minneapolis and London.

Natsume Sōseki. 1966. *Sōseki zenshū [The Complete Works of Sōseki]*, vol. 4. Tokyo.

Nava, G. 1984. 'Pascoli e il folklore', *Giornale Storico della Letteratura Italiana* 161: 507–43.

2008. *Giovanni Pascoli. Poemi conviviali*. Nuova Raccolta di Classici Italiani Annotati 21. Turin.

Neander, M. 1556. *Aristologia Pindarica graecolatina*. Basel.

Neer, R. T. 2002. *Style and Politics in Athenian Vase Painting. The Craft of Democracy, ca. 530–460 B.C.E.* Cambridge.

Neri, C. 2015. 'Il *Brothers Poem* e l'edizione alessandrina (in margine a *P. Sapph. Obbink*)', *Eikasmos* 26: 53–76.

Neri, C. (ed., transl., comm.), and Cinti, F. (transl.) 2017. *Saffo. Poesie, frammenti e testimonianze. La prima traduzione italiana di tutti i frammenti anche inediti e tutte le testimonianze*. Ariccia.

Neue, C. F. 1827. *Sapphonis Mytilenaeae fragmenta*. Berlin.

Nicholson, A. 1991. *Lord Byron. The Complete Miscellaneous Prose*. Oxford.

Nickau, K. 1974. 'Planudes und Moschopulos als Zeugen für Sappho (fr. 2,5–6 L.–P. = Voigt)', *Zeitschrift für Papyrologie und Epigraphik* 14: 15–17.

Nicosia, S. 1976. *Tradizione testuale diretta e indiretta dei poeti di Lesbo*. Filologia e Critica 19. Rome.

Nightingale, A. W. 1995. *Genres in Dialogue. Plato and the Construct of Philosophy*. Cambridge.

Nikolaidis, A. G. 2008 (ed.). *The Unity of Plutarch's Work. 'Moralia' Themes in the 'Lives', Features of the 'Lives' in the 'Moralia'*. Millennium Studies in the Culture and History of the First Millennium C.E. 19. Berlin and New York.

Nisbet, G. 2019. 'Sappho in Roman epigram', in Thorsen and Harrison 2019 (eds.), 265–87.

Norsa, M. 1937. 'Versi di Saffo in un ostrakon del sec. II a. C.', *Annali della Reale Scuola Normale Superiore di Pisa* 2nd ser. 6: 8–15.

1953. '1300. Dal primo libro di Saffo', *Papiri Greci e Latini* 13: 44–50.

<Nott, J.> 1803. *Sappho. After a Greek Romance*. London.

Nünlist, R. 2014. 'Das Schiff soll unversehrt sein, nicht voll! Zu Sapphos neuem Lied über die Brüder', *Zeitschrift für Papyrologie und Epigraphik* 191: 13–14.

Nuño, R. B. 1988. *Antología de la lírica griega*. Nuestros Clásicos 71. Mexico City.

Oakley, J. H., and Sinos, R. H. 1993. *The Wedding in Ancient Athens*. Madison.

Obbink, D. 2009. 'Sappho fragments 58–59: text, apparatus criticus, and translation', in Greene and Skinner 2009 (eds.), 7–16.

2011. 'Vanishing conjecture: lost books and their recovery from Aristotle to Eco', in Obbink and Rutherford 2011 (eds.), 20–49.

2014a. 'Two new poems by Sappho', *Zeitschrift für Papyrologie und Epigraphik* 189: 32–49.

2014b. 'Family love – new poems by Sappho', *Times Literary Supplement* 5784 (7 February): 15.

2016a. 'The newest Sappho: text, apparatus criticus, and translation', in Bierl and Lardinois 2016 (eds.), 13–33.

2016b. 'Ten poems of Sappho: provenance, authenticity, and text of the new Sappho papyri', in Bierl and Lardinois 2016 (eds.), 34–54.

2016c. 'Goodbye family gloom! The coming of Charaxos in the Brothers Song', in Bierl and Lardinois 2016 (eds.), 208–24.

Obbink, D., and Rutherford, R. B. 2011 (eds.). *Culture in Pieces. Essays on Ancient Texts in Honour of Peter Parsons*. Oxford.

Oliva Neto, J. A. 2015 (ed.). *Cadernos de literatura em tradução 15. Especial letras clássicas*. São Paulo.

Olive, P. M. de 1818. *Corina ó la Italia, sacada de la que escribió en francés Madama de Staël Holstein*, 4 vols. Madrid.

Oliveira, G. I. 2017. 'O amor na poesia de Lucas José D'Alvarenga', *Revista letras raras* 6.2: 190–211.

Olmsted, W. 2016. *The Censorship Effect. Baudelaire, Flaubert, and the Formation of French Modernism*. Oxford and New York.

Olson, S. D. 2007. *Broken Laughter. Select Fragments of Greek Comedy*. Oxford.

Or, A. 1993. *Teshuka matirat eivarim. Antologiya le-shira erotit yevanit [Limb-Loosening Desire. Greek Erotic Poetry]*. Tel Aviv.

Ormand, K. 2018. *Controlling Desires. Sexuality in Ancient Greece and Rome*. Revised edn. Austin. [1st edn 2009].

2020. 'Atalanta and Sappho: women in and out of time', in Eidinow and Maurizio 2020 (eds.), 28–48.

Orrells, D. 2015. *Sex. Antiquity and Its Legacy*. London and New York.

Osborn, J. M. 1972. *Young Philip Sidney. 1572–1577*. New Haven and London.

Ostergaard, L. 2013. '"Silent work for suffrage": the discreet rhetoric of Professor June Rose Colby and the Sapphonian Society 1892–1908', *Rhetoric Review* 32: 137–55.

Ozeki Iwaji. 1923. *Saffuo meishisen [Selected Famous Poems of Sappho]*. Tokyo.

1924. *Ren'ai shishū [Poems of Romantic Love]*. Tokyo.

Pacella, G. 1991. *Giacomo Leopardi. Zibaldone di pensieri*, 3 vols. Milan.

Page, D. L. 1955. *Sappho and Alcaeus. An Introduction to the Study of Ancient Lesbian Poetry*. Oxford.

1963. '2506. Comment on lyric poems', *The Oxyrhynchus Papyri* 29: 1–48.

1973. 'Notes on P. Oxy. XXXIX', *Classical Quarterly* NS 23: 199–201.

1974. *Supplementum lyricis Graecis. Poetarum lyricorum Graecorum fragmenta quae recens innotuerunt*. Oxford.

Paige, D. D. 1971. *The Selected Letters of Ezra Pound 1907–1941*. London. [Previously published as 1950. *The Letters of Ezra Pound 1907–1941*.]

Palacios, A. M. 2012. *Mercedes Matamoros. El último amor de Safo. Sonetos*. <Seville.>

Palamas, K. 1904. *Η ασάλευτη ζωή*. Athens.

1915. *Βωμοί*. Athens.

1931. *Περάσματα και χαιρετισμοί*. Athens.

Pallantza, E. 2005. *Der Troische Krieg in der nachhomerischen Literatur bis zum 5. Jahrhundert v. Chr.* Hermes Einzelschrift 94. Stuttgart.

Palmieri, E. M. 1998. 'Julio Herrera y Reissig: la encarnación da la palabra. Caracteres esotéricos del modernismo hispanoamericano', in Estévez 1998: 1025–59.

Papadopoulou, M. 2016. 'Textile and textual poetics in context: Callimachus' 4th *Iamb* and Theocritus' *Idyll* 28', in Fanfani *et al.* 2016 (eds.), 217–39.

Paradiso, A. 1993. 'Saffo, la poetessa', in Loraux 1993 (ed.), 39–72.

Pardini, A. 1991. 'La ripartizione in libri dell'opera di Alceo. Per un riesame della questione', *Rivista di Filologia e di Istruzione Classica* 119: 257–84.

Parker, H. N. 1993. 'Sappho schoolmistress', *Transactions of the American Philological Association* 123: 309–51. [≈ Greene 1996b (ed.), 146–83].

1997. 'The teratogenic grid', in Hallett and Skinner 1997 (eds.), 47–65.

2001. 'The myth of the heterosexual: anthropology and sexuality for classicists', *Arethusa* 34: 313–62.

2005. 'Sappho's public world', in Greene 2005 (ed.), 3–24.

Parsons, P. 2007. *City of the Sharp-Nosed Fish. Greek Lives in Roman Egypt.* London.

Paschalis, M., and Panayotakis, S. 2013 (eds.). *The Construction of the Real and the Ideal in the Ancient Novel.* Ancient Narrative Supplementum 17. Groningen.

Pascoli, G. 1895. 'Solon', *Il Convito* 3 (April). [= 1904: 5–8]

1904. *Poemi conviviali.* Poesie di Giovanni Pascoli 6. Bologna.

Patel, G. 2002. *Lyrical Movements, Historical Hauntings. On Gender, Colonialism, and Desire in Miraji's Urdu Poetry.* Stanford.

Patterson, D. 1985. 'Moving centers in modern Hebrew literature', in Abramson and Parfitt 1985 (eds.), 3–10.

Pavese, C. 1947. *Dialoghi con Leucò.* Turin.

Payne, M. 2007. 'Ideas in lyric communication: Pindar and Paul Celan', *Modern Philology* 105: 5–20.

2018. 'Fidelity and farewell: Pindar's ethics as textual events', in Budelmann and Phillips 2018 (eds.), 257–74.

Pelli, M. 1979. *The Age of Haskalah. Studies in Hebrew Literature of the Enlightenment in Germany.* Studies in Judaism in Modern Times 5. Leiden.

2010. *Haskalah and Beyond. The Reception of the Hebrew Enlightenment and the Emergence of Haskalah Judaism.* Lanham, MD etc.

Pender, E. E. 2007. 'Sappho and Anacreon in Plato's *Phaedrus*', *Leeds International Classical Studies* 6.4: 1–57.

2011. 'A transfer of energy: lyric eros in *Phaedrus*', in Destrée and Herrmann 2011 (eds.), 327–48.

Peponi, A.-E. 2004. 'Initiating the viewer: deixis and visual perception in Alcman's lyric drama', *Arethusa* 37: 295–316.

2016. 'Sappho and the mythopoetics of the domestic', in Bierl and Lardinois 2016 (ed.), 225–37.

Peri Rossi, C. <1971.> *Evohé. Poemas eróticos.* Colección la invención 1. Montevideo.

Pernigotti, C. 2001. 'Tempi del canto e pluralità di prospettive in Saffo, fr. 44 V.', *Zeitschrift für Papyrologie und Epigraphik* 135: 11–20.

Petrocchi, G. 1981. 'Foscolo traduttore di Saffo', in *Letterature comparate: problemi e metodo. Studi in onore di Ettore Paratore. Volume quarto. Letterature medievali e moderne, 1569–80.* Bologna.

Petropoulos, J. C. B. 1993. 'Sappho the sorceress – another look at fr. 1 (LP)', *Zeitschrift für Papyrologie und Epigraphik* 97: 43–56.

Pfeiffer, R. 1968. *History of Classical Scholarship. From the Beginnings to the End of the Hellenistic Age.* Oxford.

Pfeijffer, I. L. 2000a. 'Shifting Helen: an interpretation of Sappho, fragment 16 (Voigt)', *Classical Quarterly* NS 50: 1–6.

    2000b. 'Playing ball with Homer: an interpretation of Anacreon 358 PMG', *Mnemosyne* 4th ser. 53: 164–84.

Pflugfelder, G. M. 2005. '"S" is for sister: schoolgirl intimacy and "same-sex love" in early twentieth-century Japan', in Molony and Uno 2005 (eds.), 133–90.

Philips, K. 1667. *Poems.* London.

Phillips, T. 2014. 'A new Sapphic intertext in Horace', *Archiv für Papyrusforschung und verwandte Gebiete* 60: 283–9.

Piantanida, C. 2013. 'Pascoli and Sappho: two unpublished manuscripts', *Filologia Italiana* 10: 181–214.

Piccolomini, A. 1892. 'Ad Sapphus carmen in Venerem apparatus criticus auctus', *Hermes* 27: 1–10.

Pichois, C. (ed.). 1975–6. *Baudelaire. Oeuvres completes,* 2 vols. Paris.

Pierce, P. 2016. 'Letters of a poet in exile', *Meanjin* 75.4: 16–18.

Pignatari, D. 1996. *31 poetas 214 poemas. Do Rigveda e Safo a Apollinaire.* São Paulo.

    2004. *Poesia pois é Poesia. 1950–2000.* São Paulo.

Pirenne-Delforge, V., and Pironti, G. 2014. 'Héra et Zeus à Lesbos: entre poésie lyrique et décret civique', *Zeitschrift für Papyrologie und Epigraphik* 191: 27–31.

Pironti, G. 2014. '*Chrysothronos*: note in margine a un epiteto aureo', in Tortorelli Ghidini 2014 (ed.), 211–21.

Pitts, A. L. 2002. Prostitute, Muse, Lover. The Biographical Tradition of Sappho in Greek and Roman Literature. Diss. Wisconsin–Madison.

Platt, V. 2011. *Facing the Gods. Epiphany and Representation in Graeco-Roman Art, Literature and Religion.* Cambridge.

    2018. 'Silent bones and singing stones: materializing the poetic corpus in Hellenistic Greece', in Goldschmidt and Graziosi 2018 (eds.), 21–49.

Pöhlmann, E. 1994. *Einführung in die Überlieferungsgeschichte und in die Textkritik der antiken Literatur. Band I. Altertum.* Darmstadt.

Polignac, F. de 1997. 'Héra, le navire et la demeure: offrandes, divinité et société en Grèce archaïque', in La Genière 1997 (ed.), 113–22.

Pomeroy, S. B. 1991 (ed.). *Women's History and Ancient History.* Chapel Hill and London.

Pontani, F. 2001. 'Le cadavre adoré: Sappho à Byzance?', *Byzantion* 71: 233–50.

2011. 'Callimachus cited', in Acosta-Hughes *et al.* 2011 (eds.), 93–117.

2015. 'Scholarship in the Byzantine Empire', in Montanari *et al.* 2015 (eds.), II 297–455.

Poochigian, A. 2009. *Sappho. Stung with Love: Poems and Fragments*. London and New York.

Porcupine, P. [= Cobbett, W., *q.v.*]

1795. *A Kick for a Bite; or, Review upon Review; with a Critical Essay, on the Works of Mrs. S. Rowson; in a Letter to the Editor, or Editors, of the American Monthly Review*. Philadelphia.

Porro, A. 1994. *Vetera Alcaica. L'esegesi di Alceo dagli Alessandrini all'età imperiale.* Biblioteca di Aevum antiquum 6. Milan.

2004. 'Alcaeus', in Bastianini *et al.* 2004 (eds.), 75–246.

2007. 'Libri e lettori antichi di Alceo', in Bastianini and Casanova 2007 (eds.), 177–89.

Porter, J. I. 2016. *The Sublime in Antiquity*. Cambridge.

Potamiti, A. 2015. 'γρίφους παίζειν: playing at riddles in Greek', *Greek, Roman, and Byzantine Studies* 55: 133–53.

<Pound, E. (ed.)> 1914. *Des Imagistes. An Anthology*. London and New York.

Pound, E. 1916a. 'Ο Atthis', *Poetry. A Magazine of Verse* 8: 276.

1916b. *Lustra*. London.

1917. *Lustra of Ezra Pound with Earlier Poems*. New York.

Power, T. 2010. *The Culture of Kitharôidia*. Hellenic Studies 15. Cambridge, MA and London.

2020. 'Sappho's parachoral monody', in Foster *et al.* 2020 (eds.), 82–108.

Prauscello, L. 2005. '7. Note di commento a testi poetici', *Comunicazioni dell'Istituto Papirologico 'G. Vitelli'* 6: 51–67.

2006. *Singing Alexandria. Music between Practice and Textual Transmission.* Mnemosyne Supplement 274. Leiden and Boston.

2007. 'Le "orecchie" di Saffo: qualche osservazione in margine a Sapph. 31, II–12 V. e alla sua ricezione antica', in Bastianini and Casanova 2007 (eds.), 191–212.

2016. 'Sappho's book 4 and its metrical composition: the case of P.Oxy. 1787 reconsidered', *Materiali e Discussioni per l'Analisi dei Testi Classici* 76: 53–71.

Prauscello, L., and Ucciardello, G. 2015. 'Sappho 88 Voigt *P.Oxy.* 2290 + *P.Oxy.* 4411: a re-appraisal', *Zeitschrift für Papyrologie und Epigraphik* 195: 13–29.

Prescendi, F., and Volokhine, Y. 2011 (eds.). *Dans le laboratoire de l'historien des religions. Mélanges offerts à Philippe Borgeaud*. Religions en Perspective 24. Geneva.

Pretagostini, R. 1984. *Ricerche sulla poesia alessandrina. Teocrito, Callimaco, Sotade.* Filologia e Critica 48. Rome.

Prettejohn, E. 2008. 'Solomon, Swinburne, Sappho', *Victorian Review* 34: 103–28.

Priest, A.-M. 2014. 'Baby and demon: woman and the artist in the poetry of Gwen Harwood', *Hecate* 40.2: 67–83.

Primavesi, O. 2007. 'Ein Blick in den Stollen von Skepsis: vier Kapitel zur frühen Überlieferung des *Corpus Aristotelicum*', *Philologus* 151: 51–77.

Prins, Y. 1996. 'Sappho's afterlife in translation', in Greene 1996b (ed.), 36–67.

1999. *Victorian Sappho*. Princeton.

Prins, Y., and Shreiber, M. 1997 (eds.). *Dwelling in Possibility. Women Poets and Critics on Poetry*. Ithaca, NY and London.

Privitera, G. A. 2009. 'Metrica e destinataria del fr. 96 V. di Saffo', *Prometheus* 35: 97–104.

2011. 'Le colometrie di Sapph. 96 V. e di Alc. 70 V. Una risposta', *Prometheus* 37: 200–4.

Probert, P., and Willi, A. 2012 (eds.). *Laws and Rules in Indo-European*. Oxford and New York.

Prodi, E. E. 2017. 'Text as paratext: Pindar, Sappho, and Alexandrian editions', *Greek, Roman, and Byzantine Studies* 57: 547–82.

Puggioni, S. 2012. '"Di fortuna e d'amor l'avverso impero": una rivisitazione settecentesca del mito di Saffo', in Chemello 2012a (ed.), 31–44.

Puglia, E. 2008. 'P. Oxy. 2294 e la tradizione delle odi di Saffo', *Zeitschrift für Papyrologie und Epigraphik* 166: 1–8.

Pulleyn, S. 1997. *Prayer in Greek Religion*. Oxford.

Purves, A. 2014. 'Who, Sappho?', in D. Cairns and Scodel 2014 (eds.), 175–96.

Putnam, M. C. J. 1960. '*Throna* and Sappho 1.1', *Classical Journal* 56: 79–83.

2000. *Horace's Carmen Saeculare. Ritual Magic and the Poet's Art*. New Haven and London.

Quasimodo, S. 1940. *Lirici greci*. Milan.

1960. 'Saffo', in *Il poeta e il politico e altri saggi*. Milan: 99–108.

2004. *Lirici greci*. Milan.

Raaflaub, K. A. 2016. 'The newest Sappho and archaic Greek–Near Eastern interactions', in Bierl and Lardinois 2016 (eds.), 127–47.

Rabinowitz, N. S. 2002. 'Excavating women's homoeroticism in ancient Greece: the evidence from Attic vase painting', in Rabinowitz and Auanger 2002 (eds.), 106–66.

Rabinowitz, N. S., and Auanger, L. 2002 (eds.). *Among Women. From the Homosocial to the Homoerotic in the Ancient World*. Austin.

Race, W. H. 1982. *The Classical Priamel from Homer to Boethius*. Mnemosyne Supplement 74. Leiden.

1983. '"That man" in Sappho fr. 31 L–P', *Classical Antiquity* 2: 92–101.

1989. 'Sappho, *fr.* 16 L–P. and Alkaios, *fr.* 42 L–P.: romantic and classical strains in Lesbian lyric', *Classical Journal* 85: 16–33.

Ragusa, G. 2005. *Fragmentos de uma deusa. A representação de Afrodite na lírica de Safo*. Campinas.

2011. *Safo de Lesbos. Hino a Afrodite e outros poemas*. São Paulo.

2013. *Lira grega. Antologia de poesia arcaica*. São Paulo.

Rainbolt, M. 1997. 'Their ancient claim: Sappho and seventeenth- and eighteenth-century British women's poetry', *The Seventeenth Century* 12: 111–34.

Ramalho, A. C. 1965–6. 'Versões garrettianas de Safo', *Humanitas* 17–18: 211–21.

Ramfos, S. 1999. 'Σαπφώ και Ελύτης', *Kathimerini*, 3 October.

Ramien, T. 1896. *Sappho und Sokrates, oder Wie erklärt sich die Liebe der Männer und Frauen zu Personen des eigenen Geschlechts?* Leipzig.

Rauk, J. 1989. 'Erinna's *Distaff* and Sappho fr. 94', *Greek, Roman, and Byzantine Studies* 30: 101–16.

Rawles, R. 2006. 'Notes on the interpretation of the "New Sappho"', *Zeitschrift für Papyrologie und Epigraphik* 157: 1–7.

Ray, B. 1977. 'Sappho', in Chatterjee 1977 (ed.), 33–42.

Rayor, D. J. 1991. *Sappho's Lyre. Archaic Lyric and Women Poets of Ancient Greece.* Berkeley, Los Angeles, Oxford.

  2005. 'The power of memory in Erinna and Sappho', in Greene 2005 (ed.), 59–71.

  2016. 'Reimagining the fragments of Sappho through translation', in Bierl and Lardinois 2016 (eds.), 396–412.

Rayor, D. J., and Lardinois, A. 2014. *Sappho. A New Translation of the Complete Works.* Cambridge and New York.

Reed, J. D. 1995. 'The sexuality of Adonis', *Classical Antiquity* 14: 317–47.

Reichel, M., and Rengakos, A. 2002 (eds.). *Epea Pteroenta. Beiträge zur Homerforschung. Festschrift für Wolfgang Kullmann zum 75. Geburtstag.* Stuttgart.

Reichhold, K. 1975. *Attische Vasenbilder der Antikensammlungen in München nach Zeichnungen von Karl Reichhold. Band* I. *Bilder auf Krügen.* Munich.

Reiner, P., and Kovacs, D. 1993. 'Δέδυκε μὲν ἀ σελάννα: the Pleiades in mid-heaven (*PMG* frag. adesp. 976 = Sappho, fr. 168 B Voigt)', *Mnemosyne* 4th ser. 46: 145–59.

Reinsch, D. R. 2000. 'Women's literature in Byzantium? – The case of Anna Komnene', in Gouma-Peterson 2000a (ed.), 83–105.

  2006. 'Ein angebliches Sappho-Fragment (frg. 209 Lobel–Page) im Briefcorpus des Eustathios von Thessalonike', *Philologus* 150: 175–6.

Reitzammer, L. 2016. *The Athenian Adonia in Context. The Adonis Festival as Cultural Practice.* Madison and London.

Revermann, M., and Wilson, P. 2008 (eds.). *Performance, Iconography, Reception. Studies in Honour of Oliver Taplin.* Oxford.

Reynolds, M. 2000. *The Sappho Companion.* London.

  2004. 'A leap too far' (review of Jong 2004), *Guardian*, 13 November.

Richlin, A. 1991. 'Zeus and Metis: Foucault, feminism, classics', *Helios* 18: 160–80.

  1998. 'Foucault's *History of Sexuality*: a useful theory for women?', in Larmour *et al.* 1998 (eds.), 138–70.

Riera, C. 1975. *Te deix, amor, la mar com a penyora.* Barcelona.

Rigoni, M. A. 1987. *Giacomo Leopardi. Poesie e prose. Volume primo. Poesie.* Milan.

Rilke, R. M. 1907. *Neue Gedichte.* Leipzig.

  1910. *Die Aufzeichnungen des Malte Laurids Brigge,* 2 vols. Leipzig.

Ringler, W. A. Jr 1962. *The Poems of Sir Philip Sidney.* Oxford.

Rissman, L. 1983. *Love as War. Homeric Allusion in the Poetry of Sappho.* Beiträge zur klassischen Philologie 157. Königstein.

Rizaki, E. 2007. Οἱ ῾γράφουσες᾿ Ἑλληνίδες. Σημειώσεις για τη γυναικεία λογιοσύνη του 19ου αιώνα. Athens.

Robbins, E. I. 1995. 'Sappho, Aphrodite, and the Muses', *Ancient World* 26: 225–39. [= 2013: 121–44]

  2013. *Thalia Delighting in Song. Essays on Ancient Greek Poetry,* ed. B. MacLachlan. Phoenix Supplement 53. Toronto, Buffalo, London.

Robbins, R. 2013. *The Complete Poems of John Donne. Epigrams, Verse Letters to Friends, Love-Lyrics, Love-Elegies, Satire, Religion Poems, Wedding Celebrations, Verse Epistles to Patronesses, Commemorations and Anniversaries.* London and New York.

Robert, L. 1960. 'Recherches épigraphiques', *Révue des Études Anciennes* 62: 276–361. [= 1969: 792–877]

  1969. *Opera Minora Selecta. Épigraphie et antiquités grecques. Tome II.* Amsterdam.

Robinson, D. 2011. *The Poetry of Mary Robinson. Form and Fame.* New York.

Robinson, M. 1796. *Sappho and Phaon. In a Series of Legitimate Sonnets, with Thoughts on Poetical Subjects, and Anecdotes of the Grecian Poetess.* London.

Robinson, R., and Wattie, N. 1998 (eds.). *The Oxford Companion to New Zealand Literature.* Melbourne, Oxford, Auckland, New York.

Robortellus, F. 1554. *Dionysi Longini rhetoris praestantissimi liber de grandi, sive sublimi orationis genere.* Basel.

Rodríguez, M. P. 2000. *Vidas im/propias. Transformaciones del sujeto femenino en la narrativa española contemporánea.* West Lafayette, IN.

Roessel, D. 2002. *In Byron's Shadow. Modern Greece in the English and American Imagination.* Oxford and New York.

Rogers, P. 1993. *Alexander Pope.* Oxford and New York.

Rogers, V. 2009. *The Music of Peggy Glanville-Hicks.* Farnham and Burlington, VT.

Rohrbach, E. 1996. 'H.D. and Sappho: "a precious inch of palimpsest"', in Greene 1996b (ed.), 184–98.

Rosati, G. 1996. 'Sabinus, the *Heroides* and the poet-nightingale: some observations on the authenticity of the *Epistula Sapphus*', *Classical Quarterly* NS 46: 207–16.

Rosenmeyer, P. A. 1997. 'Her master's voice: Sappho's dialogue with Homer', *Materiali e Discussioni per l'Analisi dei Testi Classici* 39: 123–49.

  2006. 'Sappho's iambics', *Letras clássicas* 10: 11–36. [Appeared 2011]

  2007. 'From Syracuse to Rome: the travails of Silanion's Sappho', *Transactions of the American Philological Association* 137: 277–303.

2008. 'Greek verse inscriptions in Roman Egypt: Julia Balbilla's Sapphic voice', *Classical Antiquity* 27: 334–58.

2018. *The Language of Ruins. Greek and Latin Inscriptions on the Memnon Colossus.* Oxford.

Rösler, W. 1975. 'Ein Gedicht und sein Publikum: überlegungen zu Sappho fr. 44 Lobel–Page', *Hermes* 103: 275–85.

1976. 'Die Dichtung des Archilochos und die neue Kölner Epode', *Rheinisches Museum* NF 119: 289–310.

1980. *Dichter und Gruppe. Eine Untersuchung zu den Bedingungen und zur historischen Funktion früher griechischer Lyrik am Beispiel Alkaios.* Theorie und Geschichte der Literatur und der schönen Künste Texte und Abhandlungen 50. Munich.

1985. 'Persona reale o persona poetica? L'interpretazione dell'"io" nella lirica greca arcaica', *Quaderni Urbinati di Cultura Classica* NS 19: 131–44. [≈ Rutherford 2019 (ed.), 80–93]

2016. 'Alkaios fr. 129 und Sappho fr. 94 Voigt: wie übersetzt man Gedichtfragmente?', in Kitzbichler and Stephan 2016 (eds.), 1–62.

Ross, C. 2015. *Eccentricity and Sameness. Discourses on Lesbianism and Desire between Women in Italy, 1860s–1930s.* Italian Modernities 22. Oxford etc.

Rossi, L. E. 1998. 'Orazio, un lirico greco senza musica', *Seminari Romani di Cultura Greca* 1: 163–81.

2009. 'Horace, a Greek lyrist without music', in Lowrie 2009 (ed.), 356–77.

Rota, A. 1994. Το περιοδικό *Γράμματα* της Αλεξάνδρειας (1911–1919). Diss. Athens.

Rotstein, A. 2010. *The Idea of Iambos.* Oxford and New York.

Rowland, H. 2000. 'Anacreontic poetry', in Konzett 2000 (ed.), 114–15.

Rudd, N. 1993 (ed.). *Horace 2000: A Celebration. Essays for the Bimillennium.* London.

Rüdiger, H. 1933. *Sappho. Ihr Ruf und Ruhm bei der Nachwelt.* Das Erbe der Alten. Schriften über Wesen und Wirkung der Antike, Zweite Reihe 21. Leipzig.

1934. *Geschichte der deutschen Sappho-Übersetzungen.* Germanische Studien 151. Berlin.

Ruijgh, C. J. 2001. 'Le *Spectacle des lettres*, comédie de Callias (Athénée X 453c 455b), avec un excursus sur les rapports entre la mélodie du chant et les contours mélodiques du langage parlé', *Mnemosyne* 4th ser. 54: 257–335.

Russell, D. A. 1981. 'Longinus revisited', *Mnemosyne* 4th ser. 34: 72–86.

1990 (ed.). *Antonine Literature.* Oxford.

Russell, H. M., and Weinberg, J. 1983. *The Book of Knowledge. From the Mishneh Torah of Maimonides.* New York.

Rutherford, I. 2001. *Pindar's Paeans. A Reading of the Fragments with a Survey of the Genre.* Oxford.

2019 (ed.). *Oxford Readings in Classical Studies. Greek Lyric.* Oxford.

Ryan, L. 2001. '*Neue Gedichte* – New Poems', in Metzger and Metzger 2001 (eds.), 128–53.

<Sacy, C.-L.M. de> 1769. *Les Amours de Sapho et de Phaon.* Amsterdam.

Şahin, Ç. 1987. 'Zwei Inschriften aus dem südwestlichen Kleinasien', *Epigraphica Anatolica* 10: 1–2.

Saklatvala, B. 1968. *Sappho of Lesbos. Her Works Restored. A Metrical English Version of Her Poems with Conjectural Restorations, Together with Ovid's 'Sappho to Phaon'.* London.

Sammons, B. 2017. *Device and Composition in the Greek Epic Cycle.* Oxford and New York.

Sampson, C. M. 2016. 'A new reconstruction of Sappho 44. (*P. Oxy.* X 1232 + *P. Oxy.* XVII 2076)', in Derda *et al.* 2016 (eds.), 1 53–62.

2020. 'Deconstructing the provenances of P.Sapp.Obbink', *Bulletin of the Society of American Papyrologists* 57: 143–69.

Sanz Morales, M. 2008. 'Safo, *Poemas y Fragmentos*', in Hualde Pascual and Sanz Morales 2008 (eds.), 47–84.

Schaus, G. P. 1992. 'Archaic imported fine wares from the Acropolis, Mytilene', *Hesperia. The Journal of the American School of Classical Studies at Athens* 61: 355–74.

Scheid, J., and Svenbro, J. 1994. *Le Métier de Zeus. Mythe du tissage et du tissu dans le monde gréco-romain.* Paris.

1996. *The Craft of Zeus. Myths of Weaving and Fabric,* transl. C. Volk. Cambridge, MA and London.

Schelling, A. 1994. 'Vidya: the Sappho of India', in *Two Immortals.* Boulder: 5–11.

Schlesier, R. 2011a. 'Aphrodite reflétée: à propos du fragment 1 (LP/V) de Sappho', in Prescendi and Volokhine 2011 (eds.), 416–29.

2011b. 'Presocratic Sappho: her use of Aphrodite for arguments about love and immortality', *Scientia Poetica* 15: 1–28.

2013. 'Atthis, Gyrinno, and other *hetairai*: female personal names in Sappho's poetry', *Philologus* 157: 199–222.

2014. 'Symposion, Kult und frühgriechische Dichtung: Sappho im Kontext', in Dally *et al.* 2014 (eds.), 74–106.

2016. 'Loving, but not loved: the new Kypris Song in the context of Sappho's poetry', in Bierl and Lardinois 2016 (eds.), 368–95.

2017. 'How to make fragments: Maximus Tyrius' Sappho', in Derda *et al.* 2017 (eds.), 141–62.

Schoolfield, G. C. 2001. 'Die Aufzeichnungen des Malte Laurids Brigge', in Metzger and Metzger 2001 (eds.), 154–87.

Schrenk, L. P. 1994. 'Sappho frag. 44 and the *Iliad*', *Hermes* 122: 144–50.

Schubart, W. 1902. 'Neue Bruchstücke der Sappho und des Alkaios', *Sitzungsberichte der Königlich Preussischen Akademie der Wissenschaften zu Berlin*: 195–209.

Schweitzer, E. 2010. 'Devarim she-ba-shira: klapeichen nashim yafot, ein da'ati eyn hapakhpekha' ['Matters of poetry: for you, beautiful women, my opinion is not fickle'], *Haaretz* (3 March): online.

Sedgwick, E. K. 1990. *Epistemology of the Closet.* New York etc.

1993. *Tendencies.* Durham, NC.

Segal, C. 1974. 'Eros and incantation: Sappho and oral poetry', *Arethusa* 7: 139–60. [= Greene 1996a: 58–75]

Selle, H. 2012. Review of Caciagli 2011. *Bryn Mawr Classical Review* 2012.10.23.

Selva, S. de la 1922. *El soldado desconocido.* Mexico <City>.

Seth, V. 1993. *A Suitable Boy.* London.

Sethna, K. D. (Amal Kiran) 1998. *Sri Aurobindo and Greece.* Waterford, CT.

Shabtai, A. 1978. 'Kisma shel Sapfo' ['Sappho's charm'], *Davar* (12 December): 16.

1992. *Hipolitos [Hippolytus].* Tel Aviv.

Shachter, J., and Freedman, H. 1948. *Sanhedrin. Translated into English with Notes, Glossary, and Indices.* London.

Shao Xunmei. 2006. *Xunmei wencun [Works of Xunmei].* Shenyang.

2012a. *Rulin xinshi [A New History of the Literati].* Shanghai.

2012b. *Hua yiban de zui'e [Evil as Flowers].* Shanghai.

Sheridan, S. 2007. 'Suburban sonnets: "Mrs Harwood", Miriam Stone and domestic modernity', *Australian Literary Studies* 23: 140–52.

Shpan, S. 1953. 'Tirgumim mi-yevanit le-'ivrit' ['Greek to Hebrew translations'], *Gilyonot* 28.5–6: 276–9.

Sicherl, M. 1992. 'Die Aldina der Rhetores Graeci (1508–1509) und ihre handschriftlichen Vorlagen', *Illinois Classical Studies* 17: 109–34.

Sicking, C. M. J. 1993. *Griechische Verslehre.* Handbuch der Altertumswissenschaft II.4. Munich.

Silberschlag, E. 1977. 'Greek motifs and myths in modern Hebrew literature', *Proceedings of the American Academy for Jewish Research* 44: 151–83.

Silk, M. 2009. 'The invention of Greek: Macedonians, poets and others', in Georgakopoulou and Silk 2009 (eds.), 3–31.

2010. 'The language of Greek lyric poetry', in Bakker 2010 (ed.), 424–40.

Silva Barris, J. 2011. *Metre and Rhythm in Greek Verse.* Wiener Studien Beiheft 35. Vienna.

Silva Ramos, P. E. da 1964. *Poesia grega e latina.* São Paulo.

Simon, E. 1981. *Die griechischen Vasen*². Munich. [1st edn 1976]

Sissa, G. 1987. *Le Corps virginal. La Virginité féminine en Grèce ancienne.* Paris.

1990. *Greek Virginity,* transl. A. Goldhammer. Revealing Antiquity 3. Cambridge, MA and London.

Skinner, M. B. 1989. 'Sapphic Nossis', *Arethusa* 22: 5–18.

1996. 'Woman and language in archaic Greece, or, why is Sappho a woman?', in Greene 1996a (ed.), 175–92.

2011 (ed.). *A Companion to Catullus.* Malden, MA, Oxford, Carlton, VIC.

Slings, S. R. 1990a. 'The I in personal archaic lyric: an introduction', in Slings 1990b (ed.), 1–30.

1990b (ed.). *The Poet's I in Archaic Greek Lyric. Proceedings of a Symposium Held at the Vrije Universiteit Amsterdam.* Amsterdam.

Snell, B. 1931. 'Sapphos Gedicht φαίνεταί μοι κῆνος', *Hermes* 66: 71–90. [= 1966: 82–97]

1944. 'Zu den Fragmenten der griechischen Lyriker', *Philologus* 96: 282–92.

1966. *Gesammelte Schriften*. Göttingen.

1982. *Griechische Metrik⁴*. Göttingen. [1st edn 1955]

Snyder, J. M. 1989. *The Woman and the Lyre. Women Writers in Classical Greece and Rome*. Bristol and Carbondale, IL.

1991. 'Public occasion and private passion in the lyrics of Sappho of Lesbos', in Pomeroy 1991 (ed.), 1–19.

1997. *Lesbian Desire in the Lyrics of Sappho*. New York and Chichester.

Sommerstein, A. H., and Fletcher, J. 2007 (eds.). *Horkos. The Oath in Greek Society*. Exeter.

Sorelli, G. 1819. *Saffo. Tragedia in cinque atti del signore Francesco Grillparzer. Versione italiana di Guido Sorelli fiorentino*. Florence.

Soubiran, J. 1966. *L'Élision dans la poésie latine*. Études et Commentaires 63. Paris.

Spelman, H. 2017a. 'Sappho 44: Trojan myth and literary history', *Mnemosyne* 4th ser. 70: 740–57.

2017b. 'Borrowing Sappho's napkins: Sappho 101, Catullus 12, Theocritus 28', *Harvard Studies in Classical Philology* 109: 237–60.

Spencer, N. 1995a. 'Early Lesbos between east and west: a "grey area" of Aegean archaeology', *Annual of the British School at Athens* 90: 269–306.

1995b. 'Multi-dimensional group definition in the landscape of rural Greece', in Spencer 1995d (ed.), 28–42.

1995c. *A Gazeteer of Archaeological Sites in Lesbos*. BAR International Series 623. Oxford.

1995d (ed.). *Time, Tradition and Society in Greek Archaeology. Bridging the 'Great Divide'*. London and New York.

2000. 'Exchange and stasis in archaic Mytilene', in Brock and Hodkinson 2000 (eds.), 68–81.

Spyropoulos, I., Roussos, E., and Tsakatikas, V. 1979 (eds.), Ανθολόγιο λυρικής ποιήσεως. Athens.

Squire, D. 2018. 'Supplements for Sappho frr. 27, 4 and 98(a), 7', *Zeitschrift für Papyrologie und Epigraphik* 207: 15–18.

Squire, M. 2016. Review of Bachmann 2015, *Sehepunkte* 16.4. [15.04.2016].

Stacchini, G. 1927. *Pierre Louÿs. Lesbiche*. Milan.

Staël Holstein, Madame de. 1802. *Delphine*, 4 vols. Geneva.

1807. *Corinne ou l'Italie*, 3 vols. London.

Stählin, J. 1734. *ΣΑΠΦΟΥΣ ΜΕΛΗ. Gedichte der Sappho*. Leipzig.

Stanley, K. 1976. 'The rôle of Aphrodite in Sappho fr. 1', *Greek, Roman, and Byzantine Studies* 17: 305–21.

Stehle, E. 1996. 'Romantic sensuality, poetic sense: a response to Hallett on Sappho', in Greene 1996a (ed.), 143–9. [≈ Stehle Stigers 1979]

1997. *Performance and Gender in Ancient Greece. Nondramatic Poetry in Its Setting*. Princeton.

2009a. 'Greek lyric and gender', in Budelmann 2009 (ed.), 58–71.

2009b. '"Once" and "now": temporal markers and Sappho's self-representation', in Greene and Skinner 2009 (eds.), 118–30.

2016. 'Larichos in the Brothers Poem: Sappho speaks truth to the wine-pourer', in Bierl and Lardinois 2016 (eds.), 266–92.

Stehle Stigers, E. 1979. 'Romantic sensuality, poetic sense: a response to Hallett on Sappho', *Signs* 4: 465–71. [≈ Stehle 1996]

1981. 'Sappho's private world', *Women's Studies* 8: 47–63. [= H. Foley 1981 (ed.), 45–61]

Steiner, A. 2007. *Reading Greek Vases.* Cambridge.

Steiner, D. T. 2021. *Choral Constructions in Greek Culture. The Idea of the Chorus in the Poetry, Art, and Social Practices of the Archaic and Early Classical Period.* Cambridge.

Steinmetz, P. 1964. 'Horaz und Pindar. Hor. carm. IV 2', *Gymnasium* 71: 1–17.

Steinrück, M. 1999. 'Homer bei Sappho?' *Mnemosyne* 4th ser. 52: 139–49.

2000. 'Neues zu Sappho', *Zeitschrift für Papyrologie und Epigraphik* 131: 10–12.

2010. 'Sappho und die Wahrheit (Ergänzungen zum fr. 88 V.)', *Quaderni Urbinati di Cultura Classica* NS 94: 79–87.

Stephanus, H. 1554. *Anacreontis Teii odae.* Paris.

1556. *Anacreontis et aliorum lyricorum aliquot poëtarum odae.* Paris.

1560. *Pindari Olympia, Pythia, Nemea, Isthmia. Caeterorum octo lyricorum carmina, Alcaei, Sapphus, Stesichori, Ibyci, Anacreontis, Bacchylidis, Simonidis, Alcmanis, nonnulla etiam aliorum.* Paris.

1566. *Pindari Olympia, Pythia, Nemea, Isthmia. Caeterorum octo lyricorum carmina, Alcaei, Sapphus, Stesichori, Ibyci, Anacreontis, Bacchylidis, Simonidis, Alcmanis, nonnulla etiam aliorum.* Paris.

1586. *Pindari Olympia, Pythia, Nemea, Isthmia. Caeterorum octo lyricorum carmina, Alcaei, Sapphus, Stesichori, Ibyci, Anacreontis, Bacchylidis, Simonidis, Alcmanis, nonnulla etiam aliorum. Editio III. Graecolatina H. Steph. recognitione quorundam interpretationis locorum, et accessione lyricorum carminum locupletata.* Paris.

Stephanus, R. 1547. *Dionysii Halicarnassei De compositione, seu orationis partium apta inter se collocatione, ad Rufum. Eiusdem, artis Rhetoricae capita quaedam, ad Echecratem. Item quo genere dicendi sit usus Thucydides, ad Ammaeum.* Paris.

Stevenson, J. 2015. 'Women writers and the classics', in Cheney and P. Hardie 2015 (eds.), 129–46.

Stewart, A. 1990. *Greek Sculpture. An Exploration,* 2 vols. New Haven and London.

1998. 'Nuggets: mining the texts again', *American Journal of Archaeology* 102: 271–82.

Stewart, S. 2002. *Poetry and the Fate of the Senses.* Chicago and London.

Suárez de la Torre, E. 2008. '"Ya vienen los novios": una lectura socioantropológica del fragmento 44 V. de Safo', *Faventia* 30: 143–60.

Svenbro, J. 1975. 'Sappho and Diomedes: Some notes on Sappho 1 LP and the epic', *Museum Philologum Londiniense* 1: 37–49.

Swift, L. A. 2009. 'The symbolism of space in Euripidean choral fantasy (*Hipp.* 732–75, *Med.* 824–65, *Bacch.* 370–433)', *Classical Quarterly* NS 59: 364–82.

2015. 'Lyric visions of epic combat: the spectacle of war in archaic personal song', in Bakogianni and Hope 2015 (eds.), 93–109.

2018. 'Thinking with brothers in Sappho and beyond', *Mouseion* 59: 71–87.

Swift, L., and Carey, C. 2016 (eds.). *Iambus and Elegy. New Approaches*. Oxford.

Swinburne, A. C. 1866. *Poems and Ballads*. London.

Syndikus, H. P. 2001. *Die Lyrik des Horaz. Eine Interpretation der Oden³*, 2 vols. Darmstadt. [1st edn 1972–3]

1984–90. *Catull. Eine Interpretation*. Impulse der Forschung 46, 48, 55. Darmstadt.

Tabaki, A., and Sechopoulou, M. 2015 (eds.). *Ο ελληνικός περιοδικός τύπος του 19ου αιώνα. Ερευνητικά ζητήματα – πορίσματα της έρευνας*. Athens.

Tabaki, A., and Polykandrioti, O. 2016 (eds.). *Ελληνικότητα και ετερότητα. Πολιτισμικές διαμεσολαβήσεις και "εθνικός χαρακτήρας" στον 19ο αιώνα*, 2 vols. Athens.

Taboada, H. G. H. 2014. 'Centauros y eruditos: los clásicos en la Independencia', *Latinoamérica. Revista de estudios latinoamericanos* 59: 193–221.

Taida, I. 2015. 'A pioneer of classical studies in Japan, Shigeichi Kure: a focus on his translations', *Classical Receptions Journal* 7: 260–75.

Takayama Chogyū. 1915. *Waga sode no ki [Records of My Sleeves]*. Tokyo.

Tapscott, S. 1996 (ed.). *Twentieth-Century Latin American Poetry. A Bilingual Anthology*. Austin.

Tarrant, R. J. 1981. 'The authenticity of the letter of Sappho to Phaon (*Heroides XV*)', *Harvard Studies in Classical Philology* 85: 133–53.

Tedeschi, G. 2015. *Saffo. Frammenti. Antologia di versi con introduzione, testo, traduzione, commento*. Trieste.

Teixeira, I. 1996. *Obras poéticas de Basílio da Gama*. Texto e Arte 12. São Paulo.

Thomas, B. M. 1999. 'The rhetoric of prayer in Sappho's "Hymn to Aphrodite"', *Helios* 26: 3–10.

Thompson, E. J. 1921. 'Supplementary review', in H. Das 1921: 342–9.

Thorsen, T. S., and Harrison, S. 2019 (eds.). *Roman Receptions of Sappho*. Oxford.

Tian, X. 2003. *Safu. Yige wenxue chuantong de shengcheng [Sappho. The Making of a Literary Tradition]*. Shanghai.

Tissot, S.-A. D. 1758. *Dissertatio de febribus biliosis; seu historia epidemiae biliosae Lausannensis, an. MDCCLV. Accedit Tentamen de morbis ex manustupratione*. Lausanne.

1760. *L'onanisme; ou dissertation physique sur les maladies produites par la masturbation*. Lausanne.

1766. *Onanism: or, a Treatise upon the Disorders Produced by Masturbation: or, the Dangerous Effects of Secret and Excessive Venery*, transl. A. Hume. London.

Tomadakis, N. 1943. *Ο Σολωμός και οι Αρχαίοι*. Athens.

Topper, K. 2012. *The Imagery of the Athenian Symposium*. Cambridge.

Torrano, J. 2009. *Safo de Lesbos. Três poemas*. Rio de Janeiro.

Torres, R. R. 1970. *Bucólicos y líricos griegos*. Clásicos universales Jus 14. Mexico City.

Tortorelli Ghidini, M. 2014 (ed.). *Aurum. Funzioni e simbologie dell'oro nelle culture del Mediterraneo antico.* Studia Archaeologica 193. Rome.

Traill, A. 2005. 'Acroteleutium's Sapphic infatuation (*Miles* 1216–83)', *Classical Quarterly* NS 55: 518–33.

Traub, V. 2016. *Thinking Sex with the Early Moderns.* Philadelphia.

Treu, M. 1954. *Sappho.* Munich.

Tribulato, O. 2012 (ed.). *Language and Linguistic Contact in Ancient Sicily.* Cambridge.

2016. 'La lirica monodica', in Cassio 2016 (ed.), 197–221.

Trundle, M. 2017. 'The reception of the classical tradition in New Zealand war reporting and memory in the late nineteenth and early twentieth centuries', in D. Burton *et al.* 2017 (eds.), 313–25.

Tsagalis, C. 2017 (ed.). *Poetry in Fragments. Studies on the Hesiodic Corpus and Its Afterlife.* Trends in Classics Supplement 50. Berlin and Boston.

Tsagalis, C., and Markantonatos, A. 2017 (eds.). *The Winnowing Oar. New Perspectives in Homeric Studies. Studies in Honor of Antonios Rengakos.* Berlin and Boston.

Tsagarakis, O. 1977. *Self-Expression in Early Greek Lyric, Elegiac and Iambic Poetry.* Palingenesia 11. Wiesbaden.

Tsokhas, K. 1996. 'Modernity, sexuality and national identity: Norman Lindsay's aesthetics', *Australian Historical Studies* 27: 219–41.

Turner, E. 1987 *Greek Manuscripts of the Ancient World*², rev. P. J. Parsons. BICS Suppl. 46. London. [1st edn 1971]

Turner, J. G. 1993 (ed.), *Sexuality and Gender in Early Modern Europe. Institutions, Texts, Images.* Cambridge.

Tzamali, E. 1996. *Syntax und Stil bei Sappho.* Münchener Studien zur Sprachwissenschaft NS 16. Dettelbach.

Ucciardello, G. 2001. 'Sapph. frr. 88 e 159 V. in *POxy.* LXIV 4411', *Zeitschrift für Papyrologie und Epigraphik* 136: 167–8.

2012. 'Ancient readers of Pindar's *Epinicians* in Egypt: evidence from papyri', in Agócs *et al.* 2012 (eds.), 105–40.

Ueda Bin. 1895. 'Girishia Shichō wo ronsu' ['On Greek intellectual trends'], in *Teikoku bungaku [Empire Literature]* 1.3: 34–102.

1896. 'Saffuo no kashū' ['Lyrics of Sappho'], *Bungakukai [Literary Sphere]* 48: 1–10.

1901. *Bungei ronshū [Literary Criticisms].* Tokyo.

1922. *Ueda Bin shishū [Poems of Ueda Bin].* Tokyo.

1927a. *Ueda Bin shishū [Poems of Ueda Bin],* expanded edn. Tokyo.

1927b. *Ueda Bin shishō [Select Poems of Ueda Bin].* Tokyo.

1929. *Ueda Bin zenshū [The Complete Works of Ueda Bin],* vol. 1. Tokyo.

1978. *Teihon Ueda Bin zenshū [The Complete Works of Ueda Bin],* revised edn, vol. 1. Tokyo.

Ueding, G. 2001 (ed.). *Historisches Wörterbuch der Rhetorik. Band 5. L–Musi.* Tübingen.

Ursinus, F. 1568. *Carmina novem illustrium feminarum Sapphus Myrtidis Praxillae Erinnae Corinnae Nossidis Myrus Telesillae Anytae. Et lyricorum Alcmanis Ibyci Stesichori Anacreontis Alcaei Simonidis Bacchylidis. Elegiae Tyrtaei, et Mimnermi. Bucolica Bionis et Moschi.* Antwerp.

Valis, N. 1991. *Carolina Coronado. Poesías.* Madrid.

Vanita, R. 1996. *Sappho and the Virgin Mary. Same-Sex Love and the English Literary Imagination.* New York.

    2005. *Love's Rite. Same-Sex Marriage in India and the West.* New York and Basingstoke.

    2012. *Gender, Sex and the City. Urdu Rekhtī Poetry in India 1780–1870.* New York.

Vanita, R., and Kidwai, S. 2000 (eds.). *Same-Sex Love in India. Readings from Literature and History.* Basingstoke and London.

Varika, E. 2011. *Η εξέγερση των κυριών. Η γένεση μιας φεμινιστικής συνείδησης στην Ελλάδα 1833–1907⁶.* Athens. [1st edn 1987]

Varnalis, K. 1958. *Αισθητικά – Κριτικά Β΄.* Athens.

Vasconcellos, P. S. de 2011. 'A tradução poética e os estudos clássicos no Brasil de hoje: algumas considerações', *Scientia Traductionis* 10: 68–79.

Vassiliadou, D., Zestanakis, P., Kefala, M., and Preka, M. 2013 (eds.), *(Αντι) μιλώντας στις βεβαιότητες. Φύλα, αναπαραστάσεις, υποκειμενικότητες.* Athens.

Vasunia, P. 2013. *The Classics and Colonial India.* Oxford.

Veloudis, G. 1989. *Διονύσιος Σολωμός. Ρομαντική Ποίηση και Ποιητική. Οι γερμανικές πηγές.* Athens.

<Venette, N.> 1687. *Tableau de l'amour consideré dans l'estat du mariage.* Parma.

Venuti, L. 1998. *The Scandals of Translation. Towards an Ethics of Difference.* London and New York.

Verlaine, P. 1888. *Les Poètes maudits. Nouvelle édition. Ornée de six portraits par Luque.* Paris.

<Verri, A.> 1780. *Le avventure di Saffo poetessa di Mitilene. Traduzione dal greco originale nuovamente scoperto.* Padua. [= L. Martinelli 1975: 71–215]

Vieira, T. 2017. *Lírica grega, hoje.* São Paulo.

Vielé-Griffin, F. 1911. *Sapho.* Paris.

Vilain, R. 2016. *Rainer Maria Rilke. The Notebooks of Malte Laurids Brigge.* Oxford.

Villing, A., and Schlotzhauer, U. 2006 (eds.). *Naukratis: Greek Diversity in Egypt. Studies in East Greek Pottery and Exchange in the Eastern Mediterranean.* The Bristish Museum Research Publication 162. London.

Vitelli, G. 1913. '123. Frammenti di odi di Saffo', *Papiri Greci e Latini* 2: 21–2.

Vivien, R. 1903. *Sapho. Traduction nouvelle avec le texte grec.* Paris.

Vogliano, A. 1938. 'Nuove strofe di Saffo', *Philologus* 93: 277–86.

    1941. *Saffo, una nuova ode della poetessa.* Milan.

Voigt, E.-M. 1971. *Sappho et Alcaeus. Fragmenta.* Amsterdam.

Volger, H. F. M. 1810. *Sapphus Lesbiae carmina et fragmenta.* Leipzig.

Vossius, I. 1684. *Caius Valerius Catullus et in eum Isaaci Vossii observationes.* London.

Voulgaris, E. 1801. Ἀδολεσχία φιλόθεος ἤτοι ἐκ τῆς ἀναγνώσεως τῆς ἱερᾶς Μωσαϊκῆς Πεντατεύχου Βίβλου ἐπιστάσεις ψυχωφελεῖς τε καὶ σωτηριώδεις, 2 vols. Vienna.

Waters, W. 2003. *Poetry's Touch. On Lyric Address.* Ithaca, NY and London.

Wathelet, P. 1988. *Dictionnaire des Troyens de l'Iliade,* 2 vols. Université de Liège, Bibliothèque de la Faculté de philosophie et lettres Documenta et instrumenta 1. Liège.

Watson, L. 1991. *Arae. The Curse Poetry of Antiquity.* ARCA Classical and Medieval Texts, Papers and Monographs 26. Leeds.

Watts, E. S. 1977. *The Poetry of American Women from 1632 to 1945.* Austin and London.

Way, A. S. 1920. *Sappho and the Vigil of Venus.* London and New York.

Weigall, A. 1932. *Sappho of Lesbos. Her Life and Times.* London.

Weisbord, M. 2010. *The Love Queen of Malabar. Memoir of a Friendship with Kamala Das.* Montreal, Kingston, ON, London, Ithaca, NY.

Welcker, F. G. 1816. *Sappho von einem herrschenden Vorurtheil befreyt.* Göttingen.

West, D. 1995. *Horace Odes I. Carpe diem.* Oxford.

   1998. *Horace Odes II. Vatis amici.* Oxford.

   2002. *Horace Odes III. Dulce periculum.* Oxford.

West, M. L. 1970. 'Burning Sappho', *Maia* 22: 307–30. [= 2011–13: II 28–52]

   1977. Review of Voigt 1971, *Classical Review* NS 27: 161–3.

   1978. *Hesiod. Works and Days.* Oxford.

   1982. *Greek Metre.* Oxford.

   1983. Review of Campbell 1983, *Classical Review* NS 33: 309.

   1992. *Ancient Greek Music.* Oxford.

   2001. Review of Liberman 1999, *Classical Review* NS 51: 4–6.

   2002. 'The view from Lesbos', in Reichel and Rengakos 2002 (eds.), 207–19. [= 2011–13: I 392–407]

   2005. 'The new Sappho', *Zeitschrift für Papyrologie und Epigraphik* 151: 1–9. [= 2011–13: II 53–66]

   2007. *Indo-European Poetry and Myth.* Oxford.

   2011–13. *Hellenica. Selected Papers on Greek Literature and Thought,* 3 vols. Oxford.

   2014. 'Nine poems of Sappho', *Zeitschrift für Papyrologie und Epigraphik* 191: 1–12.

   2015. 'Epic, lyric, and lyric epic', in Finglass and Kelly 2015a (eds.), 63–80.

Wharton, H. T. 1885. *Sappho. Memoir, Text, Selected Renderings and a Literal Translation.* London.

Wilamowitz-Moellendorff, U. von 1896. Review of Louÿs 1894, *Göttingische gelehrte Anzeigen* 1896/8: 623–38. [= 1913: 63–78]

   1900. *Die Textgeschichte der griechischen Lyriker.* Abhandlungen der Königlichen Gesellschaft der Wissenschaften zu Göttingen, philologisch-historische Klasse NS 4.3. Berlin.

   1905. 'Die Griechische Literatur des Altertums', in Wilamowitz *et al.* 1905, 1–236.

1912. 'Die Griechische Literatur des Altertums', in Wilamowitz *et al.* 1912: 1–318.

1913. *Sappho und Simonides. Untersuchungen über griechische Lyriker.* Berlin.

1921. *Griechische Verskunst.* Berlin.

Wilamowitz-Moellendorff, U. von, Krumbacher, K., Wackernagel, J., Leo, F., Norden, E., and Skutsch, F. 1905. *Die griechische und lateinische Literatur und Sprache.* Die Kultur der Gegenwart 1.8. Berlin and Leipzig.

1912. *Die griechische und lateinische Literatur und Sprache. Dritte, stark verbesserte und vermehrte Auflage.* Die Kultur der Gegenwart 1.8. Leipzig and Berlin.

Willi, A. 2011. 'Language, Homeric', in Finkelberg 2011 (ed.), II 458–64.

2012a. 'Kiparsky's rule, thematic nasal presents, and athematic *verba vocalia* in Greek', in Probert and Willi 2012 (eds.), 260–76.

2012b. '"We speak Peloponnesian": tradition and linguistic identity in post-classical Sicilian literature', in Tribulato 2012 (ed.), 265–88.

Williams, C., and Williams, H. 1991. 'Excavations at Mytilene, 1990', *Échos du Monde Classique/Classical Views* NS 10: 175–91.

Williams, H. 1995. 'Investigations at Mytilene, 1994', *Échos du Monde Classique/Classical Views* NS 14: 95–100.

Williamson, M. 1995. *Sappho's Immortal Daughters.* Cambridge, MA and London.

1996. 'Sappho and the other woman', in Greene 1996a (ed.), 248–64.

2009. 'Sappho and Pindar in the nineteenth and twentieth centuries', in Budelmann 2009 (ed.), 352–70.

Wills, G. 1967. 'The Sapphic "Umwertung aller Werte"', *American Journal of Philology* 88: 434–42.

Wilson, L. H. 1996. *Sappho's Sweetbitter Songs. Configurations of Female and Male in Ancient Greek Lyric.* London and New York.

Wilson, N. G. 1996. *Scholars of Byzantium².* London and Cambridge, MA. [1st edn 1983]

Winkler, J. J. 1981. 'Gardens of nymphs: public and private in Sappho's lyrics', *Women's Studies* 8: 65–91. [= H. Foley 1981 (ed.), 63–89 ≈ Winkler 1990: 162–87 ≈ Greene 1996a (ed.), 89–109].

1990. *The Constraints of Desire. The Anthropology of Sex and Gender in Ancient Greece.* New York and London.

1991. 'Sappho and the crack of dawn (fragment 58 L–P)', *Journal of Homosexuality* 20: 227–33.

Winkler, J. J., and Zeitlin, F. I. 1990 (eds.). *Nothing to Do with Dionysos? Athenian Drama in Its Social Context.* Princeton.

Winterer, C. 2007. *The Mirror of Antiquity. American Women and the Classical Tradition, 1750–1900.* Ithaca, NY and London.

Winterson, J. 1994. *Art and Lies. A Piece for Three Voices and a Bawd.* London.

Wirth, P. 1963. 'Neue Spuren eines Sapphobruchstücks', *Hermes* 91: 115–17.

Wiseman, S. 2008. '"*Rome's* wanton Ovid": reading and writing Ovid's *Heroides* 1590–1712', *Renaissance Studies* 22: 295–306.

Wiseman, T. P. 1985. *Catullus and His World. A Reappraisal.* Cambridge.

Wittig, M. 1973. *Le Corps lesbien.* Paris.

1975. *The Lesbian Body.* London.

Wittig, M., and Zeig, S. 1976. *Brouillon pour un dictionnaire des amantes.* Paris.

1979. *Lesbian Peoples. Material for a Dictionary.* New York.

Wolf, J. C. 1733. *Sapphus, poetriae Lesbiae, fragmenta et elogia, quotquot in auctoribus antiquis Graecis et Latinis reperiuntur cum virorum doctorum notis integris.* London.

Woodman, T. 2002. '*Biformis vates*: the *Odes*, Catullus and Greek lyric', in Wiseman and Feeney 2002 (eds.), 53–64, with notes, 213–18.

Woodman, T., and Feeney, D. 2002 (eds.). *Traditions and Contexts in the Poetry of Horace.* Cambridge.

Wright, N. 1998. 'Gilbert, Ruth', in R. Robinson and Wattie 1998 (eds.), 203.

Wyke, M. 1998 (ed.). *Parchments of Gender. Deciphering the Bodies of Antiquity.* Oxford.

Wyles, R., and Hall, E. 2016 (eds.). *Women Classical Scholars. Unsealing the Fountain from the Renaissance to Jacqueline de Romilly.* Oxford.

Yang Xianyi. 1995. *Aodexiuji [Odyssey].* Beijing.

Yatromanolakis, D. 1999. 'Alexandrian Sappho revisited', *Harvard Studies in Classical Philology* 99: 179–95.

2003. 'Palimpsests of Sappho in nineteenth- and twentieth-century Greece: an overview', in Nagy and Stavrakopoulou 2003 (eds.), 171–89.

2004. 'Ritual poetics in archaic Lesbos: contextualizing genre in Sappho', in Yatromanolakis and Roilos 2004 (eds.), 56–70.

2005. 'Contrapuntal inscriptions', *Zeitschrift für Papyrologie und Epigraphik* 152: 16–30.

2006. 'A lyric "epos"', *Hellenika* 56: 381–8.

2007. *Sappho in the Making. The Early Reception.* Washington, DC and Cambridge, MA.

2008. 'P. Colon. inv. 21351+21376 and P. Oxy. 1787 fr. 1: music, cultural politics, and Hellenistic anthologies', *Hellenika* 58: 237–55.

2009. 'Alcaeus and Sappho', in Budelmann 2009 (ed.), 204–26.

Yatromanolakis, D., and Roilos, P. 2004 (eds.). *Greek Ritual Poetics.* Hellenic Studies 3. Cambridge, MA and London.

Yeats, W. B. 1899. *The Wind among the Reeds.* London.

Zachariadis, D. 1912. 'Ἡδονισμός', *Grammata* 12: 427–8.

Zarogiannis, I. 1988. Ο Βάρναλης και οι αρχαίοι. Diss. Ioannina.

Zeitlin, F. I. 1985. 'Playing the other: theater, theatricality, and the feminine in Greek drama', *Representations* 11: 63–94. [≈ 1996: 341–74 ≈ Winkler and Zeitlin 1990 (eds.), 63–96]

1996. *Playing the Other. Gender and Society in Classical Greek Literature.* Chicago and London.

Zellner, H. 2006. 'Sappho's supra-superlatives', *Classical Quarterly* NS 56: 292–7.

2010. *The Poetic Style of the Greek Poet Sappho. A Study in Word Playfulness.* Lewiston, NY, Queenston, ON, Lampeter.

Zhang, D. 2014. 'Naming the indescribable: Woolf, Russell, James, and the limits of description', *New Literary History* 45: 51–70.

Zhou Xiashou (Zhou Zuoren) 1951. *Xila nüshiren Sabo [The Greek Poetess Sappho]*. Shanghai.

Zhou Zuoren. 2009. *Zhou Zuoren sanwen quanji [The Complete Essays of Zhou Zuoren]*, 14 vols. Guilin.

Zierler, W. I. 2004. *And Rachel Stole the Idols. The Emergence of Modern Hebrew Women's Writing*. Detroit.

Zuntz, G. 1984. *Drei Kapitel zur griechischen Metrik*. Österreichische Akademie der Wissenschaften Philosophisch-historische Klasse Sitzungsberichte 443. Vienna.

Zusanek, H. 2005. *Eos. Untersuchungen zum dios-Begriff 3*, ed. M. Zusanek. Frankfurt am Main etc.

Zvelebil, K. V. 1974. *Tamil Literature (A History of Indian Literature. Volume 10)*. Wiesbaden.

General Index

Index to the Reception of Sappho